THE BEST MEAT RECIPES

A BEST RECIPE CLASSIC

THE
BEST
MEAT
RECIPES

A BEST RECIPE CLASSIC

BY THE EDITORS OF

COOK'S ILLUSTRATED

PHOTOGRAPHY

CARL TREMBLAY AND DANIEL J. VAN ACKERE

ILLUSTRATIONS

JOHN BURGOYNE

America's
TEST KITCHEN

BROOKLINE, MASSACHUSETTS

America's Test Kitchen
17 Station Street
Brookline, MA 02445

ISBN-13: 978-1-933615-32-5
ISBN-10: 1-933615-32-X
Library of Congress Cataloging-in-Publication Data
The Editors of *Cook's Illustrated*

The Best Meat Recipes: Would you sear 50 pepper-crusted filets mignons to find the ultimate recipe, one guaranteed to deliver a
perfectly browned crust and a meltingly tender interior? We did. Here are more than 300 foolproof recipes for all our favorite cuts of meat.
1st Paperback Edition

ISBN-13: 978-1-933615-32-5
ISBN-10: 1-933615-32-X
(paperback): $19.95 US/$21.50 CAN
I. Cooking. I. Title
2008

Manufactured in the United States of America

10 9 8 7 6 5 4 3 2 1

Distributed by America's Test Kitchen, 17 Station Street, Brookline, MA 02445.

Editor: Jack Bishop
Senior Editor: Julia Collin Davison
Test Cook: Sean Lawler
Assistant Test Cook: Charles Kelsey
Series Designer: Amy Klee
Jacket Designer: Richard Oriolo
Graphic Designer: Lisa Diercks
Book Production Specialist: Ronald Bilodeau
Photographers: Carl Tremblay; Daniel J. Van Ackere
Food Stylist: Mary Jane Sawyer and Marie Piraino
Illustrator: John Burgoyne
Production Manager: Jessica Lindheimer Quirk
Associate Editor: Rebecca Hays
Copyeditor: Evie Righter
Proofreader: Jessica Konopa
Indexer: Cathy Dorsey

Pictured on front of jacket: Pepper-Crusted Filets Mignons (page 53)
Pictured on back of jacket: Charcoal-Grilled Steak Tips (page 36), Charcoal-Grilled Pork Chops (page 82),
Pot Roast with Root Vegetables (page 187), Barbecued Baby Back Ribs (page 330), and Grilled Hamburgers (page 347)

Contents

WELCOME TO
AMERICA'S TEST KITCHEN

THIS BOOK HAS BEEN TESTED, WRITTEN, AND edited by the folks at America's Test Kitchen, a very real 2,500-square-foot kitchen located just outside of Boston. It is the home of *Cook's Illustrated* magazine and *Cook's Country* magazine and is the Monday-through-Friday destination for more than two dozen test cooks, editors, food scientists, tasters, and cookware specialists. Our mission is to test recipes over and over again until we understand how and why they work and until we arrive at the "best" version.

We start the process of testing a recipe with a complete lack of conviction, which means that we accept no claim, no theory, no technique, and no recipe at face value. We simply assemble as many variations as possible, test a half dozen of the most promising, and taste the results blind. We then construct our own hybrid recipe and continue to test it, varying ingredients, techniques, and cooking times until we reach a consensus. The result, we hope, is the best version of a particular recipe, but we realize that only you can be the final judge of our success (or failure).

As we like to say in the test kitchen, "We make the mistakes, so you don't have to."

All of this would not be possible without a belief that good cooking, much like good music, is indeed based on a foundation of objective technique. Some people like spicy foods and others don't, but there is a right way to sauté, there is a best way to cook a pot roast, and there are measurable scientific principles involved in producing perfectly beaten, stable egg whites. This is our ultimate goal: to investigate the fundamental principles of cooking so that you become a better cook. It is as simple as that.

You can watch us work (in our actual test kitchen) by tuning in to America's Test Kitchen (www.americastestkitchen.com) on public television or by subscribing to *Cook's Illustrated* magazine (www.cooksillustrated.com) or *Cook's Country* magazine (www.cookscountry.com), which are each published every other month. We welcome you into our kitchen, where you can stand by our side as we test our way to the "best" recipes in America.

PREFACE

VERMONT MOUNTAIN FARMS WERE LONG famous for the small scale of their operations. Each family had a cow, a couple of pigs, one or two "beefers," and a half-dozen chickens running around the yard. They boiled their own sap, grew their own vegetables, and made their own bread.

Probably because I spent summers on such a farm, our family now raises two pigs per year and owns two Herefords, half a dozen chickens (Rhode Island Reds, Speckled Wyandots, Americana, and Barred Rock), and one carrier pigeon, Homer, who adopted us about a year ago and lives in our barn. The surprise came the first year we tasted our own pork and beef. Unlike the dry, relatively insipid pork now in most supermarkets, our pork had both fat and flavor. And because the beef had been mostly grass-fed, it really tasted like something (although it was, to be fair, on the chewy side).

If you were to visit our farmhouse, you would note that our basement has three freezers full of meat. That means that we have now cooked virtually every cut of beef and pork in every conceivable way. This has led to a better understanding of which cuts work best with which cooking techniques.

Because few people have 1,000 pounds of meat in their basement to experiment with, *Cook's Illustrated* offers *The Best Meat Recipes* as a one-stop shopping spot for all of the meat recipes you may need. Our test kitchen has cooked many thousands of pounds of beef, pork, lamb, and veal in every cut and shape possible—from steaks to cutlets, from chops to roasts, from sausages to bacon. We've grilled, stir-fried, roasted, braised, barbecued, slow-cooked, pot-roasted, broiled, sautéed, and stewed. We've worked on recipes as American as barbecued ribs as well as on less familiar imports such as vitello tonnato, pork vindaloo, and lamb tagine. Why do we do it? Because we are intensely curious and want to save you the days, weeks, and months of testing necessary to determine the best methods for preparing each and every cut.

Of course, we have not included some of the meats that I have been served in Vermont, including woodchuck, squirrel, and bear. In the country, every scrap of food has a purpose—just like each and every one of my neighbors, past and present. When I was growing up, Marie Briggs was a master baker, turning out anadama bread, molasses cookies, and loaf after loaf of country white on her bright green Kalamazoo wood cookstove. Herbie and Onie did the haying in the summer and then left town in the winter. Now our local artist, Karl, is an expert on foraging for mushrooms, and if you want your car fixed, just bring it down to Dave Trachte's garage. I feel the same way about cuts of meat. Each of them has a secret locked inside, a special preparation method that suits it perfectly. Just like small town living, cooking is about nothing more than discovering the best of each ingredient and treating it such that you bring out its full potential.

Mike Thomas lives down the road from us, just over the border in New York State, and has a colorful expression for any occasion. When we first hooked up a new rototiller to the back of the tractor, he tried it out and said that it was as "slick as a mitten." When he found out what I do for a living, he suggested that testing recipes must be "about as exciting as going down to the A&P and watching them change the fruit." Maybe Mike's right, but we enjoy it. At least all of you can reap the "fruits" of our labors—recipes that are well suited to each cut and that are mostly reliable. And at least Mike is happy that he didn't have to do all of the testing.

Christopher Kimball
Founder and Editor
Cook's Illustrated and *Cook's Country*
Host, *America's Test Kitchen*

MEAT BASICS

An Illustrated
(and Opinionated)
Buying Guide for Meat

MEAT SEEMS SO SIMPLE (BUY A STEAK, THROW IT ON THE GRILL, AND SERVE), BUT as any cook knows, the process is more complex than it appears. Yes, meat cooking can be very quick, but there are many small details that can make the difference between a great meal and an average one. Which steak should you buy is a common (and perplexing) question. Many packages sport labels that say "great for grilling," but you know from experience that's not always true. We hope the pages that follow will make meat buying less daunting, whether you want to grill a couple of steaks or make a fancy roast for the holidays.

What follows are detailed buying guides for pork, lamb, veal, and beef to help you understand why we like specific cuts for specific recipes. And note that there are some cuts that we don't recommend at all. Before you choose a particular cut at the supermarket, you first must ask yourself four basic questions:

DO YOU WANT A STEAK, CHOP, OR ROAST?

The terms *steak* and *chop* refer to any relatively thin cut, with or without bone. Most steaks and chops are tender and need only a quick sear in a hot pan or a brief sizzle on the grill. Lean pork chops and moderately tough lamb chops from the shoulder can also be braised but rarely for more than half an hour.

A roast is a thick cut of meat suitable for prolonged roasting or braising. Just as you would never pot-roast a skinny flank steak, you would never grill a thick rump roast over hot coals.

DO YOU WANT BONES OR NO BONES?

The answer to this question is not always clear. For instance, you can grill steaks with or without bones. However, a stew should always be made from boneless meat. In general, bone-in cuts are more flavorful for several reasons. First, bones help meat to retain moisture. A bone-in pork chop will be juicier, especially near the bone, than a boneless chop. Also, bones can contribute flavor to sauces. For instance, when veal shanks are braised, the marrow in the bones melts into the sauce.

HOW MANY PEOPLE ARE YOU SERVING?

To answer this question, first think about how you plan to serve the meat. If you are serving a cut that naturally should be served whole (chops, small steaks) you will want to buy meat by the piece—four veal chops to feed four people. If you plan to slice or carve the meat once it has been cooked, buy between 6 and 8 ounces of meat per serving, which will yield a slightly smaller serving portion once the meat has been cooked. Note that many cuts contain bones and thick layers of fat that are trimmed or rendered during cooking and these suggested number of ounces per serving do not account for these losses. Therefore, a fatty, bone-in roast that weighs four pounds will probably feed only six to eight people.

DO YOU WANT TO COOK THE MEAT QUICKLY OR SLOWLY?

Tough cuts, which generally come from heavily exercised parts of the animal, such as the shoulder and rump, respond best to slow cooking methods, such as pot-roasting and barbecuing. The primary goal of slow cooking is to melt the collagen in the connective tissue, thereby transforming a tough piece of meat into a tender one. In addition to cooking the meat, you are changing its texture.

Tender cuts with little connective tissue respond well to quicker, dry-heat cooking, such as grilling or roasting. To make the meat palatable, you need only heat it to the desired internal temperature.

How to Buy Pork

IN 1985, AMID GROWING CONCERNS ABOUT SATURATED FAT IN THE AMERICAN DIET, Congress created the National Pork Board with the goal of helping producers provide consumers with the leaner meat they desired. Working with the board, producers developed new breeding techniques and feeding systems aimed at slimming down pigs. As a result, pigs are now much leaner and more heavily muscled than they were 20 years ago, with an average of 31 percent less fat. This is good news for our waistlines, but much of the meaty flavor, moisture, and tenderness disappeared along with the fat, causing some cuts of pork to taste like diet food. For this reason, choosing the right cut and the right cooking method make a big difference when preparing today's pork. We've rated all major cuts for flavor (★★★ being the best) and cost ($$$$ being the most expensive).

A pig is butchered into four primal cuts. The term *primal cuts* refers to the basic cuts made to an animal when it is initially butchered. Butchers turn primal cuts into the chops, roasts, and other cuts sold at the retail level. Retail cuts from the same primal cut generally share similar traits, so when shopping it helps to understand the characteristics of the four primal cuts of pork.

SHOULDER Cuts from the upper portion of the well-exercised front legs (called the blade shoulder) tend to be tough, with a fair amount of fat. The economical arm, or picnic shoulder, has characteristics similar to the blade shoulder. Shoulder hocks (used primarily as a flavoring agent in soups, slow-cooked greens, and stews) also come from this part of the pig, while ham hocks come from the hind legs of the animal. All shoulder cuts require long, slow cooking to become fork-tender.

LOIN Butchers divide this area between the shoulder and the leg into some of the most popular cuts of pork, including pork chops, tenderloin, roasts, and ribs. Because the loin area is so lean, these cuts are prone to dryness.

LEG The leg is sometimes referred to as the ham. Ham can be wet- or dry-cured or sold fresh, as a roast.

BELLY The belly, or side, of the pig is, not surprisingly, the fattiest part, home to spareribs and bacon.

THE FOUR PRIMAL CUTS OF PORK

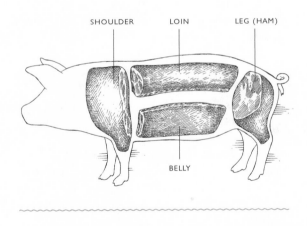

SHOULDER   LOIN   LEG (HAM)

BELLY

ENHANCED OR UNENHANCED PORK?

Because modern pork is remarkably lean and therefore somewhat bland and prone to dryness if overcooked, a product called enhanced pork has overtaken the market. In fact, it can be hard to find unenhanced pork in some areas. Enhanced pork has been injected with a solution of water, salt, sodium phosphates, sodium lactate, potassium lactate, sodium diacetate, and varying flavor agents to bolster flavor and juiciness, with the total amount of enhancing ingredients adding 7 percent to 15 percent extra weight. Pork containing additives must be so labeled, with a list of the ingredients.

After several taste tests, we have concluded that while enhanced pork is indeed juicier and more tender than unenhanced pork, the latter has more genuine pork flavor. Some tasters picked up unappealing artificial, salty flavors in enhanced pork. Enhanced pork can also leach juices that, once reduced, will result in overly salty pan sauces. If you want to add moisture and flavor to a dry cut while maintaining complete control of flavor and salt levels, we recommend that you buy unenhanced pork and brine it at home (that is, soak the meat in a saltwater solution).

PORK BUTT

Primal Cut: Shoulder
Flavor: ★ ★ ★
Cost: $ $
Alternate Names:
Boston Shoulder,
Pork Butt Roast, Boston-Style Butt

This flavorful cut, which is often used for pulled pork, has enough fat to stay moist and succulent during long, slow cooking. It is often sold boneless and wrapped in netting, as pictured here.

SHOULDER ARM PICNIC

Primal Cut: Shoulder
Flavor: ★ ★ ★ ★
Cost: $
Alternate Names:
Picnic Shoulder,
Fresh Picnic, Picnic Roast

This affordable cut contains its fair share of fat and rind, but the meat has potent pork flavor and becomes meltingly tender with cooking. Picnic roasts are sometimes sold skinless and boneless.

BLADE ROAST

Primal Cut: Loin
Flavor: ★ ★ ★
Cost: $ $
Alternate Names:
Pork 7-Rib Roast, Pork 5-Rib Roast,
Pork Loin Rib End, Rib-End Roast

The part of the loin closest to the shoulder, the bone-in blade roast can be chewy. It can also be difficult to carve because of its many separate muscles and fatty pockets. Also sold boneless (see below).

BONELESS BLADE ROAST

Primal Cut: Loin
Flavor: ★ ★ ★
Cost: $ $
Alternate Names:
Blade Roast,
Blade Loin Roast

With the bones removed, this roast is very easy to carve and we find that it has the best flavor of any boneless roast from the loin.

CENTER RIB ROAST

Primal Cut: Loin
Flavor: ★ ★ ★
Cost: $ $ $
Alternate Names: Rack of Pork,
Pork Loin Rib Half, Center-Cut Roast

Often referred to as the pork equivalent of prime rib or rack of lamb, this mild, fairly lean roast consists of a single muscle with a protective fat cap. It may be cut with anywhere from 5 to 8 ribs. It is similar to the center loin roast but slightly juicier and more flavorful.

CENTER LOIN ROAST

Primal Cut: Loin
Flavor: ★ ★ ★
Cost: $ $ $
Alternate Names: Center Cut
Loin Roast, Center Cut Pork Roast

This popular roast is juicy, tender, and evenly shaped, with somewhat less fat than the center rib roast. This roast is sometimes sold with the tenderloin attached (the round muscle on the left in this picture).

SIRLOIN ROAST

Primal Cut: Loin
Flavor: no stars
Cost: $ $ $
Alternate Name:
None

This sinuous cut with a good amount of connective tissue is difficult to cook evenly and to carve.

CROWN ROAST OF PORK

Primal Cut: Loin
Flavor: ★ ★
Cost: $ $ $
Alternate Name:
Crown Rib Roast

Butchers tie two bone-in center rib or center loin roasts together to create this impressive-looking roast. We find that a crown roast with 16 to 20 ribs is the best choice, as smaller and larger roasts are harder to cook evenly. Because of its shape and size, this roast is prone to overcooking. To minimize this risk, we recommend that you skip the customary stuffing in the middle.

TENDERLOIN

Primal Cut: Loin
Flavor: ★ ★
Cost: $ $ $
Alternate Name: None

Lean, delicate, boneless tenderloin has little marbling, cooks very quickly, and can dry out faster than fattier cuts.

BABY BACK RIBS

Primal Cut: Loin
Flavor: ★ ★ ★ ★
Cost: $ $ $ $
Alternate Names: Loin Back Ribs, Riblets

These ribs, cut with 11 to 13 bones, come from the upper end of the rib cage closest to the backbone. They are lean, tender, and smaller than other ribs. Choose meatier racks, preferably those weighing more than 1¾ pounds.

COUNTRY-STYLE RIBS

Primal Cut: Loin
Flavor: ★ ★ ★ ★
Cost: $ $ $
Alternate Name: Country Ribs

These meaty, tender ribs are cut from the upper side of the rib cage from the fatty blade end of the loin. Butchers usually cut them into individual ribs and package several together.

BLADE CHOPS

Primal Cut: Loin
Flavor: ★ ★ ★
Cost: $ $ $
Alternate Name: Pork Chop End Cuts

Cut from the shoulder end of the loin, these chops can be difficult to find at the market. They are fatty and tough, despite good flavor and juiciness. We do not recommend them.

RIB CHOPS

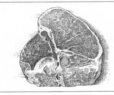

Primal Cut: Loin
Flavor: ★ ★ ★ ★
Cost: $ $ $
Alternate Names:
Rib Cut Chops, Pork Chops End Cut

Our favorite chops are cut from the rib section of the loin. They have a relatively high fat content, rendering them flavorful and unlikely to dry out during cooking. Rib chops can be distinguished by the section of rib bone running along one side.

CENTER-CUT CHOPS

Primal Cut: Loin
Flavor: ★ ★ ★
Cost: $ $ $ $
Alternate Names:
Top Loin Chops, Loin Chops

Identify these chops by the bone that divides the loin meat from the tenderloin muscle, as in a T-bone steak. The lean tenderloin section cooks more quickly than the loin section, making these chops a challenge to cook. They are sometimes available boneless and may then be referred to as America's cut.

MODERN VERSUS OLD-FASHIONED PORK

A few farmers are raising fattier pigs, yielding chops and roasts that are similar to the pork enjoyed by our grandparents. We wondered how this pork would taste to modern cooks raised on leaner modern pork. To find out, we purchased center-cut pork chops from New York farmers who raise heritage breeds the old-fashioned way (the animals are free roaming and are fed wholesome, natural diets) and tasted them alongside supermarket chops.

Tasters had an interesting response to the farm-raised pork, noting that while it was juicy, with significantly more fat than the supermarket chops, it also had unusual "mineral" and "iron" flavors. Some tasters also found that the extra fat in the old-fashioned pork left behind an unpleasant coating in their mouths. Surprisingly, most tasters favored the more familiar supermarket meat. A few tasters thought that the old-fashioned pork was delicious but definitely an acquired taste.

We wondered just how fatty this old-fashioned pork was and so sent a sample pork butt to a food laboratory to be ground and analyzed for fat content. For comparison, we also sent a supermarket sample of the same cut. As we expected, the old-fashioned pork butt had significantly more fat—50 percent more—than the supermarket butt. Old-fashioned pork chops had 210 percent more fat than the supermarket samples, but this sky-high fat level was probably due to differences in the way the two kinds of pork were trimmed; supermarkets tend to remove most external fat, pork farmers who raise heritage breeds do not.

So is it worth the effort and money to search for a local or mail-order source for old-fashioned pork? The answer may have something to do with your age. If you were raised on old-fashioned pork, you will appreciate its flavor and extra fat. If your palate is accustomed to leaner pork, you are better off shopping at the supermarket.

SIRLOIN CHOPS
Primal Cut: Loin
Flavor: no stars
Cost: $ $ $
Alternate Name: Sirloin Steaks

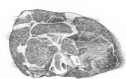

These chops, cut from the sirloin, or hip, end of the pig, are tough, dry, and tasteless. The chops contain tenderloin and loin meat, plus a slice of hipbone. We do not recommend this cut.

SPARERIBS
Primal Cut: Belly
Flavor: ★ ★ ★
Cost: $ $ $
Alternate Name: St. Louis–Style Ribs

These fatty, succulent ribs are cut from the underbelly, or lower rib cage, of the pig. A full rack contains 13 ribs and weighs about 3 pounds. St. Louis–style ribs are prepared by removing the brisket (shown on the left side of this illustration) so that the rack is more rectangular in shape.

FRESH HAM, SHANK HALF
Primal Cut: Leg
Flavor: ★ ★ ★
Cost: $ $
Alternate Name:
Shank End Fresh Ham

Fresh ham is not cured, it is simply fresh meat from the leg of the pig. We prefer the shank end (with one tapered end) over the rounded sirloin (butt) end because it is easier to carve.

FRESH HAM, SIRLOIN HALF
Primal Cut: Leg
Flavor: ★ ★ ★
Cost: $ $
Alternate Names:
Sirloin End Fresh Ham,
Butt Half Fresh Ham, Rump Half Fresh Ham

Because of its bone structure, the rounded sirloin is more difficult to carve than the shank end and is our second choice. Its flavor, however, is quite good.

SPIRAL-CUT BONE-IN HALF HAM
Primal Cut: Leg
Flavor: ★ ★ ★ ★
Cost: $
Alternate Name:
Spiral-Sliced Ham

Our favorite wet-cured ham because the ham is not pumped up with water (the label should read "ham with natural juices") and because the ham is so easy to carve. Make sure to buy a bone-in ham; it will taste better than a boneless ham. Although packages are not labeled as such, look for a ham from the shank rather than from the sirloin end. You can pick out the shank ham by its tapered, more pointed end opposite the flat cut side of the ham. The sirloin ham has more rounded or blunt ends.

COUNTRY HAM
Primal Cut: Leg
Flavor: ★ ★ ★
Cost: $ $ $
Alternate Name: None

This Southern favorite starts with the whole leg and is dry-cured like prosciutto or serrano ham. This ham has a complex, meaty, and nutty flavor. The meat is very salty and dry (even after soaking). Serve it in small pieces with biscuits or use in recipes with greens, rice, or pasta.

OTHER PORK PRODUCTS

Given the number of bacon and pork fat products available at the market, shopping can be confusing. Here are some descriptions of your main choices.

Bacon is cut from the belly of the pig, then cured with salt and sugar before smoking. It is sold in slices (thick-cut or regular) or in slabs, usually with the rind still attached.

Canadian bacon comes from the loin, not the belly, and is therefore much leaner than bacon. The meat is cured and smoked.

Fatback is unsalted, unsmoked fat from the back, not the belly, of the pig. (Salt-cured fatback is sometimes available.) Years ago, the fresh fat was commonly used to lard meat—that is, to run strips of fat through lean cuts before roasting. Today, cooks use fatback mostly to

flavor smothered greens or beans.

Lard is rendered and clarified pork fat. It is used for frying and making rich biscuits and pie crusts.

Pancetta, or Italian bacon, like regular bacon, comes from the belly of the pig. Unlike regular bacon, it is not smoked, and its cure does not contain sugar—just salt, pepper, and cloves, resulting in a subtler flavor. Pancetta is rolled into a log shape, which may then be sliced thin or thick.

Salt pork is unsmoked pork belly fat (usually with some streaks of lean). The fat is cured in salt, hence its name. Salt pork makes frequent appearances in the foods of New England (chowders and baked beans) and the South (black-eyed peas).

How to Buy Lamb

LIKE BEEF, LAMB HAS A RICH RED COLOR, BUT THE MEAT IS GENERALLY STRONGER tasting. This is because the muscle itself is quite tasty and because lamb fat has a particularly strong flavor. After cooking dozens of lamb chops and roasts, we've rated selected popular cuts for flavor (★ ★ ★ ★ being the best) and cost ($$$$ being the most expensive).

Most lamb sold in the supermarket has been slaughtered when 6 to 12 months old. (When the animal is slaughtered past the first year, the meat must be labeled mutton.) Generally, younger lamb has a milder flavor that most people prefer. The only indication of slaughter age at the supermarket is size. A whole leg of lamb weighing nine pounds is likely to have come from an older animal than a whole leg weighing just six pounds. Lamb is initially divided into five primal (or major) cuts.

SHOULDER This area extends from the neck through the fourth rib. Meat from this area is flavorful, although it contains a fair amount of connective tissue and can be tough. Chops, roasts, and boneless stew meat all come from the shoulder.

RIB The rib area is directly behind the shoulder and extends from the fifth to the twelfth rib. The rack (all eight ribs from this section) is cut from the rib. When cut into individual chops, the meat is called rib chops. Meat from this area has a fine, tender grain and a mild flavor.

LOIN The loin extends from the last rib down to the hip area. The loin chop is the most familiar cut from this part of the lamb. Like the rib chop, it is tender and has a mild, sweet flavor.

LEG The leg area runs from the hip down to the hoof. It may be sold whole or broken into smaller roasts and shanks (one comes from each hind leg).

These roasts may be sold with the bones in, or they may be butterflied and sold boneless.

FORESHANK/BREAST The final primal cut is from the underside of the animal and is called the foreshank and breast. This area includes the two front legs (each yields a shank) as well as the breast, which is rarely sold in supermarkets.

THE FIVE PRIMAL CUTS OF LAMB

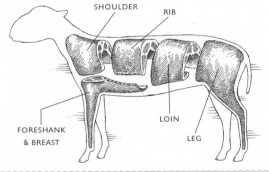

INGREDIENTS: LAMB

Lamb is a hard sell in the United States. According to the American Meat Institute, we eat less than 1 ½ pounds of lamb per person each year. Lamb gets a much more favorable reception abroad. And we wondered why. Is imported grass-fed lamb that much more tender and less "lamby" than domestic grain-fed lamb?

To find out, we held a blind taste test of imported lamb legs from New Zealand, Australia, and Iceland, along with domestic lamb. Our tasters included both lamb enthusiasts and the lamb-averse.

Tasters didn't find any of the roasts "gamey" or overly tough, and they found all of them to be juicy. The Australian lamb had the strongest lamb flavor. The meat was chewy and dark, indicating older lamb, a trait not offensive to the lamb lovers in our group. The New Zealand lamb had a bold lamb flavor, but some tasters disliked the texture, finding it "stringy" and "more like ham." The domestic lamb was milder in taste; many thought it more reminiscent of roast beef than lamb. Tasters thought that the domestic lamb's texture was a bit chewy, but not unpleasantly so. The lamb from Iceland was the smallest lamb by far. It also had the most delicate flavor—too delicate for those tasters who enjoyed a stronger lamb flavor (one referred to the Icelandic lamb as "lamb lite"). All found the texture of the Icelandic lamb to be the most tender by far. As one taster noted, it "cut like butter."

BLADE CHOPS
Primal Cut: Shoulder
Flavor: ★ ★ ★
Cost: $ $
Alternate Name:
Shoulder Chops

These roughly rectangular chops are cut from the shoulder area and contain a piece of the chine bone (the backbone of the animal) and a thin piece of the blade bone (the shoulder blade of the animal). Their texture is chewy but not tough and their flavor is gutsy. These are slightly fattier than round-bone chops and better for grilling than braising, although they can be braised if trimmed scrupulously.

ROUND-BONE CHOPS
Primal Cut: Shoulder
Flavor: ★ ★ ★
Cost: $ $
Alternate Name:
Arm Chops

These oval chops are cut from the shoulder area and are leaner than blade chops. Each chop contains a cross-section of the arm bone so that the chop looks a bit like a small ham steak. In addition to the arm bone, there's also a tiny line of riblets on the side of each chop. These chops have bold lamb flavor and aren't tough, despite some chewiness. Because these cuts are less fatty than blade chops, they can be braised as well as grilled.

RIB CHOPS
Primal Cut: Rib
Flavor: ★ ★ ★ ★
Cost: $ $ $ $
Alternate Names:
Rack Chops, French Chops

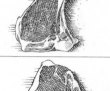

This chop has the most refined flavor and tender texture. The meat is mild and sweet. For best results, don't cook these lean chops past medium-rare. This chop is easily recognized by the bone that runs along one side. Rib chops often contain a lot of fat on the bone. Ask your butcher to "french" the chops by scraping away the fat from the end of the bone.

LOIN CHOPS
Primal Cut: Loin
Flavor: ★ ★ ★ ★
Cost: $ $ $ $
Alternate Name:
None

Like a T-bone steak, this chop has meat on either side of the bone running down the center. The small piece on the right side of the bone on this chop is very tender and fine-grained (it is akin to the tenderloin on a cow or pig). The larger piece of meat on the other side of the bone is chewier. Loin chops have a bit stronger flavor than rib chops and they are slightly firmer, although not chewy.

RACK OF LAMB
Primal Cut: Rib
Flavor: ★ ★ ★ ★
Cost: $ $ $ $
Alternate Names:
Rack Roast, Rib Roast

The equivalent to prime rib on a cow, this cut is extremely flavorful and tender. It's also very expensive. This roast usually contains either eight or nine rib bones, depending on how the meat has been butchered.

LEG OF LAMB
Primal Cut: Leg
Flavor: ★ ★ ★
Cost: $ $
Alternate Names:
Whole Leg, Sirloin-On Leg

The whole leg generally weighs 6 to 10 pounds (although smaller legs are available from younger lambs) and includes both the wider sirloin end and the narrower shank end. Make sure the butcher has removed the hipbone and aitchbone or carving will be very difficult.

LEG OF LAMB, SIRLOIN HALF
Primal Cut: Leg
Flavor: ★ ★ ★
Cost: $ $
Alternate Names:
Leg of Lamb, Butt Half

The top half of the leg is a bit more tender than the bottom half and is our preferred cut when a whole leg is too much meat.

LEG OF LAMB, SHANK HALF
Primal Cut: Leg
Flavor: ★ ★ ★
Cost: $ $
Alternate Name:
None

We generally prefer the sirloin half to this narrower half from the bottom of the leg. The one exception is when making kebabs. The smaller shank half yields less meat, just enough to serve six when the meat has been boned and trimmed for shish kebab.

HOW TO BUY VEAL

VEAL IS A COW IN MINIATURE. THE PRIMAL CUTS ARE THE SAME AS ON A COW, with the exception that the underside of the animal is grouped into one primal cut rather than three and the back half of the animal (the sirloin and leg) are combined into one primal cut. Veal cuts are generally more tender than their beef counterparts and have a milder (some might say, blander) flavor. Based on our kitchen tests, we've rated selected popular cuts for flavor (★★★ being the best) and cost ($$$$ being the most expensive).

SHOULDER This area includes the front of the animal and runs from the neck through the fifth rib. Cuts from the shoulder are moderately tough and better suited to stewing than grilling. Many markets sell cutlets cut from the shoulder but they will buckle in the pan and are not recommended.

RIB Our favorite chops come from this prime area of the calf, which includes ribs 6 through 12 along the top half of the animal. Expensive rib chops are ideal candidates for grilling.

LOIN Further back from the rib, the loin section runs along the top half of the animal and extends from the thirteenth rib back to the hipbone. Meat from this area is tender and lean. It is also very expensive and best suited to grilling.

LEG The section includes both the sirloin (the hip) and the actual leg. Cuts from this section often contain multiple muscles and connective tissue. Veal cutlets, known as scaloppine, come from this portion of the animal.

FORESHANK AND BREAST The underside of the animal yields various cuts, most of which require prolonged cooking to make tender. Veal shanks, also known as osso buco, come from this area, which is also home to the breast roast.

THE FIVE PRIMAL CUTS OF VEAL

MILK-FED VERSUS NATURAL VEAL

Many people are opposed to milk-fed veal because the calves are confined to small stalls before being butchered. "Natural" is the term used to inform the consumer that the calves are allowed to move freely, without the confines of the stalls. Natural veal is also generally raised on grass (the calves can forage) and without hormones or antibiotics.

Moral issues aside, the differences in how the calves are raised create differences in the texture and flavor of the veal. Natural veal is darker, meatier, and more like beef. Milk-fed is paler in color, more tender, and milder in flavor. When we grilled both types of veal chops in the test kitchen, each had its supporters.

Several tasters preferred the meatier, more intense flavor of the natural veal. They thought the milk-fed veal seemed bland in comparison. Other tasters preferred the softer texture and milder flavor of the milk-fed veal. They felt that the natural veal tasted like "wimpy" beef and that the milk-fed chops had the mild, sweet flavor they expected from veal.

Both natural and milk-fed veal chops grill well, so the choice is really a personal one. Milk-fed veal is sold in most grocery stores, while natural veal is available at butcher shops, specialty markets, and natural foods markets. When shopping, read labels and check the color of the meat. If the meat is red (rather than pale pink), it most likely came from an animal raised on grass rather than milk.

SHOULDER ROAST

Primal Cut: Shoulder
Flavor: ★★
Cost: $ $ $
Alternate Name:
Rolled Veal Roast

This boneless roast is usually sold in netting at the market. It is our favorite choice for stews since the roast is meaty and does not contain too much gristle or fat.

SHOULDER CHOPS

Primal Cut: Shoulder
Flavor: ★★
Cost: $ $
Alternate Names:
Round Bone Chops,
Shoulder Arm Chops

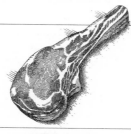

These tough, sinewy chops are not suitable for grilling (our preferred method for cooking chops). Although their texture improves when braised, their flavor does not.

RIB CHOPS

Primal Cut: Rib
Flavor: ★★★★
Cost: $ $ $ $
Alternate Name:
None

Our favorite chops because they are especially juicy and flavorful. To identify this chop, look for the bone running down the edge of the chop, with all the meat on one side.

LOIN CHOPS

Primal Cut: Loin
Flavor: ★★★
Cost: $ $ $ $
Alternate Name:
None

A good choice but a tad leaner and less flavorful than rib chops. Looks like a small T-bone steak with the bone running down the center and meat on either side.

TOP ROUND ROAST

Primal Cut: Leg
Flavor: ★★
Cost: $ $ $
Alternate Name:
Leg Round Roast

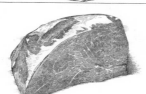

This lean, tender roast is the source for true scaloppine. Good butchers will hand-slice scaloppine from this cut but most supermarkets will not. Unless you trust your butcher, buy this boneless roast and trim cutlets yourself.

VEAL BREAST ROAST

Primal Cut: Foreshank and Breast
Flavor: ★★
Cost: $ $ $
Alternate Name:
None

The boneless roast is usually sold tied at the market. It is lean and works well in a boiled dinner, especially bollito misto.

VEAL SHANKS

Primal Cut: Foreshank and Breast
Flavor: ★★★
Cost: $ $ $
Alternate Name:
Osso Buco

Cut crosswise from the front legs, the shanks contain both meat and bone. Depending on the butcher, shanks can vary in thickness and diameter, so shop carefully. Although sometimes sold boneless, you want shanks with the marrow-packed bone, which adds flavor to the braising medium.

How to Buy Beef

BEFORE YOU CHOOSE A PARTICULAR STEAK OR ROAST, IT HELPS TO UNDERSTAND something about the anatomy of a cow. Eight different cuts of beef are sold at the wholesale level (see the illustration below). From this first series of cuts, known in the trade as primal cuts, a butcher (usually at a meat-packing plant in the Midwest but sometimes on-site at your local market) will make the retail cuts that you bring home from the market. How you choose to cook a particular piece of beef depends on where the meat comes from on the cow and how it was butchered.

CHUCK/SHOULDER Starting at the front of the animal, the chuck (or shoulder) runs from the neck down to the fifth rib. Three are four major muscles in this region, and meat from the chuck tends to be flavorful and fairly fatty, which is why ground chuck makes the best hamburgers. Chuck also contains a fair amount of connective tissue, so when the meat is not ground it generally requires a long cooking time to become tender.

RIB Moving back from the chuck, the next primal cut along the top half of the animal is the rib section, which extends from the sixth to the twelfth rib. The prime rib comes from this area, as do rib-eye steaks. Rib cuts have excellent beefy flavor and are quite tender.

SHORT LOIN The short loin (also called the loin) extends from the last rib back through the midsection of the animal to the hip area. It contains two major muscles—the tenderloin and the shell. The tenderloin is extremely tender (it is positioned right under the spine) and has a quite mild flavor. This muscle may be sold whole as a roast or sliced crosswise into steaks, called filet mignon. The shell is a much larger muscle and has a more robust beef flavor as well as more fat. Strip steaks (also called shell steaks) come from this muscle and are our favorite. Two steaks from the short loin area contain portions of both the tenderloin and shell muscles. These steaks are called the T-bone and porterhouse, and both are excellent choices.

SIRLOIN The next area is the sirloin, which contains relatively inexpensive cuts that are sold both as steaks and roasts. We find that sirloin cuts are fairly lean and tough. In general, we prefer other parts of the animal, although top sirloin makes a decent roast.

ROUND The back of the cow is called the round. Roasts and steaks cut from this area are usually sold boneless and are quite lean and can be tough. Again, we generally prefer cuts from other parts of the cow, although top round can be roasted with some success.

BRISKET/SHANK, PLATE, AND FLANK The underside of the animal is divided into the brisket/shank (near the front of the animal), the plate, and the flank. Thick boneless cuts are removed from these three parts of the cow. The brisket is rather tough and contains a lot of connective tissue. The plate is rarely sold at the retail level (it is used to make pastrami). The flank is a leaner cut that makes an excellent steak when grilled.

THE EIGHT PRIMAL CUTS OF BEEF

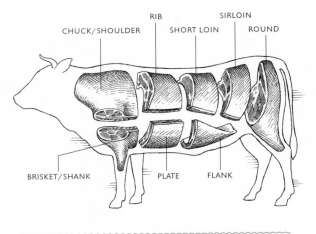

CHUCK/SHOULDER · RIB · SHORT LOIN · SIRLOIN · ROUND · BRISKET/SHANK · PLATE · FLANK

HOW TO BUY BEEF STEAKS

STEAKS GENERALLY COME FROM MANY places on the cow, although most come from the tender midsections (see the illustration on page 12). In addition to the cuts listed on the following pages, you will see many steaks cut from the round and sold as "London broil." These lean steaks are very dry and chewy and are not recommended.

For all cuts of steak, look for meat that has a bright, lively color. Beef normally ranges in color from pink to red, but dark meat probably indicates an older, tougher animal. The external fat as well as the fat that runs through the meat (called intramuscular fat) should be as white as possible. As a general rule, the more intramuscular fat (marbling), the more flavorful and juicy the steak will be. But the marbling should be smooth and fine,

running all through the meat, rather than showing up in clumps; smooth marbling melts into the meat during cooking, while knots remain as fat pockets. Stay away from packaged steaks that show a lot of red juice (known as purge). The purge may indicate a bad job of freezing; as a result, the steak will be dry and cottony.

Steaks sport different names depending on locale. We've used industry names that we feel best describe where the steaks lie on the animal; you'll find some other common names also listed. We've rated steaks for tenderness and flavor (★ ★ ★ ★ being the best) and cost ($$$$ being the most expensive). Note that tenderness is an issue with steaks because they are best cooked quickly and there is not time to transform a tough cut into something more palatable.

DOES BRANDING MATTER?

To guarantee quality, more and more people are looking beyond the confines of their local supermarket butcher case and buying their steaks through mail-order sources. These outlets promise all-star beef with a price tag to match. But do the mail-order steaks really outshine the ones you can get around the corner? And is there something you can buy locally that's better than your average supermarket steak?

We gathered seven widely available mail-order strip steaks and two from local supermarkets (Coleman Natural—hormone- and antibiotic-free—from our local Whole Foods Market and choice steak from the regular market). Our candidates included Niman Ranch, a high-end, all-natural, restaurant favorite; Peter Luger, a New York steakhouse that many consider to be the best in the country; Omaha, probably the most well-known mail-order steak company, with two steaks in the running (their "private reserve" as well as their standard); Allen Brothers, a Chicago-based company that supplies many of this country's steakhouses; and Lobel's, a New York butcher shop. In addition to Lobel's boneless strip steak we included Lobel's Wagyu, or Kobe-style, steak from Oakleigh Ranch in Australia. Kobe beef comes from Wagyu cattle raised to certain specifications in Kobe, Japan. Considered the foie gras of beef, the meat is extremely well marbled, tender, and rich. Wagyu is the more generic name for the same type of beef, but not from Japan. Although few of us could afford the hefty $68/pound price tag for Wagyu beef, we wanted to see if it was really worth that much.

Well, it was. After pan-searing three dozen steaks (four of each

type for perhaps the largest tasting turnout in the test kitchen), we found that money can buy you happiness, if happiness for you is the best steak you ever ate.

"Wow," wrote one happy taster of our first-place Wagyu steak. "This is unlike any strip that I've had." Others deemed the Wagyu steak "tender like a filet" and "very rich and meaty." But the overwhelming richness—which one taster likened to "foie gras–infused beef"—was not everyone's cup of tea. A minority of tasters agreed with the one who wrote, "This doesn't taste like beef at all."

Three steaks shared the spot for second place: Niman Ranch ($22 per pound), praised for its "good flavor" and "nice texture"; Coleman Natural, deemed "very robust"; and Peter Luger, described as having "strong beef flavor" and "great juiciness."

Unfortunately, the brand most people turn to when ordering steak through the mail took the last two spots in our tasting. The Omaha strip steak had "off flavors" and was "grainy tasting," while the Omaha Private Reserve (at almost twice the price) finished last, with tasters finding it "a little chewy" and "very dry."

The good news is that you don't have to spend a small fortune (or pay for shipping) to get a great steak. Coleman Natural steak, available at all-natural supermarkets, tied for second place and was a comparative bargain at $14 per pound (just $4 more than the low-ranked Stop & Shop beef). If you want to sample true steak greatness, however, you may want to splurge on the Wagyu beef—at least once.

SHOULDER STEAK
Primal Cut: Chuck/Shoulder
Tenderness: ★★
Flavor: ★★
Cost: $
Alternate Names: Chuck Steak, London Broil

Often labeled London broil, steaks from the shoulder of the cow are bone-less and consist of a single muscle. Buy a shoulder steak that is 1½ pounds to 2 pounds and slice it thin on the bias after cooking. We find that shoulder steaks offer the best value for cost-conscious shoppers.

TOP BLADE STEAK
Primal Cut: Chuck/Shoulder
Tenderness: ★★★
Flavor: ★★★
Cost: $
Alternate Names: Flat-iron Steak, Blade Steak

These small steaks are cut from the shoulder area of the cow. Top blade steaks are tender, but each has a line of gristle running down the center, which can be cut out when turning these steaks into kebabs.

RIB STEAK
Primal Cut: Rib
Tenderness: ★★★
Flavor: ★★★
Cost: $ $ $
Alternate Name: None

Imagine a prime rib roast at a hotel buffet or banquet. A rib steak is a steak cut from that rib roast, with the curved rib bone attached. Rib steaks are less prevalent than the boneless version, the rib eye.

RIB-EYE STEAK
Primal Cut: Rib
Tenderness: ★★★
Flavor: ★★★
Cost: $ $ $
Alternate Names:
Spencer Steak, Delmonico Steak

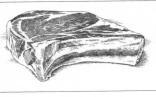

A rib-eye steak is a rib steak with the bone removed. The steak has an oval shape with a narrow strip of meat that curves around one end. Rib-eye steaks, like other steaks from the rib section, contain large pockets of fat and have a rich, smooth texture. Rib eye is often known as Spencer steak in the West and Delmonico steak in New York.

TOP LOIN STEAK
Primal Cut: Short Loin
Tenderness: ★★★
Flavor: ★★★
Cost: $ $ $
Alternate Names: Strip Steak, Shell Steak, Sirloin Strip Steak

This long, narrow, triangular steak may be sold bone-in or boneless. It is most commonly sold as "strip steak." Boneless top loin is also known as hotel steak, Kansas City strip, and New York strip. The top loin steak is a bit chewy, with a noticeable grain, and is slightly less fatty than the rib or rib-eye steak.

TENDERLOIN STEAK
Primal Cut: Short Loin
Tenderness: ★★★★
Flavor: ★
Cost: $ $ $ $
Alternate Names:
Filet Mignon,
Châteaubriand, Tournedo

The tenderloin, a long, cylindrical muscle that is the most tender meat on the cow, may be cut into a number of different steaks, each of which has its own name but all of which are very expensive, since Americans prize tenderness above all else in their steaks. Châteaubriand is a 3-inch-thick steak cut from the thickest part of the tenderloin, usually large enough to serve two. Filet, filet mignon, or tenderloin steak is typically 1 to 2 inches thick, cut from the narrow end of the tenderloin. Tournedos are the smallest tenderloin steaks, about an inch thick, cut toward the tip end. Tenderloin steaks are extremely tender but are not known for having much beefy flavor.

T-BONE STEAK
Primal Cut: Short Loin
Tenderness: ★★★
Flavor: ★★★
Cost: $ $ $
Alternate Name: None

The T-shaped bone in this steak separates the long, narrow strip of top loin and a small piece of tenderloin (on the right side of the bone in this drawing). Since it contains top loin and tenderloin meat, the T-bone is well balanced for texture and flavor.

PORTERHOUSE STEAK
Primal Cut: Short Loin
Tenderness: ★★★
Flavor: ★★★
Cost: $ $ $
Alternate Name: None

The porterhouse is really just a huge T-bone steak with a larger tenderloin section. It is cut farther back in the animal than the T-bone steak. Like the T-bone, the porterhouse, with both top loin and tenderloin sections, has well-balanced flavor and texture.

ROUND-BONE

Primal Cut: Sirloin
Tenderness: ★★
Flavor: ★★
Cost: $
Alternate Names:
New York Sirloin Steak,
Shell Sirloin Steak

Several steaks are cut from the sirloin, or hip, section; moving from the front to the rear of the steer, they are pin- or hip-bone steak, flat-bone steak, round-bone steak, and wedge-bone steak. Of these, the round bone is best; the others are rarely found in supermarkets. Shell sirloin steak is simply a round-bone sirloin steak that has had the small piece of tenderloin removed. It is most commonly found in the Northeast and is sometimes called New York sirloin. Do not confuse sirloin steaks with the superior top loin steak, which is sometimes called sirloin strip steak or New York strip steak.

TOP SIRLOIN STEAK

Primal Cut: Sirloin
Tenderness: ★★
Flavor: ★★
Cost: $
Alternate Name:
Sirloin Butt Steak

This steak is merely a boneless round-bone steak. It is sometimes sold as boneless sirloin butt steak or top sirloin butt center-cut steak. Again, do not confuse this steak with top loin steak, which is sometimes called sirloin strip steak.

FLAP MEAT SIRLOIN STEAK TIP

Primal Cut: Sirloin
Tenderness: ★★
Flavor: ★★★
Cost: $ $
Alternate Names:
Sirloin Tips,
Flap Meat, Steak Tips

This thin rectangular steak weighs about 2½ pounds and is often sold in strips or cubes. To ensure that you are buying the real thing, buy the whole steak. The meat has a distinctive longitudinal grain and a rich, deep beefy flavor. This meat can range in thickness from ½ to 1½ inches. A relatively even steak will be easier to cook than a steak with both thin and thick portions. When serving, slice the meat thinly across the grain or the meat will be tough.

CUBE STEAK

Primal Cut: Round
Tenderness: ★
Flavor: ★
Cost: $
Alternate Name:
Minute Steak

This "bumpy" steak, which usually comes from the round, is very inexpensive and chewy. The meat is partially cut (or cubed) twice, with the cuts made at right angles. We would never recommend searing this steak, but breaded and pan-fried to make chicken-fried steak, it can be quite good.

SKIRT STEAK

Primal Cut: Plate
Tenderness: ★★
Flavor: ★★★
Cost: $ $ $
Alternate Names:
Fajita Steak, Philadelphia Steak

This thin steak from the underside of the animal has an especially beefy flavor. It was the original choice for fajitas, although most cooks now use easier-to-find flank steak. Although it can be cooked like flank steak, skirt steak is fattier and juicier. Look for it at better markets and butcher shops.

FLANK STEAK

Primal Cut: Flank
Tenderness: ★★
Flavor: ★★★
Cost: $ $ $
Alternate Name:
Jiffy Steak

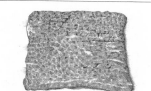

Flank steak is a large, thin, flat cut with a distinct longitudinal grain. To minimize the stringy, chewy nature of flank steak, it should not be cooked past medium and should always be sliced thinly across the grain. It is usually sold whole and weighs roughly two pounds, although some grocery stores package flank steaks cut into smaller portions.

HANGAR STEAK

Primal Cut: Flank
Tenderness: ★
Flavor: ★★
Cost: $ $ $
Alternate Names:
Hanging Tenderloin,
Butcher's Steak, Hanging Tender

This bistro favorite is actually a thick muscle attached to the diaphragm on the underside of the cow. When a cow is butchered, this steak hangs down into the center of the carcass, thus its name. Hangar steak is much tougher than flank steak and not nearly as flavorful. Don't go out of your way to find this hard-to-come-by steak.

HOW TO BUY BEEF ROASTS

ROASTS GENERALLY COME FROM SIX primal cuts (see the illustration on page 12). After identifying the roasts most commonly found in supermarkets, we cooked each in the test kitchen several times to evaluate them on a range of qualities. Given that even the toughest cut can make a great roast if cooked properly, we've focused on flavor (★★★ being the best) and cost ($$$$ being the most expensive) in our ratings.

TOP BLADE ROAST
Primal Cut: Chuck/Shoulder
Flavor: ★★★
Cost: $ $
Alternate Names:
Chuck Roast First Cut, Blade Roast, Top Chuck Roast

This broad, flat cut was far and away the best chuck roast we tasted—flavorful, juicy, and tender. Its connective tissue is unattractive but not unpleasant to eat.

CHUCK 7-BONE ROAST
Primal Cut: Chuck/Shoulder
Flavor: ★★★
Cost: $ $
Alternate Names:
Center-Cut Pot Roast,
Chuck Roast Center Cut

A bone shaped like the number seven gives this cut its name. We enjoyed the deep flavor of this thin cut, which needed less liquid and less time to cook than other cuts from the chuck.

CHUCK-EYE ROAST
Primal Cut: Chuck/Shoulder
Flavor: ★★★
Cost: $ $
Alternate Names:
Boneless Chuck Roll, Boneless Chuck Fillet

This boneless roast is cut from the center of the first five ribs (the term *eye* refers to any center-cut piece of meat). It is very tender and juicy but was criticized for its excessive fat content.

UNDER BLADE ROAST
Primal Cut: Chuck/Shoulder
Flavor: ★★★
Cost: $ $
Alternate Names:
Bottom Chuck Roast, California Roast

We found this roast's flavor to be quite similar to the 7-bone roast, but it had a bit more connective tissue. It also had a fair amount of fat, which enhanced the flavor but made the meat fall apart when carved.

CHUCK SHOULDER ROAST
Primal Cut: Chuck/Shoulder
Flavor: ★★
Cost: $ $
Alternate Names:
Chuck Shoulder Pot Roast,
Chuck Roast Boneless

Our tasters thought this roast had an unpleasantly chewy, almost bouncy texture and relatively mild flavor.

RIB ROAST, FIRST CUT
Primal Cut: Rib
Flavor: ★★★★
Cost: $ $ $ $
Alternate Names:
Prime Rib,
Loin End, Small End

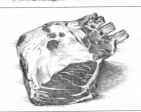

This cut consists of ribs 9 through 12, toward the back of the rib section, closer to the loin of the animal. It contains the large rib-eye muscle and was judged to be extremely tender and flavorful. The clearest way to indicate what you want when you order a rib roast is to ask for "the first four ribs from the loin end."

RIB ROAST, SECOND CUT
Prima Cut: Rib
Flavor: ★★★★
Cost: $ $ $ $
Alternate Name: Large End

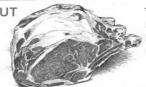

The large end of the rib roast is cut from ribs 6 though 9. Though it is still an excellent roast, we thought this cut was fattier, a little less tender, and slightly more irregularly formed than the first cut rib roast.

TENDERLOIN
Primal Cut: Short Loin
Flavor: ★
Cost: $ $ $ $
Alternate Name:
Whole Filet

The tenderloin is the most tender piece of beef you can buy. Our tasters found its flavor to be pleasantly mild, almost nonbeefy. Unpeeled tenderloins, which come with an incredibly thick layer of exterior fat still attached, also come with a tremendous amount of waste (the fat should be removed) and cost more (in both time and money) than peeled roasts, which have scattered patches of fat that need not be removed.

TOP SIRLOIN ROAST
Primal Cut: Sirloin
Flavor: ★★★★
Cost: $ $
Alternate Names:
Top Butt, Center-Cut Roast

This cut has big beefy flavor. Aside from the vein of gristle that runs through it, which we found slightly unpleasant to eat, the roast was tender and juicy.

SIRLOIN TRI-TIP ROAST
Primal Cut: Sirloin
Flavor: ★★
Cost: $ $
Alternate Name:
Triangle Roast

This cut is popular out West, but butchers on the East Coast usually cut it up into sirloin tips or "steak tips." This small, triangular roast is moist but has a strange, spongy texture and mild flavor.

TOP ROUND ROAST
Primal Cut: Round
Flavor: ★★★
Cost: $
Alternate Names:
Top Round First Cut,
Top Round Steak Roast

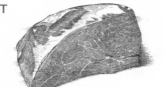

This affordable roast is the most common choice in supermarkets. Our tasters liked it, commenting that it was very similar to the top sirloin roast, with good flavor, texture, and juiciness. We like the top round roast sliced thin because it can be overly chewy if sliced thick.

BOTTOM ROUND RUMP ROAST
Primal Cut: Round
Flavor: ★★
Cost: $
Alternate Names:
Round Roast,
Bottom Round Pot Roast,
Bottom Round Oven Roast

For the money, we think this cut makes a juicy, relatively beefy roast. It was slightly less tender than the top round roast and should be sliced thin for serving.

EYE-ROUND ROAST
Primal Cut: Round
Flavor: ★
Cost: $
Alternate Name:
Round-Eye Pot Roast

This boneless roast had mediocre flavor and was considerably less juicy than any other roast we tested.

BOTTOM ROUND ROAST
Primal Cut: Round
Flavor: no stars
Cost: $
Alternate Name: None

This cut was the tasters' least favorite. It was essentially devoid of flavor and had a rubbery, chewy texture. This roast is not worth even the little that it costs.

BRISKET
Primal Cut: Brisket/Shank
Flavor: ★★★
Cost: $ $
Alternate Name: None

This large rectangular cut weighs 13 pounds so it is often divided into two sub-cuts. The flat cut (on the left in this brisket) is thinner and not quite as flavorful as the point cut (on the right). The point cut is thicker and contains more fat, which means the meat is juicier and more tender when fully cooked.

HOW TO BUY OTHER BEEF CUTS

A FEW CUTS, SUCH AS RIBS AND SHANKS, are neither steaks nor roasts. In the ratings that follow, we've focused on flavor (★★★★ being the best) and cost ($$$$ being the most expensive) since these tough cuts will become tender with prolonged cooking.

SHANKS
Primal Cut: Brisket/Shank
Flavor: ★★
Cost: $
Alternate Name: Center Beef Shanks

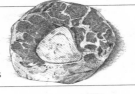

This round cut is a cross-section of the front leg and can be sold with or without the bone. The meat is fatty but flavorful and is especially good when used in soup or simmered in a boiled dinner such as pot-au-feu. This cut is the same as osso buco, but from a cow rather than a calf.

BEEF RIBS
Primal Cut: Rib
Flavor: ★★★
Cost: $ $
Alternate Name: Back Ribs

These large ribs are cut from rib bones 6 through 12—the home to prime rib. These ribs are often very large (about 8 inches long) and can be sold in smaller slabs with just three or four bones.

SHORT RIBS
Primal Cut:
Plate or Chuck/Shoulder
Flavor: ★★★
Cost: $
Alternate Name: English-Style Short Ribs

These meaty ribs can be cut from various locations on the cow, although they commonly come from the underside of the animal. In most markets, each rib bone has been separated and cut crosswise so that a large chunk of meat is attached to one side of the bone.

FLANKEN-STYLE SHORT RIBS
Primal Cut: Plate
Flavor: ★★★
Cost: $ $
Alternate Name: Flanken

Like English-style short ribs, these short ribs can be cut from various parts of the animal, although mostly commonly they come from the plate. In this case, the ribs are cut into thin cross-sections that contain two or three pieces of bone surrounded by pieces of meat. Flanken-style ribs are generally available only at butcher shops.

CHOOSING A GRADE

The U.S. Department of Agriculture (USDA) recognizes eight grades of beef, but most everything available to consumers falls into the top three: Prime, Choice, and Select. The grades classify meat according to fat marbling and age, which are relatively accurate predictors of palatability; they have nothing to do with freshness or purity. Grading is voluntary on the part of the meat packer. If the meat is graded, it should bear a USDA stamp indicating the grade, but it may not be visible. Ask the butcher when in doubt.

We pan-seared rib-eye steaks from all three grades and tasted them blind. Prime ranked first for its tender, buttery texture and rich beefy flavor; it was discernibly fattier. Choice came in second, with solid flavor and a little more chew. The Select steak was tough and stringy, with flavor that was only "acceptable." The lesson here is that you get what you pay for. Prime steaks are worth the extra money, but Choice steaks that exhibit a moderate amount of marbling are a fine and more affordable option.

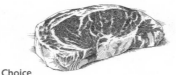

Prime
Prime meat is heavily marbled with intramuscular fat (seen as white streaks within the meat in this drawing), which makes for a tender, flavorful steak. A very small percentage (about 2 percent) of graded beef is considered Prime. Prime meats are most often served in restaurants or sold in high-end grocery stores or butcher shops.

Choice
The majority of graded beef is graded Choice. While the levels of marbling in Choice beef can vary, it is generally moderately marbled with intramuscular fat.

Select
Select beef has little marbling. Because of the small amount of intramuscular fat, Select meats are drier, tougher, and less flavorful than the two higher grades.

COOKING MEAT 101

THERE ARE BASIC COOKING METHODS THAT WE USE OVER AND OVER AGAIN WHEN cooking meat and it helps to understand how they differ from each other and why you might choose one method over another. There are a couple of issues that apply to meat cookery regardless of the method. These three points are crucial to the success of most meat recipes.

BROWN IS GOOD.

Meat with a browned exterior tastes better. If you're making a sauce, those browned bits that remain in the roasting pan or skillet will make the sauce taste better, too. So why does browned food taste so good?

When meat browns, something called the Maillard reaction occurs. This process is named after the French chemist who first described this reaction about one hundred years ago. When the amino acids (or protein components) and natural sugars in meat are subjected to intense heat, like that found in a skillet, they begin to combine and form new compounds. These compounds in turn break down and form yet more new flavor compounds, and so on and so on. The process is like rabbits multiplying and occurs both on the meat and in the cooking vessel. The browned bits left in the pan once the meat has been cooked (called *fond*) are packed with complex flavors, which in turn are carried over to the pan sauce once the fond has been dissolved.

In order to encourage browning, use sufficient heat. Steaks cooked over a wimpy fire or stew meat cooked in a cool pot will not brown properly. Many home cooks hesitate to preheat pans on the stovetop sufficiently. As a result, meat steams rather than sizzles and does not brown and, as a consequence, does not taste very good.

KNOW WHEN FOOD IS DONE.

Although professional cooks might rely on the feel of a steak to determine doneness, we find this method much too imprecise. An instant-read thermometer (see page 85) coupled with knowledge of how temperatures relate to desired doneness will ensure success in the kitchen. (The chart below lists these temperatures.)

Optimum Internal Temperatures for Meat

The chart below lists optimum internal temperatures, based on maximum juiciness and flavor. For optimum safety, all meat should be cooked until the internal temperature reaches 160 degrees.

To determine internal temperature, insert an instant-read thermometer deep into the meat away from any bone. Take two or three readings to make sure the entire piece of meat has reached the proper temperature.

Note that the temperatures that follow are at serving time. Since the internal temperature of most cuts will rise as the meat rests (the effect is called carryover cooking), you will want to remove steaks from the grill or a roast from the oven before it hits these temperatures. For instance, a roast that registers 125 degrees on an instant-read thermometer when it comes out of the oven might reach 135 degrees by the time it has rested on the counter for 15 minutes.

Unfortunately, the significance of the carryover effect will vary from recipe to recipe based on the thickness of the cut (thicker cuts hold onto heat better than thinner cuts and will experience a greater rise in temperature as they rest) as well as the heat level used during the cooking process (a roast that comes out of a 250-degree oven has less heat to hold onto and the internal temperature won't climb nearly as much a roast that comes out of a 450-degree oven). For this reason, you should follow temperatures in recipes, which have been designed to compensate for the carryover effect for that specific recipe. Recipes give temperatures at which the meat should be removed from the oven. The numbers below indicate how temperature at serving time correlates with various levels of doneness.

	RARE	MEDIUM-RARE	MEDIUM	MEDIUM-WELL	WELL-DONE
Beef	125°F	130°F	140°F	150°F	160°F
Veal	125°F	135°F	140°F	150°F	160°F
Lamb	125°F	130°F	140°F	150°F	160°F
Pork	*	*	145°F	150°F	160°F

*(Not Recommended)

Know that maximum juiciness and flavor often collides with maximum safety. Health officials generally suggest cooking all meat to 160 degrees in order to assure that any bacteria or pathogens that may be present have been killed. This is sound advice if food safety is your top concern. However, the reality is that most people (including us) prefer their meat cooked to a lower internal temperature. The reason is simple. Heating causes meat fibers to contract and expel juices. A steak cooked to 160 degrees will be significantly drier than a steak cooked to 130 degrees. In most instances, we cook meat to maximum palatability. If safety is your top concern, you should cook all meat until it is well-done (and the internal temperature registers at least 160 degrees).

Note that these temperatures apply only to lean cuts and dry-heat cooking methods such as grilling and roasting. When braising or stewing fattier cuts, the internal temperature of the meat will climb much higher, but the collagen in these cuts will protect against dryness.

LET MEAT REST AFTER COOKING.

A final but very important step when cooking meat is allowing it to rest after it comes off the heat. As the proteins in the meat heat up during cooking they coagulate, which basically means they uncoil and then reconnect, or bond with each other, in a different configuration. When the proteins coagulate, they squeeze out part of the liquid that was trapped in their coiled structures and in the spaces between the individual molecules. The heat from the cooking source drives these freed liquids toward the center of the meat.

This process of coagulation explains why experienced chefs can tell how done a piece of meat is by pushing on it and judging the amount of resistance: the firmer the meat, the more done it is. But the coagulation process is apparently at least partly reversible, so as you allow the meat to rest and return to a lower temperatures after cooking, some of the liquid is reabsorbed by the protein molecules as their capacity to hold moisture increases. As a result, if given a chance to rest, the meat will lose less juice when you cut into it, which in turn makes for much juicier and more tender meat.

This is common wisdom among cooks, but to be sure it was correct, we cooked several steaks, sliced several up immediately after they came off the fire, and allowed the second batch to rest for 10 minutes before slicing them. Not only did the first batch of steaks exude almost 40 percent more juice than the second batch when sliced, the meat also looked grayer and was not as tender. In this case, it is crucial to follow the conventional wisdom: Give your steaks a rest.

SCIENCE: COOKING PORK SAFELY

Red meat (beef, lamb, and veal) has traditionally been cooked to a lower internal temperature than pork. Guidelines for cooking pork to temperatures as high as 190 degrees originated decades ago when pork quality was inconsistent and fears of trichinosis ran high. Today, the risk of trichinosis is nearly nonexistent in the United States. According to the Centers for Disease Control and Prevention, only 13 human cases of trichinosis were confirmed in 2002, and the source of contamination for eight of those cases was wild game and for two of them privately raised pigs. What's more, even when the trichina parasite is present, it is killed when the temperature of the meat rises to 137 degrees.

Both the U.S. Department of Agriculture and the National Pork Board recommend cooking pork to a final internal temperature of 160 degrees. The Pork Board advises removing larger cuts from the oven at 150 degrees, resting the meat, and serving it at 160. Unfortunately, given the leanness of today's pork, these recommendations result in dry, tough meat. In the test kitchen, we have found cooking modern pork beyond 150 degrees to be a waste of time and money. We cook thinner cuts of pork such as chops to a slightly rosy 140 to 145 degrees; their temperature will climb about 5 degrees as they rest. We remove large cuts from the oven at about 135 degrees, tent them with foil, and allow the meat to rest, during which time the temperature rises by at least 10 degrees. (Be sure to check the final temperature before serving to make certain that it does reach 145 degrees.) If you are concerned about contamination from salmonella (which is possible in any type of meat, including beef), you must cook the pork to 160 degrees to be certain that all potential pathogens are eliminated.

Basic Cooking Methods

The following glossary explains some basic terms used throughout this book.

GRILLING Build a hot fire and cook the meat directly over the coals—nothing could be simpler. When grilling, the temperature will be in excess of 400 degrees, if not 500 degrees. As a result, meat cooks very quickly. By the time the exterior is nicely browned, the interior will be cooked through. This method works best with moderately thin steaks and chops.

If you are working with a slightly thicker steak or chop, you may need to grill over a two-level fire. When the coals are hot, pile most up on one side of the grill and then spread a few coals over the other half of the grill. You now have created a grill with two heat levels. Sear the steaks or chops over the hot part of the grill until nicely browned but then let them finish cooking through over the cooler part of the grill. This way the interior has time to cook through without the risk of burning the exterior. See pages 34 to 35 for more information about grilling.

GRILL-ROASTING A two-level fire will protect a thick steak but when trying to cook a roast on the grill you need to follow a different procedure. While grilling calls for loading the grill with charcoal or lighting all the gas burners, indirect cooking on the grill relies on a smaller fire. The lit coals are banked on one side of the grill, or one (or more) of the gas burners is turned off. Foods cooked by indirect heat are placed over the "cool" part of the grill. With the lid on to trap heat, both the exterior and interior of the food cook slowly and evenly, just as they do in an oven. We generally grill-roast at temperatures between 300 and 400 degrees and prefer to use briquettes rather than hardwood charcoal because it burns more slowly and evenly. Almost any tender cut that can roasted in the oven can be grill-roasted. See page 281 for more information about grill-roasting.

BARBECUING This traditional low- and slow-cooking method is used with ribs, pulled pork, and brisket. Because the goal is to impart as much smoke flavor as possible, a long cooking time over a relatively low fire is required. Barbecuing also provides ample time for fatty, tough cuts to become tender. The set-up is the same as for grill-roasting except there are fewer coals and less heat.

Although there is much debate among experts as to the proper cooking temperature for barbecuing, we found in our testing that it should take place between 250 and 300 degrees. While some chefs and pit masters might argue that ribs are best barbecued at 180 degrees, we found it very difficult to maintain such a low fire. Also, such low temperatures allow bacteria to multiply and increase the risk of food-borne illnesses.

ROASTING This cooking method is the perhaps the most basic. Meat is placed in a pan in a hot oven and baked until the heat of the oven has warmed the meat to the desired internal temperature.

PAN-SEARING Set a heavy-bottomed skillet over high heat and let the pan heat for several minutes, or until it very hot. Add meat and cook, without moving it (you want an nice exterior color to develop), until well browned. Next turn the meat (with tongs, not a fork, which will make holes through which juices can leak) and cook until browned on the second side. If the meat is fully browned but not cooked through, carefully slide the skillet into a hot oven for several minutes. In some cases, you may need an extremely light film of oil in the pan at the outset, but no more than a teaspoon or two. This method works well with fairly fatty steaks and chops.

SAUTÉING This cooking method is similar to pan-searing, except there's a bit more oil in the pan, usually a tablespoon or two. Also, the heat level is not quite as intense so the drippings in the pan don't burn. Therefore, once the meat has finished sautéing (cutlets are a perfect choice for this technique), it can be set aside while you build a sauce from their drippings.

PAN-FRYING Breaded cutlets are often fried in a skillet filled with a fair amount of oil. The goal here is to promote the development of an especially crisp exterior. Usually there's about one half cup of oil in the skillet and the oil comes halfway up the sides of the meat being cooked. You cook the meat until it is crisp on the first side, flip it, and then cook it on the second side. If the meat is submerged in oil (and thus there's no need to turn it), you are deep-frying.

STIR-FRYING This cooking method is very similar to sautéing. The biggest difference is that the meat is always cut into very small pieces and it is stirred as it cooks.

BRAISING Also called pot-roasting, this method starts by searing meat (to develop color and flavor) and then partially submerges the meat in liquid in a sealed pot and cooks it over gentle heat. This method is used with tough cuts, which are braised until they are fork-tender.

STEWING This method is the same as braising except the meat is boneless and in small chunks and the liquid is more abundant.

1

I WANT TO GRILL A STEAK

I Want to Grill a Steak

I WANT TO GRILL A STEAK

THERE ARE TWO MAIN AREAS THAT SEPARATE great steaks from mediocre ones. First, you have to buy the right cuts of meat. We find that some steaks, no matter how they are seasoned or grilled, are always disappointing. This chapter offers a selection of expensive and inexpensive steaks that we think are best suited to outdoor cooking.

Second, you need to use a grilling technique that is right for a particular cut. Thicker steaks must be grilled differently from thin ones. Likewise, the presence of a bone can necessitate some adjustments in technique, as can the fat content.

We found that premium steaks from the rib and short loin can be cooked and seasoned pretty much the same way, although filet mignon needs a slightly different treatment. Because of the bones and their sizes, T-bones and porterhouse steaks need slightly different treatment as well. Tougher steak tips, flank steaks, and London broil (from the shoulder) require different cooking regimens. For a detailed discussion on grilling, including information and illustrations about how to use charcoal and gas grills, see pages 34 through 35.

GRILLED PREMIUM STEAKS

GRILLED PREMIUM STEAKS HAVE MANY attractive qualities: rich, beefy flavor; a thick, caramelized crust; and almost no prep or cleanup for the cook. But sometimes a small bonfire fueled by steak fat can leave expensive steaks charred and tasting of resinous smoke. Other times the coals burn down so low that the steaks end up with pale, wimpy grill marks and almost no flavor at all. In these cases, you probably tried to leave the steaks on the grill long enough to develop flavor, but they just overcooked.

So we went to work, promising ourselves we'd figure out how to use the grill to cook the entire steak perfectly: meat seared evenly on both sides so that the juices are concentrated into a powerfully flavored, dark brown, brittle coating of crust; the juicy inside cooked a little past rare; and the outside

strip of rich, soft fat crisped and browned slightly on the edges.

We decided to focus on the steaks from the short loin and rib sections of the animal that we think are the best the cow has to offer—the T-bone and porterhouse as well as the strip and filet mignon (all from the short loin) and the rib eye (a rib steak without the bone, which is the most common way this cut is sold). We figured these steaks were bound to cook pretty much the same because they were all cut from the same general part of the cow.

Early on in our testing, we determined that we needed a very hot fire to get the crust we wanted without overcooking the steak. We could get that kind of heat by building the charcoal up to within 2 or 2½ inches of the grilling grate. But with this arrangement, we ran into problems with the fat dripping down onto the charcoal and flaming. We had already decided that a thick steak—at least 1¼ inches thick—was optimum, because at that thickness we achieved a tasty contrast between the charcoal flavoring on the outside of the steak and the beefy flavor on the inside. The problem was that we couldn't cook a thick steak over consistently high heat without burning it.

After considerable experimentation, we found the answer to this dilemma: We had to build a fire with two levels of heat. Once we realized that we needed a fire with a lot of coals on one side and far fewer coals on the other, we could sear the steak properly at the beginning of cooking, then pull it onto the cooler half of the grill to finish cooking at a lower temperature. We could also use the dual heat levels to cook thin steaks as well as thick ones properly, and the system provided insurance against bonfires as well—if a steak flared up, we simply moved it off the high heat.

We gauged the level of heat on both sides of the fire by holding a hand about five inches over the cooking grate (as explained on page 34). When the medium-hot side of the grill was hot enough for searing, we could stand to hold a hand over the grill only for three or four seconds. For the cooler side of the grill, we could count seven seconds. (This is how we adapted our recipes for a gas grill, using burners set to high and medium.)

A two-level fire is also good for cooking

porterhouse and T-bone, two of our favorite cuts, which are especially tricky to cook properly. Both consist of two muscles (strip and tenderloin) with a T-shaped bone in between. When grilled long enough to cook the strip section perfectly, the lean tenderloin is inevitably overcooked, dry, and flavorless. We found that if we grilled the steak with the tenderloin toward the cooler side of the fire, it cooked more slowly and reached proper doneness at the same time as the strip.

Common cooking wisdom suggests that bringing meat to room temperature before grilling will cause it to cook more evenly and that letting it rest for five minutes after taking it off the grill will both preserve the juices and provide a more even color. We tested the first of these theories by simultaneously grilling two similar steaks, one straight from the refrigerator and a second that had stood at room temperature for one hour. We noticed no difference in the cooked steaks except that the room temperature steak cooked a couple of minutes faster than the other. The second test was more conclusive. Letting a cooked steak rest for five minutes does indeed help the meat retain more juices when sliced and promotes a more even color throughout the meat.

We tried lightly oiling steaks before grilling to see if they browned better that way, and tried brushing them with butter halfway through grilling to see if the flavor improved. Although the oiled steaks browned a tiny bit better, the difference wasn't significant enough to merit the added ingredient. (The filet mignon cut was an exception; oiling improved browning in this leaner steak.) As for the butter, we couldn't taste any difference.

We did find that proper seasoning with salt and pepper before grilling is essential. Seasonings added after cooking sit on the surface and don't penetrate as well as salt and pepper added before cooking. Be liberal with the salt and pepper. A fair amount falls off during the cooking process. Finally, consider using coarse sea salt or kosher salt. In our tests, tasters consistently preferred steaks sprinkled with coarse salt before grilling compared with those sprinkled with table salt. The larger crystals are more easily absorbed by the meat and sprinkle more evenly. (See page 112 for more information.)

Charcoal-Grilled Strip or Rib Steaks
SERVES 4

Strip and rib steaks, on or off the bone, are our first choice for individual steaks. A steak that's between 1¼ and 1½ inches thick gives you a solid meat flavor as well as a little taste of the grill; cut any thicker and the steak becomes too thick for one person to eat. If your guests are more likely to eat only an 8-ounce steak, grill two 1-pounders, slice them, and serve each person a half steak. The most accurate way to judge doneness is to stick an instant-read thermometer through the side of the steak deep into the meat but not touching the bone, so that most of the shaft is embedded in the steak (see the illustration on page 30).

4   strip or rib steaks, with or without the bone, 1 ¼ to 1 ½ inches thick (12 to 16 ounces each), patted dry with paper towels
     Salt and ground black pepper

1. Light a large chimney starter filled with hardwood charcoal (about 6 quarts) and allow to burn until all the charcoal is covered with a layer of fine gray ash. Build a two-level fire by stacking most of the coals on one side of the grill and arranging the remaining coals in a single layer on the other side of the grill. Set the cooking rack in place, cover the grill with the lid, and let the rack heat up, about 5 minutes. Use a wire brush to scrape clean the cooking rack. The grill is ready when the pile of coals is medium-hot and the single layer of coals is medium-low. (See how to gauge heat level on page 34.)

2. Meanwhile, sprinkle both sides of the steaks with salt and pepper to taste. Grill the steaks, uncovered, over the hotter part of the fire until well browned on one side, 2 to 3 minutes. Turn the steaks; grill until well browned on the other side, 2 to 3 minutes. (If the steaks start to flame, pull them to the cooler part of the grill and/or extinguish the flames with a squirt bottle filled with water.)

3. Once the steaks are well browned on both sides, slide them to the cooler part of grill. Continue grilling, uncovered, to the desired doneness, 5 to 6 minutes more for rare (120 degrees on

an instant-read thermometer), 6 to 7 minutes for medium-rare on the rare side (125 degrees), 7 to 8 minutes for medium-rare on the medium side (130 degrees), or 8 to 9 minutes for medium (135 to 140 degrees).

4. Remove the steaks from the grill and let rest for 5 minutes. Serve immediately.

➤ VARIATION
Gas-Grilled Strip or Rib Steaks
Depending on the heat output of your gas grill, you may need to cook the steaks over the cooler part of the grill for an extra minute or two.

Turn on all burners to high, close the lid, and heat the grill until very hot, about 15 minutes. Scrape the grill grate clean with a grill brush. Leave one burner on high and turn the other burner(s) to medium. Follow the recipe for Charcoal-Grilled Strip or Rib Steaks from step 2 and cook with the lid down.

Charcoal-Grilled Filets Mignons
SERVES 4

Filet mignon steaks are cut from the tenderloin, which is, as the name indicates, an especially tender portion of

DEALING WITH MISSHAPEN FILETS

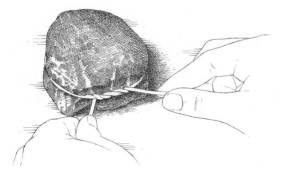

To correct for unevenly cut or oddly cut filets, tie a 12-inch piece of kitchen twine around each steak. Snip off the excess twine at the knot to make sure it does not ignite on the grill. Adjust the shape of the tied filet by gently rolling or patting it with your hand until it is more uniform in appearance and thickness.

meat. Though tender, the steaks are not extremely rich. To prevent the steaks from drying out on the grill and to encourage browning, we found it helpful to rub each steak lightly with a little oil before grilling. To serve, we suggest that you drizzle the grilled steaks with olive oil and garnish them with lemon wedges; or serve with one of the compound butters on page 29. If the filets are misshapen or unevenly cut, as supermarket steaks sometimes are, follow the illustration below to tie each one before grilling.

4   center-cut filets mignons, 1 ½ to 2 inches thick (7 to 8 ounces each), patted dry
4   teaspoons olive oil
    Salt and ground black pepper

1. Light a large chimney starter filled with hardwood charcoal (about 6 quarts) and allow to burn until all the charcoal is covered with a layer of fine gray ash. Build a two-level fire by stacking most of the coals on one side of the grill and arranging the remaining coals in a single layer on the over side of the grill. Set the cooking rack in place, cover the grill with the lid, and let the rack heat up, about 5 minutes. Use a wire brush to scrape clean the cooking rack. The grill is ready when the pile of coals is medium-hot and the single layer of coals is medium-low. (See how to gauge heat level on page 34.)

2. Meanwhile, lightly rub the steaks with the oil and sprinkle both sides of the steaks with salt and pepper to taste. Grill the steaks, uncovered, over the hotter part of the fire until well browned on one side, 2 to 3 minutes. Turn the steaks; grill until well browned on the other side, 2 to 3 minutes.

3. Once the steaks are well browned on both sides, slide them to the cooler part of the grill. Continue grilling, uncovered, to the desired doneness, 6 minutes more for rare (120 degrees on an instant-read thermometer), 7 minutes for medium-rare on the rare side (125 degrees), 8 minutes for medium-rare on the medium side (130 degrees), or 9 to 10 minutes for medium (135 to 140 degrees).

4. Remove the steaks from the grill and let rest for 5 minutes. Serve immediately.

➤ VARIATION

Gas-Grilled Filets Mignons

Depending on the heat output of your gas grill, you may need to cook the steaks over the cooler part of the grill for an extra minute or two.

Turn on all burners to high, close the lid, and heat the grill until very hot, about 15 minutes. Scrape the grill grate clean with a grill brush. Leave one burner on high and turn the other burner(s) to medium. Follow the recipe for Charcoal-Grilled Filets Mignons from step 2 and cook with the lid down.

Charcoal-Grilled Porterhouse or T-Bone Steaks

SERVES 4

How can you argue with a steak that gives you two different tastes and textures—from the strip and the tenderloin—in one cut, plus the bone? Since T-bone and porterhouse steaks are so large, it's best to have the butcher cut them thick (1½ inches) and let one steak serve two people. The key to keeping the delicate tenderloin from overcooking is to sear the steaks with the strip portions over the hottest coals and the tenderloin portions facing the cooler part of the fire.

> 2   porterhouse or T-bone steaks, 1 ½ inches thick (about 1 ¾ pounds each), patted dry
> Salt and ground black pepper

1. Light a large chimney starter filled with hardwood charcoal (about 6 quarts) and allow to burn until all the charcoal is covered with a layer of fine gray ash. Build a two-level fire by stacking most of the coals on one side of the grill and arranging the remaining coals in a single layer on the other side of the grill. Set the cooking rack in place, cover the grill with the lid, and let the rack heat up, about 5 minutes. Use a wire brush to scrape clean the cooking rack. The grill is ready when the pile of coals is medium-hot and the single layer of coals is medium-low. (See how to gauge heat level on page 34.)

2. Meanwhile, sprinkle both sides of the steaks with salt and pepper to taste. Position the steaks on the grill so the tenderloin pieces are over the cooler part of the fire but the strip pieces are over the hotter part of the fire (see the illustration on page 32). Grill the steaks, uncovered, until well browned on one side, 2 to 3 minutes. Turn the steaks; grill until well browned on the other side, 2 to 3 minutes. (If the steaks start to flame, pull them to the cooler part of the grill and/or extinguish the flames with a squirt bottle filled with water.)

3. Once the steaks are well browned on both sides, slide them completely to the cooler part of the grill. Continue grilling, uncovered, to the desired doneness, 5 to 6 minutes more for rare (120 degrees on an instant-read thermometer), 6 to 7 minutes for medium-rare on the rare side (125 degrees), 7 to 8 minutes for medium-rare on the medium side (130 degrees), or 8 to 9 minutes for medium (135 to 140 degrees).

4. Remove the steaks from the grill to a cutting board and let rest for 5 minutes. Cut the strip and filet pieces off the bones and slice each piece crosswise about ½ inch thick (see the illustrations on page 31). Serve immediately.

➤ VARIATION

Gas-Grilled Porterhouse or T-Bone Steaks

The key to preventing the delicate tenderloin portions of the steaks from overcooking is to sear the steaks with the strip portions over the burner turned to high and to keep the tenderloin facing the burner turned to medium.

Turn on all burners to high, close the lid, and heat the grill until very hot, about 15 minutes. Scrape the grill grate clean with a grill brush. Leave one burner on high and turn the other burner(s) to medium. Follow the recipe for Charcoal-Grilled Porterhouse or T-Bone Steaks from step 2 and cook with the lid down.

STEAK FIORENTINA

WHEN AMERICANS GARNISH A STEAK, IT'S often with steak sauce. The French use a flavored compound butter. But the Italians have something even better—and, arguably, easier too: olive oil and lemon. Bistecca alla Fiorentina, as it is called in Tuscany, couldn't be simpler; a thick, juicy steak is grilled rare, sliced, and served with a drizzle of extra-virgin olive oil and a squeeze of lemon. For most of us here in the test kitchen, this unexpected combination was a revelation, and we expect that any steak lover who gives it a whirl will become a convert, too. The fruity, peppery olive oil amplifies the savory nature of the beef, while the lemon provides a bright counterpoint that cuts right through the richness to sharpen the other flavors.

In a dish this direct, though, good technique can mean the difference between mediocre and magical, so we grilled our way through more than 30 pounds of steak to perfect both the grilling technique and the details of the olive oil and lemon garnish—that is, when and how to introduce it.

Thick T-bone and porterhouse steaks are recommended most often for bistecca alla Fiorentina. Both steaks feature a T-shaped bone with meat from the top loin (also known as the strip) on one

side and meat from the tenderloin on the other side. The primary difference between the two is the size of the tenderloin piece, which is larger on the porterhouse. Of course, we sampled both steaks and found them equally appealing—tender, with a robust, well-balanced flavor. There was no reason to test additional cuts. The suggested thickness, around 1½ inches, also worked well, allowing for an appealing textural contrast between the smoky crust that formed on the outside of the steak and the rare, tender interior.

As we knew from previous tests, we needed to use a two-level fire to cook these thick steaks. Starting the steaks over the hotter part of the fire allowed the exterior to sear deeply; finishing them over the cooler area allowed the inside to cook through without charring the outside.

The recipes we turned up in our research shared an odd voodoo when it came to seasoning the steaks. Several recommended using olive oil to

COMPOUND BUTTERS FOR STEAKS

Blue Cheese–Chive Butter

MAKES 4 TABLESPOONS,
ENOUGH FOR 4 STEAKS

Serve this butter with any grilled or pan-seared steaks. It is especially good with filets mignons.

3	tablespoons unsalted butter, softened
1½	ounces mild blue cheese, room temperature
⅛	teaspoon salt
2	tablespoons minced chives

Using a fork, beat the butter, blue cheese, and salt together in a small bowl until combined. Fold in the chives. Just before serving the steaks, spoon about 1 tablespoon of the butter onto each and serve.

Lemon, Garlic, and Parsley Butter

MAKES 4 TABLESPOONS,
ENOUGH FOR 4 STEAKS

This is a variation on maître d'hôtel butter, a classic French accompaniment to meat, fish, and vegetables. It works well with lean steaks.

4	tablespoons unsalted butter, softened
½	teaspoon grated lemon zest
1	tablespoon minced fresh parsley leaves
1	medium garlic clove, minced to a puree or pressed through a garlic press (about 1 teaspoon)
½	teaspoon salt
	Ground black pepper

Using a fork, beat all of the ingredients, including ground black pepper to taste, together in a small bowl until combined. Just before serving the steaks, spoon about 1 tablespoon of the butter onto each and serve.

marinate the raw steaks, a few more suggested rubbing the steaks with olive oil just before grilling
them, while one passionately declared that oiling
the meat before cooking would cause it to "taste
greasy and be nauseating." Another recipe insisted
that the steaks be both salted and drizzled with
olive oil after they had cooked but before they were
removed from the grill.

To see if any of these techniques could really
work magic, we evaluated steaks treated with oil in
five different ways: The oil was used as a marinade
before cooking, brushed on the meat before grilling, brushed on the meat as it grilled, drizzled on
the whole cooked steaks before slicing, and drizzled
over the sliced steak at serving time.

We preferred drizzling the oil over the sliced
steak for a few reasons. It was the easiest, least
fussy method; it flavored the meat most effectively,
bringing the full fruity, peppery impact of the raw
oil to the fore; and it guaranteed a hit of oil with
each bite of steak. Although the steaks that were
oiled prior to or during grilling were not nauseating, as one author had predicted, the heat of the
grill did mitigate the nuances of the oil, in a sense
deadening its flavor. The oiled steaks also caused
more flare-ups on the grill.

We tried both pure and extra-virgin olive oils,
and the extra-virgin was far and away the best for
its distinctive character and bold flavor. We went
on to try several brands of extra-virgin oil and
preferred those with bolder, fuller-bodied flavor
to the milder oils. We also experimented with the
lemon and found it easiest and best to squeeze it
over the sliced steak at the last minute. Juicing the
lemon and brushing the juice on the steaks any
earlier relieved the lemon of some of its freshness
and tang.

The use of garlic was a matter of debate in the
original recipes. Some included it, while others
decried it as nontraditional. The idea appealed to
us nonetheless, so we tried four ways of working
it into the program. We made a sauce with pureed
fresh garlic, olive oil, and lemon juice and poured it
over the sliced steak, but the garlic was overpowering. We tried rubbing both fresh and toasted garlic
cloves over the cooked steak, but tasters were not
impressed. Last, we rubbed a fresh-cut garlic clove

JUDGING WHEN STEAKS ARE DONE

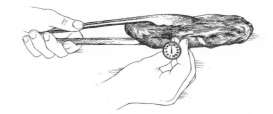

Hold the steak with a pair of tongs and push the tip of the thermometer through the edge of the steak until most of the shaft is
embedded in the meat and not touching any bone. Pull the steak off
the grill when it registers 120 degrees for rare; 125 to 130 degrees
for medium-rare; and 135 to 140 degrees for medium. Note that
the internal temperature will rise another 5 degrees or so as the
steak rests.

MINCING GARLIC TO A PUREE

There are times, such as when making a compound butter, when
you want minced garlic to be absolutely smooth. A garlic press yields
a smooth puree easily. To obtain the same effect with a chef's knife,
you will need some salt. If possible, use kosher or coarse salt; the
larger crystals do a better job of breaking down the garlic than fine
table salt.

1. Mince the garlic as you normally would on a cutting board.
Sprinkle the minced garlic with a pinch of salt.

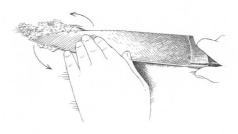

2. Drag the side of the chef's knife over the garlic-salt mixture to
form a fine puree. Continue to mince and drag the knife as necessary
until the puree is smooth.

CARVING T-BONE AND PORTERHOUSE STEAKS

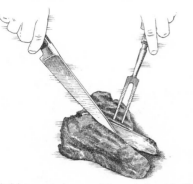

1. Once grilled, let a porterhouse or T-bone steak rest for 5 minutes before slicing. Once the meat has rested, start by slicing close to the bone to remove the strip section.

2. Turn the steak around and cut the tenderloin section off the bone.

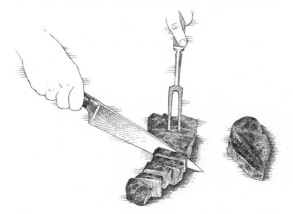

3. Slice each piece crosswise about ½ inch thick. Serve immediately.

over the bone and then the meat of the raw steak. The bone scraped the surface of the garlic, allowing small bits to cling to the meat. Once this steak was grilled, it had a faint suggestion of toasted garlic flavor that was a hit with the tasters. This became a variation on the basic recipe.

Charcoal-Grilled Tuscan Steak with Olive Oil and Lemon (Bistecca alla Fiorentina)

SERVES 4

T-Bone and porterhouse steaks are large enough to serve two. Make sure to use the finest quality oil in this recipe.

2   T-bone or porterhouse steaks, 1 ½ inches
     thick (about 1 ¾ pounds each), patted dry
     with paper towels
     Salt and ground black pepper
3   tablespoons extra-virgin olive oil
     Lemon wedges for serving

1. Light a large chimney starter filled with hardwood charcoal (about 6 quarts) and allow to burn until all the charcoal is covered with a layer of fine gray ash. Build a two-level fire by stacking most of the coals on one side of the grill and arranging the remaining coals in a single layer on the other side of the grill. Set the cooking rack in place, cover the grill with the lid, and let the rack heat up, about 5 minutes. Use a wire brush to scrape clean the cooking rack. The grill is ready when the pile of coals is medium-hot and the single layer of coals is medium-low. (See how to gauge heat level on page 34.)

2. Meanwhile, sprinkle both sides of the steaks with salt and pepper to taste. Position the steaks on the grill so the tenderloin pieces are over the cooler part of the fire but the strip pieces are over the hotter part of the fire (see the illustration on page 32). Grill the steaks, uncovered, until well browned on one side, 2 to 3 minutes. Turn the steaks; grill until well browned on the other side, 2 to 3 minutes. (If the steaks start to flame, pull them to the cooler part of the grill and/or extinguish the flames with a squirt bottle filled with water.)

3. Once the steaks are well browned on both

sides, slide them completely to the cooler part of the grill. Continue grilling, uncovered, to the desired doneness, 5 to 6 minutes more for rare (120 degrees on an instant-read thermometer), 6 to 7 minutes for medium-rare on the rare side (125 degrees), 7 to 8 minutes for medium-rare on the medium side (130 degrees), or 8 to 9 minutes for medium (135 to 140 degrees).

4. Remove the steaks from the grill and let rest for 5 minutes. Cut the strip and filet pieces off the bones and slice them each crosswise about ½ inch thick (see the illustrations on page 31). Arrange the slices on a platter, drizzle with the olive oil, and serve immediately with the lemon wedges.

➤ VARIATIONS

Gas-Grilled Tuscan Steak with Olive Oil and Lemon
Turn on all burners to high, close the lid, and heat the grill until very hot, about 15 minutes. Scrape the grill grate clean with a grill brush. Leave one burner on high and turn the other burner(s) to medium. Follow the recipe for Charcoal-Grilled Tuscan Steak with Olive Oil and Lemon from step 2 and cook with the lid down.

Grilled Tuscan Steak with Garlic Essence
Follow the recipe for Charcoal-Grilled or Gas-Grilled Tuscan Steak with Olive Oil and Lemon,

GRILLING PORTERHOUSE AND T-BONE STEAKS

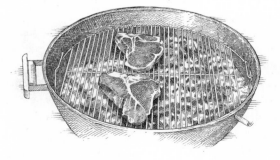

The delicate, buttery tenderloin portion must be protected when grilling porterhouse and T-bone steaks. Keep the tenderloin (the smaller portion of the left side of the bone on these steaks) over the cooler part of the fire.

rubbing a halved, peeled garlic clove over the bone and meat on each side of each steak before seasoning with salt and pepper.

GRILLED STEAK TIPS

STEAK TIPS HAVE NEVER BEEN ON OUR LIST of favorite meats. It's not that we're premium steak snobs, but we were skeptical about a cut of meat that has long been the darling of all-you-can-eat restaurant chains, where quantity takes precedence over quality. There is also some confusion about what constitutes a steak tip. Some steak tips are sautéed and served with a sauce (these are often called pub-style steak tips), some are marinated and grilled (known as tailgate tips). We were drawn to grilling and so began by testing five such recipes.

The recipes differed in the ingredients used to marinate the meat and in the marinating time. The simplest recipe marinated the tips in a bottled Italian-style salad dressing for 24 hours. The most complex marinated the meat for three days in a mixture that included aromatics and herbs. Despite such variations in time and ingredients, none of these grilled tips was very good. Some were mushy, but most were tough and dry. At this point, steak tips still seemed like a cheap cut of meat, with promising beefy flavor but poor texture.

Thinking that the problem might be the cut of meat, we went to the supermarket only to discover a confusing array of meats—cubes, strips, and steaks—labeled "steak tips." Still more confusing, these cubes, strips, and steaks could be cut from a half-dozen different parts of the cow.

After grilling more than 50 pounds of tips, it became clear that the only cut worth grilling is one referred to by butchers as flap meat. (For more information on buying steak tips, see page 33.) When we grilled whole flap meat steaks and then sliced them on the bias before serving, tasters were impressed. Although the meat was still a bit chewy, choosing the right cut was a start.

We now turned to marinades. Given the long-held belief that acidic marinades tenderize tough meat, we created four recipes using four popular acids: yogurt, wine, vinegar, and fruit juice. To determine optimal marination time, we let the meat sit in each marinade for four hours and for 24 hours. Curious about marinades' other claim to fame—flavoring—we added aromatics, spices, and herbs.

The yogurt marinade was the least favorite, producing dry meat that was chewy and tough. Tasters also panned the wine-based marinade. The meat was tough and dry, the flavors harsh and bland. Some tasters liked the complex flavor of the vinegar marinade, but everyone found the tips to be "overly chewy." The marinade prepared with pineapple juice was the favorite. Both the four-hour and 24-hour versions yielded juicy, tender, flavorful meat.

Why did pineapple juice make the best marinade? Our first thought was proteases, enzymes that help to break down proteins. Proteases are found in pineapple, papaya, and other fruits. One of them, papain, from papayas, is the active component of meat tenderizers such as Adolph's. The juice we had been using was pasteurized, however, and the heat of pasteurization is thought to disable such enzymes. To see if proteases were in fact at work, we devised three tests in which we made three more marinades: one with pasteurized pineapple juice from the supermarket; a second with pasteurized pineapple juice heated to the boiling point and then cooled; and a third with fresh pineapple pureed in a food processor.

The result? The fresh juice was a much more aggressive "tenderizer," so much so that it turned the meat mushy on the inside and slimy on the outside. We had learned: proteases do break down meat, but they don't make it any better (tasters universally disapproved of these tenderized tips); pasteurization does kill this enzyme (the fresh juice was much more powerful than the supermarket variety); and

---

INGREDIENTS: **Steak Tips**

Steak tips can come from two different parts of the cow. One type comes from tender, expensive cuts in the middle of the back of the cow, such as the tenderloin. These tips are a superior cut, but not what we consider to be a true steak tip, which should be a more pedestrian cut that is magically transformed into a desirable dish through marinating and cooking. If the steak tips at your market cost $8 to $10 per pound, the meat likely comes from the tenderloin.

True steak tips come from various muscles in the sirloin and round and cost about $5 per pound. After tasting 50 pounds of lower-priced cuts, tasters had a clear favorite: a single muscle that butchers call flap meat; with tips from this cut typically labeled "sirloin tips." A whole piece of flap meat weighs about $2\frac{1}{2}$ pounds. One piece can range in thickness from $\frac{1}{2}$ inch to $1\frac{1}{2}$ inches and may be sold as cubes, strips, or small steaks. It has a rich, deep beefy flavor and a distinctive longitudinal grain.

We found that it's best to buy flap meat in steak form rather than cut into cubes or strips, which are often taken from nearby muscles in the hip and butt that are neither as tasty nor as tender. Because meat labeling is so haphazard, you must visually identify flap meat; buying it in steak form makes this easy.

Steak tips can be cut from a half-dozen muscles and are sold in three basic forms: cubes, strips, and steaks. To make sure that you are buying the most flavorful cut (called flap meat sirloin tips by butchers and pictured below), buy whole steaks.

Cubes

Strips

Steaks

Outdoor Cooking 101

LIGHTING A CHARCOAL FIRE

Our favorite way to start a charcoal fire is with a chimney starter, also known as a flue starter. To use this simple device, fill the bottom section with crumpled newspaper, set the starter on the grill grate, and fill the top with charcoal. (A large starter can hold about six quarts of charcoal.) When you light the newspaper, flames will shoot up through the charcoal, igniting it. Match-light charcoal has been soaked in lighter fluid and we find that it imparts an off flavor to foods. Plain charcoal briquettes are a much better option. We also like hardwood charcoal, also called natural or lump charcoal. Because it burns hotter and quicker than briquettes, we prefer hardwood charcoal when grilling. However, it is too hot to be practical when cooking with indirect heat.

CHARCOAL VERSUS GAS
Our preference when grilling (that is, cooking over direct heat) is to use charcoal. We like the high heat generated and the flavor that food absorbs from hardwood charcoal (our favorite fuel for most recipes). However, when doing indirect cooking—barbecuing or grill-roasting—the differences in flavor between foods cooked over gas and charcoal diminish a bit.

TAKING THE TEMPERATURE OF THE FIRE
Use the chart below to determine the intensity of the fire. The terms hot fire, medium-hot fire, medium fire, and medium-low fire are used in all our grilling recipes. When using a gas grill, ignore dial readings such as medium or medium-low in favor of actual measurements of the temperature, as described here.

INTENSITY OF FIRE	TIME YOU CAN HOLD YOUR HAND 5 INCHES ABOVE GRATE
Hot fire	2 seconds
Medium-hot fire	3 to 4 seconds
Medium fire	5 to 6 seconds
Medium-low fire	7 seconds

Once the coals have been spread out in the bottom of the grill, put the cooking grate in place and put the cover on for five minutes to heat up the grate. (On gas grills, preheat with the lid down and all burners on high for 15 minutes.) Scrape the cooking grate clean and then take the temperature of the fire by holding your hand 5 inches above the cooking grate and counting how long you can comfortably leave it in place.

CHECKING THE FUEL LEVEL IN A GAS TANK
There's nothing worse than running out of fuel halfway through grilling. If your grill doesn't have a gas gauge, use this technique to estimate how much gas is left in the tank.

1. Bring a cup or so of water to a boil in a small saucepan or glass measuring cup (if using the microwave). Pour the water over the side of the tank.

2. Feel the metal with your hand. Where the water has succeeded in warming the tank, it is empty; where the tank remains cool to the touch, there is still propane inside.

THREE TYPES OF CHARCOAL FIRES

SINGLE-LEVEL FIRE
Arrange all the lit charcoal in an even layer. This kind of fire delivers even heat and is best for quick searing at a moderate temperature.

TWO-LEVEL FIRE
Spread some of the lit coals in a single layer over half of the grill. Leave the remaining coals in a pile that rises to within 2 or 2½ inches of the cooking grate. This kind of fire permits searing over very hot coals and slower cooking over moderate coals to cook through thicker cuts.

MODIFIED TWO-LEVEL FIRE
Pile all the lit coals into half the grill to create a hot place for searing, but leave the remaining portion of the grill empty. Some heat from the coals will still cook foods placed over the empty part of the grill, but the heat is very gentle and little browning will occur here.

BARBECUING ON A GAS GRILL

Remove part or all of the cooking grate. Place a foil tray with soaked wood chips on top of the primary burner. Make sure the tray is resting securely on the burner so it will not tip. Replace the grill rack. Light all burners and cover the grill. When you see a lot of smoke (after about 20 minutes), turn off the burner (or burners) without the chips and place the food over it (or them). If the chips flame, douse the fire with water from a squirt bottle. Cover the grill.

BARBECUING ON A CHARCOAL GRILL

1. Pile the lit coals on one half of the grill and leave the other half free of coals.

2. Place soaked and drained wood chunks or a foil packet filled with wood chips on top of the coals. Set the top grate in position, heat briefly, and then scrape the grate clean with a wire brush. You are now ready to cook over the cool part of the fire. Put the food on the grill and set the lid in place. Open the air vents as directed in individual recipes.

3. A grill thermometer inserted through the vents on the lid can tell you if the fire is too hot or if the fire is getting too cool and you need to add more charcoal. You will get different readings depending on where the lid vents are and thus the thermometer is in relation to the coals. Because you want to know the temperature where the food is being cooked, rotate the lid so that the thermometer is close to the food. Make sure, however, that the thermometer stem does not touch the food.

USING WOOD CHIPS ON A CHARCOAL GRILL

1. Place the amount of wood chips called for in the recipe in the center of an 18-inch square of heavy-duty aluminum foil. Fold in all four sides of the foil to encase the chips.

2. Turn the foil packet over. Tear about six large holes (each the size of a quarter) through the top of the foil packet with a fork to allow smoke to escape. Place the packet, with holes facing up, directly on a pile of lit charcoal.

USING WOOD CHIPS ON A GAS GRILL

Buy small rectangular disposable foil trays to hold wood chips on a gas grill or fashion your own tray out of aluminum foil.

1. Start with a 12 by 18-inch piece of heavy-duty foil. Make a 1-inch fold on one long side. Repeat three more times, then turn the fold up to create a sturdy side that measures about an inch high. Repeat the process on the other long side.

2. With a short side facing you, fold in both corners as if wrapping a gift.

3. Turn up the inside inch or so of each triangular fold to match the rim on the long sides of the foil tray.

4. Lift the pointed end of the triangle over the rim of foil and fold down to seal. Repeat the process on the other short side.

proteases were not responsible for the strong show-ing made by the original pineapple marinade. Why, then, did tasters prefer the pineapple marinade to those made with yogurt, wine, and vinegar?

After rereading the ingredient list in our pine-apple marinade, we devised a new theory. The pineapple marinade included soy sauce, an ingredi-ent that is packed with salt and that was not used in any of the other marinades. Was the soy sauce tenderizing the meat by acting like a brine of salt and water? In the past, the test kitchen has dem-onstrated the beneficial effects of brining on lean poultry and pork.

To answer these questions, we ran another series of tests, trying various oil-based marinades made with salt or soy sauce (in earlier tests, we had deter-mined that oil helped to keep the meat moist and promoted searing). To use salt in a marinade, we first had to dissolve it. Because salt doesn't dissolve in oil, we used water, but the liquid prevented the meat from browning properly. That said, brining did make these steak tips tender and juicy.

We concluded that soy sauce, not pineapple juice, was the secret ingredient in our tasters' favorite marinade. The salt in soy sauce was responsible for the improved texture of the steak tips, and the soy sauce also promoted browning. After experiment-ing with brining times, we determined that an hour was optimal. It allowed for the thicker parts of the meat to become tender while preventing the thin-ner sections from becoming too salty.

We then went to work on flavor variations, add-ing garlic, ginger, orange zest, hot pepper, brown sugar, and scallions for an Asian marinade and mak-ing a Southwest-inspired marinade that included garlic, chili powder, cumin, cayenne, brown sugar, and tomato paste. We found that a squeeze of fresh citrus served with the steak provided a bright acidic counterpoint.

Because this relatively thin cut cooks quickly, high heat is necessary to achieve a perfect crust. The uneven thickness of many tips presented a problem, though. The exterior would scorch by the time the thick portions were cooked, and the thin parts would be overcooked. A two-level fire, with more coals on one side of the grill to create hotter and cooler areas, solved the problem. We started the tips

over high heat to sear them and then moved them to the cooler area to finish cooking.

We prefer steaks grilled rare, so we were sur-prised to find that when cooked rare, the meat was rubbery, whereas longer cooking gave it a tender chew—without drying out the meat. Even when cooked until well done, the tips were exceptionally juicy. We had the brine to thank again: The salty soy marinade helped the meat hold onto its moisture.

Conventional wisdom prompted one more test. We grilled two more batches of tips and sliced one immediately after it came off the grill and the other five minutes later. Sure enough, the rested tips were both more juicy and more tender. Finally, we had a recipe for steak tips as pleasing to the palate as they are to the pocketbook.

Charcoal-Grilled Steak Tips
SERVES 4 TO 6

A two-level fire allows you to brown the steak over the hot side of the grill, then move it to the cooler side if it is not yet cooked through. If your steak is thin, however, you may not need to use the cooler side of the grill. The times in the recipe below are for relatively even, 1-inch-thick steak tips. When grilling, bear in mind that even those tasters who usually prefer rare beef preferred steak tips cooked medium-rare to medium because the texture is firmer and not quite so chewy. Serve lime wedges with the Southwestern-marinated tips and orange wedges with the tips marinated in garlic, ginger, and soy sauce.

I   recipe marinade (recipes follow)
2   pounds flap meat sirloin steak tips, trimmed of excess fat
     Lime or orange wedges for serving

1. Combine the marinade and meat in a gallon-size zipper-lock bag; press out as much air as possible and seal the bag. Refrigerate for 1 hour, flipping the bag after 30 minutes to ensure that the meat marinates evenly.

2. About halfway through the marinating time, light a large chimney starter filled with hardwood charcoal (about 6 quarts) and allow to burn until all the charcoal is covered with a layer of fine gray ash. Build a two-level fire by stacking most of the coals

on one side of the grill and arrange the remaining coals in a single layer on the other side of the grill. Set the cooking rack in place, cover the grill with the lid, and let the rack heat up, about 5 minutes. Use a wire brush to scrape clean the cooking rack. The grill is ready when the pile of coals is medium-hot and the single layer of coals is medium-low. (See how to gauge heat level on page 34.)

3. Remove the steak tips from the marinade and pat dry with paper towels. Grill, uncovered, until well seared and dark brown on the first side, about 4 minutes. Using tongs, flip the steak tips and grill until the second side is well seared and the thickest part of the meat is slightly less done than desired, 4 to 5 minutes for medium-rare (about 130 degrees on an instant-read thermometer), 6 to 8 minutes for medium (about 135 degrees); if the exterior of the meat is browned but the steak is not yet cooked through, move the steak tips to the cooler side of the grill and continue to grill to the desired doneness.

4. Transfer the steak tips to a cutting board. Tent the tips loosely with foil and let rest for 5 minutes. Slice the steak tips very thinly on the bias. Serve immediately with the lime or orange wedges.

➤   VARIATIONS

Gas-Grilled Steak Tips

Follow the recipe for Charcoal-Grilled Steak Tips through step 1. When about 15 minutes of marinating time remains, turn on all burners to high, close the lid, and heat the grill until very hot, about 15 minutes. Scrape the grill grate clean with a grill brush. Leave one burner on high and turn the other burner(s) to medium. Continue with the recipe from step 3 and cook with the lid down.

Southwestern Marinade

MAKES ENOUGH FOR 2 POUNDS OF STEAK TIPS

1/3	cup soy sauce
1/3	cup vegetable oil
3	medium garlic cloves, minced or pressed through a garlic press (about 1 tablespoon)
1	tablespoon dark brown sugar
1	tablespoon tomato paste
1	tablespoon chili powder

2	teaspoons ground cumin
1/4	teaspoon cayenne pepper

Combine all of the ingredients in a small bowl.

Garlic, Ginger, and Soy Marinade

MAKES ENOUGH FOR 2 POUNDS OF STEAK TIPS

1/3	cup soy sauce
3	tablespoons vegetable oil
3	tablespoons Asian sesame oil
3	medium garlic cloves, minced or pressed through a garlic press (about 1 tablespoon)
1	(1-inch) piece fresh ginger, peeled and minced (about 1 tablespoon)
2	tablespoons dark brown sugar
2	teaspoons grated zest from 1 orange
1/2	teaspoon red pepper flakes
1	medium scallion, sliced thin

Combine all of the ingredients in a small bowl.

GRILLED FLANK STEAK

THANKS TO FAJITAS, FLANK STEAK HAS BECOME the darling of Tex-Mex fans from New York to California and everywhere in between. But there are good reasons for the popularity of flank steak in addition to mere culinary fashion. Like other steaks cut from the chest and side of the cow, flank has a rich, full, beefy flavor. Also, because it is thin, it cooks relatively quickly. Because flank steaks are typically too long to fit into a pan, grilling makes the most sense for this cut.

Although grilling flank steak appeared to be a pretty straightforward procedure, we still had some questions about what was exactly the best way to go about it. We had two very simple goals: creating a good sear on the outside of this thin cut before it overcooked on the inside, and tenderness. We wondered whether the meat should be marinated or rubbed with spices, how hot the fire should be, and how long the meat should be cooked.

Virtually every recipe we found for flank steak called for marinating it. Most sources championed the marinade as a means of tenderizing the meat as well as adding flavor. We found that marinades with a lot of acid eventually made this thin cut mushy and unappealing. If we omitted the acid, we could flavor the meat, but this took at least 12 hours. As for tenderness, when the cooked steaks were sliced thin across the grain, there was virtually no difference between those that had been marinated and those that had not.

With marinades no longer a possibility, we turned to spice rubs. We rubbed one steak with a spice rub eight hours before cooking, one an hour before, and one just before we put it over the flames. One steak, with no spice rub at all, was cooked just like the others. The three spice-rubbed steaks all had about the same amount of flavor and all developed almost identical dark brown, very flavorful crusts. The plain steak did not develop nearly as nice a crust, but cooked in approximately the same amount of time. We noticed no differences in tenderness among the steaks.

Seeing how spice rubs created excellent crust with plenty of intense flavor, they were voted our first choice for flank steaks. That said, however, spice rubs are not good for folks who like their flank steak cooked to medium, because if you leave the steak on for that long, the spices burn. (You even have to be a bit careful to keep the spices from burning if you like your steak medium-rare.) But if you don't mind exercising a small degree of attention while grilling, we highly recommend using spice rubs for flank steak. Finally, if you want to cook flank steak beyond medium, we suggest adding flavor by passing a sauce separately at the table.

Every source we checked was in the same camp when it came to cooking flank steak, and it is the right camp. Flank steak should be cooked over high heat for a short period of time. We tried lower heat and longer cooking times, but inevitably the meat ended up being tough. Because flank steak is too thin to be checked with a meat thermometer, you must resort to a primitive method of checking for doneness: Cut into the meat to see if it is done to your liking. Remember that carryover heat will continue to cook the steak after it comes off the grill. So if you want the steak medium-rare, take it off the heat when it tests rare, and so on.

Most sources were also in the same camp when it came to letting the steak rest after cooking. During cooking, the heat drives the juices to the center of the meat. This phenomenon is particularly noticeable with high-heat cooking. If you cut the meat right after it comes off the heat, much more of the juice spills out than if you allow the meat to rest, during which time the blood becomes evenly distributed throughout the meat once again. This is common wisdom among cooks, but to be sure it was correct, we cooked two more flank steaks, sliced one up immediately after it came off the fire, and allowed the second to rest for five minutes before slicing it. Not only did the first steak exude almost twice as much juice when sliced as the second, it also looked grayer and was not as tender. So in this case, conventional wisdom prevails: Give your steak a rest.

Charcoal-Grilled Flank Steak
SERVES 4 TO 6

For this recipe, the coals are banked on one side of the grill to create an especially hot fire. Because flank steak is so thin, there's no need to use the cooler part of the grill for cooking the meat through. Also, the thinness of the meat means you have to rely on timing, touch, and/or nick-and-peek, not an instant-read thermometer, to determine doneness.

I   flank steak (about 2 ½ pounds)
    Salt and ground black pepper

1. Light a large chimney starter filled with hardwood charcoal (about 6 quarts) and allow to burn until all the charcoal is covered with a layer of fine gray ash. Build a modified two-level fire by stacking all of the coals on one side of the grill. Set the cooking rack in place, cover the grill with the lid, and let the rack heat up, about 5 minutes. Use a wire brush to scrape clean the cooking grate. The grill is ready when you have a hot fire. (See how to gauge heat level on page 34.)

2. Sprinkle both sides of the steak generously with salt and pepper to taste. Grill the steak over the coals until well seared and dark brown on one side, 5 to 7 minutes. Using tongs, flip the steak and grill until the interior of the meat when cut into is slightly less done than you want it to be when you eat it, 2 to

5 minutes more for rare or medium-rare (depending on the heat of the fire and thickness of the steak).

3. Transfer the steak to a cutting board. Tent loosely with foil and let rest for 5 minutes. Slice the steak thinly on the bias across the grain. Adjust the seasonings with additional salt and pepper and serve immediately.

➤ VARIATIONS

Gas-Grilled Flank Steak

Turn on all burners to high, close the lid, and heat the grill until very hot, about 15 minutes. Scrape the grill grate clean with a grill brush. Leave all burners on high. Follow the recipe for Charcoal-Grilled Flank Steak from step 2 and cook with the lid down.

Grilled Flank Steak Rubbed with Latin Spices

Watch the meat carefully as it cooks to ensure that the spice rub darkens but does not burn. If necessary, slide the steak to the cooler part of the charcoal grill (or reduce the heat on a gas grill) to keep the steak from charring. Flank steak can also be rubbed with Simple Spice Rub for Beef or Lamb on page 397.

2	tablespoons ground cumin
2	tablespoons chili powder
I	tablespoon ground coriander
2	teaspoons ground black pepper
1/2	teaspoon ground cinnamon
1/2	teaspoon red pepper flakes
I 1/2	teaspoons salt
I	recipe Charcoal-Grilled or Gas-Grilled Flank Steak (pages 38–39)

1. Combine all of the spices and the salt in a small bowl.

2. Follow the Charcoal- or Gas-Grilled Flank Steak recipe, omitting the salt and pepper in step 2 and rubbing the steak on both sides with the spice mixture instead.

Grilled Flank Steak with Sweet-and-Sour Chipotle Sauce

If you can't find chipotle chiles in adobo sauce, substitute a mixture of 1/2 teaspoon liquid smoke mixed with 2 minced jalapeño chiles and 3 tablespoons ketchup.

1/4	cup honey
2	tablespoons vegetable oil
3	chipotle chiles packed in adobo sauce
2	tablespoons balsamic vinegar
2	tablespoons grainy mustard
1/2	cup lime juice from 3 or 4 limes
2	medium garlic cloves, minced or pressed through a garlic press (about 2 teaspoons)
I	teaspoon ground cumin
2	tablespoons chopped fresh cilantro leaves
1/2	teaspoon salt
	Ground black pepper
I	recipe Charcoal-Grilled or Gas-Grilled Flank Steak (pages 38–39)

1. Combine the honey, oil, chiles, vinegar, mustard, lime juice, garlic, and cumin in a blender jar or the workbowl of a food processor fitted with the steel blade and puree or process until smooth. Transfer to a small bowl and stir in the cilantro, salt, and pepper to taste; set aside. (The sauce can be covered and refrigerated for 3 days.)

2. Follow the Charcoal- or Gas-Grilled Flank Steak recipe. Remove the steak from the grill and brush both sides generously with the chipotle sauce. Let the steak rest for 5 minutes. Pass the remaining sauce separately with the sliced steak.

Grilled Flank Steak with Spicy Parsley Sauce

This almost-spreadable, spicy herb sauce complements the flavor of grilled flank steak without overwhelming it. The sauce is easy to make and can be prepared in advance.

I	cup minced fresh parsley leaves
3	medium garlic cloves, minced or pressed through a garlic press (about I tablespoon)
I	medium jalapeño chile, stemmed, seeded, and minced
1/2	cup extra-virgin olive oil
3	tablespoons red wine vinegar
	Salt and ground black pepper
I	recipe Charcoal-Grilled or Gas-Grilled Flank Steak (pages 38–39)

1. Combine the parsley, garlic, chile, olive oil, vinegar, and salt and pepper to taste in a small

bowl. (The sauce can be covered and refrigerated for 3 days.)

2. Follow the Charcoal- or Gas-Grilled Flank Steak recipe. Serve the parsley sauce, passing it separately, with the sliced steak.

Classic Fajitas
SERVES 8

Although fajitas were originally made with skirt steak (a fattier cut with more flavor; for more information, see page 41), the combination of flank steak and vegetables grilled and then wrapped in warm tortillas is the one that put flank steak on the culinary map in the United States. The ingredients should go on the grill in order: the steak over a hot fire, the vegetables over a medium fire, and the tortillas around the edge of a medium-to-low fire just to warm them. Alternately, the tortillas can be stacked, then wrapped in a clean, damp dish towel, and warmed in a microwave oven at full power for about 3 minutes; keep the tortillas wrapped until serving time. Cover the grilled but unsliced flank steak with foil for the 10 minutes or so it takes for the vegetables and tortillas to cook.

   I   **recipe Charcoal-Grilled or Gas-Grilled Flank Steak (pages 38–39)**

   ¼   **cup lime juice from 4 limes**

CUTTING PEPPERS FOR THE GRILL

Remove and discard a ¼-inch-thick slice from the top and bottom of each pepper. Reach into the pepper and pull out the seeds in a single bunch. Slice down one side of the pepper, then lay it flat, skin-side down, in a long strip. Slide a sharp knife along the inside of the pepper to remove the white ribs and any remaining seeds. The flattened and cleaned pepper is now ready for grilling.

       Salt and ground black pepper

   I   **very large onion, peeled and cut into ½-inch rounds**

   2   **very large red or green bell peppers, cleaned and cut according to the illustration below**

 16   **flour tortillas (each 10 to 12 inches in diameter) Classic Red Table Salsa (page 402) and/or Chunky Guacamole (page 402)**

1. Follow the recipe for either Charcoal- or Gas-Grilled Flank Steak, sprinkling the meat with the lime juice and salt and pepper to taste before grilling.

2. Remove the steak to a cutting board and tent loosely with foil. When the charcoal fire has died down to medium or the gas grill burners have been adjusted to medium, place the onion rounds and peppers on the grill, and grill them, turning them occasionally, until the onions are lightly charred, about 6 minutes, and the peppers are streaked with dark grill marks, about 10 minutes. Remove the vegetables to a cutting board and slice them into thin strips; set aside. Arrange the tortillas around the edge of the grill and heat until just warmed, about 20 seconds per side. (Take care not to let the tortillas dry out or they will become brittle; wrap the tortillas in a towel to keep them warm, then place them in a basket.)

3. Slice the steak thinly on the bias across the grain. Arrange the sliced meat and vegetables on a large platter. Serve immediately with the tortillas and the salsa and guacamole passed separately.

GRILLED LONDON BROIL

LONDON BROIL IS A RECIPE, NOT A PARticular cut of meat. Steaks labeled London broil are usually taken from the shoulder or round and sometimes from the sirloin of the cow. Typically the steaks are thick and better suited for grilling, broiling, or pan-grilling. Slicing them thin on the bias across the grain makes the most of this often inexpensively priced beef.

It was, in fact, a thinner cut, flank steak, that set the stage for how London broil is best handled. (See pages 37 through 40 for more information on flank steak.) Flank steak is not a super-tough cut, though, and now that it costs in the environs of $7 a pound, it's not such an inexpensive cut either (especially when some cuts from the round or shoulder can cost just $2 or $3 a pound). We wanted, therefore, to figure out how to cook these cheap cuts, which are quite lean and pose certain challenges for the cook.

Before figuring out which of the cheaper cuts would work best for London broil, we needed to determine cooking technique. We were looking for a London broil grilled to a nice crisp crust with a rare to medium-rare interior. Lean meat of this kind, though, becomes intolerably dry and tough if cooked to medium or beyond. We realized we were talking a two-level fire that would allow the meat to sear on one side of the grill and cook through on the cooler, more moderate side.

To work as London broil, the cut of meat must be made up of one muscle; otherwise it simply falls apart when sliced. There are only a few cuts of beef that meet this criterion. We eliminated one of them, the tri-tip cut, because it is too difficult for most consumers to find. We also put top sirloin, along with the flank steak, out of the running as they are both too expensive. Eye of round has the wrong shape for steaks, while bottom round is almost always used for roasts.

That left two possibilities—the top round and the shoulder. When we began investigating them, we quickly made an important discovery. Although supermarkets tend to sell top round and shoulder the same way—as thick steaks labeled London broil—the cuts are very different.

If you treat a 1- or 1½-inch-thick shoulder steak like flank steak, you get good results—a chewy, flavorful steak. Not only is shoulder the least expensive steak you can buy, it also has a little bit of fat, which you want. If, however, you cook a thick cut of top round like a flank steak, you will be disappointed. The round is lean and tight-grained, with a liver-like flavor that is almost disgusting in quickly cooked muscle meat. Shoulder, we discovered, has robust beef flavor and a reasonably tender texture, both of which make it preferable. We had unraveled the case of London broil.

INGREDIENTS: Three Flat Steaks

When it comes to flat steaks, skirt and hanger steak are most similar to flank steak, and, like flank, have recently become fashionable. The similarities: Hanger and flank both come from the rear side of the animal, while skirt comes from the area between the abdomen and the chest cavity. All are long, relatively thin, quite tough, and grainy, but each has rich, deep, beefy flavor.

We soon came to realize that all flat steaks are not equal. Hanger, a thick muscle that is attached to the diaphragm of the cow, derives its name from the fact that when the animal is butchered, this steak hangs down into the center of the carcass. Because hanger steak is a classic French bistro dish, the cut is highly prized in restaurants and, therefore, difficult to find in butcher shops. We don't think this is a great loss, since the hanger steaks we sampled had the toughest texture and least flavor of the three cuts.

On the other hand, flank steak is easy to find in any supermarket. It has great beef flavor and is quite tender if cooked rare or medium-rare and sliced thin across the grain. Because of the popularity of fajitas, flank steak has recently gone up steeply in price, often retailing for $7 a pound.

Last but not least, skirt steak, which was the cut originally used for fajitas, can also be difficult to find in supermarkets and even butcher shops. This is a real pity because skirt steak has more fat than flank steak, which makes it juicier and richer-tasting. At the same time, skirt has a deep, beefy flavor that outshines both hanger or flank steak. If you see skirt steak, buy it and cook it like flank.

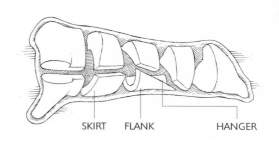

SKIRT   FLANK   HANGER

Charcoal-Grilled London Broil

SERVES 4

Because the shoulder steak is so thick, it must be grilled over a two-level fire. Do not cook it past medium-rare or this lean cut will be unpalatably dry. London broil can be seasoned with just salt and pepper or be more boldly flavored by the addition of one of the spice rubs or sauces in the preceding section on flank steak (see page 39). Because London broil is relatively lean, it is especially good when served with either of the compound butters on page 29.

I   boneless shoulder steak, I 1/2 inches thick
     (I 1/2 to 2 pounds)
     Salt and ground black pepper

1. Light a large chimney starter filled with hard-wood charcoal (about 6 quarts) and allow to burn until all the charcoal is covered with a layer of fine gray ash. Build a two-level fire by stacking most of the coals on one side of the grill and arranging the remaining coals in a single layer on the other side of the grill. Set the cooking rack in place, cover the grill with the lid, and let the rack heat up, about 5 minutes. Use a wire brush to scrape clean the cooking rack. The grill is ready when the pile of coals is medium-hot and the single layer of coals is medium-low. (See how to gauge heat level on page 34.)

2. Meanwhile, sprinkle both sides of the steak with salt and pepper to taste. Grill the steak, uncovered, over the hotter part of the fire until well browned on one side, 2 to 3 minutes. Turn the steak; grill until well browned on the other side, 2 to 3 minutes.

3. Once the steak is well browned on both sides, slide it to the cooler part of the grill. Continue grilling, uncovered, to the desired doneness, 5 to 6 minutes more for rare (120 degrees on an instant-read thermometer), 6 to 7 minutes for medium-rare on the rare side (125 degrees), or 7 to 8 minutes for medium-rare on the medium side (130 degrees).

4. Remove the steak from the grill and let rest for 5 minutes. Slice the steak thin on the bias across the grain. Adjust the seasonings with additional salt and pepper and serve immediately.

➤ VARIATION

Gas-Grilled London Broil

As in charcoal grilling, London broil should be cooked over a two-level fire.

Turn on all burners to high, close the lid, and heat the grill until very hot, about 15 minutes. Scrape the grill grate clean with a grill brush. Leave one burner on high and turn the other burner(s) down to medium. Follow the recipe for Charcoal-Grilled London Broil from step 2 and cook with the lid down.

2

I WANT TO COOK A STEAK INDOORS

I WANT TO COOK A STEAK INDOORS

JUST BECAUSE YOU CAN'T GRILL DOESN'T mean you shouldn't prepare a steak. Yes, there are few foods as perfect as a grilled steak, but there are many good ways to cook steak indoors. Recipes in the first half of this chapter explore pan-searing in a skillet over high heat (with a brief sojourn in the oven to help cook through especially thick steaks). This is how we like to cook premium steaks from the loin or rib indoors. Many of these pan-seared steaks are ideal vehicles for a rich, restaurant-quality pan sauce.

Less expensive steaks, such as flank, cube, or blade, can be used in a variety of stovetop recipes that present the steak with more rugged accompaniments. Steak pizzaiola, chicken-fried steak, teriyaki, fajitas, and Philly cheesesteak sandwiches are favorite recipes that start by cooking a less tender steak indoors and then adding some potent flavors.

PAN-SEARED PREMIUM STEAKS

STEAKS MUST BE COOKED SO THAT THE ENTIRE surface caramelizes to form a rich, thick crust. The intense heat of the grill makes it easy to obtain such a crust. But sometimes grilling is impractical. We wanted to get the same results from pan-searing.

We decided to focus on boneless steaks. Bone-in steaks, such as T-bones and porterhouses, really should be grilled; when pan-seared, it's the bone, not the meat, that makes contact with the pan, and the result is poor coloring and no crust development. We tested a dozen boneless steaks and found two that everyone in the test kitchen could agree on—rib-eye and strip steaks.

Rib steaks are cut from the rib roast (or prime rib) and come with the curved bone attached. More often, you will see boneless steaks from the rib, called rib-eye steaks. Rib eyes are tender and smooth-textured, with a distinctive, robust, beefy taste. They are very rich, with good-sized pockets of fat. Rib eye is also known as Delmonico steak in New York or Spencer steak in the West.

The strip steak is cut from the short loin part of the cow. Also called shell, Kansas City strip, New York strip, or top loin, strip steak has a noticeable grain and a moderate amount of chew. The flavor is excellent and the meat a bit less fatty than in rib-eye steaks. Strips steaks are also slightly more expensive than rib eyes.

It was obvious to us from the beginning that the key to browning the steaks was going to be preheating the pan, so that when the steaks hit the pan, the surface would be hot enough to sear them before they overcooked. In this regard, we wondered if different types of pans would heat and cook differently.

We found that a cast-iron skillet did an excellent job of browning the steaks, but we feared pan sauces would suffer. Many sources discourage the use of cast-iron pans because of the iron's tendency to react with acidic foods, giving them a metallic, off flavor. We did not find this to be a problem with *quick*-cooking sauces, as long as the skillet was well seasoned.

Next, we tried searing steaks in a nonstick skillet, but the browned bits that a good sear leaves behind in the pan and that make sauces so delicious did not materialize. The resulting sauces were anemic and weakly flavored. Pan sauces made in regular non-reactive pans were rich both in flavor and color. We had good results with heavy-bottomed pans made by All-Clad and Calphalon.

We had been searing the steaks over high heat to promote browning, but tasters noticed that the pan sauces tasted bitter. To avoid this problem, we tried heating the pan over high heat and then reducing the heat to medium-high once the steaks went into the pan. This worked fine as long as the pan was fully preheated (three minutes over high heat worked best) before the steaks were added. We found that strip and rib-eye steaks had enough fat to be seared without oil.

Over the course of testing, we noticed a few more factors that ensured a good crust on the steak and richly flavored brown bits in the pan to flavor the sauce. There should be at least ¼ inch of space between each steak if they are to sear, not steam. At the same time, the pan should not be too large because that encourages burning. A 12-inch skillet is the right size for four steaks. We also noticed that it was not a good idea to move the steaks around in the pan. This interrupted the browning process and resulted in steaks that lacked good caramelization. The steaks browned much better when moved only once, just to turn them over to the other side.

Pan-Seared Strip or Rib-Eye Steaks
SERVES 4

Serve these steaks with any of the pan sauces on pages 46–50.

> 4   boneless strip or rib-eye steaks, 1 to 1 ¼ inches thick (about 8 ounces each), patted dry with paper towels
> Salt and ground black pepper

1. Heat a heavy-bottomed, nonreactive 12-inch skillet over high heat until very hot. Meanwhile, season both sides of the steaks with salt and pepper to taste.

2. Lay the steaks in the pan, leaving ¼ inch of space between each. Reduce the heat to medium-high, and cook, not moving the steaks until they are well browned, about 4 minutes. Using tongs, flip the steaks; cook 4 minutes more for rare (120 degrees on an instant-read thermometer), 5 minutes more for medium-rare (125 to 130 degrees), and 6 minutes more for medium (135 to 140 degrees). Transfer the steaks to a large plate, tent loosely with foil, and let rest for 5 minutes while preparing a pan sauce.

PAN SAUCES FOR STEAK

A PAN SAUCE—MADE WITH JUST A HANDFUL of ingredients and in a matter of just a few minutes—can look and taste nearly as rich as a classic, labor-intensive French sauce. The base of a pan sauce is the fond, or browned bits, clinging to the bottom of the skillet after sautéing or searing meat. Once the food is removed from the skillet, aromatics such as minced shallots can be sautéed; then, in a process called deglazing, liquid (usually wine, broth, or both) is added and the fond is scraped up with a wooden spoon. The liquid is simmered and reduced to concentrate the flavors and thicken the texture and, in a final (and sometimes optional) step, the reduction is enriched and slightly thickened by the addition of butter.

If the recipe calls for canned broth (for the sake of convenience, our recipes always do), use the low-sodium variety because reduction can result in overwhelming saltiness. Also avoid the "cooking wines" sold in grocery stores. They contain considerable amounts of salt and are generally unappealing in flavor.

If you intend to make a pan sauce, opt for a traditional skillet. A nonstick skillet will not develop the fond to the same degree that a traditional skillet will, and, because fond supplies a pan sauce with richness and depth of flavor, a nonstick skillet will render a less flavorful pan sauce. Also important is the size of the skillet. It should comfortably hold the food being cooked. If it is overcrowded, the food will steam and will fail to create much fond.

If traditional (unenameled) cast iron is your cookware of choice, make sure the pan is well seasoned and free of rust. When tested in our kitchen, a sauce made in a well-seasoned cast-iron pan tasted fine. Poorly maintained cast iron, however, will yield a metallic-tasting sauce.

A great red wine pan sauce starts with the right wine (see page 47). But even the right wine can produce a poor sauce. We found that wine doesn't react well to changes in temperature, making it a tricky ingredient to handle, especially in a pan sauce where it is the dominant flavor. As wine is heated, delicate flavor compounds known as esters break apart, turning fruity flavors and aromas sour and bitter. The higher the heat, the more rapidly the esters break down.

Transferring this knowledge to cooking, it would seem reasonable to assume that low, slow heat is better for wine than hot and fast heat. To test this assumption, we made two classic steak pan sauces, one made with rapidly simmered wine, and the other made with slowly reduced wine. The results were so radically different that tasters thought the sauces had been made from different wines altogether. The rapidly simmered wine was tart and edgy, while the slowly reduced wine was smooth and round. This surprised many of us who have learned to cook pan sauces the traditional way.

Classically, wine is added to a hot pan (the same pan in which the meat was just cooked) and reduced quickly over high heat while scraping up the tasty browned bits off the pan's bottom. We found that deglazing the hot pan with stock, not wine, and finishing the sauce with wine that had been slowly reduced in a separate pan, made a much better pan sauce—one unlike any we had made before. It was rich and voluptuous, with complex layers of flavor.

As we tested a few more pan sauces using this method, we discovered another trick. The wine reduction takes on an extra dimension and polished texture when small amounts of aromatic vegetables are added. Treating the wine almost like a stock, we steeped shallots, carrots, mushrooms, and herbs in the reducing wine, then strained them out before adding the reduction to the sauce.

However, not all pan sauces with wine benefit from this extra step. For instance, we found that a sauce made with Madeira was just fine when made the conventional way (by adding the wine to the hot pan and letting it reduce).

A shallot butter sauce is even easier to prepare. It makes sense to think of this sauce as a melted version of compound butter. Compound butters are made by rolling butter (seasoned with shallots, herbs, spices, mustard, etc.) into a log, chilling the log, and then slicing off a round to melt over a cooked steak. Although delicious, a compound butter does not take advantage of the browned bits left in the pan used to sear the steaks.

For this reason, we like to add shallots to the empty skillet, then throw in the cold butter to create a quick, light sauce. Some lemon juice and parsley round out the flavor. Make sure the butter is cold when it goes into the pan. We found that cold butter gives a sauce more body than softened butter.

Classic Red Wine Pan Sauce

MAKES ENOUGH FOR 4 STEAKS

Start cooking the steaks when the wine has almost finished reducing. Use smooth, medium-bodied, fruity wine, preferably made from a blend of grapes, such as a Côtes du Rhône. For more information about choosing a red wine for cooking, see page 51. See page 48 for tips about making pan sauces.

WINE REDUCTION

- 1   small carrot, peeled and finely chopped (about 2 tablespoons)
- 1   small shallot, minced (about 2 tablespoons)
- 2   white mushrooms, finely chopped (about 3 tablespoons)
- 1   small bay leaf
- 3   sprigs fresh parsley
- 1   cup red wine

SAUCE

- 1   small shallot, minced (about 2 tablespoons)
- 1/2   cup low-sodium chicken broth
- 1/2   cup low-sodium beef broth
- 3   tablespoons cold unsalted butter, cut into 3 pieces
- 1/2   teaspoon fresh thyme leaves
    Salt and ground black pepper

1. FOR THE WINE REDUCTION: Heat the carrot, shallot, mushrooms, bay leaf, parsley, and wine in a nonreactive 12-inch skillet over low heat; cook, without simmering (liquid should be steaming but not bubbling) until the mixture reduces to 1 cup, about 15 to 20 minutes. Strain through a fine-mesh strainer and return to a clean skillet. Continue to cook over low heat, without simmering, until the liquid is reduced to 2 tablespoons, 15 to 20 minutes longer. Transfer the wine reduction to a small bowl.

2. FOR THE SAUCE: To the same skillet used to cook the steaks (do not clean the skillet or discard the accumulated fat unless there's more than 1 tablespoon in the pan), add the shallot and cook over medium-low heat until softened, about 1 minute. Turn the heat to high and add the chicken and beef broths. Bring to a boil, scraping up the browned bits

Pan Sauces 101

THE SETUP

Because pan sauces cook quickly, before you begin to cook it is essential to complete your mise en place—that is, have all necessary ingredients and utensils collected and ready to use.

Just-seared meat

After searing the meat, transfer it to a plate and tent it loosely with foil while making the sauce. A loose seal will keep any crust that has formed from turning soggy.

Small bowl

Have ready a small empty bowl or container to catch excess fat that might have to be poured off before you begin the sauce.

Aromatics

Aromatics include garlic and onions, but are most often shallots—their flavor is mild, sweet, and complex. If "minced" is specified, make sure they are fine and even; this will cause them to release maximum flavor, and their texture will be less obtrusive in the finished sauce.

Liquids

Leave liquid ingredients (such as wine, broth, juices), in a measuring cup. Once emptied, keep the measuring cup close at hand; the reduced liquid can be poured back into the measuring cup toward the end of simmering to assess its final volume and to gauge if it is adequately reduced.

Wooden utensil

A wooden utensil works best to scrape up the fond while deglazing because it is rigid (unlike a rubber spatula) and does not screech (like metal on metal). A wooden spatula is ideal because it can cover more of the surface area of the pan than the rounded tip of a spoon.

Herbs and flavorings

Herbs are sometimes used in sprig form, to be removed from the sauce before serving. Delicate herbs such as parsley and tarragon are usually chopped and added to the sauce at the end so that they do not discolor. Other flavorings such as mustard, lemon juice, capers, and chopped olives are often added at the end for maximum flavor impact.

Whisk

For maximum efficiency and easy maneuverability, use a medium-size whisk with flexible wires that can get into the rounded sides of the skillet.

Butter

Cut the butter into tablespoon-size chunks so that it will melt quickly into the sauce. Cold butter is easier to incorporate into a sauce than softened butter, and it makes a sturdier emulsion that is more resistant to separation. Butter can be omitted, but the sauce will be thinner, with little silkiness.

Salt and pepper

Tasting for and correcting seasoning is the last step before serving. Keep salt in a ramekin so that it is easy to measure out in small amounts.

THE EXECUTION

Here's how to make a pan sauce step-by-step.

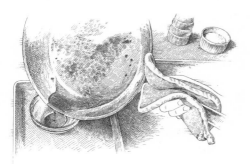

Discard excess fat

After removing the seared or sautéed items from the skillet, the first step is to discard most of the fat in the skillet, leaving just enough (several teaspoons) to cook the aromatics. With most steaks, this step is not necessary; with fatty chops, it probably is.

Sauté the aromatics

Add the aromatics to the skillet and cook them until they soften slightly, usually no more than a couple of minutes, adjusting the heat, if necessary. Be sure not to let the fond scorch, or the finished sauce will taste burnt and bitter.

Deglaze

Add the liquid to the skillet—it will sizzle and steam on contact—and scrape up the fond on the bottom of the skillet.

Reduce

The most accurate way to check the volume of the reduced liquid is to return it to the measuring cup. Some recipes ask you to reduce the liquid to an exact amount (say, 1/2 cup). Others recommend reducing the liquid by one half or two thirds.

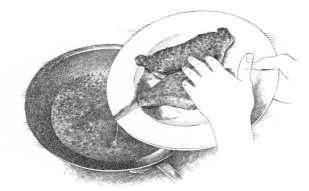

Return juices to skillet

As the meat rests, it will likely release juices; add these juices back to the skillet. If the juices should thin the sauce, allow it to simmer an additional minute or two to restore proper consistency.

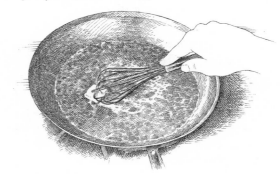

Whisk in butter

Whisk in the cold butter, one piece at a time. Grab hold of the butter with the whisk and swirl it around in the skillet until it is melted and incorporated into the sauce. Taste for seasoning before serving.

on the pan bottom with a wooden spoon until the liquid is reduced to 2 tablespoons, about 6 minutes. Turn the heat to medium-low, and whisk in the reserved wine reduction and any accumulated juices shed by the steaks. Whisk in the butter, one piece at a time, until melted and the sauce is thickened and glossy; add the thyme and season with salt and pepper to taste. Spoon the sauce over the steaks, and serve immediately.

Madeira Pan Sauce with Mustard and Anchovies

MAKES ENOUGH FOR 4 STEAKS

This sauce was inspired by one served in a Paris bistro, where the menu includes steak frites and nothing else. If you do not have Madeira on hand, dry sherry makes a fine substitute. We found no benefit to reducing Madeira slowly, so this recipe comes together much more quickly than the Classic Red Wine Sauce (see preceding recipe).

1	medium shallot, minced (about 3 tablespoons)
1	cup Madeira
2	anchovy fillets, minced to a paste (about 1 teaspoon)
1	tablespoon minced fresh parsley leaves
1	tablespoon minced fresh thyme leaves
1	tablespoon Dijon mustard
1	tablespoon juice from 1 lemon
3	tablespoons cold unsalted butter, cut into 3 pieces
	Salt and ground black pepper

To the same skillet used to cook the steaks (do not clean the skillet or discard the accumulated fat unless there's more than 1 tablespoon in the pan), add the shallot and cook over medium-low heat until softened, about 1 minute. Add the Madeira; increase the heat to high, and scrape the pan bottom with a wooden spoon to loosen the browned bits. Simmer until the liquid is reduced to about ⅓ cup, 6 to 8 minutes. Add any accumulated juices shed by the steaks and reduce the liquid 1 minute longer. Whisk in the anchovies, parsley, thyme, mustard, lemon juice, and butter, one piece at a time, until the butter has melted and the sauce is

slightly thickened; season with salt and pepper to taste. Spoon the sauce over the steaks, and serve immediately.

Shallot Butter Pan Sauce

MAKES ENOUGH FOR 4 STEAKS

This sauce requires very little time and effort to prepare.

2	medium shallots, minced (about ⅓ cup)
4	tablespoons cold unsalted butter, cut into 4 pieces
1	teaspoon juice from 1 lemon
1	teaspoon minced fresh parsley leaves
	Salt and ground black pepper

To the same skillet used to cook the steaks (do not clean the skillet or discard the accumulated fat unless there's more than 1 tablespoon in the pan), add the shallots and cook over medium-low heat until softened, about 1 minute. Stir in the butter one piece at a time, scraping up the browned bits on the pan bottom with a wooden spoon. When the butter is just melted, stir in the lemon juice and parsley; season with salt and pepper to taste. Spoon the sauce over the steaks, and serve immediately.

PAN-SEARED FILET MIGNON

WHEN IT COMES TO STEAK, AMERICANS PRIZE tenderness above all—and filet mignon is the most tender steak there is. It is also expensive, and both factors may drive its perennial popularity as a grand, splashy, celebratory restaurant meal. You've probably noticed that in a restaurant, filet mignon (also known as tenderloin steak or simply as filet) is usually served rare, with a deeply seared crust, and adorned with a rich, luxurious pan sauce or flavored butter.

Well, there is no reason to limit the fun to restaurants. Filets are available in any supermarket with a meat case, and they are not difficult to cook. We wanted to replicate the best restaurant filets at home, which meant developing a deeply browned, rich crust on both sides of each steak without overcooking the interior or scorching the drippings in the pan, which would go on to serve as the basis for a luscious sauce. To that end, we investigated the fine points of both the steaks themselves and the cooking process. Is it worth paying top dollar for superthick steaks, or would supermarket filets of any size do? And what about the best cooking method, temperature, and pan?

Filets are thick (usually 1¼ to 2 inches), boneless steaks cut from the slender, supertender, ultralean tenderloin muscle, which rests under the animal's spine. The muscle remains tender because the animal doesn't use it to move about, and it is both lean and mildly flavored because it has little marbling (ribbons of intramuscular fat that melt during cooking to provide flavor and juiciness).

We shopped for filets at six local supermarkets and were not satisfied with the butchering job

---

INGREDIENTS: Red Wines for Cooking

When a recipe calls for red wine, the tendency is to grab whatever is inexpensive, close at hand, or already open on the counter. But as with any ingredient, the type of wine you cook with can make a big difference. The wrong wine can turn a good sauce bad. Yet because wines range enormously in flavor, body, and astringency, choosing a good one for the kitchen can be a shot in the dark.

What defines a good red cooking wine? It is appropriate for a wide range of recipes, easy to find at the local store, and consistent through the years. To help determine which red wines are good cookers, we set up a series of three cooking tests—a quick tomato sauce, a long-cooked beef stew, and a pan sauce for steak—through which we could test numerous bottles.

Organizing the overwhelming body of red wine into manageable groups, we assigned four categories based on flavor, body, and style: light/fruity, smooth/mellow, hearty/robust, and nondescript jug wine. Ironically, the only type of wine not represented is the "cooking wine" found on most supermarket shelves. In the past, we found that these low-alcohol concoctions have no flavor, a high-pitched acidity, and an enormous amount of salt, which renders them both undrinkable and a very poor choice for cooking.

We began by cooking with a representative from each category: a light/fruity Beaujolais, a smooth/mellow Merlot, a hearty/robust Cabernet Sauvignon, and a jug of Paul Masson Mountain Burgundy. The results were drastically different. The Beaujolais made refreshingly fruity but wimpy sauces, while the Merlot made for balanced sauces with an overcooked, jam-like flavor. The Cabernet Sauvignon produced an astringent, woody bite that bullied other ingredients out of the way, and the Paul Masson made sweet, simple sauces that neither offended nor impressed anyone.

Although none of the four groups "won" this first round of testing, what emerged were some important attributes of a good cooking wine and some characteristics of which to be wary. The light wine made weak sauces and the hearty wine made sauces that were

too muscular. Oak flavors (from barrel aging) did not soften as they cooked but wound up tasting bitter and harsh. Fruity characteristics, on the other hand, mingled well with the other sauce ingredients and complemented their flavors.

Narrowing our focus to smooth, fruity, medium-bodied wines with little oak influence, we put four more types of wine through the trio of recipes: a Chianti, a Zinfandel, a Pinot Noir, and a Côtes du Rhône. The Chianti tasted great in the tomato sauce but made an astringent pan sauce and cardboard-tasting stews. The Zinfandel tasted overcooked and jammy in the tomato sauce and turned the pan sauce bitter. While both the Côtes du Rhône and Pinot Noir turned in impressive results across the board, the Côtes du Rhône was stellar. When compared with the sauces made with Pinot Noir (a wine made from just one type of grape), the Côtes du Rhône (a blend of grapes) had a fuller, more even-keeled flavor. The varietals within the blend compensated for each others' shortcomings. The resulting sauces were potent but well-rounded. Besides Côtes du Rhône, there are many fruity, medium-bodied, blended wines, including wines from the greater Rhône Valley, Languedoc (near the Mediterranean), Australia, and the United States.

We found a strong correlation between price and quality when it comes to red wine. Tests demonstrated that a $5 bottle cooked much differently from bottles costing $10, $20, or $30. As a wine cooks and reduces, it becomes a more intensely flavored version of itself, and defining characteristics become unbearably obvious. The sweet, bland $5 wines cooked down to a candy-like sauce, while the $10, $20, and $30 bottles were increasingly smooth, with multiple layers of flavor. Although the higher-end wines tasted slightly more balanced and refined, none of the tasters thought the flavor difference between the $10 and $20 or $30 bottles was worth the extra money. What's more, limiting the price to around $10 does not restrict your options when shopping. We found plenty of good blends from California, Australia, and France.

from a single one. The steaks were usually cut unevenly, with one end noticeably thicker than the other. Beyond that, different steaks in the same package were different sizes and weights. This was far from ideal for expensive, premium steaks. Consistency of size and thickness was important for even cooking within each steak, as well as from steak to steak, in the pan. With that in mind, we purchased a small, roughly 2-pound section of the tenderloin, called a tenderloin roast, and cut our own steaks from it. The process was easy, taking less than two minutes, and our hand-cut filets were uniform. Tenderloin roasts were available wherever we shopped, so if you can get them, too, we recommend this practice. Alternatively, ask the butcher to cut the steaks for you.

To determine the optimal thickness for filets, we cooked steaks cut 1 and 2 inches thick and at ¼-inch intervals in between. Tasters preferred the 1½-inch cut, which made for a generous (but not over-the-top) portion.

Grilling is a good option for filets, but because we also wanted to make a pan sauce, we decided to cook our filets in a pan. The recipes we looked at suggested a couple of alternatives, including broiling, high-roasting (oven-roasting at high heat), and pan-searing (stovetop cooking over high heat), all of which we tried. Pan-searing was our approach of choice because it developed the deep brown, caramelized crust critical to the flavor of both the meat and the sauce. Right off the bat, we confirmed our suspicion that filets are best cooked rare to medium-rare. In our opinion, cooking them to medium begins to compromise their tenderness, which is, after all, their raison d'être.

Our next tests involved searing well-dried filets in a dry pan and in a pan filmed with oil. (Drying the steaks thoroughly with paper towels aids development of a crust.) Not surprisingly for such lean meat, the oil was necessary to produce a deep, dark, satisfying crust, and we found that rubbing the oil right into the steaks reduced the spattering a little.

In our tests of different heat levels, we found that a crust formed over a consistently high flame was better developed than one formed over a medium-high flame. But this approach also created a problem. Over such high heat, the fond (the browned bits left in the pan after the steaks were cooked) was often scorched by the time the meat reached medium-rare, giving the sauce a bitter flavor. We tried out a couple of ideas to remedy the problem.

First, we switched from the 12-inch skillet we'd been using (for four steaks) to a smaller, 10-inch model. The decreased surface area between the steaks helped protect the fond. (A heavy-bottomed or cast-iron skillet is essential here; the All-Clad 10-inch skillets we use in the test kitchen weigh about 2½ pounds. Smaller or lighter pans, we found, overheat too easily.) Second, we revisited the high-roasting method, combining it with our searing method by finishing the seared steaks on a preheated rimmed baking sheet in a hot oven. This approach offered the double advantage of protecting the fond from the direct heat of the oven and giving us a head start on the pan sauce while the steaks finished cooking.

Throughout testing, the oven time needed to achieve a given degree of doneness varied continually, as did our thermometer readings. While internal temperature guidelines for varying stages of doneness certainly do exist, it can be difficult to achieve an accurate reading in such a small piece of meat. The reading can be way off depending on where the thermometer probe hits, and it's surprisingly easy to miss dead center when you're working fast and juggling tongs and a hot steak in one hand and a thermometer in the other. In some cases, we had readings as low as 117 degrees and as high as 140 degrees in the same steak. It all depended on the position of the thermometer probe.

What's a cook to do? Just make a small nick in the steak with the tip of a paring knife and look inside. Be sure to remove the steaks from the heat just before they are done to your liking. They will continue to cook a little off the heat, which should give them a perfect finish. This method never failed to produce steaks cooked just the way we like them.

Pan-Seared Filets Mignons
SERVES 4

If the filets are misshapen or unevenly cut, as supermarket steaks sometimes are, follow the illustration on page 27 to tie each one before cooking. Determining when the meat is cooked to your liking is key to a good steak, so pay close attention to the visual cues in step 3. We find that mild filets benefit from potent sauces, including any of the pan sauces on page 46 to 50. If you choose to serve the steaks with a pan sauce, have all the sauce ingredients ready before searing the steaks. Begin the sauce while the steaks are in the oven. Filets are also appropriate with Chimichurri (page 405), a fresh Argentinian sauce made with parsley, garlic, and vinegar. To cook six steaks instead of four, switch to a 12-inch pan and use 6 teaspoons of olive oil.

- 4 center-cut filets mignons, 1 1/2 inches thick (7 to 8 ounces each), patted dry with paper towels
- 4 teaspoons olive oil
  Salt and ground black pepper

1. Adjust an oven rack to the lower-middle position, place a rimmed baking sheet on the oven rack, and heat the oven to 450 degrees. When the oven reaches 450 degrees, heat a heavy-bottomed 10-inch skillet (not nonstick) over high heat on the stovetop until very hot.

2. Meanwhile, rub each side of the steaks with 1/2 teaspoon oil and sprinkle generously with salt and pepper to taste. Place the steaks in the skillet and cook, without moving them, until well browned and a nice crust has formed, about 3 minutes. Turn the steaks with tongs and cook until well browned and a nice crust has formed on the second side, about 3 minutes longer. Remove the pan from the heat; using tongs, transfer each steak to the heated baking sheet in the oven.

3. Roast 2 to 4 minutes for very rare (the center of the steaks will appear cherry red and feel very soft and loose when cut into with the tip of a paring knife), 4 to 6 minutes for rare (the centers will appear red and soft), 6 to 8 minutes for medium-rare (the centers will appear pink and feel firm but juicy), or 8 to 10 minutes for medium (the centers will appear light pink and feel firm and compact). (After transferring the steaks to the oven, prepare a pan sauce in the empty skillet, if desired.) Transfer the steaks to a large plate, tent loosely with foil, and let rest for about 5 minutes before serving.

➤ VARIATION
Bacon-Wrapped Filets Mignons
Wrap 1 slice bacon around the circumference of each filet, overlapping the ends and securing them to the meat with a toothpick. Follow the recipe for Pan-Seared Filets Mignons, holding the filets two or three at a time on their sides with tongs in the skillet to crisp the bacon slightly all the way around the filet before transferring the filets to the oven.

Pepper-Crusted Filets Mignons with Port-Cherry Reduction
SERVES 4

If the filets are misshapen or unevenly cut, as supermarket steaks sometimes are, follow the illustration on page 27 to tie each one before cooking. Press the plastic wrap around the top and sides of each filet to make sure the peppercorns adhere to the steak in step 2. While heating the peppercorns in oil tempers their pungent heat, this recipe is still fairly spicy. If you prefer a very mild pepper flavor, drain the cooled peppercorns in a fine-mesh strainer in step 1, toss them with 5 tablespoons of fresh oil, add the salt, and proceed. Make the Port-Cherry Reduction (recipe follows) first, then cook the steaks. Serve with Blue Cheese–Chive Butter (see page 29) for a truly decadent filet mignon.

- 5 tablespoons black peppercorns, crushed (see the illustration on page 55)
- 5 tablespoons plus 2 teaspoons olive oil
- 1 tablespoon kosher salt
- 4 center-cut filets mignons, 1 1/2 to 2 inches thick (7 to 8 ounces each), patted dry with paper towels

1. Heat the peppercorns and 5 tablespoons of the oil in a small saucepan over low heat until faint bubbles appear. Continue to cook at a bare simmer,

swirling the pan occasionally, until the pepper is fragrant, 7 to 10 minutes. Remove from the heat and set aside to cool. When the mixture is room temperature, add the salt and stir to combine.

2. Rub the steaks with the pepper mixture, thoroughly coating the top and bottom of each steak with peppercorns. Cover the steaks with plastic wrap and press gently to make sure the peppercorns adhere; let stand at room temperature for 1 hour.

3. Meanwhile, adjust an oven rack to the middle position, place a rimmed baking sheet on the oven rack, and heat the oven to 450 degrees. Heat the remaining 2 teaspoons oil in a 12-inch heavy-bottomed skillet (not nonstick) over medium-high heat until just smoking. Place the steaks in the skillet and cook, without moving them, until well browned and a nice crust has formed, 3 to 4 minutes. Turn the steaks with tongs and cook until well browned on the second side, about 3 minutes longer.

4. Remove the pan from heat; using tongs, transfer each steak to the heated baking sheet in the oven. Roast 2 to 4 minutes for very rare (the center of the steaks will appear cherry red and feel very soft and loose when cut into with the tip of a paring knife), 4 to 6 minutes for rare (the centers will appear red and soft), 6 to 8 minutes for medium-rare (the centers will appear pink and feel firm but juicy), or 8 to 10 minutes for medium (the centers will appear light pink and feel firm and compact).

5. Transfer the steaks to a large plate, tent loosely with foil, and let rest for about 5 minutes before serving.

Port-Cherry Reduction

MAKES ABOUT I CUP

The great thing about this sauce is that it can be made several hours in advance.

1½	cups port
½	cup balsamic vinegar
½	cup dried tart cherries
1	large shallot, minced (about 3 tablespoons)
2	sprigs fresh thyme
1	tablespoon unsalted butter
	Salt

1. Bring the port, balsamic vinegar, cherries, shallot, and thyme to a simmer in a medium saucepan over medium-low heat until reduced to ⅓ cup, about 30 minutes. Set aside, covered.

2. While the steaks are resting, reheat the sauce. Off the heat, remove the thyme, then whisk in the butter until melted. Season with salt to taste and serve with the steaks.

Steak au Poivre

THERE'S NOTHING COMPLICATED ABOUT steak au poivre. When well executed, the slightly sweet, smooth sauce has more than a hint of shallot and brandy, the steak is well-browned on the outside and cherry-red on the interior, and the crust of cracked peppercorns provides a pungent, slow burn, adding fire and depth to an otherwise simple steak.

That's the good news. A third-rate steak au poivre has peppercorns that fall off the steak only to reveal underbrowned meat. What's more, the peppercorn coat prevents the steak from forming drippings in the skillet that are the foundation of a rich sauce, and few home cooks have beef or veal stock on hand to give the sauce the substance and backbone it needs. Because most steak au poivre recipes make no attempt to solve these problems, the home cook is left aghast at the end result: wan, tasteless steaks covered by an insipid sauce made in a blackened skillet that is headed straight for the trash.

Our first few tests were useful only in

PROPERLY GROUND PEPPERCORNS

For steak au poivre, grind or crush whole peppercorns (left) to a very coarse texture (right). If your pepper mill cannot handle this task, see the alternate methods on page 55. In any case, do not use finely ground pepper in this recipe.

determining the best cut of steak for au poivre. Filets were tender but too mild-flavored. Rib eyes, always a favorite in the test kitchen, have abundant fat pockets and pronounced veins of gristle that separate two differently textured muscles. A peppercorn crust obscures these imperfections, requiring scrutiny and maneuvering on the part of the diner to eat around these parts. Strip steaks, however, have external lines of gristle that are easily trimmed before cooking, and their neat, tight, even grain makes them particularly well suited to steak au poivre.

We quickly determined peppercorn type. Among black, white, and a four-peppercorn blend of green, pink, black, and white, plain old black was the favorite in the test kitchen. Tasters extolled it for its sharp bite, rich and intense flavor, and elusive smokiness.

The steaks we cooked early on were crusted with a scant teaspoon of peppercorns on each side. Loose pepper fell off the steaks and scorched pitifully in the skillet. The pepper that did stick shielded the surface of the steaks, preventing browning and thereby the formation of a fond (the sticky browned bits left in a pan after sautéing) on which to build the sauce. In addition, most tasters thought we were far too liberal in our peppercorn allotment—the heat was incendiary and vicious. Our first thought was to cut back on the peppercorns, but then a light bulb went on. What if the steaks were coated on one side only? The unpeppered side would brown nicely, producing more fond for the sauce, and there would be no peppercorns on that side to singe.

Typically, steaks cook over intensely high heat. But for this new approach, we placed the skillet over medium heat until it was hot, and, after laying the steaks in the skillet—unpeppered-side down—turned up the heat to medium-high. This technique gave the steaks six minutes to brown on the first side and form a fond. Then the steaks were flipped onto their peppered side and given only three to five minutes (depending on desired doneness) to complete their cooking, this time without scorching the pepper. It worked like a charm.

The steak was done, so we turned our attention to the sauce. All steak au poivre sauces contain beef or veal stock and brandy. Most contain cream,

though some achieve a particular richness from butter only. The stock was the first problem. Most home cooks have only canned chicken and beef broth on hand, and the latter has long been considered either artificial tasting or weakly flavored in the test kitchen (see page 238 for more information). Using chicken broth alone, we cooked down the liquid to concentrate its flavor, but the sauce still lacked meatiness and depth. We tried to doctor it with dried porcini mushrooms, but the mushroom

CRUSHING PEPPERCORNS

If your pepper mill can't produce coarsely crushed peppercorns, you have two alternatives.

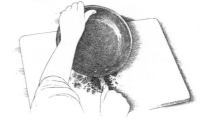

A. Use the bottom of a heavy pan and a rocking motion to crush peppercorns.

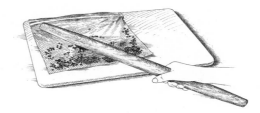

B. Or, spread the peppercorns in an even layer in a zipper-lock plastic bag and whack them with a rolling pin or meat pounder.

ADHERING THE PEPPER TO THE STEAKS

Pressing down on the steaks with a cake pan or flat pot lid once the steaks have been placed in the hot skillet promotes browning and ensures that the peppercorns adhere.

flavor was too distinct. We tried commercial veal demi-glace (superconcentrated veal stock), but the tomato paste–laden demi-glace looked and tasted unnatural. Finally, we tried low-sodium beef broth straight from the can and reduced it. This sauce was beefier, more substantial, and deeper in color—but it was plagued by the tinny flavor characteristic of canned beef broth.

On the verge of giving up, we finally hit upon a solution. We reduced almost equal amounts of chicken and beef broths with sautéed shallots to about one quarter of their original volume. Finally—a terrific, full-flavored sauce. But the long simmering time threw a wrench in the works. A typical pan sauce for steak is made by deglazing the skillet in which the steaks were cooked. This usually takes no longer than a few minutes and can be accomplished while the steaks rest. The sauce took well over 10 minutes to make, much longer than you'd want the meat to rest. The solution was straightforward: Reduce the broth mixture before cooking the steaks, then use the resulting liquid to deglaze the skillet.

Introducing brandy to the sauce was no trivial matter. We tried reducing it with the broth mixture to concentrate its flavor. This worked, but because we were also concentrating the sugar in the brandy, the resulting sauce tasted as sweet as butterscotch pudding, with no spirited bite. If we held off adding the brandy until much later in the sauce-making process, it tasted hot and raw. The time to add it was when the reduced broth mixture went into the skillet to deglaze it; the mixture simmers for about five minutes, just long enough for the brandy to reduce a bit, shake its alcoholic harshness, and meld with the broth.

Tasters voted to enrich the sauce with both cream and butter, not just butter alone. Cream made the sauce luxurious and sophisticated and gave its texture substance. Only ¼ cup was needed, and, when added at the same time as the brandy, the cream had a chance to cook down and lend body to the sauce. To finish, butter whisked in at the end brought silkiness, a bit of raw brandy gave nice bite and fresh brandy flavor, and a teaspoon of lemon juice or champagne vinegar brightened things up.

Steak au Poivre with Brandied Cream Sauce
SERVES 4

To save time, crush the peppercorns and trim the steaks while the broth mixture simmers. Many pepper mills do not have a sufficiently coarse setting. In that case, crush peppercorns with a sauté pan or rolling pin (see the illustrations on page 55). See page 54 for information about peppercorns and see page 341 for information about pepper mills, including models capable of producing crushed peppercorns. Finely ground pepper is not a substitute for the crushed peppercorns in this recipe.

SAUCE
4	tablespoons unsalted butter, cut into 4 pieces
I	medium shallot, minced (about 3 tablespoons)
I	cup low-sodium beef broth
¾	cup low-sodium chicken broth
¼	cup heavy cream
¼	cup plus I tablespoon brandy
I	teaspoon juice from I lemon or I teaspoon champagne vinegar
	Salt

STEAKS
4	strip steaks, ¾ to I inch thick and no larger than 3 inches at widest points (8 to 10 ounces each), trimmed of exterior gristle
	Salt
I	tablespoon black peppercorns, crushed

1. FOR THE SAUCE: Heat 1 tablespoon of the butter in a heavy-bottomed 12-inch skillet over medium heat. When the foaming subsides, add the shallot and cook, stirring occasionally, until softened, about 2 minutes. Add the beef and chicken broths, increase the heat to high, and boil until reduced to about ½ cup, about 8 minutes. Set the reduced broth mixture aside. Rinse and wipe out the skillet.

2. FOR THE STEAKS: Meanwhile, sprinkle both sides of the steaks with salt; rub one side of each steak with 1 teaspoon crushed peppercorns, and, using fingers, press the peppercorns into the steaks to make them adhere.

3. Place the now-empty, clean skillet over

medium heat until hot. Lay the steaks unpeppered-side down in the hot skillet, increase the heat to medium-high, firmly press down on the steaks with the bottom of a cake pan (see the illustration on page 55), and cook the steaks without moving them until well browned, about 6 minutes. Using tongs, flip the steaks, firmly press down on the steaks with the bottom of the cake pan, and cook on the peppered side, about 3 minutes longer for rare, about 4 minutes longer for medium-rare, or about 5 minutes longer for medium. Transfer the steaks to a large plate and tent loosely with foil.

4. Pour the reduced broth, cream, and ¼ cup brandy into the now-empty skillet; increase the heat to high and bring to a boil, scraping the pan bottom with a wooden spoon to loosen the browned bits. Simmer until deep golden brown and thick enough to heavily coat the back of a metal tablespoon or soup spoon, about 5 minutes. Off heat, whisk in the remaining 3 tablespoons butter, one piece at a time, the remaining 1 tablespoon brandy, lemon juice, and any accumulated meat juices. Adjust the seasonings with salt.

5. Set the steaks on individual dinner plates, spoon an equal portion of the sauce over each steak, and serve immediately.

Steak Pizzaiola

SUPPOSEDLY INVENTED BY THE WIVES OF Neapolitan pizza makers, this weeknight favorite is nothing more than steak cooked with pizza sauce—tomato sauce flavored with garlic and herbs. After making several authentic recipes, it became clear that although this classic steak dish is easy to make, it is not necessarily easy to make well.

Our first job was to find the best cut of meat. While older recipes use steaks cut from the round, we found that round steaks were too tough and dry even after they were simmered in the sauce for a long time. More modern recipes, on the other hand, call for expensive steaks such as New York strip, rib eye, and tenderloin. Although these steaks cooked up tender, their delicate flavors and fancy prices simply didn't pair well with the potency of the accompanying pizza sauce. We then tried flank steak as well as skirt steak, and we finally discovered the meat we were looking for. With a strong, beefy flavor and a reasonable price tag, these steaks cooked in only a few minutes and sliced up perfectly.

To cook the steaks, we tried the classic technique of browning them, then simmering them in the pizza sauce, but found that they overcooked easily. Flank steak and skirt steak are quite thin, and we learned it was better to brown them in a hot pan and keep them warm in the oven while we made a pizza sauce with the pan drippings.

We found that diced tomatoes tasted great but were just too chunky for this recipe. We preferred the thick, smooth sauce made from crushed tomatoes. The problem, however, is that crushed tomatoes are generally sold in 28-ounce cans, which are simply too big. We decided to crush our own tomatoes by pulsing a small (14.5-ounce) can of diced tomatoes in a food processor. Now the texture of the tomatoes was correct, and we had no leftovers.

Keeping the other flavors of the sauce simple, we added onions, garlic, oregano, red wine, and parsley. Although the sauce was perfect for pizza, it still needed a bigger flavor to stand up to the steak. We found it necessary to round out the sauce with a tablespoon of tomato paste.

Steak Pizzaiola

SERVES 4

Skirt steak is richer and beefier in flavor than flank steak, but skirt tends to fall apart when sliced. Flank steak is firmer. Both are good choices for this recipe, however.

1	(14.5-ounce) can diced tomatoes
1 ½	pounds flank or skirt steak (if using skirt steak, cut it into several 8-inch lengths)
	Salt and ground black pepper
2	tablespoons extra-virgin olive oil
1	medium onion, sliced thin
5	medium garlic cloves, minced or pressed through a garlic press (about 5 teaspoons)
	Pinch red pepper flakes
1	tablespoon tomato paste
¼	cup dry red wine

I   sprig fresh oregano
I   tablespoon minced fresh parsley leaves

1. Pulse the tomatoes and their juices in the workbowl of a food processor fitted with a metal blade to a coarse puree, about five 1-second pulses. Set the puree aside.

2. Adjust an oven rack to the middle position and heat the oven to 300 degrees. Sprinkle the meat generously with salt and pepper to taste. Heat 1 tablespoon of the oil in a heavy-bottomed 12-inch skillet over high heat until it just starts to smoke. Reduce the heat to medium, add the meat, and cook, not moving, until well browned, 4 to 5 minutes. Turn the meat with tongs and cook until well-browned on the second side, 4 to 5 minutes longer. Transfer the meat to an ovenproof plate and place the plate in the warm oven while assembling the sauce.

3. Return the empty pan to medium heat, add the remaining tablespoon oil, and swirl to coat the pan. Add the onion and cook until slightly browned around the edges, 2 to 3 minutes. Add the garlic, pepper flakes, and tomato paste and cook until aromatic, about 30 seconds. Add the wine, pureed tomatoes, and oregano, scraping any browned bits from the bottom of the pan with a wooden spoon. Cook until the sauce is slightly thickened and measures about 1½ cups, about 5 minutes. Remove the pan from the heat and stir in the parsley.

4. As the sauce finishes cooking, remove the meat from the oven and transfer it to a cutting board, adding any accumulated juices on the plate to the sauce. Slice the steak on the bias across the grain into ½-inch-thick pieces. To serve, pour the sauce onto individual plates or a large warmed serving platter and top with the sliced steak. Serve immediately.

CHICKEN-FRIED STEAK

ALTHOUGH THIS TRUCK-STOP FAVORITE often gets a bad rap, chicken-fried steak can be delicious when cooked just right. When cooked wrong, the dry, rubbery steaks snap back with each bite and are coated in a damp, pale breading and topped with a bland, pasty white sauce. When cooked well, however, thin cutlets of beef are breaded and fried until crisp and golden brown. The creamy gravy that accompanies the steaks is well seasoned and not too thick.

The first question we encountered on the road to good chicken-fried steak was what type of steak to use. By design, chicken-fried steak is a technique used with only the cheapest of cuts. No one would use strip steaks or filet mignon in this recipe, but steaks from the round, chuck, and sirloin are all contenders. We tested cube, Swiss, top round, bottom round, eye round, chuck, and top sirloin steaks and came up with one winner. The cube steak was our favorite. This steak is lean yet tender; most of the other cuts tested were either fatty or difficult to chew.

Cube steak is usually cut from the round and tenderized (cubed) by the butcher, who uses a special machine to give the steak its unique, bumpy texture. We found that this lean, tender steak required little trimming and was easy to pound out to a thin cutlet, about ⅓ inch thick. Regular top-, bottom-, and eye-round steaks, on the other hand, were thick and tough, requiring lots of muscle to pound out and chew. Swiss and chuck steaks, which come from the shoulder, were slightly less tough but still chewy and resilient. Top sirloin tasted great and had a nice texture, but the meat was laced with wide strips of gristle. Trimming the gristle turned this steak into small, awkwardly sized pieces, making for unusual portions and cooking times.

What really makes chicken-fried steak great is the coating and subsequent frying. But what kind of coating is best? To find out, we tested straight flour against various contenders, including cornflakes, Melba toast, cornmeal, matzo crumbs, ground saltines, and panko (Japanese bread crumbs). Straight flour was light and clung well to the steak but was simply too delicate for the toothsome meat and cream gravy. Cornflakes and Melba toast both burned and became tough, while the grittiness of cornmeal was simply out of place. Matzo, saltines, and panko all tasted great but quickly grew soggy under the rich cream gravy.

We figured our single-breading technique might to be blame and decided to try double (or bound) breading. With single breading, meat is dipped into egg and then into flour, while double breading starts off with an initial dip in flour, then into egg, and again into flour (or into a coating such as those we tried with the steak). In side-by-side tests, we were surprised to discover that single breading was actually messier than double. When initially dipped in flour, the meat becomes dry and talcum-smooth, allowing the egg to cling evenly to the surface. The double breading also offered a more substantial base coat on the meat that didn't become overly thick or tough. Seasoned flour and a double-breading technique yielded a much improved crust.

Although this double breading was far superior to any other breading so far, we were still left wanting a heartier and crunchier crust. We wondered if we could bolster the egg wash with some buttermilk, baking soda, and baking powder, something that we knew worked well with fried chicken. Sure enough, these ingredients turned the egg wash into a thick, foamy concoction. This created a wet yet airy layer onto which both layers of flour were able to stick and hydrate. This wet-looking, skin-like coating fried up to an impressive, dark mahogany color with a resilient texture that didn't weaken under the gravy. Because the coating is such a big part of the dish, we found it necessary to season it heavily using salt, black pepper, and cayenne.

After frying a few batches of these steaks, we found the flavor of peanut oil preferable to that of vegetable oil or even shortening. Because the steaks are thin, they fry evenly in just one inch of oil. To keep splattering to a minimum, we used a deep Dutch oven. We also noted that the steaks fried to a dark, beautiful brown without tasting too greasy when the oil was heated initially to 375 degrees. Although the thick breading offers substantial protection from the hot oil, the steaks usually cook through completely within the time it takes for the crust to brown, about 2½ minutes per side.

Equally important to the crust is the cream gravy made from the fried drippings. Not wanting to waste any time while the fried steaks were kept warm in the oven, we found it easy to strain the small amount of hot oil used to fry the steaks right away. Adding the strained bits of deep-fried crumbs back to the Dutch oven, we were ready to make gravy. Most recipes simmer the drippings with some milk and thicken it with flour. To avoid making a floury-tasting sauce, we decided to cook the flour in the fat (that is, make a roux) and then add the milk, along with a splash of chicken broth. We found this technique quick and easy, and it produced an authentic-tasting sauce.

We tested recipes using cream, half-and-half, and evaporated milk, but tasters preferred the fresh, clean flavor and lighter texture of whole milk. Onions and cayenne are traditional seasonings for the gravy, but tasters also liked small additions of thyme and garlic (neither of which is authentic). Topped with the light, well-seasoned gravy, this chicken-fried steak is the best any trucker has ever tasted.

Chicken-Fried Steak
SERVES 6

Initially heating the oil to 375 degrees is key to the success of this recipe. An instant-read thermometer with a high upper range is perfect for checking the temperature; a clip-on candy/deep-fry thermometer will also work. If your Dutch oven measures 11 inches across (as ours does), you will need to fry the steaks in two batches.

STEAK

3	cups unbleached all-purpose flour
	Salt and ground black pepper
⅛	teaspoon cayenne pepper
1	large egg
1	teaspoon baking powder
½	teaspoon baking soda
1	cup buttermilk
6	cube steaks (about 5 ounces each), pounded to ⅓-inch thickness
4–5	cups peanut oil

CREAM GRAVY

1	medium onion, minced
⅛	teaspoon dried thyme
2	medium garlic cloves, minced or pressed through a garlic press (about 2 teaspoons)
3	tablespoons all-purpose flour
½	cup low-sodium chicken broth
2	cups whole milk

¾   teaspoon salt
¼   teaspoon ground black pepper
      Pinch cayenne pepper

1. FOR THE STEAK: Measure the flour, 5 teaspoons salt, 1 teaspoon pepper, and cayenne into a large shallow dish. In a second large, shallow dish, beat the egg, baking powder, and baking soda; stir in the buttermilk (the mixture will bubble and foam).

2. Set a wire rack over a rimmed baking sheet. Pat the steaks dry with paper towels and sprinkle each side with salt and pepper to taste. Drop the steaks into the seasoned flour and shake the pan to coat. Shake the excess flour from each steak, then, using tongs, dip the steaks into the egg mixture, turning to coat well and allowing the excess to drip off. Coat the steaks with flour again, shake off the excess, and place them on the wire rack.

3. Adjust an oven rack to the middle position, set a second wire rack over a second rimmed baking sheet, and place on the oven rack; heat the oven to 200 degrees. Line a large plate with a double layer of paper towels. Meanwhile, heat 1 inch of oil in a large (11-inch diameter) Dutch oven over medium-high heat to 375 degrees. Place three steaks in the oil and fry, turning once, until deep golden brown on each side, about 5 minutes (oil temperature will drop to around 335 degrees). Transfer the steaks to the paper towel-lined plate to drain, then transfer them to the wire rack in the oven. Bring the oil back to 375 degrees and repeat the cooking and draining process (use fresh paper towels) with the three remaining steaks.

4. FOR THE GRAVY: Carefully pour the hot oil through a fine-mesh strainer into a clean pot. Return the browned bits from the strainer along with 2 tablespoons of frying oil back to the Dutch oven. Turn the heat to medium, add the onion and thyme, and cook until the onion has softened and begins to brown, 4 to 5 minutes. Add the garlic and cook until aromatic, about 30 seconds. Add the flour and stir until well combined, about 1 minute. Whisk in the broth, scraping any browned bits off the bottom of the pan. Whisk in the milk, salt, pepper, and cayenne; bring to a simmer over medium-high heat. Cook until thickened (the gravy should have a loose consistency—it will thicken as it cools slightly), about 5 minutes.

5. Transfer the chicken-fried steaks to individual plates. Spoon a generous amount of the gravy over each steak. Serve immediately, passing any remaining gravy in a bowl.

BEEF TERIYAKI

WHAT IN THE WORLD IS TERIYAKI? MOST every Asian restaurant has some version of it, generally a sickly sweet, shellac-thick sauce varnished on tough mystery meat. But teriyaki can be a well-balanced sauce napping tender pieces of flavorful beef, chicken, or fish. Despite its simplicity, however, teriyaki is prone to problems. We set out to rectify them, as it is ideal for a quick meal.

Teriyaki is a Japanese term that refers to a particular sauce and cooking style. Teri translates as "luster," and yaki is a cooking method in which food is broiled. Traditionally, the teriyaki sauce is applied toward the end of cooking. Beef teriyaki generally appears as strips of beef—on skewers or not—flash-cooked so they are pink on the inside and glossy mahogany on the outside.

When we assessed the recipes we gathered, we found little consensus about the cut of beef to use for teriyaki. Sirloin and top round appeared, but so did flank steak and even rib eye. All the choices proved acceptable, but in the end, we favored a more unorthodox choice: blade steak. Richly flavored and inexpensive, blade steak is an underutilized cut of beef. Most people dismiss it because of a minor flaw: a thick ribbon of gristle running through the middle. However, the gristle serves here as a guide for slicing the meat; keeping the knife parallel to the gristle ensures you are cutting across the grain—a job, we have found, that can be confusing for home cooks. We kept the strips thin—about ¼ inch thick—to facilitate fast cooking.

Traditional teriyaki recipes dictate that the meat be marinated in a mixture of soy and sherry for several hours. Clearly, we didn't have several hours, but we found that as little as 10 minutes in the marinade improved the meat's flavor, especially when the marinade was punched up with ginger and garlic. In addition, the seasonings cooked along with the meat, which eliminated the task of cooking them separately.

While grilling the meat is the most traditional approach, we wanted to stay indoors and use just one pan. Pan-searing was the natural choice, and a 12-inch skillet provided all the surface area necessary to spread the meat in a single layer in a single batch. (In smaller skillets, the meat overlapped and stewed when cooked in a single batch—and, for the sake of time, we wanted to avoid two batches.)

Teriyaki sauce itself is a simple combination of three to four ingredients finely balanced between sweet and salty. Soy sauce and sugar are the primary flavoring agents along with sherry or mirin, a sweetened rice wine used specifically for cooking in Japan. As the sauce is reduced to a thick glaze, attaining the proper balance of flavors was a matter of trial and error; too much soy and the sauce was inedible, but too little and the sauce was bland and one-dimensional. After several attempts came out too thin, we tried adding a small amount of cornstarch. Tasters appreciated both the thicker texture and glossier sheen a scant amount provided. We walked a fine line, however; as little as an extra ¼ teaspoon cornstarch made the sauce too viscous.

Finishing the dish was a simple matter of turning the meat in the hot sauce for a couple of minutes until each of the slices was glossy. The reduced sauce was finely balanced and lustrous, not too sweet or sticky, and the meat was tender—a perfect medium-rare.

Beef Teriyaki
SERVES 4 TO 6

See page 14 for more information about buying blade steak, which is easily recognized by the line of gristle running down the center. When slicing these steaks, cut parallel to the gristle across the grain. When you reach the gristle, turn the steak around and cut from the other side. Once all the meat is sliced away, discard the gristle. The meat and sauce may be prepared ahead of time, although the garlic and ginger are best prepared when needed. As for accompaniments, rice is a must and steamed broccoli is traditional, although nearly any blend of vegetables would be acceptable. If you have leftovers, you can make the sliced meat into a sandwich with mayonnaise and spicy greens like arugula or watercress; several test cooks swear by the combination.

2	pounds top blade steaks, 1 inch thick, sliced across the grain into ¼-inch-thick strips, gristle discarded
1	(1-inch) piece fresh ginger, peeled and grated
2	medium garlic cloves, minced or pressed through a garlic press (about 2 teaspoons)
¼	cup plus 1 tablespoon soy sauce
½	cup mirin (Japanese rice wine)
2	tablespoons sugar
½	teaspoon cornstarch
½	cup water
2	teaspoons peanut or vegetable oil
2	teaspoons sesame seeds
2	medium scallions, sliced thin on the bias

1. Toss the meat slices with the ginger, garlic, and 1 tablespoon of the soy sauce in a medium bowl and marinate for at least 10 minutes. Whisk together the remaining ¼ cup soy sauce, mirin, sugar, cornstarch, and water in a small bowl.

2. Heat the oil in a nonstick 12-inch skillet over medium-high heat until smoking. Using tongs, place the meat in a single layer in the pan (using the sloping sides, if necessary); cook, without moving, until browned, 2 to 2½ minutes. Starting with the first strips placed in the pan, flip the meat and cook until the second side is browned, about 2 minutes. Using the tongs, transfer the meat to a clean bowl.

3. Stir the sauce mixture and add it to the skillet, scraping the pan bottom with a wooden spoon to release any browned bits. Cook until the sauce is reduced by half, about 2 minutes. Reduce the heat to medium and return the meat to the pan. Cook, stirring continuously, until the sauce is reduced to a syrupy glaze and the meat is well coated, about 2 minutes.

4. Transfer the meat and sauce to a warmed serving platter. Garnish with the sesame seeds and scallions and serve immediately.

SKILLET FAJITAS

GRILLING IS THE FIRST CHOICE FOR FAJITAS (SEE page 40 for details on this technique), but what if you want to stay indoors? We followed our standard method for steaks: We heated vegetable oil in the skillet until it smoked and seared each side of the steak until it was well browned. As with smaller steaks, it was important to move the steak as little as possible as it cooked to preserve the rich brown crust. The thin steak cooked quickly, requiring less than 10 minutes to reach rare. When it was fresh from the skillet, we drizzled more lime juice over the steak.

As the steak rested, we cooked the peppers and onions in the same pan, taking advantage of the flavorful fond left by the meat. As the peppers and onions sautéed, the fond was effectively deglazed and lent the vegetables a full flavor that needed little enhancement. (A little water added to the pan helped this along.) We did, however, experiment with a variety of spices and settled on cumin seeds, which added a Southwestern touch to the mix.

Skillet Fajitas
SERVES 4 TO 6

If you like spicy food, add sliced jalapeño pepper with the red bell peppers, or a finely chopped chipotle chile once the peppers finish cooking. If you have only ground cumin, reduce the amount to ¼ teaspoon and add it for the last 30 seconds of cooking; otherwise, it could burn and turn the peppers bitter. If you can find skirt steak, by all means use it in this recipe.

1 ½	pounds flank steak, trimmed of excess fat and patted dry with paper towels
	Salt and ground black pepper
4	tablespoons juice from 2 to 3 limes
2	tablespoons vegetable oil
2	medium red bell peppers, stemmed, seeded, and sliced thin
1	large red onion, halved and sliced thin
½	teaspoon cumin seeds
2	tablespoons water
8–12	flour tortillas (each 10 to 12 inches in diameter) Classic Red Table Salsa (page 402) and/or Chunky Guacamole (page 402)

1. Sprinkle each side of the steak with a liberal coating of salt and pepper to taste, followed by 1 tablespoon lime juice (2 tablespoons in total). Heat the oil in a heavy-bottomed 12-inch skillet over medium-high heat until smoking. Lay the steak in the pan and cook, without moving, until well browned, 4 to 5 minutes. Using tongs, flip the steak. Reduce the heat to medium. Continue to cook until the second side is browned, 4 to 5 minutes. Transfer the steak to a plate, drizzle with the remaining 2 tablespoons lime juice, tent loosely with foil, and let rest for 10 minutes.

2. Meanwhile, return the skillet to medium-high heat and add the bell peppers, onion, cumin seeds, ½ teaspoon salt, and water. Cook, stirring occasionally and scraping the bottom of the skillet to release any browned bits, until the onion is very soft and browned, 5 to 6 minutes. Transfer the vegetables to a serving bowl and adjust the seasonings with salt and pepper to taste.

3. Heat a large nonstick skillet over medium heat for 2 minutes and lightly toast each tortilla in the pan for 10 to 15 seconds per side. Stack the toasted tortillas in a clean towel and wrap to keep warm.

4. To serve, slice the steak thinly on the bias across the grain and place the slices in a serving bowl. Pour any accumulated juices from the meat over the vegetables. Serve immediately with the vegetables, tortillas, and the salsa and/or guacamole passed separately.

PHILLY CHEESESTEAK SANDWICHES

THE KEY TO A GOOD PHILLY CHEESESTEAK sandwich lies in the unique texture of the meat. Making a quick study of an authentic cheesesteak, we took note of the cooking method used by most cheesesteak stands in Philly. First, a good-size roast is frozen, then sliced into credit card-thin slices on the deli slicer. The thin slices of raw meat are then thrown onto a hot, well-greased griddle over a heap of browned onions. With the help of two heavy-duty spatulas, the meat and onions are chopped together and moved around the hot griddle. As the meat finishes cooking, slices of cheese are draped over the top of the pile and allowed to melt. A few final swipes with the spatula mix the melted cheese with the steak, and the whole mixture is then placed in a toasted hoagie bun. It is the texture of this thinly sliced and spatula-chopped meat that makes this recipe so difficult to make at home.

Our first thought was to get a butcher to do the work for us. But it took only one trip to the supermarket to realize this would not be so easy. To get thin-enough slices, the butcher would have to freeze an appropriately sized roast overnight. Even after we managed to convince a butcher to do this for us, the slices of beef we procured were about ¼ inch thick. Although these steaks were relatively thin, they were simply not thin enough. Consequently, we bought several different cuts of meat (we chose steaks since roasts would produce too much meat) to see if we could slice them thinly on our own. When partially frozen, the steaks were easier to slice thin, but our knife skills were not fine enough to cut paper-thin slices. Looking at the food processor on the kitchen counter, we wondered if we couldn't use it like a deli slicer.

Using the slicing disk of the food processor, we processed several frozen steaks with a modicum of success. The meat that made it through the disk had the perfect texture. However, not much meat made it through. The solid block of frozen steak was too hard, and the blade had a difficult time cutting the meat neatly. Also, the wide mouth of the food processor opening made it easy for the steak to slip sideways and get caught. Still, knowing we were on to something, we began to fiddle with the technique. First, we tried freezing the steaks only partially, making it easier for the food processor blade to do its work. Second, we tried cutting the steaks into strips and forcing them through the feed tube. The sides of the thin tube supported the steak strips as they were processed, preventing them from falling sideways and getting caught. Using the feed tube plunger, we made quick work of the task.

With the technique nailed down, we tested

PREPARING MEAT FOR PHILLY CHEESESTEAK SANDWICHES

After preparing blade, sirloin, or round steaks, place the strips of meat on a parchment-lined baking sheet and freeze until the exterior hardens but the interior remains soft and yields to gentle pressure, about 25 to 50 minutes.

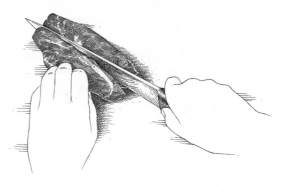

Blade Steaks

1. Cut each steak in half lengthwise, leaving the gristle attached to one half.

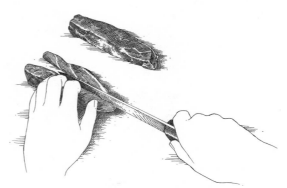

2. Cut away the gristle from the half to which it is still attached.

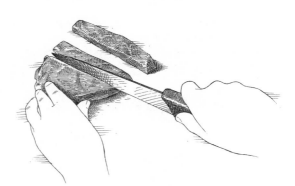

Sirloin or Round Steaks

Trim the fat from the steaks and cut into 1-inch-wide strips.

different types of steaks. Cheesesteaks should not be made with expensive cuts, so we tested blade, top sirloin, round, and chuck steaks as well as sir–loin tips. Steaks from the round, blade, and top sirloin all worked well, tasting beefy and tender. Chuck steaks, on the other hand, turned out tough and sinewy, while the sirloin tips were fibrous and livery.

Using a nonstick skillet, we easily brought the remaining sandwich ingredients in line. First, onions were quickly browned. The steak, already in bite-size pieces, was added. It did not need to be cut using a metal spatula. Once the meat was cooked through, we laid slices of cheese on top, let them melt slightly, and then quickly folded them into the meat and onions. This method worked like a charm, and several tasters native to Philadelphia were amazed at the authenticity

SHAVING MEAT FOR PHILLY CHEESESTEAK SANDWICHES

1. Once the meat has been partially frozen, place the strips in the feed tube of a food processor fitted with the slicing disk. Turn on the food processor, and use the plunger to push the meat down the tube onto the disk.

2. The food processor will shave the meat into small, paper-thin pieces.

of our homemade sandwich. They did, however, quarrel over what type of cheese to use—one claiming only American or provolone should be used, the other promoting Cheese Whiz as the authentic choice. A taste test didn't turn up a win-ner, so we decided to leave the choice up to the cook. Topped with sautéed peppers, hot peppers, sweet relish, or hot sauce and laid into a long, toasted sub roll, this rendition is by all standards a superb Philly cheesesteak sandwich.

Philly Cheesesteak Sandwiches
SERVES 4

These sandwiches are great as is, but they can be topped with pickled hot peppers, sautéed bell peppers, sweet rel-ish, or hot sauce.

- 2 pounds blade, sirloin, or round steak, trimmed (see the illustrations on page 63) and partially frozen
- 2 tablespoons vegetable oil
- I very large onion (about 20 ounces), cut into ¼-inch dice
  Salt and ground black pepper
- 6 slices American or deli-style provolone cheese, or 5 tablespoons Cheese Whiz
- 4 large fresh sub rolls, slit partially open and lightly toasted

1. Using a food processor fitted with the slicing disk, shave the partially frozen meat (see the illus-trations at left). Set the shaved meat aside.

2. Heat the oil in a nonstick 12-inch skillet over high heat until shimmering, about 2 minutes. Add the onion and sauté until softened and well browned around the edges, 4 to 5 minutes. Add the meat, ½ teaspoon salt, and ⅛ teaspoon black pepper and cook until the meat is fully cooked, 2 to 3 minutes.

3. Turn the heat to low and place the cheese slices over the meat. Allow the cheese to melt, about 1 minute. Using the tip of a heatproof rubber spatula or a wooden spoon, mix the melted cheese and meat together thoroughly. Remove the pan from the heat and spoon 1 cup of the meat mixture into each toasted bun. Serve immediately, with garnishes (see note), if desired.

3

I WANT TO COOK MEAT ON A STICK
(KEBABS AND SATAYS)

I Want to Cook Meat on a Stick

THERE'S SOMETHING UNIVERSALLY APPEALING about grilled meat on a stick. Almost every culture has some version of this dish. In many places, kebabs are street foods, eaten as snacks between meals. In this country, we generally think of kebabs as more substantial fare, appropriate for dinner. Because kebabs combine meat and vegetables, they are nearly complete meals; just add some rice, potatoes, or bread.

We prefer metal skewers to wooden ones when making kebabs. Even when soaked, wooden skewers burn on the grill. (For satays—smaller, thinner pieces of beef cooked on skewers and served as an appetizer with a Indonesian-style peanut sauce—we prefer to use slender bamboo skewers. Metal skewers are thicker than wooden ones and can tear the thin strips of meat used for satays.) Buy metal skewers once and you will own them for life. If possible, choose skewers with sharp ends (which make threading meat and vegetables much easier). Some metal skewers have wood or plastic handles. Because the handles are supposed to hang over the side of the grill, the food near the handle end of the skewer doesn't have direct contact with the cooking grate, making even cooking impossible. For this reason, we do not recommend skewers with handles. Just use tongs to turn metal skewers on the grill.

Shish kebab (made with lamb) are the most popular skewered meat although beef and pork make excellent kebabs, too.

GRILLED SHISH KEBAB

THE BACKYARD BARBECUE ALWAYS SEEMS SO familiar, so American. But grilling is practiced in almost every country around the globe. Shish kebab—skewers of lamb and vegetables—is perhaps the greatest "barbecue" dish from Turkey and the Middle East. When done right, the lamb is well browned but not overcooked and the vegetables are crisp and tender. Everything is perfumed with the flavor of smoke.

Shish kebab's components cook at different rates—either the vegetables are still raw when the meat is cooked perfectly to medium-rare, or the lamb is long overdone by the time the vegetables have been cooked properly. Our efforts to resolve this dilemma led us to explore which cut of lamb and which vegetables serve the kebab best. Getting the grill temperature just right was another challenge. Too hot, and the kebabs charred on the outside without being fully cooked; too cool, and they cooked without the benefit of flavorful browning.

Lamb can be expensive, so we searched for a cut that would give us tender, flavorful kebabs without breaking the bank. We immediately ruled out high-end cuts like loin and rib chops, which fetch upward of $14.99 per pound. These chops are just too pricey to cut up for a skewer, and they yield little meat. We had better luck with sirloin and shoulder chops, which are meatier and far more reasonable at $4.99 per pound. Each of these, however, requires cutting the meat off the bone before trimming and cubing. The best cut turned out to be the shank end of a boneless leg of lamb. It requires little trimming, yields the perfect amount of meat for four to six people, and can be purchased for about $6.99 per pound.

Lamb has a supple, chewy texture that behaves best when cut into small, dainty pieces. We found 1-inch pieces of lamb to be the optimal size for kebabs. With the meat cut and ready to go, we could now focus on the vegetables.

Many vegetables don't cook through by the time the lamb reaches the right temperature. This can be particularly ugly if you're using eggplant, mushrooms, or zucchini. We tried precooking the vegetables, but they turned slimy and were difficult to skewer. We thought about cooking them separately alongside the lamb on the grill, but that's just not shish kebab. Other vegetables, such as cherry tomatoes, initially looked great on the skewer but had a hard time staying put once cooked.

As we worked our way through various vegetables, we came up with two that work well within the constraints of this particular cooking method. Red onions and bell peppers have a similar texture and cook through at about the same rate. When cut fairly small, these two vegetables were the perfect accompaniments to the lamb, adding flavor and color to the kebab without demanding any special attention.

What these handsome kebabs needed now was seasoning, so we tried a variety of spices, dry rubs, and marinades on the meat. Spice rubs tasted good but left the surface of the meat chalky and dry; kebabs just aren't on the fire long enough for their juices to mix with the dried spices and form a glaze. Marinades, on the other hand, added a layer of moisture that kept the kebabs from drying out on the grill while their flavors penetrated the meat. Two hours in the marinade was sufficient time to achieve some flavor, but it took a good eight hours for these flavors to really sink in. Marinating for 12 hours, or overnight, was even better.

PREPARING ONIONS FOR KEBABS

1. Trim off the stem and root ends and cut the onion into quarters. Peel the three outer layers of the onion away from the inner core.

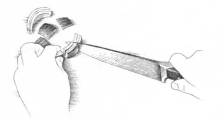

2. Working with the outer layers only, cut each quarter—from pole to pole—into three equal strips.

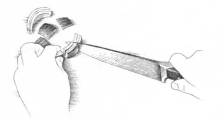

3. Cut each of the 12 strips crosswise into three pieces. You should have thirty-six 3-layer stacks of separate pieces of onion.

Charcoal-Grilled Shish Kebab

SERVES 6

Shish kebab benefits from a long marinating time, up to 24 hours, so plan ahead.

1	recipe marinade (recipes follow)
2 1/4	pounds boneless leg of lamb (shank end), trimmed of fat and silver skin and cut into 1-inch pieces
3	medium bell peppers, 1 red, 1 yellow, and 1 orange (about 1 1/2 pounds), stemmed, seeded, and cut into 1-inch pieces
1	large red onion (about 12 ounces), cut into 3/4-inch pieces (see the illustration at left) Lemon or lime wedges for serving (optional)

1. Toss the marinade and lamb in a gallon-size zipper-lock plastic bag or large nonreactive bowl. Seal the bag or cover the bowl and refrigerate until fully seasoned, at least 2 hours and up to 24 hours.

2. Light a large chimney starter filled with hardwood charcoal (about 6 quarts) and allow to burn until all the charcoal is covered with a layer of fine gray ash. Build a modified two-level fire by spreading the coals over just three quarters of the grill bottom. Set the cooking rack in place, cover the grill with the lid, and let the rack heat up, about 5 minutes. Use a wire brush to scrape clean the cooking rack. The grill is ready when you have a hot fire. (See how to gauge heat level on page 34.)

3. Meanwhile, using twelve 12-inch metal skewers, thread each skewer with one piece of meat, an onion stack (with three layers), and 2 pieces of pepper (of different colors) and then repeat this sequence two more times. Place a piece of meat on the end of each skewer.

4. Grill the kebabs, uncovered, until the meat is well browned all over, grill-marked, and cooked to medium-rare, about 7 minutes (or 8 minutes for medium), turning each kebab one-quarter turn every 1¾ minutes to brown all sides. Transfer the kebabs to a serving platter, squeeze the lemon or lime wedges over the kebabs, if desired, and serve immediately.

MARINADES FOR SHISH KEBAB

Garlic and Cilantro Marinade with Garam Masala

ENOUGH FOR 1 RECIPE OF SHISH KEBAB

1/2	cup packed fresh cilantro leaves
3	medium garlic cloves, peeled
1/4	cup dark raisins
1/2	teaspoon garam masala
1 1/2	tablespoons juice from 1 lemon
1/2	cup olive oil
1	teaspoon salt
1/8	teaspoon ground black pepper

Process all of the ingredients in the workbowl of a food processor fitted with the metal blade until smooth, about 1 minute, stopping to scrape the sides of the workbowl with a rubber spatula as needed.

Sweet Curry Marinade with Buttermilk

ENOUGH FOR 1 RECIPE OF SHISH KEBAB

3/4	cup buttermilk
1	tablespoon juice from 1 lemon
3	medium garlic cloves, minced or pressed through a garlic press (about 1 tablespoon)
1	tablespoon brown sugar
1	tablespoon curry powder
1	teaspoon red pepper flakes
1	teaspoon ground coriander
1	teaspoon chili powder
1	teaspoon salt
1/8	teaspoon ground black pepper

Combine all of the ingredients in a gallon-size zipper-lock plastic bag or large nonreactive bowl in which the meat will marinate.

Warm-Spiced Parsley Marinade with Ginger

ENOUGH FOR 1 RECIPE OF SHISH KEBAB

1/2	cup packed fresh parsley leaves
1	jalapeño chile, seeded and chopped coarse
1	(2-inch) piece fresh ginger, peeled and chopped coarse
3	medium garlic cloves, peeled
1	teaspoon ground cumin
1	teaspoon ground cardamom
1	teaspoon ground cinnamon
1/2	cup olive oil
1	teaspoon salt
1/8	teaspoon ground black pepper

Process all of the ingredients in the workbowl of a food processor fitted with the metal blade until smooth, about 1 minute, stopping to scrape the sides of the workbowl with a rubber spatula as needed.

Rosemary-Mint Marinade with Garlic and Lemon

ENOUGH FOR 1 RECIPE OF SHISH KEBAB

10	large fresh mint leaves
1 1/2	teaspoons chopped fresh rosemary
2	tablespoons juice and 1/2 tablespoon zest from 1 lemon
3	medium garlic cloves, peeled
1/2	cup olive oil
1	teaspoon salt
1/8	teaspoon ground black pepper

Process all of the ingredients in the workbowl of a food processor fitted with the metal blade until smooth, about 1 minute, stopping to scrape the sides of the workbowl with a rubber spatula as needed.

Gas-Grilled Shish Kebab

Work quickly when opening the lid to turn the kebabs; you don't want too much heat to escape.

Follow the recipe for Charcoal-Grilled Shish Kebab through step 1. Turn on all burners to high, close the lid, and heat the grill until very hot, about 15 minutes. Scrape the grill grate clean with a grill brush. Leave all burners on high. Proceed with the recipe as directed from step 3 and cook with the lid down.

GRILLED BEEF KEBABS

OUR GOALS WHEN DEVELOPING A RECIPE for beef kebabs seemed simple. We wanted meat that was nicely seared but not overcooked and vegetables that were tender but not mushy. We also wanted to cook the meat and vegetables on the same skewer so that their flavors could meld. Finally, we didn't want to spend a fortune on meat. It makes little sense to buy a premium steak and then cut it up into chunks for kebabs.

The concept behind grilled beef and vegetable kebabs is ingenious. Cut beef into small pieces, skewer along with flavorful, aromatic vegetables, and grill over a live fire—the juices emitted during cooking flavor the vegetables, and the vegetables in turn add flavor to the pieces of beef, while both are seared by the intense heat and infused with the smoke of the grill. Unfortunately, the idea of a kebab is often more appealing than the kebab itself; the pitfalls of grilling on skewers are many. To begin with, it's very easy to pick the wrong cut of beef. There are dozens of choices. It's also not very hard to overcook the meat when it's cut into smaller pieces. Or you can grill the skewers over a heat that's too intense and end up with meat that's charred on the outside and raw on the inside and vegetables that are just plain raw. When not seasoned carefully, kebabs can taste dull and bland.

We knew that choosing the right cut of beef was the most important decision we would make. Given that we didn't want to pay top price for a premium cut, we considered which cheaper cuts of meat would be tender enough to use for kebabs. We also wanted a cut of meat that wasn't too hard to cut into small pieces. In some cuts of meat, fat and sinew are abundant, making it extremely hard to prepare evenly sized pieces for the skewer. We weren't about to spend hours trimming and cutting intramuscular fat and connective tissue to make kebabs. It had to be a simple, quick process.

So we began skewering and grilling different cuts of meat from the less expensive parts of the steer. From the chuck, we tried the mock tender steak, clod steak, and top blade steak; from the round, we tested steaks cut from the top, bottom, and eye of round muscles; from the plate came the skirt and flank steak; and from the sirloin portion, we tried a top sirloin steak.

The cuts from the round portion of the cow were quite dry and chewy, with a weak, livery beef flavor. The skirt and flank steak were both flavorful and juicy, but their flat configuration and loose grain made them almost impossible to grill along with vegetables and even harder to cook to medium or medium-rare. They are much more appropriate for satay, in which long, thin strips of meat are skewered by themselves.

Not surprisingly, all but one of the nonpremium cuts from the chuck were also too tough. We say it is not surprising because this part of the steer—the neck, arm, and shoulder—is known to be flavorful but quite tough, best suited for stewing and braising. This was definitely true of the clod steak and mock tender steak. But the top blade steak was a different matter entirely—well marbled, intensely beefy, and notably tender and suitable for grilling. It was our first choice for skewers.

Our second choice was the top sirloin. This steak comes from the sirloin portion of the cow, just behind the short loin, which is the source of premium steaks such as porterhouse, filet mignon, and New York strip. The sirloin is made up of several muscles, the most tender of which is the top sirloin, from which this particular steak is cut.

So at the end of this first round of testing, we had two steaks that offered a reasonable texture and great beefy flavor at a reasonable price: top blade steak ($3.28 per pound), and top sirloin steak ($4.99

per pound). Both were also were quite easy to cut into skewerable pieces of even size.

Though the top sirloin and top blade steaks were relatively flavorful and tender on their own, we hoped that marinating the steaks would not only flavor the kebabs but also add some moisture. Thus far, we had approached the kebabs as we would a steak, seasoning with salt and pepper only. While the results were decent, the meat was a touch dry and bland. Most kebab recipes call for marinating the meat in an acidic marinade, which supposedly tenderizes it, before grilling. We tried both an acidic and a nonacidic (oil-based) marinade and left pieces of meat in both, for one hour, two hours, and four hours.

In all three cases, the acidic marinade produced meat that was mushier on the surface but not noticeably more tender than the meat in the oil-based marinade. The oil-based marinade didn't really change the texture of the meat, but the olive oil in it kept the meat from drying out on the grill and served as a great flavor vehicle for garlic, salt, and pepper. The lime juice in the acidic marinade, however, did contribute a nice flavor. We decided that instead of marinating the meat in the acid, we would marinate the meat in an oil-based marinade and squirt a little lime or lemon juice onto the kebabs after they came off the grill. We liked the results. The meat was tender yet still firm, and the lime or lemon juice tasted fresher when added to the meat just before serving.

The next step was to figure out how best to cut the steaks for skewering. As many meat connoisseurs know, beef cooked past medium becomes dry and tough. We wanted the kebabs to be cooked to medium-rare or, at most, to medium. This meant that the cubes of beef would have to be relatively large. After a few rounds of grilling, we noticed that any beef cut into pieces smaller than an inch was very hard to keep from overcooking. On the other hand, pieces of beef cut this large took quite a bit of time to marinate fully. We tried marinating overnight, and the meat still tasted a little bland because the seasoning didn't penetrate the surface very much.

After researching a number of kebab recipes, we

came upon one from Paula Wolfert's *The Cooking of the Eastern Mediterranean* (HarperCollins, 1994), in which cubes of lamb are butterflied (cut open and flattened) before being skewered for kebabs. This, we thought, might produce a more flavorful kebab. Because the pieces of meat would have more surface area, more marinade might penetrate the surface in a shorter period of time. We tested this theory out and were pleased to find the meat more flavorful; it was also easier to eat and less chewy. Unfortunately, since the meat was also thinner after being butterflied, it was getting cooked to the well-done stage. To combat this problem, we simply butterflied the meat, marinated it, and then put it on the skewer as if it were still a cube. This technique worked perfectly. Now the meat was easier to eat and packed with flavor all the way through to the center, and it was also nicely caramelized without being overcooked at the interior.

The final problem that most of us encounter when making meat and vegetable kebabs is getting both components to cook at the same rate. We noticed that if we cut the vegetables too thick, they ended up raw at the center. Our first thought was to skewer the meat and vegetables separately, but after trying a few batches of kebabs this way, we realized that both the meat and vegetables tasted much better when cooked together on the skewer.

The logical solution to the problem was to precook the vegetables. We ruled out both parboiling and presteaming because each meant dirtying another pan and making something complicated out of a dish that should be simple. The only precooking idea that made any sense was to microwave the vegetables before grilling.

After figuring out the appropriate timing in the microwave for each vegetable, we began cooking and skewering. We found this process to be extremely labor intensive; not only did we have to cut and microwave the vegetables, but the onions and peppers were slightly soft and wet, which made it hard to skewer them neatly. The kebabs already required a good deal of preparation—cutting and butterflying the meat, cutting the vegetables, and skewering both. Adding another step made it just too complicated.

Surprisingly, even though the precooked

vegetables were softer at the center after grilling, we didn't necessarily find them more appealing than those grilled from the raw stage. In fact, some of the vegetables, including the onions and bell peppers, maintained a pleasant tender-crisp texture (like that of a stir-fry) when skewered raw, and we found this to be a nice contrast with the texture of the meat. In the case of the onions and peppers, the trick is to cut them to the right dimensions (see page 68) so that they don't come off the grill undercooked.

Mushrooms and zucchini were deemed too soft to grill with beef—they work better with firmer and drier chicken and fish chunks. To add variety to meat skewers, we added chunks of pineapple; they grill well and add a nice sweetness and fruitiness to the kebabs.

There were two options when it came to grilling the kebabs: cooking over a single-level fire or over a two-level fire. Thinking that simpler is better, we started cooking the kebabs over a single-level fire. Because we wanted the kebabs to cook quickly, so that the exterior would become nicely browned while the interior retained as much juice as possible, we started with a medium-hot fire. While meat cooked this way came out relatively well browned, we thought it might be even better if cooked over a hotter fire. Instead of covering the entire grill with the hot charcoal, we used the same amount and covered only three-quarters of the grill bottom. This produced a more intense fire when cooking directly over the charcoal, searing the outside of the kebabs more successfully. The meat was richly caramelized, with a perfectly cooked, juicy interior.

Charcoal-Grilled Beef Kebabs

SERVES 4 TO 6

Our favorite cut of beef for kebabs is top blade steak (known sometimes as blade or flat-iron steak), but you can also use top sirloin. If you do, ask the butcher to cut the top sirloin steak between 1 and 1¼ inches thick (most packaged sirloin steaks are thinner). If desired, add 2 teaspoons minced fresh rosemary, thyme, basil, or oregano to the garlic and oil mixture for this marinade. For maximum efficiency, prepare the fruit and vegetables while the meat is marinating.

MEAT

¼	cup extra-virgin olive oil
3	medium garlic cloves, minced or pressed through a garlic press (about 1 tablespoon)
¾	teaspoon salt
½	teaspoon ground black pepper
2	pounds top blade steaks (about 4 to 5 steaks), trimmed of fat and prepared according to illustrations on page 73

FRUIT AND VEGETABLES

1	pineapple (about 3 ½ pounds), peeled, cored, and cut into 1-inch chunks (see the illustrations on page 405)
1	medium red bell pepper (about 8 ounces), stemmed, seeded, and cut into 1-inch pieces
1	medium yellow bell pepper (about 8 ounces), stemmed, seeded, and cut into 1-inch pieces
2	tablespoons extra-virgin olive oil
	Salt and ground black pepper
1	large red onion (about 12 ounces), peeled and cut into ¾-inch pieces (see the illustrations on page 68)
	Lemon or lime wedges for serving (optional)

1. FOR THE MEAT: Combine the oil, garlic, salt, and pepper in a gallon-size zipper-lock plastic bag or a large bowl. Add the steak cubes and toss to coat evenly. Seal the bag or cover the bowl and refrigerate until fully seasoned, at least 1 hour or up to 24 hours.

2. Light a large chimney starter filled with hardwood charcoal (about 6 quarts) and allow to burn until all the charcoal is covered with a layer of fine gray ash. Build a modified two-level fire by spreading the coals over just three quarters of the grill bottom. Set the cooking rack in place, cover the grill with the lid, and let the rack heat up, about 5 minutes. Use a wire brush to scrape clean the cooking rack. The grill is ready when you have a hot fire. (See how to gauge heat level on page 34.)

3. FOR THE FRUIT AND VEGETABLES: Meanwhile, toss the pineapple and peppers with 1½ tablespoons of the oil in a medium bowl and season with salt and pepper to taste. Brush the onion with the remaining

1½ teaspoons oil and season with salt and pepper to taste. Using eight 12-inch metal skewers, thread each skewer with a pineapple piece, an onion stack (with three layers), a cube of meat (skewering as if it were an uncut cube), and 1 piece of each kind of pepper, and then repeat this sequence two more times. Brush any oil remaining in the bowl over the skewers.

4. Grill the kebabs directly over the coals, uncovered, turning each kebab one-quarter turn every 1¾ minutes, until the meat is well browned,

---

PREPARING BEEF FOR KEBABS

Steps 1 and 2 are necessary if using top blade steaks. If using top sirloin, trim away any gristle and cut into cubes as in step 3.

1. Halve each blade steak lengthwise, leaving the gristle attached to one half.

2. Cut away the gristle from the piece to which it is still attached.

3. Cut the meat into 1¼-inch cubes, then cut each cube almost through at the center to butterfly it.

---

grill marked, and cooked to medium-rare, about 7 minutes (or about 8 minutes for medium). Transfer the kebabs to a serving platter and squeeze the lemon or lime wedges over the kebabs, if desired. Serve immediately.

➤ VARIATIONS

Gas-Grilled Beef Kebabs
Work quickly when opening the lid to turn the kebabs; you don't want too much heat to escape.

Follow the recipe for Charcoal-Grilled Beef Kebabs through step 1. Turn on all burners to high, close the lid, and heat the grill until very hot, about 15 minutes. Scrape the grill grate clean with a grill brush. Leave all burners on high. Proceed with the recipe as directed from step 3 and cook with the lid down.

Beef Kebabs with Asian Flavors
Follow the recipe for Charcoal-Grilled or Gas-Grilled Beef Kebabs, substituting 3 tablespoons vegetable oil and 1 tablespoon Asian sesame oil for the olive oil in the garlic marinade and adding 1½ teaspoons minced fresh ginger, 2 tablespoons soy sauce, 1 teaspoon sugar, ½ teaspoon red pepper flakes, and 2 minced scallions. Proceed with the recipe, substituting an equal amount of vegetable oil for the olive oil for coating the fruit and vegetables.

Southwestern Beef Kebabs
Follow the recipe for Charcoal-Grilled or Gas-Grilled Beef Kebabs, adding ½ teaspoon ground cumin, ½ teaspoon chili powder, 1 minced chipotle chile in adobo sauce, and 2 tablespoons minced fresh cilantro leaves to the oil and garlic marinade.

GRILLED PORK KEBABS

THE MAJOR ISSUE THAT MUST BE DEALT WITH when making kebabs with pork is its tendency to dry out on the grill. We wanted to develop a method that delivers moist, tender meat. The other major issue was flavor. Unlike beef and lamb, pork can be fairly bland—especially the tender cuts from the loin, which, because they cook quickly, we expected would work best for kebabs. We needed to figure out a way to boost the flavor.

We focused on two tender cuts—the loin and the tenderloin. As its name indicates, the tenderloin is plenty tender, but tasters felt it cooked up a bit mushy. We found the pork loin more appealing. It has a slightly fuller flavor, and, while still tender, it has an appealing resistance when you bite into it. A moderate degree of chew is pleasing and works well on a kebab.

Unfortunately, as expected, the loin meat dried out easily. As we often recommend when cooking meat or poultry that tends to dry out, we tried brining the loin. In addition to brining, we tested marinating the meat in an oil-based marinade to see if it would combat dryness. Side-by-side tastings showed that the marinated kebabs were tastier and just as moist and juicy as the brined meat. The marinade not only moistened the meat but also added richness of flavor that was lacking in the lean pork loin. The oil in the marinade lubricated the meat and improved its texture. The marinade also made a great vehicle for adding other flavors to the meat.

Whether marinated or not, pork that is overcooked will be dry. We found that pork kebabs should be cooked until barely pink at the center— an internal temperature of 145 degrees is ideal.

To cook the pork through at the center and get a good caramelization on the outside without singeing, we found that we needed to use a more moderate level of heat than with beef or lamb. A medium-hot fire worked like a charm. The outside of the pork was well marked, and the meat cooked through to the center. The meat also cooked through quickly, giving the moisture little time to escape from the meat and resulting in a tasty, moist kebab.

Because pork loin is neutral-tasting (some would say bland), with little fat, we wanted to infuse as much flavor and seasoning as possible into the meat before grilling. We decided to cube and then butterfly each cube, as we had done with the lamb and beef, to expose the most surface area possible to the marinade.

Charcoal-Grilled Pork Kebabs
SERVES 4 TO 6

Be sure not to overcook the pork, since this meat is prone to drying out. To make sure that the pork is done, peek into the cut that was made in the meat before skewering. It should appear opaque and just barely pink.

MEAT

1/4	cup extra-virgin olive oil
3	medium garlic cloves, minced or pressed through a garlic press (about 1 tablespoon)
3/4	teaspoon salt
1/2	teaspoon ground black pepper
1 3/4	pounds boneless center-cut pork chops, 1 1/4 inches thick (about 4 to 5 chops), cut into 1 1/4-inch cubes and butterflied (see the illustration at left)

FRUIT AND VEGETABLES

1	pineapple (about 3 1/2 pounds), peeled, cored, and cut into 1-inch chunks (see the illustrations on page 405)
1	medium red bell pepper (about 8 ounces), stemmed, seeded, and cut into 1-inch pieces
1	medium yellow bell pepper (about 8 ounces), stemmed, seeded, and cut into 1-inch pieces
2	tablespoons extra-virgin olive oil
	Salt and ground black pepper
1	large red onion (about 12 ounces), peeled and cut into 3/4-inch pieces (see the illustrations on page 68)
	Lemon or lime wedges for serving (optional)

PREPARING PORK FOR KEBABS

Cut the boneless pork chops into 1 1/4-inch cubes, then cut each cube almost through at the center to butterfly it.

1. FOR THE MEAT: Combine the oil, garlic, salt, and pepper in a gallon-size zipper-lock plastic bag or a large bowl. Add the pork cubes and toss to coat evenly. Seal the bag or cover the bowl and refrigerate until fully seasoned, at least 1 hour or up to 24 hours.

2. Light a large chimney starter filled with hardwood charcoal (about 6 quarts) and allow to burn until all the charcoal is covered with a layer of fine gray ash. Build a single-level fire by spreading the coals over the grill bottom. Set the cooking rack in place, cover the grill with the lid, and let the rack heat up, about 5 minutes. Use a wire brush to scrape clean the cooking rack. The grill is ready when you have a medium-hot fire. (See how to gauge heat level on page 34.)

3. FOR THE FRUIT AND VEGETABLES: Meanwhile, toss the pineapple and peppers with 1½ tablespoons of the oil in a medium bowl and season with salt and pepper to taste. Brush the onion with remaining 1½ teaspoons oil and season with salt and pepper to taste. Using eight 12-inch metal skewers, thread each skewer with a pineapple piece, an onion stack (with 3 layers), a cube of meat (skewering as if it were an uncut cube), and one piece of each kind of pepper, and then repeat this sequence two more times. Brush any oil remaining in the bowl over the skewers.

4. Grill the kebabs, uncovered, turning each kebab one-quarter turn every 2½ minutes, until the meat is well browned, grill marked, and cooked to medium-rare, 9 to 10 minutes. Transfer the kebabs to a large serving platter and squeeze the lemon or lime wedges over the kebabs, if desired. Serve immediately.

➤ VARIATIONS

Gas-Grilled Pork Kebabs

Work quickly when opening the lid to turn the kebabs; you don't want too much heat to escape.

Follow the recipe for Charcoal-Grilled Pork Kebabs through step 1. Turn on all burners to high, close the lid, and heat the grill until very hot, about 15 minutes. Scrape the grill grate clean with a grill brush. Leave all burners on high. Proceed with the recipe as directed from step 3 and cook with the lid down.

Grilled Pork Kebabs with West Indian Flavors

Be extremely careful handling the habañero chile pepper: Wash your hands immediately after chopping, and keep your hands away from your eyes. You may want to use disposable gloves when working with these explosively hot peppers.

3	medium scallions, sliced thin
3	medium garlic cloves, roughly chopped
½	medium habañero chile, stemmed, seeded, and roughly chopped
¼	cup lime juice from 4 limes
¼	cup vegetable oil
I	tablespoon plus 2 teaspoons brown sugar
I	teaspoon minced fresh thyme leaves
	Pinch ground allspice
I	teaspoon salt
I	recipe Charcoal-Grilled or Gas-Grilled Pork Kebabs (without marinade)

1. Place the scallions, garlic, chile, lime juice, oil, brown sugar, thyme, allspice, and salt in the workbowl of a food processor fitted with the metal blade and process until smooth.

2. Place the pork and lime juice mixture in a large nonreactive bowl and toss to coat evenly. Cover and refrigerate until fully seasoned, at least 3 hours or up to 24 hours. Proceed with the recipe, substituting an equal amount of vegetable oil instead of olive oil for coating the fruit and vegetables.

Grilled Pork Kebabs with Southeast Asian Flavors

Thai fish sauce has a more authentic flavor, but, if unavailable, soy sauce may be used in its place.

¼	cup fish sauce or soy sauce
¼	cup sugar
¼	cup vegetable oil
¼	cup lime juice from 4 limes
3	medium garlic cloves, minced or pressed through a garlic press (about I tablespoon)
I	(¾-inch) piece fresh ginger, peeled and minced (2 teaspoons)
2	medium scallions, sliced thin
2	tablespoons minced fresh cilantro leaves

I   recipe Charcoal-Grilled or Gas-Grilled Pork
     Kebabs (without marinade)

1. Combine the fish sauce, sugar, oil, lime juice,
garlic, ginger, scallions, and cilantro in a large nonreactive bowl, stirring to dissolve to the sugar.

2. Add the pork and toss to coat evenly. Cover
and refrigerate until fully seasoned, at least 1 hour
or up to 8 hours. Proceed with the recipe, substituting an equal amount of vegetable oil instead of olive
oil for coating the fruit and vegetables.

BEEF SATAY

SLENDER SLICES OF MARINATED BEEF WOVEN
onto bamboo skewers and thrown briefly on the
grill are a traditional Indonesian favorite known as
satay or sate. The meat has a sweet yet salty flavor,
and the skewers are served as an appetizer, snack,
or light main course alongside a spicy peanut sauce.
When done correctly, the tender meat is easily
pulled apart into small bites right off the skewer.
All too often, however, the beef is tough and sliced
so thickly it doesn't pull apart, leaving you with
an ungainly mouthful of meat. The peanut sauce
can be graceless with a glue-like consistency and
muddy peanut flavor. Not only would finding the
right cut of beef and slicing it correctly be key for
a tender satay, but we wondered how to make the
exotic-tasting marinade and accompanying peanut
sauce.

Starting with the beef, we surveyed the local
butcher counter for possibilities. Skipping over
the expensive cuts such as top loin, rib eye, and
tenderloin, we focused on the cheaper cuts more
appropriate for marinating and skewering—sirloin,
sirloin flap, round, skirt, flank, and blade steaks.
Bringing these cheaper cuts back to the test kitchen,
we immediately noted that slicing the raw beef into
thin strips is a difficult task. To make it easier, we
found it best to firm the meat in the freezer for
about 30 minutes. Sliced, skewered, and cooked,
these various cheaper cuts of meat produced substantially different textures. Steaks from the round
were the worst, with a tough, dry texture, followed

closely by chewy sirloin, and stringy sirloin flap (a
cut from the bottom sirloin). The blade steaks
tasted great and were fairly tender, but their small
size made it difficult to slice them into long, elegant
strips. Both the skirt and flank steak were easy to
slice and tasted best. Since skirt steak can be difficult to find and is a bit more expensive, flank steak
is the best option.

We found the key to tenderness hinges on slicing
the meat perpendicular to its large, obvious grain
(see the illustration below). Using a small, two-
pound flank steak, we could make about thirty
skewers, enough for twelve to eighteen people as
an appetizer. Although satay is classically grilled, we
found the broiler to be a simpler and more party-
friendly cooking method. Thin wooden skewers
worked better than metal skewers, which tend to
be thicker and tore up the small pieces of meat.
Protecting the bamboo skewers with foil, however,
is necessary to prevent them from burning or catch-
ing on fire. Cooked roughly six inches from the
broiler element, these thinly sliced pieces of meat
are done in only six to seven minutes.

Having found a tender cut of meat, we
focused next on adding flavor with the marinade.
Researching a variety of traditional Indonesian
recipes, we noted that most were based on a combination of fish sauce and oil. Using vegetable oil,
we tested various amounts of fish sauce, but tasters simply did not like its fermented fish flavor in

SLICING FLANK STEAK THINLY
FOR SATAYS

Using a chef's knife, cut the partially frozen flank steak across the
grain into ¼-inch-thick slices.

combination with the beef. Replacing it with soy sauce, although not traditional, worked well, lending its salty, fermented flavor without any "fishiness."

We then tried adding other flavors such as coconut milk, lime juice, Tabasco, Asian chili sauce, sugar, and an array of fresh herbs. Coconut milk dulled the beef's natural flavor, while the tart, acidic flavor of lime juice tasted out of place. Asian chili sauce added a pleasant, spicy heat without the sour, vinegary flavor that Tabasco contributed. The sweet, molasses flavor of the brown sugar added a welcome balance to the hot chili sauce and salty soy, while enhancing the beef's ability to brown under the broiler. Garlic and cilantro rounded out all of these flavors nicely. Sliced scallions tasted old and soapy when mixed into the marinade, but tasters liked their fresh flavor and color when sprinkled over the cooked skewers. Marinating the beef for more than one hour turned the texture of the thin sliced beef mushy, while less time didn't give the meat long enough to pick up the marinade flavors. One hour of marinating was perfect.

Lastly, we focused on the peanut sauce. Using creamy peanut butter, we tried spicing it up using variety of flavorings. In the end, the same ingredients used in the marinade also tasted good in the peanut sauce—soy sauce, Asian chili sauce, dark brown sugar, garlic, cilantro, and scallion. This time, however, lime juice added a welcome burst of tart acidity. We then stumbled on the obvious way to keep the sauce from being too thick or

ARRANGING THE SKEWERS

Using a narrow strip of aluminum foil, cover the exposed portion of each skewer to prevent burning. Secure the foil by crimping it tightly at the edges.

pasty: Thin it with hot water. Pairing perfectly with the flavor of the marinated beef, the peanut sauce turns these exotic-tasting skewers into an authentic satay.

Beef Satay with Spicy Peanut Dipping Sauce

SERVES 12 TO 18 AS AN APPETIZER

Meat that is partially frozen is easier to slice into thin strips. Asian chili sauce is available in most supermarkets under the name Sriracha. A chili-garlic sauce, known as sambal, could also be used; however, it is much spicier. Thirty 6-inch-long wooden skewers are required for this recipe. If you would like to halve this, buy a one pound flank steak and cut the remaining ingredients in half.

2	pounds flank steak
4	tablespoons soy sauce
4	tablespoons vegetable oil
2	tablespoons Asian chili sauce, or more to taste
¼	cup packed dark brown sugar
¼	cup minced fresh cilantro leaves
2	medium garlic cloves, minced or pressed through a garlic press (about 2 teaspoons)
4	scallions, both white and green parts, finely sliced
1	recipe Spicy Peanut Dipping Sauce (recipe follows)

1. Cut the flank steak in half lengthwise and freeze for 30 minutes.

2. Following the illustrations on page 76, slice each piece across the grain into ¼-inch-thick strips. Weave the meat onto individual bamboo skewers and lay flat in a shallow container. Combine the soy sauce, oil, chili sauce, brown sugar, cilantro, garlic, and scallions, and pour over the meat. Refrigerate for 1 hour only.

3. Adjust an oven rack to the upper position and heat the broiler. Following the illustration at left, lay the skewers on a rimmed baking sheet and cover the skewer ends with foil. Broil for 6 to 7 minutes, flipping the skewers over halfway through, until the meat is browned. Serve immediately with the peanut sauce.

Spicy Peanut Dipping Sauce

MAKES ABOUT 1 ¼ CUPS

This sauce can be made a day in advance and refrigerated. Bring the sauce to room temperature before serving.

½   cup creamy peanut butter
¼   cup hot water
1   tablespoon soy sauce
2   tablespoons lime juice from 1 lime
2   tablespoons Asian chili sauce
1   tablespoon dark brown sugar
1   medium garlic clove, minced or pressed through a garlic press (about 1 teaspoon)
1   tablespoon chopped fresh cilantro leaves
2   scallions, green and white part, sliced thin

Whisk the peanut butter and hot water together in a medium bowl. Stir in the remaining ingredients. Transfer to a small serving bowl.

EQUIPMENT: Tongs

Testing all manner of tongs, we groped and grabbed kebabs, asparagus, chicken drumsticks, and 3-pound slabs of ribs and found tong performance differed dramatically. Grill tongs by Progressive International, Charcoal, Lamson, Oxo Good Grips, and AMC Rosewood were heavy and difficult to maneuver, and their less delicate pincers couldn't get a grip on asparagus. Other problems included sharp, serrated edges that nicked the food, flimsy arms that bent under the strain of heavy food, and pincers whose spread could not even accommodate the girth of a chicken leg. The Lamson tongs had a spatula in place of one pincer, rendering its grasp almost useless.

The winner was a pair of 16-inch stainless steel kitchen tongs by Amco. Not only did they grip, turn, and move food around the grill easily, but they also were long enough to keep the cook a safe distance from the hot coals. So forget about all those flashy new grill utensils and simply bring your kitchen tongs outside.

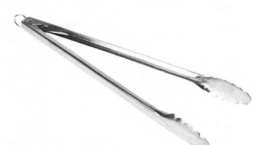

THE BEST TONGS

A pair of 16-inch stainless steel kitchen tongs made by Amco outperformed other tongs especially designed for use on the grill. Save money and use the same pair of tongs indoors and outdoors.

I WANT TO GRILL CHOPS

4

I Want to Grill Chops

THIS CHAPTER COVERS THREE KINDS OF chops—pork, lamb, and veal. As this chapter demonstrates, chops can be cut from various animals and from various parts on the same animal. Chops can come from the shoulder, rib, loin, or even sirloin areas. In general, a chop is about the size of an adult hand and contains meat and bone. (Some chops are sold boneless, but we find that cooking meat on the bone improves its flavor and so prefer to buy bone-in chops.)

Chops can vary in thickness from one-half inch to as much as two inches. We find that thick (but not gargantuan) chops are the easiest to grill. Thin chops tend to overcook by the time the exterior is seared. Really thick chops have the opposite problem—the exterior can char before the meat near the bone is done. For best results, follow the recommendations in the recipes about the thickness of the chops.

Because we prefer moderately thick chops (usually between 1 and 1½ inches), we find that they are best cooked over a two-level fire. We sear the chops over the hotter part of the grill and then drag them to the cooler part to finish cooking. Most chops are a bit fatty. This is part of their charm and what makes them so delicious. However, all that fat can cause flare-ups. The two-level fire gives you a place to drag the chops if a flare-up does occur. We also suggest keeping a spray bottle filled with water near the grill when cooking chops.

As with steaks, we like to let chops rest for about five minutes once they come off the grill. This resting time allows the juices to redistribute themselves evenly throughout the meat. Note that the internal temperature of the chop will rise by at least five degrees as it rests. For this reason, we often pull the chops from the grill at temperatures that may seem a bit low. By the time the meat reaches the table, it should be cooked to the desired doneness.

GRILLED PORK CHOPS

WE LOVE A JUICY, FLAVORFUL PORK CHOP. Too bad most pork chops are dry and bland. The pork industry has reduced the fat in pigs by 50 percent since the 1950s. Yes, pork is now the "other white meat," nearly as lean as chicken. But along with all that fat went flavor and juiciness.

The reality of many a grilled pork chop is a burnt exterior, raw interior, tough meat, nary a hint of flavor—the list goes on. We were looking for perfection: a plump, Rubenesque chop with a seared crust reminiscent of chiaroscuro and an interior that would be juicy and flavorful all the way to the bone. We wanted a chop that looked and tasted so good that it transcended the far reaches of backyard grilling and became art.

Thick pork chops usually come from the loin of the pig, which runs from the shoulder to the hip. To determine which cut would be best, we conducted a blind taste test with four different chops, starting with the blade chop, which is from the shoulder end, or front, of the loin. Because the shoulder region of the loin has the most fat and is riddled with connective tissue, tasters found the blade chops to be full of flavor but also tough and chewy. At the hip end of the loin are the sirloin chops. These were dry, somewhat tasteless, and a bit tough. Moving on to the center of the loin, we tested the center-cut chop and the rib chop. Although both were tender and flavorful, tasters preferred the rib chops, which were juicy and well marbled with fat.

Although rib chops are flavorful on their own, we wanted to see if we could boost their flavor by using a spice rub, marinade, or brine. We tested two types of rub: dry and wet. The wet rubs, made with spices and a liquid, gave the chops good flavor but also caused their exterior to turn syrupy. Tasters preferred the dry rubs, which combine potent dried spices with sugar to create big flavor and a crisp crust.

Next, we tried marinating the chops in an acidic oil mixture flavored with herbs and garlic. While the marinade succeeded in flavoring the exterior of the chops, it did little for the interior. Moreover, the meat took on a slimy texture that prohibited formation of a good crust.

Finally, we tried brining, a method we often turn to in the test kitchen, in which lean cuts of meat (usually pork or poultry) are soaked in a solution of water and salt and sometimes sugar. (Brining yields moist, well-seasoned meat and poultry that are hard to overcook, an important factor when grilling.) The brined chops were well seasoned throughout, not just on the surface. They were also extremely juicy—each bite was full of moist, seasoned pork flavor, complemented by the warm crunch of the spice rub.

It was now time to grill. As a preliminary test, we pitted hardwood charcoal against the more traditional charcoal briquettes. After grilling a few chops over each, we found we preferred the hardwood for its intensely hot fire and slightly smoky flavor. As for the fire itself, we always begin testing with a single-level fire—that is, a fire of even and generally high heat made by spreading coals evenly across the grill. We threw the chops over the fire and watched as they browned to a beautiful bronze within minutes. But when we pulled the chops off the grill and cut into one, it was rare at the bone. Moderating the temperature of the fire only drew out the cooking time and sacrificed the deep, caramelized crust we had achieved over high heat.

Moving next to a two-level fire, which is achieved by banking more hot coals on one side of the grill than on the other, we tried a multitude of temperature combinations, each time starting the chops over high heat to develop a nicely browned crust. Moving the chops from high to medium, high to low, and high to no heat were all tested, but none of these combinations produced a thoroughly cooked interior in a reasonable amount of time. Throwing the grill lid back on after the initial sear cooked the chops all the way through—a breakthrough to be sure—but the flavor of the meat was adversely affected. (The inside of most charcoal grill covers is coated with a charcoal residue that readily imparts bitter, spent flavors to foods.) Seizing on the notion of covering the chops for part of the cooking time, we turned to a handy disposable aluminum roasting pan to solve the problem. We threw the pan over the chops after searing them over high heat and moving them to the cooler part of the grill. This time we had a crisp crust, juicy meat, and no off flavors.

In our eagerness to serve these perfect chops, we cut into them right off the grill and watched as the juices ran out onto the plate. We allowed the next round of chops to sit covered under the foil pan for five minutes. When we cut into the chops this time, only a little of the juice escaped. We were surprised, however, to find that these chops were slightly tougher than the chops that did not rest. We took the internal temperature and found that it was now nearly 165 degrees—overcooked in our book. (At 145 degrees, pork is cooked, safe to eat, and still juicy. Temperatures above 150 degrees yield dry, tough meat.) We cooked one more batch of chops and this time took them off the grill earlier, once they had reached an internal temperature of 135 degrees, and let them sit under the foil pan for a good five minutes. Thanks to the residual heat left in the bone, the temperature shot up an average of 10 to 15 degrees, bringing the meat into that desirable range of 145 to 150. Magic.

Charcoal-Grilled Pork Chops

SERVES 4

Rib loin chops are our top choice for their big flavor and juiciness. Dry rubs add a lot of flavor for very little effort, but the chops can also be seasoned with pepper alone just before grilling. You will need a large disposable aluminum roasting pan to cover the chops and help them finish cooking through to the bone.

³/₄	cup kosher salt or 6 tablespoons table salt
6	tablespoons sugar
4	bone-in pork loin rib chops or center-cut loin chops, 1 ¹/₂ inches thick (about 12 ounces each)
1	recipe dry rub (page 83) or ground black pepper

1. Dissolve the salt and sugar in 3 quarts cold water in a 2-gallon zipper-lock plastic bag. Add the chops and seal the bag, pressing out as much air as possible. (Alternatively, divide the brine and chops evenly between two 1-gallon zipper-lock bags.) Refrigerate, turning the bag once, until fully seasoned, about 1 hour. Remove the chops from the brine and pat thoroughly dry with paper towels. Coat the chops with the dry rub or season generously with pepper.

2. Light a large chimney starter filled with hardwood charcoal (about 6 quarts) and allow to burn until all the charcoal is covered with a layer of fine gray ash. Build a two-level fire by stacking most of

DRY RUBS FOR GRILLED PORK

Pork benefits from assertive seasonings, especially when it is grilled and there is no opportunity to make a pan sauce. These four rubs are particularly well suited to chops and tenderloins. Consider serving pork with a fruit salsa (see pages 403 through 404) for added moisture.

Basic Spice Rub for Grilled Pork

MAKES ENOUGH FOR 4 CHOPS OR 2 TENDERLOINS

- 1   tablespoon ground cumin
- 1   tablespoon chili powder
- 1   tablespoon curry powder
- 1   teaspoon ground black pepper
- 2   teaspoons brown sugar

Combine all of the ingredients in a small bowl.

Indian Spice Rub for Grilled Pork

MAKES ENOUGH FOR 4 CHOPS OR 2 TENDERLOINS

Serve this fragrant combination with either Pineapple Salsa (page 404) or Mango Salsa (page 403).

- 1   tablespoon fennel seeds
- 1   tablespoon ground cumin
- 1   teaspoon ground coriander
- 1   teaspoon ground cardamom
- 1   teaspoon dry mustard
- 1/2   teaspoon ground cinnamon
- 1/4   teaspoon ground cloves
- 2   teaspoons brown sugar

Grind the fennel seeds to a powder in a spice grinder. Transfer to a small bowl and stir in the remaining ingredients.

Chipotle and Ancho Rub for Grilled Pork

MAKES ENOUGH FOR 4 CHOPS OR 2 TENDERLOINS

A little of this potent rub goes a long way.

- 1   dried chipotle chile (not in adobo sauce), stemmed, seeded, and broken into 1-inch pieces
- 1/2   medium ancho chile, stemmed, seeded, and broken into 1-inch pieces
- 1   teaspoon dried oregano
- 1/4   teaspoon garlic powder
- 1/4   teaspoon salt
- 2   teaspoons brown sugar

Grind both chiles to a powder in a spice grinder. Transfer to a small bowl and stir in the remaining ingredients.

Herb Rub for Grilled Pork

MAKES ENOUGH FOR 4 CHOPS OR 2 TENDERLOINS

A little salt is added to this rub to help break the dried herbs down into a powder. Do not salt the meat if using this rub.

- 1 1/2   teaspoons dried thyme
- 1 1/2   teaspoons dried rosemary
- 1 1/2   teaspoons black peppercorns
- 2   bay leaves, crumbled
- 2   whole cloves or allspice berries
- 1/2   teaspoon salt

Grind all of the ingredients to a powder in a spice grinder.

THE BEST CHOP FOR GRILLING

Pork chops come from the loin of the pig. A whole pork loin weighs 14 to 17 pounds and can be cut into blade chops, rib chops, center-cut chops, and sirloin chops. The loin muscle runs the entire length of the backbone. Starting midway back, the tenderloin muscle runs along the opposite side of the backbone. Center-cut and sirloin chops contain both kinds of muscle. (On the center-cut chop, the tenderloin is the small piece of meat on the left side of the bone in the photo below.) We found that the tenderloin cooks more quickly than the loin and can dry out on the grill. This is one reason why we prefer rib chops, which contain only loin meat. Following are tasters' impressions after sampling four different chops cut from the loin. Rib chops were tasters' top choice, followed by center-cut chops.

Blade Chop
Fattiest, toughest, juiciest, most flavor

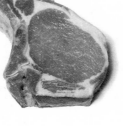

Rib Chop
Some fat, relatively tender, juicy, great flavor

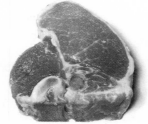

Center-Cut Chop
Little fat, relatively tender, less juicy, good flavor

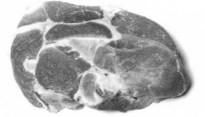

Sirloin Chop
Tough, quite dry, little flavor

the coals on one side of the grill and arranging the remaining coals in a single layer on the other side of the grill. Set the cooking rack in place, cover the grill with the lid, and let the rack heat up, about 5 minutes. Use a wire brush to scrape clean the cooking rack. The grill is ready when the pile of coals is medium-hot and the single layer of coals is medium-low. (See how to gauge heat level on page 34.)

3. Grill the chops, uncovered, over the hotter part of the fire until browned on each side, 2 ½ to 3 minutes per side. Move the chops to the cooler part of the grill and cover with a disposable aluminum roasting pan. Continue grilling, turning once, until an instant-read thermometer inserted through the side of a chop away from bone registers 135 degrees, 7 to 9 minutes longer. Transfer the chops to a platter, cover with the foil pan, and let rest for 5 minutes. (The internal temperature should rise to 145 degrees.) Serve immediately.

➤ VARIATION

Gas-Grilled Pork Chops

Because gas grill lids don't build up a residue that can impart an off flavor to foods (as charcoal grills do), they can be used to concentrate heat to cook the pork chops through; there's no need, therefore, for a disposable roasting pan.

Follow step 1 of the recipe for Charcoal-Grilled Pork Chops. Turn on all burners to high, close the lid, and heat the grill until very hot, about 15 minutes. Scrape the grill grate clean with a grill brush. Leave one burner on high and turn the other burner(s) to medium-low. Cook the chops as directed in step 3 with the lid down.

GRILLED LAMB CHOPS

LAMB CHOPS DON'T HAVE TO BE A RARE (and expensive) treat. True, loin and rib chops (together, the eight rib chops form the cut known as rack of lamb) can cost upward of $12 a pound. But we love the meaty flavor and chewy (but not tough) texture of shoulder chops. We also like the fact that they cost only about $4 per pound.

In a side-by-side taste test, we grilled loin, rib, and shoulder chops to medium-rare and let them stand about 5 minutes before tasting. The rib chop was the most refined of the three, with a mild, almost sweet flavor and tender texture. The loin chop had a slightly stronger flavor, and the texture was a bit firmer (but not chewier) than the rib chop. The shoulder chop had a distinctly gutsier flavor than the other two. While it was not at all tough, it was chewier. If you like the flavor of lamb (and we do) and are trying to keep within a budget, then try shoulder chops.

We also tried a second test in which we grilled the chops to medium, a stage at which many people prefer lamb. Both the rib and loin chops were dry and less flavorful and juicy than they were at medium-rare. The shoulder chop held its own, in both taste and texture, displaying another advantage besides price.

Shoulder chops can range in thickness from half an inch to an inch. We prefer the thicker chops; you should ask your butcher to cut them for you if necessary. Loin and rib chops are usually thicker, often close to 1½ inches.

In our testing, we found that all of these chops should be cooked over a two-level fire to bring the inside up to temperature without charring the exterior. A two-level fire also makes sense because lamb tends to flame; the cooler part of the grill is the perfect place to let flames die down. Even when cooking thinner chops, we found that the flames often became too intense on a single-level fire. When cooking lamb, it is a good idea to have somewhere to drag the meat if flames become too intense. A squirt bottle filled with water is also a handy item to have near the grill.

Charcoal-Grilled Shoulder Lamb Chops

SERVES 4

Try to get shoulder lamb chops that are at least ¾ inch thick, since they are less likely to overcook. If you can only find chops that are ½ inch thick, reduce the cooking time over the medium-low fire by about 30 seconds on each side. For information about the different kinds of shoulder chops, see page 106.

4   **shoulder lamb chops (blade or round bone), ¾ to 1 inch thick**
2   **tablespoons extra-virgin olive oil**
     Salt and ground black pepper

1. Light a large chimney starter filled with hardwood charcoal (about 6 quarts) and allow to burn until all the charcoal is covered with a layer of fine gray ash. Build a two-level fire by stacking most of the coals on one side of the grill and arranging the remaining coals in a single layer on the other side of the grill. Set the cooking rack in place, cover the grill with the lid, and let the rack heat up, about 5 minutes. Use a wire brush to scrape clean the cooking rack. The grill is ready when the pile of coals is medium-hot and the single layer of coals is medium-low. (See how to gauge heat level on page 34.)

EQUIPMENT: Instant-Read Thermometers

There are two types of commonly sold hand-held thermometers: digital and dial face. While they both take accurate readings, we prefer digital thermometers because they register temperatures faster and are easier to read. After testing a variety of digital thermometers, we preferred the Thermapen ($80) for its well-thought-out design—a long, folding probe and comfortable handle—and speed (just 10 seconds for a reading). If you don't want to spend so much money on a thermometer, at the very least purchase an inexpensive dial-face model. There's no sense ruining a $50 roast because you don't own even a $10 thermometer. Another good option is a timer/thermometer; see page 208 for details.

THE BEST INSTANT-READ THERMOMETER
The Thermapen ($80) is our top choice for its pinpoint accuracy and quick response time.

2. Rub the chops with the oil and sprinkle with salt and pepper to taste.

3. Grill the chops, uncovered, over the hotter part of the grill, turning them once, until well browned, about 4 minutes. (If the chops start to flame, drag them to the cooler part of the grill and/or extinguish flames with a squirt bottle filled with water.) Move the chops to the cooler part of the grill and continue grilling, turning once, to the desired doneness, about 5 minutes for rare (about 120 degrees on an instant-read thermometer), about 7 minutes for medium (about 130 degrees), or about 9 minutes for well-done (140 to 150 degrees).

4. Remove the chops from the grill and let rest for 5 minutes. Serve immediately.

➤ VARIATIONS

Gas-Grilled Shoulder Lamb Chops

To make sure the lamb chops aren't flaming up under the grill cover, watch for any substantial amount of smoke coming through the vents. This indicates that flare-ups are occurring and need to be extinguished.

Turn on all burners to high, close the lid, and heat the grill until very hot, about 15 minutes. Scrape the grill clean with a grill brush. Leave one burner on high and turn the other burner(s) to medium. Follow the recipe for Charcoal-Grilled Shoulder Lamb Chops from step 2 and cook with the lid down.

Grilled Shoulder Lamb Chops with Garlic-Rosemary Marinade

Garlic and rosemary are classic accompaniments with lamb.

Combine 2 tablespoons extra-virgin olive oil, 2 large garlic cloves, minced very fine or put through a garlic press, 1 tablespoon minced fresh rosemary leaves, and a pinch cayenne pepper in a small bowl. Follow the recipe for Charcoal-Grilled or Gas-Grilled Lamb Chops, rubbing the chops with the garlic-rosemary marinade instead of olive oil. Marinate in the refrigerator for at least 20 minutes or up to 1 day. Sprinkle the chops with salt and pepper to taste before grilling, then grill as directed.

Grilled Shoulder Lamb Chops with Soy-Shallot Marinade

Soy sauce works well with the gutsy flavor of shoulder chops.

Combine 2 tablespoons canola oil, ¼ cup minced shallots or scallions, 2 tablespoons each minced fresh thyme and parsley leaves, 3 tablespoons lemon juice (from 2 lemons), 2 tablespoons soy sauce, and ground black pepper to taste in a shallow dish. Follow the recipe for Charcoal-Grilled or Gas-Grilled Lamb Chops, marinating the chops in the soy marinade in the refrigerator for at least 20 minutes or up to 1 hour. (Do not marinate longer.) Follow the recipe from step 3.

Spiced Grilled Shoulder Lamb Chops with Quick Onion and Parsley Relish

You can prepare the relish a day ahead of time if you like and store it in the refrigerator. The relish combination makes a cool and refreshing foil for savory lamb chops.

Prepare Quick Onion and Parsley Relish (page 404). Follow the recipe for Charcoal-Grilled or Gas-Grilled Lamb Chops, rubbing each with oil as directed and then with 1½ teaspoons Simple Spice Rub for Beef or Lamb (page 397). Sprinkle with salt to taste but not with pepper. Grill as directed and serve with the relish.

Grilled Shoulder Lamb Chops with Near East Red Pepper Paste

This paste of fresh peppers and exotic spices lends sweet spiciness and deep color to grilled lamb.

3	tablespoons extra-virgin olive oil
½	medium red bell pepper, stemmed, seeded, and roughly chopped
½	medium serrano or jalapeño chile, stemmed, seeded, and roughly chopped
I	medium garlic clove, minced or pressed through a garlic press (about I teaspoon)
½	teaspoon ground cumin
½	teaspoon dried summer savory
¼	teaspoon ground cinnamon
½	teaspoon dried mint or I ½ teaspoons chopped fresh mint leaves

2   teaspoons juice from 1 lemon

1   recipe Charcoal-Grilled or Gas-Grilled
    Shoulder Lamb Chops (page 85)

1. Heat 1 tablespoon of the oil in a small skillet over medium-high heat until shimmering. Add the red bell pepper and chile and sauté until they start to soften, about 2 minutes. Reduce the heat to medium-low and continue to cook until softened, about 5 minutes.

2. Transfer the mixture to a food processor fitted with the metal blade. Add the garlic, cumin, summer savory, cinnamon, mint, lemon juice, and remaining 2 tablespoons oil and process until almost smooth (there will still be some chunky pieces of pepper).

3. Follow the recipe, rubbing the chops with the red pepper paste instead of the oil and marinating them in the refrigerator for at least 20 minutes or up to 1 day. Sprinkle the chops with salt and pepper to taste before grilling, then grill as directed.

Charcoal-Grilled Loin or Rib Lamb Chops

SERVES 4

While loin and rib chops are especially tender cuts of lamb, they tend to dry out if cooked past medium since they have less intramuscular fat than shoulder chops. To make these chops worth their high price, keep an eye on the grill to make sure the meat does not overcook. These chops are smaller than shoulder chops, so you will need two for each serving. Their flavor is more delicate and refined, so season lightly with just salt and pepper, or perhaps herbs (as in the variation that follows). Aggressive spices don't make sense with these rarefied chops.

8   loin or rib lamb chops, 1 1/4 to 1 1/2 inches
    thick

2   tablespoons extra-virgin olive oil
    Salt and ground black pepper

1. Light a large chimney starter filled with hardwood charcoal (about 6 quarts) and allow to burn until all the charcoal is covered with a layer of fine gray ash. Build a two-level fire by stacking most of

the coals on one side of the grill and arranging the remaining coals in a single layer on the other side of the grill. Set the cooking rack in place, cover the grill with the lid, and let the rack heat up, about 5 minutes. Use a wire brush to scrape clean the cooking rack. The grill is ready when the pile of coals is medium-hot and the single layer of coals is medium-low. (See how to gauge heat level on page 34.)

2. Rub the chops with the oil and sprinkle with salt and pepper to taste.

3. Grill the chops, uncovered, over the hotter part of the grill, turning them once, until well browned, about 4 minutes. (If the chops start to flame, drag them to the cooler part of the grill for a moment and/or extinguish the flames with a squirt bottle filled with water.) Move the chops to the cooler part of the grill and continue grilling, turning once, to the desired doneness, about 6 minutes for rare (about 120 degrees on an instant-read thermometer) or about 8 minutes for medium (about 130 degrees).

4. Remove the chops from the grill and let rest for 5 minutes. Serve immediately.

➤ VARIATIONS

Gas-Grilled Loin or Rib Lamb Chops

Turn on all burners to high, close the lid, and heat the grill until very hot, about 15 minutes. Scrape the grill grate clean with a grill brush. Leave one burner on high and turn the other burner(s) to medium-low. Follow the recipe for Charcoal-Grilled Loin or Rib Lamb Chops from step 2 and cook with the lid down.

Grilled Loin or Rib Lamb Chops with Mediterranean Herb and Garlic Paste

The delicate flavor of loin or rib lamb chops is enhanced— not overwhelmed—by this spirited Mediterranean-inspired paste.

Combine 1/4 cup extra-virgin olive oil, 3 medium garlic cloves, minced, 1 tablespoon chopped fresh parsley leaves, and 2 teaspoons each chopped fresh sage leaves, thyme leaves, rosemary leaves, and oregano leaves in a small bowl. Follow the recipe for Charcoal-Grilled or Gas-Grilled Loin or Rib Lamb Chops, rubbing the chops with the herb paste instead of the oil. Marinate in the refrigerator for at least 20 minutes or up to 1 day. Sprinkle with salt and pepper to taste before grilling, then grill as directed.

GRILLED VEAL CHOPS

VEAL CHOPS ARE NOT AS POPULAR AS PORK chops or even lamb chops. One reason is certainly price. Another reason may be flavor. Veal chops can be a bit bland, especially if you try to broil or sauté them. At upwards of $13 per pound, bland veal chops can be an expensive disappointment. Yet another reason is the way in which some of the calves used for veal are raised (see Milk-Fed versus Natural Veal on page 10).

We think that if you're going to spend the money for veal chops, you must grill them. The combination of smoky flavor and intense browning does these expensive chops justice. That said, you need the right grilling technique. Should the chops be cooked over direct heat, or do they need a two-level fire? And what about the various choices at the market? There are chops from the shoulder, loin, and rib, as well as milk-fed and natural veal.

We began by testing various types of veal chops on the grill. We quickly dismissed inexpensive shoulder chops. They were tough and chewy and seemed better suited to braising or cutting up for stews.

Both the loin and rib chops were exceptionally tender and expensive—$13 to $14 per pound in our local markets. The rib chops were a touch juicier and richer in flavor than the loin chops, so they are our first choice. However, if your market carries only loin chops, don't worry. These chops are quite good and can be grilled just like rib chops.

With our type of chops chosen, we focused on size. We found that thin chops are hard to cook correctly because they dry out before you can get any color on the exterior. Likewise, superthick chops can overbrown by the time the meat near the bone is done. We had the best luck with chops about 1¼ inches thick. Slightly thicker chops (up

to 1½ inches) are fine, and will take just an extra minute or so to grill.

It was then time to perfect our grilling technique. It quickly became clear that veal chops did not fare well when cooked solely over hot coals. The exterior burned before the center was done. Cooking over a two-level fire produced chops that were evenly cooked and nicely caramelized on the exterior. Our tasters preferred chops pulled off the grill when the internal temperature reached 130 degrees. At this stage, the chops have just a tinge of pink in the center. Do not cook veal chops past this point or they will be tough and dry.

We did have problems with flare-ups. When we trimmed away excess fat, flare-ups were reduced but not eliminated. We decided not to oil these chops to further reduce the risk of flare-ups. Keep the squirt bottle close at hand while grilling to tame any flare-ups that might occur.

Grilled veal chops are delicious with a simple seasoning of salt and pepper. If you choose to add more flavor, we suggest herbs or something fairly mild. There's no sense masking the delicate veal flavor with too many spices or chiles.

Charcoal-Grilled Rib Veal Chops
SERVES 4

Be sure to trim the veal chops of any excess fat to prevent flare-ups. Keep a squirt bottle filled with water on hand to spray on flare-ups that may still occur. Veal chops need to be cooked over a two-level fire to ensure a nicely caramelized crust and a center perfectly cooked to medium. Use an instant-read thermometer to ensure that the chops don't overcook.

4 bone-in rib veal chops, 1 ¼ inches thick (about 10 ounces each), trimmed of excess fat
   Salt and ground black pepper

1. Light a large chimney starter filled with hardwood charcoal (about 6 quarts) and allow to burn until all the charcoal is covered with a layer of fine gray ash. Build a two-level fire by stacking most of the coals on one side of the grill and arranging the

remaining coals in a single layer on the other side of the grill. Set the cooking rack in place, cover the grill with the lid, and let the rack heat up, about 5 minutes. Use a wire brush to scrape clean the cooking rack. The grill is ready when the pile of coals is medium-hot and the single layer of coals is medium-low. (See how to gauge heat level on page 34.)

2. Sprinkle the chops with salt and pepper to taste.

3. Grill the chops, uncovered, over the hotter part of the fire until browned, about 2 minutes on each side. (If the chops start to flame, drag them to the cooler part of the grill for a moment and/or extinguish the flames with a squirt bottle filled with water.) Move the chops to the cooler part of the grill. Continue grilling, turning once, until the meat is still rosy pink at the center and an instant-read thermometer inserted through the side of the chop and away from the bone registers 130 degrees, 10 to 11 minutes.

4. Remove the chops from the grill and let rest for 5 minutes. Serve immediately.

SCIENCE: Bone-In Chops Are Better

We knew from past experience that bone-in chops taste better than boneless chops, but we wanted to test this notion more systemically. To find out how boneless chops would fare on the grill, we removed the bones from several rib chops, grilled them, and compared them with their bone-in counterparts in a blind taste test. Every taster preferred the meat that had been cooked on the bone. It was much more juicy and had more pork flavor than the meat cooked without the bone. We contacted several food scientists, who offered a few explanations.

First, because bone is a poor conductor of heat, the meat next to the bone doesn't cook as quickly. Although this factor doesn't alter the cooking time significantly, having a section of the pork chop cook at a slightly slower rate contributes to a juicier end product. The bone also insulates the muscle closest to it, protecting it from exposure to the air. In a boneless chop, a larger area of muscle is exposed, so more of the flavorful juices evaporate during grilling. Finally, fat is a crucial source of flavor, and, as it melts during cooking, it also increases the perceived juiciness. In certain cuts, especially ribs and chops, deposits of fat are located next to the bone. When the bone is removed, some fat is removed as well. With less fat, the boneless chops cook up with less pork flavor and seem drier.

➤ VARIATIONS

Gas-Grilled Rib Veal Chops

Be sure to trim the veal chops of any excess fat to prevent flare-ups. Keep a squirt bottle filled with water on hand to spray on flare-ups that may still occur. Use an instant-read thermometer to ensure that the chops don't overcook.

Turn on all burners to high, close the lid, and heat the grill until very hot, about 15 minutes. Scrape the grill grate clean with a grill brush. Leave one burner on high and turn the other burner(s) to medium. Follow the recipe for Charcoal-Grilled Rib Veal Chops from step 2 and cook with the lid down.

Grilled Veal Chops with Mediterranean Herb Paste

These herb- and garlic-infused chops go very well with mashed potatoes. Because of the oil in the herb paste, these chops are prone to flare-ups, so be vigilant when grilling.

Combine ¼ cup extra-virgin olive oil, 3 medium garlic cloves, minced, 1 tablespoon chopped fresh parsley leaves, and 2 teaspoons each chopped fresh sage leaves, thyme leaves, rosemary leaves, and oregano leaves in a small bowl. Follow the recipe for Charcoal-Grilled or Gas-Grilled Rib Veal Chops, rubbing the chops with the herb paste and then sprinkling them with salt and pepper to taste. Grill as directed and serve with lemon wedges.

Porcini-Rubbed Grilled Veal Chops

Dried porcini mushrooms can be ground to a powder and then moistened with oil to form a thick paste. When spread on veal chops, the porcini paste gives the chops an especially meaty flavor. If you don't have a spice grinder, use a blender to grind the mushrooms into a fine powder. You can substitute dried shiitake or oyster mushrooms for the porcini.

Grind ½ ounce dried porcini to a powder in a spice grinder. Mix the ground mushrooms with 2 garlic cloves, minced, 6 tablespoons extra-virgin olive oil, 1 teaspoon salt, and ¼ teaspoon ground black pepper in a small bowl. Follow the recipe for Charcoal-Grilled or Gas-Grilled Rib Veal Chops, rubbing the chops with the mushroom paste. Do not sprinkle the chops with salt and pepper before grilling. Grill as directed.

Grilled Veal Chops on a Bed of Arugula

The heat of the chops wilts the arugula, rendering it toothsome and just slightly soft, as the balsamic vinegar in the dressing offsets the veal's richness—all in all, a wonderful pairing.

1	recipe Charcoal-Grilled or Gas-Grilled Rib Veal Chops
1 1/2	tablespoons balsamic vinegar
1	small garlic clove, minced to a puree (see the illustration on page 30) or pressed through a garlic press (scant 1 teaspoon)
5	tablespoons extra-virgin olive oil

Salt and ground black pepper

8   cups lightly packed, stemmed arugula, washed and thoroughly dried

1. Grill the chops as directed.

2. While the chops are cooking, whisk together the vinegar, garlic, and oil in a small bowl. Season with salt and pepper to taste. Toss the arugula and dressing in a large bowl. Transfer the arugula to a platter or divide it among individual plates.

3. As soon as the chops are done, arrange them on the arugula. Let rest for 5 minutes. Serve immediately.

EQUIPMENT: Grill Brushes

To test the brushes, we concocted a "paint"—a mixture of honey, molasses, mustard, and barbecue sauce—that we could burn onto our grates. We coated the grates four times, baking them for one hour in the test kitchen ovens between coats. The result was a charred mess that would be sure to challenge even the hardiest of brushes. The grates were put back on the grills, which were then heated so we could test the brushes under real-life conditions.

The seven brushes we tested were chosen based on the construction and design of the handle and the scrubbing head. The handle of the stainless steel model was decidedly the heaviest and looked to be the most durable, but it absorbed heat at an alarming rate. Plastic performed adequately if you didn't spend too much time in one place on the grill (melting occurred) and if the handle was long enough. One plastic-handled brush, the Grill Pro, with a skimpy 5-inch handle, didn't even make it through the first test. The handle was so short that we couldn't get the brush to the far side of the grill without getting burned. A combination plastic/aluminum brush handle was so flexible it caused burnt knuckles when pressed with any strength. The material of choice for grill brush handles is clearly wood, which is relatively comfortable and durable.

In terms of the scrubbing heads, six of the seven brushes tested had brass bristles. Among these six, those with stiffer bristles fared better than their softer counterparts, but none of them worked all that well. The bristles on most bent after a few strokes and trapped large quantities of gunk, thereby decreasing their efficiency.

In the end, only one brush was able to successfully clean our molten mess down to the grill grate in a reasonable number of strokes. The unusual but incredibly effective Grill Wizard has no brass bristles to bend, break, or clog with unwanted grease and grime. Instead, this brush comes equipped with two large woven mesh stainless steel "scrubbie" pads. The pads are able to conform to any grill grate's spacing, size, and material, including porcelain. Best of all, the pads are detachable, washable, and replaceable. The 14-inch handle, made of poplar, is smooth, with rounded edges (unlike its square-cut competitors), with a hook for easy storage.

THE BEST GRILL BRUSH

The Grill Wizard China Grill Brush ($20) has no bristles; instead, stainless steel "scrubbie" pads are held in place by stainless bars. Although it may look a bit odd, it worked far better than the other options we tested.

5

I WANT TO COOK CHOPS INSIDE

I Want to Cook Chops Inside

YOU CAN'T ALWAYS COOK PORK, LAMB, OR veal on the grill, which is our preferred method for handling these meats (see chapter 4 for details on grilling these meats). This chapter shows you how to cook chops indoors by a variety of techniques, including pan-searing, sautéing, braising, and breading.

THICK-CUT PORK CHOPS

WHEN WAS THE LAST TIME YOU HAD A really juicy, tender, thick pork chop? These days, it is likely to be something you remember but not something that you've recently enjoyed. In response to American demands for low-fat meat, the pork industry has systematically trimmed down the hefty fat-producing hogs of the past to create today's newer pig, sleek of silhouette and lean of flesh. In fact, today's pork has at least 30 percent less fat than pork had 20 years ago.

In our experience, thick-cut pork chops are less likely to dry out than thinner chops. After testing several options, we settled on rib loin chops 1½ inches thick. Thick chops require a bit more finesse than simple sautéing because the exterior will brown long before the interior comes up to temperature. Our research uncovered two options: cook the chops on the stovetop the entire time (using the cover and regulating the heat levels to produce fully cooked chops that do not burn), or start the chops on the stove and transfer them to the oven to finish cooking through to the bone.

A high-heat sear for two to three minutes per side (depending on the number of chops in the pan) followed by about 10 minutes per side of covered stovetop cooking over reduced heat yielded very good results. But we found these chops to be just slightly less tender than those that we started in the skillet and finished in the oven. There was no demonstrable advantage to using a lower oven temperature (we tried 450, 350, and 250 degrees); the chops simply took longer to cook. In the end, purely

for the sake of expediency, we settled on searing the chops in a skillet, then transferring them to a preheated, rimmed baking pan in a 450-degree oven to finish cooking.

We had found the best cooking method, but the chops were still lacking in flavor and moisture. Owing to their relative absence of fat or collagen (those classic suppliers of flavor and moisture), these chops were clearly perfect candidates for brining. Soaking the chops for an hour in a salt-and-sugar brine yielded a significant improvement in flavor and moisture.

Our final step was to determine the exact relationship between flavor and the internal temperature of the meat. The best-tasting chops we had tried had an internal reading of 140 to 145 degrees. But medium-rare pork? What would our mothers say?

One of the reasons so much pork today reaches the table dry and overcooked is the public's residual fear of the trichinosis parasite. But there is actually little cause for concern, because the United States now sees few trichinosis cases (only 230 cases nationwide from 1991 to 1996, some 40 percent of them caused by eating wild game). Moreover, the parasites that cause this disease are destroyed when the pork reaches an internal temperature of 137 degrees. So the notion of medium-rare pork needn't be met with a shudder of alarm.

After fiddling with various options, we committed to the bold maneuver of cooking the chops to a temperature of 125 to 127 degrees. We were able to do this by letting the chops complete their cooking outside the oven, covering them with aluminum

BUY THE RIGHT PORK CHOP

Supermarket chops are often cut thick at the bone and thinner at the outer edge, like the one on the left. With such chops, the thinner periphery will overcook before the thicker meat near the bone is finished. Make sure you buy chops that are of even thickness, like the one on the right.

foil while they rested to allow the juices to redistribute throughout the meat. After a five-minute rest, the chops' temperature went up to a perfect 140 to 145 degrees. Relinquishing a minimum of juice—it mostly stayed in the chops—and retaining the barest whisper of pink on their interior, the chops were succulent and highly flavorful. This was largely due, we felt, to the fact that cooking by residual heat is a gentler and more precise method of reaching the final serving temperature. Chops left to rest uncovered, on the other hand, not only lost heat but showed little escalation in their internal temperature between pan and plate.

To ensure perfectly cooked chops, an instant-read thermometer is absolutely essential. Time estimates will be just that—estimates—and no amount of prodding or poking with your finger will give you a true reading of doneness.

Pan-Seared, Oven-Roasted Thick-Cut Pork Chops

SERVES 4

Be sure to buy chops of the same thickness so that they cook consistently—see page 93 for details. If the chops aren't being cooked immediately after brining, simply wipe off the excess brine, place them on a wire rack set on top of a rimmed baking sheet, and refrigerate, uncovered, for up to three hours.

³/₄	cup packed light brown sugar
¹/₂	cup kosher salt or ¹/₄ cup table salt
4	bone-in rib loin pork chops, 1 ¹/₂ inches thick (about 12 ounces each)
¹/₂	teaspoon ground black pepper
1	tablespoon vegetable oil

1. Dissolve the sugar and salt in 6 cups of cold water in a gallon-size, zipper-lock plastic bag. Add the pork chops and seal the bag, pressing out as much air as possible. Refrigerate until fully seasoned, about 1 hour. Remove the chops from the brine, rinse, and pat thoroughly dry with paper towels. Season the chops with the pepper.

2. Adjust an oven rack to the lower-middle position, place a shallow roasting pan or rimmed baking pan on the rack, and heat the oven to 450 degrees. When the oven reaches 450 degrees, heat the oil in a heavy-bottomed 12-inch skillet over high heat until shimmering. Lay the chops in the skillet and cook until well browned and a nice crust has formed on the surface, about 3 minutes. Turn the chops over with tongs and cook until well browned and a nice crust has formed on the second side, 2 to 3 minutes longer.

3. Using the tongs, transfer the chops to the preheated pan in the oven. Roast until an instant-read thermometer inserted into the center of a chop registers 125 to 127 degrees, 8 to 10 minutes, turning the chops over once halfway through the cooking time. Transfer the chops to a platter, tent loosely with foil, and let rest for 5 minutes (use this time to make a pan sauce, if desired). Check the internal temperature; it should register 145 degrees. Serve immediately.

VARIATIONS

Thick-Cut Pork Chops with Spicy Citrus Pan Sauce

Prepare this sauce in the pan used to brown the chops. Start the sauce once the chops come out of the oven and are resting.

¹/₂	cup molasses
1 ¹/₂	teaspoons grated zest and ¹/₄ cup juice from 2 limes
1	cup juice from 2 large oranges
2	medium garlic cloves, chopped
4	chipotle chiles in adobo sauce
1	recipe Pan-Seared, Oven-Roasted Thick-Cut Pork Chops (at left)
2	tablespoons cold unsalted butter, cut into 2 pieces
	Salt and ground black pepper

1. Combine the molasses, lime zest and juice, orange juice, garlic, and chiles in the workbowl of a food processor fitted with the metal blade and puree until smooth. Transfer the puree to a bowl; set aside.

2. Brine and cook the pork chops as directed; set them aside on a platter and tent loosely with foil.

3. Pour off the fat in the skillet used to brown the chops. Place the skillet over medium-high heat and add the molasses puree, scraping the pan bottom with a wooden spoon to loosen the browned bits. Simmer until thickened and syrupy, about 2 minutes. Whisk in the butter, one piece at a time, until melted. Season the sauce with salt and pepper to taste and spoon the sauce over the chops. Serve immediately.

Thick-Cut Pork Chops with Sweet-and-Sour Pan Sauce and Bacon

Prepare this sauce in the pan used to brown the chops. Start the sauce once the chops go into the oven to roast.

I	recipe Pan-Seared, Oven-Roasted Thick-Cut Pork Chops (page 94)
5	ounces bacon (about 5 slices), cut into 1/4-inch pieces
2	large shallots, minced (about 1/2 cup) Pinch sugar
I	medium garlic clove, minced or pressed through a garlic press (about I teaspoon)
4	medium plum tomatoes, peeled, seeded, and cut into 1/4-inch pieces
1/2	cup balsamic vinegar
I	cup dry Marsala or sweet vermouth
4	tablespoons cold unsalted butter, cut into 4 pieces
I	tablespoon chopped fresh parsley leaves Salt and ground black pepper

1. Brine and pan-sear the pork chops as directed in steps 1 and 2.

2. As soon as the pork chops go into the oven (step 3), pour off the fat in the skillet used to brown the chops. Place the skillet over medium-high heat and cook the bacon until crisp, about 6 minutes. Transfer the bacon to a paper towel-lined plate; pour off all but 1 tablespoon of the bacon fat. Reduce the heat to low, add the shallots and sugar, and cook until the shallots are softened, about 1 minute (do not brown). Add the garlic and cook until fragrant, about 30 seconds. Increase the heat to medium-high, stir in the tomatoes and vinegar, and scrape the pan bottom with a wooden spoon to

loosen the browned bits. Add the Marsala and simmer until reduced by half, about 5 minutes. Whisk in the butter, one piece at a time, until melted. Stir in the parsley and season the sauce with salt and pepper to taste. Spoon the sauce over the chops and serve immediately.

PORK CHOPS WITH VINEGAR PEPPERS

THIS SIMPLE, RUSTIC DISH FEATURES PAN-seared pork chops smothered in a silky, caramelly sauce of bell peppers. Although the flavors are complex, the execution of this dish is quick and straightforward, making it easy enough for a weeknight dinner. The chops are usually browned and removed from the pan, and the vinegar and pepper sauce is built on the pan drippings.

Of course, the success of this recipe begins

SCIENCE: How Brining Works

We often soak lean cuts of pork in a saltwater solution before cooking because we have consistently found that brining keeps the meat juicier. Brining also gives meat a firmer consistency and seasons the meat down to the bone.

Brining accomplishes all of this by promoting a change in the structure of the proteins in the muscle. The salt causes protein strands to denature, or unwind. This is the same process that occurs when proteins are exposed to heat, acid, or alcohol. When protein strands unwind, they get tangled in one another and trap water in the matrix that forms. Salt is commonly used to give processed meats a better texture. For example, hot dogs made without salt would be limp.

In some cases, we add sugar to the brine to enhance flavor. We have found that brining pork chops and roasts in a solution of both salt and sugar enhances the caramelized flavor that occurs when the pork is cooked.

We usually list both kosher and regular table salt in recipes that call for brining. Because of the difference in the size of the crystals, cup for cup, table salt is about twice as strong as kosher salt. Kosher salt has the advantage of dissolving more quickly than table salt.

with properly cooked chops. We found that our recipe for thick-cut pork chops was a good place to start. The challenge was to create a heady pan sauce that would contrast with the mild flavor of pork. In almost all the traditional recipes for this combination, the peppers of choice are raw, skin-on red bell peppers that have been bottled and submerged in white vinegar and labeled "vinegar peppers," "Italian-style peppers," or "Greek-style peppers."

Some recipes called for using the liquid from the bottle, but we found the flavor to be tinny and inconsistent from manufacturer to manufacturer (some of the peppers were packed mostly in vinegar; others mostly in water), which made writing a recipe almost impossible. When we drained the peppers and replaced the vinegar mixture in the bottle with white wine vinegar, we found there was no comparison: The white wine vinegar was far brighter and clearer. Because the traditional recipe calls for white wine vinegar, we had rejected both red wine and balsamic vinegar from the start, believing that either would create an entirely different dish.

Although the combination of drained bottled peppers and fresh vinegar was a big step forward, some tinniness remained in the peppers, and their texture was slightly stiff and rubbery. We decided to try replacing the bottled peppers with fresh bell peppers. Sure enough, this was a huge improvement. Using a combination of two colors, (red and yellow), made for much more visual appeal.

We were not done with the peppers. First we quickly cooked them in vinegar alone, and they were raw and too crunchy. Next we simmered them in a covered pan, but they tasted boiled and bland. Then we decided to cook the peppers twice, first in white wine vinegar and water, and then again in plain water. Simmering them uncovered allowed the natural sugars in the peppers to caramelize and gave the peppers their characteristic caramel flavor and silky texture.

Our research recipes indicated that we had several optional ingredients still to test before the dish was final. In the end, we found that garlic, anchovies, and herbs were essential, as they made the dish bold in flavor. The net sum of our efforts? An impressive-looking, aromatic, and succulent dish

with slightly sweet, yet sour, almost tart undertones. In short, it was just what we had imagined.

Pork Chops with Bell Peppers and Vinegar

SERVES 4

Be sure to buy chops of equal thickness. See page 93 for details.

PORK CHOPS

¾	cup packed light brown sugar
½	cup kosher salt or ¼ cup table salt
4	bone-in rib loin pork chops, 1 ½ inches thick (about 12 ounces each)
½	teaspoon ground black pepper
1	tablespoon olive oil

PEPPERS

2	medium garlic cloves, minced or pressed through a garlic press (about 2 teaspoons)
2	anchovy fillets, minced
1	medium red bell pepper, stemmed, seeded, and cut into ½-inch dice
1	medium yellow bell pepper, stemmed, seeded, and cut into ½-inch dice
1	sprig fresh rosemary
1	cup water
½	cup white wine vinegar

1. FOR THE CHOPS: Dissolve the sugar and salt in 6 cups of cold water in a gallon-size, zipper-lock plastic bag. Add the pork chops and seal the bag, pressing out as much air as possible. Refrigerate until fully seasoned, about 1 hour. Remove the chops from the brine, rinse, and pat thoroughly dry with paper towels. Season the chops with the pepper.

2. Adjust an oven rack to the lower-middle position, place a shallow roasting pan or rimmed baking pan on the rack, and heat the oven to 450 degrees. When the oven reaches 450 degrees, heat the oil in a heavy-bottomed 12-inch skillet over high heat until shimmering. Lay the chops in the skillet and cook until well browned and a nice crust has formed on the surface, about 3 minutes. Turn the chops over with tongs and cook until well browned and a nice crust has formed on the second

side, 2 to 3 minutes longer.

3. Using the tongs, transfer the chops to the pre-heated pan in the oven. Roast until an instant-read thermometer inserted into the center of a chop registers 125 to 127 degrees, 8 to 10 minutes, turning the chops over once halfway through the cooking time. Transfer the chops to a platter and tent loosely with foil while you prepare the peppers.

4. FOR THE PEPPERS: As soon as you place the chops in the oven, return the skillet to medium-high heat, add the garlic, anchovies, peppers, and rosemary, and cook until the peppers begin to soften, 4 to 5 minutes. Add ½ cup of the water and the vinegar and bring to a boil, stirring and scraping any browned bits from the pan bottom. Cook until the liquid has almost evaporated, about 6 minutes. Add the remaining ½ cup water and cook until the mixture is syrupy, 3 to 4 minutes. Remove and discard the rosemary.

5. Add the pork chops to the pan and simmer, turning the chops once, until heated through and the internal temperature of the chops on an instant-read thermometer registers 145 degrees, about 2 minutes. Serve immediately.

STUFFED PORK CHOPS

A SIMPLE GARLIC AND HERB BREAD STUFF-ing seems an easy way to load flavor and richness into today's leaner pork chops. Whenever stuffing occurs, however, a host of challenges enters the kitchen. Chief among them is bringing the stuffing (often bound with raw eggs) up to a safe internal temperature without overcooking the surrounding meat. Many of the recipes we consulted employed a crude strategy to tackle this problem—surround the chops in liquid and cook them for an hour or more. This old-fashioned technique (essentially a braise) may have worked with fattier chops, but modern-day pork is lean and tender—much better suited to searing in a hot skillet, which can then be used to make a quick pan sauce.

Determining which type of chop to stuff was fairly simple. Rib chops were the obvious choice for their higher fat content (making them less likely to dry out) and wide, unbroken eye of meat. Center-cut or loin chops, on the other hand, are divided down the middle like a T-bone steak, making them tough to stuff. Thick-cut rib chops (about 1½ inches) were widely available and big enough to handle a hearty amount of filling.

Our master recipe for sautéing thick-cut pork chops pointed the way. We knew from our testing that the best results came from brining the chops beforehand and then finishing them in a hot oven instead of in the pan. As stuffed chops require more time in the oven than unstuffed ones, the brining step was crucial for retaining moisture. By first cutting a pocket in each chop, we allowed the brine to penetrate to the center of the meat.

No amount of brining could save a pork chop from 30 minutes in a 450-degree oven, however. That's about how long it took for the stuffing inside of the seared chops to reach a temperature of 160 degrees, the minimum temperature for the safe consumption of raw eggs. By that time, temperature of the meat near the edges of the chop had topped 180 degrees and was dry and tough. Using eggs to bind the stuffing was evidently out—but did we, in fact, need them?

It seemed so at first. Without the eggs, the stuffing had been loose and crumbly, spilling out all over the plate when the chops were served. Our working method for stuffing the chops had been part of the problem. We slit the pork chops open from the side and spooned loose stuffing into the middle, then tried using toothpicks to keep the chops closed. But the toothpicks interfered with the searing of the meat and did a poor job of keeping the chop closed in the heat of the oven as the pork contracted and curled open. When it came time to plate the chops, we had to dig the toothpicks out of the meat (we missed one once), which only encouraged the stuffing to come tumbling out.

Some careful knife work solved the problem. Instead of butterflying the meat, we made an inch-long cut in the side of the chop with a thin boning knife, then used the blade to clear a cavity in the center of the meat without any further cuts at the edge. We stuffed the meat through this smaller opening, and the natural shape of the chop held the stuffing in place. No eggs, no toothpicks.

STUFFING A PORK CHOP

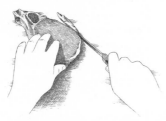

1. Using a sharp boning or paring knife, trim away the excess fat and connective tissue around the edge of the meat.

2. With the knife positioned as shown, insert the blade through the center of the side of the chop until the tip touches the bone.

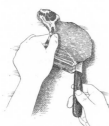

3. Holding the chop firmly, carefully swing just the tip of the blade through the middle of the chop to create a pocket.

4. Remove the knife from the chop and, if necessary, enlarge the pocket opening slit to measure one inch.

5. With your fingers, gently press the stuffing mixture into the pocket, without enlarging the opening.

Furthermore, the natural juice from the brined pork moistened the stuffing while the chop cooked.

Next, we experimented with adding bacon and sausage to our basic bread stuffing. The flavors were overbearing, tasters said, and the extra meat made the stuffing too salty. (Thanks to the brine, the juice from the pork was enough to season the stuffing without adding extra salt.) Tasters preferred the simpler version made with garlic and fresh herbs. A few tablespoons of cream added richness and enough moisture to bring the stuffing together.

The meat near the edges of the chops still tended to dry out when left in the oven until the stuffing reached 145 degrees, the temperature that recipes with nonegg stuffings recommended. Our standard operating procedure is to tent resting meat loosely with aluminum foil to allow for the juices to redistribute while the residual heat gently brings the internal temperature to the desired doneness. In this case, we were able to pull the meat from the oven when the temperature at the center of the stuffing was just 125 degrees. After 5 to 10 minutes of resting, the temperature of the pork and the stuffing had evened out around 145 degrees.

Last but not least, the drippings and fond that remained in the skillet tempted us to whip up a sweet and spicy pan sauce while the chops finished in the oven. We ended up with a simple skillet chutney made from apples, cider and spices—a pleasant change from applesauce.

Stuffed Pork Chops
SERVES 4

These stuffed pork chops may be served with applesauce, All-Purpose Gravy (page 406), or Quick Ginger-Apple Chutney (recipe follows). The chutney is made in the skillet used to cook the chops and should be started while the chops are in the oven.

CHOPS

4	bone-in rib loin pork chops, 1 1/2 inches thick (about 12 ounces each)
3/4	cup packed light brown sugar
1/2	cup kosher salt or 1/4 cup table salt
	Ground black pepper
1	tablespoon vegetable oil

STUFFING

3	tablespoons unsalted butter
1	small onion, diced small
1	medium celery rib, diced small
1/2	teaspoon salt
2	medium garlic cloves, minced or pressed through a garlic press (about 2 teaspoons)
2	teaspoons minced fresh thyme leaves
1	tablespoon minced fresh parsley leaves
2	cups 1/4-inch cubes from 1 baguette
2	tablespoons heavy cream
1/8	teaspoon ground black pepper

1. FOR THE CHOPS: Following the illustrations on page 98, cut a small pocket through the side of each chop. Dissolve the sugar and salt in 6 cups of cold water in a gallon-size, zipper-lock plastic bag. Add the pork chops and seal the bag, pressing out as much air as possible. Refrigerate until fully seasoned, about 1 hour.

2. FOR THE STUFFING: Melt the butter in a 12-inch skillet over medium heat until the foaming subsides. Add the onion, celery, and salt and cook until the vegetables are softened and beginning to brown, about 10 minutes. Add the garlic and herbs and cook until fragrant, about 1 minute. Transfer to a medium bowl, add the bread cubes, cream, and pepper, and toss well to combine. Using a rubber spatula, press the stuffing lightly against the sides of the bowl until it comes together.

3. TO STUFF, SEASON, AND COOK THE CHOPS: Adjust an oven rack to the lower-middle position, place a shallow roasting pan or jelly-roll pan on the rack, and heat the oven to 450 degrees. Remove the chops from the brine, rinse, and pat dry with paper towels. Place one quarter of the stuffing (about 1/3 cup) in the pocket of each pork chop. Season the chops with the pepper.

4. Heat the oil in a heavy-bottomed 12-inch skillet over high heat until shimmering. Lay the chops in the skillet and cook until a well browned and a nice crust has formed, about 3 minutes. Turn the chops over with tongs and cook until well browned and a nice crust has formed on the second side, 2 to 3 minutes longer.

5. Using the tongs, transfer the chops to the preheated pan in the oven. Roast until an instant-read thermometer inserted into the center of the stuffing registers 125 to 127 degrees, about 15 minutes, turning the chops over once halfway through the cooking time. Transfer the chops to a platter, tent loosely with foil, and let rest at least 5 minutes. Check the internal temperature; it should register 145 degrees. Serve with the chutney as an accompaniment.

Quick Ginger-Apple Chutney
MAKES ENOUGH FOR 4 PORK CHOPS

This chutney works well with any plain pork chops or roast pork.

1	tablespoon vegetable oil
1	small onion, cut into 1/2-inch dice
2	Granny Smith apples, peeled, cored, and cut into 1/2-inch dice
1	(1-inch) piece ginger, peeled and minced (about 1 tablespoon)
1/4	teaspoon ground allspice
1/8	teaspoon cayenne pepper
1/4	cup packed light brown sugar
1	cup apple cider
	Salt and ground black pepper

While the chops are in the oven, pour off any fat in the skillet used to sear the chops. Add the oil and heat over medium-high heat until shimmering. Add the onion and apples and cook, stirring occasionally, until softened and browned, about 10 minutes. Stir in the ginger, allspice, and cayenne and cook until fragrant, about 1 minute. Add the sugar and cider and bring to a boil, scraping the browned bits off the pan bottom, until the cider is reduced and slightly thickened, about 4 minutes. Season with salt and pepper to taste. Transfer to a serving bowl.

EASY PORK CHOPS
WE LOVE OUR THICK-CUT PORK CHOPS (page 93), but they are not the quickest or easiest of our chop recipes to prepare. You need to set aside an hour to brine the chops and then they require

a two-step cooking process that starts on the stove and finishes in the oven. They are great when you have the time to brine, sear, and roast, but is there a way to produce a good chop in less time?

Most "quick" recipes for pork chops yield meat that's dry as leather and tough as nails. There's nothing to do but open a jar of applesauce and cover the chop with it, using it to cover up a multitude of sins. Despite its drawbacks, this work-a-day pork chop has one major asset: time. From beginning to end, it's a quick fix. Could we find a simple way to create the elusive, juicy pork chop and still get it on the table in 20 minutes?

First stop was the local supermarket meat counter. We filled a shopping cart with an overwhelming number of chops and went back to the test kitchen to see if any would fit the bill. First to go were boneless chops, which cooked up much drier than their bone-in counterparts. Superthin chops (about ¼ inch thick) were axed, too, because they dried out in the time it took for us to walk them through a hot kitchen. By comparison, 1-inch-thick (or thicker) chops, which were much less apt to dry out, necessitated the use of both the stove and the oven before being fully cooked. This just wasn't quick enough to meet our 20-minute goal. The right thickness for our purposes proved to be ½ inch to ¾ inch—thin enough to keep the cooking on the stovetop and thick enough to give the chops a fighting chance for a juicy interior. As with our thick-cut pork chops, the rib chops fared best in our tests, followed by center-cut chops.

Pork chop recipes use one of three basic approaches. In the first, the chops are seared over high heat and then cooked uncovered over medium-low. The second method also starts the chops on high heat, then adds stock or water and covers the pan before reducing the heat. The third method again sears the chops over high heat but covers the pan without adding any liquid beforehand. The worst of the lot was leaving the pan uncovered, which produced unevenly cooked chops. Adding liquid and then covering the pan was not much better. After 15 minutes (about the same cooking time the other two methods required), the chops were still tough. The last method, which seared the chops over high heat

and covered the pan without first adding liquid, showed the most promise. Although still miles away from our dream of juicy, tender pork chops, we didn't need a gallon of water or the jaw strength of a bear to chew them.

Using the high-heat, covered-pan cooking method, we uncovered a few secrets of pork chop cookery. First, chops should not be cooked to an internal temperature much higher than 140 degrees—cooking them beyond this point results in tough, dry meat. We also found that when we reduced the searing time from three minutes per side to one minute per side, the chops were more moist, albeit not juicy. In fact, we needed only to look in the pan to see the enormous amount of juices that had been released. If the juices were in the pan, they weren't in the chops.

Thinking out loud, a colleague raised an interesting point—perhaps the high heat was causing the problem. Although we usually sear pork roasts and thick chops over high heat to develop flavor, perhaps these thinner chops were too quick to dry out in a hot pan. We raced back to the stove and heated the pan over a more modest medium heat before adding the chops. After a few minutes, we covered the chops and cooked them over medium-low. When we uncovered them, voilà! We found a large reduction in the amount of pan juices. We then cut into what appeared to be a pretty tender chop and happily found the juices right inside the meat, where they belonged. Progress!

Perhaps pushing our luck, we wondered what would happen if the pork chops were introduced to heat at an even slower pace. If medium heat was good, what about—you guessed it—no heat? Although it seemed strange, we placed the next batch of chops in a cold pan and then turned the heat to medium. After the chops had cooked for a few minutes on each side, we covered them and cooked them through over low heat while uttering a silent prayer. Our hopes ran high when we noticed that there were barely any pan juices in the skillet. We plated a chop, bit down, and was met with the juiciest and most tender chop yet.

The only drawback was color—or lack thereof. Without enough heat to promote browning, these pork chops were as blond as the ubiquitous bombshell. Using a little sugar in addition to salt and pepper to season them went a long way toward helping to color the chops. We also found that instead of splitting the browning time and the sugar evenly between the two sides of the chops, it was better to sugar one side and let it develop a more substantial color. This side, the first side to come in contact with the pan, then became the presentation side.

Although starting meat in a cold pan was odd—if not downright weird—it made quick-cooking a weeknight pork chop almost foolproof. Would these pork chops win any beauty contest? We doubted it. We did know, though, that we didn't have to serve them in a sea of applesauce. It could, and would be served on the side.

Easy Pork Chops
SERVES 4

In this recipe, "natural" pork chops—that is, pork chops that are not "enhanced"—work best (for more information on enhanced pork, see page 4); the liquid injected into enhanced pork inhibits browning. Electric burners are slower to heat than gas burners, so, if using one, begin heating the burner before seasoning the chops. If you don't hear a gentle sizzle after the pork chops have been cooking for two minutes over medium heat, your stovetop is running at a low heat output. Raise the heat to medium-high to cook the pork chops uncovered (as directed in the recipe). Then reduce the heat to medium-low instead of low, cover the chops, and continue with the recipe as directed. When cooking the first side of the chops, use color as an indicator of when to flip the chops; then, to determine doneness, use an instant-read thermometer—do not go solely by cooking times. Serve these very simple pork chops with chutney or applesauce, or try one of the recipe variations that follow.

4　bone-in rib or center-cut pork chops, 1/2 to 3/4 inch thick (about 7 ounces each), patted dry with paper towels and scored according to the illustration at right)
1　teaspoon vegetable oil
　　Salt and ground black pepper
1/2　teaspoon sugar

1. If using an electric stove, turn the burner to medium heat. Rub both sides of each chop with 1/8 teaspoon of the oil and sprinkle with salt and pepper to taste. Sprinkle the meat portion on one side of each chop evenly with 1/8 teaspoon sugar, avoiding the bone.

2. Place the chops, sugared-side down, in a non-stick 12-inch skillet, positioning the chops so that the ribs point to the center of the pan. Using your hands, press the meat on each chop into the pan. Set the skillet over medium heat; cook until lightly browned, 4 to 9 minutes (the pork chops should be sizzling after 2 minutes; if not, see note above). Using tongs, flip the chops, positioning them in same manner, with the ribs pointing to the center of the skillet. Cover the skillet, reduce the heat to low, and cook until the center of each chop registers 140 to 145 on an instant-read thermometer, 3 to 6 minutes (begin checking internal temperature after only 2 minutes); the chops will barely brown on the second side. Transfer the chops to a platter, tent loosely with foil, and let rest for 5 minutes. Do not discard the liquid in the skillet.

3. Add any juices accumulated on the platter to the skillet. Set the skillet over high heat and simmer vigorously until reduced to about 3 tablespoons, 30 seconds to 90 seconds; adjust the seasonings with salt and pepper to taste. Off heat, return the pork chops to the skillet, and turn them to coat with the reduced juices. Serve the chops immediately, browned-side up, pouring any remaining juices over them.

SCORING THE CHOPS

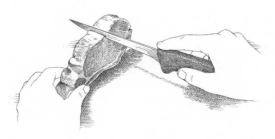

Using a sharp knife, cut two slits, about 2 inches apart, through the outer layer of fat and connective tissue. This will keep the chops from curling as they cook.

➤ VARIATIONS

Pork Chops with Mustard-Sage Sauce

This sauce and the brandy and prune one that follows it both start out thick and are thinned by the juices released by the chops as they rest.

Follow the recipe for Easy Pork Chops; after transferring the chops to a platter and tenting them loosely with foil, pour the pan juice in the skillet into a small bowl and reserve. While the chops rest, add 1 teaspoon vegetable oil and 1 medium garlic clove, minced (about 1 teaspoon), to the now-empty skillet; set the skillet over medium heat and cook until fragrant, about 30 seconds. Add ¼ cup low-sodium chicken broth; increase the heat to high and simmer until reduced to about 2 tablespoons, about 3 minutes. Add the pork chop juice accumulated in the bowl to the skillet. Off heat, whisk in 1 tablespoon Dijon mustard and 3 tablespoons cold unsalted butter, one piece at a time, until melted and combined. Stir in 1 teaspoon minced fresh sage leaves and adjust the seasonings with salt and pepper to taste. Spoon the sauce over the chops and serve immediately.

Pork Chops with Brandy and Prunes

Cover ⅓ cup chopped pitted prunes with ¼ cup brandy and let stand. Follow the recipe for Easy Pork Chops; after transferring the chops to a platter and tenting them loosely with foil, pour the pan juice in the skillet into a small bowl and reserve. While the chops rest, add 1 teaspoon vegetable oil and 1 medium shallot, minced (about 3 tablespoons), to the now-empty skillet; set the skillet over medium heat and cook, stirring occasionally, until the shallot has softened, about 2 minutes. Off heat, add the brandy and prunes; set the skillet over medium-high heat and cook until the brandy is reduced to about 2 tablespoons, about 3 minutes. Add the pork chops juices accumulated in the bowl to the skillet. Off heat, whisk in 2 teaspoons minced fresh thyme leaves and 3 tablespoons cold unsalted butter, one piece at a time, until melted and combined. Adjust the seasonings with salt and pepper to taste. Spoon the sauce over the chops and serve immediately.

SMOTHERED PORK CHOPS

SMOTHERED PORK CHOPS, A HOMEY DISH of chops braised in deeply flavored onion gravy, are folksy, not fancy; denim, not worsted wool. The cooking process is straightforward: You brown the chops, remove them from the pan, brown the onions, return the chops to the pan, cover them with the onions and gravy—hence the term smothered—and braise them until tender. Inarguably easy, but initial recipe tests produced bland, dry pork, and near-tasteless gravies with woeful consistencies ranging from pasty to processed to gelatinous to watery.

Poor texture and shallow flavor robs smothered pork chops of their savory-sweet glory. To get it right, we knew we'd have to identify the best chop and the best way to cook it. And the gravy was no less important.

Some of our research recipes specified sirloin chops, which are cut from the rear end of the loin. Our tasters found this cut a little dry and often unavailable. Blade chops, cut from the far front end of the loin, were juicier but suffered the same spotty availability. Of the two remaining types of chops, center-cut loin and rib, we found the latter to be the juiciest and most flavorful because it had a bit more fat.

We tried rib chops as thick as 1½ inches and as thin as ½ inch and were shocked when tasters unanimously chose the thin ½-inch chops. Thick chops overwhelmed the gravy, which we believed should share equal billing with the meat. Thin chops also picked up more onion flavor during cooking. We also tried boneless chops, but they cooked up dry, so we decided to stick with bone-in for optimum juiciness.

Still in pursuit of the maximum juiciness, we indulged our passion for brining, by soaking the chops in a simple salt-sugar-water solution before cooking them. It turned out that brining was ill-suited to this dish for two reasons. First, these chops cook in a moist environment provided by the gravy, so why spend time instilling extra moisture? We would not be using the harsh, dry heat of grilling, searing, or roasting, which makes brining a viable and often necessary option. Second, no matter how we adjusted the salinity of the brine, the salt-infused meat caused the gravy to become intolerably salty.

Last we tackled the question of cooking time. Although we prefer to slightly undercook pork to ensure tenderness, this is one application where further cooking was necessary since we wanted to infuse the meat with the flavor of the gravy and onions. After their initial browning, the chops registered a rosy 140 degrees on an instant-read thermometer. They were cooked through and tender, but since they had yet to be smothered, they had none of the onion flavor we wanted. Fifteen minutes of braising in the gravy boosted the flavor but toughened the chops, which now registered almost 200 degrees. At that temperature, the meat fibers have contracted and expelled moisture, but the fat and connective tissue between the fibers, called collagen, have not had a chance to melt fully and turn into gelatin. It is this gelatin that makes braised meats especially rich and tender. Another 15 minutes of braising time solved the problem. At this point, the chops registered 210 degrees; the extra time allowed the fat and collagen to melt completely, so the meat was tender and succulent as well as oniony from the gravy.

It was important that the gravy build on the flavor of the browned pork chops. The canned, condensed soup called for in some of the research recipes produced gravies that tasted processed and gluelike. Water produced a weak, thin gravy, but chicken broth improved the picture, adding much-needed flavor.

For liquid to morph into gravy, it must be thickened. Cornstarch is an easy option, but it resulted in a gelatinous, translucent sauce that looked and felt wrong. Next we tried adding flour, in three different ways. Flouring the chops before browning them turned their exteriors gummy and left the gravy with a chalky mouthfeel. Flouring the onions left the gravy tasting of raw flour. Last, we called upon a roux, a mixture of flour and fat (in this case, vegetable oil) cooked together. This occasioned the need for an extra pan, which that we'd hoped to avoid having to use, but the results were fantastic. The roux was simple to make, and it thickened the sauce reliably without adding the taste of raw flour, lending the gravy both a smooth finish and another layer of flavor that was slightly nutty.

SCIENCE: Low and Slow for Pork Chops

Pork chops, which may go from succulent to leathery with the most minor differences in cooking technique, pose a challenge for the cook. According to one Canadian study, for example, pork cooked to an internal temperature of 180 degrees in a 400-degree oven can lose between two and three times the moisture of pork cooked to 160 degrees in a 250-degree oven. Curious about this and about the unconventional cold-pan method of cooking chops in our recipe, we decided to investigate the effect of heat on pork meat. What we discovered was that the secret to juicy pork resided in the structure of its muscle proteins.

Proteins are long chains of linked amino acids that fold into a huge variety of three-dimensional shapes. Folded muscle protein also holds and immobilizes a considerable amount of water in an ordered fashion. Introduce heat, though, and this organized state of affairs is thrown into disarray as the proteins unfold. Thermal analysis of pork has shown that there are three approximate temperatures at which groups of pork proteins come undone: 126 degrees, 145 degrees, and 168 degrees. As each of these temperatures is reached, more water is freed from the proteins. Meat proteins also tend to compact as they cook, squeezing out the freed-up water.

To better understand these effects, we took cubes of pork and cooked them to 100 degrees, 140 degrees, and 180 degrees. At the highest temperature, the meat not only shrank more but the muscle fibers became tighter and more pronounced. When we went ahead and seared a cube on one side in a very hot pan, we found that the edge touching the pan contracted and looked similar to the cube cooked to 180 degrees, even though the rest of the cube was raw.

All cooks focus on the temperature reached at the middle of a piece of meat to determine doneness, but this may be too myopic. The means by which the middle gets to that temperature is at least as important. High-heat cooking methods, such as searing, guarantee that the outer layer of meat will be very well done before the inside is just done. Brining can compensate for this but this method just won't work with regular (unbrined) chops. By keeping the heat level low, water loss on the outside of the chop is minimized and more of the juice that is bound inside the meat remains there.

The roux was good, but we tried to improve it with two oft-used refinements. First, we fried a couple of slices of bacon and substituted the rendered fat for the vegetable oil in the roux. What a hit! The sweet/salty/smoky bacon flavor underscored and deepened all of the other flavors in the dish. Beyond that, we followed in the footsteps of many a gravy master who has eked out even more flavor from a roux by browning it for five minutes to the shade of peanut butter. Cooking the flour this way unlocks a rich, toasty flavor that builds as the shade deepens. Both techniques are widespread and justly popular, as they turned out to be huge flavor builders.

The onions play a title role in the gravy. We tried them minced, chopped, and sliced both thick and thin. Thin-sliced onions cooked to a melting texture that was our favorite. We tried different quantities of onions, from one to four, for four pork chops and found that two was best. We tried simply softening the onions until they were translucent versus cooking them for a few more minutes until their edges browned, a winning technique that accentuated their natural sweetness. Perhaps the most important onion test was trying different types, including standard-issue supermarket yellow onions, red onions, and sweet Vidalia onions. The yellow onions triumphed for their "deep brown hue" and "balanced flavor." By comparison, tasters found the red onions to be harsh tasting and ugly and the Vidalias to be "bland" and "wan" looking.

The onions cook in the same pan used to brown the chops. We wanted to make sure that the onions released enough moisture to dissolve (or deglaze) the flavorful, sticky, brown bits (called fond) left in the pan by the chops, so we salted them lightly. The heat and salt worked together to jumpstart the breakdown of the onions' cell walls, which set their juices flowing. We also added two tablespoons of water to the pan for insurance.

Our last flavor tweak was an unusual one for us—we eliminated the salt we customarily use to season chops. Tasters agreed that the salt added to the onions, along with the naturally salty bacon and chicken broth and the garlic, thyme, and bay used to build extra flavor in the gravy, seasoned the dish adequately. These chops were hearty, deeply flavored, and comforting.

Smothered Pork Chops
SERVES 4

Use low-sodium chicken broth in this recipe; regular chicken broth can result in an overseasoned sauce. Serve smothered chops with a starch to soak up the rich gravy. Simple egg noodles was the test kitchen favorite, but rice or mashed potatoes also work well.

3	ounces bacon (about 3 slices), cut into $1/4$-inch pieces
2	tablespoons all-purpose flour
1 $3/4$	cups low-sodium chicken broth
	Vegetable oil
4	bone-in rib loin pork chops, $1/2$ to $3/4$ inch thick (about 7 ounces each), patted dry with paper towels
	Ground black pepper
2	medium yellow onions, halved and sliced thin (about 3 $1/2$ cups)
	Salt
2	tablespoons water
2	medium garlic cloves, minced or pressed through a garlic press (about 2 teaspoons)
1	teaspoon minced fresh thyme leaves
2	bay leaves
1	tablespoon minced fresh parsley leaves

1. Fry the bacon in a small saucepan over medium heat, stirring occasionally, until lightly browned and the fat is rendered, 8 to 10 minutes. Using a slotted spoon, transfer the bacon to a paper towel–lined plate and reserve, leaving the fat in the pan (you should have 2 tablespoons bacon fat; if not, supplement with vegetable oil). Reduce the heat to medium-low and gradually whisk the flour into the fat until smooth. Cook, whisking frequently, until the mixture is light brown, about the color of peanut butter, about 5 minutes. Whisk in the chicken broth in a slow, steady stream; increase the heat to medium-high and bring to a boil, stirring occasionally. Cover and reserve off heat.

2. Heat 1 tablespoon oil in a 12-inch skillet over high heat until smoking. Meanwhile, sprinkle the pork chops with ½ teaspoon pepper. Brown the chops in a single layer until deep golden on the first side, about 3 minutes. Flip the chops and cook until

browned on the second side, about 3 minutes longer. Transfer the chops to a large plate and set aside.

3. Reduce the heat to medium and add 1 tablespoon oil, onions, ¼ teaspoon salt, and water to the now-empty skillet. Using a wooden spoon, scrape up the browned bits on the pan bottom; cook, stirring frequently, until the onions are softened and browned around the edges, about 5 minutes. Stir

DEVELOP FLAVOR IN EVERY STEP

Brown is good when it comes to flavor. Cooking each component fully contributes greater flavor to the finished dish. For instance, the blond roux is not particularly deep of flavor, whereas its counterpart is bronze and nutty (see below, top photos). The well-browned chop tastes more savory than the poorly browned, pale chop (middle photos). The onions with the brown edges are sweeter and softer than the light, crunchy onions (bottom photos).

Brown roux versus blond roux

Well-browned pork chop versus poorly browned pork chop

Caramelized, softened onions versus blond, crunchy onions

in the garlic and thyme and cook until fragrant, about 30 seconds. Return the chops to the skillet in a single layer, and cover them with the onions. Pour in the reserved sauce and any juices released by the pork chops; add the bay leaves. Cover, reduce the heat to low, and simmer until the pork is tender and a paring knife inserted into the chops meets very little resistance, about 30 minutes.

4. Transfer the chops to a warmed serving platter and tent with foil. Increase the heat to medium-high and simmer the sauce rapidly, stirring frequently, until thickened to a gravy-like consistency, about 5 minutes. Discard the bay leaves, stir in the parsley, and adjust the seasonings with salt and pepper to taste. Cover the chops with the sauce, sprinkle with the reserved bacon, and serve immediately.

➤ VARIATIONS

Smothered Pork Chops with Cider and Apples

Follow the recipe for Smothered Pork Chops, substituting apple cider for the chicken broth and 1 large or 2 small Granny Smith apples, peeled, cored, and cut into ⅓-inch wedges, for 1 of the onions, and increasing the salt to ½ teaspoon in step 2.

Smothered Pork Chops with Spicy Collard Greens

Follow the recipe for Smothered Pork Chops, increasing the oil in step 3 to 2 tablespoons, omitting 1 of the onions, and increasing the garlic to 4 cloves, minced. Just before returning the browned chops to the pan in step 3, add 4 cups thinly sliced collard greens and ½ teaspoon red pepper flakes.

BRAISED LAMB CHOPS

IN OUR TESTS, WE FOUND THAT GRILLING is the best method for cooking most lamb chops. They are too fatty for broiling (unless, of course, your kitchen has a professional ventilation system); our kitchen filled with smoke every time we tried this technique. Sautéing is not much better. The chops render so much fat that they are swimming in grease in no time and do not brown all that well since the edges tend to curl up as the chops cook. For best results, we prefer to grill lamb chops.

There are two exceptions to this rule. We love pan-fried lamb chops coated with Parmesan. (For more information on this Italian classic, see page 107.) We are willing to deal with some mess to prepare this dish. The other indoor preparation we like for lamb chops calls for braising somewhat chewy shoulder chops, which respond especially well to this cooking method. (Don't braise rib or loin chops; they lose their distinctive flavor when braised.)

Our first test in this arena was a stovetop braise using a minimal amount of liquid that could be quickly reduced and thickened for a sauce. We browned the chops with sliced onion in a deep sauté pan large enough to hold the chops in a single layer. Then we deglazed with white wine, herbs, a little

tomato, and water to barely cover the chops and simmered the whole thing, covered, for an hour and a half, until the meat was tender. We were surprised at how long the relatively thin chops took to cook, and the results were disappointing. The lamb had a sticky, gummy quality that we attributed to the scant quantity of liquid.

Next time, we switched to red wine (and more of it) and braised the chops just to medium. We decided to try this experiment after it occurred to us that grilled chops are tender when cooked medium—maybe we needn't actually stew the chops at all—just briefly braise them. The red wine improved the flavor, and cooking the meat to a lesser degree of doneness vastly shortened the cooking time. Using chops about ¾ inch thick, we found that we now had a delicious stovetop braise that cooked in just 15 to 20 minutes—a true weeknight supper dish for the winter months.

INGREDIENTS: Shoulder Lamb Chops

Lamb shoulder is sliced into two different cuts, blade and round bone chops. You'll find them sold in a range of thicknesses (from about ½ inch to more than 1 inch thick), depending on who's doing the butchering. (In our experience, supermarkets tend to cut them thinner, while independent butchers cut them thicker.) Blade chops are roughly rectangular in shape, and some are thickly striated with fat. Each blade chop includes a piece of the chine bone (the backbone of the animal) and a thin piece of the blade bone (the shoulder blade of the animal).

Round bone chops, also called arm chops, are more oval in shape and as a rule are substantially leaner than blade chops. Each contains a round cross-section of the arm bone so that the chop looks a bit like a mini ham steak. In addition to the arm bone, there's also a tiny line of riblets on the side of each chop.

As to which chop is better, we didn't find any difference in taste or texture between the two types except that the blade chops generally have more fat. We grill both blade and round bone chops. We like the way the fat in the blade chop melts on the grill, flavoring and moistening the meat, and we love the grilled riblets from the round bone chop. For braising, though, we always prefer round bone chops because they add less fat to the sauce. That said, blade chops vary quite a bit in fat content; those with little intramuscular fat will work fine if well trimmed. See page 84 for illustrations of these two chops.

Braised Shoulder Lamb Chops with Tomatoes and Red Wine
SERVES 4

Because they are generally leaner, round bone chops, also called arm chops, are preferable for this braise. If available, however, lean blade chops also braise nicely. See box at left for more information on different shoulder chops.

4   shoulder lamb chops, about ¾ inch thick, trimmed of excess fat
     Salt and ground black pepper
2   tablespoons olive oil
1   small onion, chopped fine
2   small garlic cloves, minced or pressed through a garlic press (about 1 ½ teaspoons)
⅓   cup dry red wine
1   cup canned diced tomatoes with juice
2   tablespoons minced fresh parsley leaves

1. Sprinkle the chops with salt and pepper to taste. Heat 1 tablespoon of the oil in a heavy-bottomed nonreactive 12-inch skillet over medium-high heat. Cooking in batches if necessary to avoid overcrowding, add the chops and sauté until brown on both sides, 4 to 5 minutes. Remove the chops from the pan to a plate and set aside.

2. Pour off the fat in the pan. Return the pan to medium heat and add the remaining tablespoon oil. Add the onion and cook until softened, about 4 minutes. Add the garlic and cook until fragrant, about 1 minute. Add the wine and simmer until reduced by half, scraping the browned bits from the pan bottom with a wooden spoon, 2 to 3 minutes. Stir in the tomatoes, then return the chops to the pan. Reduce the heat to low, cover, and simmer until the chops are cooked through but tender, 15 to 20 minutes.

3. Transfer 1 chop to each of 4 plates. Stir the parsley into the braising liquid in the skillet and simmer until the sauce thickens, 2 to 3 minutes. Adjust the seasonings with salt and pepper, spoon the sauce over the chops, and serve immediately.

➤ VARIATIONS

Braised Shoulder Lamb Chops with Tomatoes, Rosemary, and Olives

Follow the recipe for Braised Shoulder Lamb Chops with Tomatoes and Red Wine, adding 1 tablespoon minced fresh rosemary leaves with the garlic and stirring in ⅓ cup pitted and sliced Kalamata olives with the tomatoes in step 2.

Braised Shoulder Lamb Chops with Red Peppers, Capers, and Balsamic Vinegar

Follow the recipe for Braised Shoulder Lamb Chops with Tomatoes and Red Wine, adding 1 medium red bell pepper, stemmed, seeded, and diced, with the onion in step 2 and stirring in 2 tablespoons drained capers and 2 tablespoons balsamic vinegar with the parsley in step 3.

Braised Shoulder Lamb Chops with Figs and North African Spices

Serve this with couscous.

⅓	cup stemmed dried figs
4	shoulder lamb chops, about ¾ inch thick, trimmed of excess fat
	Salt and ground black pepper
2	tablespoons olive oil
1	small onion, chopped fine
2	small garlic cloves, minced or pressed through a garlic press (about 1 ½ teaspoons)
1	teaspoon ground coriander
½	teaspoon ground cumin
½	teaspoon ground cinnamon
⅛	teaspoon cayenne pepper
1	cup canned diced tomatoes with juice
2	tablespoons honey
2	tablespoons minced fresh parsley leaves

1. Place the figs and ⅓ cup warm water in a bowl and soak for 30 minutes. Drain, reserving the water. Cut the figs into quarters and reserve.

2. Sprinkle the chops with salt and pepper to taste. Heat 1 tablespoon of the oil in a heavy-bottomed nonreactive 12-inch skillet over medium-high heat. Cooking in batches if necessary to avoid overcrowding, add the chops and cook until brown on both sides, 4 to 5 minutes. Remove the chops from the pan to a plate and set aside.

3. Pour off the fat in the pan. Return the pan to medium heat and add the remaining tablespoon oil. Add the onion and cook until softened, about 4 minutes. Add the garlic and spices and cook until fragrant, about 1 minute. Add the reserved soaking liquid from the figs and simmer until reduced by half, scraping the browned bits from the pan bottom with a wooden spoon, 2 to 3 minutes. Stir in the tomatoes and honey, then return the chops to the pan. Reduce the heat to low, cover, and simmer until the chops are cooked through but tender, 15 to 20 minutes.

4. Transfer 1 chop to each of 4 plates. Stir the parsley into the braising liquid in the skillet and simmer until the sauce thickens, 2 to 3 minutes. Adjust the seasonings with salt and pepper, spoon the sauce over the chops, and serve immediately.

PARMESAN-BREADED LAMB CHOPS

THIS EMBLEMATIC ITALIAN DISH IS SAVORED throughout Italy and can be easily, elegantly, and authentically reproduced at home. The idea and the execution are quite simple. Take the finest lamb chops, coat them with Parmesan cheese and bread crumbs, and sauté the breaded chops until the coating turns golden brown and crisp. At $14 to $16 per pound for lamb, there is almost no main course so costly to prepare. After making it numerous times, our conclusion is that it is more than worth the price. But if you don't follow some basic rules, you can make costly mistakes along the way.

There was no question that a dish of this delicacy needed the youngest and smallest loin or rib chops we could find; such chops are more widely available at butchers and natural foods markets than at grocery stores. While many of the recipes we saw in Italian books called for flattening the lamb chops, we discovered that it was not necessary with the single-rib chops less than 1 inch thick. However, it is essential to buy chops of the same thickness so that they will cook consistently. When we bought chops of different sizes, we ended up with some perfectly cooked chops and some that were either overcooked or undercooked.

For this recipe, the lamb chops are prepared in the classic breading style (first dredged in flour, then dipped in eggs and then in bread crumbs—except here, true to the tradition of the recipe, we dusted them with finely grated Parmesan cheese instead of flour. After almost grinding Parmesan cheese into butter in the food processor, we realized that it needed to be done by hand with either a microplane or a box grater in order to grate the cheese fine enough. We did try coating the chops with the coarser Parmesan and, although we liked it, all the tasters preferred the delicacy of more finely grated cheese. We determined that ½ cup of cheese was enough to coat lightly 12 chops. (Because these chops are so thin, tasters agreed that three chops, rather than the standard two, made a generous serving.)

After determining the right amount of cheese, our next task was to work on the bread crumbs. As we expected, dry bread crumbs did not do justice to the lamb. Fresh homemade crumbs are a must here. Toasting the crumbs first didn't work, as we were then essentially retoasting and therefore burning them when we cooked the chops—yet we found the fresh bread crumbs a tad bland. Adding more Parmesan cheese to the crumbs produced a burnt crust, whereas the addition of rosemary and mint,

classically paired with lamb, enhanced the dish and made it more striking.

Last, we found it essential to let the chops rest after being breaded. When we sautéed the chops right away parts of the coating peeled off, taking with them flavor and beauty. When we let the chops rest, refrigerated, for as little as 30 minutes and as much as four hours, the coating stayed on, producing a tastier and more attractive dish. The succulent and delicate chops had a crisp crust and a tender, slightly pink interior.

The actual cooking procedure turned out to be simple. The chops should be sautéed in enough oil to come halfway up their sides. A 12-inch skillet can accommodate six chops and requires four tablespoons of oil. For the best results, the oil should be very hot before the chops are added. Cooking time is just five minutes. As for serving the chops, we could find nothing to beat the classic choice—lemon wedges.

Parmesan-Breaded Lamb Chops
SERVES 4
Make sure the oil is good and hot before adding the chops. You want them to brown quickly because these thin chops will overcook if left in the pan too long.

- ½ cup finely grated Parmesan cheese
- 2 large eggs
- 1 tablespoon plus ½ cup extra-virgin olive oil
- 1½ cups fresh bread crumbs (page 125)
- 1 teaspoon finely chopped fresh rosemary leaves
- 2 teaspoons finely chopped fresh mint leaves
- 12 loin or rib lamb chops, ¾ to 1 inch thick, trimmed of excess fat and patted dry with paper towels
- ½ teaspoon salt
- ¼ teaspoon ground black pepper
- 1 lemon, cut into wedges, for serving

1. Place the cheese in a shallow dish or pie plate. Beat the eggs and the 1 tablespoon oil in a second shallow dish. Combine the bread crumbs, rosemary, and mint in a third shallow dish. Sprinkle the chops with the salt and pepper.

2. Working with one chop at a time, dredge the chops in the cheese, patting them to make the cheese adhere. Using tongs, dip both sides of the chops in the eggs, taking care to coat thoroughly and allowing the excess to drip back into the dish to ensure a very thin coating. Dip both sides of the chops in the bread crumb mixture, pressing the crumbs with your fingers to form an even, cohesive coat. Place the breaded chops in a single layer on a wire rack set over a baking sheet and refrigerate for at least 30 minutes or up to 4 hours.

3. Adjust an oven rack to the lower-middle position, set a large heatproof platter on the rack, and heat the oven to 200 degrees.

4. Heat ¼ cup of the oil in a nonstick 12-inch skillet over medium-high heat until it is shimmering but not quite smoking. Add half the chops (the oil should go halfway up the sides) and cook, turning once, until well browned on both sides and medium-rare in the center (the internal temperature should register 125 degrees on an instant-read thermometer), about 5 minutes. Line the heated platter with paper towels, transfer the chops to the platter, and keep them warm in the oven.

5. Discard the used oil. Wipe the skillet clean using tongs and a large wad of paper towels. Repeat step 4, using the remaining ¼ cup oil and the now-clean skillet to cook the remaining chops. Blot the second batch of chops with paper towels. Remove the platter from the oven, remove the paper towels, add the just-cooked chops, and serve immediately with the lemon wedges.

Pan-Seared Veal Chops

TOSSING PRICEY VEAL CHOPS INTO A SMOKing hot pan takes a bit of courage on the part of the cook. Without precise timing and a properly heated pan, a lot can go wrong in a hurry. But a perfectly pan-seared veal chop, with a thick, brown crust yielding to a juicy, creamy interior, is well worth the careful stove-side attention it requires.

Choosing the right chops at the store is easily as important as the proper cooking technique. When it comes to choosing veal chops, we have found rib chops to possess the fullest flavor and juiciest, most tender meat. Loin chops, which look like little T-bone steaks, tasted good but were difficult to cook evenly in the pan. The meat close to the center bone stayed rare while the edges overcooked, and the tenderloin section cooked at a different rate than the rest of the chop. Some variation in doneness is fine, even desirable, in a T-bone steak, but veal's delicate texture is not as forgiving. Served rare or even medium-rare, we find veal to be soft and unappealing, with a mushy texture like raw chicken. We prefer to eat veal that is cooked medium, cooked through but still very juicy and with a faint trace of pink at the center.

The importance of even cooking places limits on the thickness of the chop. A high-end butcher sold us huge 2-inch-thick chops, which weighed in at close to a pound each. Supermarket chops, on the other hand, are often half as thick and weigh as little as eight ounces. The larger chops simply didn't work in the pan—even after 20 minutes of cooking, there was a very clear line of undercooked meat at the center, while the rest of the chop was well done and dry. This test emphasized just how quickly lean veal crosses the line between undercooked and overcooked, especially without the even, ambient heat of an oven. At the other end of the spectrum, chops that were thinner than 1 inch overcooked before we could get a dark, even crust. We settled on a weight range of eight to 12 ounces, and an ideal thickness of 1 to 1½ inches. Chops in this size range could be nicely seared and then cooked to the proper doneness by adjusting the cooking time in the pan.

We knew the secrets to successful pan-searing were simple: the skillet must be smoking hot and the cook patient. The best indication of a pan ready to sear meat is smoking vegetable oil. A thin slick of oil across the skillet bottom is all that's necessary; once smoke is wafting from the surface, the pan is ready. On most ranges, this takes about four minutes. If the chops are added too early, the meat will take too long to form a crust and is liable to overcook—something not worth risking with meat this expensive.

Once the chops are in the pan, patience comes into play again. It is crucial to not move the chops for at least 3 minutes; otherwise, the meat may stick to the pan and its surface will be marred. After about four or five minutes, we found, the perfect crust is formed and the chop is ready to be flipped. As the chops would have to cook for almost twice as long on the second side, we found it important to reduce the pan temperature to medium.

When were the chops done? We tried cooking chops to various temperatures and found that chops were done to perfection when cooked to an internal temperature of 130 degrees, then allowed to rest, tented with foil, for five minutes. Do not cook veal chops beyond this point, or they will be tough and dry.

Pan-Seared Veal Chops
SERVES 4

The best way to judge doneness is with an instant-read thermometer—the center of the chops should measure 130 degrees. If you don't own an instant-read thermometer, use the tip of a paring knife to nick into the center of a chop, then peek—the very center should contain a very thin strip of pink, translucent meat. Make sure to let the cooked chops rest, tented with foil, for 5 minutes before serving.

4   bone-in rib veal chops, 1 to 1 ½ inches thick (8 to 12 ounces each), trimmed of excess fat and patted dry with paper towels
    Salt and ground black pepper
2   teaspoons vegetable oil
1   lemon, cut into wedges, for serving

1. Season the chops liberally with salt and pepper. Heat the oil in a 12-inch skillet over medium-high heat until smoking. Lay the chops in the pan and cook without moving until well browned, 4 to 5 minutes. Using tongs, flip the chops. Reduce the heat to medium, and continue to cook until the chops reach an internal temperature of 130 degrees on an instant-read thermometer (the center of the chop should still have a very thin strip of pink, translucent meat), 8 to 12 minutes.

2. Transfer the chops to a large plate, tent with foil, and let rest for 5 minutes. Serve immediately with the lemon wedges.

➤ VARIATION
Pan-Seared Veal Chops with Wilted Spinach and Gremolata

Make gremolata, a classic Italian garnish of garlic, lemon zest, and parsley, before searing the chops. Then, while the chops rest, you can wilt spinach in the skillet used for the chops. You will need three bunches of flat-leaf spinach, each weighing about 10 ounces, washed, dried, and torn into pieces (about 4 quarts).

For the gremolata, combine 2 tablespoons extra-virgin olive oil, 1 teaspoon finely minced lemon zest, 1 medium garlic clove, minced (about 1 tablespoon), and 2 tablespoons minced fresh parsley leaves in a small bowl. Set aside. Follow the recipe for Pan-Seared Veal Chops. While the chops rest, add 1 tablespoon extra-virgin olive oil to the skillet used to cook the chops and set the pan over medium-high heat. By the handful, add 4 quarts washed, dried, and torn flat-leaf spinach leaves with salt to taste. Use tongs to stir and coat the spinach with the oil. Continue stirring with the tongs until the spinach is uniformly wilted, about 2 minutes. Sprinkle the spinach with 2 teaspoons lemon juice and adjust the seasonings with salt and pepper. Divide the spinach among 4 plates, top each with a chop, and top each chop with some of the gremolata. Serve immediately.

BREADED VEAL CHOPS
NOT MEANT FOR A WEEKNIGHT SUPPER, delicate and pricey veal chops are usually reserved for special occasions and good company. However, their mild flavor is often disappointing when they are merely sautéed or broiled, especially when they cost anywhere from $14 to $16 a pound. Breading the chops before quickly pan-frying them, as cooks do in Milan, adds flavor and texture as well as a protective coating that shields the delicate meat. Of course, this recipe is not without its pitfalls. The breading often turns soggy, falls off the meat, or, worse, tastes stale and old.

As we did for grilled chops, we found rib chops preferable to shoulder chops, which are tough and chewy, and loin chops, which have a bone in the middle and two smaller portions of meat on either side. Cooking chops of varying thickness, we found medium-thick chops (roughly 1 inch thick) fried up best. Thinner chops overcooked before the bread crumbs had a chance to brown, while thicker chops were simply too bulky and took too long to cook through. We unearthed several recipes that called for pounding the meat around the bone with a mallet; however, our tests found the step unnecessary.

When it came to breading, we far preferred the flavor of homemade bread crumbs to any we could buy. Compared to the light flavor of fresh bread processed into crumbs, the packaged commercial varieties tasted stale and of plastic. A thin coat of beaten egg (mixed with a bit of oil to help the excess slide off the meat) acted as a glue between the meat and crumbs, and a sheer film of flour applied to the meat just beforehand allowed the egg to cling. We tried to do without the initial flour coating, but the egg would not adhere to the meat without it, leading to a flimsy coating.

The highlight of these chops, besides the rare and delicate flavor of the veal, is the crisp, golden crust that results from the pan-frying. After cooking batches of these chops several times, we realized that the key to a good crust is using enough hot oil. It is crucial that the oil reach halfway up the chops as they cook, ensuring an evenly colored, crisp coating. When less oil is used, the chops turn out blotchy, with both charred and blond spots. A 12-inch skillet requires about ½ cup of oil to pan-fry 1-inch-thick chops. The large skillet can cook only two chops at a time, and we found it necessary to use fresh oil when frying the second batch. When we didn't change the oil, small crumbs fell off the chops in the first batch, burned, then stuck to the coating of the second batch, making them taste scorched. Last, we found that letting the breaded chops rest in the refrigerator for at least 30 minutes before they were cooked helped the coating adhere better.

Using enough heat is also important when frying breaded veal chops. When the oil was not hot enough, the crust turned greasy and took too long to brown, overcooking the meat. Cooking the chops so that the meat at the very center retained some of its rosy hue (medium to medium-rare) took only five to six minutes. To get the oil hot enough to brown the crumbs within this timeframe, we found it necessary to heat it in the pan over high heat for about two minutes before adding the chops.

To prevent the first batch of chops from getting soggy or cold while the second batch fried, we found it best to let them rest in a warm oven. Served with wedges of lemon, these crisp, delicate veal chops are an interesting and welcome change of pace that will leave you looking for special occasions on which to serve them.

Breaded Veal Chops
SERVES 4 TO 6
Good sliced sandwich bread works best for making the crumbs for this recipe. For uniformity in color and crumb texture, we found it necessary to remove the crust.

- ½ cup unbleached all-purpose flour
- 3 cups fresh bread crumbs (page 125)
- 2 large eggs
- 1 tablespoon plus 1 cup vegetable oil
- 4 bone-in rib veal chops, 1 inch thick (about 8 ounces each), trimmed of excess fat and patted dry with paper towels
  Salt and ground black pepper
- 1 lemon, cut into wedges, for serving

1. Spread the flour in a shallow dish or pie plate. Place the bread crumbs in a second dish. Beat the eggs with the 1 tablespoon oil in a third dish.

2. Sprinkle the chop liberally with salt and pepper to taste. Working with one chop at a time, dredge the chops thoroughly in the flour, shaking off the excess. Using tongs, dip both sides of the chops in the egg mixture, allowing the excess to drip back into the dish to ensure a very thin coating. Dip both sides of the chops in the bread crumbs, pressing the crumbs with your fingers to form an even, cohesive coat. Place the breaded chops in a single layer on a wire rack set over a baking sheet and refrigerate for at least 30 minutes or up to 4 hours.

3. Adjust an oven rack to the lower-middle position, set a large heatproof plate on the rack, and heat the oven to 200 degrees. Heat ½ cup of the

oil in a nonstick 12-inch skillet over medium-high heat until shimmering. Place 2 chops in the skillet and fry until crisp and deep golden brown on the first side, gently pressing down on them with a wide metal spatula to help ensure even browning and checking partway through, about 3 minutes. Using tongs, flip the chops and reduce the heat to medium. Continue to cook until the meat feels firm when pressed gently and the second side is deep golden brown and crisp, again checking partway through, 2 to 3 minutes longer. Line the warmed plate with a double layer of paper towels and set the chops on top; return the plate to the oven.

4. Discard the used oil and wipe the skillet clean using tongs and a large wad of paper towels. Repeat step 3, using the remaining ½ cup oil and the now-clean skillet and preheating the oil 2 minutes to cook the remaining 2 chops. Blot the second batch of chops with paper towels. Remove the plate from the oven, remove the paper towels, add the just-cooked chops, and serve immediately with the lemon wedges.

INGREDIENTS: Salt

The food press has exalted exotic sea salts. We wondered if a pinch here or a smidgen there is really worth as much as $36 a pound. Will your food taste better if you spend more money on salt?

To find out, we embarked on a two-month odyssey, testing nine brands of salt in five different kitchen applications. Each was dissolved in spring water, dissolved in chicken stock, dissolved in water used to cook pasta, baked in biscuits, and sprinkled onto pieces of roast beef tenderloin. For each test, we measured salt by weight rather than volume. The results were, to say the least, surprising.

Tasters loved the crunch of the large sea salt flakes or crystals when sprinkled over slices of roast tenderloin. Here, Maldon Sea Salt was the clear winner, followed by Fleur de Sel de Camargue and Light Grey Celtic Sea Salt.

Although tasters had a clear preference in the meat test, we found that all brands and types of salt taste pretty much the same. Why didn't the fancy sea salts beat the pants off plain table salt in these tests? The main reason is dilution. Yes, sea salts sampled right from the box (or sprinkled on meat at the table) did taste better than table salt. But dissolve that salt in a pot of stock or stew and you'll never be able to tell the difference.

One final (and very important) point. Our results should not be taken to mean that all salts behave in the same way in the kitchen. For example, salts with a fine texture may seem saltier than coarse salts because of the way the crystals pack down in a teaspoon when measured. For instance, a teaspoon of coarse Maldon Sea Salt contains just half as much salt as a teaspoon of fine table salt.

What, then, can we conclude from the results of these tests? For one, expensive sea salts are best saved for the table, where their delicate flavor and great crunch can be appreciated. Don't waste $36-a-pound sea salt when making stew. If you like to keep coarse salt in a ramekin next to the stove where you can pick up a pinch, choose a kosher salt, which costs just pennies per pound. If you measure salt by the teaspoon when cooking, you might as well use table salt, which is also the best choice for baking.

6
I WANT TO COOK CUTLETS

I Want to Cook Cutlets

TENDER CUTLETS OF EITHER PORK OR VEAL are a favorite weeknight meal because most recipes can be on the table in less than 30 minutes. Pork cutlets usually start with the tenderloin, a small, boneless, torpedo-shaped muscle nestled against the rib bones in the loin section, which is roughly equivalent to a position deep inside the midback on a human being. The cut is notable for its remarkable lack of marbling, those ribbons of intramuscular fat that run through meat, as well as its tenderness. To make cutlets, the tenderloin is sliced and pounded into ½-inch-thick rounds.

Veal cutlets are usually cut even thinner from the round. Although many markets sell cutlets, they are often poorly butchered. If your market sells misshapen, uneven, or overly small veal cutlets, take several minutes to cut your own cutlets from the round.

Given their size, it's no surprise that both pork and veal cutlets cook quickly. They are best sautéed in a film of oil or pan-fried. The latter cooking method is a must when cooking cutlets that have been coated with bread crumbs.

BREADED PORK CUTLETS

THERE'S SOMETHING FEW PEOPLE CAN RESIST about a properly fried pork cutlet. Spartanly adorned with a spritz of lemon juice or gussied up with fixings nestled in a sandwich, the juicy, tender meat is perfectly accented by the sweet, crisp crunch of the breading. A pork cutlet is all about technique—proper breading and frying are crucial to the best results. Luckily, good technique need not take long. We found perfect fried cutlets were entirely possible even when time is tight and are a worthy centerpiece for several different meals.

The natural place to commence testing was the pork itself. In the recipes we researched, boneless pork chops and tenderloin were the most common cuts and, after the first test, tasters overwhelmingly preferred the sweeter, moister tenderloin. The tenderloin cutlets we purchased, however,

were uneven and raggedly cut, broadly ranging in thickness; evidently, we would have to prepare our own cutlets. Making our own cutlets gave us complete control over portion size and thickness, something that would prove to be the secret to success. A 1- to 1¼-pound tenderloin yielded six portions, two cutlets per person for a typical entrée or one cutlet per sandwich.

The trick was finding a thickness at which the pork would cook through by the time the crumbs browned, which, as we found, was easier said than done. Pounded very thin, under a ¼ inch, the pork was tough and chewy by the time the coating cooked. When only lightly pounded to about an inch thick, the pork was blushing pink at the center when the coating was just shy of burnt. Aiming for a happy medium, we pounded the cutlets to a thickness of ½ inch and met with success. Both the coating and meat were cooked to near perfection—the meat was juicy and tender, and the crust crisp and golden.

While the cutlet thickness was tantamount to success, there were a few other minor points that helped. When breading the cutlets, we found that it was crucial to remove as much excess flour as possible prior to dipping the cutlet into the egg. For the crumbs, its important to make sure each cutlet is thoroughly coated, but not to pack it on, which can make for a dense exterior. We normally prefer freshly ground crumbs made from white sandwich bread, but for the sake of time in this case, we chose panko (Japanese-style bread crumbs). They are very crisp and a much better choice than other commercial bread crumbs. And the final step prior to frying was a quick rest to allow the breading to adhere firmly to the meat; otherwise, it is liable to slough off during frying.

For pan-frying, we prefer the clean flavor of vegetable oil. It also has a fairly high smoke point when compared with olive oil, so it's much safer for frying and there's little risk that the oil will turn acrid. Pan-frying takes much less oil than most people imagine. After frying three cutlets in varying depths of oil in a 12-inch skillet, we found that the oil needed to reach just halfway up the sides of the cutlets was ½ cup. So the recipe requires a total of just 1 cup of oil to fry all six cutlets.

Pan-Fried Breaded Pork Cutlets

SERVES 3

Look for panko where other Asian products are shelved at the supermarket. For an Asian touch, replace the lemon wedges with tonkatsu sauce, a ketchup-based sweet brown sauce that can be prepared in just minutes with pantry items (see the variation below). If you can't find panko, use fresh bread crumbs (page 125) rather than other commercial crumbs. See the illustrations on page 126 for tips on breading cutlets.

½   cup unbleached all-purpose flour
2   large eggs
1   tablespoon plus 1 cup vegetable oil
2   cups panko (Japanese-style bread crumbs)
1   pork tenderloin (1 to 1 ¼ pounds), trimmed of the silver skin, cut crosswise into 6 pieces, and pounded to a thickness of ½ inch (see the illustrations on page 117)
       Salt and ground black pepper
1   lemon, cut into wedges, for serving

1. Adjust an oven rack to the lower-middle position, set a large heatproof plate on the rack, and heat the oven to 200 degrees. Spread the flour in a wide shallow dish or pie plate. Beat the eggs with the 1 tablespoon oil in a second dish. Spread the panko in a third dish. Position the flour, egg, and bread crumbs in a row on the work surface.

2. Blot the cutlets dry with paper towels and sprinkle both sides thoroughly with salt and pepper to taste. Working one at a time, dredge the cutlets thoroughly in the flour, shaking off the excess. Using tongs, dip both sides of cutlets in the egg mixture, allowing the excess to drip back into the pie plate to ensure a thin coating. Dip both sides of the cutlets in the panko, pressing the crumbs with your fingers to form an even, cohesive coat. Place the breaded cutlets in a single layer on a wire rack set over a baking sheet and allow the coating to dry for 5 minutes.

3. Meanwhile, heat ½ cup of the oil in a heavy-bottomed nonstick 12-inch skillet over medium-high heat until shimmering but not smoking. Lay 3 cutlets in the skillet. Fry until deep golden brown and crisp on the first side, gently pressing down on the cutlets with a wide metal spatula to help ensure even browning and checking the browning partway through, about 2½ minutes (smaller cutlets from the tail end of the tenderloin may cook faster). Using tongs, flip the cutlets, reduce the heat to medium, and continue to cook until the meat feels firm when pressed gently and the second side is deep golden brown, again checking browning partway through, about 2½ minutes longer. Line the warmed plate with a double layer of paper towels and set the cutlets on top; return the plate to the oven. Discard the oil in the skillet and wipe the skillet clean using tongs and a large wad of paper towels.

4. Repeat step 3 using the remaining ½ cup oil and the now-clean skillet to cook the remaining cutlets. Serve immediately with the lemon wedges or tonkatsu sauce (see variation) or use the cutlets as directed in one of the recipes on the following pages.

➤ VARIATION

Breaded Pork Cutlets with Tonkatsu Sauce

While the breaded cutlets are resting, mix ½ teaspoon dry mustard powder with 1 teaspoon water in a small bowl until smooth. Stir in ½ cup ketchup, 2 tablespoons Worcestershire sauce, and 2 teaspoons soy sauce. Cut the fried cutlets into ¾-inch-wide strips and drizzle with the sauce.

BREADED PORK CUTLETS WITH PEPPER AND ONION SAUTÉ

WITH A HOT SKILLET LEFT FROM FRYING the cutlets, we knew it would be easy to make a quick sauce. The trick was to come up with a sauce that could be cooked in minutes, just long enough to let the cutlets rest in a warm oven and still retain their crisp crust. The sauce had to meet certain criteria, however. It needed to be fairly "dry" as to not impact the crust (the whole point of pan-frying the cutlets). Our thoughts gravitated toward a mixture of peppers and onions—something like pipérade from the Basque region of France. The peppers and onions were easy to prepare, and their sweetness would complement the pork. Most important, it did not make the cutlets soggy.

In essence, the "sauce" was nothing but a quick vegetable sauté. As a cooking medium, we turned to flavorful extra-virgin olive oil. We started the garlic first, so that it would lightly brown and develop a mild nutty flavor, ideally suiting pork's sweet flavor. In next went the onion and peppers to soften and brown. Red bell peppers were our tasters' favorite, though yellow or a combination of the two worked fine as well.

To flavor the vegetables, tasters were divided between the piney flavor and aroma of rosemary and the simple freshness of parsley. Both had their own charms, so we left both as an option. The rosemary was left whole on the sprig, so that it could be removed when the flavor was potent enough. From experience, we knew that rosemary could overpower a dish all too quickly.

We wanted the "sauce" to remain on the dry side, but it needed some liquid to release the flavorful bits that adhered to the surface of the skillet as the vegetables browned. Stock accomplished little, and water even less, but white wine added a pleasant acidity that sharpened the flavors. A scant half cup quickly reduced in the hot skillet, leaving just enough liquid to moisten the vegetables.

TURNING ONE TENDERLOIN INTO SIX CUTLETS

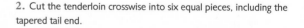
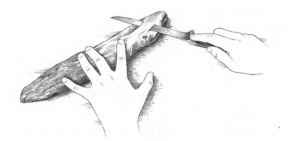

1. Slip a knife under the silver skin, angle it slightly upward, and use a gentle back-and-forth motion to remove the silver skin. Discard the skin.

2. Cut the tenderloin crosswise into six equal pieces, including the tapered tail end.

3. Lay one piece of tenderloin at a time cut-side down on a piece of plastic wrap or parchment paper, cover with a second piece, and pound gently with a mallet or meat pounder to an even thickness of 1/2 inch.

4. The thin tail piece of the tenderloin requires some finessing to produce a cutlet. Fold the tip of the tail under the cut side and pound between two sheets of plastic wrap or parchment paper.

Breaded Pork Cutlets with Pepper and Onion Sauté

SERVES 3

For a little heat in the dish, add a pinch of red pepper flakes with the garlic-the chile flavor will become intensified by the "toasting." A sprig of marjoram or oregano would be a suitable replacement for the rosemary.

1	recipe Pan-Fried Breaded Pork Cutlets (page 116)
2	tablespoons extra-virgin olive oil
3	medium garlic cloves, slivered
2	small red bell peppers, stemmed, seeded, and sliced thin
1	small onion, halved and sliced thin
1	small sprig rosemary, optional
	Salt
½	cup dry white wine
2	tablespoons chopped fresh parsley leaves
	Ground black pepper

1. Once the second batch of cutlets is finished, thoroughly wipe the skillet clean using tongs and a wad of paper towels. Add the olive oil and garlic to the skillet and heat over medium–high heat, sliding the pan back and forth over the burner to cook the garlic evenly. Cook until the garlic is just beginning to turn golden brown, 1 to 1½ minutes. Add the bell peppers, onion, and rosemary sprig (if using), and ¼ teaspoon salt. Cook, stirring frequently, until the onion and peppers have softened and begun to brown, about 7 minutes.

2. Remove the skillet from the heat and add the white wine, scraping the pan bottom with a wooden spoon to release any browned bits. Discard rosemary, if using, and stir in the parsley. Adjust the seasonings with salt and pepper to taste and serve alongside (or on top) of the pork cutlets.

MAKING PORK CUTLET SANDWICHES

BREADED PORK CUTLETS ARE OFTEN used in sandwiches. They take well to a range of garnishes, traditional and not. Try any combination of the following: lettuce, thin-sliced tomato or red onion (raw or pickled), coleslaw, mustard, barbecue sauce, tartar sauce, pickle relish, or prepared chutney. Mayonnaise is also traditional; if you feel adventurous, flavor it by mixing ½ cup mayonnaise with 1 minced anchovy fillet (about ½ teaspoon) or 1 small minced chipotle chile in adobo sauce (about 1 teaspoon). Or, for an Asian-inspired mayo, stir in 2 teaspoons soy sauce and ½ teaspoon each grated ginger and minced garlic. Soft white sandwich bread or hamburger buns are the breads of choice.

BREADED PORK CUTLETS, PO'BOY STYLE

NEW ORLEANS HAS A CERTAIN REPUTATION for satisfying the more carnal desires, be it jazz, booze, bordellos, or—most importantly from our standpoint—food. Cajun and Creole cooking represent some of this country's finest indigenous cooking, from humble street snacks to fine dining feasts. Even the lowly sandwich is given royal treatment. Po'boys, probably the most famous New Orleans sandwich (if not the most colorfully named), is simple at heart, but worthy of kings, despite its origins as a filling snack of the "poor." Po'boys (a contraction of "poor boys") come in all stripes, from grilled steak and fried oysters to a seemingly oddball combination of French fries and roasted pork.

A pork cutlet sandwich takes very little work beyond frying the cutlets. Essentially, the po'boy is little more than what in other regions may be called a hoagie, torpedo, grinder, or submarine: It's a Dagwood-size sandwich constructed on a long roll or baguette. We favor our po'boys "dressed," which, in local patois, means the sandwich comes laden with lettuce, tomato, mayonnaise, and pickles.

As to be expected, there was very little technique involved with making a po'boy—it's all about the ingredients. For bread, a very fresh, crusty baguette is essential. The crisp exterior serves to retain all the juices of the filling ingredients and provides textural contrast. The soft, chewy crumb acts as a blotter. Honoring tradition, we scooped out a portion of the crumb to make room for the filling—there is a lot of filling to pack in there.

First things first: A layer of mayonnaise is thickly slathered on the bread. Next comes the pickle so that the juices may mingle with the mayonnaise and lubricate the otherwise dry sandwich. With the pork cutlet, tasters preferred the sweet and sour bite of bread-and-butter pickles, though dill came in a close second. Pickle chips work fine, but the "planks" make assemblage even easier. On top of the pickle comes lettuce. Sweet, hearty romaine worked well, though green leaf lettuce was a close second. We preferred the lettuce sliced into ribbons.

To finish off the po'boy we needed only the cutlet itself and thin slices of ripe tomato. To fit a whole cutlet into the sandwich, we found it best to cut it into three pieces and squeeze them into place, laid diagonally across the width of the baguette. The tomato, wedged into place, added a mild sweetness and a bit more juice to lubricate the roll. With a stack of napkins and a bottle of cold beer, dinner (or lunch) was served.

Breaded Pork Cutlet Po'Boys

SERVES 6

See page 118 for other ideas on turning breaded pork cutlets into quick sandwiches.

2	baguettes, cut into 3 equal pieces each (crusty end pieces removed), each piece slit open horizontally
¾	cup mayonnaise
12	bread-and-butter pickle "planks," or 20 to 25 pickle slices
4	cups lightly packed thinly sliced romaine or green leaf lettuce leaves
1	recipe Pan-Fried Breaded Pork Cutlets (page 116), each cutlet sliced lengthwise into 3 pieces
2	medium tomatoes, cored and sliced thin
	Salt and hot pepper sauce

Using your fingers, evenly pull out a 1-inch-wide channel of interior crumb from the top and bottom of each piece of baguette. Spread 2 tablespoons mayonnaise over the inside of each piece of baguette. Into each bottom baguette piece, layer pickles, lettuce, a pork cutlet, and tomatoes. Adjust the seasonings with salt and hot pepper sauce to taste, top with a remaining piece of baguette, and serve immediately.

SAUTÉED PORK TENDERLOIN MEDALLIONS

THERE'S NO REASON WHY PORK TENDERLOIN cutlets have to be breaded and pan-fried. They can be cut a bit thicker, sautéed, and then finished with a pan sauce.

We started our testing by cutting the tenderloin into 1-inch-thick slices and pounded them down to ¾ inch with the flat side of a chef's knife blade (to increase the surface area for searing). We then sautéed the medallions in a bit of sizzling oil for about one minute per side. At the end, every single slice was seared beautifully on both sides, and the pan drippings were perfectly caramelized and ready to deglaze for a flavorful, simple sauce. The whole operation, from refrigerator to table, took only 15 minutes. Beneath the seared crust on each slice was juicy, succulent meat that met all our expectations for this extra-tender cut.

While testing and retesting our chosen method, we came up with a few pointers to help ensure successful sautéing. First, trim the pearlescent membrane, called the silver skin, from the tenderloin before cutting the medallions. If left on, the silver skin shrinks in the heat of the pan, pulling the meat up and out of the hot fat, thereby inhibiting browning. Second, do not overcook the meat. There should be just a tinge of pink when you peek into a piece with the tip of a paring knife. The meat will not be completely cooked at the end of the searing time, but that is fine because you later return it to the pan to reheat and meld with the sauce.

There is one drawback to sautéing. We found that sautéing four batches of medallions (the amount derived from two tenderloins) in the same pan caused the pan drippings to burn. We found it best to sauté just two batches of medallions (the amount that one tenderloin yields) and then make the pan sauce. For this reason, sautéing is ideal when cooking for three. You may cook medallions from two tenderloins in two sauté pans at the same time and then make pan sauces in each pan, but grilling or roasting is probably easier when trying to cook pork tenderloin for a crowd.

Sautéed Pork Tenderloin Medallions

SERVES 3 (3 OR 4 SLICES PER PERSON)

To promote even cooking, cut your slices to a uniform thickness. If it helps, lay a ruler in front of the loin and slice at the one-inch marks. If you've got one, cover the pan with a splatter screen to keep the fat from splattering. Serve with one of the pan sauce variations that follow.

I	teaspoon salt
1/2	teaspoon ground black pepper
I	pork tenderloin (about I pound), trimmed of the silver skin (see the illustrations on page 117), cut into I-inch slices, each pounded to 3/4 inch with flat side of chef's knife blade
2	tablespoons olive oil

Sprinkle the salt and pepper over both sides of the pork slices. Heat the oil in a large heavy-bottomed skillet until shimmering. Working in batches of no more than six slices to avoid overcrowding, sear the medallions without moving them until brown on one side, about 80 seconds (the oil should sizzle but not smoke). Turn the medallions with tongs to avoid scraping off the sear; sear until the meat is mostly opaque at the sides, firm to the touch, and well browned, about 80 seconds. Transfer the pork to a plate; continue with one of the pan sauce recipes that follow, using the drippings in the pan as the base for the sauce.

➤ VARIATIONS

Sautéed Pork Tenderloin Medallions with Port, Dried Cherries, and Rosemary

I	recipe Sautéed Pork Tenderloin Medallions (at left)
1/3	cup port
1/2	cup dried cherries
2/3	cup low-sodium chicken broth
2	teaspoons minced fresh rosemary leaves
	Salt and ground black pepper

1. Prepare the pork as directed and transfer it to a plate.

2. Set the now-empty skillet used to cook the pork over medium-high heat and add the port and cherries. Cook, scraping the pan bottom with a wooden spatula to loosen the browned bits, until the liquid reduces to about 2 tablespoons, 2 to 3 minutes. Increase the heat to high and add the broth, rosemary, and any accumulated pork juices from the plate. Cook until the liquid reaches the consistency of maple syrup, about 2 minutes. Add salt and pepper to taste.

3. Reduce the heat to medium and return the pork to the pan, turning the meat to coat. Simmer to heat the pork through, about 3 minutes. Adjust the seasonings with salt and pepper to taste. Transfer the pork to a serving plate and spoon the sauce over the meat. Serve immediately.

Sautéed Pork Tenderloin Medallions with Cream, Apples, and Sage

I	recipe Sautéed Pork Tenderloin Medallions (at left)
I	tablespoon unsalted butter
I	Granny Smith apple, peeled, cored, and cut into 12 slices
1/2	medium onion, sliced thin (about 1/2 cup)
1/3	cup apple cider
3	tablespoons applejack or brandy
1/2	cup low-sodium chicken broth
2	tablespoons minced fresh sage leaves
1/4	cup heavy cream
	Salt and ground black pepper

1. Prepare the pork as directed and transfer it to a plate.

2. Set the now-empty skillet used to cook the pork over medium-high heat and add the butter. Swirl the pan until the butter melts. Add the apple and onion and sauté until the apple starts to brown, about 4 minutes. Add the cider and applejack and simmer, scraping the pan bottom with a wooden spatula to loosen the browned bits, until the liquid reduces to a glaze, about 2½ minutes. Increase the heat to high and add the broth, sage, and any accumulated pork juices from the plate. Cook until the liquid reaches the consistency of maple syrup, about 3 minutes. Add the cream and cook until reduced by half, about 2 minutes.

3. Reduce the heat to medium and return the pork to the pan, turning the meat to coat. Simmer to heat the pork through and blend the flavors, about 3 minutes. Adjust the seasonings with salt and pepper to taste. Transfer the pork to a serving plate and spoon the sauce over the meat. Serve immediately.

Sautéed Pork Tenderloin Medallions with Red Wine Vinegar, Warm Spices, and Raisins

1	recipe Sautéed Pork Tenderloin Medallions (page 120)
½	teaspoon ground cinnamon
¼	teaspoon ground cloves
⅛	teaspoon cayenne pepper
2	teaspoons sugar
1	tablespoon olive oil
1	medium onion, sliced thin (about 1 cup)
¼	cup dry sherry
¼	cup red wine vinegar
½	cup low-sodium chicken broth
¼	cup raisins
	Salt

1. Prepare the pork as directed and transfer it to a plate.

2. Mix the cinnamon, cloves, cayenne, and sugar in a small bowl; set aside. Set the now-empty skillet used to cook the pork over medium-high heat, add the oil, and heat briefly. Add the onion and

sauté until softened and starting to color, about 2 minutes. Add the spice mixture, sherry, and vinegar and cook, scraping the pan bottom with a wooden spatula to loosen the browned bits, until the liquid reduces to a glaze, about 2½ minutes. Increase the heat to high and add the broth, raisins, and any accumulated pork juices from the plate. Cook until the liquid reaches the consistency of maple syrup, about 3 minutes.

3. Reduce the heat to medium and return the pork to the pan, turning the meat to coat. Simmer to heat the pork through and blend the flavors, about 3 minutes. Adjust the seasonings with salt and pepper to taste. Transfer the pork to a serving plate and spoon the sauce over the meat. Serve immediately.

Sautéed Pork Tenderloin Medallions with Orange, Fennel, and Green Olives

See the illustrations on page 163 for tips on preparing the fennel.

1	recipe Sautéed Pork Tenderloin Medallions (page 120)
1	tablespoon olive oil
½	medium fennel bulb, fronds and stems discarded, root end trimmed, cored, and sliced thin (about 1 cup)
2	medium garlic cloves, minced or pressed through a garlic press (about 2 teaspoons)
1	teaspoon grated zest and ⅓ cup juice from 1 large orange
⅔	cup low-sodium chicken broth
¼	cup pitted green olives, sliced
2	tablespoons chopped fresh parsley leaves Salt and ground black pepper

1. Prepare the pork as directed and transfer it to a plate.

2. Set the now-empty skillet used to cook the pork over medium-high heat, add the oil, and heat briefly. Add the fennel and sauté until softened and starting to color, about 2 minutes. Add the garlic and cook until fragrant, about 30 seconds. Add the orange juice and cook, scraping the pan bottom with a wooden spatula to loosen the browned bits, until the liquid reduces to a glaze, about 2½ minutes. Increase the heat to high and add the broth and

any accumulated pork juices from the plate. Cook until the liquid reaches the consistency of maple syrup, about 3 minutes.

3. Reduce the heat to medium and return the pork to the pan, turning the meat to coat. Add the orange zest, olives, and parsley and simmer to heat the pork through and blend the flavors, about 3 minutes. Adjust the seasonings with salt and pepper to taste. Transfer the pork to a serving plate and spoon the sauce over the meat. Serve immediately.

VEAL SCALOPPINE

THIS CLASSIC DISH IS FAST, EASY, AND tastes impressive when done right. Thin pieces of veal are quickly sautéed, leaving tasty drippings in the pan that are perfect for building an accompanying sauce. The problem, however, is that the cutlets are so thin that it is difficult for them to acquire a brown crust without overcooking. Also, we noted that many cutlets buckle and turn tough as they cook, while others remain flat and tender.

Beginning our testing at the meat counter, we found most packaged cutlets inaccurately butchered. Proper scaloppine should be cut from the top round, the upper portion of the leg, which is lean and has no muscle separation. The packaged cutlets we found were obviously cut from the shoulder and other parts of the animal, resulting in shaggy, fatty pieces that fell apart and cooked unevenly.

We also found that many of these cutlets were cut with the grain of the muscle instead of across it (see the illustrations at right). When cut with the grain of the muscle, the cutlet contracts and puckers as it cooks, turning tough. If cut across the grain of the muscle, the cutlet remains flat as it cooks and stays tender. Although most butchers were obliging when we asked them to slice cutlets for us in this manner, we also found the cutlets easy to cut ourselves from a veal top round roast (see the illustrations at right).

Before turning to the stove, we had one outstanding detail to test—pounding. Although both pounded and unpounded cutlets worked well,

BUYING VEAL CUTLETS

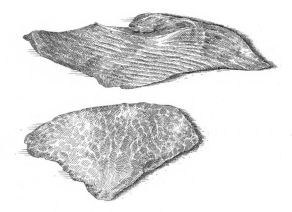

Veal cutlets should be cut from the top round. Most supermarkets use the leg or sirloin and do not butcher the meat properly, cutting it with the grain, not across the grain, as is best. When shopping, look for cutlets in which no linear striation is evident. The linear striation in the top cutlet is an indication that the veal has been cut with the grain and will be tough. Instead, the cutlet should have a smooth surface, like the cutlet on the bottom, in which no lines are evident. If your market doesn't offer cutlets that look this, consider cutting your own cutlets from a piece of top round, following the illustration below.

CUTTING VEAL CUTLETS

1. With a boning knife, remove the silver skin, the white membrane that covers the meat in places, from a piece of veal top round. Discard the skin.

2. Using a long, inflexible slicing knife, cut the round on the bias across the grain into cutlets between $1/4$ and $1/2$ inch thick.

tasters preferred the lightly pounded cutlets for their delicate texture and elegant thinness.

Next, we focused on how to achieve a crust on the cutlets without overcooking them. Using a hot pan, we were surprised to find that pounded cutlets cooked in merely two minutes—one minute on each side. When cooked any longer, the meat turned dry and stringy. In an effort to produce some sort of brown crust within that short cooking time, we tried flouring the cutlets. Compared to cutlets that were unfloured, the floured pieces browned in spots and had a crisp exterior that nicely contrasted with the soft interior. The flour also acted as a barrier that helped protect the delicate meat as it cooked. We tried using a nonstick pan but found the floured cutlets didn't brown as readily and produced almost no drippings with which to make a sauce.

We then put the cutlets in a warm oven to help them retain their heat while we made a quick pan sauce. We found, however, that the five minutes it took to make the sauce was too long for the thin cutlets to rest in the oven; they overcooked. To avoid this, we simply set them off to the side, covered, while we focused our attention on the sauce. Using only onions, lemon juice, parsley, butter, and either white wine or Marsala (both are traditional), we were able to make a simple, classic sauce, culminating in a wonderful—and authentic—veal scaloppine.

Veal Scaloppine

SERVES 4

White wine or Marsala can be used in this recipe. When made with white wine, the sauce is light and crisp. With Marsala, the sauce is dark and sweet. Refer to the illustration on page 122 for tips on buying veal cutlets, or see the illustrations on page 122 if you want to cut your own cutlets from a roast.

6	veal cutlets cut from the round, 1/2 inch thick (about 4 ounces each)
	Salt and ground black pepper
1/2	cup unbleached all-purpose flour
3	tablespoons extra-virgin olive oil
1/2	small onion, minced
1/2	cup dry white wine or Marsala
2	tablespoons unsalted butter, cut into 2 pieces
1	tablespoon juice from 1 lemon
1	tablespoon minced fresh parsley leaves

1. Place the cutlets between two sheets of parchment or wax paper and pound to a thickness of ¼ inch. Season both sides of the cutlets liberally with salt and pepper to taste. Measure the flour into a wide shallow dish or pie plate. Working with one at a time, dredge the cutlets in the flour and shake to remove the excess.

2. Heat 1 tablespoon of the oil in a heavy-bottomed 12-inch skillet over high heat until just smoking. Lay 3 cutlets in the pan, making sure they do not overlap. Reduce the heat to medium-high and cook, not moving, until browned, about 1 minute. Turn the cutlets with tongs and sauté until the meat feels firm when pressed, about 30 seconds. Remove the pan from the heat and transfer the cutlets to a clean plate and cover with foil. Add another tablespoon of oil to the pan, return the heat to medium-high, and allow the oil to heat for 5 to 10 seconds. Cook the remaining 3 cutlets in the same manner, transferring them to the foil-covered plate to keep warm while making the sauce.

3. Add the remaining 1 tablespoon oil to the now-empty skillet and return the pan to medium heat. Add the onion and cook, scraping the pan bottom with a wooden spoon to loosen the browned bits, until softened, about 1 minute. Add the wine and cook, scraping up the browned bits, until well reduced and syrupy, 3 to 4 minutes. Whisk in the butter, lemon juice, parsley, and any accumulated veal juices from the plate. Remove the pan from the heat and season the sauce with salt and pepper to taste. To serve, arrange the cutlets on either a large platter or individual plates and pour the sauce over them. Serve immediately.

> VARIATIONS
Veal Cutlets with Tomato and Caper Sauce

Follow the recipe for Veal Scaloppine through step 2. Heat the 1 remaining tablespoon oil in the empty skillet set over medium heat. Add 2 medium garlic cloves, minced, and cook until fragrant, about 15 seconds. Increase the heat to high; add ½ cup dry white wine, ½ cup canned diced tomatoes, drained, and 1 tablespoon drained capers and scrape the pan bottom with a wooden spoon to loosen the browned bits. Boil until well reduced, 3 to 4 minutes. Whisk in 2 tablespoons softened butter and 1 teaspoon chopped fresh oregano and adjust the seasonings with salt and pepper to taste. Pour the sauce over the cutlets and serve immediately.

Veal Cutlets with Olive, Anchovy, and Orange Sauce

Follow the recipe for Veal Scaloppine through step 2. Heat the 1 remaining tablespoon oil in the empty skillet set over medium heat. Add 2 minced anchovy fillets, 1 medium garlic clove, minced, and 1 teaspoon grated orange zest and cook until fragrant, about 15 seconds. Increase the heat to high; add ¼ cup dry vermouth and ¼ cup low-sodium chicken broth and scrape the pan bottom with a wooden spoon to loosen the browned bits. Boil until well reduced, 3 to 4 minutes. Whisk in 2 tablespoons softened butter, ¼ cup pitted and halved oil-cured black olives, and 2 teaspoons chopped fresh basil and adjust the seasonings with salt and pepper. Pour the sauce over the cutlets and serve immediately.

VEAL SALTIMBOCCA

SALTIMBOCCA IS ROME'S SIMPLE VARIATION on veal scaloppine, the name literally meaning "jump in the mouth." Thin slices of prosciutto and sage leaves are pressed into the cutlets, then quickly sautéed. The combination is so good that it is said the cutlets jump into your mouth.

Having already deduced what veal to buy for scaloppine and how to cook the cutlets properly, it was nothing to add on prosciutto and sage to our basic recipe. Although many of the recipes we researched for authenticity called for pounding the prosciutto and sage into the cutlets, this didn't work very well for us. The pounding tore the thin prosciutto and fragile sage to shaggy pieces. Instead, we used our hands to press the prosciutto into the

already pounded cutlets, topped it with a sage leaf, then secured the whole with a toothpick.

Just like scaloppine, these cutlets browned better when they were floured, and they cooked quickly—in less than two minutes. Finished with a simple white wine pan sauce, veal saltimbocca is both simple and elegant. It's also amazingly delicious.

Veal Saltimbocca

SERVES 4

See the illustration on page 122 for information on cutting your own cutlets, then see page 125 for how to attach the prosciutto and sage to the individual pieces of meat.

6	veal cutlets cut from the round, ¹/₂ inch thick (about 4 ounces each)
6	thin prosciutto slices (about 3 ounces)
6	large fresh sage leaves
	Salt and ground black pepper
¹/₂	cup unbleached all-purpose flour
3	tablespoons extra-virgin olive oil
¹/₂	small onion, minced
¹/₂	cup dry white wine
2	tablespoons unsalted butter, cut into 2 pieces
I	tablespoon lemon juice from I lemon
I	tablespoon minced fresh parsley leaves

1. Place the cutlets between two sheets of parchment or wax paper and pound to a thickness of ¼ inch. Place 1 slice of prosciutto on top of each cutlet and lay 1 sage leaf in the center of each cutlet, pressing them into the veal with the palm of your hand. Secure the prosciutto and sage with a toothpick. Season both sides of the cutlets liberally with salt and pepper to taste. Measure the flour into a wide shallow dish or pie plate. Working with one at a time, dredge each cutlet in flour and shake to remove the excess.

2. Heat 1 tablespoon of the oil in a heavy-bottomed 12-inch skillet over high heat until just smoking. Lay 3 cutlets, prosciutto-side down, in the pan, making sure they do not overlap. Reduce the heat to medium-high and cook, not moving, until browned, about 1 minute. Turn the cutlets with tongs and sauté until the meat feels firm when pressed, about 30 seconds. Remove the pan from the heat and

MAKING VEAL SALTIMBOCCA

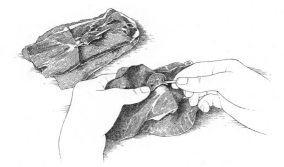

Using a wooden toothpick as if it were a stickpin, secure the prosciutto and sage leaf to the veal cutlet by poking the toothpick down through the three layers, then back out again. The toothpick should be parallel to the cutlet and as flat as possible.

transfer the cutlets to a clean plate and cover with foil. Add another tablespoon oil to the pan, return the heat to medium-high, and allow the oil to heat for 5 to 10 seconds. Cook the remaining 3 cutlets in the same manner, transferring them to the foil-covered plate to keep warm while making the sauce.

3. Add the remaining 1 tablespoon oil to the now-empty skillet and return the pan to medium heat. Add the onion and cook, scraping the pan bottom with a wooden spoon to loosen the browned bits, until softened, about 1 minute. Add the wine and cook, scraping up the browned bits, until well reduced and syrupy, 3 to 4 minutes. Whisk in the butter, lemon juice, parsley, and any accumulated veal juices from the plate. Remove the pan from the heat and season the sauce with salt and pepper to taste. To serve, arrange the cutlets, prosciutto-side up, on either a large platter or individual plates and pour the sauce over them. Serve immediately.

BREADED VEAL CUTLETS

VEAL CUTLETS PAN-FRIED WITH A CLOAK of mild-flavored crumbs have universal appeal. Almost every cuisine has such a dish. In Italy, grated Parmesan is added to the coating, and the dish is called veal Milanese. In Austria, the cutlets are often cooked in butter and the dish is called wiener schnitzel (see page 128 for details on this recipe). Though simple, this dish can fall prey to a host of problems. The veal itself may be rubbery and tasteless, and the coating (called a bound breading and arguably the best part of the dish) often ends up uneven, greasy, pale, or even burnt.

The ideal breading should taste mild and comforting but not dull and certainly not greasy. To explore the possibilities, we pan-fried cutlets coated with fine, fresh bread crumbs (made from fresh sliced white sandwich bread ground fine in the food processor) and dry bread crumbs. The dry bread crumbs had an unmistakably stale flavor. The fresh bread crumbs swept the test, with a mild, subtly sweet flavor and a light, crisp texture. We went on to test crumbs made from different kinds of white bread, including premium sliced sandwich bread, Italian, French, and country-style. Crumbs from the sliced bread were the sweetest and appealed most to our tasters. (That said, fresh crumbs made from all of these breads were good.) See the box below for more information on homemade bread crumbs.

During the crumb testing, we made several important observations about the breading process.

FRESH BREAD CRUMBS

WE LOVE THE CRISP TEXTURE OF panko, Japanese-style bread crumbs sold in Asian markets and some supermarkets, for coating cutlets. Panko crumbs far outperform the dry, stale-tasting bread crumbs widely available in supermarkets. However, there are times when you want the flavor and softness that only fresh bread crumbs provide. Although you can turn almost any plain white bread (baguette, rustic country-style, peasant) into crumbs, we prefer the sweetness of high-quality white sandwich bread. No, we don't mean squishy white bread, but something decent, such as Pepperidge Farm.

To make homemade bread crumbs, tear the bread into pieces and grind them in a food processor fitted with the metal blade until evenly textured, 20 to 30 seconds. Figure on three or four slices of bread (depending on thickness) to yield one cup fresh crumbs.

First, we learned that the cutlets had to be thoroughly dry. We also learned that we could not dispense with the coating of flour that went onto the cutlet before the egg wash and crumbs. If the cutlets were even slightly moist, or if we skipped the flour coat, the breading would peel off the finished cutlets in sheets. Dry cutlets also produced the thinnest possible coating of flour, which eliminated any floury taste when the cutlets were cooked and served. In addition, we found that it was essential to press the crumbs onto the cutlets to assure an even, thorough cover. Finally, we discovered that it was best to let the breaded cutlets rest for about five minutes before frying them, again to help bind the breading to the meat.

The bread crumbs adhere to the floured cutlets by virtue of a quick dip into two beaten eggs. But beaten eggs are thick and viscous, and they formed too heavy a layer on the meat, giving the breading a thick, indelicate quality. Thinning the egg with oil, water, or both is a common practice that allows excess egg to slide off the meat more easily, leaving a thinner, more delicate coat. We tried all three routines, and honestly, we couldn't detect much difference in the flavor or texture of the finished breading. In repeated tests, we did notice that the breading made with oil-thinned egg wash seemed to brown a little more deeply than that made with water-thinned wash, so we added a tablespoon of oil to our eggs.

BREADING CUTLETS

1. Dredge the cutlets thoroughly in flour, shaking off the excess.

2. Using tongs, dip both sides of the cutlets in the egg mixture, taking care to coat them thoroughly and allowing the excess to drip back into the dish to ensure a very thin coating. Tongs keep the breading from coating your fingers.

3. Dip both sides of the cutlets in the bread crumbs, pressing the crumbs with your fingers to form an even, cohesive coat.

4. Place the breaded cutlets in a single layer on a wire rack set over a baking sheet and allow the coating to dry for about 5 minutes. This drying time stabilizes the breading so that it can be sautéed without sticking to the pan or falling off.

Last, we explored the details of pan-frying. In any breaded preparation, the oil in the pan should reach one third to one half of the way up the food for thorough browning. Nothing could be simpler or more delicious.

Breaded Veal Cutlets

SERVES 4

Six cutlets is a realistic number to serve four people. (Allow one cutlet per person, then halve the remaining two cutlets after cooking to yield four smaller additional servings.) If you'd rather not prepare fresh bread crumbs, use panko, Japanese bread crumbs, which cook up extra-crisp. The veal is cooked in two batches because the crust is noticeably crisper if the pan is not overcrowded. To cut your own cutlets from a roast refer to the illustrations on page 122.

½	cup unbleached all-purpose flour
2	large eggs
1	tablespoon plus 1 cup vegetable oil
2	cups fresh bread crumbs (page 125)
6	veal cutlets cut from the round, ½ inch thick (about 4 ounces each)
	Salt and ground black pepper
1	lemon, cut into wedges

1. Adjust an oven rack to the lower-middle position, set a large heatproof plate on the rack, and heat the oven to 200 degrees. Spread the flour in a wide shallow dish or a pie plate. Beat the eggs with the 1 tablespoon oil in a second dish. Spread the bread crumbs in a third dish. Position the flour, egg, and bread crumbs in a row on the work surface.

2. Place the cutlets between two sheets of parchment or wax paper and pound to a thickness of ¼ inch. Blot the cutlets dry with paper towels and season both sides of the cutlets with salt and pepper to taste.

3. Working with one at a time, dredge the cutlets thoroughly in the flour, shaking off the excess. Using tongs, dip both sides of the cutlets in the egg mixture, taking care to coat them thoroughly and allowing the excess to drip back into the pie plate to ensure a very thin coating. Dip both sides of the cutlets in the bread crumbs, lightly pressing the crumbs with your fingers to form an even, cohesive coat. Place the breaded cutlets in a single layer on a wire rack set over a baking sheet and allow the coating to dry for 5 minutes.

4. Meanwhile, heat ½ of the cup oil in a heavy-bottomed nonstick 12-inch skillet over medium-high heat until shimmering but not smoking. Lay 3 cutlets in the skillet. Fry until deep golden brown and crisp on the first side, gently pressing down on the cutlets with a wide metal spatula to help ensure even browning and checking browning partway through, about 2½ minutes. Using tongs, flip the cutlets, reduce the heat to medium, and continue to cook until the meat feels firm when pressed gently and the second side is deep golden brown, again checking the browning partway through, about 2½ minutes longer. Line the warmed plate with a double layer of paper towels and set the cutlets on top; return the plate to the oven. Discard the oil in the skillet and wipe the skillet clean using tongs and a large wad of paper towels.

5. Repeat step 4 using the remaining ½ cup oil and the now-clean skillet to cook the remaining cutlets. Serve immediately with the lemon wedges.

> VARIATION
Veal Milanese
Replace some of the bread crumbs with grated Parmesan cheese and you have veal Milanese.

Follow the recipe for Breaded Veal Cutlets, reducing the bread crumbs to 1½ cups and mixing ½ cup grated Parmesan cheese with the crumbs.

VEAL PARMESAN

VEAL PARMESAN (BREADED VEAL CUTLETS topped with cheese and tomato sauce—is beloved by many American families. Although the dish has its roots in Italy, the execution and the excess are purely American. The veal is usually covered with way too much cheese and sauce, and it is served with a full portion of spaghetti.

We wanted to remain true to the hearty nature of

this dish, but we also wanted to use some restraint. At the outset, we made several decisions. First, the veal would take center stage, and the pasta portion would be modest. (We figured on eight ounces of dried spaghetti for four servings, not the pound called for in many recipes.) Second, we would cover the veal with a modest amount of cheese and tomato sauce. You spend a lot of time breading and cooking the veal; why bury it under a mountain of molten cheese and sauce? We also wanted to avoid a problem common with this dish (soggy cutlets).

Based on our previous experience, we knew the best way to bread and cook a cutlet. However, we wondered if sautéing would be the right route here, as the cheese that coats the cooked cutlets would be melted under the broiler or in the oven. We figured it was worth trying to cook the veal under the broiler and save a step. Unfortunately, broiling resulted in inconsistently and unimpressively browned cutlets. In contrast, sautéing produced a beautiful, evenly golden-brown color and rich, satisfying flavor.

Some recipes, especially older ones, instruct the reader to top cooked cutlets with mozzarella cheese and bake them on a bed of tomato sauce, covered, until the cheese melts. As far as we are concerned, this step not only added several minutes to the preparation time, it also destroyed the crisp, delicious coating and turned the cutlets into soggy mush. We simply sprinkled the cooked cutlets with mozzarella and Parmesan (a scant 3 tablespoons mozzarella and 1 tablespoon Parmesan per cutlet was sufficient) and broiled them until the cheeses melted and turned spotty brown. They were now ready for tomato sauce and the accompanying pasta, or for layering into a hoagie roll.

As for the sauce, veal Parmesan requires a smooth, thick sauce that comes together in a flash. Crushed tomatoes were the obvious choice. We found that a little garlic and herbs enlivened their flavor and kept the recipe simple.

Veal Parmesan

SERVES 4

Serve the cutlets alongside half a pound of spaghetti for dinner, or tuck them inside hoagie rolls to make sandwiches. There will be plenty of extra sauce for the spaghetti.

SMOOTH TOMATO SAUCE

2	medium garlic cloves, minced or pressed through a garlic press (about 2 teaspoons)
¼	cup extra-virgin olive oil
1	(28-ounce) can crushed tomatoes
½	teaspoon dried basil
¼	teaspoon dried oregano
¼	teaspoon sugar
	Salt and ground black pepper

1	recipe Veal Milanese (page 127)
1	cup (4 ounces) shredded mozzarella cheese
6	tablespoons grated Parmesan cheese

1. FOR THE SAUCE: Heat the garlic and oil together in a large saucepan over medium-high heat until the garlic starts to sizzle. Stir in the tomatoes, basil, oregano, sugar, a pinch of salt, and two grinds of pepper and bring to a simmer. Continue to simmer until the sauce thickens a bit and the flavors meld, 10 to 12 minutes. Taste the sauce, adjusting the salt if necessary. Cover and keep warm.

2. Adjust the oven rack to the top position and heat the broiler. Transfer the cooked cutlets to a clean wire rack set over a clean baking sheet (or broiler pan top set over a broiler pan bottom). Top each cutlet with scant 3 tablespoons mozzarella and 1 tablespoon Parmesan cheese. Place the baking sheet under the broiler and broil until the cheeses melt and are spotty brown, about 3 minutes. Transfer the cutlets to individual plates (or into rolls for sandwiches) and spoon sauce over part of each cutlet. Serve immediately.

WIENER SCHNITZEL

IT HAS BEEN SAID THAT COOKING PROPER wiener schnitzel takes years of practice. Large, sweet tasting, veal cutlets (schnitzel) are pounded incredibly thin and then breaded using ultra-fine bread crumbs. Fried to a crisp, buttery, light golden, the coating magically wrinkles as it cooks to form a dramatic, rumpled appearance. Requiring far more attention than a simple breaded veal cutlet, we wondered if we could skip the requisite years of practice and uncover the secrets of authentic wiener schnitzel in the test kitchen.

Focusing first on the veal, we found some recipes that used special schnitzel cut from the loin, as opposed to being cut from the round, which is more common. Costing roughly $27 per pound at our local market, however, the loin cutlets were quickly omitted from our testing. Working with cutlets from the round, we found that flavor depends largely on freshness. Look for veal with a bright, rosy pink color, and stay away from any that looks dull or slightly gray.

Buying cutlets that are cut big enough, we discovered, can be a tricky business. Most butchers slice the cutlets as thinly as possible, usually weighing in around two ounces. But we wanted them to be twice as big and found it best to either cut them ourselves from a large piece of veal round, or special order them as "four-ounce veal cutlets" from a trusted butcher. Pounded to an even thickness between ⅛ and ¼ inch, the four-ounce cutlets become quite large, and it is customary to serve just one per person.

Moving onto the coating, we determined that the fresh bread crumbs we usually prefer for breading (made from processing fresh bread in the food processor) were not quite right. Their texture was too coarse and in order to be crisp they needed to be fried to a darker brown than what is appropriate for wiener schnitzel. Using dried bread crumbs made it easier to achieve a crisp texture and light golden color, however, premade dried bread crumbs tasted terrible compared to homemade. In order to make the crumbs very fine and absolutely uniform, we found it necessary to process fresh slices of sandwich bread into crumbs using the food processor and dry them out in the oven, before processing them again to a superfine consistency.

The standard method for adhering the crumbs to the cutlet includes three steps: first the veal is dredged in flour, then egg, and finally bread crumbs. A few of the recipes we researched skipped the flouring step or replaced it with an additional layer of bread crumbs. We determined that the standard method worked best. We also found it important that both the flour and egg layers be as thin as possible to prevent the coating from being too thick or lumpy. Dusting the extra flour off thoroughly and thinning the egg out with a little oil helped.

Next, we tested frying the cutlets in oil versus butter. Tasters liked the flavor of the butter but preferred the ultra-crisp texture of the schnitzel fried in oil. By using a combination of oil and a little butter we managed to find the best of both. Heating the oil/butter combination until really hot (375 degrees) proved key in preventing the crust from becoming soggy. At this high temperature, the schnitzels cook through in only 2½ to 3 minutes, crucial to us because the schnitzels are so large only two can be cooked at time, which means that they need to be cooked in batches.

Last, we fussed with various techniques to encourage the breading to wrinkle into its hallmark Shar Pei-like texture. Using enough oil and butter so that the schnitzels actually floated in the skillet proved key. Shaking the pan constantly as they cooked, a method recommended by some recipes, also proved worthwhile. Finding that these tricks did a nice job at wrinkling the first batch, we were disappointed when the second batch turned out completely flat (although they tasted fine). Using fresh oil and butter to cook the second batch was the only way around this dilemma and, thus, we found it necessary to keep the first batch warm in a low oven.

Requiring just a brief pat dry with paper towels to remove any excess oil before being served, these authentic wiener schnitzel take only about 30 minutes (as opposed to several years) to master, and taste best when served simply with wedges of lemon.

Wiener Schnitzel
SERVES 4

Using fresh oil and butter for cooking the second batch of schnitzel is only necessary if you desire the authentic, wrinkled texture on the finished cutlets. To ensure ample room for the schnitzels as they fry, it is necessary to use a 12-inch skillet. We prefer frying in a nonstick pan for easier clean up; however, a traditional skillet can be used. See the illustrations on page 126 for tips on breading the cutlets.

8 slices high-quality white bread, torn into large pieces

½ cup unbleached all-purpose flour

2 large eggs

1 tablespoon plus 1 ½ cups vegetable oil
Salt and ground black pepper

4 veal cutlets cut from the round, ½-inch-thick (about 4 ounces each)
Salt and ground black pepper

4 tablespoons unsalted butter

1 lemon, cut into wedges

1. Adjust an oven rack to the middle position and heat the oven to 300 degrees. Process the bread in a food processor to very fine crumbs, about 30 seconds. Transfer the crumbs to a rimmed baking sheet and bake, stirring them and shaking the pan occasionally, until dried but not browned, 15 to 20 minutes. Process the crumbs again in the food processor until evenly texture, 5 to 10 seconds. Spread the crumbs in a wide shallow dish or pie plate. Spread the flour in a second pie plate. Beat the eggs with the 1 tablespoon oil in a third pie plate.

2. Meanwhile, place the cutlets between two sheets of parchment or wax paper and pound to a thickness between ⅛ and ¼ inch. Season both sides of the cutlets with salt and pepper to taste.

3. Lower the oven temperature to 200 degrees. Set a heatproof plate on the middle rack. Working with one at a time, dredge the cutlets thoroughly in the flour, shaking off the excess. Using tongs, dip both sides of the cutlets in the egg mixture, taking care to coat them thoroughly and allowing the excess to drip back into the dish to ensure a very thin coating. Dip both sides of the cutlets in the bread crumbs, lightly pressing the crumbs with your fingers to form an even, cohesive coat. Place the breaded cutlets in a single layer on a wire rack set over a baking sheet and allow the coating to dry for 5 minutes.

4. Heat ¾ cup of the oil and 2 tablespoons of the butter in a 12-inch skillet over high heat until it measures 375 degrees on an instant-read thermometer (or the edge of a cutlet bubbles wildly when dipped into the oil), 2 to 4 minutes. Lay 2 cutlets, without overlapping them, in the skillet and cook, continuously shaking the pan gently, until wrinkled and a light golden brown on the first side, 1 to 1½ minutes. Using tongs, flip the cutlets and continue to cook, shaking the pan, until the second side is wrinkled and lightly golden, 1 to 1½ minutes. Line the warmed plate with paper towels and set the cutlets on top; flip the cutlets several times to blot up any excess oil. Return the plate to the warm oven. Discard the oil in the skillet and wipe the skillet clean using tongs and a wad of paper towels.

5. Repeat step 4 using the remaining ¾ cup oil, 2 tablespoons butter, and the now-clean skillet to cook the remaining cutlets. Serve immediately with the lemon wedges.

VITELLO TONNATO

THIS UNUSUAL, LIGHT SUMMER DISH OF thinly sliced veal "marinated" in a tuna and garlic mayonnaise may sound odd at first, but it makes sense when you picture eating it seaside in Italy with a chilled glass of white wine. Wanting to reproduce this warm-weather classic here in the United States, we set out to uncover its secrets in our test kitchen.

All of the authentic recipes we found called for the same cut of veal and cooked it similarly. Using a top round veal roast, these recipes poached the meat for hours in a watery broth, then pulled the pot off the heat, letting the roast cool until it could be sliced and layered with the sauce. Although this method sounded strange to us (and chancy), we gave it a whirl. While the tuna sauce tasted surprisingly good, the veal turned out as we expected—dry and bland, leaving much of its moisture and flavor behind in the broth.

Focusing our attention on the meat, we decided not to try other cuts of veal but rather to use the traditional top round roast and work on improving the poaching technique. First, we noted that most recipes threw only a handful of vegetables into the poaching liquid. Thinking that the liquid needed more flavor if the veal were to emerge from it tasting like anything, we added several carrots, ribs of celery, and onions along with garlic, bay leaves, parsley, and peppercorns. Although this made a huge difference in the flavor of the veal, its texture was still too dry and chewy.

Turning our attention to the cooking time, we wondered if we could correct the tough meat problem by cooking the veal less. We wondered if poaching the veal for several hours was necessary. Poaching two roasts side by side, we pulled one out of the liquid when it reached an internal temperature of 155 degrees (after about 55 minutes in the simmering water), and cooked the other for the standard two hours (it reached an internal temperature in excess of 200 degrees). After they were cooled and sliced, we found the veal cooked to 155 degrees was far more tender and juicy.

We weren't finished. All the old recipes let the veal cool in its poaching liquid, allowing the moisture to soak into the meat as it comes to room temperature. Wanting to try this technique but worried that the residual heat from the poaching liquid would raise the temperature of the veal above 155 degrees, we tried cooking the roast to 125 degrees before pulling the pot off the heat. This final trick worked like a charm, and the veal roast emerged from an hour in the cooling liquid with an internal temperature of 155 degrees. Not only did the veal have a full, round flavor, it was moist and tender, with only the slightest toothsome bite.

It was time to address the tuna sauce. Based on a mayonnaise-like emulsion, the sauce is made classically by blending a raw egg yolk slowly with olive oil (making an emulsion), then flavoring it with tuna, anchovies, capers, and lemon juice. Although this sounds strange, the resulting flavor is mild and elegant, and it pairs amazingly well with the poached veal. We tried making the sauce with extra-virgin olive oil but found its flavor was overly bitter and fruity, preferring instead the simple flavor of regular olive oil. As for the tuna, we vastly preferred the flavor of olive oil–packed tuna to any of the water-packed varieties, and good-quality tuna made all the difference.

As for the assembly method, we tried several techniques and wound up liking the easiest one best. After making a loose emulsion in the food processor with a whole egg and 1 cup of olive oil, we simply pulsed in the tuna and flavorings along with some water to adjust the consistency. Rather than making the sauce with just a yolk, as most recipes do, we found that it was easier to use a whole egg. The yolk slipped under the blades of the processor, making it difficult to process, while the whole egg blended in easily, with no discernible difference in either the texture or the flavor.

Last, we combined the thinly sliced veal and tuna sauce and let it sit until the flavor of the tuna and moisture of the olive oil permeated the veal. It took at least four hours for the veal to take on the flavor of the sauce, but the dish tasted much better when allowed to "marinate" overnight. Garnished with lemon wedges, capers, and minced parsley, this unusual dish is light, refreshing, and elegant. It requires only a glass of crisp, white wine and a warm, sunny day to be complete.

Vitello Tonnato
SERVES 4

Tying the roast makes it easier to carve uniform slices after it has cooled—ask your butcher to do this for you. Although the poaching liquid in this recipe is not used after the veal is cooked, it has great flavor and would make a delicious base for soups. If saving the broth, strain it after removing the veal, then refrigerate or freeze it until needed.

2	medium carrots, diced medium
2	medium celery ribs, diced medium
3	medium onions, diced medium
1	head garlic, smashed, with loose, papery skins removed
2	bay leaves
5	fresh parsley stems
5	black peppercorns
1	top round veal roast (about 1 1/2 pounds), tied Cold Tuna Sauce (recipe follows)
1	lemon
1	tablespoon capers, rinsed and patted dry
1	teaspoon minced fresh parsley leaves

1. Bring the carrots, celery, onions, garlic, bay leaves, parsley, peppercorns, and 5 quarts water to a boil in a large stockpot over high heat. Add the veal and bring to a gentle simmer. Reduce the heat

to low, cover, and cook until the internal temperature on an instant-read thermometer registers 125 degrees, 25 to 30 minutes. Remove the pot from the heat, place it on a sturdy cooling rack on the counter, uncover, and allow the veal to cool in its broth, about 1 hour.

2. When the meat has cooled, remove it from the cooking liquid and slice it as thinly as possible using either a sharp slicing or serrated knife. Reserve the cooking liquid for another use (see the note at the beginning of the recipe).

3. To assemble, spread a thin layer of the tuna sauce on a large serving platter. Lay slices of veal, side by side but not overlapping, on top of the sauce. Repeat with the remaining sauce and veal (the number of layers will depend on the size of the platter). When topping the final layer with sauce, leave ¼ inch of the outer edge of the meat unsauced. Cover with plastic wrap and refrigerate for at least 4 hours or overnight.

4. Just before serving, cut the lemon into quarters. Slice 2 quarters into very thin slices and arrange them around the edge of the platter. Sprinkle the capers and parsley over the top as a garnish and spritz with lemon juice to taste from the remaining 2 lemon quarters. Serve immediately.

Cold Tuna Sauce

MAKES A GENEROUS 2 CUPS

We prefer the mellow flavor of regular olive oil (as opposed to extra-virgin oil) in this recipe. To minimize (but not eliminate) the risk of salmonella, be sure to use a very fresh egg for this recipe.

1	large egg
	Salt and ground black pepper
1	cup olive oil
3	tablespoons lemon juice from 2 lemons
1	(6-ounce) can tuna packed in olive oil, drained
6	anchovy fillets
3	tablespoons capers, rinsed and patted dry
½	cup water

Place the egg, ¼ teaspoon salt, and a pinch of pepper in the workbowl of a food processor fitted with a metal blade. Process until the mixture turns light yellow, about 30 seconds. With the motor running, pour the oil in a thin steady, stream through the feed tube until fully incorporated, about 1 minute. Turn the machine off and add the lemon juice, tuna, anchovies, capers, and water. Pulse until the tuna is well broken up and the sauce is loose but well mixed, about ten 1-second pulses. Transfer the sauce to a bowl and season with salt and pepper to taste. The sauce can be refrigerated in an airtight container for up to 1 day.

7

I WANT TO STIR-FRY

I Want to Stir-Fry

ORDERING CHINESE TAKE-OUT IS LIKE playing Russian roulette. Once in a great while, those little white cartons deliver tasty morsels of stir-fried meat and vegetables in a lightly thickened, potent, and savory sauce, with the flavors of garlic and ginger clean and invigorating. Unfortunately, the reality is usually something quite different. The meat is tough, the vegetables are overcooked, and the sauce is thick and gloppy. The garlic and ginger taste scorched and the sauce is bland, greasy, or overly sweet.

We think the best stir-fries are made at home, where it's easier to pay attention to detail and the food can be served immediately. Over the years, the test kitchen has developed some foolproof guidelines that guarantee great stir-fries.

To stir-fry properly, you need plenty of intense heat. The pan must be hot enough to caramelize sugars, deepen flavors, and evaporate unnecessary juices. All this must happen in minutes. The problem for most American cooks is that the Chinese wok and American stovetop are a lousy match that generate moderate heat at best.

Woks are conical because in China they traditionally rest in cylindrical pits containing the fire. Food is cut into small pieces to shorten cooking time, thus conserving fuel. Only one vessel is required for many different cooking methods, including sautéing (stir-frying), steaming, boiling, and deep-frying.

Unfortunately, what is practical in China makes no sense in America. A wok was not designed for stovetop cooking, where heat comes only from the bottom. On an American stove, the bottom of the wok gets hot but the sides are only warm. A horizontal heat source requires a horizontal pan. Therefore, for stir-frying at home, we recommend a large skillet, 12 to 14 inches in diameter, with a nonstick coating. If you insist on using a wok for stir-frying, choose an electric model (see page 144 for more details) that will maintain heat better than a traditional wok used on a flat cooktop.

American stoves necessitate other adjustments. In Chinese cooking, intense flames lick the bottom and sides of a wok, heating the whole surface to extremely high temperatures. Conventional stoves simply don't generate enough British Thermal Units (BTUs) to heat any pan (whether a wok or flat skillet) sufficiently. American cooks must accommodate the lower horsepower on their stoves. Throw everything into the pan at one time and the ingredients will steam and stew, not stir-fry.

One solution is to boil the vegetables first so that they are merely heated through in the pan with the other stir-fry ingredients. We prefer to cut the vegetables quite small and add them to the pan in batches. By adding a small volume of food at a time, the heat in the pan does not dissipate. Slow-cooking vegetables such as carrots and onions go into the pan first, followed by quicker-cooking ones such as zucchini and bell peppers. Leafy greens and herbs go in last. Vegetables that require some moisture (such as broccoli) are stir-fried, then water is added to the pan and the pan is covered so that the vegetables can steam.

We found that vegetable cooking times will be affected by how they are prepared. For instance, sliced mushrooms will cook more quickly than whole mushrooms. In some cases, we found it necessary to remove cooked vegetables from the pan before adding the next batch. This is especially important if you are cooking a large volume of vegetables.

All meat must be cut into bite-size pieces. We find it best to freeze beef and pork for 20 or 30 minutes to making slicing easier. We marinate all meat, once sliced, in soy sauce (sometimes flavored with other ingredients). Just make sure to drain the meat before stir-frying. If you add the marinating liquid, the protein will stew rather than sear.

Many stir-fry recipes add the aromatics (garlic, ginger, and scallions) too early, causing them to burn. In our testing, we found it best to add the aromatics after cooking the vegetables. When the vegetables are done, we push them to the sides of the pan, add the aromatics (oiled earlier) to the center of the pan, and cook them until fragrant but not colored, about 20 seconds. To keep the aromatics from burning and becoming harsh-tasting, we stir them into the vegetables. Then the seared meat is added back to the pan followed by the sauce.

A stir-fry for four people needs only ¾ to 1 pound of meat to 1½ pounds of prepared vegetables. This ratio keeps the stir-fry from becoming too heavy and is also more authentic, since protein is a luxury used sparingly in China. The recipes in this chapter are designed to serve four as a main course. Serve the following recipes with plenty of rice or over boiled noodles, especially thin Chinese egg noodles (which resemble linguine) or thin cellophane noodles (which look like transparent angel hair pasta).

STIR-FRIED BEEF AND BROCCOLI

ORDER BEEF AND BROCCOLI IN MOST RES-taurants and you are served a pile of chewy, gray "beef" surrounded by a forest of giant, overcooked army-issue broccoli. Worst of all is the thick-as-pudding brown sauce (more suitable for meatloaf than stir-fry), which, aside from being flavored with burnt garlic, is otherwise tasteless.

We turned to several recipes in cookbooks for help. Although most produced that gloppy, tasteless mass of beef and broccoli that we were trying to avoid, a couple of recipes showed promise. In these recipes, we found that each component of the dish—the beef, the broccoli, and even the sauce—was distinct and cooked to the best of its ability. Grateful for this glimmer of hope, we grabbed a nonstick 12-inch skillet (our pan of choice when it comes to stir-frying because its flat surface perfectly matches the surface of the American stovetop) and started cooking.

Although flank steak—a chewy cut from the underbelly beneath the loin—is most often called for in this stir-fry, we also tested a few other boneless cuts. Tender and expensive filet mignon (from the tenderloin) was mushy and dull flavored in this application. Strip steak (from the loin) was good, but not as good as the flank. A blade steak (cut from the shoulder blade area of the chuck) was similar to the tenderloin—too soft and too mild-tasting. Flank steak clearly offered the biggest beefy taste. Slicing the steak thinly across the grain made it tender, but when we used a less than razor-sharp knife (like the knives found in most home kitchens), the steak tugged on the blade. We put the steak in the freezer for 20 minutes to stiffen it up enough to make slicing easier.

Having recently discovered that using soy sauce in a marinade aids in tenderizing meat (see steak tips on page 36), we tested one batch of nonmarinated flank steak against batches marinated in soy sauce for two hours, one hour, and ten minutes. The results were dramatic. Two hours was overkill; the steak became gummy and spongy. One hour was perfect. The steak was tender and full of great soy flavor. Just a few minutes of marinating, however, made a big difference, which is good news if you don't have the full hour to marinate the steak.

Cooking the broccoli evenly was the next test, and our first decision here was to get rid of those gargantuan pieces of broccoli we found in both the restaurant and recipe versions of this dish. Fork-friendly 1-inch pieces of broccoli floret seemed right, and by trimming the tough exterior from the broccoli stems and slicing them into thin ⅛-inch slices, we were able to cook the stems right along with the florets.

Most recipes cook the broccoli by either straightforward stir-frying or by steaming or blanching. While the former technique produced unevenly cooked broccoli, steaming or blanching made for tender broccoli every time. Unfortunately, this technique required an additional pan. In an effort to avoid this, we modified our use of the pan we'd already been using. After cooking the beef and removing it from the skillet, we stir-fried the broccoli for a few seconds, added water to the pan, and covered it tightly in hopes of steaming the broccoli. This greatly simplified the recipe and produced superior broccoli—steamed to perfect tenderness and a brilliant emerald hue.

As for other vegetables, tasters wanted to keep this dish true to its name, save for the addition of red bell pepper, which added sweetness and vivid color. After removing the broccoli, we tossed the peppers into the hot pan and cooked them briefly to retain their crispness.

Garlic was a must, but we had to figure out the best way to add it to the mix. Added to the marinade, the garlic scorched in the skillet as it cooked with the beef. Added with the broccoli, it tasted raw. In the end, we added minced garlic (along with some well-received ginger) to the skillet when the red peppers were nearly finished cooking.

Oyster sauce is the typical base for the sauce in this dish. Indeed, in some restaurants, it is referred to as "beef and broccoli in oyster sauce." We found no need to depart from the tradition of oyster sauce, as its deep, earthy notes provided the right flavor base and its thick consistency (think ketchup) added great body to the sauce. Soy sauce was next up for consideration, but we found it to be an unnecessary addition; there was already enough in both the oyster sauce and the beef marinade. Rice vinegar and sherry are common additions, but only the latter was approved for its warm flavor. Chicken broth also passed muster to balance the flavors. Just a little Asian sesame oil and light brown sugar and the sauce took a sweet and nutty turn for the better.

Finally satisfied with the sauce, we added it to the pan with the browned beef and steamed broccoli. We tossed the mixture, but the sauce pooled on the bottom of the skillet. Clearly the sauce wasn't thick enough, so we reluctantly returned to an often used but frequently troublesome ingredient: cornstarch. While many recipes (including some used in our early failed tests) called for a tablespoon or more of this thickener, we started more modestly. With a tentative hand, we stirred in the cornstarch until we had used only one teaspoon.

And now we had it: a sensuous sauce that barely clung to the deeply browned, tender beef and perfectly cooked jade-green broccoli. The kitchen was awash with the heady aroma of garlic, and we knew that we had brought in Chinatown, just as we'd hoped.

Stir-Fried Beef and Broccoli with Oyster Sauce

SERVES 4 WITH RICE

This basic recipe can be altered in countless ways by changing the vegetables and/or sauce. The variations offer two possibilities. See page 140 for more information about oyster sauce.

1	pound flank steak, sliced according to the illustrations on page 138
3	tablespoons soy sauce
1	tablespoon dry sherry
2	tablespoons low-sodium chicken broth
5	tablespoons oyster sauce
1	tablespoon light brown sugar
1	teaspoon Asian sesame oil
1	teaspoon cornstarch
6	medium garlic cloves, minced or pressed through a garlic press (about 2 tablespoons)
1	(1-inch) piece ginger, peeled and minced (about 1 tablespoon)
3	tablespoons peanut or vegetable oil
1 1/4	pounds broccoli, florets cut into bite-size pieces, stems trimmed, peeled, and cut into 1/8-inch-thick slices on the diagonal
1/3	cup water
1	small red bell pepper, stemmed, seeded, and diced
3	medium scallions, sliced 1/2 inch thick on the diagonal

1. Combine the beef and soy sauce in a medium bowl; cover with plastic wrap and refrigerate at least 10 minutes or up to 1 hour, stirring once. Meanwhile, whisk the sherry, chicken broth, oyster sauce, sugar, sesame oil, and cornstarch in a measuring cup. Combine the garlic, ginger, and 1½ teaspoons peanut oil in a small bowl.

2. Drain the beef and discard the liquid. Heat 1½ teaspoons of the peanut oil in a nonstick 12-inch skillet over high heat until smoking. Add half of the beef to the skillet and break up the clumps; cook without stirring, 1 minute, then stir and cook until the beef is browned about the edges, about 30 seconds. Transfer the beef to a medium bowl. Add 1½ teaspoons peanut oil to the skillet, heat until just smoking, and repeat with the remaining beef.

3. Add 1 tablespoon peanut oil to the now-empty skillet; heat until just smoking. Add the broccoli and cook 30 seconds; add the water, cover the pan, and lower the heat to medium. Steam the broccoli until tender-crisp, about 2 minutes; transfer to a paper towel-lined plate.

4. Add the remaining 1½ teaspoons peanut oil to the skillet; increase the heat to high and heat until just smoking. Add the bell pepper and cook, stirring frequently, until spotty brown, about 1½ minutes.

5. Clear the center of the skillet; add the garlic and ginger to the clearing and cook, mashing the

mixture with a spoon, until fragrant, about 15 to 20 seconds, then stir the mixture into the peppers. Return the beef and broccoli to the skillet and toss to combine. Whisk the sauce to recombine, then add to the skillet; cook, stirring constantly, until the sauce is thickened and evenly distributed, about 30 seconds. Transfer to a serving platter, sprinkle with the scallions, and serve.

➤ VARIATIONS

Stir-Fried Beef and Eggplant with Oyster Sauce

If you like, add 1 teaspoon minced fresh chile with the garlic and ginger.

Follow the recipe for Stir-Fried Beef and Broccoli with Oyster Sauce through step 2. Omit the broccoli. Add 1 tablespoon peanut oil to the now-empty skillet and heat until just smoking. Add 1 pound eggplant, cut into ¾-inch cubes, and cook, stirring every 30 seconds, until browned and no longer spongy, about 5 minutes; transfer to the bowl with the beef. Proceed with the recipe as

SLICING FLANK STEAK FOR STIR-FRIES

1. To make slicing flank steak easier, freeze the meat until firm, 20 to 30 minutes. Slice the meat lengthwise (with the grain) into 2-inch-wide strips.

2. Slice each 2-inch strip thinly on the bias across the grain.

directed from step 4, returning the eggplant to the skillet with the beef.

Stir-Fried Beef and Snow Peas with Ginger Sauce

This classic stir-fry has a clean, bright ginger flavor. Snow peas require so little cooking that one pound may be cooked in a single batch.

1	pound flank steak, sliced according to the illustrations below
6	tablespoons soy sauce
1	tablespoon dry sherry
3	tablespoons low-sodium chicken broth
1	teaspoon Asian sesame oil
½	teaspoon sugar
1	teaspoon cornstarch
6	medium garlic cloves, minced or pressed through a garlic press (about 2 tablespoons)
1	(3-inch) piece ginger, peeled and minced (about 3 tablespoons)
2	tablespoons plus 1 ½ teaspoons peanut or vegetable oil
1	pound snow peas, strings removed
1	(8-ounce) can sliced bamboo shoots in water, drained
3	medium scallions, sliced ½ inch thick on the diagonal

1. Combine the beef and 3 tablespoons of the soy sauce in a medium bowl; cover with plastic wrap and refrigerate at least 10 minutes or up to 1 hour, stirring once. Meanwhile, whisk the remaining 3 tablespoons soy sauce, sherry, chicken broth, sesame oil, sugar, and cornstarch in a measuring cup. Combine the garlic, ginger, and the 1½ teaspoons peanut oil in a small bowl.

2. Drain the beef and discard the liquid. Heat 1½ teaspoons of the peanut oil in a nonstick 12-inch skillet over high heat until smoking. Add half of the beef to the skillet and break up the clumps; cook without stirring, 1 minute, then stir and cook until the beef is browned about the edges, about 30 seconds. Transfer the beef to a medium bowl. Add 1½ teaspoons peanut oil to the skillet, heat until just smoking, and repeat with the remaining beef.

3. Add the remaining 1 tablespoon peanut oil to

Stir-Frying 101

There are six key steps you should follow to turn out a perfect stir-fry. Use a minimum of oil, preferably peanut oil, in each of the steps called for below—no more than one tablespoon and less when possible.

1. Preparing the ingredients in advance is key. While the meat is marinating, whisk the sauce ingredients together in a measuring cup and add a small amount of oil to the garlic and ginger.

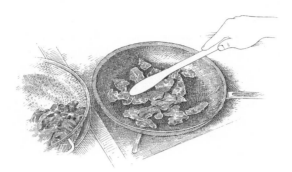

2. Heat the oil in a nonstick 12-inch skillet until smoking. Drain the meat and add half to the pan. Cook until well browned. Remove to a large bowl and repeat with more oil and the remaining meat.

3. Stir-fry long-cooking vegetables—such as broccoli, asparagus, or green beans—in oil in the empty pan; add a little water, cover, and then steam. Once the vegetables are crisp-tender, transfer them to a bowl.

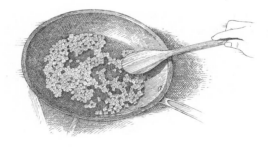

4. Stir-fry short-cooking vegetables—such as peppers, snow peas, or onions—for a minute or two in oil in the empty pan.

5. When the vegetables are slightly browned, push them to the sides of the pan, and add the garlic and ginger to the center of the pan. Cook until fragrant (15 to 20 seconds), then stir the aromatics into the vegetables.

6. Return the meat and long-cooking vegetables to the skillet. Whisk the sauce to recombine, pour it into the skillet and toss with the meat and vegetables. When all of the ingredients are heated through (30 to 60 seconds), serve immediately.

Oyster sauce, called oyster-flavored sauce in actuality, is a rich, concentrated mixture of oyster extracts, soy sauce, brine, and assorted seasonings. This brown sauce is thick, salty, and strong-tasting. Most often, it is used sparingly, to enhance the flavor of a variety of different dishes, including those—like some of the stir-fries in this chapter—without seafood.

A trip to our local grocery store and Asian market turned up five different brands of bottled oyster sauce. Lee Kum Kee dominated the shelves with three varieties: Choy Sun, Panda Brand, and Premium Brand. Coin Tree and Sa Cheng rounded out the list. Although oyster sauce is too strong to be used as a condiment, we thought it important to take note of the raw, unadulterated flavor of each bottle before using it in a recipe. Each brand of the potent sauce received the same standard comments: "salty," "biting," and "fishy." However, when we mixed the bottled oyster sauces with other ingredients—sherry, soy sauce, sesame oil, sugar, and freshly ground black pepper—and then made simple stir-fries, our tasters were able to detect a wider range of flavors.

The most authentic of the group was undoubtedly Lee Kum Kee's Premium Brand Oyster Flavored Sauce with Dried Scallop. Intense and somewhat fishy, it was the only sauce with true depth of flavor; its saltiness was balanced by sweet caramel undertones, and the oyster flavor was strong. However, this sauce is not for the faint of heart, as one taster proclaimed, "My American tastebuds can't take it." According to Jason Wong, president of AsiaFoods.com, Lee Kum Kee's Premium sauce is the favorite among the Asian-American population and the "only one" used in restaurants. It is also the most expensive sauce we tested ($5.79 for an 18-ounce bottle). All of this notwithstanding, the other favorite among tasters was Sa Cheng Oyster Flavored Sauce ($1.59 for a 15-ounce bottle), preferred because it was mild and "gravylike." The other three bottled sauces we tried didn't seem to add much to our stir-fries. As one taster put it, they "may just as well have been soy sauce."

the now-empty skillet; heat until just smoking. Add the snow peas and cook until crisp-tender, about 1 minute. Add the bamboo shoots and cook until sizzling, about 30 seconds.

4. Clear the center of the skillet; add the garlic and ginger to the clearing and cook, mashing the mixture with a spoon, until fragrant, about 15 to 20 seconds, then stir the mixture into the snow peas. Return the beef to the skillet and toss to combine. Whisk the sauce to recombine, then add to the skillet; cook, stirring constantly, until the sauce is thickened and evenly distributed, about 30 seconds. Transfer to a serving platter and sprinkle with the scallions. Serve immediately.

PORK STIR-FRIES

FROM A PORK AND VEGETABLE STIR-FRY—homemade or ordered out—we usually expect nothing more than tough, tasteless pork and barely cooked vegetables in a thick, slithery sauce. We set out to make pork and vegetable stir-fries that were both tasty and tender without being labor-intensive.

Pork shoulder is often called for in authentic pork stir-fry recipes, but because pieces weighing less than several pounds can be difficult to find and because most Western cooks would be loath to deal with the accompanying gristle and intramuscular fat, we excluded pork shoulder as a possibility. Instead, we tried stir-frying the more sensible options: boneless loin chops and tenderloin, both cut into strips thin enough to eat with a piece or two of vegetable. The pork loin cooked into dry, tight, tough pieces not unlike shoe leather. The tenderloin was the uncontested winner. Tender and yielding, it had the textural quality of a filet mignon.

The next task was to determine whether marinating the pork was worth the trouble. We tossed one plain batch of tenderloin strips unceremoniously into the skillet; we marinated a second batch with some soy sauce and sherry to a few minutes before cooking. The version with the marinade, which boosted flavor quickly and easily, was the clear winner. But it also dealt us a setback when the pork failed to brown properly, even in the hottest skillet. The reason? Pork tenderloin is almost always sold in shrink-wrapped packages and therefore contains a lot of moisture (and we were adding more). We discovered that the answer was to cook the pork in batches over high heat. This way, the moisture that the pork released evaporated rapidly, and, after it did, the pork was free to take on color. Each batch needed to cook for only two minutes—quite a flash in the pan.

With the pork out of the skillet and set aside in a

bowl, we worked on the vegetables and flavorings. Because different vegetables cook at different rates, batch cooking was necessary (batch cooking also prevents overcrowding, so that the vegetables, too, can brown their way to good flavor). We added various mixes of aromatics (such as garlic and ginger) using our standard stir-fry method (add at the end of cooking to a clearing in the center of the skillet, where they can cook long enough to develop their flavors but not long enough to burn).

We were not after an abundance of sauce, just enough light-bodied liquid to cling to the pork and vegetables and provide succulence. If we added enough soy sauce or fish sauce to provide the bulk of the sauce, saltiness or fishy pungency prevailed. If we added water, the flavor was hollow. Chicken broth was the solution. It provided a liquid element that gave the sauce backbone and did not dilute flavor. We also found that a small addition of acid—lime juice or rice vinegar—did a lot to brighten flavors. Finally, just a teaspoon of cornstarch prompted the sauce to cloak the meat and vegetables lightly instead of pooling at the bottom of the pan.

Stir-Fried Pork, Eggplant, and Onions with Garlic and Black Pepper

SERVES 4 WITH RICE

This Thai stir-fry is not for those with timid palates.

12	ounces pork tenderloin, sliced according to the illustrations above
1	teaspoon plus 2 ½ tablespoons fish sauce
1	teaspoon plus 2 ½ tablespoons soy sauce
2	tablespoons low-sodium chicken broth
2	teaspoons juice from 1 lime
2 ½	tablespoons light brown sugar
1	teaspoon cornstarch
9	medium garlic cloves, minced or pressed through a garlic press (about 3 tablespoons)
2	teaspoons ground black pepper
3 ½	tablespoons peanut or vegetable oil
1	pound eggplant, cut into ¾-inch cubes
1	large onion, cut into ¼- to ⅜-inch wedges
½	cup loosely packed fresh cilantro leaves, chopped very coarse

SLICING PORK TENDERLOIN FOR STIR-FRIES

1. Freeze the tenderloin until firm, 20 to 30 minutes. Cut the tenderloin crosswise into ⅓-inch-thick medallions.

2. Slice each medallion into ⅓-inch-wide strips.

1. Combine the pork, the 1 teaspoon fish sauce, and the 1 teaspoon soy sauce in a small bowl. Whisk the remaining 2½ tablespoons each fish sauce and soy sauce, chicken broth, lime juice, sugar, and cornstarch in a measuring cup. Combine the garlic, pepper, and 1 tablespoon of the peanut oil in a small bowl.

2. Heat 1½ teaspoons peanut oil in a nonstick 12-inch skillet over high heat until smoking; add half of the pork to the skillet and cook, stirring occasionally and breaking up the clumps, until well browned, about 2 minutes. Transfer the pork to a medium bowl. Repeat with an additional 1½ teaspoons peanut oil and the remaining pork.

3. Add 1 tablespoon peanut oil to the now-empty skillet; add the eggplant and cook, stirring every 30 seconds, until browned and no longer spongy, about 5 minutes; transfer to the bowl with the pork.

4. Add the remaining 1½ teaspoons peanut oil to the skillet; add the onion and cook, stirring occasionally, until beginning to brown and soften, about 2 minutes.

5. Clear the center of the skillet; add the garlic and pepper mixture to the clearing and cook, mashing the mixture with a spoon, until fragrant and beginning to brown, about 1½ minutes, then stir the mixture into the onion. Return the pork and eggplant to the skillet and toss to combine. Whisk the sauce to recombine, then add to the skillet; cook, stirring constantly, until the sauce is thickened and evenly distributed, about 30 seconds. Transfer to a serving platter and sprinkle with the cilantro. Serve immediately.

Stir-Fried Pork, Green Beans, and Red Bell Pepper with Gingery Oyster Sauce

SERVES 4 WITH RICE

See page 140 for more information on oyster sauce.

12	ounces pork tenderloin, sliced according to the illustrations on page 141
2	teaspoons soy sauce
2	teaspoons plus 1 tablespoon dry sherry
⅓	cup low-sodium chicken broth
2 ½	tablespoons oyster sauce
2	teaspoons Asian sesame oil
1	teaspoon rice vinegar
¼	teaspoon ground white pepper
1	teaspoon cornstarch
2	medium garlic cloves, minced or pressed through a garlic press (about 2 teaspoons)
1	(2-inch) piece ginger, peeled and grated (about 2 tablespoons)
3	tablespoons peanut or vegetable oil
12	ounces green beans, cut into 2-inch lengths on the diagonal
¼	cup water
1	large red bell pepper (about 8 ounces), stemmed, seeded, and cut into ¾-inch squares
3	medium scallions, sliced thin on the diagonal

1. Combine the pork, soy sauce, and 2 teaspoons sherry in a small bowl. Whisk the remaining 1 tablespoon sherry, chicken broth, oyster sauce, sesame oil, rice vinegar, white pepper, and

---

INGREDIENTS: Broccoli Relations

In addition to the standard supermarket variety of broccoli, which we all (well, almost all) know and love, we tested some other "broccoli" options in our beef and broccoli recipe and found that all worked well.

Chinese Broccoli

Chinese broccoli, sometimes referred to as Chinese kale, or gai lan, is the broccoli called for in many authentic Chinese recipes. With thick stems topped with leaves, it tastes of bell pepper that is mildly bitter. Trim off any yellowed or bruised leaves and the bottom inch of stem from one pound of Chinese broccoli, then cut it into 2-inch-long pieces. Chinese broccoli can be substituted for the broccoli called for in the recipe and should be cooked exactly the same way.

Broccoli rabe, also known as rapini, is actually a type of turnip green. Similar in appearance to Chinese broccoli, but with thinner stems, broccoli rabe has a much stronger flavor, which some people find very bitter. Cut off the bottom 2 inches of the stems from one pound of broccoli rabe, then cut the stems into 2-inch-long pieces. Cook according to the recipe instructions, increasing the steaming time to three minutes.

Broccoli Rabe

Baby broccoli, sold under the names Broccolini or Asperation, resembles a cross between broccoli and asparagus, but is, in fact, a cross between broccoli and Chinese broccoli. Very mild in flavor, the stalks are tender and do not need to be peeled, as do the stalks on regular broccoli. Remove any leaves from one pound of baby broccoli, then cut it into 2-inch-long pieces. Cook baby broccoli exactly as directed in the recipe.

Baby Broccoli

cornstarch in a measuring cup. Combine the garlic, ginger, and 1½ teaspoons of the peanut oil in a small bowl.

2. Heat 1½ teaspoons peanut oil in a nonstick 12-inch skillet over high heat until smoking; add half of the pork to the skillet and cook, stirring occasionally and breaking up the clumps, until well browned, about 2 minutes. Transfer the pork to a medium bowl. Repeat with an additional 1½ teaspoons peanut oil and the remaining pork.

3. Add 1 tablespoon peanut oil to the now-empty skillet; add the green beans and cook, stirring occasionally, until spotty brown, about 2 minutes. Add the water, cover the pan, and lower the heat to medium. Steam until the beans are tender-crisp, 2 to 3 minutes; transfer beans to the bowl with the pork.

4. Add the remaining 1½ teaspoons peanut oil to the skillet; add the bell pepper and cook, stirring frequently, until spotty brown, about 2 minutes.

5. Clear the center of the skillet; add the garlic and ginger mixture to the clearing; cook, mashing the mixture with a spoon, until fragrant, about 45 seconds, then stir the mixture into the peppers. Return the pork and green beans to the skillet and toss to combine. Whisk the sauce to recombine, then add to the skillet; cook, stirring constantly, until the sauce is thickened and evenly distributed, about 30 seconds. Transfer to a serving platter and sprinkle with the scallions. Serve immediately.

Spicy Stir-Fried Pork, Asparagus, and Onions with Lemon Grass

SERVES 4 AS WITH RICE

See the illustrations on page 318 for tips on mincing the lemon grass.

12	ounces pork tenderloin, sliced according to the illustrations on page 141
1	teaspoon plus 2 tablespoons fish sauce
1	teaspoon soy sauce
⅓	cup low-sodium chicken broth
2	teaspoons juice from 1 lime
1	tablespoon light brown sugar
1	teaspoon cornstarch
2	medium garlic cloves, minced or pressed through a garlic press (about 2 teaspoons)
¼	cup minced lemon grass from 2 stalks
¾	teaspoon red pepper flakes
3 ½	tablespoons peanut or vegetable oil
1	pound asparagus, cut into 2-inch pieces on the diagonal
¼	cup water
1	large onion, cut into ¼- to ⅜-inch wedges
¼	cup chopped fresh basil leaves

1. Combine the pork, the 1 teaspoon fish sauce, and soy sauce in a small bowl. Whisk the remaining 2 tablespoons fish sauce, chicken broth, lime juice, sugar, and cornstarch in a measuring cup. Combine

INGREDIENTS: Soy Sauce

Few condiments are as misunderstood as soy sauce, the pungent, fragrant, fermented flavoring that's a mainstay in Asian cooking. Its simple, straightforward composition—equal parts soybeans and a roasted grain, usually wheat, plus water and salt—belies the subtle, sophisticated contribution it makes as an all-purpose seasoning, flavor enhancer, tabletop condiment, and dipping sauce.

The three products consumers are likely to encounter when buying soy sauce are: regular soy sauce; light soy sauce (made with a higher percentage of water and hence lower in sodium); and tamari (made with fermented soybeans, water, and salt—no wheat). Tamari, which generally has a stronger flavor and thicker consistency than soy sauce, is traditionally used in Japanese cooking.

In a tasting of leading soy sauces, we found that products aged according to ancient customs were superior to synthetic sauces, such as La Choy's, which are made in a day and almost always contain hydrolyzed vegetable protein. Our favorite soy sauce, Eden Selected Shoyu Soy Sauce (shoyu is the Japanese word for soy sauce), is naturally brewed and aged for three years. Tasters also liked products made by San-J and Kikkoman.

THE BEST SOY SAUCE

Eden Selected Shoyu Soy Sauce was described by tasters as "toasty, caramel-y, and complex." The saltiness was tangible but not overwhelming. Among the 12 brands tested, it was the clear favorite.

the garlic, lemon grass, red pepper flakes, and 1 tablespoon of the peanut oil in a small bowl.

2. Heat 1½ teaspoons peanut oil in a nonstick 12-inch skillet over high heat until smoking; add half of the pork to the skillet and cook, stirring occasionally and breaking up the clumps, until well browned, about 2 minutes. Transfer the pork to a medium bowl. Repeat with an additional 1½ teaspoons peanut oil and the remaining pork.

3. Add 1 tablespoon peanut oil to the now-empty skillet; add the asparagus and cook, stirring every 30 seconds, until lightly browned, about 2 minutes. Add the water, cover the pan, and lower the heat to medium. Steam the asparagus until tender-crisp, about 2 minutes; transfer the asparagus to the bowl with the pork.

4. Add the remaining 1½ teaspoons peanut oil to the skillet; add the onion and cook, stirring occasionally, until beginning to brown and soften, about 2 minutes.

5. Clear the center of the skillet; add the garlic and lemon grass mixture to the clearing and cook, mashing the mixture with a spoon, until fragrant, about 1 minute, then stir the mixture into the onion. Return the pork and asparagus to the skillet and toss to combine. Whisk the sauce to recombine, then add to the skillet; cook, stirring constantly, until the sauce is thickened and evenly distributed, about 30 seconds. Transfer to a serving platter and sprinkle with the basil. Serve immediately.

EQUIPMENT: Electric Woks

We've said it plainly several times: We don't like woks. The relatively small base of a wok means only modest burner contact, which translates to less than maximal heat. Quite simply, the design of a wok is not meant for cooking on a Western stovetop, where a large open skillet is much more successful at achieving optimum sizzle and sear.

We wondered, however, if electric woks offered advantages over stovetop woks. We collected six of them, ranging in price from $30 to $100, then stir-fried and deep-fried in each, looking for differences in heating ability and design. We were surprised to find one wok—and a modestly priced one—that excelled in all areas, and another that did quite well.

The runaway winner was the Maxim Nonstick Electric Wok with Dome Cover ($60). Stir-frying in it was commensurate with stir-frying in a skillet, and it heated oil for deep-frying to a fault. The temperature dial was accurate and easy to read. The size of this wok is generous (14 inches in diameter, with a 6 ½-quart capacity), and the long-handled design makes it possible to simultaneously empty and scrape ingredients out of the wok when cooking in batches.

The runner-up was the Toastmaster High Performance Electric Wok ($30). This wok had the heat output of the winner, but it was not nearly as commodious (12 ¾ inches in diameter, with a 4 ½-quart capacity). With use, its temperature dial became hot to the touch, and its two short handles were less than ideal for cooking in batches, making it impossible to scrape out food while turning the wok to empty it.

The remaining four woks tested—Rival Stainless Steel Electric Wok ($90), West Bend Electric Wok ($48), Martin Yan Professional Wok ($90), and Circulon Hard Anodized Electric Wok ($100)—weren't worth the space they occupied on the countertop. Problems included flimsy construction, odd design, and hot spots. Moreover, not one of these woks had good heat output—in fact, three couldn't get the oil for deep-frying above 350 degrees, though their thermostats were set for 375 and indicated that the temperature had been reached. (In one, the oil hovered at 312 degrees.) In comparison, our favorite woks maintained oil temperatures of 365 to 375 degrees, ideal for deep-frying.

Should you purchase an electric wok? Probably, if you're a frequent fryer or like to use a bamboo steamer. However, if stir-frying is your limit, stick with a large, heavy, totally utilitarian nonstick skillet.

THE BEST ELECTRIC WOK
The Maxim Nonstick Electric Wok ($60) was the best of the six models we tested. We particularly like the long handle (which makes it easy to pick up) and no-fuss cleanup. It's great for deep-frying and stir-fries, on par with a large, nonstick skillet.

8

I WANT TO MAKE A STEW

I Want to Make a Stew

THIS CHAPTER COVERS STEWS MADE WITH beef, veal, lamb, and pork. Although each kind of meat and each stew has its own requirements, there are a few general points to keep in mind. First and foremost, start with the right cut of meat.

In our testing, we found that meat from the shoulder area of the animal usually has the best combination of flavor and texture. This meat is well marbled with fat, so it won't dry out during the stewing process. Other cuts are simply too lean to use in stews. They will become tough if cooked this way.

So why does shoulder meat generally make the best stews? Its intramuscular fat and connective tissue make it amenable to long, slow, moist cooking. When cooked in liquid, the connective tissue melts down into gelatin, making the meat tender. The fat in the meat helps as well, in two important ways. Fat carries the chemical compounds that our taste buds perceive as beef, lamb, pork, or veal flavor, and it also melts when cooked, lubricating the meat fibers as it slips between the cells, increasing tenderness.

In our tests, we found that buying roasts or chops and cutting them up for stew ourselves had distinct advantages over buying precut meat. Packages labeled "stew meat" in supermarkets often contain misshapen or small bits of meat. In addition, these packages may have scraps from various parts of the animal. To make sure that you have purchased the proper cut of meat and that it is divided into evenly sized chunks, take the five extra minutes to cut the meat yourself.

Browning the meat well is another key point to keep in mind. Meat stews generally begin by seasoning the chunks of meat with salt and pepper and then sautéing them in a film of oil. Don't rush this step. In our tests, meat that was only spottily browned didn't taste as good. Browning the meat and some of the vegetables, especially onions, adds flavor to the final dish.

How does browning work? In vegetables it is largely sugars and in meat sugars and proteins that caramelize, or brown, making the meat and vegetables taste better. In addition to flavoring the meat, proper browning covers the bottom of the pan with browned bits called fond. When liquid is added to the pot, the fond loosens and dissolves,

adding flavor to the stew. This process is called deglazing. Wine and stock are the most common choices for deglazing the pan, but water works, too. Because the foundation of a stew's flavor comes from the fond and deglazing liquid, it is crucial that the meat be browned properly. In most recipes, to ensure proper browning, we sauté the meat in two batches. If all of the meat is put into the pot at once, the pieces crowd one another and steam, thus turning a pallid gray color rather than brown.

Contrary to popular belief, browning does not "seal in" the juices in meat. After browning, when the meat is slow-cooked, more and more juices are expelled as the internal temperature of the meat rises. By the time the meat is fork-tender, it has in fact shed most of its juices. As odd as it sounds, this is the beauty of a stew, since the surrounding liquid, which is served as a sauce, is enriched by these juices.

Our tests revealed that the temperature of the stewing liquid was crucial. We found it essential to keep the temperature of the liquid below 212 degrees. Boiled meat remains tough, and the outside becomes especially dry. Keeping the liquid at a simmer (rather than a boil) allows the internal temperature of the meat to rise slowly. By the time it is actually fork-tender, much of the connective tissue will have turned to gelatin. The gelatin, in turn, helps to thicken the stewing liquid.

To determine whether stews cook best on the stovetop or in the oven, we tried both, simmering a basic beef stew on the stovetop over low heat (with and without a flame-taming device to protect the pot from direct heat) and in a moderate oven. The flame-tamer device worked too well in distancing the pot from the heat; the stew juices tasted raw and boozy. Putting the pot right on the burner worked better, but we found ourselves constantly adjusting the burner to maintain a gentle simmer, and this method is prone to error. We had the most consistent results in the oven. We found that putting a covered Dutch oven in a 300-degree oven ensures that the temperature of the stewing liquid will remain below the boiling point, at about 200 degrees. (The oven must be kept at a temperature higher than 200 degrees because ovens are not completely efficient in transferring heat; a temperature of 300 degrees recognizes that some heat will be lost as it penetrates through the pot and into the stew.)

The beef, veal, lamb, and one of the pork recipes in this chapter are conventional stews—large chunks of boneless meat accompanied by vegetables in a thickened sauce. The chapter includes also several dishes that don't fit this definition.

For pozole (Mexico's most famous pork stew),

CUTTING STEW MEAT

For stew meat pieces that are cut from the right part of the animal and regularly shaped, we suggest buying a boneless roast and cutting the meat yourself. A three-pound roast, once trimmed, should yield 2 ¾ pounds of beef, the maximum amount that can be correctly browned in two batches in a large Dutch oven.

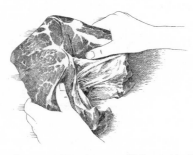

1. Pull apart the roast at its major seams (delineated by lines of fat and silver skin). Use a knife as necessary.

2. With a paring knife, trim off excess fat and silver skin.

3. Cut the meat into cubes or chunks as directed in specific recipes.

a picnic roast is simmered, cooled, and then shredded. Cassoulet is a classic French dish that combines stewed meat, beans, sausage, and toasted bread crumbs. We've radically simplified this recipe, making it possible to prepare this grand dish at home.

A final note about our choice of liquids for use in meat stews. Few home cooks have meat stock on hand. They might make beef stock for beef soup because there's no other alternative, but they generally make only what they need for a particular recipe. In stews, with their many components, the liquid element is usually not as central as it is in soup. Beef stock is too much work for such recipes. We find that low-sodium canned chicken broth (which tastes better than canned beef broth; see page 238) is a fine option. If you have homemade chicken stock on hand, you can use some in these recipes. However, we have found that the differences between meat stews made with homemade chicken stock and those made with canned chicken broth are minimal.

HEARTY BEEF STEW

BEEF STEW SHOULD BE RICH AND SATISFYing. Our goal in developing a recipe for it was to keep the cooking process simple without compromising the stew's deep, complex flavor. We focused on these issues: What cuts of beef respond best to stewing? How much and what kind of liquid should you use? When and with what do you thicken the stew?

Experts tout different cuts as being ideal for stewing. We browned 12 different cuts of beef, marked them for identification, and stewed them in the same pot. Chuck proved to be the most flavorful, tender, and juicy. Most other cuts were too stringy, too chewy, too dry, or just plain bland. The exception was rib-eye steak, which made good stew meat but is too expensive a cut for this purpose.

Our advice is to buy a steak or roast from the chuck and cube it yourself. The names given to different cuts of chuck vary, but the most commonly used names for retail chuck cuts include boneless chuck-eye roasts, cross-rib roasts, blade steaks and roasts, shoulder steaks and roasts, and arm steaks and roasts. We particularly like chuck-eye roast, but all chuck cuts are delicious when cubed and stewed.

Having settled on our cut of beef, we started to explore how and when to thicken the stew. Dredging meat cubes in flour is a roundabout way of thickening stew. The floured beef is browned, then stewed. During the stewing process, some of the flour from the beef dissolves into the liquid, causing it to thicken. Although the stew we cooked this way thickened up nicely, the beef cubes had a "smothered steak" look.

We also tried two thickening methods at the end of cooking—a beurre manié (softened butter mixed with flour) and cornstarch mixed with water. Both methods are acceptable, but the beurre manié lightened the stew liquid's color, making it look more like pale gravy than rich stew juices. Also, the extra fat did not improve the stew's flavor enough to justify its addition. For those who prefer thickening at the end of cooking, we found that cornstarch dissolved in water did the job without compromising the stew's dark, rich color.

Pureeing the cooked vegetables is another thickening method. Once the stew is fully cooked, the meat is pulled from the pot and the juices and vegetables are pureed to create a thick sauce. Tasters felt this thickening method made the vegetable flavor too prominent.

Ultimately, though, we opted for thickening the stew with flour at the beginning—stirring it into the sautéing onions and garlic, right before adding the liquid. Stew thickened this way did not taste any better than that thickened at the end with cornstarch, but it was easier. There was no last-minute work; once the liquid started to simmer, the cook was free to do something else.

We next focused on stewing liquids. We tried water, wine, canned beef broth, canned chicken broth, combinations of these liquids, and beef stock. Stews made with water were bland and greasy. Stews made entirely with wine were too strong. The stew made from beef stock was delicious, but we decided that beef stew, which has many hearty ingredients contributing to its flavor profile, did not absolutely need beef stock, which

is time-consuming to make. When we turned to canned broths, the chicken outscored the beef broth. The stew made entirely with chicken broth was good, but we missed the acidity and flavor provided by the wine. In the end, we preferred a combination of chicken broth and red wine.

We tested various amounts of liquid and found that we preferred stews with a minimum of liquid, which helps to preserve a strong meat flavor. With too little liquid, however, the stew may not cook evenly, and there may not be enough "sauce" to spoon over starchy accompaniments. A cup of liquid per pound of meat gave us sufficient sauce to moisten a mound of mashed potatoes or polenta without drowning them. We tested various kinds of wine and found that fairly inexpensive fruity, full-bodied young wines, such as Chianti or Zinfandel were best.

To determine when to add the vegetables, we made three different stews, adding carrots, potatoes, and onions to one stew at the beginning of cooking and to another stew halfway through the cooking process. For our final stew, we cooked the onions with the meat but added steamed carrots and potatoes when the stew was fully cooked.

The stew with vegetables added at the beginning was thin and watery. The vegetables had fallen apart and given up their flavor and liquid to the stew. The beef stew with the cooked vegetables added at the last minute was delicious, and the vegetables were the freshest and most intensely flavored. However, it was more work to steam the vegetables separately. Also, vegetables cooked separately from the stew didn't really meld all that well with the other flavors and ingredients. We preferred to add the vegetables partway through the cooking process. They didn't fall apart this way, and they had enough time to meld with the other ingredients. There is one exception to this rule. Peas were added just before serving the stew to preserve their color and texture.

One final note: The meat passes from the tough to tender stage fairly quickly. Often at the 1¾-hour mark, we found that the meat would still be chewy. Fifteen minutes later it would be tender. Let the stew go another 15 minutes and the meat starts to dry out. Taste the meat often as the stew nears completion to judge when it's just right.

⨳
Hearty Beef Stew
SERVES 6 TO 8

Make this stew in an ovenproof Dutch oven, preferably with a capacity of 8 quarts but nothing less than 6 quarts. Choose a Dutch oven with a wide bottom; this will allow you to brown the meat in just 2 batches. See page 151 for information about choosing a red wine for use in this dish.

3	pounds beef chuck roast, trimmed and cut into 1 1/2-inch cubes (see the illustrations on page 148)
	Salt and ground black pepper
3	tablespoons vegetable oil
2	medium onions, chopped coarse (about 2 cups)
3	medium garlic cloves, minced or pressed through a garlic press (about 1 tablespoon)
3	tablespoons unbleached all-purpose flour
1	cup full-bodied dry red wine
2	cups low-sodium chicken broth
2	bay leaves
1	teaspoon dried thyme
4	medium red potatoes (about 1 1/2 pounds), peeled and cut into 1-inch cubes
4	large carrots (about 1 pound), peeled and sliced 1/4 inch thick
1	cup frozen peas (about 6 ounces), thawed
1/4	cup minced fresh parsley leaves

1. Adjust the oven rack to lower-middle position and heat the oven to 300 degrees. Dry the beef thoroughly on paper towels, then season it generously with salt and pepper to taste. Heat 1 tablespoon of the oil in a large ovenproof Dutch oven over medium-high heat until shimmering. Add half of the meat so that the individual pieces are close together but not touching. Cook, not moving the pieces until the sides touching the pot are well browned, 2 to 3 minutes. Using tongs, turn each piece and continue cooking until most sides are well browned, about 5 minutes longer. Transfer the beef to a medium bowl, add another 1 tablespoon oil to the pot, and swirl to coat the pan bottom. Brown the remaining beef; transfer the meat to the bowl and set aside.

2. Reduce the heat to medium, add the remaining tablespoon oil to the now-empty Dutch oven, and swirl to coat the pan bottom. Add the onions and 1/4 teaspoon salt. Cook, stirring frequently and vigorously, scraping the pot bottom with a wooden spoon to loosen the browned bits, until the onions have softened, 4 to 5 minutes. Add the garlic and continue to cook for 30 seconds. Stir in the flour and cook until lightly colored, 1 to 2 minutes. Add the wine, scraping up the remaining browned bits from the bottom and edges of the pot and stirring until the liquid is thick. Gradually add the broth, stirring constantly and scraping the pan edges to dissolve the flour. Add the bay leaves and thyme and bring to a simmer. Add the meat and return to a simmer. Cover and place the pot in the oven. Cook for 1 hour.

3. Remove the pot from the oven and add the potatoes and carrots. Cover and return the pot to the oven. Cook until the meat is just tender, about 1 hour. Remove the pot from the oven. (The stew can be covered and refrigerated for up to 3 days. Bring to a simmer over medium-low heat.)

4. Add the peas, cover, and allow to stand for 5 minutes. Stir in the parsley, discard the bay leaves, adjust the seasonings, and serve immediately.

BEEF GOULASH

THIS SIMPLE EASTERN EUROPEAN STEW has been around for centuries. The word goulash comes from the Hungarian gulyas, which means "herd of cattle." Originally, cattlemen seared and stewed beef until the liquid evaporated and then dried the meat in the sun. When needed, the meat was rehydrated with water and, depending on how much liquid was added, goulash, stew or soup was created. Goulash stew—without the drying step—is the more popular version in the United States.

There are several versions of modern goulash stew. Beef, onions, garlic, and paprika are constants. Other possible ingredients include potatoes, tomatoes, and bell peppers. Our goal was to create a very simple stew with tender, flavorful beef and browned onions in an intensely flavored, rich sauce. The sauce would be thick and brownish red in color, both from the paprika and the good browning that the meat and onions would receive.

As with our Hearty Beef Stew (see page 148), we found that chuck meat was the best choice because it cooks up tender and flavorful. Traditional recipes brown the beef in lard, and we found that the gentle pork flavor of good lard does add something to this dish. Given the fact that most cooks don't have lard on hand, we tried bacon fat as substitute. Tasters reacted negatively to goulash made with bacon fat. They said the smoky flavor imparted by the bacon was at odds with this stew. Vegetable oil turned out to be a better choice. Although not as flavorful as lard, oil will suffice.

On a related subject, we found that leaving a little fat attached to the pieces of meat boosts flavor and helps compensate for the missing pork flavor if lard is not used. (You will need to defat the stew before serving, but this is easily done with a spoon.)

INGREDIENTS: Red Wine for Stew

When making a dish that uses red wine, our tendency is to grab whichever inexpensive, dry red is on hand, usually the leftover contents of a recently opened bottle. But we began to wonder what difference particular wines would make in the final dish and decided to investigate.

We called on the advice of several local wine experts, who gave us some parameters to work with when selecting red wines to use in a braise such as Hearty Beef Stew. (The rules are slightly different when making some dishes, such as Beef Burgundy, that traditionally rely on a particular kind of wine. See page 158 for more details on choosing a red wine for this dish.)

When selecting a red wine for a basic stew, look for one that is dry (to avoid a sweet sauce) and with good acidity (to aid in breaking down the fibers of the meat). Keep in mind that any characteristic found in the uncooked wine will be concentrated when cooked.

From tests we ran, we found that softer, fruity wines such as Merlot yielded a "grape jelly" flavor, which most tasters thought was too sweet for beef stew or cacciatore. We also learned that it's best to avoid wines that have been "oaked," usually older wines; the oak flavor tends to become harsh and bitter as the wine is cooked.

In these early tests, we found that browning the meat well is essential to flavor development in goulash. The hearty, rich flavor and color of goulash is dependent on browning of the meat and onions and then deglazing the crusty, deep brown bits stuck to the bottom of the Dutch oven.

We found that adding a little salt with the onions caused them to release moisture and kept them from scorching. This moisture also helped to loosen the browned bits, a process that is completed once the liquid is added to the pan. Although onions are a must, the recipes we looked at were divided on the question of garlic. Tasters, however, were not. Everyone in the test kitchen liked garlic in this stew. Six cloves added depth and also balanced the sweetness of the paprika and onions.

Once the garlic was fragrant, it was time for the paprika to go into the pot. Sweet Hungarian paprika is essential in this recipe. We added the flour (to thicken the stew) at the same time.

Recipes uncovered in our research used an assortment of liquids, including water, beef stock, and chicken stock. We found that water created a bland stew. Homemade beef stock was delicious in this dish but required a large investment of time. We wondered if we could substitute canned broth without compromising the flavor too much. Canned beef broth tasted tinny and did not work in goulash. We had better results with canned chicken broth and, in fact, with homemade chicken stock. Both gave the stew good body, and the chicken flavor faded behind the beef and spices.

Some recipes also include wine in the mix, although authentic recipes do not. We tried varying amounts of red wine, and tasters felt that its flavor was too overpowering. Goulash should be soft and mellow; while red wine added complexity, it also made the stew acidic and a bit harsh. A few sources suggested white wine, but again tasters were unimpressed.

Our recipe was coming together—browned beef and onions, garlic and paprika for flavor, and chicken stock or canned broth as the liquid. We had two major issues to resolve—tomatoes and vegetables. We started with the tomatoes.

Many goulash recipes contain tomato, although the original dish (which dates back several centuries before the arrival of tomatoes from the New World) certainly did not. We decided to make four batches of goulash—one with canned diced tomatoes, one with plain tomato sauce, one with tomato paste, and one with no tomato product. The diced tomatoes and tomato sauce proved to be too dominant and made the stew reminiscent of beef cacciatore. Tomato paste, however, blended into the background and enhanced other flavors in the dish. Compared with the stew made without any tomatoes, the version with tomato paste was more complex and appealing. In fact, the tomatoes functioned a bit like wine in terms of adding depth, but they were also much more subtle than wine and thus more in tune with the spirit of goulash.

Vegetables were easy to incorporate into the dish. Tasters liked large chunks of red and green bell peppers, especially when added to the stew near the end of the cooking time. When added earlier (just after the onions are browned is a common choice), the peppers become mushy and fell apart. We found that if they are added to the stew while it is in the oven, the peppers soften without turning mushy.

We tested carrots, cabbage, celery, and green beans (ingredients used in some of the recipes we had collected) but did not like any of them in goulash. Potatoes were a different story. Several recipes added them to the stew pot with the liquid so they would fall apart and thicken the stew. Although we did not like this approach, we did like potatoes simmered in the stew until tender. Adding the potatoes partway through the oven cooking time yielded this result, so we decided to make the goulash with potatoes a variation (see page 153).

Many Hungarian goulash recipes do not include sour cream, which seems more popular in German and Austrian versions. But our tasters all felt that the sour cream mellowed and enriched this stew. To prevent the sour cream from curdling, we combined the sour cream with a little hot stewing liquid to temper it and then stirred the mixture back into the stew pot.

Goulash is traditionally served over buttered egg noodles or spaetzle. Egg noodles require almost no effort to cook and were our first choice. Mashed potatoes are not traditional, but they made an excellent accompaniment, too.

Beef Goulash

SERVES 6 TO 8

Goulash is like the Merlot of beef stews—mellow, with sweet overtones. If your tastes run more toward Zinfandel, add a pinch of hot paprika or cayenne pepper for a more complex, spicy version. The flavor from the beef fat adds something to this stew, so don't trim the meat too closely. We recommend removing external fat from the chuck roast but leaving internal fat alone unless it is excessively thick. Serve the stew over 1 pound of buttered egg noodles. Try tossing the noodles with 1 tablespoon of toasted caraway seeds for a distinctive and delicious flavor combination. (Caraway is an unusual and authentic touch.)

3	pounds beef chuck roast, trimmed and cut into 1 1/2-inch cubes (see the illustrations on page 148)
	Salt and ground black pepper
3	tablespoons vegetable oil or lard
3	medium-large onions, chopped coarse (about 5 cups)
6	medium garlic cloves, minced or pressed through a garlic press (about 2 tablespoons)
5	tablespoons sweet paprika
1/4	cup unbleached all-purpose flour
3	cups low-sodium chicken broth
2	tablespoons tomato paste
2	bay leaves
1	teaspoon dried marjoram
1	large red bell pepper, stemmed, seeded, and chopped coarse
1	large green bell pepper, stemmed, seeded, and chopped coarse
1/2	cup sour cream
1/4	cup minced fresh parsley leaves

1. Adjust the oven rack to the lower-middle position and heat the oven to 300 degrees. Dry the beef thoroughly on paper towels, then season it generously with salt and pepper to taste. Heat 1 tablespoon of the oil in a large ovenproof Dutch oven over medium-high heat until shimmering. Add half of the meat so that the individual pieces are close together but not touching. Cook, not moving the pieces until the sides touching the pot are well browned, 2 to 3 minutes. Using tongs, turn each

piece and continue cooking until most sides are well browned, about 5 minutes longer. Transfer the beef to a medium bowl, add another 1 tablespoon oil to the pot, and swirl to coat the pan bottom. Brown the remaining beef; transfer the meat to the bowl and set aside.

2. Reduce the heat to medium, add the remaining tablespoon oil to the now-empty Dutch oven, and swirl to coat the pan bottom. Add the onions and ¼ teaspoon salt. Cook, stirring frequently and vigorously, scraping the pot bottom with a wooden spoon to loosen the browned bits, until the onions have softened and browned, about 8 minutes. Stir in the garlic and cook until fragrant, about 30 seconds. Add the paprika and flour and stir until the onions are evenly coated and fragrant, 1 to 2 minutes.

3. Stir in 1½ cups broth, scraping the pot bottom with a wooden spoon to loosen the remaining browned bits and stirring until the flour is incorporated and the liquid thickened. Gradually add the remaining 1½ cup of broth, stirring constantly and scraping the pan edges to dissolve the flour. Stir in the tomato paste, bay leaves, marjoram, and ¾ teaspoon salt. Add the browned beef and accumulated juices, stir to blend, and submerge the meat under the liquid. Increase the heat to medium, bring to a simmer, cover the pot, and place it in the oven. Cook for 1 hour and 20 minutes.

4. Remove the pot from the oven and stir in the red and green peppers. Cover and return the pot to the oven. Cook until the meat is just tender, about 40 minutes. Remove the pot from the oven. If serving immediately, spoon off the fat that rises to the top. (The stew can be covered and refrigerated for up to 3 days. Spoon off the congealed fat and bring the stew back to a simmer over medium–low heat.)

5. Place the sour cream in a medium bowl and stir in about ½ cup of the hot stewing liquid. Stir the sour cream mixture back into the stew. Stir in the parsley and season with salt and pepper to taste. Serve immediately.

➤ VARIATION

Beef Goulash with Potatoes and Caraway
With potatoes added, there's no need to serve this stew over noodles. Caraway is a traditional addition to Hungarian goulash.

Follow the recipe for Beef Goulash, reducing the amount of beef to 2½ pounds, adding 1 teaspoon caraway seeds with the paprika and flour, and adding ¾ pound red potatoes, peeled and cut into 1-inch dice, after the stew has cooked in the oven for 1 hour. Proceed with the recipe as directed.

CARBONNADE

A BASIC BEEF STEW CAN BE ALTERED IN dozens of ways, usually by adding more ingredients to the pot. But you can also go the other way and strip beef stew down to its bare bones (to its beef). If you also trade in the carrots and potatoes for a plethora of onions and add a good dose of beer, you've created a Belgian beef stew called carbonnade à la flamande.

Beef, beer, and onions have an affinity—they're an ensemble with great appeal (think burger, onion rings, and a beer). In a carbonnade, the heartiness of beef melds with the soft sweetness of sliced onions in a broth that is deep and rich with the malty flavor of dark beer.

We made several versions of carbonnade and found that despite the simple and few ingredients, making a poor one is quite easy to do. We wound up with several batches of tough, tasteless beef and onions in a pale, insipid broth. Not quite what we had in mind.

We used the framework of our recipe for hearty beef stew to arrive at an improved carbonnade. The operations were as follows: The beef is browned in batches and set aside, the onions are sautéed in the empty pot, the flour is sprinkled over the onions, the liquid is added, the beef is returned to the pot, and the covered pot goes into the oven where it simmers until the beef is fork-tender.

In developing a recipe for carbonnade, the first departure from our beef stew recipe came with the selection of beef. For a basic beef stew, we prefer a chuck roast cut into 1½-inch chunks. A chuck roast is composed of a number of different muscles interwoven with intramuscular fat and connective tissue. This fat and tissue make for good texture and flavor, and the different muscles make for pieces of meat with uneven or differing textures, even when cooked.

The substance of carbonnade is purely beef and onion—there are no chunks of potatoes or carrots with which the beef competes. Consequently, we wanted smaller pieces of beef of a uniform texture that would be a better match for the soft, thinly sliced onions. Enter 1-inch-thick blade steaks (also called top blade or flatiron steaks)—small, long, narrow steaks cut from the shoulder (or chuck) area of the animal. Most blade steaks have a decent amount of fat marbling, which gives them good flavor as well as a tender texture. One taster described the blade steak in carbonnade as "buttery," a quality that is well suited to this stew. The trade-off is that these smaller steaks are a bit more time-consuming to trim of silver skin and gristle, but they are well worth it.

Onions—and a good deal of them—go into a carbonnade. Two pounds was the right amount in relation to the amount of beef. We tried both white and red onions, but both were cloyingly sweet. Yellow onions tasted the best. After browning the beef, the floor of the pot was crusty with fond (browned bits). Do not underestimate the importance of the fond—it furnishes the stew with color and flavor. As we had done with goulash, we added ¼ teaspoon salt along with the thinly sliced onions to help release their moisture. This assists in keeping the fond from burning and in loosening it from the pot when deglazing. Garlic is not an ingredient in all carbonnade recipes, but we liked its heady essence; a small amount is added to the onions only after they are cooked so that the garlic does not burn.

The right beer is key to achieving a full, robust carbonnade. Beers of the light, lager persuasion, those commonly favored in America, lack guts—they result in light-colored, watery-tasting stews. We tried a number of different beers and found that reasonably dark ales, very dark ales, and stouts made the richest and best-tasting carbonnade. A few of our favorites were Chimay (a Trappist ale from Belgium), Newcastle Brown Ale, Anchor Steam (this beer cannot technically be classified as an ale), Samuel Smith Taddy Porter, and Guinness Extra Stout.

We tried making carbonnade with beer as the only liquid, but they lacked backbone and sometimes had an overwhelming bitterness, depending on the type of beer used. Equal parts chicken stock or canned broth and beer made a deeper, more solid-tasting stew. The addition of dried thyme and a bay leaf added herbal notes that complemented the other flavors. Just a bit of cider vinegar perked everything up, and a bit of dark brown sugar rounded out the flavors.

Carbonnade à la Flamande
SERVES 6 TO 8

To make sure the beef browns well, dry the pieces thoroughly on paper towels. Don't bother making this stew with a light-colored beer—both the color and flavor will be insipid. We particularly liked Newcastle Brown Ale, Anchor Steam, and Chimay. For those who like a heavier beer, with a slightly bitter flavor, porter and stout are good. Top blade steaks are cut from the shoulder area of the cow. They are tender, but each steak has a line of gristle running down the center that should be removed. Top blade steaks are often called flatiron steaks or blade steaks.

3–3 ½   **pounds top blade steaks, gristle removed (see the illustrations on page 63) and cut into 1-inch pieces**
     Salt and ground black pepper
3   **tablespoons vegetable oil**
2   **pounds medium onions, halved and sliced thin**
2   **medium garlic cloves, minced or pressed through a garlic press (about 2 teaspoons)**
3   **tablespoons unbleached all-purpose flour**
1 ½   **cups low-sodium chicken broth**
1 ½   **cups dark beer (see note)**
¾   **teaspoon dried thyme**
1   **bay leaf**
1   **tablespoon dark brown sugar**
1   **tablespoon cider vinegar**

1. Adjust the oven rack to the lower-middle position and heat the oven to 300 degrees. Dry the beef thoroughly on paper towels, then season it generously with salt and pepper to taste. Heat 1 tablespoon of the oil in a large ovenproof Dutch oven over medium-high heat until shimmering.

Add half of the meat so that the individual pieces are close together but not touching. Cook, not moving the pieces until the side touching the pot is well browned, 2 to 3 minutes. Using tongs, turn each piece and continue cooking until most sides are well browned, about 5 minutes longer. Transfer the beef to a medium bowl, add another 1 tablespoon oil to the pot, and swirl to coat the pan bottom. Brown the remaining beef; transfer the meat to the bowl and set aside.

2. Reduce the heat to medium-low, add the remaining tablespoon oil to the now-empty Dutch oven, and swirl to coat the pan bottom. Add the onions and ¼ teaspoon salt and cook, stirring occasionally and vigorously, scraping the pot bottom with a wooden spoon to loosen the browned bits, until the onions have released some moisture, about 5 minutes. Increase the heat to medium and cook, stirring occasionally and scraping the pot bottom, until the onions are limp, softened, and lightly browned, 12 to 14 minutes. Stir in the garlic and cook until fragrant, about 30 seconds. Add the flour and stir until the onions are evenly coated.

3. Stir in the broth, scraping the pot bottom and edges with a wooden spoon to loosen the browned bits. Gradually add the beer, stirring constantly and scraping the pan edges to dissolve the flour. Add the thyme, bay leaf, sugar, and vinegar as well as the browned beef and accumulated juices, pushing down on the beef to submerge the pieces; sprinkle with salt and pepper to taste, bring to a simmer, cover, and place in the oven. Cook until the beef is fork-tender, 1½ to 2 hours. Remove and discard the bay leaf. Adjust the seasonings with salt and pepper to taste and serve. (The stew can be covered and refrigerated for several days. Bring back to a simmer over medium-low heat.)

BEEF BURGUNDY

IF THE LOUVRE WERE JUST A MUSEUM, THEN boeuf à la bourguignonne might be just beef stew. Both are French and utterly extraordinary, but only one can be enjoyed at home. We liken beef Burgundy more to a fabulous prime steak napped with a rich, silken red wine reduction sauce than to a mundane beef stew. The beef in beef Burgundy is cut into satisfyingly large chunks that become utterly tender. The braising liquid, brimming with voluptuous wine and infused with aromatic vegetables, garlic, and herbs, is finessed into a sauce of burgundy velvet studded with mushrooms and pearl onions. Beef Burgundy is earthy, big, robust, warm, and welcoming in a brooding sort of way.

At least that's what it is at its best. We have had versions that fell far short of this, with tough meat or a dull sauce with no flavor complexity. We wanted to find a way to bring this classic dish to its full potential in a home kitchen.

Recipes for beef Burgundy are very much alike. Aromatic vegetables (onions, garlic, and carrots), red wine, stock, herbs, mushrooms, and pearl onions are all requisite ingredients; their combinations and proportions and the variations in preparation and technique are where the recipes diverge.

We started by completing four recipes, and from these four we made several important observations. First, marinating the beef in the red wine and herbs that will later go into the braise—a common recommendation in recipes—does not improve the flavor of the cooked meat. Second, the braising liquid requires straining to rid it of bits of aromatic vegetables and herbs so that it may become a silky sauce. We found that bundling in cheesecloth all the goods that must eventually come out of the pot made their extraction possible in one easy step. When wrapped in cheesecloth, however, the aromatic vegetables cannot first be sautéed—a customary step, the omission of which we feared would adversely affect the flavors of the braise. Remarkably, it did not. But perhaps this is why it took such generous amounts of chopped onions, carrots, and garlic as well as parsley, thyme, peppercorns, and bay leaves to create a balanced mélange of flavors.

The cut of beef best suited to the long braise of beef Burgundy is a chuck roast. It's the cut that almost every recipe calls for and the one we preferred in a regular beef stew because of its rich, meaty flavor. Because the beef in a beef Burgundy is cut into chunks larger than those in a beef stew—a good 1½ to 2 inches—we found it necessary to take extra care to trim off as much fat and silver skin as possible; larger pieces of beef also mean larger, more detectable bites of these undesirables.

Each and every beef Burgundy begins with either salt pork or bacon cut into lardons, or small strips, and fried to a crisp; the fat that results is used to brown the beef chunks. The crisped pork is added to the pot to simmer alongside the beef so that it can relinquish its flavors to the braise, providing a subtle, sweet underpinning and lending the sauce roundness and depth. We tried both bacon and salt pork and favored the cleaner, purer, more honest flavor of salt pork. Moreover, the thicker, more toothsome strips of salt pork had better texture than the lifeless, thin pieces of bacon. Salt pork can be a challenge to find in grocery stores, so we reasoned that just as blanching salt pork removes excess salt that would otherwise crystallize on the surface during frying, blanching thick-cut bacon ought to calm the smoke and sugar and make it appropriate for beef Burgundy. This worked well. The thick-cut bacon had more textural appeal than regular bacon and was an acceptable substitute for salt pork.

As for the stock that goes into the braise, most recipes call for beef, preferably homemade. Because making beef stock is so time-consuming, we wanted to try canned broth. From past experience we knew that canned beef broth does not make an acceptable substitute for homemade beef stock. Therefore, in all subsequent tests, we used what we have found to be the next best option—canned chicken broth—with excellent results. Still, beef Burgundy necessitates a good amount of liquid for braising, and too much chicken broth tasted too chickeny. Water was a fine filler, especially since the braising liquid is later reduced to create the sauce. We then tried something a bit unorthodox to boost flavor. Just a small amount of dried porcini mushrooms wrapped into the cheesecloth package brought the meatiness and savory quality that homemade beef stock would conceivably have added. A modicum of tomato paste added color and sprightliness.

Wine was the next issue. Beef Burgundy does not exist without a healthy dose of it. We concluded after several batches that anything less than a whole bottle left the sauce lacking and unremarkable.

After numerous experiments, we had determined that a Burgundy, or at least a decent Pinot Noir, is indeed the wine of choice (see page 158 for more details). Though most recipes indicate that all of the wine should be added at the outset, one recipe, as well as one wine expert, recommended saving just a bit of the wine to add at the very end, just before serving. This late embellishment of raw wine vastly improved the sauce, brightening its flavor, giving it resonance, and making it sing.

Midway through testing, we decided we needed an alternative to browning the meat in the Dutch oven, where it would eventually be braised. Browning in batches took too long, and the drippings, or fond, that are essential flavor providers frequently burned. Evidently, the small cooking surface of even a large Dutch oven was a liability. We took to browning the beef in two batches in a heavy, large 12-inch skillet. To keep the fond from going to waste, we deglazed the pan with a bit of water and poured it directly into the braising pot, where it would eventually marry with the broth and wine.

Next we went to work to find the best means of adding flour to thicken the braising liquid that must blossom into a velvety sauce. Tossing the beef in flour before browning interfered with the color the beef could attain and ultimately affected its flavor. We found it preferable to make a roux in the skillet and add broth and water to it, then have it join the beef, wine, and vegetable and herb bouquet in the braising pot. This afforded us the opportunity to cook the roux until it achieved a toasty brown color, which made a favorable impact on the flavor of the dish.

With everything assembled in the Dutch oven, into the oven it went, where the constant, all-encompassing heat produced an even simmer that required little attention. This was the time to prepare the mushrooms and pearl onions, both of which would later join the sauce. Peeling fresh pearl onions is a nuisance, but opening a bag isn't. We embraced already-peeled frozen pearl onions that, contrary to expectations, are not inferior in flavor or texture to fresh when browned, as they are when boiled. A brisk simmer in a skillet with some water, butter, and sugar, and then a quick sauté with the mushrooms, created glazed beauties that were ready to grace the sauce. The final flourish, a little brandy, added richness and warmth to an already magnificent boeuf à la bourguignonne.

Beef Burgundy

SERVES 6

If you cannot find salt pork (see page 158 for more information), thick-cut bacon can be substituted. Cut it crosswise into ¼-inch pieces and treat it just as you would the salt pork, but note that you will have no rind to include in the vegetable and herb bouquet. To make this dish a day or two in advance, see Do-Ahead Beef Burgundy on page 159. Boiled potatoes are the traditional accompaniment, but mashed potatoes or buttered noodles are nice as well.

BEEF BRAISE

6	ounces salt pork, trimmed of rind (see the illustration on page 158), rind reserved, and salt pork cut into ¼ inch by ¼ inch by 1-inch pieces
10	sprigs fresh parsley, torn into quarters
6	sprigs fresh thyme
2	medium onions, chopped coarse
2	medium carrots, chopped coarse
1	medium head garlic, cloves separated and crushed but unpeeled
2	bay leaves, crumbled
½	teaspoon black peppercorns
½	ounce dried porcini mushrooms, rinsed (optional)
4–4 ¼	pounds beef chuck roast, trimmed and cut into 2-inch chunks (see the illustrations on page 148)
	Salt and ground black pepper
4	tablespoons unsalted butter, cut into 4 pieces
⅓	cup unbleached all-purpose flour
1 ¾	cups low-sodium chicken broth
1 ½	cups water
1	bottle (750 ml) wine, red Burgundy or Pinot Noir
1	teaspoon tomato paste

ONION AND MUSHROOM GARNISH

36	frozen pearl onions (about 7 ounces)
1	tablespoon unsalted butter
1	tablespoon sugar
½	teaspoon salt
10	ounces white mushrooms, whole if small, halved if medium, quartered if large
2	tablespoons brandy
3	tablespoons minced fresh parsley leaves

1. FOR THE BRAISE: Bring the salt pork, reserved salt pork rind, and 3 cups water to a boil in a medium saucepan over high heat. Boil 2 minutes, then drain well.

2. Cut two 22-inch lengths of cheesecloth. Following the illustrations on page 159, wrap the parsley, thyme, onions, carrots, garlic, bay leaves, peppercorns, porcini mushrooms (if using), and blanched salt pork rind in the cheesecloth and set in an large ovenproof Dutch oven. Adjust the oven rack to the lower-middle position and heat the oven to 300 degrees.

3. Put the salt pork in a 12-inch skillet and set the skillet over medium heat; sauté until lightly brown and crisp, about 12 minutes. With a slotted spoon, transfer the salt pork to the Dutch oven. Pour off all but 2 teaspoons fat and reserve. Dry the beef thoroughly on paper towels, then season it generously with salt and pepper to taste. Increase the heat to high and brown half of the beef in a single layer, turning once or twice, until deep brown, about 7 minutes; transfer the browned beef to the Dutch oven. Pour ½ cup water into the skillet and scrape the pan with a wooden spoon to loosen the browned bits. When the pan bottom is clean, pour the liquid into the Dutch oven.

4. Return the skillet to high heat and add the 2 teaspoons reserved pork fat; swirl to coat the pan bottom. When the fat begins to smoke, brown the remaining beef in a single layer, turning once or twice, until deep brown, about 7 minutes; transfer the browned beef to the Dutch oven. Pour ½ cup water into the skillet and scrape the pan with a wooden spoon to loosen the browned bits. When the pan bottom is clean, pour the liquid into the Dutch oven.

5. Set the now-empty skillet over medium heat and add the butter. When the foaming subsides, whisk in the flour until evenly moistened and pasty. Cook, whisking constantly, until the mixture has

INGREDIENTS: Does It Have to Be Burgundy?

Beef Burgundy is rightfully made with true Burgundy wine. This means a red wine made from the Pinot Noir grape grown in the French province of Burgundy. Characteristically, these wines are medium-bodied but also deep, rich, and complex, with earthy tones and a reticent fruitiness. They are also expensive. Throughout our testing, into each batch of beef Burgundy, we emptied a $12 bottle of Burgundy—the least expensive we could find. Quite frankly, it was making outstanding beef Burgundies. Nonetheless, we tried more costly, higher-quality Burgundies and found that they bettered the dish—a $30 bottle gave a stellar, rousing performance. We thought it worth exploring other wines, but, wanting to remain faithful to the spirit of the dish, we limited ourselves to Pinot Noirs made on the West Coast of the United States, which are slightly less expensive than French Burgundies. We made beef Burgundies with domestic Pinot Noirs at three different price points, and even the least expensive wine—a $9 bottle—was perfectly acceptable, although its

flavors were simpler and less intriguing than those of its Burgundian counterpart.

Both the Burgundies and the Pinot Noirs exhibited the same pattern—that is, as the price of the wine increased, so did the depth, complexity, and roundness of the sauce. We can advise with some confidence to set your price, then seek out a wine—either Burgundy or Pinot Noir—that matches it. But if your allegiance is to a true Burgundy, be warned that they can be difficult to find because production is relatively limited. We also caution you to beware of several very inexpensive mass-produced wines from California of questionable constitutions that are sold as "Burgundy." They are usually made from a blend of grape varieties, and whether or not they actually contain so much as a drop of Pinot Noir is a mystery. We made beef Burgundy with one of these wines, and it resulted in a fleeting, one-dimensional, fruity, sweet sauce that, though palatable, lacked the deep, lavish flavors we have come to expect in a beef Burgundy.

---

toasty aroma and resembles light-colored peanut butter, about 5 minutes. Gradually whisk in the broth and water. Increase the heat to medium-high and bring to a simmer, stirring frequently, until thickened. Pour the mixture into the Dutch oven. Add 3 cups of the wine, the tomato paste, and salt and pepper to taste to the Dutch oven and stir to combine. Set the Dutch oven over high heat and bring to a boil. Cover and place the pot in the oven. Cook until the meat is tender, 2½ to 3 hours.

6. Remove the Dutch oven from the oven and,

TRIMMING THE RIND FROM SALT PORK

Salt pork is usually sold with rind, and you must remove this tough rind before slicing or chopping the salt pork. Steady the salt pork with one hand, and with the other hand slide the blade of a sharp chef's knife between the rind and the fat, using a wide sawing motion to cut away the rind in one piece.

using tongs, transfer the vegetable and herb bouquet to a mesh strainer set over the pot. Press the liquid back into the pot and discard the bouquet. With a slotted spoon, transfer the beef to a medium bowl; set aside. Allow the braising liquid to settle about 15 minutes, then, with wide shallow spoon, skim the fat off the surface and discard.

7. Bring the liquid in the Dutch oven to a boil over medium-high heat on the stovetop. Simmer briskly, stirring occasionally to ensure that the bottom is not burning, until the sauce is reduced to about 3 cups and thickened to the consistency of heavy cream, 15 to 25 minutes.

8. PREPARE THE GARNISH: While the sauce is reducing, bring the pearl onions, butter, sugar, ¼ teaspoon of the salt, and ½ cup water to a boil in a medium skillet over high heat. Cover, reduce the heat to medium-low, and simmer, shaking the pan occasionally, until the onions are tender, about 5 minutes. Uncover, increase the heat to high, and simmer until all liquid evaporates, about 3 minutes. Add the mushrooms and the remaining ¼ teaspoon salt. Cook, stirring occasionally, until the liquid released by the mushrooms evaporates and the vegetables are browned and glazed, about 5 minutes. Transfer the vegetables to a large plate and set aside. Add ¼ cup water to the skillet and stir with a wooden spoon to loosen the browned bits. When

the pan bottom and sides are clean, add the liquid to the reducing sauce.

9. When the sauce in the Dutch oven has reduced to about 3 cups and thickened to the consistency of heavy cream, reduce the heat to medium-low. Stir the beef, mushrooms and onions (and any accumulated juices), the remaining wine, and the brandy. Cover the pot and cook until just heated through, 5 to 8 minutes. Adjust the seasonings with salt and pepper to taste and serve, sprinkling the individual servings with some of the minced parsley.

MAKING THE VEGETABLE AND HERB BOUQUET

1. Cut two 22-inch lengths of cheesecloth and unfold each piece once lengthwise so that each forms a 2-ply, 22 by 8-inch piece.

2. Lay the cheesecloth in a medium bowl, stacking the sheets. Place the designated ingredients in the cheesecloth-lined bowl.

3. Gather together the edges of the cheesecloth and fasten them securely with kitchen twine. Trim any excess cheesecloth with scissors if necessary.

➤ VARIATION
Do-Ahead Beef Burgundy

The braise can be made a day or two ahead, and the sauce, along with the onion and mushroom garnish, can be completed the day you intend to serve the dish.

1. Follow recipe for Beef Burgundy through step 5. Using tongs, transfer the vegetable and herb bouquet to a mesh strainer set over the Dutch oven. Press the liquid back into pot and discard the bouquet. Let the beef cool to room temperature in the braising liquid in the Dutch oven. The braise can be kept covered in the refrigerator for 1 to 2 days.

2. To complete the dish, use a slotted spoon to skim the congealed fat off the top and discard. Set the pot over medium-high heat and bring to a simmer. With a slotted spoon, transfer the beef to a medium bowl and set aside. Simmer the sauce briskly, stirring occasionally to ensure that the bottom is not burning, until reduced to about 3 cups and thickened to the consistency of heavy cream.

3. Continue with the recipe from step 8.

BEEF STROGANOFF

BEEF STROGANOFF LOOKS LIKE A STEW. IT tastes like a stew. It is served like a stew. But it is not a stew. Deconstructed, beef stroganoff is a simple sauté and pan sauce combo in which meat and mushrooms are sautéed and then held on the side while a quick sauce is made. They are all reunited and joined with egg noodles in holy matrimony. The meat that goes into a stroganoff is tender stuff like filet mignon and sirloin rather than braising cuts such as chuck or brisket, which need time and patience to grow tender under a lid.

Stroganoff is nevertheless a tough dish to get right for a couple of reasons. Because stroganoff is a pan sauce, it is a light proposition and hasn't time to gather the intensity of flavor a braise might; and, since it is served over noodles, the sauce must be thinner and cleaner than a microreduced buttery pan sauce. Matters in the flavor department would be much simplified by the addition of homemade demi-glace—a highly concentrated sauce that takes hours to reduce—clearly not an option—and the easier alternative of canned chicken broth plus 10 minutes or so of cooking doesn't do it, either.

Beef, mushrooms, onions, and sour cream are classic ingredients in a stroganoff. Beyond that there seem to be no standard seasonings, probably because the dish itself did not evolve naturally from Russian cuisine but was introduced to the Russian aristocracy by a French chef. The sour cream seems to have been thrown in as an afterthought to put a Russian spin on things.

There is an almost desperate "anything goes" feeling in some recipes for beef stroganoff. Different combinations of ingredients such as prepared mustard, paprika, Worcestershire sauce, cider vinegar, tomato paste, brown sugar, brandy, and sherry ultimately antagonized each other. Still, our impulse, like everyone else's, was to use as many flavor-building ingredients as possible in hopes of getting a little flirtation into the whole affair.

We first set up a basic recipe using 1 pound of beef, 6 ounces of mushrooms, ¼ quarter cup of minced onions, 1 tablespoon of flour, 1 cup of chicken broth, and ½ cup of sour cream, then went off to test cuts of beef (all steaks, really). Though we knew beef tenderloin was favored in stroganoff, we thought other steak cuts might bring more flavor to the pan. Toward that end, we made four stroganoffs, sautéing strips of sirloin, rib eye, blade steak, and tenderloin. Our assumption proved faulty. While the improved flavor of fattier cuts is striking in a simple grilled format, it was altogether lost in a sauce rich with dairy. The other steaks were also unpleasantly chewy and at odds with the plush, velvety sauce and mushrooms, and the lush noodles.

Many recipes for stoganoff flour the meat to promote browning and thicken the sauce. But flouring left the sautéed meat lying in the sauce look like swathed mummies. What worked far better was adding a single tablespoon of flour to the pan after the meat had been sautéed. We also found that broader strips of tenderloin (we were cutting them about a half inch thick to begin) often had a livery taste—even with the sour cream. By slicing them as thin as ⅛ inch, we were able to reduce the total weight of the meat to ¾ pound and surround each bite with flavorful browned edges. Since most beef stroganoff recipes feature strips of meat that appear to have been browned very little, if at all, we thought it would be only be fair to try a batch of meat tossed in a skillet with no attention to browning. Sure enough, it looked just like the stroganoff we had seen in hotel chafing dishes. Unfortunately, it tasted like them, too.

As for the mushrooms, we knew they would benefit from hot, dry heat, which would brown their edges and leave their insides silky and flavorful. There is no greater injustice wrought upon a mushroom than being sliced thin and boiled off in a sauce. We also wanted the mushrooms to have a presence equal to the beef, so we decided to use button mushrooms and quarter or halve them (depending on their size) rather than slice them.

We knew that the fond, or browned bits left in the pan after sautéing, would be critical to a flavorful sauce and that the sequence of the sauté would be key. We found it was better to start with the mushrooms (which, by the time they were finished, had barely colored the pan bottom), remove them from the pan, and then sauté the beef. By the time the beef had been browned and set aside with the mushrooms, a beautiful brown film covered the pan bottom. It needed only to be lifted from the pan with a little liquid, or deglazed. Here red wine did the job nicely.

Aromatics were up next. We gave minced onions and shallots equal play. Surprisingly, though we favor sautéed shallots over onions in sauces 90 percent of the time for their mildness, in this case we found the shallots muted and ineffective and liked the bright flavor of the onions.

Now came the gypsy caravan of flavorings and the finishing touch of liquid. In different combinations, singly, doubly, and in groups, we tried all the seasonings listed earlier. Despite our desire to pump flavor into the sauce, the only survivors were 1 teaspoon of tomato paste and 1½ teaspoons of dark brown sugar. We kept just a splash of chicken stock and added two jiggers of red wine and a big dollop of sour cream. This at last was stroganoff, recognizably retro, and, in the company of a bowl of hot, buttered noodles, pretty irresistible.

Beef Stroganoff

SERVES 4

Stroganoff is an elegant dish made with tender pieces of beef tenderloin and finished with a swirl of sour cream. Sour cream can curdle if added directly to hot liquid. To prevent this, temper the sour cream by stirring a little of the stewing liquid into it and then stirring the warmed sour cream mixture back into the pan of stroganoff. Buttered egg noodles are the classic accompaniment. You'll need about ½ pound of noodles.

2	teaspoons vegetable oil
12	ounces button mushrooms, cleaned and halved or quartered depending on their size
	Salt and ground black pepper
¾	pound beef tenderloin (about 2 filets), cut into ⅛-inch strips (see the illustrations at right)
¾	cup dry red wine
1	tablespoon unsalted butter
1	small onion, minced (½ cup)
1	teaspoon tomato paste
1½	teaspoons dark brown sugar
1	tablespoon unbleached all-purpose flour
½	cup low-sodium chicken broth
⅓	cup sour cream

1. Heat 1 teaspoon of the oil in a heavy 12-inch skillet over high heat until shimmering. Add the mushrooms and cook over high heat, without stirring, for 30 seconds, thereafter shaking the pan occasionally until the mushrooms have browned lightly, about 3 minutes more. Season the mushrooms with salt and pepper to taste and transfer them to a large bowl.

2. Return the pan to high heat, add the remaining 1 teaspoon oil, and swirl the pan to coat the bottom. Place the tenderloin strips carefully in the pan in a single layer, taking care that the strips are not touching, and sear them without turning until the meat is well browned on one side, 2 to 2½ minutes. Turn the strips and sear the other side until well browned, about 1 minute more. Season the meat with salt and pepper to taste and transfer it to the bowl with the mushrooms.

3. Return the pan to high heat and add ¼ cup of the wine to deglaze the pan, scraping up the browned bits on the pan bottom with a wooden spoon. Simmer and reduce the wine until it is syrupy and glazed, about 30 seconds. Transfer the glaze to the bowl with the mushrooms and beef, using a rubber spatula to scrape the pan clean.

4. Set the pan over medium heat and add the butter. When the butter foams, add the onion, tomato paste, and sugar, and cook, stirring frequently, until the onion is lightly browned, about 3 minutes. Stir in the flour until well incorporated. Add the remaining ½ cup wine and the broth and whisk vigorously until the liquid simmers and has thickened, about 1½ minutes. Add any accumulated juices from the mushrooms and the beef to the sauce and simmer just to incorporate. Stir about ½ cup of the hot sauce into the sour cream, then stir the mixture back into the sauce. Add the mushrooms

SLICING TENDERLOIN FILET

For stroganoff, we usually buy two 6-ounce tenderloin filets and cut them into thin strips as shown.

1. Turn each filet on its side and cut it in half lengthwise to yield two ½-inch-thick medallions.

2. Cut the medallions across the grain into ⅛-inch strips.

and beef, and heat to just warm through, about 1 minute. Season with salt and pepper to taste. Serve over buttered egg noodles, if desired.

VEAL STEW

WITH A PERFUMED FLAVOR AND DELICATE texture, veal stew is a welcome change of pace from beef. The most familiar veal stew is a snowy white, French blanquette de veau, which demands that the veal, sauce, and colorless vegetables (pearl onions and mushrooms) all be prepared separately. Less well known is an Italian recipe in which the veal is first browned, then the stew is built progressively in the same pot, like a beef stew (see page 148 for details on this recipe.) We began by looking at which cuts are appropriate for veal stew.

Researching multiple recipes and options at the meat counter left us with three possible cuts—veal breast, shoulder, and round. Tasters found that meat cut from the round tasted dry and tough, while meat cut from the breast was extremely chewy (and was difficult to cut into stew meat). Unanimously choosing veal shoulder for its tenderness and ability to remain juicy, we found it easy to buy a 2-pound boneless veal shoulder roast and cut the stew meat ourselves. We trimmed between 4 and 8 ounces of fat and gristle from the roast and the resulting meat cooked more evenly than any precut generic veal stew meat we could buy.

It was time to start developing the first of our two very different veal stew recipes. Beyond the multiple pots and hours of cooking, it is the clean flavor and delicate, creamy texture that make a traditional blanquette de veau memorable. Wanting to make a similarly delicate and elegant stew, we directed our focus on how to trim both the cooking time and number of dirty dishes as we developed an updated variation.

Traditional blanquette recipes begin by blanching the veal for several minutes to rid it of a gray "scum" that would otherwise mar the pristine, white-colored stew (this is not an issue if the meat is browned). More modern blanquette recipes that omit this step chose one of three options: Add the raw veal right to the stew liquid, cook the veal gently in batches with butter over low heat and then add it to the stew, or sweat the veal with butter in a covered pot over low heat, rinse it, and then add the meat to the stew. We tried all three modern options as well as the traditional method.

Adding the raw meat straight to the stew was the worst option, producing an overwhelming stinky flavor and dirty, gray-colored sauce. The gently sweated meat had an awful, chewy texture and also produced a dull-colored sauce. Cooking the meat with a little butter in batches tasted OK, yet it turned the sauce an odd khaki color. Blanching the veal for a few minutes in simmering water was the clear favorite because it yielded a pure white sauce and wonderfully clean, delicate veal flavor. After bringing the veal and water to a simmer in a Dutch oven, we found it only needed to be simmered for five minutes for all of the scum to be released. (The scum will float to the top of the water and it is necessary to pour it off before completely draining the veal into a colander.) A quick rinse also ensures that any residual scum doesn't make its way into the stew.

With the blanched, rinsed veal resting off to the side, we rinsed out the Dutch oven and returned it to the stove to begin building the stew. Traditional blanquettes simmer the blanched veal in a plain broth until tender, then strain off the broth and turn it into a sauce. Wanting to simplify this process, we decided to simmer the veal in the sauce (like a traditional stew). We softened mild shallots in a little butter before adding some flour and chicken broth. Tasters liked the addition of either dry white wine or dry vermouth. We rounded out the flavors with garlic and bay leaves, then stirred in the blanched meat and let the stew cook in a moderate (300-degree) oven until tender.

Since the veal required at least 1½ hours to become tender, we needed to stir the vegetables in partway through the cooking to prevent them from overcooking and turning to mush. We found the clean, sweet flavors of fennel, carrots, and peas compatible with the veal, shallots, and white wine. Finished with fresh tarragon, parsley, and a splash of fresh cream, this elegant, stew is a simplified, flavorful alternative to the classic blanquette.

Veal Stew with Fennel, Tarragon, and Cream

SERVES 6

Serve this elegant, updated rendition of classic veal stew with buttered egg noodles or mashed potatoes.

2	pounds boneless veal shoulder roast, trimmed and cut into 1-inch pieces
3	tablespoons unsalted butter
4	large shallots, minced
	Salt
2	medium garlic cloves, minced or pressed through a garlic press (about 2 teaspoons)
2	tablespoons unbleached all-purpose flour
¾	cup dry white wine or dry vermouth
1 ½	cups low-sodium chicken broth
2	bay leaves
1	large head fennel, fronds and stems discarded, root end trimmed, halved, cored, and cut into ¼-inch-thick strips (see the illustrations at right)
3	medium carrots, peeled and sliced ¼ inch thick
1	cup frozen peas
½	cup heavy cream
1	tablespoon minced fresh parsley leaves
2	teaspoons minced fresh tarragon leaves
2	teaspoons lemon juice from 1 lemon
	Ground black pepper

1. Adjust an oven rack to the middle position and heat the oven to 300 degrees.

2. Bring the veal and 8 cups water to a simmer in a large ovenproof Dutch oven over high heat. Reduce the heat to medium–low and simmer for 5 minutes. Pour off any foamy scum, then drain the veal in a colander, discarding the liquid. Rinse the veal briefly and set aside to drain.

3. Rinse and dry the Dutch oven and return it to the stove. Melt the butter in the Dutch oven over medium heat. Add the shallots and ¼ teaspoon salt and cook until the shallots have softened, 3 to 5 minutes. Stir in the garlic and cook until fragrant, 30 seconds. Stir in the flour and cook for 30 seconds. Add the wine, scraping up any bits from the pan bottom with a wooden spoon; simmer until thickened.

Increase the heat to high and add the broth, stirring constantly and scraping the pan edges. Add the bay leaves and meat and bring to a simmer. Cover and place the pot in the oven. Cook for 1 hour.

4. Remove the pot from the oven and stir in the fennel and carrots. Cover the pot and return it to the oven. Cook until the meat and vegetables are just tender, 30 to 45 minutes.

PREPARING FENNEL

1. Trim and discard the feathery fronds and stems.

2. Trim a thick slice from the base and remove the blemished outer layers. Cut the bulb in half through the base and use a paring knife to remove the pyramid-shaped core in each half.

3. Lay the cored fennel flat on a work surface and cut in half crosswise, holding the knife parallel to the work surface. Cut the fennel lengthwise into ¼-inch-thick strips.

5. Remove the pot from the oven. Stir in the peas, cream, parsley, and tarragon. Cover and let stand for 5 minutes. Remove and discard the bay leaves and stir in the lemon juice. Season with salt and pepper to taste and serve immediately.

Italian Veal Stew

OSSO BUCO, BRAISED VEAL SHANKS, IS ONE of Italy's most renowned dishes. Veal shanks can be large, however, and we've found that such generous, albeit rustic, portions can actually be limiting—you must serve everyone one shank, which is often too much food. Our goal? To create an osso buco-style stew using boneless veal stew meat.

We started with a 2-pound boneless veal shoulder roast and cut the stew meat ourselves. Following our own instructions for osso buco (page 207), we immediately noticed that shanks and shoulder stew meat do not brown similarly. The shanks are able to achieve a nice, dark brown crust; the boneless veal shoulder meat, on the other hand, released a lot of moisture and steamed rather than browned. Wanting to avoid having to sear the meat in many small batches and risk burning the pot, we found an easier approach: Cook the meat in just two batches over high heat, stirring often and letting the juices reduce and caramelize. Stirring is usually discouraged when browning meat; however, we found that, in this case, it helped the juices evaporate more quickly and redistribute the intense heat throughout the pot. Equally important, the meat never achieves a dark, crisp crust, but rather becomes coated with a uniform, golden brown glaze.

Following our osso buco recipe but using our glazed stew meat, we next found it necessary back off on the wine. Veal shanks have a much stronger, richer flavor than boneless veal shoulder, which could not tolerate more than ¾ cup of dry white wine. We also found that we had to reduce the amount of broth and add a little flour in order to thicken the sauce to more of a stew-like consistency. Last, rather than sprinkling each portion of the finished stew with the gremolata, as is done with traditional osso buco, we simply stirred this

mixture of minced garlic, lemon zest, and parsley into the stew before serving. Ecco! We had deconstructed osso buco and in the de-shanking created a succulent stew.

Italian Veal Stew

SERVES 6

Serve over polenta, mashed potatoes, risotto, or buttered noodles.

STEW
2	pounds boneless veal shoulder roast, trimmed and cut into 1-inch pieces
	Salt and ground black pepper
3	tablespoons olive oil
2	medium onions, cut into ½-inch dice
2	medium carrots, peeled and cut into ½-inch dice
2	medium celery ribs, cut into ½-inch dice
6	medium garlic cloves, minced or pressed through a garlic press (about 2 tablespoons)
2	tablespoons unbleached all-purpose flour
¾	cup dry white wine
1 ½	cups low-sodium chicken broth
1	(14.5-ounce) can diced tomatoes, drained
2	bay leaves

GREMOLATA
1	large garlic clove, minced or pressed through a garlic press (about 1 ½ teaspoons)
2	teaspoons minced lemon zest
¼	cup minced fresh parsley leaves

1. FOR THE STEW: Adjust the oven rack to the middle position and heat the oven to 300 degrees.

2. Season the veal generously with salt and pepper to taste. Heat 1 tablespoon of the oil in a large ovenproof Dutch oven over high heat until smoking. Add half of the veal and cook, stirring frequently, until it has released its juices and is lightly browned, 4 to 6 minutes. Transfer the veal to plate and set aside. Add another tablespoon oil to the pot and repeat with the remaining veal. Transfer the second batch of veal to the plate.

3. Add the remaining 1 tablespoon oil to the now-empty pot and heat it over medium heat until

shimmering. Add the onions, carrots, and celery and cook, scraping the pot bottom occasionally with a wooden spoon, until the onions are soft and lightly browned, 6 to 10 minutes. Add the garlic and cook until fragrant, 10 to 30 seconds. Add the flour and cook for 20 seconds. Add the wine, scraping up any bits on the pot bottom, and simmer until thickened. Increase the heat to high and add the broth, stirring constantly and scraping the pan edges. Add the tomatoes, bay leaves, and meat along with any accumulated juices on the plate, and bring to a simmer. Cover and place the pot in the oven. Cook for 1½ to 1¾ hours, until the veal is tender

4. For the gremolata: Combine the garlic, lemon zest, and parsley together in a small bowl and set aside.

5. Remove the pot from the oven and stir in the gremolata. Let stand, covered, for 5 minutes. Season with salt and pepper to taste and serve immediately.

Irish Stew

IRISH STEW IS A SIMPLE LAMB STEW THAT has sustained countless generations. At its most basic, Irish stew is made with just lamb, onions, potatoes, and water. There's no browning or pre-cooking. The raw ingredients are layered in the pot and cooked until tender.

We prepared several variations of this basic dish and identified a couple of problems. First, by modern standards, it is bland. With no browning and so few ingredients, authentic Irish stew can't even compete with a good bowl of beef stew. Second, the potatoes break down and lose their shape after several hours of simmering. Although the potatoes do thicken the stew, modern palates generally prefer vegetables that are not so overcooked.

Our goals for this recipe were clear. While remaining true to the dish's humble roots—lamb and potatoes—we wanted to pump up the flavors (especially of the lamb) and find a way to thicken the stew without overcooking the potatoes.

We started with boneless lamb shoulder meat,

figuring that the equivalent cut had worked well with beef stews. We browned the meat, replaced the water with chicken broth, added carrots and Worcestershire sauce for flavor (this ingredient was suggested in a number of recipes), and thickened everything with flour. The results were better but not great. Browning helped intensify the lamb's flavor, but the chicken broth, carrots, and Worcestershire sauce tended to diminish this effect. The flour was a good idea, though, creating a nicely textured sauce.

For the next test, we browned the chunks of boneless shoulder meat, removed the meat from the pan, added some onions, and cooked them until tender. We added some flour for thickening power and then some water. We returned the meat to the pot and let the stew cook for an hour before adding the potatoes (so they would not overcook). This stew was better—there were few distractions—but the lamb flavor was a bit weak. With so little else in the pot, the lamb has to carry the day, and this meat was not up to the task.

We started to think that shoulder meat was the wrong choice. We tested some boneless leg of lamb (the cut commonly sold as stew meat), and the results were extremely disappointing. The meat cooked up dry, tough, and not very flavorful. This cut has far less fat than the shoulder, making it a poor choice for stewing.

We were ready to throw in the towel when James Beard came to the rescue. In the course of our research, we found his recipe for Irish stew, which called for leaving the meat on the bone. We tested his recipe and were pleasantly surprised. The water and lamb bones had, in fact, created a rich-tasting stock. The meat itself was especially tasty, no doubt because it was cooked on the bone. Cooking whole chops (as Beard suggested) made this dish seem more like a braise than a stew. Also, Beard did not brown the meat, a step we had grown fond of in earlier tests.

We took a Chinese cleaver and cut shoulder chops into 2-inch pieces. Although this idea seemed promising, the hacked-up bones created some small splinters, which tasters felt were unappealing and even dangerous. Our next idea was to remove the meat from the bones and cut it into stew-size chunks. The meat would be browned and then removed from the pot so that the onions could be cooked. When the meat was added back to the stew pot, we would throw in the uncooked lamb bones as well. As we had hoped, this strategy gave us excellent results.

Cutting the lamb meat into medium-size chunks made this dish seem like a stew. Browning added flavor to the meat as well as the stew. The bones, which still had bits of meat attached to them, created a rich, heady sauce. Some tasters liked to gnaw on the meaty bones; others felt that bones have no place in a finished stew and should be discarded just before serving. The choice is yours.

We found it worthwhile to buy shoulder chops from the butcher. In most supermarkets, lamb shoulder chops are thin—often about ½ inch thick. At this thickness, the stew meat is too insubstantial. Ideally, we like chops cut 1½ inches thick, but 1-inch chops will suffice.

We had a few more tests to run. Although traditional recipes often layer raw onions into the pot with the meat, potatoes, and water, we knew that cooking the onions would be key. Tasters had liked stews made with softened onions, but further tests proved that browning the onions added even more depth to the final dish.

We generally prefer low-starch, red-skinned potatoes in stews because they hold their shape well. However, in this dish the potatoes traditionally act as a thickener. Even though we had added some flour to the browned onions to thicken the sauce, we wondered if a higher-starch potato would be more appropriate in Irish stew. We decided to try this dish with russets and Yukon Golds as well as red potatoes.

Russets fell apart into a soupy mess and were universally panned. The red potatoes were fine, but the Yukon Golds stole the show. Their buttery, rich flavor was appreciated by tasters in this simple stew. Tasters also liked the soft, creamy texture of the Yukon Gold potatoes.

Thyme and parsley are often added to Irish stew, and we saw no need to deviate from tradition. The parsley is best stirred in just before serving to maintain its bright, fresh flavor. At last, a hearty Irish stew worth eating.

Irish Stew

SERVES 6

The secret to the success of this Irish stew is the addition of lamb bones to the pot. Bone-in shoulder chops weighing 4½ pounds will yield about 2½ pounds of boneless meat as well as a pile of bones. Some meat will cling to the bones, and the choice is yours whether to remove the bones just before serving for a more refined dish or to include them for a casual eating experience. True Irish stew includes just meat and potatoes with some onions. We've added a recipe for a popular variation with carrots and turnips.

4 ½	pounds lamb shoulder chops, 1 to 1 ½ inches thick
	Salt and ground black pepper
3	tablespoons vegetable oil
3	medium-large onions, chopped coarse (about 5 cups)
4	tablespoons unbleached all-purpose flour
3	cups water
1	teaspoon dried thyme
6	medium Yukon Gold or red potatoes (about 2 pounds), peeled and cut into 1-inch cubes
¼	cup minced fresh parsley leaves

1. Adjust the oven rack to the lower-middle position and heat the oven to 300 degrees. Cut the meat from the bones and reserve the bones. Trim the meat of excess fat and cut it into 1½-inch cubes. Season the meat generously with salt and pepper to taste.

2. Heat 1 tablespoon of the oil in a large oven-proof Dutch oven over medium-high heat until shimmering. Add half the meat to the pot so that the individual pieces are close together but not touching. Cook, not moving the pieces until the side touching the pot is well browned, 2 to 3 minutes. Using tongs, turn each piece and continue cooking until most sides are well browned, about 5 minutes longer. Transfer the meat to a medium bowl, add another 1 tablespoon oil to the pot, and swirl to coat the pan bottom. Brown the remaining lamb in the same manner; transfer the meat to the bowl and set aside.

3. Reduce the heat to medium, add the remain-

ing tablespoon oil, and swirl to coat the pan bottom. Add the onions and ¼ teaspoon salt and cook, stirring frequently and vigorously, scraping the pot bottom with a wooden spoon to loosen any browned bits, until the onions have softened, about 5 minutes. Add the flour and stir until the onions are evenly coated, 1 to 2 minutes.

4. Stir in 1½ cups of the water, scraping the pan bottom and edges with the wooden spoon to loosen the remaining browned bits. Gradually add the remaining 1½ cups water, stirring constantly and scraping the pot edges to dissolve the flour. Add the thyme and 1 teaspoon salt and bring to a simmer. Add the bones and then the meat and accumulated juices in the bowl. Return to a simmer, cover the pot, and place it in the oven. Cook for 1 hour.

5. Remove the pot from the oven and place the potatoes on top. Cover, return the pot to the oven, and cook until the meat is tender, about 1 hour. If serving immediately, stir the potatoes into the liquid, wait for 5 minutes, and spoon off any fat that rises to the top. (The stew can be covered and refrigerated for up to 3 days. Spoon off the hardened fat and bring back to a simmer over medium-low heat.)

6. Stir in the parsley and adjust the seasonings. Remove the bones, if desired. Serve immediately.

➤ VARIATIONS

Irish Stew with Carrots and Turnips

Follow the recipe for Irish Stew, substituting ½ pound carrots, peeled and sliced ¼ inch thick, and ½ pound turnips, peeled and cut into 1-inch cubes, for 1 pound of the potatoes. Proceed as directed.

Italian-Style Lamb Stew with Green Beans, Tomatoes, and Basil

This peasant-style lamb stew has its roots in Sicily. The approach to preparing it, though, is identical to that of Irish stew. Garlic, wine, and rosemary add the flavors of the Mediterranean, and tomatoes and green beans replace some of the potatoes to lighten the dish.

4 ½	pounds lamb shoulder chops, 1 to 1 ½ inches thick
	Salt and ground black pepper
3	tablespoons vegetable oil
3	medium-large onions, chopped coarse (about 5 cups)
3	medium garlic cloves, minced or pressed through a garlic press (about 1 tablespoon)
4	tablespoons unbleached all-purpose flour
½	cup dry white wine
1 ¾	cups water
1	tablespoon minced fresh rosemary leaves
1	(14.5-ounce) can diced tomatoes
4	medium Yukon Gold or red potatoes (about 1 ¼ pounds), peeled and cut into 1-inch cubes
¾	pound green beans, ends trimmed and halved
¼	cup minced fresh basil leaves

1. Adjust the oven rack to the lower-middle position and heat the oven to 300 degrees. Cut the meat from the bones and reserve the bones. Trim the meat of excess fat and cut it into 1½-inch cubes. Season the meat generously with salt and pepper to taste.

2. Heat 1 tablespoon of the oil in a large oven-proof Dutch oven over medium-high heat until shimmering. Add half of the meat to the pot so that the individual pieces are close together but not touching. Cook, not moving the pieces until the side touching the pot is well browned, 2 to 3 minutes. Using tongs, turn each piece and continue cooking until most sides are well browned, about 5 minutes longer. Transfer the meat to a medium bowl, add another 1 tablespoon oil to the pot, and swirl to coat the pan bottom. Brown the remaining lamb in the same manner; transfer the meat to the bowl and set aside.

3. Reduce the heat to medium, add the remaining 1 tablespoon oil, and swirl to coat the pot bottom. Add the onions and ¼ teaspoon salt and cook, stirring frequently and vigorously, scraping the pot bottom with a wooden spoon to loosen any browned bits, until the onions have softened, about 5 minutes. Add the garlic and cook until fragrant, about 30 seconds. Add the flour and stir until the onions are evenly coated, 1 to 2 minutes.

4. Stir in the wine and 1 cup of the water, scraping the pot bottom and edges with the wooden spoon to loosen the remaining browned bits. Gradually add the remaining ¾ cup water, stirring constantly and scraping the pan edges to dissolve

the flour. Add the rosemary, tomatoes, and 1 teaspoon salt and bring to a simmer. Add the bones and then the meat and accumulated juices in the bowl. Return to a simmer, cover the pot, and place it in the oven. Cook for 1 hour.

5. Remove the pot from the oven and place the potatoes and green beans on top. Cover, return the pot to the oven, and cook until the meat is tender, about 1 hour. If serving immediately, spoon off any fat that rises to the top. (The stew can be covered and refrigerated for up to 3 days. Spoon off the hardened fat and bring back to a simmer over medium-low heat.)

6. Stir in the basil and adjust the seasonings. Remove the bones, if desired. Serve immediately.

LAMB TAGINE

TAGINES ARE FUNDAMENTAL TO THE CUISINES of Morocco, Algeria, and other North African countries. The term comes from the earthenware pot with a conical cover that has traditionally been used to prepare stews in this region. Most tagines are highly aromatic and feature a blend of sweet and savory ingredients. Most also contain some sort of fruit (often dried) as well as a heady mixture of ground spices, garlic, and cilantro. Lamb tagines are especially popular, although chicken or vegetable tagines have their advocates, too.

Tagines differ widely from region to region. We decided to start with a classic, slow-simmering recipe typically prepared in Morocco. Our goal was to develop a dish that kept the authentic flavors of Morocco but eliminated most of the fuss.

Many tagine recipes have incredibly long ingredient lists or call for pieces of equipment (such as the above-mentioned earthenware pot) that are unlikely to be found in American kitchens. We wanted to make this dish in a Dutch oven. As for the tagine itself, we wanted the lamb to be moist and succulent. The flavors and aromas would be heady, with a medley of spices blending together harmoniously. A few vegetables and fruits would provide depth and offer the characteristic sweet and savory components.

Given our results with Irish stew, we were leery of using boneless lamb shoulder meat. However, our fears were unfounded. Given the abundance of flavors in this recipe, tasters did not miss the extra oomph provided by the lamb bones we had included in our recipe for Irish stew. Shoulder meat was plenty tasty when seasoned so liberally with the spices of a tagine.

Using our recipe for beef stew as a template, we realized right off that some changes would have to be made. Although we found it necessary to pat the beef dry with paper towels before browning it, the same step caused problems with lamb. Unlike beef, which can be moist, lamb tends to be sticky, and the paper towels "glued" onto it. Picking off the bits of paper was tedious, so we quickly abandoned the step.

Next we focused on the spices. Sweet, warm spices are typically used in North African cooking. Ground cinnamon and ginger were quickly voted in by tasters, as were paprika and cumin. Most everyone liked the addition of some fragrant coriander but tasters were divided about cayenne—some liked a little heat, but others did not. We decided to make this spice optional.

Although some sources suggested tossing the meat with the spices before browning it, we found that this caused the spices to burn. Other recipes add the spices with the liquid, but we found sautéing the spices in a little oil helps to bring out their flavor. It made sense to add the spices to the pot along with the flour—that is, once the onions and garlic were sautéed.

Adding the spices with the flour creates a thick coating on the pan bottom. We found it is essential to scrape the pan bottom when the liquid is added to incorporate the spices into the stew and develop their full flavor potential.

As for the liquid in a tagine, some traditional recipes call for lamb stock. We wondered how canned chicken broth would perform instead. Thankfully, canned chicken broth proved more than adequate in this dish. It adds body to the stew but doesn't compete with the lamb flavor (the way it did in Irish stew). We also tested water in this recipe, but tasters felt that the stew suffered a bit, especially in terms of body.

Tomatoes are another constant in most tagines. We found that canned diced tomatoes provide an acidic contrast that heightens the other flavors. We tested several other vegetables, including summer squash, sweet potatoes, and potatoes. All are delicious, but none seemed essential in a basic tagine—the tomatoes and onions are more than enough. We did like the addition of chickpeas, another common addition to many tagines. Canned chickpeas are fine in this dish; just make sure to add them near the end of the stewing time to keep them from becoming mushy.

As for fruits, we liked the soft texture and sweet flavor of most every dried fruit tested. Apricots were a unanimous favorite, but prunes, raisins, and currants are other good options.

Finally, we found that it's best to use a strong hand with the seasonings. Plenty of garlic and cilantro punch up the flavor and keep the sweet elements in check.

Lamb Tagine

SERVES 6 TO 8

If you can't find boneless lamb shoulder, you can purchase blade or arm chops and remove the meat yourself. Figure that 4½ pounds of chops will yield the 2½ pounds of boneless meat needed for this recipe. A variety of dried fruits—pitted prunes, raisins, golden raisins, or currants—can be substituted for the apricots. Serve this exotic fare over couscous or basmati rice.

2 ½	pounds boneless lamb shoulder, trimmed and cut into 1 ½-inch cubes
	Salt and ground black pepper
3	tablespoons olive oil
2	medium-large onions, chopped coarse (about 3 cups)
4	medium garlic cloves, minced or pressed through a garlic press (about 4 teaspoons)
3	tablespoons unbleached all-purpose flour
1 ½	teaspoons ground cumin
1	teaspoon ground cinnamon
1	teaspoon ground ginger
½	teaspoon ground coriander
⅛	teaspoon cayenne pepper (optional)
2 ¼	cups low-sodium chicken broth
1	(14.5-ounce) can diced tomatoes
1	cup dried apricots, roughly chopped
2	bay leaves
6	fresh cilantro sprigs (optional), plus ¼ cup minced fresh cilantro or parsley leaves
1	(15-ounce) can chickpeas, drained and rinsed
¼	cup toasted slivered almonds (optional)

1. Adjust the oven rack to the lower-middle position and heat the oven to 300 degrees. Season the lamb generously with salt and pepper to taste.

2. Heat 1 tablespoon of the oil in a large ovenproof Dutch oven over medium-high heat until shimmering. Add half of the meat so that the individual pieces are close together but not touching. Cook, not moving the pieces until the side touching the pot is well browned, 2 to 3 minutes. Using tongs, turn each piece and continue cooking until most sides are well browned, about 5 minutes longer. Transfer the meat to a medium bowl, add another 1 tablespoon oil to the pot, and swirl to coat the pan bottom. Brown the remaining lamb in the same manner; transfer the meat to the bowl and set aside.

3. Reduce the heat to medium, add the remaining tablespoon oil, and swirl to coat the pan bottom. Add the onions and ¼ teaspoon salt and cook, stirring frequently and vigorously, scraping the pot bottom with a wooden spoon to loosen any browned bits, until the onions have softened, about 5 minutes. Stir in the garlic and cook until fragrant, about 30 seconds. Add the flour, cumin, cinnamon, ginger, coriander, and cayenne (if using) and stir until the onions are evenly coated and fragrant, 1 to 2 minutes.

4. Gradually add the broth, scraping the pot bottom and edges with the wooden spoon to loosen the remaining browned bits and spices, and stirring until the flour is dissolved and the liquid thick. Stir in the tomatoes, apricots, bay leaves, and cilantro sprigs and bring to a simmer. Add the browned lamb and accumulated juices in the bowl, pushing down the meat to submerge the pieces. Return to a simmer, cover the pot, and place it in the oven. Cook for 1 hour and 15 minutes.

5. Remove the pot from the oven and stir in the chickpeas. Cover and return the pot to the oven. Cook until the meat is tender and the chickpeas

are heated through, about 15 minutes. If serving immediately, spoon off any fat that rises to the top. (The stew can be covered and refrigerated for up to 3 days. Spoon off the hardened fat and bring back to a simmer over medium-low heat.)

6. Discard the bay leaves and cilantro sprigs. Stir in the cilantro leaves and adjust the seasonings. Serve immediately, garnishing each bowl with almonds, if desired.

PORK VINDALOO

VINDALOO HAS ITS ROOTS IN GOA, A REGION on India's western coast that was once a Portuguese colony. Many local dishes, including vindaloo, are a blend of Indian and Portuguese ingredients and techniques. Vindaloo is most often made with pork but sometimes with chicken, beef, or vegetables. The word vindaloo is derived from a combination of Portuguese words vinho, for wine vinegar, and alhos, for garlic. This stew is usually made with a mixture of warm spices (such as cumin and cardamom), chiles (usually in the form of cayenne and paprika), tomatoes, mustard seed, and vinegar.

When this stew is correctly prepared, the meat is tender, the liquid is thick and deep reddish-orange in color, and the flavors are complex. The heat of chiles is tamed by the sweetness of the aromatic spices and the acidity of the tomatoes and vinegar. Onions and garlic add pungency, while mustard seeds lend their unique flavor and crunch.

Most vindaloo recipes we tested were pretty good but we noticed two recurring problems— meat that was dry and/or tough and flavors that were muddled. We decided to start with the meat component in this dish and then test the flavoring option.

Given our results with beef, we figured that pork shoulder would make the best stew. To test this proposition, we stewed various cuts of pork from the shoulder and loin, including several kinds of chops. The shoulder cuts were far superior to the loin. Like beef chuck, pork shoulder has enough fat to keep the meat tender and juicy during the long cooking process.

Pork shoulder is often called Boston butt or Boston shoulder in markets. The picnic also comes from the shoulder. For vindaloo, a boneless Boston butt is your best option because there is less waste. (You can use a picnic roast, but the bone, skin, and thick layer of fat will need to be discarded.) As with beef, we recommend buying a boneless roast and cutting it into cubes yourself. When we purchased precut pork labeled "stew meat," the results were disappointing. The pieces were irregularly sized and seem to have come from several parts of the animal. The resulting stew had pieces that were dry and others that were overcooked.

As expected, we found that browning enhances the flavor of the pork and the stewing liquid. Make sure to leave a little room in the pot between pieces of meat and plan on a total of at least seven minutes to get each pork cube well browned. We found that 2¾ pounds of pork cubes could be browned in two batches in a large Dutch oven and decided to limit the meat to this amount.

Spices are the cornerstones of this stew. Classic recipes included a combination of sweet and hot ground spices. We had the best results when we used small amounts of many spices, rather than larger amounts of fewer spices. For chile flavor, we used sweet paprika and cayenne. To give the stew its characteristic earthy qualities, we added cumin, cardamom, and cloves. The cardamom and cloves are highly sweet and aromatic, while the cumin hits lower, earthier notes. Mustard seeds, a spice used frequently in the cooking of South India, add pungency. Bay leaves bring a deep, herbaceous flavor to this stew and a hit of cilantro just before serving adds freshness.

With our meat and spices chosen, we turned our attention to the liquid component. Most of the recipes we uncovered in our research called for water. The theory is that water is a neutral medium that allows the flavors of the meat and spices to come through as clearly as possible. We wondered, though, if chicken broth would add richness and body to the stewing liquid. We prepared two batches—one with water, the other with canned chicken broth. Tasters felt that the chicken broth added complexity and fullness without calling attention to itself.

Only the flavoring remained. A blend of sweet and sour flavors predominate in this stew. Diced canned tomatoes, with their juices, were far less work than fresh tomatoes (which needed to be peeled and seeded) and the canned tomatoes performed admirably. Two tablespoons of red wine vinegar and a teaspoon of sugar provided the right balance of sour and sweet. We tried adding the vinegar at the end of the cooking time (a step suggested in a few recipes), but tasters felt this stew was harsh. The vinegar needs time to soften and mix with the other flavors.

Although vindaloo is not fiery, it is spicy and is therefore best served over rice to help temper the intensity of flavors. Basmati rice is the ideal partner for this dish but steamed long-grain rice will do nicely.

Pork Vindaloo

SERVES 6 TO 8

This stew of Portuguese ancestry is a full of hot, sweet, spicy, and pungent flavors that come together in a tantalizing way. A piece of boneless Boston butt is easy to trim and cut into cubes. However, a bone-in picnic roast will also work in this recipe. In addition to the bone, a picnic roast typically is covered with skin and a thick layer of fat. When trimmed, a 5-pound picnic roast will yield the same amount of meat (about 2¾ pounds) as a 3-pound Boston butt. Premeasure the flour with the spices to assist in adding them easily to the pot. Serve with basmati rice.

3	pounds boneless Boston butt roast, trimmed and cut into 1 ½-inch cubes
	Salt and ground black pepper
3	tablespoons vegetable oil
3	medium-large onions, chopped coarse (about 5 cups)
8	medium garlic cloves, minced or pressed through a garlic press (scant 3 tablespoons)
3	tablespoons unbleached all-purpose flour
1	tablespoon sweet paprika
¾	teaspoon ground cumin
½	teaspoon ground cardamom
¼	teaspoon cayenne pepper
¼	teaspoon ground cloves
1 ½	cups low-sodium chicken broth
1	(14.5-ounce) can diced tomatoes
2	bay leaves
1	teaspoon sugar
2	tablespoons red wine vinegar
1	tablespoon mustard seeds
¼	cup minced fresh cilantro leaves

1. Adjust the oven rack to lower-middle position and heat oven to 300 degrees. Season the meat generously with salt and pepper to taste. Heat 1 tablespoon of the oil in a large ovenproof Dutch oven over medium-high heat until shimmering. Add half of the meat to the pot so that the individual pieces are close together but not touching. Cook, not moving the pieces until the side touching the pot is well browned, 2 to 3 minutes. Using tongs, turn each piece and continue cooking until most sides are well browned, about 5 minutes longer. Transfer the meat to a medium bowl, add another 1 tablespoon oil to the pot, and swirl to coat the pan bottom. Brown the remaining meat in the same manner; transfer the meat to the bowl and set aside.

2. Reduce the heat to medium, add the remaining tablespoon oil to the now-empty Dutch oven, and swirl to coat the pan bottom. Add the onions and ¼ teaspoon salt and cook, stirring frequently and vigorously, scraping the pot bottom with a wooden spoon to loosen any browned bits, until the onions have softened, about 5 minutes. Stir in the garlic and cook until fragrant, about 30 seconds. Add the flour, paprika, cumin, cardamom, cayenne, and cloves. Stir until the onions are evenly coated and fragrant, 1 to 2 minutes.

3. Gradually add the broth, scraping the pot bottom and edges with the wooden spoon to loosen the remaining browned bits and dissolve the flour. Add the tomatoes, bay leaves, sugar, vinegar, and mustard seeds and bring to a simmer. Add the browned pork and accumulated juices in the bowl, submerging the meat under the liquid. Return to a simmer, cover the pot, and place it in the oven. Cook for 2 hours.

4. Remove the pot from the oven. If serving immediately, spoon off any fat that rises to the top. (The stew can be covered and refrigerated for up to

3 days. Spoon off the hardened fat and bring back to a simmer over medium-low heat.) Remove the bay leaves, stir in the cilantro, and adjust the seasonings. Serve immediately.

PORK TINGA

WHILE THE NAME SOUNDS LIKE A TUESDAY-night special at Trader Vic's, pork tinga is actually a stew-like pork dish from Mexico. Fiercely spiced with chorizo sausage, chipotle chiles, and garlic, this is heady stuff.

Authentic pork tinga is composed of stewed or braised shredded pork shoulder that is simmered with chorizo in a tomato-based "sauce." The texture is fairly dry, more like a saucy stir-fry than a stew. But thinly sliced and sautéed pork could fill its role—not quite authentic, but by our reckoning, the sauce was the star of the show anyhow. By turning this slow-simmering stew into a quick sauté with pan sauce, the recipe changes from an all-day project to a prepared-at-the-last-minute weeknight supper.

We experimented with several different cuts of pork and tenderloin proved the easiest to prepare and the most flavorful. To cook the meat as quickly as possible, we cut it as for a stir-fry, thinly slicing it from a whole tenderloin into cutlets and then "shredding" them into thin strips. (A brief spell in the freezer firmed the pork, making it easier to cut.) The meat browned within a couple of minutes in a large smoking-hot skillet, both improving the pork's overall flavor and lending depth to the final dish.

While the pork was easy to figure out, the sauce took some effort. The best versions of pork tinga we tasted were finely balanced between hot and sweet, suffused with smoky heat from chorizo and chiles and lightened with fresh oregano. Onion, tomatoes, and garlic rounded out the flavors, providing resonance.

The first step, then, was to sauté the chorizo, which would provide the fat necessary to soften the onion and garlic. Chorizo is integral to both Mexican and Spanish cooking, and is now available in many markets. We found it in medium-size links as well as thicker ones. For the skinnier links, we cut them into small pieces; fatter sausages must have the casings removed and the meat diced. The sausage browned quickly and rendered plenty of fat in which to cook the onion and garlic. We sautéed the onion until soft, then added a large amount of garlic so that it maintained its sharp bite.

It was time to address the chipotle chiles, the star of the show. Chipotles, also known as smoked jalapeños, are searingly hot and very smoky tasting. They are available dried as well as rehydrated and packed in an adobo sauce, which includes tomato, onion, oil, and herbs. Whereas the dried chiles must be toasted and rehydrated, the canned version in adobo was ready to use, saving valuable preparation time. Chipotle chiles are very hot and discretion is important. After multiple tries, tasters favored 1½ chiles—any more and it was hard to taste anything beneath the spiciness. Canned diced tomatoes tempered the whole and were easy to use as they needed no prep work outside of a quick drain.

We simmered the sauce for about 10 minutes, just long enough to blend the flavors, break down the tomatoes, and reduce the liquid. We found it necessary to add additional liquid for a smoother flavor and texture and canned chicken broth filled the bill. Where's the pork, you ask? It is not added until the final moments to prevent it overcooking, always a risk when simmering thin pieces of meat.

Pork Tinga
SERVES 4 TO 6

This recipe is best made with thin chorizo sausage, about 1 inch thick. If you can find only plump links, remove the casings and crumble the meat before cooking it. If you can't find chorizo at all, substitute kielbasa, though the flavor won't be quite as intense. Pork tinga can be served over rice, with tortillas, on even tucked into French bread or a roll as a sandwich. If you choose to use it in a sandwich, melt a soft cheese, like Monterey Jack or Colby, over top of the meat.

I   pork tenderloin (I to I ¼ pounds), cut into thin strips (see the illustrations on page I4I)
Salt and ground black pepper

4   teaspoons vegetable oil

8   ounces chorizo, quartered lengthwise and
     then cut crosswise ¼ inch thick

1   medium onion, chopped fine

4   medium garlic cloves, minced or pressed
     through a garlic press (about 4 teaspoons)

1 ½ chipotle chiles in adobo sauce, minced

1   (14.5-ounce) can diced tomatoes, drained

1 ¾ cups low-sodium chicken broth

1   tablespoon brown sugar

1 ½ teaspoons coarsely chopped fresh oregano
     leaves

1. Toss the pork with salt and pepper to taste in a medium bowl. Heat 2 teaspoons of the oil in a large skillet over medium-high heat until smoking. Add the pork in a single layer and cook, without stirring, until browned, 1½ to 2 minutes. Using tongs, flip the pork strips and brown on the second side, 1½ to 2 minutes. Transfer the pork to a bowl and cover with aluminum foil to keep warm.

2. Add the remaining 2 teaspoons oil and the sausage to the now-empty skillet. Cook, stirring infrequently, until lightly browned, about 2 minutes. Add the onion, ¼ teaspoon salt, and 2 tablespoons water to loosen the browned bits on the pan bottom. Cook, stirring frequently, until the onion has softened, 2 to 3 minutes. Stir in the garlic and chipotles and cook until fragrant, about 30 seconds. Add the tomatoes, broth, and brown sugar and bring to a boil. Reduce the heat to medium-low and simmer until the liquid is reduced by half and the flavors have blended, about 10 minutes. Stir in the pork and oregano and cook until just heated through, 2 to 3 minutes. Serve immediately.

POZOLE

POZOLE IS THE MEXICAN NAME FOR BOTH hominy (dried field corn kernels treated with lime and boiled until tender but still chewy) and the stew made with hominy and pork. The stew is made throughout Mexico, in several quite distinct incarnations. Pozole blanco (white pozole) is prepared without any chiles. Pozole rojo (red pozole)

is made with dried red chiles and pozole verde (green pozole) with tomatillos, fresh green chiles, and cilantro. Pozole blanco seems fairly bland compared with the red and green versions, so we decided to focus on the latter two styles.

Whether red or green, pozole should have a complex, richly flavored broth with lots of body. The meat, which is shredded, must be exceedingly tender, while the hominy is toothsome and sweet. A garnish of chopped raw vegetables (lettuce, radishes, and herbs) is added at the table.

Although pozole has become popular in the United States, especially in the Southwest, most American cooks balk at preparing traditional recipes, many of which take 12 hours or more to execute. One of the culprits here is the hominy. If you begin with dried field corn, you must boil it with slaked lime to loosen the hulls. The corn is then washed to remove the hulls, and the germ is pinched off from each kernel by hand. Preparing hominy can take an entire afternoon. We wanted to figure out how to use canned, or precooked, hominy to save time.

Another concern when making pozole is the meat. In Mexico, pozole is traditionally made with cuts rarely sold in American supermarkets (unsmoked pig's feet and pig's head, for example). We would have to find an acceptable substitute.

With these goals in mind, we started work on a red pozole recipe. (We figured that green pozole could be a variation of our red pozole.) The meat issue seemed like the first one to tackle.

Authentic pozole is made with bones from the head, neck, shank, and feet of the pig, supplemented with some boneless meat from the shoulder or loin. We wondered how important bones were to this dish. We prepared one batch with boneless shoulder meat only and another with a bone-in shoulder roast. (We chose the shoulder not only because of availability but because it has consistently proven to be the best cut for stewing.) The liquid of the pozole prepared without bones was weak in flavor and thin in texture. The version made with the bone-in shoulder roast had a distinctive, satisfying pork flavor. It was obvious to tasters that bones are key to developing rich, full-bodied pork flavor. In addition, the bones released a large amount of gelatin that gave the pozole a voluptuous body.

There are two cuts from the shoulder. Since Boston butt is typically sold without the bone, we decided to use the picnic roast. We found that a 5-pound roast, once trimmed of its thick skin and fat, yielded just less than 3 pounds of boneless meat—enough for the stew.

Pozole differs from other meat stews in that the meat is shredded rather than cubed. The meat is usually stewed in large chunks until it is tender enough to pull apart by hand. Just to make sure that tradition is best, we trying cubing the meat and then shredding it after cooking, but this process proved quite tedious. We then tried cooking the roast whole, but this increased the cooking time dramatically. Finally, we tried cutting the meat into large chunks, following the natural lines of the muscles as we removed the meat from the bone. This approach worked best—the stewing time was not excessive (two hours did the trick) and the meat was easy to shred. The sizes and shapes of these chunks varied from 3- by 1-inch strips to 4-inch cubes. From a 5-pound roast we cut eight or nine randomly shaped chunks plus the bones, which had some pieces of meat tightly attached.

Pozole differs from most stews in another regard. Stew meat is typically browned to enhance the flavor of both the meat and the stewing liquid. In many pozole recipes, the meat is simply added raw to the simmering liquid. The reason is simple: Browning inhibits the shredding process and creates a firmer, crustier texture on the outside of each piece of meat. Another choice is to sweat the meat with some onions. We tried both simmering and sweating and found that the latter developed more flavor in the liquid without firming up the texture of the meat. Just make sure to cook the onions first so they will release some liquid and thus prevent the meat from burning or scorching on the outside.

In addition to onion, garlic is the other aromatic ingredient typically added at the outset when making pozole. Once the onion is soft, the garlic goes into the pot and cooks just until fragrant. We found that gentle sweating, rather than browning, works best for the alliums.

Once the meat has been sweated, it's time to add the liquid and other seasonings. We tested water and canned chicken broth (figuring that homemade stock, while always good, wouldn't be necessary in such a highly flavored dish). Although the water was fine, the broth was superior, adding not only depth of flavor but body to the stewing liquid. Tomatoes would also add moisture. Although some versions of red pozole reserve the tomatoes as part of the garnish, our tasters liked the tomatoes cooked right into the stew. The acidity of the tomatoes created a more lively mix. (Note that for green pozole, the tomatoes should be used as a garnish.)

Oregano is another main ingredient in pozole. Several varieties are grown in Mexico, all of which differ from the Mediterranean oregano popular in this country. Mexican oregano does not have the anise compounds found in Mediterranean varieties. Its flavor is more earthy and more potent. We tested pozole with dried Mexican, dried Mediterranean, and fresh Mediterranean oregano. (We were unable to purchase fresh Mexican oregano.) The dried Mediterranean oregano had a strong pizza-parlor flavor that was out of place in pozole. The fresh Mediterranean oregano was a better substitute for the dried Mexican oregano, which we prefer but can be difficult to find.

The final component of the pozole to examine was the chiles. The red color comes from dried chiles, so we tested several possibilities—anchos, New Mexico reds, and pasillas. We removed stems and seeds from the dried chiles, soaked them in boiling water, and then pureed the chiles and soaking liquid to create a thick paste. (We tested toasting the chiles before soaking but found this step added little to this dish.) The paste was added to the pot once the meat was tender. We liked all three chiles but preferred the deep reddish brown color and rich, sweet, raisiny flavor of the anchos.

We also tested chili powder, sprinkling some into the pot once the onions, garlic, and meat had been sweated. Although the results weren't terrible, everyone in the test kitchen agreed that the pozole made with powder instead of a puree of whole chiles was less complex-tasting, and less appealing. It's worth spending the extra few minutes soaking and pureeing the anchos as directed in our recipe.

We found that it can be difficult to create a stew that pleases all tasters, especially when it comes to an agreed-upon spiciness. For this reason, we think it makes sense to mix three quarters of the ancho chile puree into the pozole and serve the remaining puree at the table with the garnishes. Those who like spicy food can add puree; those who don't, won't.

It was time to deal with the hominy. We started by preparing one batch of pozole with freshly rehydrated hominy (which took hours to prepare) and another batch with canned hominy (which took seconds to drain and rinse). The pozole with freshly cooked hominy was superb, but the pozole with canned hominy was pretty good. It was chewy (as hominy should be) and relatively sweet.

After a few more tests, we found that cooking the canned hominy in the stew for 40 to 45 minutes allows the hominy to soak up some of the flavorful broth. Don't try to cook canned hominy any longer. We found that the texture will suffer and the hominy will become soggy if simmered for an hour or more.

Canned hominy comes in white and yellow varieties, depending on the type of field corn used. We tested white and yellow hominy and found that both types are fine. Flavor isn't much of an issue; white and yellow hominy are both sweet and "corny" tasting. In terms of appearance, yellow hominy looks a bit better in green pozole, but the difference is slight. (The chile puree used to make red pozole makes it impossible to tell the difference between white and yellow hominy in this version.)

Our pozole recipe turned out to be remarkably simple—no more than an hour of hands-on work and a start-to-finish time of about three hours. Do take the 10 minutes to prepare all the suggested garnishes. The lettuce, radishes, cilantro, oregano, and lime juice all brighten the stew and turn it into a one-dish meal.

Pozole Rojo
SERVES 8 TO 10

This earthy-tasting, full-flavored pork and hominy stew originated in Mexico, although it is now extremely popular in the American Southwest. This stew is typically accompanied by an assortment of crunchy toppings (each in a small bowl) and warm tortillas. Ancho chiles (see page 302) are used to create the rich flavor and color in this dish. Mexicans use oregano liberally, but varieties of Mexican oregano are different from Mediterranean oregano. If available, use dried Mexican oregano; fresh Mediterranean oregano is a better substitute than dried Mediterranean oregano.

STEW
- 1   bone-in picnic shoulder roast (about 5 pounds)
    Salt and ground black pepper
- 2   tablespoons vegetable oil
- 2   medium-large onions, chopped coarse (about 3 cups)
- 5   medium garlic cloves, minced or pressed through a garlic press (about 5 teaspoons)
- 1   (14.5-ounce) can diced tomatoes
- 1   tablespoon chopped fresh oregano leaves or 1 teaspoon dried Mexican oregano
- 6   cups low-sodium chicken broth
- 2   ounces dried ancho chiles (about 3 large)
- 3   (15-ounce) cans white or yellow hominy, drained and rinsed

GARNISHES
- 2   limes, cut into quarters
- 1/2   head romaine lettuce, sliced crosswise into thin strips
- 6   medium radishes, sliced thin
- 1   small onion, minced
    Roughly chopped fresh cilantro leaves
    Chopped fresh oregano or dried Mexican oregano
- 1/4   cup pureed ancho chiles (prepared with the stew)
    Flour or corn tortillas, warmed

1. Adjust the oven rack to the lower-middle position and heat the oven to 300 degrees. Trim the thick skin and excess fat from the meat and cut along the muscles to divide the roast into large pieces of various sizes; reserve the bones. Season the meat generously with salt and pepper to taste.

2. Heat the oil in a large ovenproof Dutch oven over medium heat until shimmering. Add the onions and 1/4 teaspoon salt. Cook, stirring frequently, until the onions have softened, about 4 minutes. Stir in the garlic and cook until fragrant, about 30 seconds.

3. Add the meat and bones and stir often until it is no longer pink on the outside, about 8 minutes. Add the tomatoes, oregano, broth, and ½ teaspoon salt. Increase the heat to medium-high and bring to a simmer. With a large spoon, skim off any scum. Cover the pot, and place it in the oven. Cook until the meat is very tender, about 2 hours.

4. Meanwhile, remove the stem and seeds from the ancho chiles; soak the chiles in a medium bowl with 1½ cups boiling water until soft, about 20 minutes. Puree the chiles and soaking liquid in a blender until smooth. Pour the puree through a strainer into a bowl and reserve ¼ cup of the pureed anchos for garnish.

5. Remove the pot from the oven and remove the meat and bones to a cutting board. Stir in the hominy and the remaining ¾ cup ancho chile puree. Cover and bring the stew to a simmer on top of the stove over medium-low heat. Cook until the hominy is hot and the flavors meld, about 30 minutes.

6. When the meat is cool, shred it using your fingers or the tines of 2 forks; discard the bones. Stir the shredded meat into the stew. If serving immediately, spoon off any fat that rises to the top and then simmer until the meat is hot, about 10 minutes. (The stew can be covered and refrigerated for up to 3 days. Spoon off the hardened fat and bring back to a simmer over medium-low heat.) Adjust the seasonings. Ladle the stew into individual bowls and serve immediately with the garnishes.

➤ VARIATION
Pozole Verde

Verde means green in Spanish and green pozole, not surprisingly, is lighter and refreshing than red pozole. Green pozole is prepared with lots of cilantro, fresh jalapeños, and tomatillos. These ingredients are cooked for a very short time; the flavors are bigger, brighter, and fresher-tasting than pozole with red sauce. A slightly different set of garnishes accompanies green pozole as well: diced tomato, diced avocado, and minced jalapeño. In other words, forego the cilantro, oregano, and ancho chile puree garnishes suggested for Pozole Rojo.

Follow the recipe for Pozole Rojo, eliminating the tomatoes and ancho chiles. While the pozole is simmering, puree 1 pound tomatillos, husked, washed, and quartered; 3 medium jalapeños, stemmed, seeded, and chopped coarse; ½ small onion, chopped coarse; and ½ cup water in a blender until smooth, 2 to 3 minutes. Add 2 bunches (about 5 cups) fresh cilantro leaves and stems and puree until smooth, about 2 minutes. When the pozole comes out of the oven in step 5, remove the meat and bones and stir in the hominy. Simmer as directed. Stir the tomatillo mixture into the stew along with the shredded cooled meat and simmer until heated through, 10 to 15 minutes. Serve with the garnishes noted above.

CASSOULET

EVERY ONCE IN A WHILE, A DISH COMES around that is so robust, so satisfying to every sense that we deem it comfort food. It warms us from the inside out and assures us that this winter, too, shall pass. Cassoulet is such a dish. But for most cooks, the reasons to eat cassoulet outnumber the reasons to make it. Cassoulet can take three days to make, and the ingredients can be both hard to find and difficult to prepare.

Cassoulet originated in Languedoc, France, and each area of the region touts its recipe as "the real thing." All versions of the dish contain white beans, but that is where the agreement ends. Some prefer pork loin in their cassoulet, others use a shoulder of lamb, while still others use a combination of both. Mutton, duck, pheasant, garlic sausage, and even fish can be found in the different variations.

But the best-known and most often replicated cassoulet comes from Toulouse. This cassoulet must start with the preparation of confit. Meat or poultry, most often goose legs (the region of Toulouse is also home to the foie gras industry, which means that goose is plentiful), is placed in a large container, sprinkled heavily with salt, and cured for 24 to 48 hours. This both preserves and tenderizes the meat. After this, the meat is simmered slowly in its own fat, so that the flavor of the fat penetrates the spaces previously occupied by the juices. The finished confit may be used immediately or stored in an airtight container, covered in its own fat, to prevent contamination.

The challenge of making cassoulet doesn't end with preparing confit, however. Pork loin and mutton must be slow-roasted for hours to become fully tender, and garlic sausages freshly made. The beans must be presoaked and then simmered with pork rinds to develop flavor. Finally, the entire mixture has to be combined in an earthenware pot, topped with bread crumbs, and placed in a low-temperature oven to simmer slowly for several hours.

The result is nothing short of divine. But while this classic French peasant dish can be replicated by restaurants, it is definitely not a dish for the casual home cook. The time investment alone is impractical, and it can be difficult to achieve a perfect balance of flavors. On more than one occasion we have eaten cassoulets that were overwhelmed by salt or swimming in fat, most often because of the confit and sausages. All the same, we love this dish so much that we decided it would be worth the effort to try to streamline it without compromising its essential nature.

We decided to accept the hardest of the challenges first and conquer the confit component. We eliminated the notion of confit made from scratch as far too time-consuming. Assessing our other options, we created three cassoulets. One was prepared with braised duck leg confit (goose leg confit is less widely available) purchased through our butcher. The others we made with no confit at all, starting one version with sautéed and braised duck legs and the other with sautéed and braised chicken legs, which we wanted to use because they're so easy to find in the supermarket. The results were disheartening, although not surprising. The cassoulet made with the purchased confit was the clear favorite. Those made without it produced dishes more reminiscent of duck and chicken stews.

Unfortunately, ready-made confit is not widely available, so we wanted to develop a recipe that wouldn't rely on it. Somewhat ironically, we arrived at the solution to the problem with some help from the confit itself.

Because confit is salt-cured and then cooked in its own fat, it retains an intense duck flavor when

added to the cassoulet, contributing a rich, slightly smoky flavor that was noticeably absent from the dishes prepared with the sautéed duck and chicken. The texture of the dish made with confit was superior as well, the flesh plump with flavor yet tender to the bite; the sautéed and braised duck and chicken became tough and gave up all of their flavor to the broth. Taking an educated guess, we decided to adopt an approach often used in the test kitchen and brine the chicken. Because we had found when making other dishes that brining resulted in poultry that was both more moist and more flavorful, we reasoned that brining the chicken might bring it closer to the tender texture of confit. To approximate the confit's light smokiness, we decided to cook the legs in bacon fat.

We quick-soaked the chicken thighs for one hour in a concentrated salt and sugar solution, sautéed them quickly in rendered bacon fat, then braised them with the rest of the cassoulet ingredients. What resulted was just what we were hoping for: a suitable substitute for duck confit. The bacon added smoky flavor, and it enhanced the flavors of the pork and sausage added later. The texture and flavor were spot on; the chicken thighs were plump and juicy; and the broth became well seasoned because of the brine. With this "mock" confit in hand, we proceeded.

Our next test involved figuring out which meats to use and how to avoid slow roasting. We knew that we wanted to be true to the original recipe and use either fresh pork or lamb. We decided to try stewing the meat in liquid entirely on top of the stove. This method yielded great results in terms of tenderness, but the meat had none of the depth of flavor that occurs with roasting. Searing the meat in some of the rendered bacon fat that we had used with the chicken thighs took care of that problem.

Because we were now stewing the meat, we needed to use cuts that were appropriate for this method. We tried pork loin, the choice in so many cassoulet recipes, but the loin became waterlogged and tasteless during stewing. A suggestion from our butcher led us to try a blade-end roast, which is the part of the loin closest to the shoulder. The blade-end roast, which has more internal fat than the center loin, retained the moisture and flavor. To facilitate quicker cooking, we cut the roast into 1-inch pieces. We used similar testing with the lamb. Lamb shoulder is the best cut for stewing, but it can be difficult to find in markets. We bought thick shoulder lamb chops instead, which we boned and also cut into 1-inch pieces. Finally, perfectly tender meat—and a choice of meats, at that!—without the effort of roasting.

Cassoulets traditionally use white beans. We wanted to make sure that the beans would retain their shape while adding a soft texture to the dish. Canned beans fell apart quickly, so we opted for dried. We tested four varieties, and the winner was the pale green flageolet bean. These small, kidney-shaped French beans have a creamy, tender texture and delicate flavor that perfectly enhanced the cassoulet. We also cooked the beans on top of the stove along with some bacon and the aromatics to let them absorb as much flavor as possible, an effort to duplicate the depth of flavor in the original dish.

The last major decision we had to make concerned the sausage. After ruling out the use of hard-to-find French sausages (and not willing to take the time to make our own), we found that both kielbasa and andouille sausages intensified the smoky flavor that we so desired.

With the major problems out of the way, we

SORTING DRIED BEANS WITH EASE

It is important to pick over and rinse dried beans to remove any stones or debris before cooking. To make this easier, sort dried beans on a white plate or cutting board. The neutral background makes any unwanted matter easy to spot and remove.

were able to concentrate on streamlining the technique used to cook the dish. This proved to be quite simple. With the chicken, meat, and beans now modified for cooking on the stovetop, oven braising became unnecessary. Cooking the dish entirely on the stove at a low simmer, with a quick finish in the oven to brown the bread crumbs, produced perfect results in a short amount of time. At last we had it: a quick cassoulet that was worthy of the name.

Simplified Cassoulet with Pork and Kielbasa

SERVES 8

Although this dish can be made without brining the chicken, we recommend that you do so. To ensure the most time-efficient preparation of the cassoulet, while the chicken is brining and the beans are simmering, prepare the remaining ingredients. Look for dried flageolet beans in specialty food stores. If you can't find a boneless blade-end pork loin roast, a boneless Boston butt makes a fine substitution. Additional salt is not necessary because the brined chicken adds a good deal of it. If you skip the brining step, add salt to taste before serving.

CHICKEN

1 cup kosher salt or 1/2 cup table salt

1 cup sugar

10 bone-in chicken thighs (about 3 1/2 pounds), excess fat removed

BEANS

1 pound dried flageolet or great Northern beans, picked over and rinsed (for easy sorting see the illustration at left)

1 medium onion, peeled and left whole

1 medium head garlic, papery outer skin removed and top 1/2 inch sliced off

1 teaspoon salt

1/2 teaspoon ground black pepper

6 ounces (about 6 slices) bacon, chopped medium

1 pound boneless blade-end pork loin roast, trimmed of excess fat and cut into 1-inch pieces

1 small onion, chopped fine

2   medium garlic cloves, minced or pressed
     through a garlic press (about 2 teaspoons)
1   (14.5 ounces) can diced tomatoes, drained
1   tablespoon tomato paste
1   large sprig fresh thyme
1   bay leaf
¼   teaspoon ground cloves
     Ground black pepper
3 ½ cups low-sodium chicken broth
1 ½ cups dry white wine
½   pound kielbasa, halved lengthwise and cut
     crosswise into ¼ -inch slices

CROUTONS
6   slices good-quality white sandwich bread, cut
     into ½-inch dice (about 3 cups)
3   tablespoons unsalted butter, melted

1. FOR THE CHICKEN: In a gallon-size zipper-lock plastic bag, dissolve the salt and sugar in 1 quart cold water. Add the chicken, pressing out as much air as possible; seal and refrigerate until fully seasoned, about 1 hour. Remove the chicken from the brine, rinse thoroughly under cold water, and pat dry with paper towels. Refrigerate until ready to use.

2. FOR THE BEANS: Bring the beans, whole onion, garlic head, salt, pepper, and 8 cups water to a boil in a stockpot or large Dutch oven over high heat. Cover, reduce the heat to medium-low, and simmer until the beans are almost fully tender, 1¼ to 1½ hours. Drain the beans and discard the onion and garlic. Return the cooked beans to the Dutch oven.

3. While the beans are cooking, fry the bacon in another Dutch oven over medium heat until just beginning to crisp and most of the fat has rendered, 5 to 6 minutes. Using a slotted spoon, add half of the bacon to the pot with the beans; transfer the remaining bacon to a paper towel–lined plate and set aside. Increase the heat to medium-high. When the bacon fat is shimmering, add half of the chicken thighs, fleshy-side down; cook until lightly browned, 4 to 5 minutes. Using tongs, turn the chicken pieces and cook until lightly browned on the second side, 3 to 4 minutes longer. Transfer the chicken to a large plate; repeat with the remaining thighs and set aside. Drain off all but 2 tablespoons

fat from the pot. Return the pot to medium heat; add the pork pieces and cook, stirring occasionally, until lightly browned, about 5 minutes. Add the chopped onion and cook, stirring occasionally, until softened, 3 to 4 minutes. Add the minced garlic, tomatoes, tomato paste, thyme, bay leaf, cloves, and pepper to taste; cook until fragrant, about 1 minute. Stir in the broth and wine, scraping up the browned bits on the pot bottom with a wooden spoon. Add the chicken thighs to the pot, with any accumulated juices, and submerge them in the liquid. Increase the heat to high and bring to a boil. Then reduce the heat to low, cover, and simmer about 40 minutes. Remove the cover and continue to simmer until the chicken and pork are fully tender, 20 to 30 minutes more. Using tongs and a slotted spoon, remove and discard the skin on the chicken thighs.

4. FOR THE CROUTONS: While the chicken and pork simmer, adjust an oven rack to the lower-middle position and heat the oven to 400 degrees. Mix the bread crumbs and butter in a small baking dish. Bake, tossing occasionally, until light golden brown and crisp, 8 to 12 minutes. Cool to room temperature; set aside.

5. Gently stir the kielbasa, drained beans and bacon, and the reserved bacon into the pot with the chicken and pork; remove and discard the thyme sprig and bay leaf and adjust the seasonings with salt and pepper to taste. Sprinkle the croutons evenly over the surface and bake, uncovered, until the flavors have melded and the croutons are deep golden brown, about 15 minutes. Let stand 10 minutes and serve.

BLADE VERSUS CENTER LOIN PORK

Because the pork is stewed, the blade end of the loin is preferable to the leaner center loin.

➤ VARIATION

Simplified Cassoulet with Lamb and Andouille Sausage

Lamb, with its robust, earthy flavor, makes an excellent substitute for the pork. Andouille sausage adds a peppery sweetness that our tasters loved.

Follow the recipe for Simplified Cassoulet with Pork and Kielbasa, substituting 2 pounds shoulder lamb chops, trimmed, boned, and cut into 1-inch pieces, for the pork, and substituting 8 ounces andouille sausage for the kielbasa.

INGREDIENTS: Chicken Broth

Few of the commercial broths in our tasting came close to the full-bodied consistency of a successful homemade stock. Many lacked even a hint of chicken flavor. Interestingly, the four broths we rated best were all products of the Campbell Soup Company, of which Swanson is a subsidiary. In order, they were Swanson Chicken Broth, Campbell's Chicken Broth, Swanson Natural Goodness Chicken Broth (with 33 percent less sodium than regular Swanson Chicken Broth), and Campbell's Healthy Request Chicken Broth (with 30 percent less sodium than regular Campbell's Chicken Broth). The remaining broths were decidedly inferior and hard to recommend.

A few national brands of chicken broth have begun to offer their products in aseptic packaging (cartons rather than cans). Compared with traditional canning, in which products are heated in the can for up to nearly an hour to ensure sterilization, the process of aseptic packaging entails a flash heating and cooling process that is said to help products better retain both their nutritional value and their flavor.

We decided to hold another tasting to see if we could detect more flavor in the products sold in aseptic packaging. Of the recommended broths in the tasting, only Swanson broths are available in aseptic packaging. We tasted Swanson's traditional and Natural Goodness chicken broths sold in cans and in aseptic packages. The results fell clearly in favor of the aseptically packaged broths; both tasted cleaner and more chickeny than their canned counterparts. So if you are truly seeking the best of the best in commercial broths, choose one of the two Swanson broths sold in aseptic packaging. An opened aseptic package is said to keep in the refrigerator for up to two weeks (broth from a can is said to keep, refrigerated, for only a few days).

9

I WANT TO MAKE POT ROAST

I Want to Make Pot Roast

BRAISING—SEARING MEAT, PARTIALLY SUB-merging it in liquid in a sealed pot, and then cooking it until fork-tender—is a classic technique used for tough cuts of meat. Pot roast is the most familiar of these dishes, but this category also includes braised brisket (both plain and corned) as well as other boiled dinners (bollito misto, from Italy, and pot-au-feu, from France) as well as braised ribs (especially beef short ribs) and shanks (veal or lamb).

A variety of cooks have put forward theories about why and how braising (as opposed to roasting or boiling) works. We set out to devise a series of experiments that would explain the mystery of braising.

Before kitchen testing began, we researched the meat itself to better understand how it cooks. Meat (muscle) is made up of two major components: muscle fibers, the long thin strands visible as the "grain" of meat, and connective tissue, the membranous, translucent film that covers the bundles of muscle fiber and gives them structure and support. Muscle fiber is tender because of its high water content (up to 78 percent). Once meat is heated beyond about 120 degrees, the long strands of muscle fiber contract and coil, expelling moisture in much the same way that it's wrung out of a towel. In contrast, connective tissue is tough because it is composed primarily of collagen, a sturdy protein that is in everything from the cow's muscle tendons to its hooves. When collagen is cooked at temperatures exceeding 140 degrees, it starts to break down to gelatin, the protein responsible for the tender, rich meat and thick sauces of braised dishes such as pot roast.

In essence, then, meat both dries out as it cooks (meat fibers lose moisture) and becomes softer (the collagen melts). That is why (depending on the cut) meat is best either when cooked rare or pot-roasted—cooked to the point at which the collagen dissolves completely. Anything in between is dry and tough, the worst of both worlds.

This brings us to why braising is an effective cooking technique for tough cuts of meat. To determine the relative advantages of roasting, braising, and boiling, we constructed a simple test. One roast was cooked in a 250-degree oven, one was braised, and one was simmered in enough liquid to cover it.

The results were startling. The dry-cooked roast never reached an internal temperature of more than 175 degrees, even after four hours, and the meat was tough and dry (see Roasting versus Braising on page 189). To our great surprise, both the braised and boiled roasts cooked in about the same amount of time, and the results were almost identical. Cutting the roasts in half revealed little difference—both exhibited nearly full melting of the thick bands of connective tissue. As far as the taste and texture of the meat, tasters were hard-pressed to find any substantial differences between the two. Both roasts yielded meat that was exceedingly tender, moist, and infused with rich gelatin.

The conclusion? Dry heat (roasting) is ineffective because the meat never gets hot enough to fully melt the collagen. It does not appear that steam heat (braising) enjoys any special ability to soften meat over boiling. Braising has one advantage over simmering or boiling, however—half a pot of liquid reduces to a sauce much faster than a full pot.

POT ROAST

POT ROAST, A SLOW-FOOD SURVIVOR OF generations past, has stubbornly remained in the repertoire of Sunday-night cookery, but with few good reasons. The meat is often tough and stringy and so dry that it must be drowned with the merciful sauce that accompanies the dish.

A good pot roast by definition entails the transformation of a tough (read cheap), nearly unpalatable cut of meat into a tender, rich, flavorful main course by means of a slow, moist cooking process called braising. It should not be sliceable; rather, the tension of a stern gaze should be enough to break it apart. Nor should it be pink or rosy in the middle—save that for prime rib or steak.

The meat for pot roast should be well marbled with fat and connective tissue to provide the dish with the necessary flavor and moisture. Recipes typically call for roasts from the sirloin (or rump), round (leg), or chuck (shoulder). When all was said and done, we cooked a dozen cuts of meat to find the right one.

The sirloin roasts tested—the bottom rump roast and top sirloin—were the leanest of the cuts and needed a longer cooking to be broken down to a palatable texture. The round cuts—top round, bottom round, and eye of round—had more fat running through them than the sirloin cuts, but the meat was chewy. The chuck cuts—shoulder roast, boneless chuck roast, cross rib, chuck mock tender, seven-bone roast, top-blade roast, and chuck-eye roast—cooked up the most tender, although we gave preference to three of these cuts (see page 187 for more information). The high proportion of fat and connective tissue in these chuck cuts gave the meat much-needed moisture and superior flavor.

Tough meat, such as brisket, can benefit from the low, dry heat of oven roasting, and it can be boiled. With pot roast, however, the introduction of moisture by means of a braising liquid is thought to be integral to the breakdown of the tough muscle fibers. (We also tried dry-roasting and boiling pot roast just to make sure. See page 187 to find out why braising was the winner.) It was time to find out what kind of liquid and how much was needed to best cook the roast and supply a good sauce.

Before we began the testing, we needed to deal with the aesthetics of the dish. Because pot roast is traditionally cooked with liquid at a low temperature, the exterior of the meat will not brown sufficiently

HOW TO TIE A TOP-BLADE ROAST

1. Slip a 6-foot piece of twine under the roast and tie a double knot.

2. Hold the twine against the meat and loop the long end of twine under and around the roast.

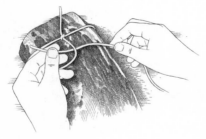

3. Run the long end through the loop.

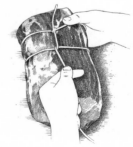

4. Repeat this procedure down the length of the roast.

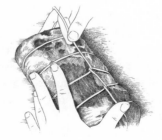

5. Roll the roast over and run the twine under and around each loop.

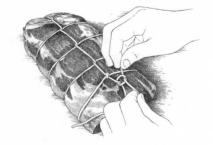

6. Wrap the twine around the end of the roast, flip the roast, and tie to the original knot.

unless it is first sautéed in a Dutch oven on the stovetop. High heat and a little oil were all that were needed to caramelize the exterior of the beef and boost both the flavor and appearance of the dish.

Using water as the braising medium, we started with a modest ¼ cup, as suggested in a few recipes. This produced a roast that was unacceptably fibrous, even after hours of cooking. After increasing the amount of liquid incrementally, we found that the moistest meat was produced when we added liquid halfway up the sides of the roast (depending on the cut, this amount could be between 2 and 4 cups). The greater amount of liquid also accelerated the cooking process, shaving nearly one hour off the cooking time needed for a roast cooked in just ¼ cup of liquid. Naively assuming that more is always better, we continued to increase the amount of water but to no better effect. We also found it necessary to cover the Dutch oven with a piece of foil before placing the lid on top. The added seal of the foil kept the liquid from escaping (in the form of steam) by means of the loose-fitting lid and eliminated any need to add more liquid to the pot.

Next we tested different liquids, hoping to add flavor to the roast and sauce. Along with our old standby, water, we tested red wine, low-sodium canned chicken broth, and low-sodium canned beef broth. Red wine had the most startling effect on the meat, penetrating it with a potent flavor that most tasters agreed was "good, but not traditional pot roast." However, tasters did like the flavor of a little red wine added to the sauce after the pot roast was removed from the pan. Each of the broths on their own failed to win tasters over completely—the chicken broth was rich but gave the dish a characteristic poultry flavor, while the beef broth tasted sour when added solo. In the end, we found that an equal amount of each did the job, with the beef broth boosting the depth of flavor and the chicken broth tempering any sourness. Because different amounts of liquid would have to be added to the pot depending on the size and shape of each individual roast, we chose to be consistent in the amount of chicken and beef broth used—1 cup each—and to vary the amount of water to bring the liquid level halfway up the sides of the roast.

Trying to boost the flavor of the sauce even

more, we added the basic vegetables—carrot, celery, onion, and garlic—to the pot as the meat braised. Unfortunately, the addition of raw vegetables made the pot roast taste more like a vegetable stew. We then tried sautéing them until golden brown and found that the caramelized flavor of the vegetables added another layer of flavor to the sauce. Tomato paste, an ingredient found in several recipes, was not a welcome addition. Tasters appreciated the sweetness it added but not the "tinny" flavor. A little sugar (2 teaspoons) added to the vegetables as they cooked gave the sauce the sweetness tasters were looking for.

Some recipes thicken the sauce with a mixture of equal parts butter and flour (beurre manié); others use a slurry of cornstarch mixed with a little braising liquid. Both techniques made the sauce more gravy-like than we preferred, and we didn't care for the dilution of flavor. We chose to remove the roast from the pot, then reduce the liquid over high heat until the flavors were well concentrated and the texture more substantial.

As for the best cooking method for pot roast, there are two schools of thought: on the stove or in the oven. After a few rounds of stovetop cooking, we felt that it was too difficult to maintain a steady, low temperature, so we began pot-roasting in the oven, starting out at 250 degrees. This method required no supervision, just a turn of the meat every 30 to 40 minutes to ensure even cooking. We then tested higher temperatures to reduce the cooking time. Heat levels above 350 degrees boiled the meat to a stringy, dry texture because the exterior of the roast overcooked before the interior was cooked and tender. The magic temperature turned out to be 300 degrees—enough heat to keep the meat at a low simmer while high enough to shave a few more minutes off the cooking time.

As noted above, pot roast is well-done meat—meat cooked to an internal temperature above 165 degrees. Up to this point, we were bringing the meat to an internal temperature of 200 to 210 degrees, the point at which the fat and connective tissue begin to melt. In a 300-degree oven, the roast came up to that temperature in a neat 2½ hours, certainly by no means a quick meal but still a relatively short time in which to cook a pot roast. But we still had not achieved our goal of fall-apart tenderness. We went back and reviewed our prior testing to see what we might have missed.

Once in a great while in the test kitchen we happen upon a true "Eureka!" moment, when a chance test result leads to a breakthrough cooking technique. Some days before, we had forgotten to remove one of the roasts from the oven, allowing it to cook one hour longer than intended. Racing to the kitchen with our instant-read thermometer, we found the internal temperature of the roast was still 210 degrees, but the meat had a substantially different appearance and texture. The roast was so tender that it was starting to separate along its muscle lines. A fork poked into the meat met with no resistance and nearly disappeared into the flesh. We took the roast out of the pot and "sliced" into it. Nearly all the fat and connective tissue had dissolved into the meat, giving each bite a soft, silky texture and rich,

SCIENCE: What's So Special about Collagen?

Collagen is the predominant protein in connective tissue and is quite difficult to chew. It is found in abundance in tough cuts of meat, such as those used to make pot roast. Braising is a slow cooking technique that is applied to tough cuts of meat. The meat is submerged halfway in cooking liquid, covered, and heated at a low temperature. By the time the meat reaches 150 degrees, the muscle tissue has tightened fully and has expelled a great deal of its moisture into the braising liquid. If the meat is pulled from the pot at this temperature it will be dry and tough, but the braising liquid will be rich and flavorful.

With further heating, the collagen in the muscle will break down progressively into soft gelatin. The tightened muscle tissue strands can then separate a little, and moisture from the cooking liquid will accumulate between the fibers. Now, though the finished product still is tough muscle tissue, it is more succulent, owing to the conversion of collagen to soft gelatin and to the resultant opening of gaps between the tough strands of muscle.

Since collagen won't completely melt until the internal temperature of the meat reaches 200 degrees, you must really cook tough cuts of meat to make full use of this phenomenon. In fact, when making pot roast you really can't overcook the meat. Excessive cooking might cause the meat to fall apart, but, in general, the longer the meat is pot-roasted, the more tender it will become.

succulent flavor. We "overcooked" several more roasts. Each roast had the same great texture. The conclusion? Not only do you have to cook pot roast until it reaches 210 degrees internally, but the meat has to remain at that temperature for a full hour. In other words, cook the pot roast until it's done—and then keep on cooking!

Simple Pot Roast
SERVES 6 TO 8

Our favorite cut for pot roast is a chuck-eye roast. Most markets sell this roast with twine tied around the center (see the photo on page 187); if necessary, do this yourself. Seven-bone and top-blade roasts are also good choices for this recipe. Remember to add only enough water to come halfway up the sides of these thinner roasts, and begin checking for doneness after 2 hours. If using a top-blade roast, tie it before cooking (see the illustrations on page 184) to keep it from falling apart. Mashed or boiled potatoes are a good accompaniment to pot roast.

1	boneless chuck-eye roast (about 3 $1/2$ pounds), patted dry with paper towels
	Salt and ground black pepper
2	tablespoons vegetable oil
1	medium onion, chopped medium
1	small carrot, chopped medium
1	small celery rib, chopped medium
2	medium garlic cloves, minced or pressed through a garlic press (about 2 teaspoons)
2	teaspoons sugar
1	cup low-sodium chicken broth
1	cup low-sodium beef broth
1	sprig fresh thyme
1–1 $1/2$	cups water
$1/4$	cup dry red wine

1. Adjust an oven rack to the middle position and heat the oven to 300 degrees. Sprinkle the roast generously with salt and pepper to taste.

2. Heat the oil in a large ovenproof Dutch oven over medium-high heat until shimmering but not smoking. Brown the roast thoroughly on all sides, reducing the heat if the fat begins to smoke, 8 to 10 minutes. Transfer the roast to a large plate; set aside.

3. Reduce the heat to medium; add the onion, carrot, and celery to the pot and cook, stirring occasionally, until beginning to brown, 6 to 8 minutes. Add the garlic and sugar; cook until fragrant, about 30 seconds. Add the chicken and beef broths and thyme, scraping the pan bottom with a wooden spoon to loosen the browned bits. Return the roast and any accumulated juices on the plate to the pot; add enough water to come halfway up the sides of the roast. Cover with a lid, bring the liquid to a simmer over medium heat, then transfer the pot to the oven. Cook, turning the roast every 30 minutes, until fully tender and a meat fork or sharp knife slips easily in and out of the meat, 3½ to 4 hours.

4. Transfer the roast to a carving board; tent with foil to keep warm. Allow the liquid in the pot to settle about 5 minutes, then use a wide spoon to skim the fat off the surface; discard the thyme sprig. Boil over high heat until reduced to about 1½ cups, about 8 minutes. Add the wine and reduce to 1½ cups, about 2 minutes. Season with salt and pepper to taste.

5. Using a chef's or carving knife, cut the meat into ½-inch-thick slices, or pull apart into large pieces; transfer the meat to a warmed serving platter and pour about ½ cup of the sauce over the meat. Serve, passing the remaining sauce separately.

➤ VARIATIONS
Pot Roast with Root Vegetables
In this variation, carrots, potatoes, and parsnips are added near the end of cooking to make a complete meal.

1. Follow the recipe for Simple Pot Roast. In step 2, when the roast is almost tender (a sharp knife should meet little resistance), transfer the roast to a cutting board. Pour the braising liquid through a mesh strainer and discard the solids. Return the liquid to the empty pot and let it settle for 5 minutes; use a wide spoon to skim the fat off the surface. Return the roast to the liquid and add 1½ pounds (about 8 medium) carrots, peeled and sliced ½ inch thick (about 3 cups), 1½ pounds small red potatoes, halved if larger than 1½ inches in diameter (about 5 cups), and 1 pound (about 5 large) parsnips, peeled and sliced ½ inch thick (about 3 cups), submerging them in the liquid. Continue to cook until the vegetables are almost tender, 20 to 30 minutes.

2. Transfer the roast to a carving board; tent with foil to keep warm. Add the wine and salt and pepper to taste; boil over high heat until the vegetables are fully tender, 5 to 10 minutes. Using a slotted spoon, transfer the vegetables to a warmed serving bowl or platter; using a chef's or carving knife, cut the meat into ½-inch-thick slices or pull apart into large pieces; transfer to the bowl or

CHUCK ROASTS

Seven-Bone Pot Roast   **Top-Blade Pot Roast**   **Chuck-Eye Roast**

The seven-bone pot roast (left) is a well-marbled cut with an incredibly beefy flavor. It gets its name from the bone found in the roast, which is shaped like the number seven. Because it is only 2 inches thick, less liquid and less time are needed to braise this roast. Do not buy a seven-bone pot roast that weighs more than 3 1/2 pounds, as it will not fit into a Dutch oven. This roast is also sometimes referred to as a seven-bone steak.

The top-blade pot roast (middle) is also well marbled with fat

and connective tissue, which make this roast very juicy and flavorful. Even after thorough braising, this roast retains a distinctive strip of connective tissue, which is not unpleasant to eat. This roast may also be sold as a blade roast.

The chuck-eye roast (right) is the fattiest of the three roasts and the most commonly available. Its high proportion of fat gives pot roast great flavor and tenderness. Because of its thicker size, this roast takes the longest to cook.

platter and pour about ½ cup of the sauce over the meat and vegetables. Serve, passing the remaining sauce separately.

Stracotto (Pot Roast with Mushrooms, Tomatoes, and Red Wine)

This is the Italian version of pot roast.

I	boneless chuck-eye roast (about 3 ½ pounds), patted dry with paper towels Salt and ground black pepper
2	tablespoons vegetable oil
I	medium onion, chopped medium
I	small carrot, chopped medium
I	small celery rib, chopped medium
10	ounces white button mushrooms, quartered
2	medium garlic cloves, minced or pressed through a garlic press (about 2 teaspoons)
2	teaspoons sugar
½	cup low-sodium chicken broth
½	cup low-sodium beef broth
½	cup dry red wine
I	(14.5-ounce) can diced tomatoes
I	sprig fresh thyme
I–I ½	cups water
I	sprig fresh rosemary

1. Adjust an oven rack to the middle position and heat the oven to 300 degrees. Sprinkle the roast generously with salt and pepper to taste.

2. Heat the oil in a large ovenproof Dutch oven over medium–high heat until shimmering but not smoking. Brown the roast thoroughly on all sides, reducing the heat if the fat begins to smoke, 8 to 10 minutes. Transfer the roast to a large plate; set aside.

3. Reduce the heat to medium, add the onion, carrot, celery, and mushrooms to the pot, and cook, stirring occasionally, until the vegetables begin to brown, 6 to 8 minutes. Add the garlic and sugar and cook until fragrant, about 30 seconds. Add the chicken and beef broths, wine, tomatoes and their juices, and thyme, scraping the pan bottom with a wooden spoon to loosen the browned bits. Return the roast and any accumulated juices on the plate to the pot. Add enough water to come halfway up the sides of the roast. Bring the liquid to a simmer over

medium heat, then place a large piece of foil over the pot and cover tightly with the lid. Transfer the pot to the oven. Cook, turning the roast every 30 minutes, until fully tender and a meat fork or sharp knife slips easily in and out, 3½ to 4 hours.

4. Transfer the roast to a carving board and tent with foil to keep warm. Allow the liquid in the pot to settle for about 5 minutes, then use a wide spoon to skim the fat off the surface. Add the rosemary and boil over high heat until reduced to about 1½ cups, about 8 minutes. Discard the thyme and rosemary sprigs. Season with salt and pepper to taste.

5. Using a chef's or carving knife, cut the meat into ½-inch-thick slices or pull it apart into large pieces. Transfer the meat to a warmed serving platter and pour the sauce and vegetables over it. Serve immediately.

BEEF BRAISED IN BAROLO

ALTHOUGH SIMILAR TO POT ROAST, THIS Italian recipe doesn't use stock in the braising liquid, only fine Barolo wine. Barolo is made from the Nebbiolo grape and is produced in the northern region of Piedmont. This red wine is known for its hearty aromas of oak, licorice, plum, roses, and violets. As the meat slowly cooks in the Barolo, the flavors meld and mellow; the dish emerges from the oven with a heady aroma and potent flavor unlike any pot roast you've ever had. The problem, however, is that Barolo is a tannic, full-bodied wine that produces a harsh, astringent-tasting pot roast if not handled correctly.

Starting with our recipe for Simple Pot Roast, we focused our attention on the best way to add the Barolo and eliminate the broth and water. Many recipes we researched soaked the roast in the wine for several hours before braising it, however, we found this made the meat taste musty and fermented. Simply replacing the three cups of stock, wine, and water in our Stracotto recipe (at left) with a bottle of Barolo was quicker and better. However, our work was not done. This second method produced a raw-tasting sauce with mouth-puckering intensity.

To temper the Barolo, we tried increasing the amount of vegetables—onions, carrots, and celery. Although this helped round out the flavor of the roast itself, the sauce was still a bit overpowering. Tasters wanted a smoother, rounder sauce, which we finally achieved by using a little tomato paste and a few spices. Cinnamon, cloves, bay leaves, thyme, and parsley added complexity to the sauce and helped bring the big flavors in the wine under control.

Lastly, unlike our previous pot roast, the spent vegetables and spices in this version are strained out of the beautiful, dark sauce before serving. The sauce for beef in Barolo is usually thickened slightly and glossy. We found that adding flour to the sautéed vegetables as well as reducing the sauce once the meat was removed from the pot helped achieve the correct consistency.

Beef Braised in Barolo

SERVES 6 TO 8

There is no such thing as a cheap Barolo (prices start at $30 a bottle at our local wine shops), but there's no need to spend more for a reserve wine. Chuck-eye roast is our choice for this recipe because the meat holds together nicely and slices better than similar cuts. Most markets sell this roast with twine tied around the center (see the photo on page 187). If necessary, do this yourself.

I	boneless chuck-eye roast (about 3 ½ pounds), patted dry with paper towels
	Salt and ground black pepper

2	tablespoons vegetable oil
2	medium onions, chopped medium
2	medium carrots, chopped medium
2	medium celery ribs, chopped medium
3	medium garlic cloves, minced or pressed through a garlic press (about 1 tablespoon)
½	teaspoon sugar
I	tablespoon tomato paste
I	tablespoon unbleached all-purpose flour
I	(750-milliliter) bottle Barolo (see note)
3	bay leaves
I	cinnamon stick
3	whole cloves
2	sprigs fresh thyme
10	sprigs fresh parsley

1. Adjust an oven rack to the middle position and heat the oven to 300 degrees. Sprinkle the roast generously with salt and pepper to taste.

2. Heat the oil in a large ovenproof Dutch oven over medium-high heat until shimmering but not smoking. Brown the roast thoroughly on all sides, reducing the heat if the fat begins to smoke, 8 to 10 minutes. Transfer the roast to a large plate; set aside.

3. Reduce the heat to medium, add the onions, carrots, and celery to the pot, and cook, stirring occasionally, until the vegetables begin to brown, 6 to 8 minutes. Add the garlic, sugar, tomato paste, and flour and cook until fragrant, about 30 seconds. Add the wine, scraping the pan bottom with a wooden spoon to loosen the browned bits. Return the roast and any accumulated juices on the plate to the pot. Add the bay leaves, cinnamon, cloves,

ROASTING VERSUS BRAISING

A distinctive pattern of fat and connective tissue runs through the meat of a chuck roast (left). When cooked in dry heat, or roasted (middle), the fat and sinew do not break down sufficiently, even after many hours in the oven. Cooking the meat in moist heat, or braising (right), promotes a more complete breakdown of the fat and connective tissue, yielding very tender meat.

and thyme and parsley sprigs. Bring the liquid to a simmer over medium heat, then place a large piece of foil over the pot and cover it tightly with the lid. Transfer the pot to the oven. Cook, turning the roast every 30 minutes, until fully tender and a meat fork or sharp knife slips easily in and out, 3½ to 4 hours.

4. Transfer the roast to a carving board and tent with foil to keep warm. Allow the liquid in the pot to settle for about 5 minutes, then use a wide spoon to skim the fat off the surface. Bring to a boil over high heat. Cook, whisking vigorously to help the vegetables dissolve, until the sauce is well thickened and measures about 2 cups, 5 to 6 minutes. Strain the sauce through a fine-mesh sieve and season with salt and pepper to taste (you should have about 1 cup sauce).

5. Using a chef's or carving knife, cut the meat into ½-inch-thick slices or pull it apart into large pieces. Transfer the meat to a warmed serving platter and pour about half the sauce over it. Serve immediately, passing the remaining sauce separately.

Braised Brisket

BRAISED BRISKET IS A WORKHORSE MEAL. It is cheap, can serve many people (or just a few with great leftovers), and is usually cooked with straightforward, universally appealing flavors. The all-too-common problem with brisket, however, is that the meat turns out extraordinarily dry and chewy.

Whole briskets weigh roughly 12 to 13 pounds, yet butchers usually sell them cut in half or even smaller. If cut in half, one end of the brisket is called the "first" or "flat" cut and the other is called the "second" or "point" cut. We prefer pieces from the second (point) cut because they tend to be thicker, more tender, and more flavorful. Braising requires that the meat lay flat in a covered pot, and we noted that a three-pound brisket was the largest any of our covered pots could accommodate (serving six to eight people).

The method for braising brisket is the same as for other stews and braises. The meat is first browned, then set off to the side while the browned bits left behind in the pot are used to make a flavorful sauce. The browned beef is nestled back into the pot with the sauce, the liquid is brought to a gentle simmer, and the meat is cooked until tender.

Using this basic method as our starting point, we noted that there are three keys to cooking brisket so that it doesn't taste dry or chewy. First (taking a cue from our pot roast recipe) it is easier to maintain a consistent simmer in a 300-degree oven than on top of the stove. Oven temperatures higher than 300 degrees turn the simmer into a boil (which dries out the meat), while oven temperatures lower than 300 degrees simply added unnecessary hours to the cooking time. Second, we found it takes several hours of constant simmering for the brisket to turn tender. A three-pound piece of brisket requires 2½ to 3 hours in the oven, at which point, a dinner fork should slide in and out of its center with little resistance. Third, it is necessary to slice the brisket thinly across the grain when serving.

Core to the universal appeal of brisket is the simple flavored sauce that accompanies it. Many brisket recipes we researched base the sauce around the flavor of caramelized onions (the meat is almost smothered by the onions as it cooks). Giving this idea a try, we found it easy to lightly caramelize some onions in the drippings left over from browning the meat. To build a flavorful, well-rounded sauce around the onions, it is important to add both brown sugar and tomato paste to develop their sweet onion flavor. A combination of beef and chicken broth also proved crucial, as did the addition of red wine, garlic, bay leaves, and fresh thyme. Lastly, we refreshened the flavor of this well-simmered sauce by adding a dash of cider vinegar just before serving. With an ample amount of sauce to serve alongside the sliced brisket, no one will ever complain that this version tastes chewy or dry.

Braised Beef Brisket
SERVES 6 TO 8

Make sure to use an ovenproof pot that is large enough so that the brisket lays flat. Leftover brisket can be refrigerated in the sauce for a day or two. Reheat the brisket in the sauce in a covered pot over medium-low heat.

1   beef brisket (about 3 pounds), preferably point cut (see the illustration on page 192), trimmed of excess fat and patted dry with paper towels

2   tablespoons vegetable oil
Salt and ground black pepper

3   pounds yellow onions, sliced thin (about 6 large onions)

2   tablespoons brown sugar

6   medium garlic cloves, minced or pressed through a garlic press (about 2 tablespoons)

1   teaspoon tomato paste

1/4   cup unbleached all-purpose flour

1/2   cup dry red wine

1   cup low-sodium beef broth

1   cup low-sodium chicken broth

4   bay leaves

4   sprigs fresh thyme

1   tablespoon cider vinegar

1. Adjust an oven rack to the middle position and heat the oven to 300 degrees.

2. Sprinkle the brisket generously with salt and pepper to taste. Heat the oil in a large ovenproof Dutch oven over high heat until smoking. Cook the brisket until dark brown on the first side, about 5 minutes. Flip the brisket and cook until well browned on the second side, about 5 minutes longer. Transfer the brisket to a large plate; set aside.

3. Reduce the heat to medium. Add the onions,

EQUIPMENT: Dutch Ovens

We find that a Dutch oven (also called a lidded casserole) is almost essential to making stews and braises such as pot roast. A Dutch oven is nothing more than a wide, deep pot with a cover. It was originally manufactured with ears on the side (small, round tabs used for picking up the pot) and a top that had a lip around the edge. The latter design element was important because a Dutch oven was heated by coals placed both underneath and on top of the pot. The lip kept the coals on the lid from falling off. One could bake biscuits, cobblers, beans, and stews in this pot. It was, in the full sense of the word, an oven. This oven was a key feature of chuck wagons and essential in many Colonial American households, where all cooking occurred in the fireplace. This useful pot supposedly came to be called "Dutch" because at some point the best cast iron came from Holland.

Now that everyone in the United States has an oven, the Dutch oven is no longer used to bake biscuits or cobblers. However, it is a requisite for dishes that start on top of the stove and finish in the oven, as many stews do. To make recommendations about buying a modern Dutch oven, we tested 12 models from leading makers of cookware.

We found that a Dutch oven should have a capacity of at least six quarts to be useful. Eight quarts is even better. As we cooked in the pots, we came to prefer wider, shallower Dutch ovens because it's easier to see and reach inside them, and they offer more bottom surface area to accommodate larger batches of meat for browning. This reduces the number of batches required to brown a given quantity of meat and, with it, the chances of burning the flavorful pan drippings. Ideally, the diameter of a

Dutch oven is twice as great as its height.

We also preferred pots with a light-colored interior finish, such as stainless steel or enameled cast iron. It is easier to judge the caramelization of the drippings at a glance in these pots. Dark finishes can mask the color of the drippings, which may burn before you realize it. Our favorite pot is the eight-quart All-Clad Stainless Stockpot (despite the name, this pot is a Dutch oven). The seven-quart Le Creuset Round French Oven, which is made of enameled cast iron, also tested well. These pots are quite expensive, costing at least $150 even on sale. A less expensive alternative is the seven-quart Lodge Dutch Oven, which is made from cast iron. This pot is extremely heavy (making it a bit hard to maneuver), it must be seasoned (wiped with oil) regularly, and the dark interior finish is not ideal, but it does brown food quite well and costs just $45.

THE BEST DUTCH OVENS
Our favorite pot is the eight-quart All-Clad Stainless Stockpot (left). Despite the name, this pot is a Dutch oven. Expect to spend nearly $200 for this piece of cookware. A less expensive alternative is the seven-quart Lodge Dutch Oven (right), which costs about $45 (right). However, since this pot is made from cast iron, it may react with acidic sauces and is not appropriate with all recipes, especially those that contain significant amounts of tomatoes or wine.

sugar, and ¼ teaspoon salt. Using a wooden spoon, scrape the browned bits from the pan bottom. Cook, stirring frequently, until the onions are softened and lightly browned, about 10 minutes. Stir in the garlic and tomato paste and cook until fragrant, about 30 seconds. Stir in the flour and cook for 1 minute. Slowly stir in the wine to dissolve the flour and cook until almost dry, about 1 minute. Stir in the beef broth, chicken broth, bay leaves, and thyme. Return the brisket to the pot, nestling it in the liquid, and bring to a simmer. Cover the pot, transfer it to the oven, and cook until a fork slides easily in and out of the center of the roast, 2½ to 3 hours.

4. Transfer the brisket to cutting board, tent with foil, and let rest for 15 minutes. Remove and discard the bay leaves and thyme from the sauce, stir in the vinegar, and adjust the seasonings with salt and pepper to taste. Slice the brisket thinly across the grain. Arrange the meat on a warmed platter and spoon some of the sauce over it. Serve, passing the remaining sauce at the table.

LOCATING THE BRISKET

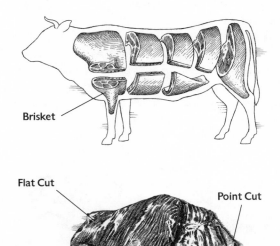

Butchers often separate the whole brisket into two parts, the flat end (left portion) and the point cut (right portion). The point cut is a bit thicker and contains more fat. It is more tender than the flat cut and is our first choice.

➤ VARIATION
Braised Brisket with Sauerkraut and Prunes

This traditional German recipe offers a good balance between sweet and sour.

Follow the recipe for Braised Beef Brisket, reducing the amount of onions to 1½ pounds (about 3 large onions). Stir in 2 pounds packaged sauerkraut, well rinsed and drained (about 3 cups), and 1 cup pitted prunes along with the broths in step 3. Proceed with the recipe as directed.

CORNED BEEF AND CABBAGE

CORNED BEEF AND CABBAGE, THE VENERable one-pot meal of boiled corned beef, cabbage, and other winter vegetables (also known in parts of the country as New England boiled dinner), has struck us less as a dish with big flavor and genuine dinner-table appeal than as a symbol of the stalwart Yankee ethics of hard work and thrift. That misconception, however, was the first of several to be busted during our testing. In the course of tasting umpteen dishes of corned beef and cabbage, we came to realize that this dish needn't be mushy, overwhelmingly salty, or one-dimensional, as it had always seemed. Instead, it can be a full-flavored medley of meaty, tender, well-seasoned beef, subtle spice, and sweet, earthy vegetables, each distinct in flavor and texture.

We commenced our research and testing with the usual spate of recipes, most of which were based on a four- to six-pound piece of corned beef. The term corned refers to the curing of meat with salt, often used as a method of preservation before refrigeration became widespread. Legend has it that the salt grains were roughly the same size as corn kernels, hence the name corned beef. The cut of beef most commonly corned is boneless brisket, which is a trimmed, 12- to 13-pound piece taken from the front part of the cow's breast. For retail sale, the whole brisket is usually split into two parts, called the first, or flat, cut and the second, or point, cut. Of the two, the point cut is thicker, fattier, and, to our taste, more flavorful and more tender than the flat cut. Both cuts can be trimmed further into smaller pieces of meat, and both are available as commercially corned beef.

At the supermarket, we found more commercial corned beef options than we had anticipated from reading the recipes we had researched. In addition to "low-sodium" corned beef, there were regular and "gray," each in both flat and point cuts in sizes ranging from three to six pounds. We were told by a representative from Mosey's, a national producer of corned beef, that the gray style is popular only in, and therefore limited to, New England. The difference between regular and gray is made clear on the package. The brine for gray corned beef contains only water and salt, whereas the "regular" corned beef brine also contains sodium nitrite, which helps the meat retain its red color by reacting with purple color pigments and turning them to pink and red.

We brought back an example of each type and took to the stove. Cooking directions on the packages and in our research recipes did not vary by much. Generally, instructions were to cover the meat with one to three inches of water and simmer until tender, anywhere from 2½ to 3½ hours, depending on the size of the brisket.

To our surprise, the regular corned beef choices disappointed us across the board. Though they remained an appealing pink even when cooked, our tasters described the flavor of both the full- and low-salt versions as "sharp and somewhat chemical," most likely from the nitrite. In addition, the texture was deemed grainy, with a noticeably chalky mouthfeel. By comparison, the gray corned beef looked, well, gray, because it lacked the color boost given to regular brisket by the nitrite. The flavor, however, was superior, and for that, we'll gladly trade the pink color. Whereas the chemical qualities we noted in the regular versions obscured the flavor of the beef, the gray corned beef tasted cleaner and beefier. The salt had a stronger presence than we preferred, and the spice we look for in ideal corned beef was nonexistent, but we knew we wanted to stick with the gray for further testing.

But because the gray corned beef we preferred is a product limited to a small region of the country, we decided to try corning our own brisket. We

figured that this would also make it easier to control the saltiness. Our research turned up two methods of corning—the wet cure and the dry cure. Both methods require close to a week, but they are also mindlessly easy. All you need to do is prepare the meat and its cure. Beyond that, there is no work whatsoever. We tested each method, using 5-pound fresh briskets in both flat and point cuts.

Because meat preservative is readily available in drugstores in the form of the potassium nitrate called saltpeter, we still had the option of producing regular and gray corned beef. Even in our home-corned beef, though, the preservative added a harshness to the flavor that competed with the taste of the beef. Because the color of the meat was less important to us than the flavor, we dropped the saltpeter from further testing.

Testing the wet method for our gray corned beef involved tasting briskets cured in a brine of 2 cups of salt and 3 quarts of water for 14, 12, 10, 7, and 5 days. Among all of them, we liked the 5-day brisket best, noting a pleasing saltiness alongside the distinctive flavor of beef. We also confirmed our preference for the fattier point cut of brisket. Fat carries flavor in all cuts of meat, and beef brisket is no different. The flat cut is especially lean and therefore less flavorful and moist than the point cut.

At this point, we also gave the dry-cure method a go. Adapting a recipe from Julia Child's *The Way to Cook* (Knopf, 1989), we rubbed our 6-pound, point-cut brisket with ½ cup salt and a few crushed herbs and spices, placed it in a 2-gallon zipper-lock bag, weighted the meat with a brick, and let it sit for 5 days in the fridge. Lo and behold, the result was the best corned beef of them all, even better than the 5-day wet-cured corned beef, with a concentrated beef flavor, assertive yet not overpowering saltiness, and a pleasant spiciness. Curing the brisket for 2 extra days, 7 in total, brought out the flavor of the spices a little more, without affecting the saltiness.

Julia Child's recipe suggested desalting the dry-cured meat by soaking it in several changes of water for at least 24 hours or up to 3 days, depending on the size of the brisket. To be honest, we initially overlooked this step; we simply rinsed the surface of the meat to remove shards of crumbled bay leaf and cracked peppercorns and went ahead with the cooking. When we finally did try the full desalting, we found that the meat tasted slightly richer because of the diminished salt presence, but not so much better that it justified a 24-hour soak as opposed to a quick rinse.

With the corned beef tasting just the way we wanted it, we turned our attention to the cooking method, then to the vegetables. Though most recipes call for cooking corned beef and cabbage on the stove, we did try a couple of tests in the oven. Our advice is to stick to the stove, on which the meat cooked faster and was easier to monitor. Also, we found that adding the vegetables and adjusting the heat to compensate was easier with the pot on top of the stove.

On the stove, we noticed that the meat emerged from the pot tender and flaky if cooked at a lively simmer, as opposed to tight and tough when cooked at a full boil. We also preferred to cook the meat covered to prevent water evaporation and a resulting overconcentration of salt in the broth. We experimented with different quantities of water in the pot, covering the corned beef by ½ inch to 3 inches and found that it makes no difference in terms of the meat or vegetables. The amount of water does matter to the broth, though. The broth produced from covering the meat by ½ inch to an inch (8 to 10 cups over a 4½-pound brisket in our 8-quart pot) and cooking it with the pot lid on was nicely seasoned and suitable for use on its own or in a soup.

The last, though not insignificant, variable was the vegetables. We tested a wide variety of vegetables, from the familiar to the exotic, and settled on the traditional green cabbage, with the added interest of carrots, parsnips, potatoes, turnips, rutabagas, onions, and Brussels sprouts, all borrowed from the New England boiled dinner, as our favorites. We tried cooking the vegetables along with the meat, but there were two distinct disadvantages to this approach. First, it was difficult to judge when the vegetables were properly done. Second, it would require a pot larger than any we had in the test kitchen or in our own homes.

The best method turned out to be removing the meat from the broth when done, then cooking the vegetables in the broth. This not only benefited the vegetables, giving them a full, round flavor from the salt and rendered fat in the broth, but it also allowed us time to let the meat rest before cutting it.

Home-Corned Beef Brisket and Cabbage, New England Style

SERVES 8 WITH LEFTOVERS

If you prefer a leaner piece of meat, feel free to use the flat cut. In fact, we found more flat-cut than point-cut briskets in supermarket meat cases, so you'll probably have to ask the meat department attendant or butcher to bring you a point cut. Leave a bit of fat attached for better texture and flavor. The meat is cooked fully when it is tender, the muscle fibers have loosened visibly, and a skewer slides in with minimal resistance. Serve this dish with horseradish, either plain or mixed with whipped or sour cream, or with grainy mustard. Use any leftover meat to make Corned Beef Hash (page 370).

½	cup kosher salt
1	tablespoon black peppercorns, cracked
¾	tablespoon ground allspice
1	tablespoon dried thyme
½	tablespoon paprika
2	bay leaves, crumbled
1	beef brisket (4 to 6 pounds), preferably point cut (see the illustration on page 192), trimmed of excess fat and patted dry with paper towels
7–8	pounds prepared vegetables of your choice (see page 195)

1. Mix the salt and seasonings in a small bowl.

2. Spear the brisket about 30 times per side with a meat fork or metal skewer. Rub each side evenly with the salt mixture; place in a 2-gallon zipper-lock bag, forcing out as much air as possible. Place in a pan large enough to hold it (a rimmed baking sheet works well), cover with a second, similar-size pan, and weight with 2 bricks or heavy cans of similar weight. Refrigerate 5 to 7 days, turning once a day. Rinse the meat and pat dry.

3. Bring the brisket to a boil with water to cover by ½ to 1 inch in a large Dutch oven or stockpot (at

least 8 quarts), skimming any impurities that rise to the surface. Cover and simmer until a skewer inserted in the thickest part of the brisket slides out with ease, 2 to 3 hours.

4. Heat the oven to 200 degrees. Transfer the meat to a large platter, ladling about 1 cup of the cooking liquid over it to keep it moist. Cover with aluminum foil and set in the oven.

5. Add the vegetables from category 1 (below) to the pot and bring to a boil; cover and simmer until the vegetables begin to soften, about 10 minutes. Add the vegetables from category 2 (below) and bring to a boil; cover and simmer until all the vegetables are tender, 10 to 15 minutes longer.

6. Meanwhile, remove the meat from the oven and cut it across the grain into ¼-inch slices. Return the meat to the platter.

7. Transfer the vegetables to the meat platter, moisten with additional broth, and serve.

BOLLITO MISTO

SERVED ON MANY SPECIAL OCCASIONS, the classic Italian dish bollito misto is a large platter of various boiled meats accompanied by salsa verde—a bright green sauce of chopped parsley, capers, anchovies, lemon juice, and olive oil. Meats simmer together in a large pot of flavorful broth until tender, juicy, and tasty. We set out to discover how American home cooks could make a good bollito misto.

We began with the ingredient list. The authentic recipes we found read more like a butcher's daily chalkboard than a recipe: beef tongue, brisket, veal breast, pigs' feet, chicken, pork sausage—and the list goes on. To update this recipe for the American palate (and supermarket), we decided to include only mainstream meats such as beef brisket, veal breast, chicken, and pork sausage.

The cooking method for all these meats,

Vegetables for Corned Beef and Cabbage

The vegetables listed below are some of our favorites. However, if you love potatoes but cannot abide parsnips, choose vegetables to suit your tastes. To make sure that the vegetables are evenly cooked, we trim them all to sizes appropriate for their density and cooking characteristics and add them to the pot in two batches.

CATEGORY 1

Once the meat has been removed from the pot, add the desired selection and quantity of vegetables from this category. Return the liquid to a boil and simmer for 10 minutes before adding vegetables from category 2.

VEGETABLE	PREPARATION
Carrots	Peeled and halved crosswise; thin end halved lengthwise, thick end quartered lengthwise.
Rutabagas (small)	Peeled and halved crosswise; each half cut into six chunks.
White turnips (medium)	Peeled and quartered.
New potatoes (small)	Scrubbed and left whole.

CATEGORY 2

At the 10-minute mark, add selected vegetables from this category, return cooking liquid to boil, then continue to simmer until all vegetables are just tender, 10 to 15 minutes longer.

Boiling onions	Peeled and left whole.
Green cabbage, uncored (small head)	Blemished leaves removed and cut into six to eight wedges.
Parsnips	Peeled and halved crosswise; thin end halved lengthwise, thick end quartered lengthwise.
Brussels sprouts, whole	Blemished leaves removed, stems trimmed, and left whole.

however, is universal. A water-based broth is seasoned and brought to a simmer. The meat is then added to the broth and poached until it is fully cooked and tender. Because the different meats require different cooking times, they are added to the pot sequentially so that they are all done at the same time. Figuring out this timing, we realized, is the trick to a good bollito misto.

Beginning with the broth, we figured we needed five to six quarts of liquid to be able to cook the brisket, veal, and chicken together in the same pot. (The fatty sausage is always cooked separately so as not to ruin the flavor of the broth.) To make the broth, all the recipes we found added just one carrot, one celery rib, and one onion to the water. Realizing that this small amount of vegetables would not add enough flavor to five or six quarts of water, we doubled the amount of carrot and celery, tripled the amount of onion, and added a head of garlic, some parsley, bay leaves, peppercorns, and salt. With five to six quarts of this flavorful broth brought to a simmer in a 10- to 12-quart pot, we were ready to start adding the meat.

To ensure that all the meat emerges from the broth perfectly cooked at the same time, all the recipes we found cooked the various items according to the following schedule: Cook the brisket for two hours, add the veal breast and cook for half an hour longer, then add the chicken for a final hour. The result of this classic bollito misto schedule, however, was disappointing. All of the meat was far overcooked; the brisket began to shred apart on its own, while the veal and chicken turned bone dry. To correct this, we needed to find out exactly how long it would take each of the meats to cook. Cooking them separately, we determined that a 2-pound piece of brisket requires about two hours, a 2-pound veal roast about one hour, and a 3½-pound chicken about 30 minutes. Combining these times, it was easy to organize an accurate cooking schedule for the bollito misto. The sausage, which we cooked separately in a pot of water, required 15 to 20 minutes to cook through.

We next focused on making enough salsa verde to accompany the meat. The sauce, made mostly from parsley and olive oil, is seasoned with capers, garlic, anchovies, and lemon juice. Salsa verde is usually hand chopped to yield a slightly chunky texture, but due to the volume we needed, it was easier to make the sauce in a food processor. We found that a slice of lightly toasted bread muted harsh flavors and prevented the sauce from separating. We processed the bread with the oil and lemon juice, then pulsed the parsley, capers, garlic, and anchovies. This clean, crisp sauce is the perfect accompaniment to the tender, juicy meats.

Bollito Misto

SERVES 10 TO 12

The leftover broth used to cook the meat should not be discarded but rather strained and reserved for use as a stock or soup base. (The liquid used to cook the sausage is very fatty and should be discarded.) If you want to prepare this recipe in advance, follow the recipe through step 1, then remove the meat from the broth and refrigerate both separately for up to 2 days. When reheating, bring the broth to a simmer, then return the cooked brisket and veal to the broth and continue with steps 2 and 3. Ask your butcher to tie the veal roast so it won't fall apart as it cooks. Serve with a double batch of the Salsa Verde on page 405.

3	medium onions, chopped coarse
2	medium carrots, chopped coarse
2	medium celery ribs, chopped coarse
I	head garlic, smashed, with loose, papery skins discarded
3	bay leaves
5	sprigs fresh parsley
5	black peppercorns
I	tablespoon salt
I	beef brisket (about 2 pounds), preferably point cut (see the illustration on page 192), trimmed of excess fat
I	boneless veal breast roast (about 2 pounds), tied
I	whole chicken (about 3 ½ pounds)
2	pounds cotechino, garlic-pork sausage, or sweet Italian sausage
I ½	cups Salsa Verde (page 405) at room temperature

1. Place the onions, carrots, celery, garlic, bay leaves, parsley, peppercorns, and salt in a 10- or 12-quart stockpot and fill halfway with water. Bring to a boil over high heat and add the beef brisket. Bring the liquid back to a simmer, cover the pot, and reduce the heat as necessary to maintain the simmer. Cook for 1 hour. Add the veal roast, return the liquid to a simmer, cover the pot, and cook for 30 minutes.

2. Add the chicken and return the liquid to a simmer. Cover and cook until an instant-read thermometer inserted in the chicken breast registers 160 degrees, 25 to 30 minutes.

3. Meanwhile, bring 2 quarts of water to a boil in a separate pot. Prick the sausages several times with the tines of a fork and add them to the water. Bring to a simmer and cook over medium-low heat until the sausage is cooked through, 15 to 20 minutes. Remove the sausages and discard the cooking liquid.

4. To serve, remove the meats from the hot broth, slice, and arrange them on a large platter. Sprinkle the sliced meats with several tablespoons cooking liquid to help keep them moist. (Alternatively, you can strain the broth, place it in a tureen large enough to hold all the meats, and slice to order at the table.) Serve immediately with the Salsa Verde.

POT-AU-FEU

NOT LONG AFTER MAN DISCOVERED FIRE, he (or she) discovered the boiled dinner. This primal and simplest of cooking methods is nothing more than simmering meat and vegetables in a pot of water, and the technique is used around the world, from Mongolian hotpot to New England corned beef and cabbage. Literally translated as "pot on fire" (referring to the stovetop simmering method and not some unfortunate cooking accident), pot-au-feu is France's version. The resulting broth is often elegant enough to serve as its own course with crusty bread, followed by the sliced, meltingly tender beef and an assortment of vegetables, all of which are presented family-style, with condiments such as horseradish and mustard.

As exotic ingredients and chef-inspired recipes have taken hold of American cooks, traditional recipes such as pot-au-feu have fallen out of favor. But there is something appealing about this relic from the golden age of French country cooking. Pot-au-feu is straightforward fare that uses neither strange ingredients nor complicated cooking methods, and, although it requires a substantial investment of time (it takes hours to make tough, cheap meat tender), this recipe can produce a spectacular complete meal for a crowd. As we also found out, bad pot-au-feu recipes (unfortunately, we tried quite a few) are shockingly disappointing.

Because it is so simple (there is no potent ingredient or sauce to mask mistakes), pot-au-feu has to be perfectly executed. If the meat is tough and fibrous or if the vegetables are bloated from overcooking, the dish has little appeal. Each ingredient must be perfectly seasoned and cooked. We reasoned that choosing the right ingredients—from the cut of beef to the proper vegetables—would greatly enhance the flavor of the dish. When to add the ingredients and how long they should cook would also be key.

To offer a mix of meat textures, pot-au-feu uses at least two types of beef, usually a boneless roast as well as a bone-in cut such as short ribs or beef shanks. Our first attempts to use only one cut provided either an anemic broth (all roast and no bones) or lack of meat (all bones, no roast). It was clear that we would need to use both. For the roast, we tested cuts from the round (leg) and chuck (shoulder) as well as brisket and preferred the chuck roasts, which get their big flavor and velvety texture from the good amount of fat and collagen running through them. All of the chuck roasts tested were good, but the chuck-eye was our favorite. As for bony cuts, we loved the richly decadent meat from short ribs, but this cut didn't add much flavor to the broth. Beef shanks are packed with flavorful marrow that melted into the broth during our next test, but shank meat was not as satisfying as that from the short ribs. We decided to include both bony cuts to produce a beefy broth and rich-tasting meat.

A barely simmering pot gave us fall-apart tender meat in more than six hours. We turned up the heat from barely bubbling to a healthy simmer, and our next batch was done in 3½ hours. Could we speed things up even more? In a word, No. Even though it's called "boiled dinner," we found that pot-au-feu does not respond well to constant boiling; the meat turns stringy (the violent agitation of the liquid literally tears the meat apart) and the resulting broth is a murky mess. In addition, chuck roasts cooked for less time were tough—this meat needs time to become fork-tender.

As for which vegetables to include, tasters were most comfortable with more conservative additions, such as carrots, parsnips, new potatoes, and green beans, although pearl onions, fennel, cabbage, leeks, turnips, butternut squash, and sweet potatoes were also well received. A few vegetables were disliked. Zucchini and summer squash were watery and spongy, and broccoli was too stinky. Most recipes call for adding the vegetables to the broth all at once, but this produced overcooked vegetables every time. We discovered that batch cooking—potatoes go in for a few minutes, then the carrots and parsnips, then the green beans—ensures that each vegetable cooks perfectly.

Perfectly cooked—but, unfortunately, also perfectly bland. In addition, the pounds of vegetables made the broth taste like vegetable soup. We decided to cook the vegetables separately from the beef in highly salted water (2 tablespoons of salt per 4 quarts of water), hoping that this would season the vegetables sufficiently. And did it ever! Each vegetable now tasted brighter and cleaner, and the whole dish took a giant leap forward.

While we weren't looking for vegetable soup, we admitted that the broth could use a little more flavor. Herbs and spices were a natural addition, and we found that a few bay leaves, peppercorns, and whole cloves gave the broth depth, while parsley and thyme added freshness. A whole head of garlic improved things greatly, but still we wanted more.

We added a little carrot, celery, and onion back to the broth (not enough to overpower the beef flavor), and we had a definite improvement in flavor. We tried sweating the vegetables in a minute amount of oil until they began to exude their juices. This extra step took all of 10 minutes, but now the broth tasted full and complex. And yet . . . we still wanted a richer, more concentrated broth.

Like many pot-au-feu recipes, ours now called for about seven quarts of water, enough to cover the pounds of beef and vegetables. Because we had decided to cook our vegetables separately, however, we realized that this much water was now probably too much. We cut 1 quart of water and knew we were on the right track. We thought that cutting another quart might be pushing the envelope, as the water barely covered the meat, but this was no problem; the once sizable roast reduced in mass as it cooked. With the lid left off the pot, our 5 quarts of water reduced down to 3 quarts of rich broth.

With our heady broth ladled over the fall-apart-tender roast, melt-in-your mouth ribs and shanks, and perfectly cooked and seasoned vegetables, our pot-au-feu was now simple cooking at its best. This French classic didn't seem that dated anymore. In fact, with its emphasis on presenting each ingredient in its most natural form, it was downright chic—well, almost.

Pot-au-Feu

SERVES 8 TO 10

A large stockpot, one with at least a 12-quart capacity, is necessary for this recipe. Cheesecloth is ideal for straining the broth, although a quadruple layer of paper towels will do in a pinch. Once the beef braise reaches a boil, reduce the heat to maintain a steady simmer (see page 200 for more information); if left to boil, the resulting broth will be murky, even after straining. For serving, arrange the components on a large warmed platter and give diners individual shallow soup bowls in which to plate their portions. It is not compulsory to serve all of the condiments listed below; mustard and cornichons are traditional choices.

BEEF BRAISE

1   medium celery rib, chopped medium

2   medium carrots, chopped medium

2   medium onions, chopped medium

2   teaspoons vegetable oil

1   beef chuck roast (about 3 pounds), preferably chuck eye, tied according to the illustration on page 199

3   pounds beef short ribs (about 5 large ribs), trimmed of excess fat and tied according to the illustration on page 199

2   pounds beef shanks, about 1 ½ inches thick,
    tied according to the illustration below
5   quarts water
3   large bay leaves
1   teaspoon whole black peppercorns
5   whole cloves
1   large garlic head, outer papery skins
    removed and top third of head cut off
    and discarded
10 fresh parsley stems
8   sprigs fresh thyme
1   tablespoon salt

    VEGETABLES
2   pounds small red new potatoes, scrubbed and
    halved if larger than 1 ½ inches
2   tablespoons salt
1 ½ pounds carrots (about 7 medium),
    peeled, halved crosswise, thicker half
    quartered lengthwise, thinner half halved
    lengthwise
1 ½ pounds parsnips (4 to 5 medium), peeled,
    halved crosswise, thicker half quartered
    lengthwise, thinner half halved lengthwise
1   pound green beans, stem ends trimmed

    GARNISHES AND CONDIMENTS
¼   cup chopped fresh parsley leaves
1   baguette, thickly sliced
    Dijon or whole-grain mustard
    Sea salt
    Cornichons
    Prepared horseradish

1. FOR THE BEEF BRAISE: Stir together the celery, carrots, onions, and oil in a 12-quart stockpot. Cook, covered, over low heat, stirring frequently, until the vegetables are softened but not browned and have released their moisture, 8 to 10 minutes. (If the vegetables begin to color before softening, add 1 tablespoon water and continue to cook.) Add the chuck roast, short ribs, beef shanks, water, bay, peppercorns, and cloves; increase the heat to medium-high and bring to a boil, using a large shallow spoon to skim any foam and fat that rises to surface. Reduce the heat to low and simmer, uncovered, for 2½ hours, skimming the surface of

fat and foam every 30 minutes.

2. Add the garlic, parsley stems, thyme, and salt. Simmer for additional 1 to 1½ hours or until the tip of a paring knife inserted into the meats gets little resistance.

3. Using tongs, transfer the roast, ribs, shanks, and garlic to a large cutting board and tent with foil. Strain the broth through a mesh strainer lined with a doubled layer of cheesecloth into a large container (you should have about 3 quarts liquid). Let the broth settle for at least 5 minutes, then skim the fat off using a large shallow spoon.

TYING THE MEAT

Chuck roast: Cut two 2-foot pieces of butcher's twine. Wrap one piece around roast about 1 inch from bottom and tie with double knot. Snip off excess and repeat with second piece about 1 inch from top.

Short ribs: Cut two 1-foot pieces of butcher's twine for each rib. Wrap one piece about 1 inch from top and tie with double knot. Snip off excess and repeat with second piece about 1 inch from bottom.

Shanks: Cut four 1-foot pieces of twine for each shank. Wrap each piece of twine around shank and tie in center.

4. FOR THE VEGETABLES: While the broth settles, rinse out the stockpot and add the potatoes, salt, and 4 quarts water; bring to a boil over high heat, then boil 7 minutes. Add the carrots and parsnips and cook 3 minutes longer. Add the green beans and cook 4 minutes longer. Using a slotted spoon, transfer the vegetables to a large warmed serving platter, arranging them as desired; tent with foil.

5. TO SERVE: Using tongs, squeeze the garlic into a small serving bowl. Remove the twine from the roast and separate the roast at its seams; cut the roast across the grain into ½-inch-thick slices and arrange on the platter with the vegetables. Remove the twine from the shanks and ribs and arrange on the platter. Ladle about 1 cup strained broth over the meat and vegetables to moisten; sprinkle with the parsley. Serve, ladling additional broth over individual servings and passing the garlic, baguette slices, and condiments separately.

STEADY (AND NOT SO SLOW) WINS

We found that the rate at which the pot-au-feu cooks can greatly influence the end product and simmering time. The best choice is a steady simmer, which is strong enough to cook the meat in about 3½ hours but gentle enough not to damage the meat or broth.

GENTLE SIMMER: 198°–205°
Cooking time: 6 hours
Very few bubbles break the surface of the broth, appearing mostly around the sides of the pot. Broth is perfectly clear.

STEADY SIMMER: 206°–211°
Cooking time: 3½ hours
Larger bubbles break the surface of the broth at a more rapid rate, especially around the sides of the pot. Broth is fairly clear.

RAPID BOIL: 212°
Cooking time: 1½ hours
Large bubbles appear all over the surface and begin to "roll over." Violent churning breaks apart meat and turns broth cloudy.

BRAISED SHORT RIBS

IN THE SUPERMARKET MEAT CASE, SHORT ribs are often overlooked, seldom understood, rather intimidating hunks of meat and bone that are frequently shunned. But braise them, and they become yielding, tender, and succulent. Then douse them with a velvety sauce containing all the rich, bold flavors from the braise, and they are as satisfying as beef stew, but with much more panache. All of this, however, comes at a price: short ribs are outrageously fatty. The challenge is to get them to give up their fat.

The first step in most braises is browning the meat. Browning adds color and flavor, but in the case of short ribs it also presents an opportunity to render some of the fat. We tried browning both on the stovetop and in the oven and quickly became a proponent of oven browning. As long as you own a roasting pan large enough to hold all of the ribs in a single layer, you can use the oven to brown them in just one batch. This eliminates the need to brown in multiple batches on the stove, which can create a greasy, splattery mess and result in burnt drippings in the bottom of the pot. In the oven, the ribs can brown for a good long time to maximize rendering. (Because they can brown unattended, you can use that time to prepare the other ingredients for the braise). The single inconvenience of oven browning is deglazing the roasting pan on the stovetop, which makes a burner-worthy roasting pan a prerequisite.

Like a beef stew, short ribs need aromatic vegetables. After having made a couple of batches with onions only, we chose to use a combination of onions, carrots, celery, and garlic for full, round flavor.

Braising liquids required only a cursory investigation. Homemade beef stock was out of the question because just about no one makes it. Based on previous tastings in the test kitchen, we also discounted canned beef broth. Canned chicken broth, however, offered sufficient backbone and, when enriched by the flavor and body contributed by the short ribs themselves, made for a rich, robust sauce. We began using a combination of red wine, chicken broth, and water. We eventually eliminated the water, but the sauce, despite the abundance of aromatics and herbs, remained strangely hollow and lacking. All along we had been using a cheap, hardly potable wine. After stepping up to a good, solid one worthy of drinking, the sauce improved dramatically; it had the complexity and resonance that we were seeking.

If the braising liquid were to transform itself into the sauce we were after, it would need some thickening. After various experiments, we found that adding flour to the sautéed vegetables before pouring in the liquid resulted in a sauce that was lustrous and had the perfect consistency.

As they braise, the browned short ribs continue to release fat, which means that the braising liquid must be defatted before it is palatable. We found the easiest technique to be a two-day process, necessitating some forethought. Braise the ribs, let them cool in the liquid so that the meat does not dry out, remove them, strain the liquid, and then chill the ribs and the liquid separately. The next day, spoon the solidified fat off the liquid's surface, and heat the liquid and the ribs together.

Short Ribs Braised in Red Wine with Bacon, Parsnips, and Pearl Onions
SERVES 6

If braising and serving the ribs on the same day, bypass cooling the ribs in the braising liquid; instead, remove them from the pot straight out of the oven, strain the liquid, then let it settle so that the fat separates to the top. With a wide shallow spoon, skim off as much fat as possible and continue with the recipe. Though this recipe and the one that follows call for widely available English-style short ribs, both recipes will also work with flanken-style

short ribs. We like to serve these short ribs with mashed potatoes, but they also taste good over egg noodles.

6	pounds bone-in English-style short ribs, trimmed of excess fat and silver skin, or bone-in flanken-style short ribs (see page 202)
	Salt and ground black pepper
3	cups dry full-bodied red wine
3	large onions, chopped medium
2	medium carrots, chopped medium
1	large celery rib, chopped medium
9	medium garlic cloves, chopped (about 3 tablespoons)
1/4	cup unbleached all-purpose flour
4	cups low-sodium chicken broth
1	(14.5-ounce) can diced tomatoes, drained
1 1/2	tablespoons minced fresh rosemary leaves
1	tablespoon minced fresh thyme leaves
3	medium bay leaves
1	teaspoon tomato paste

BACON, PEARL ONION, AND PARSNIP GARNISH

6	ounces (about 6 slices) bacon, cut into 1/4-inch pieces
8	ounces frozen pearl onions (do not thaw)
4	medium parsnips (about 10 ounces), peeled and cut diagonally into 3/4-inch pieces
1/4	teaspoon sugar
1/4	teaspoon salt
6	tablespoons minced fresh parsley leaves

1. Adjust an oven rack to the lower-middle position and heat the oven to 450 degrees. Arrange the short ribs, bone-side down, in a single layer in a large flameproof roasting pan; season with salt and pepper to taste. Roast until the meat begins to brown, about 45 minutes; drain off all liquid and fat with a bulb baster. Return the pan to the oven and continue to cook until the meat is well browned, 15 to 20 minutes longer. (For flanken-style short ribs, arrange the ribs in a single layer in a large roasting pan; season with salt and pepper. Roast until the meat begins to brown, about 45 minutes; drain off all liquid and fat with a bulb baster. Return the pan to the oven and continue to cook until browned,

about 8 minutes; using tongs, flip each piece and cook until the second side is browned, about 8 minutes longer). Transfer the ribs to a large plate; set aside. Drain off fat to a small bowl and reserve. Reduce the oven temperature to 300 degrees. Place the roasting pan on 2 stovetop burners set at medium heat; add the wine and bring to a simmer, scraping up the browned bits on the pan bottom with a wooden spoon. Set the roasting pan with the wine aside.

2. Heat 2 tablespoons reserved fat in a large ovenproof Dutch oven over medium-high heat; add the onions, carrots, and celery. Sauté, stirring occasionally, until the vegetables soften,

INGREDIENTS: Short Ribs

Short ribs are just what their name says they are: "short ribs," cut from any part along the length of the cow's ribs. They can come from the lower belly section or higher up toward the back, from the shoulder (or chuck) area, or the forward midsection.

When we started testing short ribs, we went to the local grocery store and bought out their supply. What we brought back to the test kitchen were 2- to 4-inch lengths of wide flat rib bone, to which a rectangular plate of fatty meat was attached (see photo below left). We also ordered short ribs from the butcher. Imagine our confusion when these turned out to be long, continuous pieces of meat, about 3/4 inch thick, that had been cut across the ribs and grain and that included two or three segments of rib bone (see photo below right). The former, we learned, are sometimes called English-style short ribs, and the latter are called flanken-style ribs.

We began by braising both types of ribs. The ones from the butcher were favored by most tasters because the relatively thin, across-the-grain cut made the meat more pleasant to eat; the supermarket ribs were a bit stringier because they contained longer segments of "grain." Both types were equally tender and good, but considering the cost ($5.99 versus $2.99 per pound) and effort (special order) required to procure the butcher-cut specimens, we decided to go with the supermarket variety.

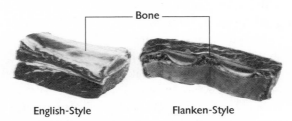

Bone

English-Style   Flanken-Style

about 12 minutes. Add the garlic and cook until fragrant, about 30 seconds. Stir in the flour until combined, about 45 seconds. Stir in the wine from the roasting pan, chicken broth, tomatoes, rosemary, thyme, bay leaves, tomato paste, and salt and pepper to taste. Bring to a boil and add the short ribs, completely submerging the meat in the liquid; return the liquid to a boil, cover the pot, place it in the oven, and simmer until the ribs are tender, about 2 to 2½ hours. Transfer the pot to a wire rack and cool, partially covered, until warm, about 2 hours.

3. Transfer the ribs from the pot to a large plate, removing the excess vegetables that may cling to the meat; discard loose bones that have fallen away from the meat. Strain the braising liquid into a medium bowl, pressing out the liquid from the solids; discard the solids. Cover the ribs and liquid separately with plastic wrap and refrigerate overnight. (Can be refrigerated up to 3 days.)

4. TO PREPARE THE GARNISH AND FINISH THE DISH: Cook the bacon in a Dutch oven over medium heat until just crisp, 8 to 10 minutes; remove with a slotted spoon to a plate lined with paper towels. Add the pearl onions, parsnips, sugar, and salt to the Dutch oven; increase the heat to high and sauté, stirring occasionally, until browned, about 5 minutes. Meanwhile, spoon off and discard the solidified fat from the reserved braising liquid. Add the defatted liquid to the Dutch oven and bring to a simmer, stirring occasionally; adjust the seasonings with salt and pepper to taste. Submerge the ribs in the liquid and return to a simmer. Reduce the heat to medium and cook, partially covered, until the ribs are heated through and the onions and parsnips are tender, about 5 minutes longer; gently stir in the bacon. Divide the ribs, vegetables, and sauce among individual bowls, sprinkle each with 1 tablespoon parsley, and serve.

➤ VARIATION

Porter-Braised Short Ribs with Prunes, Brandy, and Lemon Essence

Brandy-soaked prunes take the place of vegetables here, so this version is particularly suited to a mashed root vegetable or potato accompaniment. Use a dark, mildly assertive beer, not a light lager.

PRUNE, BRANDY, AND LEMON ESSENCE
GARNISH

½	cup brandy
8	ounces pitted prunes, each prune halved
2	teaspoons brown sugar
2	teaspoons grated zest from 1 lemon
6	tablespoons minced fresh parsley leaves

1. Follow the recipe for Short Ribs Braised in Red Wine with Bacon, Parsnips, and Pearl Onions, substituting 3 cups porter beer for the red wine, eliminating the rosemary, and substituting 2 tablespoons Dijon mustard and 2 teaspoons Worcestershire sauce for the tomato paste. Continue with the recipe through step 3.

2. To prepare the garnish and finish the dish: Bring the brandy to a boil in a small saucepan; off heat, add the prunes and let stand until plump and softened, about 15 minutes. Meanwhile, spoon off and discard the solidified fat from the braising liquid. Bring the braising liquid to a boil in a Dutch oven over medium-high heat, stirring occasionally. Add the prunes and the brandy and the brown sugar; adjust the seasonings with salt and pepper to taste. Submerge the ribs in the liquid and return to a simmer. Reduce the heat to medium-low and cook, partially covered, until the ribs are heated through, about 5 minutes longer; gently stir in the lemon zest. Divide the ribs and sauce among individual bowls, sprinkle each with 1 tablespoon parsley, and serve.

Braised Lamb Shanks

ONE OF THE GREAT PLEASURES OF COOK-ing is turning relatively tough cuts of meat into meltingly tender dishes. Among the most richly flavored of these tougher cuts is the lamb shank, which is simply the bottom portion of the fore or hind leg of a lamb.

Like other cuts of meat that come from the joints of animals, such as oxtails or short ribs, lamb shanks are extremely flavorful when properly cooked. This is because they contain a high proportion of connective tissue and fat, which break down during cooking and add flavor to the meat.

However, the presence of all this connective tissue and fat means that shanks can only be cooked using a long, slow, moist cooking method that will cause the connective tissue to disintegrate and render the fat without drying out the meat. The only practical cooking method for achieving this goal is braising, which means cooking the meat partially covered in liquid, usually in a closed container. Braising keeps the temperature of the meat relatively low—around the boiling point of water—for a long period, which is exactly what is needed to convert the tough collagen to tender gelatin.

While we obtained satisfactory results by braising shanks on top of the stove, we preferred braising in an oven because of its unique heating properties. With the heat coming from all directions, the meat cooks more evenly. This is a particular advantage, given that many pans have hot spots that cause them to heat unevenly on a burner.

Because of the high fat content of this cut, several straightforward precautions are necessary to keep the level of fat in the final product to a minimum. First, if your butcher has not already done so, take the time to trim the lamb shanks of the excess fat that encases the meat. Even a long, slow braise will not successfully render all of the exterior fat on a lamb shank. Trimming it helps you get a jump on that potential problem.

Browning the shanks well before braising them also helps render some of the exterior fat. Browning also offers the advantage of providing a great deal of flavor to the dish. Be sure to drain the fat from the pan after browning.

The third important step is to remove the fat from the braising liquid after the shanks have been cooked. To do this, take the shanks out of the braising liquid, strain out the vegetables, and allow the sauce to rest undisturbed for a short while. Then, using a ladle, carefully skim the fat that has risen to the surface and discard it. This process can be facilitated by transferring the sauce to a taller, narrower container before setting it aside to rest. If, after skimming the liquid, you find that it still has too much fat, you may repeat this step after 10 more minutes, although with most shanks, this will not be necessary. Further, if the braise is prepared well in advance of serving, you may refrigerate the braising liquid, then lift off the solidified fat from the top of the liquid.

The braising liquid, along with the aromatics you add to it, will greatly enhance the flavor of the entire dish. Stock is the traditional braising liquid because it adds textural richness as well as depth of flavor. As we have said many times before in these pages, making homemade stock is not practical. We recommend, therefore, using canned chicken broth, not beef broth, for this braise. The chicken broth complements the flavor of the lamb shanks.

Wine is a particularly good addition to the braising liquid, adding complexity and acid to the sauce. The acid is particularly important because of the richness of the lamb. Too little acid creates a dull, rather flat-tasting dish. On the other hand, too much acid results in a harsh, off-putting flavor. After trying different ratios, we found that 2 parts wine to 3 parts stock gives the best flavor. We found that either white wine or red works well, the difference being that red wine will give you a richer, deeper finish.

Whatever liquid you use for braising, we discovered, it should cover all but the top inch of the shanks. This is a departure from classic braising, where less liquid is used. We adopted this method after leaving shanks to braise in the oven, then returning some time later to find that the liquid had boiled away and the shanks were burned. Unless you are using a true braising pan with an extremely tight-fitting lid, a fair amount of liquid will escape over the cooking process. Using more liquid prevents the pan from drying out, no matter how loose the seal is.

Lamb shanks need not be served whole, though we prefer them this way for their dramatic appeal. Once the shanks are cooked and cooled, you may remove the meat from the bone before reincorporating it with the vegetables and sauce. The resulting stew-type dish will be less dramatic in presentation but equally delicious. You may also vary the choice of herbs and spices according to your taste; in the following recipes, we have included suggestions.

Lamb Shanks Braised in Red Wine
SERVES 6

If you're using smaller shanks than the ones called for in this recipe, reduce the initial braising time in step 3 from 1½ hours to 1 hour. Serve these braised shanks over mashed potatoes or polenta. If you want to prepare the dish ahead of time, make the recipe through step 3, then cool and refrigerate the shanks and braising liquid (still in the pot) overnight. When ready to serve, remove the solidified fat on the surface, then warm the dish over medium heat.

1	tablespoon extra-virgin olive oil
6	lamb shanks (¾ to 1 pound each), trimmed of excess fat
	Salt and ground black pepper
2	medium onions, sliced thick
3	medium carrots, cut crosswise into 2-inch pieces
2	celery ribs, cut crosswise into 2-inch pieces
4	medium garlic cloves, peeled
2	tablespoons tomato paste
2	teaspoons minced fresh thyme leaves
2	teaspoons minced fresh rosemary leaves
2	cups dry red wine
3	cups low-sodium chicken broth

1. Adjust an oven rack to the lower-middle position and heat the oven to 350 degrees. Heat the oil in a large ovenproof Dutch oven over medium-high heat until it is shimmering. Meanwhile, sprinkle both sides of the shanks generously with salt and pepper to taste. Swirl to coat the pan bottom with the oil. Place 3 shanks in a single layer in the pan and cook, turning once, until nicely browned all over, about 7 minutes. Transfer the shanks to a plate and set aside. Brown the remaining shanks and transfer them to the plate.

2. Drain all but 2 tablespoons fat from the pot. Add the onions, carrots, celery, garlic, tomato paste, herbs, and a light sprinkling of salt. Cook until the vegetables soften slightly, 3 to 4 minutes. Add the wine, then the stock, stirring with a wooden spoon to loosen the browned bits on the pan bottom. Bring the liquid to a simmer. Add the shanks and season with salt and pepper to taste.

3. Cover the pot and transfer it to the oven. Braise the shanks for 1½ hours. Uncover and continue braising until the shank tops are browned, about 30 minutes. Turn the shanks and braise until the other side is browned and the meat is fall-off-the-bone tender, 15 to 30 minutes longer.

4. Remove the pot from the oven and let the shanks rest in the sauce for at least 15 minutes. With tongs, carefully transfer the shanks to individual plates. Arrange a portion of the vegetables around each shank. With a large spoon or ladle, skim the excess fat from the braising liquid and adjust the seasonings. Spoon some of the braising liquid over each shank and serve immediately.

➤ VARIATION

Braised Lamb Shanks with Lemon and Mint

Grate the zest from 1 lemon, then cut the lemon into quarters. Follow the recipe for Lamb Shanks Braised in Red Wine, replacing the thyme and rosemary leaves with 1 tablespoon minced fresh mint leaves and replacing the red wine with dry white wine. Add the quartered lemon to the braising liquid in step 2. Proceed as directed, stirring the lemon zest and an additional 1 tablespoon minced fresh mint leaves into the sauce just before serving.

OSSO BUCO

OSSO BUCO, OR ITALIAN BRAISED VEAL shanks, is too venerable a recipe to fiddle with. We decided the best way to approach the dish was to perfect (and simplify, if possible) the cooking technique and to extract the most flavor from the simple ingredients: veal shanks (which are browned), aromatics (onions, carrots, and celery, all sautéed), and liquids (a blend of wine, stock, and tomatoes).

To start, we gathered three classic recipes and prepared each in the test kitchen. At the tasting, there was little consensus about the recipes, although white wine was clearly preferred to red wine. Tasters did, however, offer similar ideas as to what constituted the perfect osso buco; it would be rich in flavor and color and somewhat brothy but not stewy. This first goal is the reason why we

prefer osso buco to veal stews made with boneless shoulder meat. While shoulder meat can be a bit wan, the shank is robust, and the bone adds tremendous flavor to the stewing liquid. With these traits in mind, we created a rough working recipe and set out to explore the two main components in this dish—the veal shanks and the braising liquid.

Most recipes we reviewed called for shanks from the upper portion of the hind leg, cut into pieces between 1 and 1½ inches thick. We found that purchasing shanks is tricky, even when we special-ordered them. From one market, we received stunning shanks with a lovely pinkish blush, which were ideal except for the weight. Each shank weighed between 12 and 16 ounces—too large for individual servings. Part of the charm of osso buco is receiving an individual shank as a portion. We concluded that shanks should weigh 8 to 10 ounces (with the bone) and no more. At another market, the shanks were generally in the ideal weight range, but the butchering job was less than perfect. In the same package, shank widths varied from 1 to 2½ inches and were occasionally cut on an extreme bias, making tying difficult (see explanation below) and searing uneven.

The first step, then, is to shop carefully. We found a thickness of 1½ inches and a weight of 8 ounces ideal. Make sure all the shanks you buy are close to these specifications. Each shank should have two nicely cut, flat sides to facilitate browning.

Preparing the meat for braising was the first step. Most recipes called for tying the shanks and dredging them in flour before searing. We found that tying a piece of butcher's twine around the equator of each shank does prevent the meat from falling apart and makes for a more attractive presentation. When we skipped this step, the meat fell off the bone and floated about in the pot.

Although we do not generally dredge meat in flour before browning, we felt we should at least try it, considering that the majority of osso buco recipes include this step. Tasters felt that the meat floured before searing was gummy and lacked depth. The flour on the meat browns rather than the meat itself, and the flour coating may peel off during the long braising time.

To develop the best flavor in the shanks, we

seasoned them heavily with salt and pepper and seared them until a thick, golden brown crust formed. We seared the shanks in two batches (even if they could all fit in the pan at the same time) so that we could deglaze the pan twice with wine, thereby enriching the braising liquid doubly.

The most difficult part of developing this recipe was attaining an ideal braising liquid and sauce. Braising, by design, is a relatively inexact cooking method because the rate at which the liquid reduces can vary greatly. Some of the initial recipes we tried yielded far too much liquid, which was thin in flavor and texture. In other cases, the liquid nearly evaporated by the time the meat was tender. We needed to create a foolproof, flavorful braising liquid and cooking technique that produced a rich sauce in a suitable volume and did not need a lot of last-minute fussing.

We experimented with numerous techniques to attain our ideal liquid, including reductions before braising and after braising (with the aromatics and without) and a reduction of the wine to a syrup during the deglazing process. In the end, we settled on the easiest method: natural reduction in the oven. The seal on most Dutch ovens is not perfectly tight, so the liquid reduces as the osso buco cooks. We found further simmering on the stovetop unnecessary as long as we started with the right amount of liquid in the pot.

The braising liquid traditionally begins with meat stock and adds white wine and tomatoes. As few cooks have homemade meat stock on hand and canned versions are often unappealing, we knew that canned chicken broth would be our likely starting point. Two cups (or one can) seemed the right amount, and tests confirmed this. To enrich the flavor of the broth, we used a hefty amount of diced onion, carrot, and celery. Tasters liked the large amount of garlic in one recipe, so we finely minced about five cloves and added it in to the pot prior to the broth. We rounded out the flavors with two bay leaves.

We hoped to write the recipe in even amounts, using whole vegetables, one can of stock, one bottle of wine, and so on. But an entire bottle of wine proved overwhelming. The resulting sauce was dominated by acidity. Some testers also felt that

the meat was tougher than previous batches with less wine. We scaled the wine back to 2½ cups, about two thirds of a bottle, and were happy with the results. More than half of the wine is used to deglaze the pot between searing batches of veal shanks and thus the final dish is not as alcoholic or liquidy as it might seem.

With the wine and broth amounts settled, we needed to figure out how to best incorporate tomatoes. Most tasters did not like too much tomato because they felt it easily overwhelmed the other flavors. Fresh tomatoes are always a gamble outside of the summer months, so we chose canned diced tomatoes, thoroughly strained of their juice. This approach worked out well, and the tomatoes did not overwhelm the sauce.

We still needed to determine the ideal braising time. Several sources suggested cooking osso buco almost to the consistency of pulled pork. Tasters loved the meat cooked this way, but it was less than attractive—broken down and pot roast-like. We wanted compact meat firmly attached to the bone, so we cooked the meat until it was just fork-tender but still clinging to the bone. Two hours in the oven produced veal that was meltingly soft but still attached to the bone. With some of the larger shanks, the cooking time extended to about 2½ hours.

We experimented with oven temperature and found that 325 degrees reduced the braising liquid to the right consistency and did not harm the texture of the meat. While beef stews are best cooked at 300 degrees, veal shanks have so much collagen and connective tissue that they can be braised at a slightly higher temperature.

Just before serving, osso buco is sprinkled with gremolata, a mixture of minced garlic, parsley, and lemon zest. We were surprised to find variations on this classic trio. A number of recipes included orange zest mixed with lemon zest or on its own. Other recipes included anchovies. We tested three gremolatas: one traditional, one with orange zest mixed in equal part with lemon zest, and one with anchovies. Tasters liked all three, but favored the traditional version.

In some recipes the gremolata is used as a garnish, and in others it is added to the pot just before serving. We chose a compromise approach, stirring half the gremolata into the pot and letting it stand for five minutes so that the flavors of the garlic, lemon, and parsley permeated the dish. We sprinkled the remaining gremolata on individual servings for a hit of freshness.

Osso Buco

SERVES 6

To keep the meat attached to the bone during the long simmering process, tie a piece of twine around the thickest portion of each shank before it is browned. Use a zester, vegetable peeler, or paring knife to remove the zest from a single lemon, then mince it with a chef's knife. Osso buco is traditionally served with risotto alla Milanese although mashed potatoes or polenta are good options, too.

OSSO BUCO

6	tablespoons vegetable oil
6	veal shanks, 1 1/2 inches thick (8 to 10 ounces each), patted dry with paper towels and tied around the equator with butcher's twine
	Salt and ground black pepper
2 1/2	cups dry white wine
2	medium onions, cut into 1/2-inch dice (about 2 cups)
2	medium carrots, cut into 1/2-inch dice (about 1 1/2 cups)
2	medium celery ribs, cut into 1/2-inch dice (about 1 cup)
6	medium garlic cloves, minced or pressed through a garlic press (about 2 tablespoons)
2	cups low-sodium chicken broth
2	small bay leaves
1	(14.5-ounce) can diced tomatoes, drained

GREMOLATA

3	medium garlic cloves, minced or pressed through a garlic press (about 1 tablespoon)
2	teaspoons minced lemon zest
1/4	cup minced fresh parsley leaves

1. FOR THE OSSO BUCO: Adjust an oven rack to the lower-middle position and heat the oven to 325 degrees. Heat 2 tablespoons of the oil in a large ovenproof Dutch oven over medium-high heat until shimmering. Meanwhile, sprinkle both sides of the shanks generously with salt and pepper to taste. Swirl to coat the pan bottom with the oil. Place 3 shanks in a single layer in the pan and cook until they are golden brown on one side, about 5 minutes. Using tongs, flip the shanks and cook on the second side until golden brown, about 5 minutes longer. Transfer the shanks to a bowl and set aside. Off the heat, add 1/2 cup of the wine to the Dutch oven, scraping the pan bottom with a wooden spoon to loosen any browned bits. Pour the liquid into the bowl with the browned shanks. Return the pot to medium-high heat, add 2 tablespoons oil, and heat until shimmering. Brown the remaining shanks, about 5 minutes for each side. Transfer the shanks to the bowl. Off the heat, add an additional 1 cup wine to the pot, scraping the bottom to loosen the browned bits. Pour the liquid into the bowl with the shanks.

2. Set the pot over medium heat. Add the remaining 2 tablespoons oil and heat until shimmering. Add the onions, carrots, and celery and cook, stirring occasionally, until soft and lightly browned, about 9 minutes. Add the garlic and cook until lightly browned, about 1 minute longer. Increase the heat to high and stir in the broth, remaining 1 cup wine, accumulated veal juices in the bowl, and bay leaves. Add the tomatoes; return the veal shanks to the pot (the liquid should just cover the shanks). Cover the pot and transfer it to the oven. Cook the shanks until the meat is easily pierced with a fork but not falling off the bone, about 2 hours. (Can be refrigerated for up to 2 days. Bring to a simmer over medium-low heat.)

3. FOR THE GREMOLATA: Combine the garlic, lemon zest, and parsley in a small bowl. Stir half of the gremolata into the pot, reserving the rest for garnish. Adjust the seasonings with salt and pepper to taste. Let the osso buco stand, uncovered, for 5 minutes.

4. Using tongs, remove the shanks from the pot, cut off and discard the twine, and place 1 veal shank in each of 6 bowls. Ladle some of the braising liquid over each shank and sprinkle each serving with gremolata. Serve immediately.

BRACIOLE

BEEF BRACIOLE IS A CLASSIC SUNDAY DIN-ner in many Italian-American households. The recipe has its roots in southern Italy. For braciole, thin slices of meat are filled with aromatics, rolled, and braised in a tomato sauce often referred to as Sunday gravy or Sunday sauce. Although recipes for braciole call for a range of fillings from sausage and prosciutto to spinach and provolone, the classic (and, we think, best) filling consists of raisins, pine nuts, herbs, grated cheese, and garlic. We began our testing with an authentic recipe from an editor's Italian grandmother who is known for her good food. (The editor also swore by this family recipe.) This treasured recipe immediately set the parameters for our testing.

A good braciole doesn't require the use of a knife at the table; it should fall apart under the light pressure of a fork. Although most recipes call for thin slices of meat cut from the round, we tried making braciole using two other common cuts of beef. Chuck steaks turned out to be too fatty, leaving a greasy slick on top of the sauce, while steaks cut from the loin turned tough and dry after being simmered in the tomato sauce. Returning to thin steaks cut from the round, we then tested whether or not they should be pounded. The unpounded steaks turned out dense and a bit too chewy, while the pounded steaks emerged from the sauce absolutely tender. For the best results, we discovered that the meat should be pounded to a thickness of ¼ inch.

For the filling, we tried several approaches using the basic mixture of raisins, pine nuts, parsley, basil (tasters liked both herbs rather than just one),

---

pecorino cheese (which tasters preferred over milder Parmesan), and garlic. Some recipes call for binding the mixture with oil, eggs, fresh bread crumbs, or cubes of bread soaked in milk. However, our tasters preferred the clean, herbaceous flavor of the mixture without any binding. The oil-soaked stuffing added unnecessary fat to the sauce, while the egg, bread crumbs, and milk-soaked cubes turned it heavy, soggy, and leaden. Left alone, the loose, dry mixture of herbs, nuts, and raisins acted like an aromatic paste, infusing flavor into both the meat and the sauce.

To help this loose mixture of fruit and nuts stick to the meat, we brushed the pounded steaks with a little oil before sprinkling the mixture evenly over the meat. We also found it helpful to press the mixture lightly into the meat with our hands.

Several recipes call for a slice of provolone to be rolled up in the braciole, but the result was met with mixed reviews. Many of the tasters liked the texture and flavor of gooey cheese in the filling, while others preferred it without (we made it optional). Just 1½ tablespoons of the mixture was needed to fill one braciola, and we noted that a total of 12 braciole served 6 people.

Cooking braciole is a straightforward procedure. The rolls are browned and removed from the pan. A simple tomato sauce is then built using the drippings left behind in the pan. Finally, the rolls are simmered in the sauce until they are fork-tender. The recipes we researched called for a range of simmering times from 15 minutes to several hours, but our grandmother's recipe nailed the time perfectly. The beef rolls took exactly two hours to cook through. When cooked less, the braciole required a sharp knife and a strong jaw to eat, while more time in the pan simply caused the beef (and the rolls) to fall apart.

To make the simple tomato sauce, we first discarded the spent oil left over from browning the braciole. Using fresh extra-virgin olive oil, we sautéed onion and garlic, then added some red wine and two large cans of crushed tomatoes. (The sauce for braciole is traditionally smooth, so crushed tomatoes are the best choice here.) Seasoned with fresh basil, red pepper flakes, and a bay leaf, the sauce turned out flavorful and ample for both our authentic braciole and a pound of freshly cooked pasta, its classic accompaniment.

Braciole
SERVES 6

Many supermarkets sell meat specifically labeled "for braciole." If yours does not, the butcher should be able to cut it for you. Steaks that measure 5 inches across by 7 inches long are ideal. This recipe makes enough extra sauce to coat 1 pound of pasta. We like to serve braciole with a hearty pasta shape, such as ziti or rigatoni.

BRACIOLE

- 2 medium garlic cloves, minced or pressed through a garlic press (about 2 teaspoons)
- ½ cup raisins
- ½ cup pine nuts, toasted in a dry skillet until fragrant
- ½ cup minced fresh parsley leaves
- ¼ cup minced fresh basil leaves
- ⅓ cup grated Pecorino Romano cheese
- 6 steaks cut from the widest part of a top round roast, ½ inch thick (about 2 pounds total)
- 5 tablespoons extra-virgin olive oil
  Salt and ground black pepper
- 6 thin slices provolone cheese, cut in half (optional)

SIMPLE TOMATO SAUCE

- 2 tablespoons extra-virgin olive oil
- ½ small onion, minced
- 5 medium garlic cloves, minced or pressed through a garlic press (about 5 teaspoons)
- ¼ teaspoon red pepper flakes
- ⅓ cup dry red wine
- 2 (28-ounce) cans crushed tomatoes
- 1 bay leaf
- 2 tablespoon minced fresh basil leaves
  Salt and ground black pepper

1. FOR THE BRACIOLE: Combine the garlic, raisins, pine nuts, herbs, and cheese in a medium bowl. Cut each steak in half crosswise to yield 12 pieces in total. Place the meat between 2 sheets of parchment or wax paper and pound with a meat mallet or pounder to a thickness of ¼ inch. Lay the meat flat on a cutting board, brush the top of each piece with a little oil (use 3 tablespoons oil in total), and season with salt and pepper to taste. If using, lay

a slice of provolone on top of each piece of meat. Sprinkle 1½ tablespoons filling evenly over each piece of meat, leaving a clean ½-inch border. Press the filling lightly into the meat to help it adhere. Starting at the narrow end, roll each piece of meat to form a tidy bundle; secure the end with a metal turkey trussing skewer, long toothpick, or bamboo skewer cut to a 4-inch length. Season the rolls with salt and pepper to taste.

2. Heat the remaining 2 tablespoons oil in a large nonreactive sauté pan or Dutch oven over medium-high heat until shimmering with wisps of smoke, about 2 minutes. Add half the braciole to the pan, reduce the heat to medium, and cook, turning several times, until well browned on all sides, 5 to 6 minutes. Transfer the braciole to a plate. Add the remaining braciole to the pan and cook in the same manner, adjusting the heat as necessary to prevent the pan drippings from burning. Transfer the second batch to the plate.

3. FOR THE SAUCE: Discard any oil left in the pan, but retain the browned bits. Add 2 tablespoons oil to the pan and return the pan to medium heat. When the oil is hot, add the onion and sauté, scraping up the browned bits, until the onion is soft, about 2 minutes. Add the garlic and pepper flakes and cook until aromatic, about 30 seconds. Add the wine, scraping up any browned bits. Add the tomatoes and bring to a simmer. Stir in the bay leaf and basil and return the braciole to the pan. Bring to a simmer, cover, and reduce the heat to low. Cook, turning the braciole occasionally, until the meat is fork-tender, about 2 hours.

4. Transfer the braciole to a large serving platter and tent with foil. Bring the sauce to a boil over medium-high heat. Cook until the sauce is thickened and measures 5 cups, 10 to 15 minutes. Discard the bay leaf. Season with salt and pepper to taste. Pour 3 cups sauce around the braciole on the platter and serve. The remaining 2 cups tomato sauce are for the pound of cooked pasta that serves as an accompaniment.

BARBECUED BABY BACK RIBS **PAGE 330**

BEEF KEBABS **PAGE 72**

GRILLED PORK TENDERLOIN **PAGE 289**

GRILLED HAMBURGERS **PAGE 347**

TUSCAN-STYLE ROAST PORK LOIN WITH GARLIC AND ROSEMARY **PAGE 263**

ROASTED RACKS OF LAMB **PAGE 271**

ROAST FRESH HAM **PAGE 381**

217

STEAK AU POIVRE WITH BRANDIED CREAM SAUCE **PAGE 56**

STIR-FRIED PORK, RED BELL PEPPER, AND GREEN BEANS WITH GINGERY OYSTER SAUCE **PAGE 142**

MAPLE-GLAZED PORK ROAST **PAGE 253**

BEEF BURGUNDY **PAGE 157**

POT ROAST WITH ROOT VEGETABLES **PAGE 187**

ROAST BONELESS LEG OF LAMB WITH GARLIC, HERB, AND BREAD CRUMB CRUST **PAGE 277**

POT-AU-FEU **PAGE 198**

224

GRILLED STEAK TIPS **PAGE 36**

ROAST CURED RACK OF PORK **PAGE 268**

10

I WANT TO COOK A ROAST

I WANT TO COOK A ROAST

THIS CHAPTER COVERS A WIDE RANGE OF beef, pork, and lamb roasts, each of which relies on a very distinct cooking method. There are, however, several points to keep in mind. In general, lower oven temperatures guarantee more evenly cooked roasts. At a high oven temperature, the exterior layers of meat will overcook before the interior comes up to temperature. This problem is especially severe when you are talking about a huge roast, such as prime rib or crown roast of pork. For this reason, we generally favor oven temperatures between 250 and 350 degrees.

There is one downside to a low oven temperature—little or no browning. For this reason, we often sear roasts in a hot skillet on the stovetop before placing them in the oven. (If the roast is too large to fit in a large skillet, you can crank up the oven temperature during the final minutes of cooking to promote better browning.)

We would never spend big money on a huge roast and then ruin the meat by overcooking it. An instant-read thermometer, inserted deep into the center of the roast and away from any bones, is a must. Remember that the internal temperature will rise as the meat rests on the counter. With large roasts, this effect is especially pronounced. The internal temperature can rise 10 or even 15 degrees as you wait for the juices in the meat to redistribute themselves. Be patient. While a steak might require just five minutes of resting time, a big roast needs 15 or 20 minutes, or more.

PRIME RIB

A PRIME RIB IS A LITTLE LIKE A TURKEY: You probably cook only one a year, usually for an important occasion such as Christmas. Although you know there are alternative cooking methods that might deliver a better roast, they're too risky. You don't want to be remembered as the cook who carved slices of almost raw standing rib roast or delayed dinner for hours waiting for the roast to finish cooking. Rather than chance it, you stick with the standard 350 degrees for X minutes per pound. A roast cooked this way, you decide, will at least not embarrass you.

Other than using general terms like juicy and tender, we weren't quite sure how to define perfect prime rib when we started testing, so we had no preconceived ideas about what techniques or methods would deliver a superior roast. In addition to our normal cookbook research, we decided to interview a few of the thousands of chefs who cook prime rib every day. Between what we found in books and what we learned from these chefs, we came up with a dozen or so fairly different methods. Although there were minor issues, such as whether the roast needed to be tied or whether it should be roasted on a rack, one big question needed answering: At what temperature should prime rib be roasted?

We started with oven temperatures. Suggested roasting temperatures ranged from a tepid 250 degrees to a bold 425 degrees. Other recipes recommended an initial high-temperature sear (450 to 500 degrees), then reduced the oven temperature to a more moderate 350 degrees for actual roasting. Wanting to test the full range, we roasted prime ribs at temperatures ranging from 250 to 500 degrees.

All prime ribs roasted at oven temperatures exceeding 300 degrees looked pretty much the same. Each slice of carved beef was well done around the exterior, medium toward the center, and a beautiful, pink medium-rare at the center. We might have been tempted to report that roasting temperature doesn't much matter if we hadn't tried cooking prime rib at oven temperatures under 300 degrees. The results surprised us, although it certainly wasn't love at first sight.

About halfway through the cooking time of the first roast tested at 250 degrees, we wrote in our notes, "Though the meat looks virtually raw, the internal temperature registers 110 degrees, and very little of its fat has rendered." But we changed our minds quickly as soon as we carved the first slice. This roast was as beautiful on the inside as it was anemic on the outside. Unlike the roasts that cooked at higher temperatures, this one was rosy pink from the surface to the center—the juiciest and most tender of all the roasts we had cooked. This was restaurant prime rib at its best.

In addition to being evenly cooked, the prime rib roasted in a 250-degree oven had another thing

TYING UP PRIME RIB

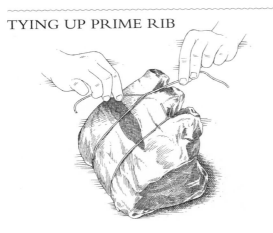

It is imperative to tie prime rib before roasting. If left untied, the outer layer of meat will pull away from the rib-eye muscle and overcook. To prevent this problem, tie the roast at both ends, running the string parallel to the bone.

CARVING PRIME RIB

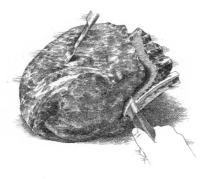

1. Using a carving fork to hold the roast in place, cut along the rib bones to sever the meat from the bones.

2. Set the roast cut-side down; carve the meat across the grain into thick slices.

going for it: Its internal temperature increased only a degree or two during its resting period. (Roasts are allowed to rest when they come out of the oven both to distribute the heat evenly and to allow the juices to reabsorb back into the outer layers of the meat.) A roast cooked to 128 degrees, for example, moved only to 130 degrees after a 45-minute rest.

Not so with the roasts cooked at higher temperatures. Their internal temperatures increased much more dramatically out of the oven. As a matter of fact, we noticed a direct correlation between oven temperature and the increase in the temperature of the roast while resting. Prime ribs roasted at moderate temperatures (325 to 350 degrees) increased, on average, 14 degrees during resting. In other words, if pulled from the oven at a rare 126-degree internal temperature, these roasts moved up to a solid medium (140 degrees) by the end of the resting period. Meanwhile, the prime rib roasted at 425 degrees increased a whopping 24 degrees (from 119 to 143) during its rest. We considered a smaller increase in postcooking temperature a definite advantage. It let us pull the roast from the oven at the temperature we wanted instead of having to speculate as to how many degrees the temperature would climb during resting.

In addition to its more stable internal temperature, prime rib roasted at 250 degrees lost less weight during cooking than prime rib roasted at higher temperatures. A 6¾-pound roast cooked in a 250-degree oven weighed just over 6¼ pounds when it came out of the oven, a loss of less than half a pound. By contrast, similar roasts cooked in a 325-degree oven lost just more than a pound, while roasts cooked at 350 degrees lost 1½ pounds. The prime rib cooked at 425 degrees lost a shocking 2 pounds. Part of the weight loss is fat, but certainly a good portion is juice. This test confirmed our suspicions that the beef roasted at 250 degrees was indeed juicier than that roasted at higher temperatures.

Because members of the National Cattlemen's Beef Association would not endorse an oven-roasting temperature below 300 degrees, we decided to check the safety of this low-heat method before getting too sold on it. After conversations with a number of food scientists across the country, we determined that low-temperature roasting is as safe a cooking method as higher-temperature roasting, especially if you brown the roast first, which should kill any bacteria on the exterior. And though the odds of finding bacteria inside a prime rib roast are close to nil, the only way to guarantee a bacteria-free slab of prime rib is to cook it to an internal temperature of 160 degrees, no matter what cooking method is used, low temperature or high. Unfortunately, at 160 degrees, the meat is gray, tough, and unappetizing.

So were we willing to brown the roast first to kill any bacteria on the exterior. Yes, in fact, we thought this step was necessary for other recipes. The only thing that bothered us about the slow-roasted prime rib was its raw-looking, fatty exterior. Searing the meat on top of the stove before low-roasting it gave it a beautiful crusty brown exterior.

As nebulous as the meaning of "perfect prime rib" had been to us at the beginning of our tests, it became crystal clear the moment we carved off that first slice of low-roasted prime rib. We immediately recognized it as the beef you get at a great prime rib restaurant. As it turns out, many such restaurants slow-roast their meat. They use special ovens that roast the meat at 250 degrees until it reaches an internal temperature of 120 degrees. At that time, the oven heat is decreased to 140 degrees, causing the meat's internal temperature to increase to 130 degrees and remain there until ready to serve (up to 24 hours later). Unfortunately, few home cooks can use this method since most home oven thermostats

do not go below 200 degrees. But by following our recipe, home cooks can very closely approximate the superb prime rib served in the country's best restaurants.

Prime Rib

SERVES 6 TO 8

If you purchase the roast several days ahead of time, you might want to try aging the meat in the refrigerator to improve its flavor and texture. (See page 234 for more information on aging beef.) For information on buying a rib roast, see the box below.

I   (3- or 4-rib) standing rib roast (about 7 pounds), aged up to 4 days (if desired), tied with kitchen twine at both ends, twine running parallel to bone (see the illustration on page 230)
    Salt and ground black pepper

1. An hour before cooking, remove the roast from the refrigerator to bring it to room temperature.

2. Adjust an oven rack to the low position and heat the oven to 250 degrees. Heat a large, heavy-bottomed roasting pan set over two burners set at medium-high heat on the stovetop. Place the roast in the hot pan and cook on all sides until nicely browned and about ½ cup fat has rendered, 6 to 8 minutes.

3. Remove the roast from the pan. Set a wire

INGREDIENTS: Two Rib Roasts

A whole rib roast (aka prime rib) consists of ribs 6 through 12. Butchers tend to cut the roast in two. We prefer the cut further back on the cow, which is closest to the loin. This cut is referred to as the first cut, the loin end, or sometimes the small end because the meat and ribs get larger as they move up toward the shoulder. The first cut can include anywhere from two to four ribs. Sometimes we like a large roast for the holidays and in this case we prefer a roast with four ribs. At other times, a slightly smaller roast, with just three ribs, is fine. When ordering the former, be sure to specify the first four ribs from the loin end—ribs 9 through 12—to receive the first cut. When ordering a three-rib roast, ask for the first three ribs from the loin end—ribs 10 through 12.

Either way, the first cut is more desirable because it contains the large, single rib-eye muscle and is less fatty. The less desirable cut, which is still an excellent roast, is closer to the chuck (or shoulder) end and is sometimes called the second cut. The closer to the chuck, the less tender the roast becomes.

First Cut   **Second Cut**

rack in the pan, then set the roast on the rack. Generously season with salt and pepper to taste.

4. Place the roast in the oven and roast until the meat registers 130 degrees (for medium-rare), 3 to 3½ hours. Remove the roast from the oven and tent with foil. Let stand 20 to 30 minutes to allow the juices to redistribute themselves evenly throughout the roast.

5. Remove the twine and set the roast on a cutting board, rib bones at a 90-degree angle to the board. Carve (see the illustrations on page 230), and serve immediately.

ROAST BEEF WITH YORKSHIRE PUDDING

ROAST BEEF WITH YORKSHIRE PUDDING can be simple or elaborate. The English tend to make it Sunday afternoon with a cheap cut of beef from the shoulder or round. In America, we use an expensive rib roast and promote it as a holiday recipe. We decided to pursue the latter, assuming that most American cooks would want to save this dish for special occasions.

When we tested a half dozen sample recipes for this dish, however, we were disappointed. Too often the meat was dry, chewy, and unevenly cooked. The accompanying jus was bland, thin, and pale. The recipes for Yorkshire pudding seemed fickle: Sometimes the pudding failed to rise and its texture was too dense; other times it cooked unevenly. But these tests helped us figure out what we wanted. We envisioned a roast beef with a browned, flavorful exterior complementing an evenly cooked, juicy, tender, and rosy red interior. The ideal jus, made from the beef drippings, would be rich in beef flavor and deep mahogany in color, with plenty of body. As for the perfect Yorkshire pudding, it would be dramatically high and have a crisp and lightly browned outer crust with a tender, moist, and airy interior. Unlike the popover, Yorkshire pudding should be richly flavored with beef fat.

We started with a first-cut rib roast but wondered whether we needed to use a bone-in or boneless roast. A blind taste test revealed the bone-in roast as the unanimous favorite. Tasters said this roast was juicier and had a beefier flavor. In comparison, the boneless roast was chewy and dry. We concluded that the bones must be protecting the non-fatty side of the meat, helping to retain the juices and bringing forth a meatier flavor. Discussing this discovery with our butcher, he suggested a way to have the best of both worlds—the superior meat from cooking on the bone and the ease of serving a boneless roast. He cut the meat from the bones and tied it back on (most any butcher and many supermarkets will provide this service), and we cooked the whole thing. This was the first important step toward a great roast beef dinner, as we got the flavor we wanted along with quick and easy carving. Just snip the twine after roasting, set the bones aside, and start slicing.

Most roast beef recipes utilize a moderate oven temperature of about 350 degrees. Often the roasting process begins or ends with a blast of high heat—upward of 400 degrees. The intention is to have the high heat brown the outside of the roast and the moderate heat cook the inside. The problem with this standard approach is that the outer layers of meat overcook, while the slices from the middle are unevenly cooked, the center being red and the remainder gray and unappealing. After considerable testing, we found that a boneless roast is like a bone-in prime rib, it benefits from a quick sear on the stovetop to develop the crust and then a low oven heat of 250 degrees. A roast cooked at 250 degrees will be rosy pink from the surface to the center, juicy, and tender.

A minor obstacle appeared during the searing step when the rendered beef fat melted the twine that held the meat to the bones. We tried again, this time separating the meat from the bones and searing just the fatty top and sides of the meat. We let the meat cool briefly, tied it back onto the bones, and then roasted the meat at 250 degrees. Finally, a perfectly prepared roast beef. The exterior was crusty, browned, and flavorful; the inside juicy, tender, evenly cooked, and brimming with beef flavor.

But still there were problems to contend with. Slow-roasting succeeds so well at keeping the juices inside the meat that there were no pan drippings for the jus or rendered beef fat for the Yorkshire pudding. We tried using the fat rendered from the searing on the stovetop, but it was overly seasoned, and the puddings were inedible. Seasoning the meat after searing, which would have produced usable fat, also failed because the low oven temperature did not dissolve the salt into the meat. We now had a perfectly cooked roast beef, but we also had to face the challenges of where to find the flavor for the jus and the fat for the Yorkshire pudding.

Traditionally, a jus is prepared after a roast is cooked. The roasting pan is placed on the stovetop, and some liquid, typically wine, is added to deglaze the pan, a process in which all of the flavorful browned bits get lifted off the pan bottom. Broth is then added to the pan and reduced by simmering to concentrate the flavors and improve the texture. Vegetables and aromatics are often added to the pan prior to roasting to add flavor to a jus, so this is where we began our next batch of tests.

EQUIPMENT: Roasting Pans

Though most cooks haul out their roasting pan infrequently, when you do need this large pan, nothing else will do. A roasting pan is a must for prime rib and other roasts.

A roasting pan should promote deep, even browning of food. It should be easy to maneuver in and out of the oven. And it should be able to travel from oven to stovetop, so that you can deglaze the pan and loosen drippings.

Roasting pans can be made from stainless steel, enameled steel, nonstick-coated aluminum, or anodized aluminum, all of which we tested. We decided not to test pans lined with copper, which are prohibitively expensive; cast-iron pans, which when loaded with food are too heavy to lift; and pans made from Pyrex, ceramic, or stoneware, all of which seem better suited to lasagna and casseroles because they can't be used on top of the stove.

We tested eight roasting pans and preferred the materials we like in other cookware—stainless steel and anodized aluminum. These materials are heavy (though not prohibitively so) and produce good browning. Although nonstick coatings made cleanup easier, roasting racks slid around in these pans. For instance, when one test cook tilted a nonstick pan ever so slightly to remove it from the oven, a turkey and rack slid sharply to one side, which threw off her balance and nearly landed the hot turkey in her lap.

Roasting pans generally come in two different styles—upright handles and side handles (see the photos below). Upright handles tend to be square in shape, while side handles are generally oval loops. We found upright handles to be easier to grip. The problem with side handles is that their position, coupled with the large size of the pan, can cause you to bring your forearms perilously close to the hot oven walls. We tested one pan without handles, which was by far the most difficult to take out of the oven.

We tested pans ranging in length from 16 to 20 inches and in width from 11 to 14 inches. We preferred pans that measured about 16 inches long and 12 to 14 inches across. Larger pans made for an awkward fit in the oven, and, because of their large surface area, tended to burn pan drippings more easily.

In terms of weight, heavier pans performed better in all tests, especially on top of the stove. Lightweight pans buckled, and the meat browned quite spottily.

To summarize, heavy-duty pans made from stainless steel or anodized aluminum work best to brown foods, especially if the pan is to be used on top of the stove as well as in the oven, as is the case with our prime rib recipe.

THE BEST ROASTING PANS

The All-Clad Stainless Steel Roti ($200), left, is our favorite roasting pan. The handles on the roasting pan are upright and easy to grasp. More important, this heavy pan conducts heat well and works on both the stovetop and in the oven. The Granite Ware Oval Roaster, right, is the best inexpensive option, priced at just $20. The side handles on this pan are more difficult to grasp than upright handles and seem more likely to cause burns. Also, this lightweight pan does not perform well on the stovetop, often causing foods to burn if the pan is set over high heat. You should sear roasts in a heavy skillet and only use the roasting pan for the oven portion of the cooking process. But given the difference in price, it's worth considering this lightweight option.

We threw in onions, carrots, celery, thyme, and a bit of water with the roast at the beginning of oven cooking. The vegetables steamed and the jus was terrible. We eliminated the water, but still no browning occurred because of the low oven temperature. (One taster said this jus was like dishwater.) Because browning brings out flavor, we considered using the time that the raw roast rests out of the refrigerator to roast the vegetables at high heat, using the same pan in which we'd cook the beef. This jus was better, but too vegetal tasting. We tried adding tomatoes and garlic, ingredients that are sometimes added to meat stocks to add richness and base notes. "Where's the beef?" asked one taster, thereby giving us an idea. We tossed in some oxtails (a readily available and inexpensive cut) with the vegetables in the next test. Oxtails are not only loaded with beef flavor but are also very fatty. We had struck gold! Our search for flavor for the jus had also unearthed fat for the pudding.

It took a few more tests to determine that the jus was actually improved when we used oxtails and onions alone. We had eliminated the carrots and celery because they detracted from the rich beef flavor. The garlic was too strong, and the thyme proved more pleasing if we added it when making the jus on the stovetop. The jury was out on the tomatoes. Some thought they rounded out the flavor, while other tasters thought they were too harsh and acidic. We tried another test, employing a technique used when roasting veal bones for stock: We rubbed the oxtails with a bit of tomato paste. "Wow, what did you do?" the tasters exclaimed. Not only was the rich beefy flavor more intense, but the texture of the jus was now thicker and silkier. Now on a roll, we had one more idea to try. We snipped the twine on the cooked roast and tossed the rib bones into the simmering jus. Perfection at last.

Finally, we used the fat from the oxtails to create the best Yorkshire pudding. Now we had a superior

SCIENCE: Why Aging Tenderizes Beef

Meat is aged to develop its flavor and improve its texture. This process depends on certain enzymes, whose function while the animal is alive is to digest proteins. After the animal is slaughtered, the cells that contain these enzymes start to break down, releasing the enzymes into the meat where they attack the cell proteins and break them down into amino acids, which have more flavor. The enzymes also break down the muscles, so the tissue becomes softer. This process can take a few days or a few weeks. (For the sake of safety, meat should not be aged for more than four days at home; beyond that time it must be done under carefully controlled conditions.)

Traditionally, butchers have hung carcasses in the meat locker to age their beef. Today, some beef is still aged on hooks (this process is called dry aging), but for the most part beef is wet-aged in vacuum-sealed packets. We wondered if it was worth it to the home cook to go the extra mile for dry-aged beef, so we ordered both a dry-aged and wet-aged prime rib roast from a restaurant supplier in Manhattan. The differences between the two roasts were clear-cut.

Like a good, young red wine, wet-aged beef tasted pleasant and fresh on its own. When compared with the dry-aged beef, though, we realized its flavors were less concentrated. The meat tasted washed out. The dry-aged beef, on the other hand, engaged the mouth. It was stronger, richer, and gamier-tasting, with a pleasant tang. The dry-aged and wet-aged beef were equally tender, but the dry-aged beef had an added buttery texture.

Unfortunately, most butchers don't dry-age beef anymore because hanging the quarters of beef eats up valuable refrigerator space. Dry-aged beef also dehydrates (loses weight) and requires trimming (loses more weight). That weight loss means less beef costs more money. Wet-aged beef loses virtually no weight during the aging process, and it comes prebutchered, packaged, and ready to sell. Because beef is expensive to begin with, most customers opt for the less expensive wet-aged beef. Why does dry aging work better than wet aging? The answer is simple: air. Encased in plastic, wet-aged beef is shut off from oxygen—the key to flavor development and concentration.

Because availability and price pose problems, you may simply want to age beef yourself. It's just a matter of making room in the refrigerator and remembering to buy the roast ahead of time, up to four days before you plan on roasting it. When you get the roast home, pat it dry and place it on a wire rack set over a paper towel–lined cake pan or plate. Set the racked roast in the refrigerator and let it age until you are ready to roast it, up to four days. (Aging begins to have a dramatic effect on the roast after three days, but we also detected some improvement in flavor and texture after just one day of aging.) Before roasting, shave off any exterior meat that has completely dehydrated. Between the trimming and dehydration, count on a 7-pound roast losing at least half a pound during aging.

recipe, albeit one that takes a bit more work than the standard English version. This is a dish worth serving on a special occasion, not just for Sunday dinner.

Prime Rib Roast Beef with Jus
SERVES 10 TO 12

Ask the butcher to cut the meat off the ribs, but make sure to keep the ribs because the meat is tied back onto them for roasting. Letting the roast stand at room temperature for 1 hour before roasting helps it cook evenly. Plan on removing the roast from the refrigerator about 4½ hours before serving.

1	(4-rib) standing rib roast (about 8 pounds), meat removed from the bone, ribs reserved (see note), and meat patted dry with paper towels
1 ½	pounds oxtails (4 pieces, each about 3 inches in diameter)
1	tablespoon tomato paste
3	medium onions, cut into eighths
3	tablespoons vegetable oil
	Salt, preferably kosher
2	tablespoons ground black pepper
1	cup medium-bodied red wine, such as a Côtes du Rhône
1 ¾	cups low-sodium beef broth
1 ¾	cups low-sodium chicken broth
2	sprigs fresh thyme

1. Remove the roast and ribs from the refrigerator and let stand at room temperature for 1 hour. Meanwhile, adjust an oven rack to the lowest position and heat the oven to 400 degrees. Rub the oxtails with the tomato paste and place in a large, heavy-bottomed roasting pan. Toss the onions with 1 tablespoon of the oil, then scatter the onions in the roasting pan. Roast until the oxtails and onions are browned, about 45 minutes, flipping the oxtails halfway through the cooking time. Remove from the oven and set the roasting pan with the oxtails aside; reduce the oven temperature to 250 degrees.

2. When the roast has stood at room temperature for 1 hour, heat a heavy-bottomed 12-inch skillet over medium heat until hot. Meanwhile, rub the ends and fat side of the roast with the remaining

2 tablespoons oil, then sprinkle with 1½ teaspoons kosher salt (or ¾ teaspoon table salt) and the pepper. Place the roast, fat-side down, in the hot skillet and cook until well browned, 12 to 15 minutes. Using tongs, stand the roast on end and cook until well browned, about 4 minutes. Repeat with the other end. Do not brown the side where the ribs were attached. Place the roast, browned-side up, on a cutting board and cool 10 minutes. Following illustration 1 below, tie the browned roast to the

PREPARING BONELESS PRIME RIB

1. Position the meat back on the bones exactly from where it was cut. Using 4 individual lengths of twine, tie the meat back onto the bones, running the strings parallel to the bones.

2. Use a metal spatula to push the oxtails and onions to the sides of the pan. Place the roast, bone-side down (seared fatty-side up) in the center of the roasting pan.

3. When it comes time to check the temperature of the roast, insert a thermometer through the top of the roast until you reach the center.

ribs. Set the roast, bone-side down, in the roasting pan (illustration 2), pushing the oxtails and onions to the sides of the pan.

3. Roast for 1 hour, then remove from the oven and check the internal temperature; the center of the roast should register about 70 degrees on an instant-read thermometer. (If the internal temperature is higher or lower adjust the total cooking time.) Return the roast to the oven (prepare Yorkshire pudding batter now, if making), and cook 1¼ to 1¾ hours longer, until the center of meat registers about 122 degrees for rare to medium-rare or about 130 degrees for medium-rare to medium (illustration 3). Transfer the roast to a cutting board and tent loosely with foil. If making Yorkshire pudding, increase the oven temperature to 450 degrees.

4. While the roast rests, spoon off the fat from the roasting pan, reserving 3 tablespoons for the Yorkshire pudding; set the roasting pan aside while preparing the puddings for baking. While the puddings bake, set the roasting pan over 2 burners at high heat. Add the wine to the roasting pan; using a wooden spoon, scrape up the browned bits and boil until reduced by half, about 3 minutes. Add the beef broth, chicken broth, and thyme. Cut the twine on the roast and remove the roast from the ribs; transfer the meat to the cutting board and re-tent with the foil. Add the ribs to the roasting pan and continue to cook, stirring occasionally, until the liquid is reduced by two thirds (to about 2 cups), 16 to 20 minutes. Add any accumulated juices from the meat and cook to heat through, about 1 minute longer. Discard the ribs and oxtails; strain the jus through a mesh strainer into a gravy boat, pressing on the onions to extract as much liquid as possible.

5. Set the meat, browned-side up, on the cutting board and cut into ⅜-inch-thick slices; sprinkle lightly with salt. Serve immediately, passing the jus separately.

Yorkshire Pudding

YORKSHIRE PUDDING IS MADE WITH FLOUR, salt, eggs, milk, and fat rendered from the roast beef, which gives it flavor and distinguishes it from the popover, which is generally made with butter. The eggy batter rises dramatically in the oven, and, as this happens, the center becomes airy and custardy and the crust crisps and browns.

Yorkshire pudding is often prepared in a roasting pan and then cut into individual pieces. Initial tests revealed problems with this approach. The pieces from the center of the pan were squat and lacked enough of the delectable browned crust, while those from the edges of the pan were missing a pleasing amount of the tender, soft, airy interior. Tasters were more smitten by individual puddings. They are uniform in shape, consistent in contrasting components, and much easier to serve. Because a popover pan makes only six and most people do not have one we decided to try a muffin pan and got excellent results.

With the question of the proper baking pan settled, we focused on several other fine points. The biggest challenge would be getting the right height and texture. Yorkshire pudding can be notoriously fickle, rising beautifully sometimes and other times falling flat. We started our tests by leaving the batter lumpy (a common recipe directive). When this approach failed, we tried the less popular instruction: whisking the ingredients until smooth. These puddings rose higher and the texture became more airy.

Next we tried the common practice of using room-temperature ingredients and letting the batter rest before baking. This gives the batter a bit of a head start when it enters the oven, having to rise up from a base temperature of about 70 degrees rather than a chilly 40 or 50 degrees. Sure enough, a rested, room-temperature batter enhanced the height and inner texture of the puddings.

Experimenting with oven temperatures was next. We tried constant, moderate oven temperatures ranging from 325 to 375. These puddings looked more like muffins because the large crown was missing. Constant high temperatures, ranging from 400 to 450 also failed. These puddings had the desired height, but they were too dark on the outside and undercooked on the inside. Some Yorkshire pudding recipes call for starting with a hot oven (450 degrees in most recipes) and then lowering the heat about halfway through baking (to 350 degrees). We tried this approach, and these puddings were excellent. The intense 450-degree heat not only browns the puddings nicely but quickly turns the moisture in the batter to steam, causing it to rise. The interior then cooks through at 350 degrees. Curious during the next test, we peeked inside the oven while the puddings were baking, and the inflow of cool air caused the puddings to collapse. (Hence the first rule of making Yorkshire pudding: No peeking!)

Additional testing showed that an accurate oven temperature is essential. If your oven is 25 degrees too high, the outer crust will darken and taste burnt; if it is 25 degrees too low, the inside of the puddings will not cook fully. Since most home ovens are not well calibrated, it makes sense to purchase a good oven thermometer before making this recipe.

Following through on the idea that an initial blast of high heat is good, we also tried preheating the greased muffin tin. The beef fat was smoking hot, and the batter sizzled when it hit the tin. This worked like a charm. We thought we were done until we noticed that the leftovers fell slightly as they sat. Remembering a technique used to preserve popover height, we pierced the next batch of puddings with a skewer as soon as they came out of the oven. This allowed the steam to escape instead of condensing inside the puddings, turning the interiors soft and overly moist, which causes collapse.

YORKSHIRE PUDDING, FLAT OR FULL?

If the batter does not rest to give the gluten in the flour time to relax or if the oven door is opened during baking, the puddings will fall (left). Proper mixing and resting of the batter and an undisturbed bake in the oven ensure huge crowns with crisp, golden brown exteriors and tender, moist, airy interiors (right).

As for flavor, recipes for Yorkshire pudding are remarkably consistent in terms of using beef fat, although amounts vary. We prepared a batch using 4 tablespoons of fat from the rendered oxtails. Although these puddings were flavorful, they were dripping in fat. Three tablespoons proved ideal.

Individual Yorkshire Puddings
SERVES 12

Prepare the Yorkshire pudding batter after the beef has roasted for 1 hour, then, while the roast rests, add beef fat to the batter and get the puddings into the oven. While the puddings bake, complete the jus. A hot, accurate oven temperature is key for properly risen and perfectly browned puddings. Work quickly to fill the muffin tin with batter, and do not open the oven door during baking.

3	large eggs, at room temperature
1 1/2	cups whole milk, at room temperature
1 1/2	cups (7 1/2 ounces) unbleached all-purpose flour
3/4	teaspoon salt
3	tablespoons beef fat (reserved from the roasting pan)

1. Whisk the eggs and milk together in a large bowl until well combined, about 20 seconds. Whisk the flour and salt together in a medium bowl and add to the egg mixture; whisk quickly until the flour is just incorporated and the mixture is smooth, about 30 seconds. Cover the batter with plastic wrap and let stand at room temperature for at least 1 hour or up to 3 hours.

2. After removing the roast from the oven, whisk 1 tablespoon of beef fat into the batter until bubbly and smooth, about 30 seconds. Transfer the batter to a 1-quart liquid measuring cup or other pitcher.

3. Measure 1/2 teaspoon of the remaining 2 tablespoons beef fat into each cup of a standard (12-cup) muffin pan. When the roast is out of oven, increase the oven temperature to 450 degrees and place the muffin pan in the oven to heat for 3 minutes (the fat will smoke). Working quickly, remove the muffin pan from the oven, close the oven door, and divide the batter evenly among the 12 muffin cups, filling each about two-thirds full. Immediately return the

pan to the oven. Bake, without opening the oven door, for 20 minutes; reduce the oven temperature to 350 degrees and bake until deep golden brown, about 10 minutes longer. Remove the pan from the oven and pierce each pudding with a skewer to release the steam and prevent collapse. Using your hands or a dinner knife, lift each pudding out of the pan. Serve immediately.

ROAST BEEF TENDERLOIN

FOR LARGE HOLIDAY PARTIES, FEW CUTS can top beef tenderloin. The tenderloin, which comes from the short loin, starts out very tender and can be cooked at a high oven temperature. This elegant roast thus cooks quickly, and its rich, buttery slices are always fork-tender. Despite its many virtues, however, beef tenderloin is not without its liabilities. Price, of course, is the biggest. Even at a local warehouse-style supermarket, the going rate for a whole beef tenderloin is $7.99 a pound—making for an average sticker price of about $50.

There is good reason for the tenderloin's hefty price. Because it sits up under the spine of the cow, it gets no exercise at all and is therefore the most tender piece of meat. It is one of the two muscles in the ultra-premium steaks known as the porterhouses and T-bone, so when it is removed from the cow as a whole muscle, it is going to sell for an ultra-premium price. We confirmed this by heading to the supermarket and the local butcher and purchasing $550 worth of beef tenderloin—which bought us just 11 roasts.

A whole beef tenderloin can be purchased "unpeeled," with an incredibly thick layer of exterior fat left attached, but it's usually sold "peeled," or stripped of its fat. Because of our many bad experiences with today's overly lean pork and beef, we

---

INGREDIENTS: Beef Broth

Beef stock is a traditional European and American staple, a key ingredient in many classic sauces. However, almost no home cook has homemade stock around the kitchen. Commercial beef broth is the only realistic choice, or is it?

When we tasted a dozen commercial beef broths, tasters were pretty horrified. Although few of us in the test kitchen like commercial chicken broth, a few brands are decent and actually taste like chicken. Not so when it comes to commercial beef broth. None of the brands we sampled had any real beef flavor. We wondered, "Where's the beef?"

As things stand, U.S. regulations for beef broth do not require much beef. A commercial beef broth need contain only 1 part protein to 135 parts moisture, according to the U.S. Department of Agriculture's standards. That translates to less than about an ounce of meat (or about one quarter of a hamburger) to 1 gallon of water. Most commercial products are very close to that limit, strictly because of economics. Generally, manufactured beef broth derives its flavor from bare beef bones and a boost of various additives. A glance at the label on the side of any canned broth or boxed bouillon cubes will confirm this.

We wanted to talk to the manufacturers of beef broths to verify our impressions of the way they make their products, but calls to broth giants Hormel Foods and Campbell Soup Company were dead ends. Both declined to answer questions as to how their commercial beef broths are made. But beef bones plus additives would certainly explain why none of the commercial broths we tasted came even close to the full-bodied, beefy flavor of homemade.

What seems to distinguish most supermarket broths from homemade is a riddling of flavor additives. Monosodium glutamate (MSG) can be found in nearly all supermarket beef broths. Disodium guanylate and disodium isonate, which are both yeast-based, hydrolyzed soy protein, are also typically added to commercial broths. Other yeast extracts also find their way into most of these broths. All approved by the U.S. Food and Drug Administration (FDA), these additives are intended to "enhance" flavor. As one FDA spokesperson explained, "You've got something that's kind of 'blah,' so to give it a little more taste they add these things."

Salt—and lots of it—also adds to the flavor of these broths. Most beef broth products contain about 35 percent of the daily allowance for sodium per serving. Salt is also added to help extract the needed protein from the beef bones.

Over the years, we've found that a little beef broth can be mixed with chicken broth to create a good pan sauce, but don't use beef broth straight from the can—it needs to be doctored.

purchased six of the 11 roasts unpeeled, determined to leave on as much fat as possible. However, after a quick examination of the unpeeled roasts, we realized that the excessively thick layer of surface fat had to go. Not only would such a large quantity of rendering fat smoke up the kitchen, it would also prohibit a delicious crust from forming on the meat. We dutifully peeled the thick layer of fat from the six tenderloins, but even after removing the sheaths of fat, there were still large pockets of fat on the interior as well as significant surface fat.

Does it make sense to buy an unpeeled roast and trim it yourself? We think not. We paid $6.99 a pound at the butcher for our unpeeled tenderloins, each weighing about 8 pounds. After cleaning them up, the peeled tenderloins weighed about 5 pounds, with a whopping 3 pounds of waste. We purchased peeled tenderloins of similar quality from another source for only $7.99 per pound. Clearly, the unpeeled tenderloins were more expensive with no benefits. And although we don't like tenderloins that have been picked clean, right down to the meat, we recommend buying peeled roasts, with their patches of scattered fat, and letting them be.

The tenderloin's sleek, boneless form makes for quick roasting, but its torpedo-like shape—thick and chunky at one end, gradually tapering at the other end—naturally roasts unevenly. For those looking for a range of doneness, this is not a problem, but for cooks who want a more evenly cooked roast, something must be done.

Folding the tip end of the roast under and tying it bulks up the tenderloin center to almost the same thickness as the more substantial butt end. This ensures that the tenderloin cooks more evenly. (Even so, the tip end is always a little more well done than the butt.) Tying the roast at approximately 1½-inch intervals further guarantees a more uniform shape and consequently more even slices of beef. Snipping the silver skin (the translucent sheath that encases certain cuts of beef) at several points also prevents the meat from bowing during cooking. This occurs when the silver skin shrinks more than the meat to which it is attached.

Over the years, we've come to like slow-roasting for large roasts. The lower the heat, we've found, the more evenly the roast cooks. To develop a rich brown crust on these low-roasted larger cuts, we pan-sear them first or increase the oven temperature for the last few minutes of roasting—or we may do both.

PREPARING A BEEF TENDERLOIN

1. To keep the meat from bowing as it cooks, slide a knife under the silver skin and flick the blade upward to cut through the silver skin at five or six spots along the length of the roast.

2. To ensure that the tenderloin roasts more evenly, fold the thin tip end of the roast under about 6 inches.

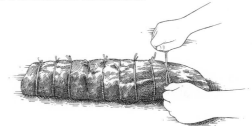

3. For more even cooking and evenly sized slices, use 12-inch lengths of kitchen twine to tie the roast every 1½ inches.

4. Set the meat on a sheet of plastic wrap and rub it all over with oil. Sprinkle with salt and pepper, then lift the plastic wrap up and around the meat to press on the excess. This last step guarantees even coverage.

But a beef tenderloin is a different proposition. Though relatively large, its long, thin shape would seem to dictate a relatively quick cooking time. To determine the ideal roasting temperature, we started at the two extremes, roasting one tenderloin at 200 degrees, the other at 500. As expected, the roast cooked at 500 degrees not only created a very smoky kitchen from the rendering fat, it was also overcooked at each end and around the perimeter. However, the high oven heat had formed a thick, flavorful crust. A good crust is crucial to this rich yet mild-tasting roast, whose flavor is sometimes barely recognizable as beef. Despite the even, rosy pink interior of the beef cooked at 200 degrees, this roast lacked the all-important crust. Neither oven temperature was ideal, so we kept roasting.

Because the higher roasting temperature provided the rich flavor this roast desperately needs, we decided to roast it at as high a temperature as possible. A 450-degree oven still gave us smoke and uneven cooking, so we moved down to 425 degrees. For comparison, we roasted another tenderloin at 200 degrees, this time increasing the oven temperature to 425 degrees at the end of cooking to develop a crust. Both roasts emerged from the oven looking beautiful, and their meat looked and tasted almost identical. Because the tenderloin roasted at 425 degrees was done in just 45 minutes (compared with the slow-roasted tenderloin, which took just about twice as long), we chose the high-heat method.

Although all roasts should rest 15 to 20 minutes after cooking, we found that beef tenderloin improves dramatically if left uncarved even longer. If cut too soon, its slices are soft and flabby. A slightly longer rest—we settled on 30 minutes—allows the meat to firm up to a texture we found much more appealing. Before carving, we preferred removing the big pockets of excess fat, which become more obvious at warm and room temperatures.

Roast Beef Tenderloin

SERVES 12 TO 16

To give the tenderloin a more pronounced pepper crust, increase the amount of pepper to 6 tablespoons and use a mixture of strong black and white and mild pink and green peppercorns. Be sure to crush the peppercorns with a mortar and pestle or with a heavy-bottomed saucepan or skillet. Do not use a coffee or spice grinder, which will grind the softer green and pink peppercorns to a powder before the harder black and white peppercorns begin to break up. See the illustrations on page 239 for more information on preparing the tenderloin. Serve with Parsley Sauce with Cornichons and Capers (page 405), Salsa Verde (page 405), or Chimichurri (page 405). Make a double recipe of the last two sauces to accompany such a large piece of meat.

1	whole peeled beef tenderloin (5 to 6 pounds), patted dry with paper towels, silver skin cut, tip end tucked under, and tied (see illustrations 1 through 3 on page 239)
2	tablespoons olive oil
1	tablespoon kosher salt or 2 teaspoons table salt
2	tablespoons coarsely ground black pepper (see note)

1. Remove the tenderloin from the refrigerator 1 hour before roasting to bring the meat to room temperature.

2. Adjust an oven rack to the upper-middle position and heat the oven to 425 degrees. Set the roast on a sheet of plastic wrap and rub it all over with the oil. Sprinkle with the salt and pepper and then lift the wrap to press the excess seasoning into the meat (see illustration 4 on page 239).

3. Transfer the prepared tenderloin from the wrap to a wire rack set in a shallow roasting pan.

LEARNING TO TIE BUTCHER'S KNOTS

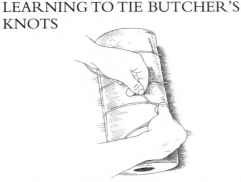

Many cooks have trouble tying roasts properly. If that's the case, practice with a roll of paper towels and strands of butcher's twine. It's a lot neater than practicing on a roast.

Roast until an instant-read thermometer inserted into the thickest part of the roast registers about 125 degrees (the meat will range from medium-rare to medium in different areas when it finishes resting), about 45 minutes. Remove from the oven and tent loosely with foil. Let stand for about 30 minutes before carving. (The cooled tenderloin can be wrapped in plastic, refrigerated up to 2 days, sliced, and served chilled.)

4. Cut the meat into ½-inch-thick slices. Arrange on a platter and serve.

BEEF WELLINGTON

EVEN READERS ON THE NOD DURING THE early 1960s will recognize beef Wellington, the substantial piece of tenderloin swathed in fine pâté and duxelles (a heady mix of mushrooms, shallots, herbs, and butter) and bundled up in a cloak of puff pastry. A pitcher of dark, glossy sauce should be on hand to carry red wine and rich meat juices to the earthy brown of mushrooms and pâté, and onward over buttery, rare beef. The most appealing part of the story is the flaky, golden pastry that holds things in place. Is this a big, aging dinosaur of a dish? Yes. But its interplay of flavors and star presentation make it peerless party fare. Too often, of course, beef Wellington is all dry gray meat, grainy, overcooked pâté, and soggy bottoms or—still worse—served with a metallic tinned jus or packet of thick gravy mix. Even the best claret in the world would bring little comfort.

After examining a couple dozen cookbooks, we found that recipes for beef Wellington showed a consensus as to ingredients—pâté, standard duxelles, preseared beef, and commercial puff pastry—and a uniform lack of detail around the assembly of the beast. Given the potentially irreconcilable differences between a thick log of raw beef and a thin sheet of raw pastry, we had our work cut out for us. Our hope was to minimize and secure the efforts

---

EQUIPMENT: Boning Knives

The slim, flexible blade of a boning knife may look eccentric, but it is perfectly designed to slide nimbly through joints and between bones. It is an essential tool for such tasks as removing cutlets from a whole chicken breast and can also be used to remove fat and silver skin from a beef tenderloin. The slim blade creates less drag through the meat, and the slices made are neater than those possible with the wider blade on a chef's knife.

Because most home cooks are likely to use a boning knife infrequently, we wondered if a cheaper knife would do. To find out, we tested six leading knives with blades between 5 and 7 inches long and prices between $9 and $71. Both large- and small-handed testers used each knife to butcher a whole chicken and to trim beef ribs of fat and silver skin. Each knife was evaluated for handle comfort, slipperiness (hands become very greasy when butchering), agility (including flexibility), and sharpness.

The winning Forschner (Victorinox) Fibrox boning knife, priced at $17.90, received high marks for its uniquely designed ergonomic handle as well as its slim, highly maneuverable blade and razor-sharp edge. The plastic handle nestled comfortably into both large and small hands, and it stayed there even when our hands became slick with fat. The blade was the narrowest of the lot, which made it very agile. And while all the knives arrived with razor-sharp edges, the

Forschner seemed exceptionally keen, gliding effortlessly through tough tendon and thick skin.

The J.A. Henckels Professional S boning knife ($49.99) finished a close second. Its blade was nearly as agile as the Forschner, but the handle was somewhat slippery. The Wüsthof-Trident Grand Prix boning knife ($54) was "fiendishly sharp," but the wide blade was not as agile as the top models and the handle became slippery when coated with chicken fat. The textured metal handle of the Global boning knife ($70.99) received mixed reviews, and testers did not like the boxy handle on the Chicago Cutlery boning knife ($14.99) or the flimsy blade on the Farberware Professional boning knife ($8.99).

THE BEST BONING KNIFE
The Forschner (Victorinox) Fibrox knife boasts a handle that testers found "easy to grip" and a narrow blade that shows "great flexibility around bones." Everyone raved about the "amazing" sharpness of this knife straight out of the box.

needed to deliver the roast to the table in perfect condition: crust golden, meat rare, accompanying flavors rich and compatible, and no leaky pastry. We also wanted a simple, respectable sauce at its side.

Beginning with the beef, we discovered that there were multiple issues to work through before even setting the oven. The first were size and shape. Unquestionably company dinner, to serve eight to 10, beef Wellington requires a piece of tenderloin in the 3- to 4-pound range (untrimmed tenderloins can weigh anywhere between 8 and 10 pounds). Trips to the market turned up surprisingly different shapes and sizes of tenderloin in this weight range. And aesthetics were not the only problem. The shape and diameter of the meat were crucial to recipe consistency as well. To get the proper weight and number of portions, we would need—in the argot of the industry—a center-cut Châteaubriand.

The tenderloin wanted a brief but high-impact pan-sear before assembly. Wrapping raw meat in dough left the finished Wellington with a spongy texture and unappealing steamed flavor. We found that a sear of one minute per side in a very hot pan afforded depth of flavor and an attractive color contrast in the sliced presentation as well.

Because tenderloin is a watery cut, many recipes suggest dry-aging the meat in the refrigerator before cooking it. Though we did not expect dry-aging to solve the problem of excessive moisture altogether, we hoped it would, at the very least, evaporate moisture from the meat's surface—creating a more interesting surface texture—and improve the meat's flavor as well. Two days proved ideal: The meat's surface, though leathery, was still malleable enough to accept a pan-sear without needing a trim, and its exterior, once roasted, had a nice chew, tender insides, and meatier flavor.

We moved on to the Wellington's accessories, the pâté and duxelles. It took only a couple of attempts at a quick chicken liver pâté to convince us that we could not get close to the smooth richness of an authentic pâté de foie gras. Our "homemade" attempts were grainy and disappointing. A smooth, commercial pâté, on the other hand, wafted with cognac and truffles and melted sweetly, playing to the mushrooms and the meat.

Duxelles hearken back to classical French culinary times and, in truth, have not changed much since the days of Escoffier. Chopped and sautéed with butter and shallots or onions, the mushrooms cook down into an intense, nubby hash inside of 15 minutes. The food processor brought a pound of them into line very quickly. We chose shallots over onions for their nuanced delicacy. Two tablespoons of heavy cream, directed into the pan once the

ANATOMY OF A BEEF TENDERLOIN

Butt End
Tip End
Center-Cut Chateaubriand

A whole beef tenderloin is comprised of these sections: The thicker end of the roast is called the butt end; the middle portion—which is virtually an even thickness—is called the center-cut Chateaubriand or short tenderloin; and the tapering tip end is sold as part of the whole tenderloin or removed and sold as tenderloin tips.

LOCATING THE TENDERLOIN

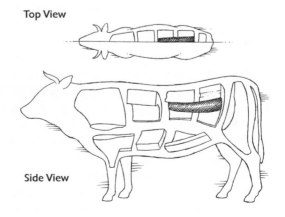

Top View
Side View

The tenderloin muscle is extremely tender because it is never used to move any part of the cow.

mushrooms had cooked down, a splash of Madeira, and a toss of fresh thyme gave the duxelles a moist, supple texture and an earthy perfume.

At first, we weren't eager to envelope this masterpiece in commercial puff pastry. We resisted, using instead our recipe for quick puff pastry with great success. The major advantages of homemade puff pastry are flavor and ease of shaping. Nevertheless, we knew most cooks would prefer to get on with the business at hand and duly gave store-bought Dufour all-butter puff pastry a turn. Though problematic to handle when completely thawed—its high water content caused it to pull and stick like chewing gum on hot pavement—Dufour responded well to a leisurely refrigerator thaw that left it still semifrozen, and relatively manageable, after about three hours. The dough's slim dimensions were well suited to the tenderloin: The 10 by 13-inch rectangle had to be extended only a bit; pressure from a rolling pin repaired cracks along the fold lines.

With each component at the ready, it was time to assemble. Potential clashes between texturally and temperamentally different ingredients were mitigated by making everything dead cold. The seared tenderloin, for example, required a minimum of four hours in the refrigerator to become cold enough to stiffen up and get slathered top and sides with pâté. We discovered that flattening the hot duxelles with a spatula into a thin, compatibly sized rectangle on a parchment-lined baking pan, then chilling them, allowed us to invert them onto the center of the rolled-out dough, then peel off the parchment. The pâté-slathered tenderloin could then be neatly inverted onto the duxelles, avoiding messy double-layering of pâté and duxelles on the meat. The chilled but malleable dough was simply folded up snugly over the roast and set right-side-up on a parchment-lined baking sheet. The assembled, unbaked Wellington also benefited from advance chilling. Thirty minutes in the fridge helped set and seal the dough.

Though beef Wellington is often shown with leaf and vine decorations made from its own dough scraps, we settled for simple dough ribbons (trimmed in strips from the rolled-out rectangle) draped across the Wellington halfway through baking.

Though we experimented with temperatures between 400 and 450 degrees, as well as lower oven adjustments midway through baking, both meat and dough enjoyed a nice, hot oven. It was 450 all the

MAKING PUFF PASTRY

1. Turn the shaggy dough mass out onto the work surface and press it together with both hands.

2. Use the heel of one hand braced against the work surface to drag a small portion of the dough forward in a short, brisk stroke. Repeat with the remaining portions of dough.

3. Gather the dough together with a bench scraper and repeat step 2 a second time. Press the dough into an 8 by 4-inch rectangle, wrap in plastic, and refrigerate at least 30 minutes.

way. Lesser temperatures produced melting, slippage, and half-baked dough. The bottom oven rack was the place to be. Because juices flow downward, the pastry bottom needed hot, searing heat to fight off sogginess. A low rack also allowed the top of the Wellington to keep its distance from scarring heat.

When baking the Wellington, 30 minutes will get you rare and 35 minutes will cook the meat medium-rare. At this point, the dough has seen enough of the oven, making higher meat temperatures inadvisable. The finished Wellington needs a full 10 minutes to rest before being sliced—otherwise the red seas will run. (The internal temperature of the meat will also climb as the roast rests.) Its arrival on the counter in the test kitchen always drew a crowd—many of whom were born after Wellington was already out of style. Beef Wellington, meet the new generation.

Dry-Aged Beef Tenderloin for Beef Wellington

MAKES ENOUGH FOR I RECIPE BEEF
WELLINGTON

Ask the butcher to trim excess fat and the silver skin and to the roast at regular intervals. See page 242 for information on identifying a center-cut Châteaubriand at the market. Ideally you want a roast about 12 inches long and 4 inches in diameter.

I   beef tenderloin center-cut Châteaubriand
     (3 to 4 pounds), silver skin cut and tied
     (see illustrations I and 3 on page 239)

Place the roast on a wire rack set on a rimmed baking sheet and refrigerate, uncovered, for 48 hours.

Duxelles

MAKES ENOUGH FOR I RECIPE BEEF
WELLINGTON

The duxelles can be made 1 day in advance.

I   pound button mushrooms, brushed of dirt and
     broken into rough pieces by hand
3   tablespoons unsalted butter

2–3 large shallots, minced (about ½ cup)
2   tablespoons heavy cream
I   teaspoon Madeira (optional)
I   teaspoon salt
½   teaspoon ground black pepper
I   tablespoon minced fresh thyme leaves

1. Process half of the mushrooms in the workbowl of a food processor fitted with the steel blade until chopped uniformly fine, about ten 1-second pulses, stopping to scrape down the bowl after 5 pulses (the mushrooms should not be ground so fine as to release liquid). Transfer the chopped mushrooms to a medium bowl and repeat with the remaining mushrooms.

2. Heat the butter in a 12-inch skillet over medium-low heat until foaming; add the shallots and cook, stirring frequently, until softened, 3 to 5 minutes. Stir in the mushrooms, increase the heat to medium-high, and cook, stirring frequently, until most of the liquid given off by the mushrooms has evaporated, 7 to 10 minutes. Add the cream, Madeira (if using), salt, and pepper; cook until the mixture is dry, about 3 minutes longer. Off heat, stir in the thyme.

3. Line a rimmed baking sheet with parchment paper; turn the duxelles onto the baking sheet and, with a rubber spatula, spread into an 8 by 10-inch rectangle of even thickness (see illustration 1 on page 247). Cover with plastic wrap, pressing it directly onto the surface, then refrigerate until completely cold, at least 2 hours or up to 24.

Quick Puff Pastry

MAKES ABOUT I POUND, ENOUGH FOR I
RECIPE BEEF WELLINGTON

If well wrapped, puff pastry will keep in the refrigerator for 2 days or in the freezer for 1 month.

2   cups (10 ounces) unbleached all-purpose flour
I   tablespoon sugar
I   teaspoon salt
16   tablespoons (2 sticks) cold unsalted butter,
     cut into ¼-inch cubes
6   tablespoons ice water
I   teaspoon juice from I lemon

1. In the workbowl of a food processor fitted with the steel blade pulse the flour, sugar, and salt to combine. Add one quarter of the butter cubes and cut the butter into the flour until the butter is in dime-sized pieces, four 1-second pulses. Add the remaining butter and pulse to coat the cubes with flour, two 1-second pulses. Transfer the mixture to a medium bowl.

2. Combine the ice water and lemon juice in a small bowl. Add half the liquid to the flour and butter mixture and toss until just combined. Keep adding the liquid, 1 tablespoon at a time, until the dough will clump together in your hand. Turn the dough out onto a work surface. The dough will be quite dry and shaggy at this point. Following along with the photos on page 243, press the dough mass together with both hands. Use the heel of one hand braced against the work surface to drag a small portion of the dough forward in a short, brisk stroke. Repeat with the remaining portions of dough.

TURNING PUFF PASTRY

1. Place the dough on a lightly floured piece of parchment paper and roll into a 15 by 10-inch rectangle. Fold the dough lengthwise into thirds, like a business letter.

2. Starting from the narrow end, loosely roll up the dough as illustrated. Press it to form a 6 by 5-inch rectangle. Repeat steps 1 and 2.

Gather the dough together with a bench scraper and repeat the dragging and kneading process a second time. Press the dough into an 8 by 4-inch rectangle, wrap in plastic, and refrigerate for 1 hour.

3. Unwrap the dough and follow the illustrations below for turning the dough twice. (If the dough becomes soft and sticky after the first turn, wrap it in plastic and refrigerate 30 minutes until workable, then repeat rolling and pressing.) When the second rolling and folding is complete, wrap the dough in plastic and chill for at least 1 hour.

Beef Wellington
SERVES 8 TO 10

Be sure to use a smooth-textured pâté, not a coarse country pâté. Our Quick Puff Pastry recipe (page 244) takes just minutes to prepare. If you prefer to use store-bought pastry, look for the Dufour brand in the freezer section of better grocery stores. One 14-ounce package will be enough; defrost it in the refrigerator for 3 hours before using it in this recipe. Pepperidge Farm frozen puff pastry comes in smaller sheets and you will need to roll two together for this recipe (see the illustrations on page 246) before using this puff pastry in this recipe.

1	Dry-Aged Beef Tenderloin for Beef Wellington (page 244)
2	tablespoons olive oil
2	teaspoons salt
2	teaspoons ground black pepper
5	ounces fine-textured pâté, mashed until smooth
	Flour for dusting work surface
1	pound puff pastry, preferably homemade (see note)
1	large egg
1	recipe Duxelles (page 244)
1	recipe Red Wine Sauce for Beef Wellington (recipe follows)

1. Heat a heavy-bottomed 12-inch skillet over high heat until very hot. Meanwhile, rub the tenderloin with the oil, then sprinkle with the salt and pepper and lightly rub into the meat.

2. Set the tenderloin in the hot skillet, curving it to fit if necessary, and sear on the first side without moving, until well browned, about 1 minute,

pressing down on the meat so that the bottom of the roast makes full contact with the pan. Using tongs, rotate the tenderloin and brown on all sides, about 1 minute per side. Remove from the skillet, wrap the hot tenderloin tightly in plastic wrap, and refrigerate at least 4 hours or up to 24.

3. Unwrap the tenderloin and cut off and discard the twine. Using a small spatula, spread the pâté over the top and sides of the tenderloin (see illustration 2 on page 247); set aside.

4. Dust a large sheet of parchment paper with flour. Unwrap the puff pastry and place it on the parchment; dust the puff pastry lightly with flour and cover with a second large sheet of parchment. Roll into 13 by 14½-inch rectangle, mending cracks as you roll. Remove the top sheet of parchment and with a sharp knife trim the edges to form a neat rectangle that measures 12½ by 14 inches. (If the dough is soft and sticky or tears easily, slide the parchment with the pastry onto a baking sheet and freeze until firm, about 10 minutes.)

5. Line a rimmed baking sheet with parchment paper and spray lightly with nonstick cooking spray; set aside. Beat the egg with 1 tablespoon water; set aside.

6. Remove the plastic wrap from the duxelles. Following illustration 3, invert the duxelles onto the puff pastry; peel off the parchment. Following illustration 4, place the tenderloin pâté-side down onto the duxelles-covered dough. Brush the edges of the dough lightly with beaten egg. Following illustrations 5 and 6, encase the tenderloin in the dough, wrapping tightly. (There should be about 1-inch overlap forming a seam; if the overlap is excessive, trim with scissors.) Carefully invert the dough-wrapped tenderloin onto the prepared baking sheet and brush the dough lightly with beaten egg; refrigerate, uncovered, 30 minutes.

WORKING WITH SUPERMARKET PUFF PASTRY

Dufour puff pastry, sold in the freezer case, at better markets, is our first choice for beef Wellington. This all-butter brand tastes good and the one large sheet is easily rolled into the large rectangle needed for our recipe. However, if you can't find this brand and don't want to make homemade puff pastry, you can use widely available Pepperidge Farm puff pastry, but you will need to roll the two sheets sold in each one-pound package together to form the 12½ by 14-inch rectangle that our Wellington recipe requires. Follow these steps to fuse two sheets of Pepperidge Farm puff pastry into one large rectangle. If you are using Dufour puff pastry, skip these steps.

1. Unfold two pieces of thawed puff pastry onto a piece of parchment liberally dusted with flour. Brush some beaten egg along one edge of one sheet of puff pastry.

2. Overlap with the second sheet of dough by 1 inch and press to seal together.

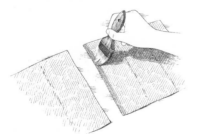

3. With a rolling pin, smooth out the seam, and continue to roll the dough until it measures 13 by 14½ inches.

4. With a pizza wheel or knife and ruler, trim the edges of the dough to form a tidy rectangle that measures 12½ inches by 14 inches.

7. Adjust an oven rack to the lowest position and heat the oven to 450 degrees. Bake the Wellington until deep golden brown and an instant-read thermometer inserted into the center registers between 113 and 115 degrees for rare, about 30 minutes, or around 120 degrees for medium-rare, about 35 minutes. Let stand 10 minutes, transfer to a carving platter, and cut crosswise into ½-inch-thick slices. Serve with the sauce.

Red Wine Sauce for Beef Wellington

MAKES ABOUT 1¼ CUPS

Developing a robust, satiny sauce proved much easier than we had imagined. It took only a package of oxtails, a decent red wine, and some judicious simmering to produce this richly flavorful and full-bodied sauce, which doesn't even require thickening. The stock that is the base of this *sauce can—and should—be made in advance. But do not finish the sauce (step 5, below) until the beef Wellington is in the oven.*

2 ½	pounds beef oxtails, trimmed of excess fat
2	medium carrots, chopped into 1-inch pieces (about 1 cup)
2	medium celery ribs, chopped into 1-inch pieces (about 1 cup)
4	small onions, chopped coarse (about 3 cups)
1	large garlic head, broken into cloves, unpeeled
2	teaspoons tomato paste
1	bottle (750 ml) dry red wine
4–6	large shallots, minced (about 1 cup)
1	bay leaf
10	sprigs fresh thyme
1 ¾	cups low-sodium beef broth
1 ¾	cups low-sodium chicken broth
7	cups water

ASSEMBLING BEEF WELLINGTON

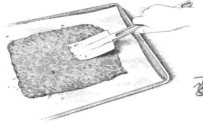

1. Turn the duxelles onto a parchment-lined baking sheet and spread into an 8 by 10-inch rectangle. Chill thoroughly.

2. Cut off the twine from the seared roast and discard. Spread the pâté evenly on the top and sides of the tenderloin.

3. Invert the duxelles onto the dough and peel back the parchment carefully.

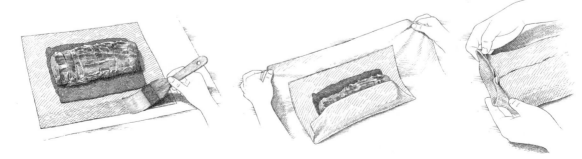

4. Place the tenderloin, bare-side-up, on the dough and brush the dough edges with the egg wash.

5. Lift the dough edges up to encase the tenderloin tightly, allowing for a 1-inch overlap. Pinch the seam to seal.

6. Turn the dough corners up, as when wrapping a gift, and press to seal.

1   teaspoon whole black peppercorns

6   parsley stems

1/4   cup ruby port

4   tablespoons cold unsalted butter, cut into 4
      pieces
      Salt and ground black pepper

1. Adjust an oven rack to the lower-middle position and heat the oven to 450 degrees. Combine the oxtails, carrots, celery, onions, and garlic together in a large flameproof roasting pan; spray lightly with cooking spray and toss to combine. Roast, stirring every 10 minutes, until the beef and vegetables are well browned, 40 to 50 minutes, adding the tomato paste to the roasting pan after 30 minutes.

2. While the oxtails and vegetables roast, bring the wine, shallots, bay leaf, and thyme to a simmer over medium heat in a heavy-bottomed 8-quart stockpot or Dutch oven; reduce the heat to low, and simmer slowly, uncovered, until reduced to about 1 ½ cups, about 30 minutes. Set the pot aside.

3. Place the roasting pan over burner(s) set at high; add the beef and chicken broths and bring to a boil, scraping up the browned bits on the pan bottom with a wooden spoon.

4. Transfer the contents of the roasting pan to the stockpot with the wine reduction. Add the water, peppercorns, and parsley stems, and bring to a boil over high heat; reduce the heat to low and simmer, uncovered, until richly flavored and full-bodied, 3 to 4 hours. Strain the stock into a large glass measuring cup or container (you should have about 2 cups), discarding the solids in the strainer. Cool to room temperature; cover with plastic wrap, and refrigerate at least 1 hour or up to 2 days.

5. While the beef Wellington bakes, skim the hardened fat from the surface of the stock using a soup spoon; discard. Transfer the stock to a small saucepan and simmer over medium-low heat until reduced to about 1 cup, 10 to 15 minutes. Add the port; set aside off heat.

6. While the beef Wellington rests, return the stock to a simmer over medium heat and whisk in the butter, 1 piece at a time. Season the sauce with salt and pepper to taste and serve with the beef Wellington.

BASIC ROAST BEEF

SOMETIMES YOU JUST WANT ROAST BEEF. Not a bank account busting holiday rib roast, not a dainty and delicate tenderloin, but an honest, everyman's slice of Tuesday night beef, served with mashed potatoes, gravy, and green vegetables. Most supermarket meat departments are loaded with inexpensive roasts that would seem to fit the bill, but their labels can be a bit baffling. What's the difference between a bottom rump round roast and a bottom butt sirloin? Lots of these names would make an eight-year-old snicker, but they are not all that helpful.

Determined to get to the bottom of this, we gathered armloads of these cheap roasts and went to work. We decided to develop a technique first and then examine the various cuts that might (or might not) work with our final technique. To start, we cooked five separate roasts, each at a different oven temperature, ranging from 250 to 500 degrees. The results were disappointing, but we learned two things. First, the lowest oven temperature was best. The meat that was roasted at 500 degrees became dry, with most of the outer layers of the meat overcooked. The roast cooked at 250 degrees, however, was more tender and juicy and had better flavor. Second, and most important, we found that the internal temperature of the meat does not necessarily determine the juiciness or texture of the roast. A roast cooked at 250 degrees until it reaches an internal temperature of 120 degrees is definitely more tender and juicy than meat cooked to the same internal temperature in a 500-degree oven. In other words, it's not just where you are going, but how you get there.

Why is this true? To fully understand what was happening inside the meat, we examined four different roasts prepared at different temperatures—250, 350, 400, and 500 degrees. All were cooked to the same internal temperature—130 degrees—and allowed to sit for an additional 10 minutes after they were removed from the oven. The roasts were then cut in half. When we compared the roasts, the answer was immediately apparent. The 500-degree roast was almost entirely overcooked. That is, the center was still red, but 70 percent of the remainder was gray and unappealing. By comparison, the roast cooked at 250 degrees was light red throughout, with only 10 percent of the outer layer gray and overcooked. The roasts cooked at the in-between temperatures varied between these two extremes. Lower oven temperatures allow sufficient time for the even conduction of heat to the center of the roast. At higher oven temperatures, the outside and the inside of the roast have a much larger temperature differential.

The meat developed very little exterior flavor or color when roasted at a constant low temperature, however. Our options for producing the desired crispy brown crust were to crank up the oven, either at the beginning or end of the cooking time, or to sear the roast on the stovetop. We experimented with these methods, alone and in combination, and first eliminated the variations with an initial high oven temperature. Even after turning the temperature back down to 250 degrees, the oven retained enough of the extra heat to spoil our slow, evenly cooked center. Turning the oven up towards the end of the cooking time was much more successful: The meat did not overcook at the edges, but the color was still not as dark as we wanted. When combined with an initial sear in a hot roasting pan or Dutch oven, this method ultimately delivered the best results. The meat had a crisp crust when it went into the oven, and it developed a deeper, more even color during the final blast of oven heat.

The key to making sense of the confusing labels found on supermarket roasts is to identify the larger section, or primal, from which the roast was cut. In this category of inexpensive roasts, the relevant sections are the chuck (or shoulder), round (or back leg), and sirloin (or lower back). Many different roasts can be cut from each of these sections, and butchers in different parts of the country are liable to call the same roast by different names. Thus, every roast is different, but meat cut from each of these three main sections is similar enough to allow us to make some useful generalizations. While the top round is certainly different from the bottom round, for the purposes of this recipe, we've found that all "round roasts" will behave in much the same way, which is to say differently from "chuck roasts" or "sirloin roasts." (See pages 16 to 17 for more specific information on beef roasts.)

Sirloin roasts were our favorite for this cooking method. They had big, beefy flavor, enough fat to stay juicy, and a tender texture. Cheaper round roasts were decidedly second best: not bad at all, but generally tougher, drier and less flavorful than the sirloin. Both sirloin and round roasts will sometimes be labeled "rump" roasts; this means that the roast was cut from the area near the dividing line between the round and the sirloin. As such, any kind of rump roast falls somewhere between the two in our ranking: better than a "bottom round" roast, for example, but not quite as nice as a "top sirloin."

Chuck roasts were a dilemma. We love the flavor of the chuck, and in many cases even preferred it to that of the sirloin. But since the chuck is crisscrossed with so many connective fibers, it is not a pretty roast to look at, and veins of tough gristle can make it tough to chew. Chuck is an excellent choice for pot-roasting and stewing, which allow the connective tissue to break down and dissolve. Since it is scarce in some supermarkets anyway, we recommend choosing one of these other cooking methods when lucky enough to obtain a nice chuck roast.

Slow-Roasted Beef

SERVES 6 TO 8

Our favorite roast for this recipe is the top sirloin but any roast from the sirloin will work well. Round roasts are also an option, but they are definitely a second choice. If you have time, refrigerate the roast on a wire rack set over a paper towel-covered plate for up to three days. This aging process delivers a tender, more flavorful roast. Make sure, however, that before roasting you trim off the parts of the roast that have dehydrated and turned leathery. Tying the roast makes it compact and promotes even cooking. Leftovers make excellent roast beef sandwiches. This roast works well with All-Purpose Gravy (page 406) and potatoes.

I   boneless beef roast (3 to 4 pounds), preferably from the sirloin, aged (see note), if desired, and tied crosswise with twine at 1-inch intervals
    Salt and ground black pepper
I   tablespoon vegetable oil

1. Adjust an oven rack to the lower-middle position and heat the oven to 250 degrees. Season the roast liberally with salt and pepper to taste. Heat the oil in an ovenproof Dutch oven or flameproof heavy-duty roasting pan over medium-high heat until just smoking. Sear the roast until well browned, about 2 minutes on each side.

2. Transfer the pot to the oven and cook, uncovered, until an instant-read thermometer inserted into the thickest part of the roast registers 110 degrees, 45 minutes to 1 hour. Increase the oven temperature to 500 degrees and cook until the internal temperature reaches 120 degrees for rare, 125 degrees for medium-rare, or 130 degrees for medium, 10 to 20 minutes longer. (Cooking times can vary depending on the size and shape of the roast.) Remove the roast from the pot and transfer to a cutting board. Tent the roast loosely with foil and let stand for 20 minutes. Snip the twine off the roast, cut crosswise into thin slices, and serve.

ROAST PORK LOIN

UNASSUMING AND SIMPLE TO PREPARE, A boneless pork roast is hearty weeknight fare for a casual family feast. The practical advantages of this supermarket cut are many: It is affordable and widely available; the mild, sweet flavor of roast pork pairs well with most any side dish; and leftovers make great sandwiches.

The two types of boneless roasts from the loin are the common center loin roast, which contains a lean, unbroken eye of meat, and the blade-end loin roast, which has a section of the shoulder's blade muscle attached. Both are fine, although tasters preferred the flavor and juiciness of the blade-end roast, which benefits from a deposit of fat that separates the two muscles. A blade-end roast is also thicker and shorter in length than a center loin roast of equal weight, which means a center loin roast may cook unevenly due to its elongated shape.

As is the custom in our test kitchen, we tried brining the meat (soaking it in a saltwater solution to season and boost juiciness), and brining did, indeed, yield tender, juicy, well-seasoned pork. On the other hand, the unbrined pork was almost

as good (as long as we took care not to overcook it), and it was nice to dispense with the 2½-hour brining time. (Serve the roast with a pan sauce, which was our plan, also made brining less imperative.) We also ran a series of tests using "enhanced" pork, a common supermarket product that has been injected with a solution of water, salt, and sodium phosphate to season the meat and add moisture. Tasters were put off by the flood of liquid these roasts released when they were sliced, as well as by the overly wet, spongy texture of the meat.

Today's leaner pork may be pleasing to health-conscious carnivores, but its low fat content makes it exceptionally prone to overcooking. Pork is best served at a temperature of 145 to 150 degrees, rather than the 160 degrees (or higher) recommended by many older recipes. If, however, you take the roast out of the oven once it reaches this temperature, it will be overcooked. The temperature of the roast will continue to rise, by as much as 15 degrees, once it has been taken out of the oven. The thing to do is to remove the roast when it registers 135 degrees, and then let it rest on the cutting board before slicing.

Just as important as the final temperature of the roast is how quickly it gets there. We roasted pork loins at a variety of oven temperatures and found that roasting slow and low is the key to juicy, evenly cooked meat. Roasts cooked at high temperatures were dried out near the edges before the center was done. However, even large roasts (where the disparity in cooking rates between the exterior and interior is greatest) were tender and juicy throughout when cooked at in a 300-degree oven.

Innumerable tests have proven that roasts with a deep brown, caramelized crust both look and taste better than those without. Trying to brown the meat using high oven heat at the beginning or end of the roasting produced marginal results, so we decided to sear it on the stovetop. Because the meat was tied into a neat bundle, it fit well in a skillet on the stovetop, which gave us great browning and lots of control over the process. Tying a roast may seem fussy to some, but we discovered that this small investment of time is amply rewarded. The uniform shape of a tied roast promotes even cooking and yields attractive round slices.

After searing the roast on the stovetop there were plenty of drippings and crusty brown bits, or fond, leftover in the skillet—perfect for making a quick pan sauce. After searing several roasts, however, we discovered that the amount and color of the fond varied greatly. Sometimes the pan was quite dark, almost black in spots, and the resulting sauce tended to be bitter. Other times there was very little stuck to the pan, and the sauce turned out pale and bland. By adjusting the heat as needed during the searing process we were able to keep the pan from burning, but how could we make sure enough fond would stick to the pan in the first place? The key was to control the amount of fat in the skillet. Pork loin roasts have a layer of fat on just one side, which is usually presented as the "top." When we placed the roast in the skillet with the fat side down first, as we were naturally inclined to do, much of that fat layer quickly rendered into the pan and prevented the meat from sticking to the surface. The meat browned, but the pan stayed fairly clean. Conversely, when we browned the fat side last, the other sides had plenty of time to brown in a relatively dry pan, and thus left behind lots of fond for our sauce.

Roast Pork Loin

SERVES 4 TO 6

This recipe can be made with roasts as large as 4½ pounds, which should serve 8 to 10 people. This recipe makes enough jus for a larger roast. Because of the addition of vegetables, the variations will only accommodate a 2½-pound roast. A thin (⅛-inch) layer of fat will result in a delicious crispy crust, but this recipe will also work with a roast that has been completely trimmed.

ROAST

1   boneless blade-end pork loin roast (about 2½ pounds), tied at even intervals along the length with 5 pieces butcher's twine (see the photo on page 252) and patted dry with paper towels
    Salt and ground black pepper
1   tablespoon vegetable oil

JUS

1   tablespoon vegetable oil (if needed)
2   small shallots, minced (about ¼ cup)

2   cups low-sodium chicken broth
2   bay leaves
2   sprigs fresh thyme
¼   teaspoon sugar
2   teaspoons juice from 1 lemon

1. Adjust an oven rack to the middle position and heat the oven to 300 degrees. Sprinkle the roast evenly with salt and pepper. Heat the oil in a 12-inch skillet over medium-high heat until smoking. Add the roast, fat-side up, and brown on all sides (fat-side last), 8 to 10 minutes, lowering the heat to medium if necessary to prevent the roast from burning. Transfer the roast to a V-rack set inside a roasting pan, but do not wash the skillet.

2. Transfer the roasting pan to the oven and cook until an instant read thermometer inserted into the center of the roast registers 135 degrees, 45 to 55 minutes. (If cooking a larger roast, increase the time to 65 to 75 minutes.) Remove the roast from the oven and transfer it to a cutting board. Tent lightly with foil and let rest 15 to 20 minutes (the center of the roast should register 145 to 150 degrees).

3. While the roast is resting, make the jus. Either pour off fat or add oil to the skillet so that there is about 1 tablespoon of fat in the pan. Heat the skillet over medium heat until the oil is shimmering. Add the shallots and cook, scraping the browned bits from the pan bottom, until softened, 4 to 5 minutes. Add the broth, bay leaves, thyme, and sugar and simmer until reduced by half, about 15 minutes. Remove the pan from the heat and stir in the lemon juice. Discard the bay leaves and thyme and adjust the seasonings with salt and pepper to taste.

4. Snip the twine off the roast and cut the pork crosswise into thin slices. Serve immediately with the jus.

➤ VARIATIONS

Roast Pork Loin with Carrots, Fennel and Honey

Toss 2 medium bulbs fennel (about 1½ pounds), halved, cored, and cut into ½-inch-thick pieces, and 1½ pounds carrots, peeled and cut on the bias into 1½-inch pieces, with 2 tablespoons melted butter, 2 tablespoons honey, ½ teaspoon salt, and ⅛ teaspoon ground black pepper in a large roasting pan. Place a V-rack in the pan over the vegetables. Follow the recipe for Roast Pork Loin, placing the seared roast on the rack in the pan with the vegetables. After the roast is removed from the oven in step 2, return the roasting pan with the vegetables to the oven, increase the temperature to 500 degrees, and roast the vegetables, stirring occasionally, until browned, 15 to 20 minutes longer. Prepare the jus as directed in step 3, replacing the sugar with ¼ teaspoon honey. Serve the roasted vegetables with the pork.

Roast Pork Loin with Potatoes and Sage

Toss 3 pounds large red potatoes, cut into 1-inch wedges, with 2 tablespoons olive oil, 1 teaspoon salt, and ¼ teaspoon ground black pepper in a large roasting pan. Place a V-rack in the pan over the potatoes. Follow the recipe for Roast Pork Loin, placing the seared roast on the rack in the pan with the potatoes. After the roast is removed from the oven, add 2 teaspoons chopped fresh sage leaves to the potatoes, increase the oven temperature to 500 degrees, and roast the potatoes, stirring occasionally, until browned and crisp, 15 to 20 minutes. Serve the roasted potatoes with the pork.

MAPLE-GLAZED PORK ROAST

FROM PANCAKES TO PINEAPPLE, NEW Englanders will slather maple syrup on just about anything. Among the multitude of dishes done right by a dash of maple, classic New England maple-glazed pork roast is one of our favorites. Sweet maple, with its delicate flavor notes of smoke, caramel, and vanilla, makes an ideal foil for pork, which has a faint sweetness of its own. The result of this marriage is a glistening maple-glazed pork roast, which, when sliced, combines the juices from tender, well-seasoned pork with a rich maple glaze to create complex flavor in every bite.

When we tested five different recipes, however, we found that this dish often falls short of its savory-sweet promise. Of course, many of the roasts turned out dry (a constant concern when cooking today's lean pork), but we were surprised to discover that the glazes presented even bigger problems. Most of them were too thin to coat the pork properly, some were so sweet that they required a hotline to the dentist's office, and none of them had a pronounced maple flavor.

Good maple-glazed roast pork starts out as good plain roast pork. We wanted a boneless cut and tested four options. Tasters preferred the blade-end loin roast for its flavor and juiciness, which it receives in part from a deposit of fat that separates the two muscle sections at one end of the roast. As with our basic recipe for roasting this cut, we found that brining was not necessary but that a stovetop sear followed by roasting in a moderate oven were key.

With the roast in the oven, it was time to get serious about developing maple flavor. The recipes we had researched touted dozens of glaze concoctions and methods for marrying them to the pork. Most of the flavoring ingredients added to the maple syrup either diluted it (so that it was too thin to use as a glaze) or were simply unwelcome. This list included soy sauce, vinegar, lemon juice, cranberry juice, cider, and bourbon for liquid ingredients and herbs, spices, jams, jellies, brown sugar, maple sugar, mustards, and chiles for flavor boosters. (We reserved the best of these flavorings for recipe variations). Everyone agreed, however, that small amounts of complementary spices added subtle dimension to the maple, thus cinnamon, ground cloves, and cayenne all found their way into

TYING A PORK LOIN

Straight from the supermarket packaging, most pork loins will lie flat in the pan and cook unevenly (left). Tying the roast not only yields more attractive slices but ensures that the roast will have the same thickness from end to end so that it cooks evenly (right).

the glaze recipe. Still, we wanted more maple flavor and a glaze that would really stick to the meat. We even tried brining one loin in maple syrup and wrapping another with maple-flavored bacon. The former added no discernible maple flavor, while the latter tasted mildly artificial. We finally hit upon a simple solution to enhance flavor when we reduced the maple syrup in a saucepan. But we were frustrated when it dripped down off the roast onto the bottom of the roasting pan and burned.

Then we had an idea. Remember the hot pan we had left from searing the roast? How about putting it to additional use? We decided to use it to flash-reduce the maple syrup. We removed the loin from the pan after searing, poured off the excess fat, added the syrup, and let it heat for 30 seconds. This allowed us to use the drippings that had formed in the pan when the meat seared and also eliminated the extra pan we had been using to reduce the syrup. Next we decided to lose the roasting pan (and basting brush, which we invariably trashed with the sticky glaze) in favor of the same skillet. Instead of pouring the glaze mixture over the pork in the roasting pan, where it would run to the edges and scorch, we returned the seared loin to the skillet with the syrup, twirled the pork around in the glaze a couple of times with tongs, and popped the whole thing into the oven, with the skillet serving as the roasting pan.

The smaller surface area of the skillet prevented the glaze from spreading out and burning. This pan also made it easier to coat the pork thoroughly because it was sitting right in the glaze, like a belle in her bath. The roast emerged from the oven with a thick, uniform, glistening coating of glaze and an impressive, concentrated maple flavor. We had the best results with fairly small roasts (about 2½ pounds); the sauce tended to burn when we tried to cook through larger roasts. An oven temperature of 325 degrees (which is 25 degrees higher than our standard roasting temperature for this cut of meat) was fine given the small size of the roast, and it helped speed up the roasting time a bit, too.

In the end, we had managed to turn this into a one-pan dish by searing, reducing the glaze, and roasting all in the same skillet. And there was yet another bonus. Starting with a hot skillet shaved a little time off the whole process. This skillet-roasted, burnished beauty was now out of the oven in 45 minutes or less.

THE PROBLEM WITH ENHANCED PORK

Juices Lost from Enhanced Pork   **Juices Lost from Regular Roast**

Many markets sell enhanced pork, which has been injected with a water/salt/sodium phosphate solution meant to season the meat and improve juiciness. During testing, we found that an enhanced roast exuded nearly one-and-a-half times as much liquid as a regular roast when carved. We recommend buying regular pork.

Maple-Glazed Pork Roast
SERVES 4 TO 6

A nonstick ovenproof skillet will be much easier to clean than a traditional one. Whichever you use, remember that the handle will be blistering hot when you take it out of the oven, so be sure to use a pot holder or oven mitt. Note that you should not trim the pork of its thin layer of fat. The flavor of grade B maple syrup (sometimes called "cooking maple") is stronger and richer than grade A, but grade A syrup will work well, too. This dish is unapologetically sweet, so we recommend side dishes that take well to the sweetness. Garlicky sautéed greens, braised cabbage, and soft polenta are good choices.

⅓	cup maple syrup, preferably grade B
⅛	teaspoon ground cinnamon
	Pinch ground cloves
	Pinch cayenne pepper
1	boneless blade-end pork loin roast (about 2 ½ pounds), tied at even intervals along the length with 5 pieces butcher's twine (see the photo on page 252) and patted dry with paper towels
¾	teaspoon salt
½	teaspoon ground black pepper
2	teaspoons vegetable oil

1. Adjust an oven rack to the middle position and heat the oven to 325 degrees. Stir the maple syrup, cinnamon, cloves, and cayenne together in a measuring cup or small bowl; set aside. Sprinkle the roast evenly with the salt and pepper.

2. Heat the oil in a heavy-bottomed ovenproof nonstick 10-inch skillet over medium-high heat until just beginning to smoke. Place the roast fat-side down in the skillet and cook until well browned, about 3 minutes. Using tongs, rotate the roast one-quarter turn and cook until well browned, about 2½ minutes; repeat until the roast is well browned on all sides. Transfer the roast to a large plate. Reduce the heat to medium and pour off the fat from the skillet; add the maple syrup mixture and cook until fragrant, about 30 seconds (the syrup will bubble immediately). Off the heat, return the roast to the skillet; using tongs, roll to coat the roast with glaze on all sides.

3. Transfer the skillet to the oven and roast until the center of the roast registers about 135 degrees on an instant-read thermometer, 35 to 45 minutes, using tongs to roll the roast to coat with glaze twice during roasting time. Transfer the roast to a carving board; set the skillet aside to cool slightly to thicken the glaze, about 5 minutes. Pour the glaze over the roast and let rest for 15 minutes (the center of the roast should register 145 to 150 degrees). Snip the twine off the roast, cut into ¼-inch slices, and serve immediately.

➤ VARIATIONS

Maple-Glazed Pork Roast with Rosemary

Follow the recipe for Maple-Glazed Pork Roast, substituting 2 teaspoons minced fresh rosemary leaves for the cinnamon, cloves, and cayenne.

Maple-Glazed Pork Roast with Orange Essence

Follow the recipe for Maple-Glazed Pork Roast, adding 1 tablespoon grated orange zest to the maple syrup along with the spices.

Maple-Glazed Pork Roast with Star Anise

Follow the recipe for Maple-Glazed Pork Roast, adding 4 star anise pods to the maple syrup along with the spices.

Maple-Glazed Pork Roast with Smoked Paprika

Follow the recipe for Maple-Glazed Pork Roast, adding 2 teaspoons smoked hot paprika to the maple syrup along with the spices.

ROAST STUFFED PORK LOIN

WHEN MOST AMERICANS THINK OF A PORK roast, it's a boneless center-cut loin roast that comes to mind. Though this cut is particularly well suited for stuffing and roasting because it is both tender and evenly shaped and cooks quickly, our past experiences with roast stuffed pork loin have been fraught with the same problems every time. First is the danger that the meat will become dry, tough, and overcooked by the time the stuffing is done. Second is a stuffing with dull flavor or poor texture. Third is a sloppy appearance and stuffing that oozes out from the ends of the roast during cooking, both the result of haphazard tying of the roast.

When we consulted our library for recipes that might deal with these problems, though, all we found was confusion. Methods for stuffing and cooking the meat were as disparate as the ingredients in the recipes, which varied wildly from meat to bread to fruit to nuts to greens—and countless combinations thereof. A few rounds in the test kitchen, we hoped, would clear the way to a tender, juicy, flavorful, substantial, and neat roast stuffed pork loin.

Boneless loin roasts are the typical and—according to our testing—best choice for stuffing because they consist largely of a single, uniformly shaped muscle that is easy to stuff and roast neatly. When we started testing, though, our first few trips to the market revealed that not all boneless loin roasts are the same. We had to communicate clearly and specifically with the supermarket meat manager or butcher to get roasts with a large circumference, which was key for manageable stuffing and roasting (see page 257 for more information).

Even when we got the roast we wanted, though,

our first few tests turned out dry, tough, tasteless meat. It's no secret that today's pork is considerably leaner, and therefore less flavorful and juicy, than that of a generation ago. The effects of this lack of fat are compounded in the loin, which is in any case one of the leaner cuts from the animal.

To solve our problems, we had to embrace two proven test kitchen techniques, while eschewing a third. Soaking the meat in a salt and sugar brine was one technique we welcomed. This treatment offered dual benefits: The salt and sugar seasoned the meat and helped to keep it juicy as it cooked. The second useful technique was butterflying and pounding. Butterflying, or cutting the roast in the center and opening it like a book, proved to be the best way to prepare it for stuffing. We were determined to provide every diner with a generous amount of stuffing, and butterflied loins hold more of the mixture than roasts stuffed by means of the other methods we tried, including boring a hole through the center of the roast with a knife and sharpening steel, making a "Y" cut to create space in the center, slitting the loin from the bottom, and studding the meat with its filling. Pounding the butterflied roast further maximized the amount of stuffing we could use by increasing the meat's surface area. Pounding also helped to even out the thickness of the meat and, in test after test, proved to tenderize it as well.

The one common cooking technique recommended for this recipe that we discarded was to sear the stuffed roast in a pan on the stovetop to brown the meat before roasting. Not only did the large roasts we were using complicate this process, but a series of tests revealed that putting this now-thin cut of meat in direct contact with a blazing-hot pan toughened it. Instead, we developed an alternative means of coloring the roast—brushing it with a sweet glaze that caramelized in the oven. The glaze also added flavor and moisture.

Our last hedge against tough pork was to avoid overcooking it. As we usually do in the test kitchen, we aimed for a final internal temperature of 145 to 150 degrees, at which point the meat would be fully cooked yet retain a slightly rosy hue inside.

Having successfully completed our inquiries into matters of the meat, we turned our efforts to the stuffing. We tried all the usual stuffing bases, including ground meat, sausage, bread (fresh and dried, crumbs and cubes), fruit (dried and fresh, whole and pureed), ground nuts, greens, and herbs. Stuffings based on fruit, nuts, greens, or herbs struck us as unsubstantial. They didn't add the panache that the star of a holiday meal needs. We preferred to use dried fruit and nuts as accents in a heartier mixture.

We tried sausage, but found it was seasoned too assertively. Ground pork showed promise. The problem with the ground pork stuffing was that it had to reach an internal temperature of 160 degrees to eliminate the possibility of bacterial contamination. If harmful bacteria are present at all, they settle on the exterior of a cut of meat. When that cut is ground, however, the bacteria spread throughout the meat, inside and out. Hence the need for a high internal temperature. Unfortunately, by the time the stuffing was at 160 degrees, the meat around it had reached almost 195 degrees and was tough as a tire. We tried precooking the meat stuffing, but this caused it to develop an unpleasantly loose, crumbly texture and a gritty mouthfeel.

Undaunted, we developed a fresh bread stuffing with terrific flavor and a firm, sliceable, but still supple texture. This stuffing did its part for the roast's appearance, too, refraining from the leaking and oozing characteristic of many of the other mixtures we tried. Good as it was, though, safety concerns about its use of egg as a binder still necessitated a finished internal temperature of 160 degrees. When eggs are cooked alone, any bacteria present are killed at a lower temperature. In stuffing, however, other ingredients buffer the bacteria from the heat, so the final temperature must be higher (that is, 160 degrees). This was a problem because the dense bread stuffing heated more slowly than the meat stuffing had. No matter what oven temperature or rack position we tried, the stuffing lagged behind the pork by roughly 30 degrees. When the stuffing had reached 140 degrees, the meat was overcooked at 170 degrees.

With a single bold move, we were able to eliminate that temperature differential completely. Recalling that the reason our previous efforts at precooking stuffing had failed was because of the meat, we decided to precook our bread stuffing. We used the time during which the pork was resting in its brine to mix up the stuffing and shape it into a log that would fit easily into the butterflied meat. We then baked the log for 45 minutes in a moderate oven.

This technique was a coup. The prebaked stuffing reached a temperature of 200 degrees with its flavor and texture undamaged, thus taking care of any safety concerns. Even though the idea of handling hot stuffing was off-putting, it was surprisingly easy. Because we had preshaped the stuffing into a cylinder, we could roll it right off the baking sheet and onto the meat without even touching it. And even though the temperature of the stuffing dropped about 70 degrees during the stuffing process, the meat and stuffing kept an almost equal pace when they began to heat up in the oven, finishing within just 5 degrees of each other. This technique makes careful timing an important element in the recipe, but the results are well worth the effort.

The first few roasts we stuffed and tied looked more like something from a flaky midnight monster movie than dinner in a classic holiday rerun. For the uninitiated, packaging the stuffed roast into a neat cylinder can be quite the challenge. So we came up with an easier method. We found that bamboo skewers, broken in half and used to fasten the sides of the meat around the stuffing, provided terrific temporary support. The skewers also helped to hold the stuffed roast together when we tied it.

Our final refinement came in the tying itself. Many cooks (including some in our test kitchen) are all thumbs when it comes to manipulating a single long piece of twine into a series of butcher's knots around a roast. But with the roast held together by its skewers, we could actually cut separate, shorter pieces of twine and tie them one at a time at even intervals along the length of the roast.

Roast Pork Loin with Apricot, Fig, and Pistachio Stuffing
SERVES 8 TO 10

Timing is important. The goal is to coordinate the timing of the brining and the stuffing so that the pork is out of the brine and ready to be stuffed when the precooked stuffing comes out of the oven. To achieve this, begin preparing the stuffing ingredients immediately after setting the pork

in the brine. Bamboo skewers, available in supermarkets, are our favorite way to fasten the roast around the stuffing. Alternatively, use poultry lacers (though they are generally sold only six to a package). The apricot preserves for the glaze can be melted in the microwave instead of on the stovetop. To do so, heat the preserves in a small, microwave-safe bowl, covered loosely with plastic wrap, at full power until melted, about 40 seconds.

ROAST

1	boneless blade-end pork loin roast (about 4 1/2 pounds)

BRINE

3/4	cup sugar
3/4	cup kosher salt or 6 tablespoons table salt
3	bay leaves, crumbled
1	tablespoon whole allspice berries, lightly crushed
1	tablespoon whole black peppercorns, lightly crushed
10	medium garlic cloves, lightly crushed and peeled

STUFFING

5	cups roughly torn 1-inch pieces baguette (not sourdough) (7 to 8 ounces)
1/2	cup dried apricots
1	medium garlic clove, peeled
	Pinch ground cumin
	Pinch ground coriander
	Pinch ground cinnamon
	Pinch cayenne
2	tablespoons grated onion from 1 small onion
1/2	cup dried figs, halved lengthwise
1/2	cup shelled pistachios, toasted in a medium skillet over medium heat until the color deepens slightly, then cooled and chopped coarse
2	teaspoons minced fresh thyme leaves
2	tablespoons minced fresh parsley leaves
1 1/2	teaspoons kosher salt or 1 teaspoon table salt
	Ground black pepper
2	large eggs
1/2	cup heavy cream

GLAZE

1/2	cup apricot preserves

1. Following illustrations 1 through 4 (below), trim, butterfly, and pound the pork loin to an even 1-inch thickness with a mallet or the bottom of a heavy skillet.

2. FOR THE BRINE: In a large, wide bowl, dissolve the sugar and salt in 8 cups cold water. Add the bay leaves, allspice, peppercorns, and garlic, and stir to combine. Add the butterflied and pounded pork; cover the bowl with plastic wrap and refrigerate

until fully seasoned, about 1½ hours. Remove the pork from the brine, pick the spices off the meat, and dry the pork thoroughly with paper towels.

3. FOR THE STUFFING AND GLAZE: Once the pork is in the brine, adjust an oven rack to the lower-middle position and heat the oven to 325 degrees. Process half the bread pieces in the workbowl of a food processor fitted with the steel blade until broken into crumbs with few pieces no larger than

STUFFING A PORK ROAST

1. Using a boning knife, trim the tough silver skin from the pork loin.

2. Lay the loin on the cutting board and begin to slice laterally through the center, starting at the thinner edge.

3. As you slice, open the meat as you would a book. Stop slicing 1 inch shy of the edge to create a "hinge."

4. Cover the surface with plastic wrap and pound the meat to a 1-inch thickness.

5. Cut eight 24-inch pieces of kitchen twine. Break nine 10- or 12-inch bamboo skewers in half.

6. Roll the hot stuffing onto the center of the butterflied pork, over the hinge.

7. Bring both sides of the meat together over the stuffing and fasten at the center with one skewer. Fasten the roast with the remaining skewers placed at regular intervals.

8. Shimmy lengths of twine one by one down under the roast and tie them between the skewers, as shown. Trim the twine and remove the skewers before roasting.

about ¼ inch, about 45 seconds; transfer to a large mixing bowl and set aside. Repeat the process with the remaining bread pieces (you should have about 4 cups crumbs total).

4. In the now-empty workbowl, process the apricots, garlic, cumin, coriander, cinnamon, and cayenne until finely ground, about 30 seconds; add the mixture to the reserved bread crumbs. Add the onion, figs, pistachios, thyme, parsley, salt, and pepper to taste to the crumb and apricot mixture; toss until well distributed, breaking up any apricot clumps as necessary. Beat the eggs and cream in a small bowl; pour over the bread and apricot mixture and toss with your hands until evenly moistened and a portion of the mixture holds together when pressed.

5. On a parchment paper–lined cookie sheet or inverted rimmed baking sheet, form the stuffing into a log shape equal in length to butterflied pork. Cover the stuffing with foil and bake until firm and cooked through and the butterflied pork has been removed from the brine and prepared for stuffing, about 45 minutes. Remove the stuffing from the oven; increase the oven temperature to 450 degrees.

6. While the stuffing bakes, heat the apricot preserves in a small saucepan over medium–low heat, stirring occasionally, until melted but not liquefied,

5 to 7 minutes. Strain through a small strainer into a small bowl (you should have about ⅓ cup) and set aside; discard the solids in the strainer.

7. TO STUFF, ROAST, AND GLAZE THE ROAST: Line a shallow roasting pan or rimmed baking sheet with foil, position a flat wire roasting rack over the foil, and set aside. Following illustrations 5 through 8 on page 257, stuff, roll, fasten, and tie the pork loin. Place the stuffed roast on the rack, brush half of the apricot glaze evenly over the exposed surface of the meat, and roast for 20 minutes. Remove the roast from the oven and, with tongs, rotate the roast so that the bottom side faces up. Brush the exposed surface with the remaining apricot glaze; return the roast to the oven and roast for 25 minutes longer (the glaze should be medium golden brown and the internal temperature of both the meat and stuffing should register 145 to 150 degrees on an instant-read thermometer). Transfer the roast to a carving board, tent with the foil, and let rest for 5 minutes. Cut off the twine, slice, and serve.

➤ VARIATIONS

Roast Pork Loin with Apricot, Cherry, and Pecan Stuffing

Follow the recipe for Roast Pork Loin with Apricot, Fig, and Pistachio Stuffing, substituting

---

INGREDIENTS: Pork Loin Roasts

The pork loin runs from the shoulder of the hog down the back to the ham in the rear. While every hog is different, most whole boneless loins measure roughly 30 inches long and weigh in the range of 8 to 12 pounds when they reach the butcher shop or supermarket meat department. There they are broken down into the 2- to 3-pound roasts typically available in the meat case. Most important for this recipe is the loin's shape, which is wide near the shoulder, or blade, end, and tapers to a thinner silhouette at the center.

In the process of cooking more than 50 loin roasts, we learned from experience that boneless loin roasts of the same weight can have entirely different dimensions, depending on the section of the loin from which they were cut. To be successful in our efforts, we had to use roasts cut from the wider blade end of the loin. These blade-end loin roasts offered more surface area once butterflied and were much easier to stuff than those from the slender center section. Both of the roasts shown here, for example, weigh 4 ½ pounds, but the center-cut roast, right, has a circumference of 3 inches at its widest point and a whopping 19-inch length, making it a poor choice for

stuffing. With its generous 4-inch circumference and shorter 13-inch length, the blade-end loin roast, left, is a much better choice for this recipe. Because large, 4 ½-pound roasts are rare in the meat case, you'll probably have to ask the butcher to cut it for you. Ask for the blade end of the largest loin available.

Good Roast for Stuffing

Bad Roast for Stuffing

½ cup dried tart cherries for the figs and ½ cup coarsely chopped toasted pecans for the pistachios in the stuffing mixture.

Roast Pork Loin with Apricot, Prune, and Pine Nut Stuffing

Follow the recipe for Roast Pork Loin with Apricot, Fig, and Pistachio Stuffing, substituting ½ cup pitted prunes, halved lengthwise, for the figs and ½ cup toasted pine nuts for the pistachios in the stuffing mixture.

Roast Pork Tenderloin

QUICK COOKING, LEAN, AND MODERATELY priced, pork tenderloin is one of our favorite cuts of pork. It is easily turned into a variety of dishes, from roasts to cutlets, all easy to prepare and ready in minutes. Roasted pork tenderloins are appealing because they are so quick to cook. However, they can be dry. We find they are best served with a sweet sauce, which improves the mild flavor of the pork and keeps the meat moist.

One of our favorite pork preparations is a Chinese dish called char siu, roasted pork marinated in a variety of seasonings. Most Americans have had char siu at one point or another, whether they've recognized it or not. This roasted pork is used in many Chinese restaurant dishes, such as fried rice, pork stir-fries, and dim sum variations. The meat's exterior is a characteristically vibrant red or pinkish hue from a combination of caramelized sugar and red food color. The flavor is both sweet and salty, with a deep hoisin flavor and backnotes of Chinese five-spice power, ginger, and garlic. Generally, char siu is purchased from Asian specialty markets, where it is roasted in large cuts in intensely hot ovens designed for the purpose. Char siu is typically used in things, not on its own, and is therefore potently flavored. Our goal, then, was to tone down the seasoning and make the dish into a main course meal, suitable on its own, though good in things too, if there happened to be leftovers.

From the start, we had a game plan for our char siu. In hopes of keeping things easy, we wanted to sear the tenderloins on the stovetop for flavor and color and then finish them in a very hot oven. Then, once the meat was cooked through, we would coat it with the thick sauce with all the flavors normally present in the marinade. We borrowed the technique from our beef teriyaki (page 61). Tenderloins couldn't be easier to prepare, requiring a minimal amount of trimming. For this dish, we found it important to remove the silver skin (the tough connective tissue striating the tenderloin's exterior) so that it didn't roll up onto itself—the silver skin tightens more than the meat and causes the meat to arc. As for the untrimmed fat, we left it alone. Tenderloins are so lean that they need all the help they can get, and most of the fat renders off the meat as it cooks.

After consulting a tall stack of recipes, we reckoned the base flavors of char siu marinade (therefore for our sauce) were five-spice powder, ginger, garlic, hoisin sauce, soy sauce, and a sweetener of some sort. Our testing, then, centered on the proper proportions for each ingredient and how to best flavor the pork with the seasonings. One thing we learned right from the start was how important it was to expose the five-spice powder to direct, dry heat. When we added it to the other sauce components, its potent flavor dominated the mix, even when it was scaled back significantly. The cinnamon was too potent, tasting like a cheap cookie. But after toasting, the powder—especially the cinnamon—took a backseat and lent mystery to the sauce's sweet edge without a distinct presence. To save on cooking steps, we found we could use the five-spice powder (combined with salt) as a spice rub on the tenderloin, thereby "toasting" the spices as the meat seared.

The rest of the sauce ingredients proved easier to nail, though balancing sweet and salty took some work. What tasted balanced raw didn't always taste correct once reduced. After starting off with plain white sugar for a sweetener, we found honey a better choice as its floral tones emphasized the flavor of the hoisin sauce and thick honey also added luster to the sauce.

Building the sauce in the skillet, post roast, also allowed us to use any fond that built up—an easy and effective way to bolster flavor. Because the pork was so lean, we needed to add additional oil to sauté the garlic and ginger, and then added the rest of the sauce components to reduce and blend. Once the sauce was syrupy, we returned the tenderloins to the skillet and turned them to coat. The result was stunning—the meat was thickly glossed with a mahogany glaze. Yes, it lacked the trademark scarlet red hue (nobody in the test kitchen complained), but the flavor was just as good.

Roast Pork Tenderloins, Chinese Style

SERVES 4 TO 6

Serve the pork with steamed white rice. Leftover pork may be used to flavor a stir-fry, in fried rice, or in a sandwich with spicy greens like watercress.

1 ½	teaspoons Chinese five-spice powder
	Salt
2	pork tenderloins (about 1 pound each), trimmed of the silver skin (see the illustration on page 117) and patted dry with paper towels
4	teaspoons vegetable oil
1	tablespoon honey
1	tablespoon soy sauce
¼	cup hoisin sauce
½	cup water
2	medium garlic cloves, minced or pressed through a garlic press (about 2 teaspoons)
1	(1-inch) piece fresh ginger, peeled and minced (1 tablespoon)

1. Adjust an oven rack to the middle position and heat the oven to 425 degrees. Combine the five-spice powder and 1 teaspoon salt in a small bowl. Thoroughly rub the tenderloins with the spice mixture. Heat 2 teaspoons of the oil in a large ovenproof skillet over medium-high heat until smoking. Add the tenderloins to the skillet and cook until browned on the bottom, 1 to 1½ minutes. Using tongs, rotate the tenderloin a quarter turn and cook until well browned, 1 to 1½ minutes. Repeat 2 more times until the tenderloins are well browned on all sides. Transfer the skillet to the oven and cook until an instant-read thermometer registers 135 to 140 degrees, 15 to 18 minutes.

Remove the skillet from the oven, transfer the tenderloins to a cutting board, and tent them with foil to keep warm.

2. While the tenderloins are in the oven, mix the honey, soy sauce, hoisin sauce, and water together in a small bowl and set aside.

3. Return the now-empty skillet to medium-high heat, add the remaining 2 teaspoons oil, and swirl to coat the pan. Add the garlic and ginger and cook, stirring frequently, until very aromatic, about 30 seconds. Add the sauce mixture and cook, stirring frequently and scraping the pan bottom with a wooden spoon to remove any browned bits, until syrupy, 3 to 4 minutes. Return the tenderloins to the pan and, using tongs, roll them several times to coat thoroughly with the sauce. Transfer the meat to a cutting board and cut the tenderloins crosswise into thin slices. Arrange the slices on a platter and pour the sauce over the top. Serve immediately.

TUSCAN PORK ROAST WITH GARLIC AND ROSEMARY

TUSCAN-STYLE ROAST PORK IS A DISH WITH lore reaching back to the 15th century. This simple roasted pork loin is served boneless and sliced thick, often accompanied by the pan juices. The meat is succulent, the crust crisp, and the roast is infused with the appealing flavor combination of rosemary and garlic. It's great hot from the oven or cold sliced in sandwiches, and it is surprisingly inexpensive. This is a roast that can be a showpiece for a special occasion or a family meal with leftovers.

But for such a simple roast, problems abound. The meat can be dry, tough, and unevenly cooked; the crust can be absent, resulting in a pale and unappealing dish; and the rosemary and garlic flavors can be either too bland or too harsh. Our research revealed that there is no consensus on the cut of meat, the best way to flavor the pork, or the oven temperature at which to roast it.

We began by testing the cut of meat. Recipes called for a wide range of choices, the most popular being a boneless center-cut pork loin. Preparing and tasting 12 recipes convinced us to use a bone-in loin. These roasts had a richer pork flavor and were noticeably juicier. The boneless loins, in comparison, failed on the taste test, but we noted that they were easier to carve. We also observed that the boneless roasts cooked on a rack, assuring that the meat on the bottom roasted rather than steamed. With this information in hand, we continued testing to determine which of the bone-in choices was best.

Visualizing the anatomy of a pig helps in understanding the choices. Working from shoulder to midsection, first comes the blade roast, then the rib roast, next the loin roast, and finally the sirloin roast. We eliminated the blade roast and the sirloin roast, both of which are composed of many separate muscles and fatty deposits. Tests showed that these cuts were difficult to cook evenly, flavor well, and carve.

Both the rib roast and the loin roast seemed worthy candidates. Each of these roasts consists largely of the same single, uniformly shaped muscle, so we prepared them side by side. You can imagine our delight at discovering that the cut of choice, the rib roast, provided not just the tastiest meat but also the most natural and ideal rack to cook the loin on—the rib bones.

We asked several butchers to explain why the meat was so much better from the rib roast despite the similarity of the loin roast. We learned that the meat on the rib roast includes a protective cap of fat and muscle and is marbled with more fat than the loin roast. The marbling (threads of intramuscular fat) and the fat in the cap melt during cooking and flavor the meat as well as ensure juiciness. The loin roast has less marbling, lacks a protective cap of fat and muscle, and does not have as many rib bones.

The bones of the rib roast make an important contribution to the success of this dish. They protect the meat, which helps keep it moist, and they enhance the pork flavor. The rib bones also lift the meat off the floor of the roasting pan, which allows for the circulation of air and, hence, even cooking, and prevents mushy bottom meat. The backbone, called the chine bone, is sometimes attached to the rib bones, and it also provides stability. After much testing, we concluded that the cut of choice was a rib roast with the chine bone attached.

Purchasing a rib roast requires an understanding of the distinction between the rib roast and the loin roast because sometimes these roasts are labeled exactly the same: "center cut, bone-in roast." If you are looking in a meat case, refer to the photographs on page 262, or simply ask your butcher. Know that this is the same prized cut of meat sold as rack of lamb or prime rib of beef—it just comes from a pig.

With the cut of meat decided, we turned our attention to the traditional Tuscan flavors. Rosemary, garlic, and olive oil are strong characters, and we were determined to harness and marry their flavors so that the roast would be perfumed with their essence. We identified the classic approaches and began testing.

Stuffing slivers of garlic, with or without rosemary, into slits on the outside of the roast failed to impress. The flavors did not permeate deeply (even when we refrigerated the loin overnight before cooking), and the garlic and rosemary were not pleasant to eat. Garlic and rosemary rubbed on the outside tended to burn and become bitter. Rosemary sprigs tied to the outside looked appealing, but the flavor did not penetrate and the crust did not brown evenly. In an attempt to flavor the center of the meat, some recipes called for creating a hole in the middle of the loin and then stuffing it, while other recipes have you slit open the loin and spread a rosemary garlic mixture on the inside. These approaches held promise, but the garlic was often undercooked and harsh and the rosemary overpowering.

We were convinced that putting a paste in the center of the meat was the answer. We tried using a mini food processor to make the paste, but the garlic did not break down into small enough pieces. The bigger chunks were undercooked and sharp tasting in the cooked pork. Making the paste by hand with the help of a garlic press gave the best results. Equal parts rosemary and garlic was most pleasing, and tests showed that including olive oil helps heat and cook the garlic and rosemary paste, which facilitates the infusion of flavor.

We were on our 26th roast and still having problems using the paste to infuse the meat with flavor. Our search for creative solutions led us to remove the meat from the bone, cut it open in the center, and open it like a book, a technique called butterflying. We spread the paste in the cut and then tied the roast back together. This roast was very flavorful, but there was too much paste, which was unpleasant and overpowering to eat. We tried another butterflied loin with the intention of using less of the paste in the cut when the naked bones gave us an idea. We slathered the bones with two thirds of the paste and spread the rest in the cut, then tied the meat back onto the bones. This technique worked like a charm. The rosemary and garlic flavors infused the meat, but the paste stayed on the bones when the roast was sliced and served. The bonus of deconstructing the roast to apply the paste was that carving was no longer an issue. By simply cutting the twine after cooking, the bone-in roast was now as easy to slice and serve as the boneless roasts we had tried at the beginning. Our search for flavor had served up convenience as well.

We now had a very good-tasting roast, but we were looking for the best. We wanted to address the fact that pigs are bred leaner these days, and less fat means less flavor and less moisture. We decided to try brining—soaking the pork (both the meat and the bones) in a saltwater and sugar solution. Brining causes the protein cells within the meat to unravel and thus capture and retain both moisture and seasoning. Sure enough, tests confirmed that this technique produced a roast that was better seasoned and juicier. We added rosemary and garlic to the brine along with brown sugar for depth and caramelization. This created a terrific and aromatic roast, with complex flavors that were both strong and savory.

We were in the home stretch and ready to experiment with roasting methods. Our goal—a crispy and flavorful crust combined with tender and moist morsels of meat—was in sight. Older recipes call for cooking the loin until the internal temperature reaches 160 degrees. Especially with today's lean pork, this produces a roast that is dry and gray. With concerns about the trichinosis parasite largely eliminated, the Pork Board now recommends cooking pork until it is just slightly rosy in the center and registers 150 degrees on an instant-read thermometer. The test kitchen suggests a final temperature of 145 to 150 degrees—the meat will be juicier and the temperature is sufficient to kill trichinosis, however remote the possibility that the parasite is present. Because the internal heat will keep cooking the meat and cause the temperature to rise while the roast is resting, the meat should be removed from the oven at 135 degrees.

Roasting at a constant temperature was not ideal. A low temperature (325 degrees or lower) produced the best meat, while high heat (400 degrees or higher) produced the best crust. A moderate oven temperature produced neither delectable meat nor an appealing crust.

We resisted dividing the cooking between the stovetop and the oven, trying every imaginable combination of high heat and low heat in the oven instead. But this approach also failed. The high heat dried out the meat or even worse; occasionally, the high heat resulted in billows of smoke pouring out of the oven from the pork fat.

The answer came easily once we let go of our resolve to limit cooking to the oven. Restaurant training taught us that searing on the stovetop and then cooking in the oven is a fail-safe method for producing an excellent crust and perfectly cooked meat. A constant 325-degree oven subsequent to stovetop searing gave the best results.

Finally, we had developed a recipe for a Tuscan-

TWO CENTER-CUT PORK ROASTS

Loin Roast   **Rib Roast**

Both the rib roast and loin roast can be labeled "center-cut roast" at the market, but they are not the same. The meat on the pork rib roast includes a protective cap of fat and muscle and is marbled with more fat than the loin roast. The marbling (threads of intramuscular fat) and the fat in the cap melt during cooking and flavor the meat as well as ensure its juiciness. The loin roast has less marbling, lacks a protective cap of fat and muscle, and does not have as many rib bones, so the meat is more likely to dry out in the oven. For these reasons, we recommend a rib roast, not a loin roast.

style roast pork loin that lives up to its reputation. The approach of using a bone-in roast, removing the meat to brine it and flavor it, then tying the meat back to the bone for roasting is a bit unconventional—but the process is easy and ensures a roast that reveals why the love affair with Tuscan-style roast pork began 600 years ago.

Tuscan–Style Roast Pork Loin with Garlic and Rosemary

SERVES 6 TO 8

The roasting time is determined in part by the shape of the roast; a long, thin roast will cook faster than a roast with a large circumference. Though not traditionally served, the ribs are rich with flavor. If you'd like to serve them or enjoy them yourself, after untying the roast and removing the loin, scrape the excess garlic-rosemary paste from the ribs, set the ribs on a rimmed baking sheet, and put them in a 375-degree oven for about 20 minutes or until they are brown and crisp (the roast is resting at this point). See page 262 for tips on buying the right pork roast for this recipe.

ROAST

2	cups kosher salt or 1 cup table salt
2 1/3	cups packed (1 pound) dark brown sugar
10	large garlic cloves, lightly crushed and peeled
5	sprigs fresh rosemary, each about 6 inches long
1	bone-in, center-cut pork loin roast with chine bone cracked, preferably from the rib end (about 4 pounds), prepared according to illustrations 1 and 2 on page 264

GARLIC-ROSEMARY PASTE

8–10	garlic cloves, pressed through a garlic press or minced to a paste (about 3 tablespoons)
1 1/2	tablespoons finely chopped fresh rosemary leaves
1	teaspoon ground black pepper
1	tablespoon extra-virgin olive oil
1/8	teaspoon kosher salt or pinch table salt
1	cup dry white wine
1	teaspoon ground black pepper
1	medium shallot, minced (about 3 tablespoons)
1 1/2	teaspoons minced fresh rosemary leaves
1 3/4	cups low-sodium chicken broth

2	tablespoons unsalted butter, cut into 4 pieces and softened

1. FOR THE ROAST: Dissolve the salt and brown sugar in 1½ quarts hot tap water in a large stockpot or clean bucket. Stir in the garlic and rosemary. Add 2½ quarts cold water and submerge the meat and bones in the brine. Refrigerate until fully seasoned, about 3 hours. Rinse the meat and ribs under cold water and dry thoroughly with paper towels.

2. FOR THE PASTE: While the roast brines, mix the garlic, rosemary, pepper, olive oil, and salt together in a small bowl to form a paste; set aside.

3. FOR COOKING THE ROAST: When the roast is out of the brine, adjust an oven rack to the middle position and heat the oven to 325 degrees. Heat a heavy-bottomed 12-inch skillet over medium heat until hot. Place the roast, fat side down, in the skillet and cook until well browned, about 8 minutes. Transfer the roast, browned side up, to a rimmed baking sheet and set aside. Pour off the fat from the skillet and add the wine. Increase the heat to high and bring to a boil, scraping the browned bits on the pan bottom with a wooden spoon until loosened. Set the skillet with the wine aside.

4. Make a lengthwise incision in the pork loin and rub with one-third of the garlic-rosemary paste (see illustrations 3 and 4 on page 264). Rub the remaining paste on the cut side of the ribs where the meat was attached (see illustration 5). Tie the meat to the ribs (see illustration 6); sprinkle the browned side of the roast with the pepper. Pour the reserved wine and browned bits from the skillet into the roasting pan. Roast, basting the loin with the pan

THE TEMPERATURE MATTERS

Juicy Roast	Dried-Out Roast

At a final internal temperature (after resting) of 145 degrees, the meat is just slightly rosy at the center and moist (left photo). Let the roast reach an internal temperature of 160 degrees (as recommended in many older recipes) and the meat will be gray and dry (right).

drippings every 20 minutes, until the center of loin registers about 135 degrees on an instant-read thermometer, 65 to 80 minutes. (If the wine evaporates, add about ½ cup water to the roasting pan to prevent scorching.) Transfer the roast to a carving board and tent loosely with foil. Let stand until the center of the loin registers about 145 degrees on an instant-read thermometer, about 15 minutes.

5. While the roast rests, spoon most of the fat from the roasting pan and place the pan over 2 burners at high heat. Add the shallot and rosemary. Using a wooden spoon, scrape up the browned bits and boil the liquid until reduced by half and the shallot has softened, about 2 minutes. Add the chicken broth and continue to cook, stirring occasionally, until reduced by half, about 8 minutes. Add any accumulated pork juices from the carving board

and cook 1 minute longer. Off the heat, whisk in the butter. Strain the jus into a gravy boat.

6. Cut the twine on the roast and remove the roast from the bones. Set the roast, browned-side up, and cut into ¼-inch thick slices. Serve immediately, passing the jus separately.

➤ VARIATIONS

Tuscan-Style Roast Pork Loin with Potatoes

Instead of making a jus from the roasting pan drippings, use them to flavor roasted potatoes to serve with the pork.

Follow the recipe for Tuscan-Style Roast Pork Loin with Garlic and Rosemary, reducing the wine to ¾ cup and omitting the shallot, chicken broth, and butter. When the pork has roasted 15 minutes, quarter 2 pounds red potatoes (each

PREPARING A TUSCAN PORK ROAST

1. Position the loin so that the rib bones are perpendicular to the cutting board. Using a sharp knife and starting from the far end and working toward you, separate the meat from the rib bones by pressing—almost scraping—the knife along the rib bones.

2. Use a series of small, easy strokes to cut all along the bones, following the rib bones along the curve to the backbone until the meat is free of the bones. You will have a compact eye of the loin, with a small flap attached to the side.

3. Slice through the center of the entire length of the eye, stopping 1 inch shy of the edge.

4. Open the eye up so it is spread flat like butterfly wings and rub one third of the garlic-rosemary paste in an even layer on one side of the cut, leaving ½ inch on each end bare.

5. Spread the remaining garlic-rosemary paste evenly along the bones from where the meat was cut, leaving ½ inch on each end bare. Fold the eye back together and secure the meat on the bones exactly from where it was cut.

6. Use seven lengths of butcher's twine to tie the meat back onto the bones.

about 2½ inches in diameter); toss the potatoes with 2 tablespoons olive oil in a medium bowl and season generously with salt and pepper to taste. After the pork has been roasting for 30 minutes, add the potatoes to the roasting pan; stir to coat the potatoes with the drippings. After transferring the roast to a carving board, turn the potato pieces with a wide metal spatula and spread them in an even layer. Increase the oven temperature to 400 degrees, return the potatoes to the oven, and continue to roast until tender and browned, 5 to 15 minutes longer. Serve the potatoes with the roast.

Tuscan-Style Roast Pork Loin with Fennel

Fennel is a common addition to the classic garlic-rosemary–flavored pork roast. Fennel seeds and the delicate, wispy fronds are used in the paste, and sliced fennel roasts in the pan alongside the pork.

1. Trim 2 medium fennel bulbs of stalks and fronds; finely chop 2 teaspoons fronds. Cut each bulb lengthwise into eighths. Toss the fennel with 1 tablespoon olive oil in a medium bowl and season generously with salt and pepper to taste.

2. Follow the recipe for Tuscan-Style Roast Pork Loin with Garlic and Rosemary, adding 1 teaspoon finely chopped fennel seeds and the chopped fennel fronds to the garlic-rosemary paste. Reduce the wine to ¾ cup and omit the shallot, chicken broth, and butter. Add the sliced fennel to the roasting pan along with the wine. After transferring the roast to the carving board, return roasting pan with the fennel to the oven and continue to roast until tender, 5 to 15 minutes. Serve the fennel with the roast.

CROWN ROAST OF PORK

FEW THINGS LOOK MORE IMPRESSIVE THAN a crown roast of pork on the holiday table. But looks can be deceiving. Beyond being a gorgeous centerpiece with the ability to feed a room full of guests, this traditional roast often has little to offer

in the way of flavor and can be incredibly dry. We set out to find a way to make a crown roast taste as good as it looks.

Researching a number of existing recipes, we noted that many offer instructions for tying two racks of pork loin into a crown. Involving band saws, sewing needles large enough to accommodate butcher's twine, and a strong sense of confidence, we decided that this is one task best left to the butcher. We recommend that you buy a roast already tied and ready to cook. Talking to several butchers around town, we learned that crowns can be ordered in different sizes, and easiest being by the number of ribs. (Figure on roughly 1 rib per person with a few extra for good measure.) Depending on the size, the butcher may have to cut small incisions between each rib in order to bend the racks into a round.

After cooking crown roasts made with varying numbers of ribs, we found that size does matter. Small crowns made with fewer than 16 ribs were simply too tight and compact to cook through evenly (if you're serving just a few people, it is easier to cook a rack of pork, see the recipe on page 267). At the other extreme, huge crowns with over 20 ribs were difficult to handle as were roasting pans large enough to hold them. Crowns with 16 to 20 ribs (weighing 9 to 12 pounds) worked best and can serve from 14 to 20 people.

Moving onto the cooking method, we set aside the idea of stuffing the roast (a method many recipes employ) in order to focus more closely on the meat itself. Cooking three roasts side by side, we compared a brined (soaked in a salt and sugar solution) and an unbrined crown roast against one that was cooked upside down (a method a few recipes tout). The least favorite of the three was the unbrined roast, which was tough and overcooked around the outside of the ring, yet slightly pink and underdone around the inside. The brined roast turned out good and juicy; however, it also was unevenly cooked. The crown roast cooked upside down (that is, with the bones facing down) was the favorite, offering juicy, flavorful, evenly cooked meat and a fantastic, crisp brown crust around the bottom. Because the meat is propped up on its ribs (see the illustration on 266), the hot air of the oven was able to circulate around the roast and cook it more evenly. Testing oven temperatures ranging from 300 to 425 degrees, we found the differences substantial. Increasing the oven temperatures resulted in tougher, drier meat that was unevenly cooked. A gentle 300-degree oven produced the best results.

A beautiful crust does form on the bottom of the crown as it roasts upside down, but the top (the presentation side) remains somewhat pale and unattractive. In order to brown it, we found it necessary to make two significant alterations: stand the roast right side up for the last 30 minutes of roasting time, and boost the oven temperature to 500 degrees. We also found it necessary to wrap the ends of the ribs in foil to prevent them from burning.

Our research revealed that overcooking the meat, even if just a little, quickly turns a juicy, flavorful roast dry and bland. With the curved shape of a crown roast, it can difficult to take an accurate temperature reading. Depending on where the probe of the thermometer is placed, readings can vary up to 15 degrees. To simplify the matter, we decided to monitor the temperature of the roast only in the center of the eye of the meat (see the illustration below). Other recipes that we used for reference gave a range of finish temperatures, from 145 to 175 degrees. We determined that the roast should be removed from the oven when the center registers 140 degrees (the temperature in the center will continue to rise outside the oven to 150 to 155 degrees). At this temperature, all the nooks and crannies on the outside and inside of the crown will be cooked through, yet none will be overcooked.

To further ensure a tender, juicy and evenly cooked roast, we availed ourselves of a few other trustworthy tricks. Letting the meat sit at room temperature for an hour before cooking helped ease its transition from the cold refrigerator to a hot oven. It was also helpful to rotate the roasting pan halfway through cooking to accommodate any hot spots in the oven. Last, sometimes it was necessary to tighten a loose or wobbly roast into a more uniform shape by wrapping it several times with extra twine.

As for flavoring, we tried several herb and spice

PREPARING CROWN ROAST OF PORK

1. Wrap butcher's twine tightly around the circumference of the crown roast.

2. Flip the crown roast upside down, and, if unsteady, tie more twine around the circumference to stabilize it.

3. Place the inverted crown roast in a roasting pan. Roast as directed.

4. To measure the temperature accurately, insert an instant-read thermometer into the center of the eye of the meat.

5. When the thermometer registers 110 degrees, flip the crown roast right-side up, using 2 wads of paper towels to protect your hands.

6. Brush the meat with melted butter and wrap a narrow band of foil around the tips of the ribs to prevent them from burning. Finish roasting as directed.

based rubs only to find that a simple sprinkling of salt, pepper, and sugar (which also promotes browning) tasted best. Having tasted many crowns, we realized one unavoidable fact: "Unenhanced" pork is worth tracking down. This roast is only worth making if you start with high-quality meat.

Crown Roast of Pork

SERVES 14 TO 20

Ask your butcher to do as much work as possible—that is, to tie the roast and cut the chine bone. Ideally, the butcher will totally remove the chine bone to facilitate easy carving. Some butchers may keep the chine bone attached and just cut through the bones between each rib. Although you can use a roast that has been prepared this way, our preference is for a crown roast with the chine bone removed before roasting. You will still need to tie extra twine around many roasts. Note that the frilly papers some butchers put on the ends of the ribs should be removed. This roast is traditionally served with stuffing and gravy. Our All-Purpose Gravy (page 406) is ideal. If you prefer, serve with cranberry or apple chutney instead.

1	(16- to 20-rib) crown roast of pork (9 to 12 pounds)
4	teaspoons salt
2	teaspoons ground black pepper
1	tablespoon sugar
2	tablespoons unsalted butter, melted

1. Unwrap the pork roast and let it stand at room temperature for 1 hour. Mix the salt, pepper, and sugar together in a small bowl; set aside.

2. Adjust an oven rack to the lower-middle position and heat the oven to 300 degrees. Rub the salt mixture evenly over the pork. Following illustrations 1 through 3 on page 266, tie the crown roast with extra twine and set it, bone-side down, in a roasting pan. Place in the oven and cook until an instant-read thermometer inserted into the center of the eye registers 110 degrees (see illustration 4), 2 to 2½ hours, rotating the roasting pan halfway through the cooking time.

3. Remove the crown roast from the oven and increase the oven temperature to 500 degrees. Following illustrations 5 and 6, invert the crown roast, bone-side up, brush the meat with the butter, and cover the tips of the ribs with a small band of foil to protect them from burning. Return the crown roast to the oven and continue to cook until the instant-read thermometer inserted in the center of the eye registers 140 degrees, about 30 minutes.

4. Remove the crown roast from the oven and transfer it to a cutting board. Tent with foil and allow to rest for 15 to 20 minutes (as it rests, the internal temperature should rise to between 150 and 155 degrees in all spots). Snip off the twine. Transfer the crown roast to a serving platter and slice between the ribs into individual portions. Serve immediately.

RACK OF PORK

CROWN ROAST OF PORK CAN BE A LOT OF work and a plain pork roast just doesn't seem festive enough. Is there something that's festive but also easy to prepare? The answer is yes—a rack of pork. In this recipe, two bone-in pork loins are roasted separately, then presented at the table with frenched ribs crossed.

Because this cooking configuration allows the loins to roast independently of each other, browning on all sides was ensured. Roasts from the rib end (rather than from the center or loin end of the whole loin) also guaranteed better flavor: Located close to the more flavorful shoulder, this part of the loin is multimuscled, with much-needed fat separating the muscles.

Bones also add flavor to meat. To fashion racks into a crown roast, the chine bone (the backbone) is sometimes removed, thus further robbing the meat of much-needed flavor. A rack of pork, however, does not require complete removal of the chine bone, so the loin can roast on the bone.

To improve the roast's flavor even more, we decided to mimic the pork industry's meat-marinating technique. Using a gadget we found at a local cooking shop, we injected each of three roasts with a different flavor. Dying each mixture blue so that it could be tracked as it traveled through the meat, we made one of salt and water; one of salt, sugar, and water; and one of salt, water, and oil. We roasted these three roasts along with a fourth seasoned on the surface only. The results were quite amazing. The injected flavorings permeated the roasts, gravitating to the center and making the loin muscle much more flavorful and juicy than the surface-seasoned roast. This instant marinating step takes about 10 minutes, and the results make it worth the effort.

We still had one more test to go. From working with corned beef, we knew that dry curing (rubbing meat with salt and aging it in the refrigerator) could improve the flavor of beef (see page 193). It seemed to us that pork might react the same way. So we bought a two more roasts, coated each with 2 tablespoons kosher salt, put them on a wire rack over a paper towel–lined plate, and set them in the refrigerator for 4 days. After thoroughly brushing off all the remaining salt and removing thin slices of dried-out pork from each end of the roasts, we roasted this rack. The flavor and texture was even better than the injected roast. Even though it was a little too salty, this roast tasted like real pork, with a smooth, buttery texture. Reducing the salt in a second test gave us still better results.

For those who buy their rack of pork the afternoon before they want to serve it, we recommend the injection method as a means of flavoring it. For those who think three or four days ahead, salting and aging the roast is the ticket.

Roast Cured Rack of Pork

SERVES 6 TO 8

In order to dry cure the meat, you will need to purchase the rack of pork 3 to 5 days prior to serving it. Then you must make space for the rack in the refrigerator for up to a 4-day cure. If you don't have that kind of time, try the optional marinade below. Or, if you're in a real rush, skip both, knowing that choosing the right roast and cooking it according to the suggested method will deliver better-than-average results.

For a festive presentation, french the bones—remove the meat from between each rib with a paring knife. So that the bones will cross at presentation, have the butcher remove the tip of chine. To make carving easier, have the butcher cut the chine bone between each rib.

2   bone-in, center-cut pork loin roasts (5 to 6 ribs each), preferably from the rib end, tip of chine removed, chine bone cut between each rib, and "frenched" (see illustrations 1 through 4 on page 269)

2   tablespoons kosher or 1 tablespoon table salt

3   medium garlic cloves, minced or pressed through a garlic press (1 tablespoon)

2   teaspoons ground black pepper

2   tablespoons minced fresh thyme, sage, or rosemary leaves

2   tablespoons olive oil, plus extra for tossing vegetables

1   small carrot, cut into 1-inch chunks

1   small onion, chopped coarse

3   tablespoons Madeira

1. Scrape the rib bones with a paring knife to remove any scraps of meat or fat the butcher might have missed until the bones are absolutely clean (see illustration 5 on page 269). Rinse the roasts and pat dry with paper towels.

2. Rub 1 tablespoon kosher or 1½ teaspoons table salt evenly over each roast. Place on a wire rack set over a paper towel–lined baking or roasting pan and refrigerate, uncovered, for 3 to 4 days.

3. Adjust an oven rack to the lower-middle position and heat the oven to 250 degrees. Brush the salt from the roasts and shave off a very thin exterior layer of the hardened, dehydrated meat. Mix the garlic, pepper, herb, and oil together in a small bowl to make a thick paste, and rub half evenly over each roast. Scatter the vegetables in the roasting pan, toss lightly with oil, place the loins on a large roasting rack, and set in the pan over the vegetables. Roast until an instant-read thermometer registers 120 degrees, 1¼ to 1½ hours. Increase the oven temperature to 425 degrees. When the drippings turn brown and just start to smoke, 8 to 10 minutes, add 1 cup water to the roasting pan. Continue roasting until the meat registers 145 degrees, about 20 minutes longer

4. Transfer the loins to a serving platter, arranging them so that the ribs cross (see illustration 6 on page 269). Cover loosely with foil. To make the sauce, strain the pan drippings into a measuring cup, pressing on the vegetables to release their liquid, and

spoon off the excess fat. Add more water, if necessary, to measure 1 cup. Transfer the cooking liquid to a small saucepan, add the Madeira, and simmer to blend the flavors, about 5 minutes. Carve the roast, cutting between each rib, and serve the sauce passed separately.

➤ VARIATION

Roast Marinated Rack of Pork

After curing, the next best (and at just 10 minutes, significantly speedier) way to improve the flavor and mouthfeel of the meat is to inject it with this simple marinade. The injector looks like a large doctor's syringe, somewhat shocking in appearance but very effective. (Look for this item in kitchenware shops.) For a hint of sweetness in the meat, dissolve 1 tablespoon brown sugar along with the salt in the marinade.

Follow the recipe for Roast Cured Rack of Pork, omitting step 2 and instead dissolving 2 teaspoons salt in ⅓ cup lukewarm water in a lidded container. Add ¼ cup canola oil and shake to emulsify. Fill the syringe and inject each loin, shaking the injector occasionally to ensure that the oil and water do not separate (oil alone is difficult to inject). Rub ½ teaspoon salt, then the garlic-herb paste, evenly over each rack. Proceed with the recipe to roast the pork.

RACK OF LAMB

THE WORD "MOUTHWATERING" MUST HAVE been coined to describe rack of lamb. The meat is ultratender and luscious tasting, more refined in flavor than almost any other cut of lamb, but no less satisfying.

But, at $17 to $18 a pound, there's hardly a cut of meat more expensive. And like other simple but

PREPARING A RACK OF PORK

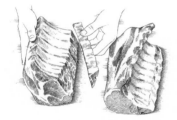

1. The success of this roast starts with good shopping. Select a roast from the rib end of the pork loin. (Whole roast is at right.) To make it possible to cross the frenched bones at the table, have the butcher remove the tip of the chine (chine has been removed from the roast on the left).

2. So that chops can be easily carved from the roast, have the butcher cut the chine bone between each rib. When you pull the roast apart, you should be able to see the cuts between the individual chops.

3. Before the ribs can be frenched, the fatty piece that covers the ribs must be removed. Ask your butcher to do this, or do it yourself.

4. Use a paring knife to remove the meat from between each rib. Again, have the butcher do this, if possible.

5. Scrape the bones with the paring knife to remove any remaining pieces of meat or fat. The butcher should do this, unless you are frenching the bones yourself.

6. For a dramatic presentation, arrange roasted loins on a serving platter so that ribs cross.

fabulous dishes (roast chicken comes to mind), there's nothing to cooking it except that there's no disguising imperfection. You want the meat to be perfectly pink and juicy, the outside intensely browned to boost flavor and provide contrasting texture, and the fat to be well enough rendered to encase the meat in a thin, crisp, brittle shell.

With all of this in mind, we set out to find a foolproof way to roast this extravagant cut. And because it's such a good choice for a party, we wanted a sauce to serve with it. A traditional jus is easy to make from pan drippings if your butcher gives you bones from butchering and trimming the rack. But you don't get bones if you buy a rack from a supermarket or one that's been vacuum sealed, and two racks on their own, cooked only to medium-rare, just don't produce enough jus for four people. We had to figure out a new way to make a sauce.

Since good exterior caramelization is critical to the taste of any roast meat, we needed to find out whether the rack would brown adequately in the oven or would need to first be browned on top of the stove. We hoped for the former; we like the ease of simply shoving the rack into the oven. So we decided to test four racks that had been trimmed and frenched (rib bones cleaned of meat and fat for an attractive presentation) at four different temperatures in a preheated oven: 425 degrees, 475 degrees, 500 degrees, and, finally, 200 degrees.

Unfortunately, none of the high oven temperatures gave us the quality of crust we were looking for, even when we preheated the roasting pan. We knew that the conditions of our remaining test—roasting at 200 degrees—would not make for a nicely browned lamb; the meat wouldn't form a crust at such a low temperature. So we started this test by searing the fat side of the rack in a little vegetable oil in a skillet on top of the stove to get a crust before putting it in a 200-degree oven. The slow-roast technique was a bust: the meat was no more tender than when cooked at a high heat, it had a funny, murky taste and mushy texture that we didn't like, and it took much too long to cook. But the searing technique was terrific. The only refinement we needed was to find a way to brown the strip of eye meat that lies below the bones on the bony side of the rack. After some experimentation we came up with the system of leaning two racks upright one against the other in the pan; this allowed us to brown all parts of the meat before roasting.

Now we went back to testing oven temperatures. Once the rack was seared, we roasted it at 350, 425, and 475 degrees. We ended up taking the middle road. At 425 degrees, the lamb tasted at least as good as (if not better than) it did when cooked at a lower temperature, and there was more room for error than when it cooked at a higher heat.

But now we were running into an unexpected problem. Surprisingly, the racks we were cooking were too fatty. They looked great when they came out of the oven, but once carved the chops were covered with a layer of fat that was browned only on the exterior. Some chops also had a second layer of internal fat, separated by a thin piece of meat, called the cap, that didn't get browned at all. We didn't want to forfeit this little flap of meat (particularly at the price we paid for it), but there seemed no help for it: We needed to get rid of some of the fat. So we trimmed the flap and all the fat underneath it, leaving only a minimal amount at the top of the eye and covering the bones to give the cut its characteristic rounded shape.

The meat tasted great, needing only one final adjustment: We removed the silver skin that we had exposed in trimming the fat. (The silver skin is the pearlescent membrane found on certain cuts of

BROWNING RACKS OF LAMB

To achieve a good crust on a rack of lamb, brown it on both sides on top of the stove before placing it in the oven in a preheated roasting pan. Start by placing 2 racks in a hot pan with the meat in the center and the ribs facing outward (left). Once browned, stand the racks up in the pan and lean them against each other to brown the bottoms (right).

meat. It is very tough and, if not removed, can cause meat to curl during cooking.)

Satisfied with our roasting technique, we were now ready to work on a sauce. We wanted a separate sauce, ready just as soon as the lamb was done, so that we weren't starting from scratch with the pan drippings at the last minute. First we made a separate jus (a very concentrated, reduced stock made with meat, onions, carrots, garlic, and a little water), using lamb stew pieces on the bone bought separately at the supermarket. The jus tasted good, but making it was too much work; we didn't want to complicate a simple meal. So we went back to the pan drippings. If we transferred the rack to a second pan after browning on top of the stove, we could make a pan sauce while the lamb roasted. As it turned out, we got the best results by preheating the roasting pan in the oven so that it was hot when the lamb hit it.

Roasted Racks of Lamb

SERVES 4 TO 6

Have your butcher french the racks (that is, remove excess fat from the rib bones) for you; inevitably, the ribs will need some cleaning up, but at least the bulk of the work will be done. Should you choose to make one of the accompanying pan sauces, have all the ingredients ready before browning the lamb on the stovetop and start to make the sauce just as the lamb goes into the oven. This way, the sauce will be ready with the meat. See the photos on page 270 for tips on browning the racks of lamb.

> 2   (8- or 9-rib) racks of lamb (1 ¼ to 1 ½ pounds each), rib bones frenched, meat trimmed of fat and silver skin (see the illustrations at right), and patted dry with paper towels
>   Salt and ground black pepper
> 2   tablespoons vegetable oil

1. Adjust an oven rack to the lower-middle position, place a shallow roasting pan or jelly-roll pan on the oven rack, and heat the oven to 425 degrees.

2. Season the lamb generously with salt and pepper to taste. Heat the oil in a heavy-bottomed 12-inch skillet over high heat until shimmering. Place the racks of lamb in the skillet, meat-side down, in the center of the pan, with the ribs facing outwards. Cook until well browned and a nice crust has formed on the surface, about 4 minutes. Using tongs, stand the racks up in the skillet, leaning them against each other to brown the bottoms; cook until the bottom sides have browned, about 2 minutes longer.

3. Transfer the lamb to the preheated roasting pan. (Begin a pan sauce, if making.) Roast until an instant-read thermometer inserted into the center of each rack registers about 125 degrees for medium-rare or 130 degrees for medium, 12 to 15 minutes, depending on the size of the rack. Remove the racks from the oven, cover the meat loosely with foil, and

PREPARING RACK OF LAMB

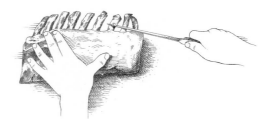

1. Using a boning or paring knife, scrape the ribs clean of any scraps of meat or fat.

2. Trim off the outer layer of fat, the flap of meat underneath it, and the fat underneath that flap.

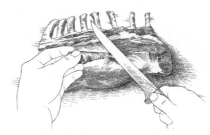

3. Remove the silver skin by sliding the boning knife between the silver skin and the flesh.

let rest about 10 minutes. Carve, slicing between each rib into individual chops Serve immediately with an additional sprinkling of salt and pepper or with one of the following sauces.

➤ VARIATIONS

Roasted Racks of Lamb with Red Wine Pan Sauce and Rosemary

1	recipe Roasted Racks of Lamb (page 271)
2	medium shallots, minced
1	cup dry red wine
2 1/2	teaspoons minced fresh rosemary leaves
1	cup low-sodium chicken broth
2	tablespoons cold unsalted butter, cut into 2 pieces
	Salt and ground black pepper

1. Prepare the lamb as directed.

2. After transferring the browned lamb to the roasting pan, pour off all but 1½ tablespoons fat from the skillet. Add the shallots and place the skillet over medium heat. Sauté the shallots until softened, about 1 minute. Add the red wine and rosemary; increase the heat to medium-high and simmer, scraping up the browned bits on the pan bottom, until dark and syrupy, about 7 minutes. Add the chicken broth and simmer until reduced to about ¾ cup, about 5 minutes longer. Swirl in the butter, 1 piece at a time, and season with salt and pepper to taste. Serve the sauce with the lamb, passing it separately at the table.

Roasted Racks of Lamb with Sweet-and-Sour Mint Sauce

This simple sauce should be made before you begin cooking the lamb so the sugar has time to dissolve while the lamb cooks.

1/2	cup loosely packed fresh mint leaves, chopped
1/4	cup red wine vinegar
1	tablespoon sugar
	Salt
1	recipe Roasted Racks of Lamb (page 271)

1. Stir the mint, vinegar, and sugar together in a small bowl. Let stand about 20 minutes to allow the sugar to dissolve. Season with salt to taste.

2. Prepare the lamb as directed. Serve the sauce with the lamb, passing it separately at the table.

Roasted Racks of Lamb with Orange Pan Sauce and Middle Eastern Spices

1	recipe Roasted Racks of Lamb (page 271)
2	medium shallots, minced
1	teaspoon ground cumin
1/4	teaspoon ground black pepper
1/4	teaspoon ground cinnamon
1/4	teaspoon ground cardamom
1/8	teaspoon cayenne pepper
2	teaspoons sugar
3	tablespoons red wine vinegar
1/4	cup juice from 1 medium orange
1 1/2	cups low-sodium chicken broth
1	tablespoon minced fresh cilantro leaves
	Salt

1. Prepare the lamb as directed.

2. After transferring the browned lamb to the roasting pan, pour off all but 1½ tablespoons fat from the skillet. Add the shallots and place the skillet over medium heat. Sauté the shallots until softened, about 1 minute. Stir in the cumin, pepper, cinnamon, cardamom, cayenne, and sugar; cook until fragrant, about 1 minute. Stir in the vinegar, scraping up the browned bits on the pan bottom. Add the orange juice, increase the heat to medium-high, and simmer until very thick and syrupy, about 2 minutes. Add the chicken broth and simmer until slightly thickened and reduced to about ¾ cup, 8 to 10 minutes. Off heat, stir in the cilantro and season with salt to taste. Serve the sauce with the lamb, passing it separately at the table.

ROAST LEG OF LAMB

THE MAIN PROBLEM WE HAVE HAD WITH roast leg of lamb is that it cooks unevenly. In the past, no matter what we have tried, the outer part became dry and gray, while the meat around the bone remained almost raw. The uneven thickness of the leg is the most formidable obstacle to even

TWO SAUCES FOR LAMB

You can serve lamb plain or with mint jelly, but we find that these two sauces are far superior.

Piquant Caper Sauce

MAKES ENOUGH TO ACCOMPANY 1 LEG
OF LAMB

If making this sauce, ask the butcher for the hipbone and aitchbone and reserve any meat scraps that have come off the lamb during the cleaning process. Make sure to remove the fat from these scraps. You can also use the hinged part of the shank bone. To accommodate the hipbone, you will need a wide saucepan or deep sauté pan. Start the sauce as soon as the lamb goes into the oven.

1	tablespoon olive oil
	Lamb bones and meat scraps (see note)
1	medium onion, chopped coarse
3	cups low-sodium chicken broth
1/3	cup dry white wine or dry vermouth
2	tablespoons unsalted butter, softened
2	tablespoons unbleached all-purpose flour
1/3	cup (3 ounces) small capers, drained, bottling liquid reserved
1	teaspoon balsamic vinegar

1. Heat the oil in a large, heavy-bottomed saucepan over medium heat until shimmering. Add the reserved bones and meat scraps and onion and sauté, turning the bones several times, until well browned, about 10 minutes. Add the broth, scraping the pan bottom to loosen the browned bits; bring to a boil. Reduce the heat to low; simmer, partially covered, until the bones and meat have given up their flavor to the broth, about 1 hour. Add a little water if the bones are more than half exposed during cooking.

2. While the roasted leg of lamb is resting, set the now-empty pan used to roast the lamb over medium heat. Add the wine and scrape with a wooden spoon until the browned bits dissolve. Pour the mixture into the lamb stock, then strain everything into a 2-cup glass measure. Let sit until the fat rises, then skim off the fat. Add water, if necessary, to make 1½ cups of liquid. Pour the liquid back into the saucepan and bring to a boil.

3. Mix the butter and flour in a small bowl to form a smooth paste. Gradually whisk the butter-flour mixture into the stock. Stir in the capers, vinegar, and any juices released by the lamb as it rested. Simmer to blend the flavors, about 3 minutes. Add more vinegar or caper bottling liquid to achieve a piquant, subtly sharp-sweet sauce. Serve the sauce with the lamb, passing it separately at the table.

Mint Sauce

MAKES ENOUGH TO ACCOMPANY 1 LEG
OF LAMB

This sauce has a refreshing mint flavor without the cloying sweetness of mint jelly. The texture is much thinner than jelly, similar to maple syrup. This sauce is remarkably easy to make and does not require any bones since no stock is necessary. If making this sauce, eliminate the rosemary from the lamb recipe and just rub the meat with olive oil and salt and pepper and stud with garlic. Mince the mint right before adding it to the sauce to preserve its fresh flavor.

1	cup white wine vinegar
6	tablespoons sugar
1/4	cup minced fresh mint leaves

1. Bring the vinegar and sugar to a simmer in a nonreactive medium saucepan over medium heat and cook until slightly syrupy, 8 to 10 minutes. (The liquid should be reduced to about ½ cup.)

2. Remove the pan from the heat, let cool for 5 minutes, and stir in the mint. Pour the sauce into a bowl and cover with plastic wrap. Set aside for at least 1 hour. (The sauce can be set aside for several hours.) Serve at room temperature with the lamb.

cooking. At the thicker sirloin end, the meat surrounding the flat, twisting hipbone is very thin. The center of the leg, which consists of the top half of the thigh, is fleshy, but the thigh then tapers dramatically toward the knee joint, and the shank itself is a mere nub of meat.

The only way to deal with this problem is to remove the hipbone and aitchbone entirely and then tie the leg into as compact a shape as possible. Once you have done this, by the way, you will understand why it is not smart to buy the sirloin end of the leg as a separate small roast, no matter how attractive the price. After the hipbone has been removed, there is barely enough meat at the sirloin end to serve two people.

Boning and tying, however, do not by themselves guarantee even cooking, as we discovered. Special procedures must be followed in roasting the leg to ensure that all parts are exposed to the same amount of heat and will thus reach similar internal temperatures at the same time.

We started out by roasting a 7½-pound leg at 400 degrees, with the meat resting directly on the roasting pan. After approximately one hour, the top of the leg, which had been facing up, registered 120 degrees on a meat thermometer, which to our taste is underdone for leg of lamb. The meat around the thigh bone, meanwhile, was practically raw, while the bottom of the leg, which had been resting on the hot pan, had reached a temperature of around 135 degrees, which is a little overcooked for our taste.

We have always resisted roasting on a rack because, when cooked only to rare or medium-rare, meat produces virtually no brown bits for gravy unless it rests directly on the pan. With leg of lamb, however, we surmised that a rack might be useful, for it would protect the downward-facing side of the leg from becoming overcooked by the heat of the pan.

To test this theory, we rack-roasted another leg. After cooking it at 500 degrees for 30 minutes (high initial heat promotes browning) and then at 300 degrees for about 45 minutes longer, the leg was done on the top side; the thermometer registered a consistent 130 degrees whether inserted sideways, into the exterior portion of the top side, or poked deep into the middle. Alas, the bottom side of the

roast proved undercooked. Evidently the rack had been too effective in keeping the bottom of the leg cool.

But this experiment, while only partially successful, pointed toward a solution. Perhaps turning the leg during cooking would promote more even cooking by allowing the top and the bottom sides equal exposure to both the cool rack and the hot oven roof. We further reasoned that setting the pan on the bottom shelf of the oven would slightly heat up the rack side, which was too cool, while mitigating the glare from the oven roof.

This is how we roasted our next lamb leg, and the results were near perfect. The outermost slices were a little closer to medium than to medium-rare and the bone meat was still a bit underdone, but most of the roast was the way we wanted it, deep pink and juicy.

Roast Leg of Lamb

SERVES 8 TO 12, DEPENDING ON SIZE OF LEG

Legs come in a variety of sizes. Our recipe starts with a semiboneless (the butcher should remove the hipbone and aitchbone) leg that weighs between 6 and 8 pounds. (The weight of the whole, untrimmed leg is about 1½ pounds more.) Smaller legs have a sweeter, milder flavor, so you may want to search for a petite leg if you don't like a strong "sheepy" flavor. If roasting a smaller leg, reduce the cooking time at 325 degrees by at least 10 minutes.

We find it best to cook lamb by internal temperature. We like our lamb medium-rare, or about 135 degrees when carved. Since the internal temperature will rise while the lamb rests, pull the leg out of the oven when the temperatures reaches 130 degrees. If you like lamb on the rarer side, pull it out of the oven at 120 degrees (the temperature will rise to 125 degrees by carving time). If you like lamb more well done, pull it out at 135 degrees (the temperature will rise above 140 degrees).

Salt and ground black pepper
1   teaspoon finely minced fresh rosemary leaves (omit if making Mint Sauce on page 273)
1   semiboneless leg of lamb (6 to 8 pounds), trimmed of excess fat (see illustrations 1 through 4 on page 275)

3 medium garlic cloves, peeled and cut into thin slivers

2 tablespoons olive oil
Piquant Caper Sauce or Mint Sauce (page 273)

1. Mix 2 teaspoons salt, 2 teaspoons pepper, and the rosemary together in n a small bowl.

2. Sprinkle a portion of the rosemary mixture over the inner surface of the cleaned and boned meat. Tie the lamb according to illustrations 5 and 6 below. Cut slits into the roast with the tip of a paring knife. Poke the garlic slivers inside. Brush the exterior with oil, then rub the remaining seasoning onto all surfaces of the meat. Place the leg, meaty side up, on a roasting pan fitted with a flat rack; let stand 30 minutes. Adjust an oven rack to the lowest position and heat the oven to 450 degrees.

3. Pour ½ cup water into the bottom of the roasting pan. Roast the lamb for 10 minutes. With a wad of paper toweling in each hand, turn the leg over. Roast 10 minutes longer. Lower the oven temperature to 325 degrees. Turn the leg meaty side up and continue roasting, turning the leg every 20 minutes, until an instant-read thermometer inserted in several locations registers 130 degrees for medium, 60 to 80 minutes longer. Transfer the roast to another pan; cover with foil and set aside in a warm spot to complete cooking and to allow the juices to reabsorb into the meat, 15 to 20 minutes. Reserve the roasting pan if making the Piquant Caper Sauce.

4. When the sauce is ready, remove the string from roast and carve by cutting slices parallel to the bone, each about ¼-inch thick. When the meat on top has been removed, flip the leg over and carve the bottom in the same fashion. To facilitate carving

PREPARING A LEG OF LAMB FOR ROASTING

1. The butcher should remove the aitchbone and hipbone (right front); you should save it so you can make stock. If the shank bone has been partially detached by the butcher, remove it with a knife and save it, too, for stock.

2. Lamb fat is strong flavored and unpleasant to chew. Remove large pieces of fat, using a knife and your hands to cut and then pull the fat off the leg. It's fine to leave a few streaks of fat to moisten the roast.

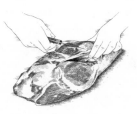

3. The strong-tasting lymph node (a ½-inch round, grayish flat nodule) and surrounding fat should be removed. Set the leg meaty side up and cut into the area that separates the broad, thin flap of meat on one side of the leg with the thick, meaty lobe.

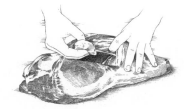

4. Use both hands and the knife to widen the incision, exposing the lymph node and surrounding fat. Reach in and grasp the nugget of fat. Pull while cutting the connective tissue, being very careful not to cut into the gland itself. Pull the fat and other matter free.

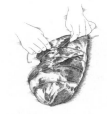

5. Set the leg meaty side up and smooth the flap of meat at the sirloin end so that it folds over and neatly covers the tip of the thigh bone. Tie several short lengths of twine around the leg, placing each piece of twine parallel to the next.

6. Tie several more short lengths of twine around the leg, running pieces of twine perpendicular to those in step 5.

the side of the leg, grasp the narrow end of the leg and hold it perpendicular to the work surface and slice as before. Serve the sliced lamb with either sauce or plain.

ROAST BONELESS LEG OF LAMB

WE LOVE TO GRILL BUTTERFLIED LEG OF lamb but wondered if there was a good way to prepare this cut indoors. We started with the easiest method possible—we seasoned the lamb, put it in the oven, and checked on it occasionally. But the roast, to our disappointment, cooked to a brown, rubbery mass. Even worse, the outer layer of fat began to smoke, filling the kitchen with an odious aroma that penetrated the meat, giving it that familiar and offensive "gamey" flavor. This was not acceptable. We knew how fabulous grilled lamb leg tasted. Now we wanted great flavor, but we also wanted a roast elegant enough for a small dinner party, something more reminiscent of lamb chops—tender and juicy, with a crust to complement the delicately flavored meat. Could we really get all that from a boneless leg of lamb?

Whole boneless legs can weigh 8 to 9 pounds; great for a crowd, but impractical for a small, elegant dinner. More practical were boneless half legs, which weigh 3 to 5 pounds. We found the sirloin (top) to be more tender than the shank (lower) end, but both roast beautifully.

After settling on the half leg, we decided to experiment with oven temperatures. We usually roast lamb at 375 degrees. But since we had been successful in slow-roasting beef, we wanted to give it a try with lamb, too. But lamb cooked at 250 degrees turned to mush. After some investigation, we learned that this transformation was due to an enzyme found in meat that targets myosin, a substance that gives meat its firmness. The enzyme breaks down the myosin when the internal temperature of the meat is between 95 and 135 degrees. Slow-roasting at 250 degrees allows for the complete collapse of the myosin. Because lamb is so tender to begin with, this turns the meat to mush.

A 450-degree oven, on the other hand, overcooked the lamb exterior. The best lamb was the half leg roasted at 400 degrees. But because we

PREPARING ROAST BONELESS LEG OF LAMB

1. Cover the lamb with plastic wrap and pound to a uniform ³/₄-inch thickness.

2. Cover with the herb mixture, leaving a one inch border around the edge, then roll lengthwise into a tight cylinder.

3. Tie the roast into a neat package, following the directions on page 278.

4. Holding the leg with tongs, sear the two ends until well browned.

5. When the lamb is almost midway through cooking, remove it from the oven and carefully remove the twine.

6. Coat the lamb with the herb and bread crumb mixture, pressing it on well to ensure that it sticks.

wanted a crisp crust, we cooked the lamb at 450 to 500 degrees to start and then reduced the temperature to 375 degrees to finish.

This oven-searing method brought us closest to our goal, but the exterior fat still smoked and gave the meat that unwanted gamey flavor. Taking a cue from our roasted rack of lamb recipes, we tried pan-searing the lamb on the stovetop before putting it into the oven to finish. The results were perfect. The direct heat jump-started the cooking of the lamb's exterior, producing a crisp crust in a matter of minutes. The flesh, meanwhile, remained very tender, and although there was still a little smoke, the meat picked up none of the gamey flavor produced with oven-searing. Using a roasting rack allowed the lamb to cook evenly on all sides once transferred to the oven.

With our cooking method of choice established, we were ready to test flavorings. We started out intending to stuff the roast but soon dispensed with that idea. This was not only too much work, the stuffing also overshadowed the lamb. Instead, we found that a simple rub of aromatics worked best; just enough herbs and garlic to enhance but not overpower the flavor of the lamb. A savory crumb crust also proved to be a perfect addition to the roast, making it reminiscent of the delicate lamb chops that we love. Unlike chops, however, lamb leg is tied, which means that a crust will disintegrate when you cut the string after the roast comes out of the oven. We solved this problem by cutting the twine and placing the crust on the lamb midway through cooking, after it had roasted long enough to hold its shape.

Roast Boneless Leg of Lamb with Garlic, Herb, and Bread Crumb Crust

SERVES 4 TO 6

Our preference is for the sirloin end of the leg, however, the shank end can be used in the recipe, too.

3   tablespoons olive oil
3   medium garlic cloves, peeled
3   tablespoons fresh rosemary leaves
2   tablespoons fresh thyme leaves
¼   cup packed fresh parsley leaves
⅓   cup grated Parmesan cheese (about 1 ounce)
1   cup coarse fresh bread crumbs (page 125)
1   boneless half leg of lamb (3 ½ to 4 pounds), untied (if tied when purchased), trimmed of surface fat, and pounded to even ¾-inch thickness (see illustration 1 on page 276), at room temperature
    Salt and ground black pepper
1   tablespoon Dijon mustard

1. Adjust an oven rack to the lower-middle position and heat the oven to 375 degrees. Meanwhile, in the workbowl of a food processor fitted with the steel blade, process 1 teaspoon of the oil with the garlic, rosemary, thyme, and parsley until minced, scraping down the bowl with a rubber spatula as necessary, about 1 minute. Remove 1½ tablespoons herb mixture to a small bowl and reserve. Scrape the remaining mixture into a medium bowl; stir in the cheese, bread crumbs, and 1 tablespoon oil, and set aside.

2. Lay the lamb with the rough interior side (which was against the bone) facing up on a work surface; rub with 2 teaspoons oil, and season generously with salt and pepper to taste. Spread the reserved 1½ tablespoons herb mixture evenly over the meat, leaving a 1-inch border around the edge. Following illustrations 2 and 3 (page 276), roll the roast and tie (see the illustrations on page 278). Season the tied roast generously with salt and pepper, then rub with the remaining 1 tablespoon oil.

3. Place a roasting rack on a rimmed baking sheet. Heat a heavy-bottomed 12-inch skillet over medium-high heat until very hot. Sear the lamb until well browned on all sides, about 2 minutes per side; then, using tongs, stand the roast on each end to sear (see illustration 4), about 30 seconds per end. Transfer to the rack and roast until an instant-read thermometer inserted into the thickest part registers 120 degrees, 30 to 35 minutes. Transfer the lamb to a cutting board; following illustration 5, remove and discard the twine. Brush the lamb exterior with the mustard, then, following illustration 6, carefully press the herb and bread crumb mixture onto the top and sides of the roast

with your hands, pressing firmly to form a solid, even coating that adheres to the meat. Return the coated roast to the rack; roast until an instant-read thermometer inserted into the thickest part of roast registers 130 to 135 degrees (medium-rare), 15 to 25 minutes longer. Transfer the meat to a cutting board, tent with foil, and let rest for 10 to 15 minutes. Cut into ½-inch slices and serve.

➤ VARIATION

Indian-Spiced Roast Boneless Leg of Lamb with Herbed Almond-Raisin Crust

Garam masala, an Indian spice blend, can be found in specialty food stores and well-stocked grocery stores.

3	medium garlic cloves, peeled
¼	cup packed fresh mint leaves
¼	cup packed fresh cilantro leaves
1	piece fresh ginger (about 1 inch), peeled and quartered
1	teaspoon garam masala (see note)
¼	teaspoon ground coriander
¼	teaspoon ground cumin
2	tablespoons olive oil
¼	cup slivered almonds
¼	cup raisins
1	tablespoon plain yogurt
1	boneless half leg of lamb (3 ½ to 4 pounds), untied (if tied when purchased), trimmed of surface fat, and pounded to even ¾-inch thickness (see illustration 1 on page 276), at room temperature
	Salt and ground black pepper

1. Adjust an oven rack to the lower-middle position and heat the oven to 375 degrees. Meanwhile, in the workbowl of a food processor fitted with the steel blade, process the garlic, mint, cilantro, ginger, ½ teaspoon of the garam masala, ⅛ teaspoon of the coriander, ⅛ teaspoon of the cumin, and 1 teaspoon of the oil until the herbs are minced, scraping down the bowl with a rubber spatula as necessary, about 1 minute. Remove 1½ tablespoons herb mixture to a small bowl and reserve. Add the almonds and raisins to the food processor workbowl; continue processing until finely ground, about 45 seconds, and transfer to a small bowl. Combine the yogurt with the remaining ½ teaspoon garam masala, ⅛ teaspoon coriander, and ⅛ teaspoon cumin; set aside.

2. Follow the recipe for Roast Boneless Leg of Lamb with Garlic, Herb, and Bread Crumb Crust from step 2, substituting the yogurt mixture for the mustard in step 3 and the almond-raisin crust for the herb and bread crumb mixture.

HOW TO TIE A BONELESS LAMB ROAST

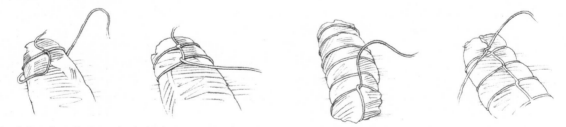

Slip a 5-foot piece of twine under the lamb roast and tie a double knot, then loop the long end of twine under and around the roast. Run the long end through the loop and repeat this procedure down the length of the roast. Roll the roast over and run the twine under and around each loop. At the end, tie to the original knot.

11

I WANT TO GRILL A ROAST

I Want to Grill a Roast

CUTS OF MEAT THAT ARE TOO LARGE TO grill over direct heat can be cooked over a two-level fire (page 34) or roasted in a covered grill. Thinner cuts, such as pork tenderloin, rack of lamb, and butterflied leg of lamb are best cooked over a two-level fire. Thicker roasts should be grill-roasted.

Since grill-roasting involves fairly high temperatures and occurs fairly quickly (relative to barbecuing, that is—see page 21 for definitions of grill-roasting and barbecuing), tender cuts are a must. This means roasts taken from the rib or loin area of the animal. On the cow, this translates to the rib roast (also known as prime rib) or the tenderloin. On the pig, the loin roast and is the best choice.

A prime rib is a massive cut with bones. It requires nearly two hours on the grill to cook through. Beef tenderloin, pork loin, rack of lamb, and butterflied leg of lamb are easier to prepare and take less time to cook. These cuts are not terribly thick and can be done in as little as 30 minutes. A skinny pork tenderloin cooks through in even less time.

Grill-Roasted Prime Rib

PRIME RIB IS THE ULTIMATE MEAT DISH FOR entertaining—it's impressive and it feeds a crowd. But if you're making prime rib, you're probably make a lot of other food. We think it's worth considering the grill when cooking prime rib. Rather than tying up your oven for hours on end (and thus making the preparation of side dishes a real hassle), let the meat cook outside. Besides convenience, a grilled prime rib has two advantages over a roasted prime rib—a better crust and some smoky flavor. But whether you are cooking prime rib in an oven or on the grill, we think the goal is the same: Slices should be rosy pink from the surface to the center, and the meat should be juicy and tender.

We started our testing by examining the issues of trimming fat and tying the roast. We found that it is best to leave about one-quarter inch of fat on the roast to prevent it from drying out on the grill. Most of this fat drips off of the rib roast as it cooks,

basting the meat. Tying the meat before grilling is essential. Two pieces of twine keep the surrounding muscles from separating from the main part of the roast and thus improve the appearance of the grilled roast. In addition, these smaller, thin pieces of meat will overcook if they detach from the main muscle during grill-roasting.

We wondered just how few coals we could get away with. From our work in the past with prime rib cooked in the oven, we knew that a low oven temperature is kinder to prime rib, helping the meat to retain its juices and promoting even cooking. We figured the same would be true on the grill.

After much testing, we found 45 briquettes to be optimum. This was the least amount of coals we could use to make it possible to cook the whole roast properly without adding more briquettes. With 45 briquettes, the fire reaches an initial temperature of about 375 degrees and eventually burns down to about 300 degrees by the time the roast is finished (the last 45 minutes or so). Using the indirect method, you still get a lovely surface caramelization, while the interior is almost entirely pink, except for the outer half inch or so.

We wanted to add some wood to the fire to flavor the meat, but not enough to overpower its own delicious flavor. You don't want prime rib to taste like ribs. Adding two cups of chips or two larger wood chunks to the fire creates a rib roast with a nice contrast between the smoky caramelized exterior and savory, beefy interior meat.

The next issue to examine was at what internal temperature the roast should be removed from the grill. We knew that the temperature inside the roast would continue to rise as the meat rested before carving. For the perfect medium-rare, we found it best to take the meat off the grill when it hit an internal temperature of 125 degrees. When taken out at 125 degrees and then allowed to rest for 20 minutes, the temperature jumped another 12 to 13 degrees. As with rack of lamb, it is imperative with prime rib to use an instant-read thermometer. There is no really good way of telling how cooked the meat is at the very center of a rib roast without one, and if you spent about $50 for a seven-pound roast, you don't want to mess up by over- or undercooking. Also, using a thermometer to determine doneness will keep you from cutting into the meat to check doneness before it's had a chance to rest; if you cut into the meat too soon (before it's rested off the grill for 20 minutes), you will lose a good amount of the juices. (During the rest period, the juices evenly redistribute themselves throughout the meat.)

Grill-Roasted Prime Rib on a Charcoal Grill

SERVES 6 TO 8

You may or may not have to trim some fat off your rib roast, depending on how well it was butchered at the store. Just be sure to leave at least ¼ inch of fat on the side opposite the bones to keep the meat from drying out; the fat will slowly render, basting the meat as it melts. If you purchase the roast several days in advance, see page 234 to learn more about the benefits of aging the roast in the refrigerator before cooking it.

1	(3- or 4-rib) standing rib roast (about 7 pounds), aged up to 4 days (if desired), and tied with kitchen twine at both ends, twine running parallel to bone (see the illustration on page 235)
2	(3-inch) wood chunks or 2 cups wood chips
1	tablespoon vegetable oil
	Salt and ground black pepper

1. An hour before cooking, remove the roast from the refrigerator to bring it to room temperature.

2. Meanwhile, soak the wood chunks in cold water to cover for 1 hour and drain, or place the wood chips on an 18-inch square of aluminum foil, seal to make a packet, and use a fork to create about 6 holes to allow smoke to escape (see the illustrations on page 35).

3. Light a large chimney starter filled halfway with charcoal briquettes (about 3 quarts or 45 coals) and allow to burn until covered with a thin layer of gray ash. Transfer the coals from the chimney to one side of the grill, piling them up in a mound 2 or 3 briquettes high. Keep the bottom vents completely open. Lay the wood chunks or the wood chip packet on top of the charcoal. Put the cooking

grate in place, open the grill lid vents completely, and cover, turning the lid so that the vents are opposite the wood chunks or chips to draw smoke through the grill. Let the grate heat for 5 minutes. Clean the grate with a wire brush.

4. Rub the rib roast with the oil. Season generously with salt and pepper to taste.

5. Position the rib roast, bone-side down, on the grate opposite the fire, with the meaty eye of the roast closest to the fire. Cover the grill, turning the lid so that the vents are opposite the fire to draw smoke through the grill. Grill-roast without removing the lid for 1 hour. (The initial temperature will be about 375 degrees.) Remove the lid and turn the roast so that the bone side of the roast is facing up. Replace the lid and continue grill-roasting until an instant-read thermometer inserted into the center of the roast registers 125 degrees (for medium-rare), 30 to 60 minutes. (The temperature inside the grill will gradually fall to about 300 degrees by the time the roast is done.)

6. Transfer the roast to a cutting board and tent loosely with foil. Let stand at least 20 minutes to allow the juices to redistribute themselves evenly throughout the roast.

7. To carve (see the illustrations on page 230), remove the twine and set the roast on a cutting board with the rib bones perpendicular to the board. Using a carving fork to hold the roast in place, cut along the rib bones to sever the meat from the bones. Set the roast cut-side down; carve the meat across the grain into thick slices. Serve immediately.

➤ VARIATIONS

Grill-Roasted Prime Rib on a Gas Grill

The gas grill variation mimics the temperatures of the charcoal grill. To make sure the wood chips begin to smoke, the grill is quite hot—550 degrees—when you first put the meat on the fire. Once you turn off all but the primary burner (which is left on medium-high), the temperature of the grill averages out to about 350 degrees. The roast cooks at this heat level for 1 hour. The primary burner is then turned down once again to medium heat, and the average temperature of the grill hovers around 300 degrees for the rest of the cooking time, which should be between 1 hour and 1 hour and

15 minutes, until the internal temperature of the roast is 125 degrees. Be sure not to open the lid of the gas grill too often during cooking; the temperature of the grill will drop significantly each time you open it, and then take some time to come back up to temperature. If you prefer a roast with a less smoky flavor, gas grilling is the right option (as opposed to charcoal grilling). In fact, if you are simply cooking on the grill to save oven space and don't care to taste the smoky flavor of the grill, omit the use of wood chips altogether.

Follow the recipe for Grill-Roasted Prime Rib on a Charcoal Grill, letting the roast come to room temperature, rubbing it with oil, and seasoning it with salt and pepper as directed in steps 1 and 4. Meanwhile, soak 2 cups wood chips in a bowl of water to cover for 15 minutes. Place the wood chips in a foil tray (see the illustrations on page 35). Place the foil tray with the soaked wood chips on top of the primary burner (see the illustration on page 35) and replace the cooking grates. Turn all burners to high and preheat with the lid down until the chips are smoking heavily, about 15 minutes. Carefully open the grill (there may be some smoke), scrape the grill grate clean with a grill brush, and turn the primary burner down to medium-high; turn all other burners off. Place the rib roast over the cooler side of the grill, bone-side down. Cover and cook until an instant-read thermometer inserted through to the center of the roast reads between 80 and 85 degrees, about 1 hour. (During this hour the temperature inside the grill will initially be very hot, 550 degrees, and then it will drop off to about 350 degrees.) Turn the primary burner down to medium and continue cooking, covered, until the instant-read thermometer inserted through to the center of the roast reads 125 degrees (for medium-rare), about 60 to 75 minutes longer. (During this period of time, keep the average temperature of the grill at about 300 degrees.) Transfer the roast to a cutting board and proceed as directed in steps 6 and 7.

Grill-Roasted Prime Rib with Garlic and Rosemary Crust

Rosemary and garlic are a simple embellishment for the roast and won't overwhelm the beefy flavor of the meat.

Mix together 6 medium garlic cloves, minced, 2 tablespoons chopped fresh rosemary leaves, 2 teaspoons ground black pepper, and 1 teaspoon salt together in a small bowl. Follow the recipe for Grill-Roasted Prime Rib (charcoal or gas), oiling the roast as directed in step 4. Instead of sprinkling the oiled roast with salt and pepper, rub it with the garlic and rosemary mixture. Proceed as directed.

GRILL-ROASTED BEEF TENDERLOIN

BEEF TENDERLOIN IS A TENDER CUT OF meat that can be grill-roasted at a high temperature. This roast cooks quickly, and its rich, buttery slices are fork-tender. The challenge is to create a good crust on the meat while not overcooking the interior.

As with our oven-roasted tenderloin, we quickly decided that a peeled tenderloin with its thin tip end folded under and tied was the best choice for the grill. As for the actual cooking process, we found that a beef tenderloin cooks well over indirect heat. To build a nice thick crust on the meat, the initial charcoal fire should be fairly hot—400 to 425 degrees is ideal. We also found that searing the meat briefly over the hot coals and then moving it to the cool side of the grill improved the crust. We tried turning the roast as it cooked over indirect heat but found that opening the lid caused the fire to lose heat and that the roast was browning evenly anyway. Keep the lid on and don't check the roast until you think it is done.

Once the roast reaches an internal temperature of 125 degrees, it should be pulled off the grill and allowed to rest. The internal temperature will rise another 5 degrees, ensuring meat that is perfectly medium-rare. If you want rare meat, remove the roast earlier (at 120 degrees); for meat that is closer to medium, remove the roast at 130 to 135 degrees. It seems a shame to cook this meat any further as it begins to dry out once it reaches higher internal temperatures. As with oven-roasted tenderloin, the grilled roast should rest for 30 minutes so to allow this soft cut to firm up.

Grill-Roasted Beef Tenderloin on a Charcoal Grill

SERVES 10 TO 12

If you can't find a whole tenderloin with the tip end attached (see the photo on page 242), use a smaller tenderloin and omit the tucking step. The cooking time will be about the same for the smaller roast because it is just as thick. Serve as is or with Parsley Sauce with Cornichons and Capers (page 405) or Salsa Verde (page 405)—you will want to make a double batch of the latter.

- 1   whole peeled beef tenderloin (about 5 pounds), patted dry with paper towels, silver skin cut, tip end tucked under, and tied (see illustrations 1 through 3 on page 239)
- 2   (3-inch) wood chunks or 2 cups wood chips
- 2   tablespoons olive oil
- 2   teaspoons salt
- 2   tablespoons coarsely ground black pepper

1. Remove the tenderloin from the refrigerator 1 hour before cooking to bring the meat to room temperature.

2. Meanwhile, soak the wood chunks in cold water to cover for 1 hour and drain, or place the wood chips on an 18-inch square of aluminum foil, seal to make a packet, and use a fork to create about 6 holes to allow smoke to escape (see the illustrations on page 35).

3. Set the tenderloin on a sheet of plastic wrap and rub all over with the oil. Sprinkle with the salt and pepper, then lift the wrap to press the excess seasoning into the meat (see illustration 4 on page 239).

4. Light a large chimney starter filled with charcoal briquettes (about 6 quarts) and allow to burn until all the charcoal is covered with a layer of fine gray ash. Transfer the hot coals to one side of the grill, piling them up in a mound 3 briquettes high. Keep the bottom vents completely open. Lay the wood chunks or the wood chip packet on top of the charcoal. Put the cooking grate in place, open the grill lid vents completely, and cover, turning the lid so that the vents are opposite the wood chunks

or chips to draw smoke through the grill. Let the grate heat for 5 minutes. Use a wire brush to scrape clean the grill grate.

5. Roll the tenderloin off the plastic wrap onto the grate directly over the hot coals so that the long side of the loin is perpendicular to the grill rods. Sear the meat for 2½ minutes on the first side, then give the roast a one-quarter turn and sear another 2½ minutes. Repeat 2 more times to sear all four sides of the tenderloin directly over the coals. Move the tenderloin to the side of the grill opposite the fire and cover the grill, turning the lid so that the vents are opposite the fire to draw smoke through the grill, and so that the long side of the loin is perpendicular to the grill rods. (The initial temperature inside the grill should be about 425 degrees.) Grill-roast the tenderloin, covered, until an instant-read thermometer inserted into the thickest part registers about 125 degrees (for medium-rare), 25 to 30 minutes longer.

6. Transfer the tenderloin to a cutting board and tent loosely with foil. Let rest for 30 minutes. (The whole tenderloin can be wrapped in plastic, refrigerated up to 2 days, and served chilled.) Cut the roast into ½-inch-thick slices and serve.

➤ VARIATIONS

Grill-Roasted Beef Tenderloin on a Gas Grill

This version will be less smoky than a roast cooked over charcoal. If you prefer not to add any smoke flavor, omit the wood chips.

Follow the recipe for Grilled-Roasted Beef Tenderloin on a Charcoal Grill, letting the meat first come to room temperature, rubbing it with oil, and seasoning it with salt and pepper as directed in steps 1 and 3. Meanwhile, soak 2 cups wood chips in a bowl of cold water for 15 minutes. Drain the chips and place them in a foil tray (see the illustrations on page 35). Place the foil tray with the soaked wood chips on top of the primary burner (see the illustration on page 35), and replace the cooking grates. Turn all burners to high and preheat with the lid down until very hot, about 15 minutes. Carefully open the preheated grill (there may be some smoke), scrape the grill grate clean with a grill brush, and place the tenderloin on the side opposite the primary burner. Sear the tenderloin for 3 minutes on the first side, then give the meat a one-quarter turn and sear that side. Repeat, searing all four sides for 3 minutes each, or until dark grill marks appear. Leave the primary burner on high but turn off all other burners. Cover with the lid and grill-roast until an instant-read thermometer inserted into thickest part of the tenderloin registers about 125 degrees (for medium-rare), 25 to 30 minutes longer. (The temperature inside the grill should average between 375 and 400 degrees; adjust the lit burner as necessary.) Transfer the tenderloin to a cutting board and proceed as directed in step 6.

Grill-Roasted Beef Tenderloin with Mixed Peppercorn Crust

Buy a mixture of peppercorns at the supermarket or create your own mixture at home. Black and white peppercorns are much stronger than the pink and green varieties, so adjust the blend to suit your personal taste.

Coarsely crush 6 tablespoons black, white, pink, and green peppercorns with a mortar and pestle or with a heavy-bottomed saucepan or skillet. Follow the recipe for Grill-Roasted Beef Tenderloin (charcoal or gas), replacing the coarsely ground black pepper with the peppercorn mixture. Proceed as directed.

Grill-Roasted Beef Tenderloin with Garlic and Rosemary

Studding the tenderloin with slivered garlic and fresh rosemary gives it an Italian flavor.

Follow the recipe for Grill-Roasted Beef Tenderloin (charcoal or gas), making the following changes: After tying the roast, use a paring knife to make several dozen shallow incisions around the surface of the roast. Stuff a few fresh rosemary needles and 1 thin sliver of garlic into each incision. (Use a total of 1 tablespoon rosemary and 3 large garlic cloves, peeled and slivered.) Oil the roast as directed. Sprinkle with salt, pepper, and an additional 2 tablespoons minced fresh rosemary, pressing the herb into the meat with the plastic wrap. Proceed as directed.

GRILL-ROASTED PORK LOIN

A BONELESS PORK LOIN IS AN IDEAL CANdidate for grill-roasting. As opposed to barbecued pulled pork (see page 332), which starts out with a very fatty cut from the shoulder or leg, lean loin roasts are the best choice for relatively quick grill-roasting since they are already tender. However, unlike a thin pork tenderloin, the loin is too thick to cook over direct heat. The exterior chars long before the interior comes up to temperature.

Unlike a beef tenderloin, a pork center loin has a fairly even thickness from end to end, so there is no need to tuck up one side or the other. To make the meat perfectly even and ensure proper cooking, we found it helpful to tie the roast at regular intervals.

A pork loin can be grill-roasted much like a beef tenderloin, although it does not need an initial searing period over direct heat. (The meat stays on the grill longer because it must be cooked to a higher internal temperature, so there's plenty of time for a nice crust to form when the roast is cooked strictly over indirect heat.)

The biggest challenge when grill-roasting pork loin is keeping the meat moist. Beef tenderloin can be pulled from the grill at 125 degrees and eaten medium-rare. Pork must be cooked to a higher temperature to make the meat palatable (rare pork has an unappealing texture).

Using the kettle grill, we tried a couple of different setups for indirect cooking. We tried putting the roast in the center of the grill, with two piles of charcoal on opposite sides. This worked reasonably well, but the crust was a bit weak. Banking a full chimney of coals on one side of the grill and placing the roast over the other side worked better. To get the best crust, put the roast close to, but not directly over, the coals.

After testing various temperatures, we found that center loin roasts should be taken off the grill when the internal temperature registers 135 degrees on an instant-read thermometer. After the meat rests for 15 minutes, the temperature will rise to about 150 degrees. The meat will have a slight pink tinge, but it will be far juicier than roasts cooked to an internal temperature that is just 10 degrees higher. (A temperature of 150 degrees is high enough to kill the parasite that causes trichinosis. However, the U.S. Department of Agriculture recommends cooking all meat to an internal temperature of 160 degrees to kill bacteria such as salmonella. If safety is your primary concern, follow the USDA's guidelines.) Because the diameter of a pork loin can vary from one roast to another, allow a window of 30 to 45 minutes to cook the roast through.

While we had little trouble getting the meat properly cooked on the grill, we found pork loin to be a bit bland and not as moist as we might have liked. Both problems stem from the fact that most of the internal fat has been bred out of the pig in recent years. We hit upon several strategies for making the meat taste better and juicier when cooked.

Like poultry, lean pork responds well to brining. A brined pork roast will cook up juicier and more flavorful than a regular roast. Aggressive seasoning is also a good idea. A potent spice rub or a heady mixture of garlic and rosemary will improve the flavor of the meat. A rich mustard-maple glaze, applied when the roast is nearly cooked through, is another option.

Grill-Roasted Pork Loin on a Charcoal Grill

SERVES 4 TO 6

We find that the blade-end roast is a bit more flavorful than the center-cut roast but either works well in this recipe. To make sure the roast doesn't dry out during cooking, look for one covered with a layer of fat on one side that is at least ⅛ inch thick. Because the diameter of pork loins varies significantly from one to another, check the internal temperature of the loin with an instant-read thermometer at 30 minutes, then every 5 minutes or so thereafter, to make sure that your pork cooks to the optimum temperature of 140 degrees. Do not overcook the pork, as it dries out easily. Let the roast rest for at least 15 minutes in order for its internal temperature to rise to a safe temperature—about 150 degrees. Use leftover meat for sandwiches.

¾ cup kosher salt or 6 tablespoons table salt
1 boneless blade-end or center-cut pork loin roast (2 ½ to 3 pounds), tied with twine at 1 ½-inch intervals
2 (3-inch) wood chunks or 2 cups wood chips
2 tablespoons olive oil
1 ½ tablespoons coarsely ground black pepper

1. At least 8 hours before grill-roasting, dissolve the salt in 3 quarts of cold water in a large container. Place the pork loin in the saltwater mixture, cover, and refrigerate for at least 8 hours or overnight.

2. An hour before cooking, remove the roast from the brine, rinse, and pat dry; let the roast stand to come to room temperature.

3. Meanwhile, soak the wood chunks in cold water to cover for 1 hour and drain, or place wood chips on an 18-inch square of aluminum foil, seal to make a packet, and use a fork to create about 6 holes to allow smoke to escape (see the illustrations on page 35).

4. Set the roast on a sheet of plastic wrap and rub all over with the oil. Sprinkle with the pepper and then lift the plastic wrap to press the excess seasoning into the meat (see the illustration on page 239).

5. Light a large chimney filled with charcoal briquettes (about 6 quarts) and allow to burn until all the charcoal is covered with a thin layer of gray ash. Transfer the hot coals from the chimney to one side of the grill, piling them up in a mound 3 briquettes high. Keep the bottom vents completely open. Lay the soaked wood chunks or the wood chip packet on top of the charcoal. Put the cooking grate in place and open the grill lid vents halfway. Let the grate heat for 5 minutes. Clean the grate with a wire brush.

6. Roll the pork loin off the plastic wrap and onto the grate opposite, but close to the fire; the long side of the loin should be perpendicular to the grill rods. Cover with the lid, turning the lid so the vents are opposite the fire to draw smoke through the grill. (The initial temperature inside the grill will be about 425 degrees.) Grill-roast the pork loin, covered, until an instant-read thermometer inserted into the thickest part of the roast registers about 135 degrees, 30 to 45 minutes, depending on the thickness of the loin.

7. Transfer the loin to a cutting board. Tent

loosely with foil and let stand for about 15 minutes. (The internal temperature should rise to about 150 degrees.) Cut the roast into ½-inch-thick slices and serve.

➤ VARIATIONS

Grill-Roasted Pork Loin on a Gas Grill

When using the gas grill for this recipe, the meat must be seared over direct heat. This is because the gas grill's maximum temperature using indirect heat is about 400 degrees, which is not quite hot enough to give the loin a deep crust in the amount of time it takes to cook through over indirect heat.

Follow the recipe for Grilled-Roasted Pork Loin on a Charcoal Grill, brining the roast, letting it come to room temperature, rubbing it with oil, and seasoning it with salt and pepper as directed in steps 1, 2, and 4. Meanwhile, soak 2 cups wood chips in a bowl of cold water for 15 minutes. Drain the chips and place them in a foil tray (see the illustrations on page 35). Place the foil tray with the soaked wood chips on top of the primary burner (see the illustration on page 35) and replace cooking grates on the gas grill. Turn all burners to high and preheat with the lid down until very hot, about 15 minutes. Carefully open the preheated grill (there may be some smoke), scrape the grill grate clean with a grill brush, and place the roast, fat-side down, on the side opposite the primary burner. Cover and grill until the meat is grill marked, about 4 minutes. Turn the roast over, cover again, and grill for another 4 minutes. Leave the primary burner on high, but turn off all other burners. Cover with the lid and grill-roast until an instant-read thermometer reads 135 degrees at the thickest part of the roast, 30 to 45 minutes. (The temperature inside the grill should average between 375 and 400 degrees; adjust the lit burner as necessary). Transfer the loin to a cutting board and proceed as directed in step 7.

Grill-Roasted Pork Loin with Garlic and Rosemary

Other fresh herbs, especially sage or thyme, can be used in place of the rosemary.

Follow the recipe for Grill-Roasted Pork Loin (charcoal or gas), making the following changes: After tying the roast, use a paring knife to make several dozens of shallow incisions around the surface of the roast. Stuff a few fresh rosemary needles and 1 thin sliver of garlic into each incision. (Use a total of 1 tablespoon rosemary and 3 large garlic cloves, peeled and slivered.) Oil the roast as directed. Sprinkle with salt, pepper, and an additional 2 tablespoons minced fresh rosemary, pressing the excess seasoning into the meat with the plastic wrap. Proceed as directed.

Grill-Roasted Pork Loin with Barbecue Rub and Fruit Salsa

Because of its mild flavor, pork loin benefits greatly from spice rubs. Fruit salsa adds both moisture and a sweetness that is naturally compatible with pork.

Follow the recipe for Grill-Roasted Pork Loin (charcoal or gas), replacing the pepper with 2 tablespoons Dry Rub for Barbecue (page 397). Proceed as directed, serving the sliced meat with Peach Salsa (page 404) or Mango Salsa (page 403).

Grill-Roasted Pork Loin with Maple-Mustard Glaze

This glaze can literally be prepared in seconds.

Mix ½ cup pure maple syrup, ½ cup whole-grain mustard, and 1 teaspoon soy sauce together in a medium bowl. Reserve half of the glaze in a separate bowl. Follow the recipe for Grill-Roasted Pork Loin (charcoal or gas), brushing the loin with half of the glaze about 5 minutes before it reaches the designated internal temperature. Slice the pork and serve it with the remaining glaze passed at the table.

GRILLED PORK TENDERLOIN

ALTHOUGH A PORK TENDERLOIN IS TOO small to grill-roast, it is a roast and it can be grilled. In fact, grilling is a terrific way to cook pork tenderloin, a sublimely tender cut that benefits especially from the flavor boost provided by fire. But grilling a tenderloin does have its challenges. The chief problem is how to achieve a rich, golden, caramelized crust without destroying the delicate texture of the meat by overcooking it. What level of heat is best, and exactly how long should a tenderloin cook? Will grilling alone adequately flavor the meat, or should you pull another flavor-building trick from your culinary magic hat?

As the name suggests, tenderness is the tenderloin's main appeal. Anatomically speaking, the tenderloin is a small, cylindrical muscle located against the inside of the pig's rib cage. (In a human being, the equivalent muscle is in the midback area.) Because this muscle doesn't get much use, it remains very tender. Also, because the tenderloin is small, usually weighing 12 to 16 ounces, it cooks very quickly. So it is great for fast, easy weeknight dinners.

Another reason for the tenderloin's popularity is its natural leanness. Though this is good news for diners concerned about fat intake, it can cause problems for the cook. The cut has almost no marbling, the threads of intramuscular fat that contribute a great deal of flavor to meat. Marbling also helps ensure juiciness, since the fat between the muscle fibers melts during cooking. Without that extra measure of protection, the long, slender, quick-cooking tenderloin can overcook and dry out much faster than fattier cuts.

To guard against this possibility, the tenderloin should be cooked to medium so it will retain a slightly rosy hue in the center. The internal temperature should be 145 to 150 degrees, which is just short of the 160 degrees recommended by the U.S. Department of Agriculture. In the time it takes this cut to reach 160 degrees, the meat becomes dry, chewy, grayish white, and unappetizing. (For information on safe internal temperatures when cooking pork, see page 20.)

Before setting match to charcoal, we reviewed numerous grilled tenderloin recipes and found most to be more confusing than enlightening. Many recipes were vague, offering ambiguous directions such as "grill the tenderloins for 10 to 12 minutes, turning." Those which did provide details disagreed on almost every point, from method (direct or indirect heat, open or covered grill) to heat level (hot, medium-hot, medium, or medium-low), timing (anywhere from 12 to 60 minutes), and internal temperature (from 145 to 160 degrees).

Direct grilling over hot, medium-hot, medium,

and medium-low fires constituted our first series of tests. While the meat certainly cooked over all of these fires, it didn't cook perfectly over any of them. The medium-low fire failed to produce the essential crust. Each of the other fires produced more of a crust than we wanted by the time the internal temperature of the tenderloins had reached 145 degrees. Even the medium fire, which took 16 minutes to cook the tenderloin to 145 degrees, charred the crust a little too much by the time the meat had cooked through. The more intense medium-hot and hot fires cooked the meat a little faster, which meant less time on the grill, but the crust was still overly blackened in some spots.

It was clear at this point that building a two-level fire and some indirect cooking on a cooler area of the grill would be necessary to allow the tenderloin to cook through without becoming charred. Cooking over a medium-hot fire seared the meat steadily and evenly in 2½ minutes on each of four sides, but the internal temperature at this point usually hovered around 125 degrees. To finish cooking, we moved the tenderloin to the cooler part of the grill and waited for the internal temperature to climb. And we waited, and waited some more. About 10 seemingly endless minutes and countless temperature checks later, the meat arrived at 145 degrees. Since this took so long, we tried speeding up the process up by covering the tenderloin with

INGREDIENTS: Preflavored Pork Tenderloin

The fact that today's leaner pork is less flavorful is recognized by the industry as well as by consumers. This development, coupled with sheer convenience, may be why some distributors now offer various superlean cuts, including the tenderloin and the center cut loin filet, vacuum-packed in their own "flavoring solutions." The flavoring choices in our local market were peppercorn and teriyaki for tenderloins and lemon-garlic and honey-mustard for center-cut loin filets.

Curious, we bought one of each and grilled them carefully for a test kitchen tasting. The results fell far short of the mark. Sitting in the flavor solutions for who knows how long obliterated the texture of the meat, making it soft, wet, and spongy. In addition, these flavorings tasted genuinely awful; none allowed the taste of the pork itself to come through.

a disposable aluminum roasting pan.

We seared the meat directly over medium-hot coals for 2½ minutes per side, then moved it to a cooler part of the grill and covered it with a pan. In just 2½ minutes under the pan, the tenderloin reached 145 degrees internal without picking up additional char on the crust.

The well-developed crust did the tenderloin a world of good, but we knew there were other flavor development methods to try, including marinating, dry and wet flavor rubs, and brining. Marinating, which required at least 2 to 3 hours and often up to 24, simply took too long, especially for an impromptu weeknight meal. Next we tried both dry and wet flavor rubs. Our tasters' favorite dry spice rubs for pork were quick to throw together and gave the tenderloin a fantastic, flavorful crust. We also had good luck with wet rubs. They are also easy to make, have strong flavors, and give the pork a lovely, crusty, glazed effect.

As good as these methods are, though, the meat still lacked seasoning at its center. So we tried brining. Since it takes close to an hour to make a rub and any side dishes, prepare the fire, and heat the grill rack, we reasoned that the tenderloins could spend that time—but no more—sitting in a brine. We started out with a simple saltwater brine, which seasoned the meat nicely throughout. Then, picking up on the subtle sweetness we liked in the dry and wet rubs, we added some sugar to the brine. The results were spectacular. The sweetness enhanced the flavor of the pork, and the brine ensured robust flavor in every bite of every slice of meat.

Grilled pork tenderloin, then, can be more than just a tender, lean cut of meat that cooks up quickly. With a combination of brining to season the interior of the meat, a rub to season the exterior, and careful grilling to produce a glistening, caramelized crust without overcooking, it is a real treat to eat, too.

Charcoal-Grilled Pork Tenderloin

SERVES 6 TO 8

Pork tenderloins are often sold two to a package, each piece usually weighing 12 to 16 ounces. The cooking times below are for two average 12-ounce tenderloins; *if necessary, adjust the cooking times to suit the size of the cuts you are cooking. For maximum time efficiency, while the pork is brining, make the flavor rub and then light the fire. If you opt not to brine, bypass step 1 in the recipe below and sprinkle the tenderloins generously with salt before grilling. Use a spice rub whether or not the pork has been brined—it adds extra flavor and forms a nice crust on the meat. If rubbing tenderloins with dry spices, consider serving with a fruit salsa (pages 403 to 404) for added moisture and flavor. You will need a disposable aluminum roasting pan for this recipe.*

3	tablespoons kosher salt or 1 ½ tablespoons table salt
¾	cup sugar
2	pork tenderloins (1 ½ to 2 pounds total), trimmed of silver skin (see the illustration on page 117)
1	recipe wet spice rub (page 290) or 2 tablespoons olive oil and 1 recipe dry spice rub (page 83)

1. Dissolve the salt and sugar in 4 cups cold water in a medium bowl. Add the tenderloins, cover the bowl with plastic wrap, and refrigerate until fully seasoned, about 1 hour. Remove the tenderloins from the brine, rinse well, and dry thoroughly with paper towels. Set aside.

2. Light a large chimney starter filled with hardwood charcoal (about 6 quarts) and allow to burn until all the charcoal is covered with a layer of fine gray ash. Build a modified two-level fire by spreading the coals out over half of the grill bottom. Set the cooking rack in place, cover the grill with the lid, and let the rack heat up, about 5 minutes. Use a wire brush to scrape clean the cooking rack. The grill is ready when the coals are medium-hot. (See how to gauge heat level on page 34.)

3. If using a wet spice rub, rub the tenderloins with the mixture. If using a dry spice rub, coat the tenderloins with the oil and then rub with the spice mixture.

4. Cook the tenderloins, uncovered, over the hotter part of the grill until browned on all four sides, about 2½ minutes on each side. Move the tenderloins to the cooler part of the grill and cover with a disposable aluminum roasting pan. Grill,

WET SPICE RUBS FOR PORK TENDERLOIN

A spice rub helps develop the crust on a pork tenderloin and adds some much-needed flavor. If using a wet rub (with spices and liquid ingredients), simply massage the mixture into the meat. If using a dry rub (with spices only), massage the meat with olive oil and then coat with the rub. See page 83 for dry rub recipes.

Orange, Sage, and Garlic Wet Rub

MAKES ABOUT ⅓ CUP, ENOUGH FOR 2 TENDERLOINS

If you have no orange marmalade, substitute an equal amount of honey.

- 3   medium garlic cloves, minced or pressed through a garlic press (about 1 tablespoon)
- 1   tablespoon grated zest from 1 orange
- 1   tablespoon chopped fresh sage leaves
- ½   teaspoon ground black pepper
- ¼   teaspoon salt
- 1   tablespoon orange marmalade
- 1   tablespoon extra-virgin olive oil

Mix all ingredients together in a small bowl.

Caribbean Wet Rub

MAKES ABOUT ⅓ CUP, ENOUGH FOR 2 TENDERLOINS

Scotch bonnet chiles are extremely hot, so be certain to wash your hands thoroughly with soap and hot water right after chopping it or, better yet, wear rubber gloves.

- ½   medium Scotch Bonnet or habanero chile, stemmed, seeded, and minced (about 1 teaspoon)
- 1   tablespoon chopped fresh thyme leaves
- 2   medium scallions, white and green parts, minced
- 1   large garlic clove, minced or pressed through a garlic press (about 1½ teaspoons)
- 1   tablespoon grated zest from 1 lime
       Pinch ground allspice
- 1   tablespoon light brown sugar
- 1   teaspoon dry mustard powder
- 1   tablespoon extra-virgin olive oil

Mix all ingredients together in a small bowl.

Asian Wet Rub

MAKES ABOUT ⅓ CUP, ENOUGH FOR 2 TENDERLOINS

If you don't have hoisin sauce on hand, use an equal amount of soy sauce in its place.

- 3   medium garlic cloves, minced or pressed through a garlic press (about 1 tablespoon)
- 1   (2-inch) piece fresh ginger, peeled and minced (about 2 tablespoons)
- 2   medium scallions, white and green parts, minced
- 2   tablespoons light brown sugar
- ½   teaspoon red pepper flakes
- ¼   teaspoon Chinese five-spice powder
- ¼   teaspoon salt
- 1   tablespoon hoisin sauce
- 1   tablespoon Asian sesame oil

Mix all ingredients together in a small bowl.

Mustard, Garlic, and Honey Wet Rub

MAKES ABOUT ⅓ CUP, ENOUGH FOR 2 TENDERLOINS

You can substitute 1 teaspoon dried rosemary for the fresh herb if desired.

- 3   medium garlic cloves, minced or pressed through a garlic press (about 1 tablespoon)
- 2   teaspoons honey
- 2   teaspoons Dijon mustard
- 2   teaspoons chopped fresh rosemary leaves
- 1   teaspoon grated zest from 1 lemon
- ½   teaspoon black pepper
- ¼   teaspoon salt
- 1   tablespoon extra-virgin olive oil

Mix all ingredients together in a bowl.

turning once, until an instant-read thermometer inserted into the thickest part of the tenderloin registers 145 degrees or until the meat is slightly pink at the center when cut with a paring knife, 2 to 3 minutes longer. Transfer the tenderloins to a cutting board, cover with the disposable aluminum pan, and let rest about 5 minutes. Slice crosswise into 1-inch thick pieces and serve.

➤ VARIATION

Gas-Grilled Pork Tenderloin

A gas grill runs slightly cooler than a charcoal fire so the tenderloins can be cooked over direct heat for the entire time.

Follow step 1 of Charcoal-Grilled Pork Tenderloin. Preheat the grill with all burners set to high and the lid down until the grill is very hot, about 15 minutes. Scrape the grill grate clean with a grill brush. Coat the tenderloins with the spice rub of choice and grill, with the lid down, until browned on all four sides, about 3 minutes per side.

GRILLED RACK OF LAMB

A RACK OF LAMB IS A PERFECT CANDIDATE for grilling. This fatty cut is actually easier to cook outdoors and the meat develops an excellent crust.

We started our tests by focusing on trimming the racks. Rack of lamb has a lot of excess fat, and we wondered how much would have to be removed before grilling. We found that racks sold at butcher shops and higher-end grocery stores tend to be frenched—that is, the butcher has removed the fat and gristle between each chop to expose the ends of the bones. The chine bone had been removed from most racks that we purchased at butcher shops. At many supermarkets, we found racks that were not frenched and still had the chine bone attached. If the chine bone is left on, it is very hard to separate the grilled rack into individual chops. Since it is quite difficult to remove the chine bone at home, ask the butcher to do this. (Also, why pay $17 a pound for useless bone?) We found that most frenched racks with the chine bone removed weigh in at about 1½

pounds or so, and that racks weighing 2 pounds or more usually need more butchering. If you are about to purchase a rack that is this heavy, ask the butcher to make sure that the chine bone has been removed.

Even if you buy a frenched rack with the chine bone removed, you will still have some work to do. A typical rack is thicker at one end. At the thicker end, there is a layer of fat covering a thin layer of meat, called the cap. Another thin layer of fat rests underneath the cap. Trying to save as much meat as we could on the rack, we trimmed off only the first layer of fat. Unfortunately, however, the thin layer of meat was not really worth saving—the extra layer of fat underneath caused flare-ups on the grill, and we found the meat hard to eat because there was just too much fat surrounding it. We also found that leaving on the extra layer of meat and fat made the rack cook unevenly—the small end was overdone by the time the thicker end cooked to medium-rare. So we trimmed the cap and all the fat underneath it, leaving only a minimal amount of fat at the top of the rack and covering the bones to give the cut its characteristic rounded shape.

With our trimming tests completed, we turned to grilling. Our research uncovered three options: grilling the racks directly over the coals, searing the racks over hot coals and then sliding them to a cooler part of the grill to cook by indirect heat, or cooking the racks completely over indirect heat.

Direct heat was unsuccessful when cooking the racks over a medium-hot fire as well as over a medium fire. We found that the racks charred on the outside, while the inside was still raw. Grilling over direct heat using a cooler fire just doesn't make sense; there are too few coals, which will burn out too quickly.

A combination of direct and indirect heat worked better. First, we seared the racks directly over a hot fire and then moved the meat to indirect heat on the other side of the grill. The racks were satisfactorily cooked to medium-rare at the center. However, the outer layers of meat were a tad overdone.

We were surprised to find that cooking completely by indirect heat worked best. The racks slowly developed a rich crust, and the interior was more evenly cooked to medium-rare than by the direct/indirect method. On charcoal, we had to use disposable aluminum pie plates to cover each of the racks to prevent the meat from drying out (total grill time is 17 to 18 minutes) and to speed up grilling time. The racks must also be placed quite close to but not directly over the pile of coals. To ensure even cooking, the racks must be turned 180 degrees on each side in addition to being flipped over. Some sources suggest covering the protruding bones with foil to keep them from charring. We didn't have a problem with bones burning, so we feel that this extra step is not necessary.

Our final tests concerned flavoring. Rack of lamb is so tasty (that's why we are willing to pay so dearly for it) that it doesn't need much help, just a little salt and pepper to heighten its natural flavor. For variety, though, we found that both dry rubs and pastes work equally well to flavor the exterior of the meat. Rack of lamb has a tendency to be soft and mushy, and we found that marinades only exacerbated this problem.

One final note. We strongly recommend using an instant-read thermometer when grilling rack of lamb. There is no other reliable way to tell if the rack is properly cooked. No one wants to ruin $50 worth of meat because they overcooked it. Simply slide an instant-read thermometer through the end of the meat, toward the center but away from any bones, to gauge the temperature at the center of the rack.

We found that cooking the meat to 125 degrees is perfect for medium-rare, as long as the meat is allowed to rest, tented with foil, after coming off the grill. Carry-over cooking brings the temperature of the meat up to between 135 and 140 degrees after 10 minutes. For those who like their rack cooked further, 130 degrees is right for medium. After resting, the meat will reach 140 to 145 degrees. Keep in mind that the chops closer to the ends of the rack will cook somewhat ahead of the chops at the center. For example, when the chops are medium-rare at the center, you can expect those toward the ends to be cooked to medium, and for racks where the center chop is medium, the chops at the end will be medium-well to well-done.

Charcoal-Grilled Rack of Lamb

SERVES 4

Have your butcher french the racks of lamb for you (this means that part of the rib bones is exposed). If the racks are available already frenched, chances are there is still a good deal of fat on one side. Be sure to trim this excess fat away (according to the illustrations on page 271) to prevent flare-ups on the grill. Also, make sure that the chine bone (the bone running along the bottom of the rack) has been removed to ensure that it will be easy to cut between the ribs after cooking. Ask the butcher to do it; it's very hard to cut the chine bone off at home. You will need two 9-inch disposable pie plates for this recipe.

2   racks of lamb (about 1 ½ pounds each), trimmed according to the illustrations on page 271
     Salt and ground black pepper

1. Light a large chimney starter ¾ full with hardwood charcoal (about 4½ quarts or 70 coals) and allow to burn until all the charcoal is covered with a layer of fine gray ash. Build a modified two-level fire by spreading the coals over half the grill bottom. Set the cooking rack in place, cover the grill with the lid, and let the rack heat up, about 5 minutes. Use a wire brush to scrape clean the cooking rack. The grill is ready when the coals are medium-hot. (See how to gauge heat level on page 34.)

2. Meanwhile, sprinkle both sides of the trimmed racks with a generous amount of salt and pepper to taste.

3. Place the racks of lamb, bone-side up, on the grill, with the meaty side of the racks very close to, but not quite over, the hot coals. Cover with pie plates and grill until a deeply colored crust develops, about 8½ minutes, rotating the racks halfway through the cooking time so that the protruding bones are closer to the coals. Turn the racks over, bone-side down, and cover with the pie plates. Grill, rotating the racks halfway through for even cooking, until an instant-read thermometer inserted from the side of the rack through to the center, but away from any bone, reads 125 degrees for medium-rare or 130 degrees for medium, another 8½ to 10 minutes.

4. Remove the racks from the grill to a cutting board and allow to rest, tented with foil, for 10 minutes (the racks will continue to cook while resting). Cut between each rib to separate chops and serve immediately.

➤ VARIATIONS

Gas-Grilled Rack of Lamb

Preheat the grill with all burners set to high and the lid down until very hot, about 15 minutes. Scrape the grill grate clean with a grill brush. Leave one burner on high and turn the other burner(s) to medium-low. Follow the recipe for Grilled Rack of Lamb (charcoal or gas), seasonings the racks as directed in step 2 and cooking the racks with the lid down as directed in step 3. Let rest as directed in step 4 before serving.

Grilled Rack of Lamb with Garlic and Herbs

Mix 4 teaspoons chopped fresh rosemary leaves, 2 teaspoons chopped fresh thyme leaves, 2 garlic cloves, minced, and 4 teaspoons extra-virgin olive oil together in a small bowl. Follow the recipe for Grilled Rack of Lamb (charcoal or gas), rubbing the herb/garlic mixture over the lamb after seasoning it with salt and pepper.

Grilled Rack of Lamb with Turkish Spice Rub

Pickling spice is a spice blend sold in many supermarkets.

Grind 1 tablespoon pickling spice in a spice grinder. Mix the ground pickling spice, 1 teaspoon dried summer savory, ½ teaspoon ground black pepper, ½ teaspoon ground cumin, ¼ teaspoon grated nutmeg, ¼ teaspoon ground cinnamon, and ¾ teaspoon salt together in a small bowl. Follow the recipe for Grilled Rack of Lamb (charcoal or gas), rubbing the meat with the pickling spice rub instead of sprinkling it with salt and pepper in step 2. Proceed with the recipe.

GRILLED BUTTERFLIED LEG OF LAMB

A LEG OF LAMB CAN BE GRILLED IF THE LEG is boned and then butterflied, a technique in which several cuts are made in the boned flesh to open and flatten the leg so that its uneven topography is smoothed to an even thickness. A butterflied leg of lamb is a large, unwieldy piece of meat, about ¾ inch thick and covered with a thin layer of fat. You can butterfly a leg of lamb yourself or buy a butterflied leg of lamb at the supermarket (see pages 295 to 296 for more detailed information on both of these options).

For our first test, we used a kettle grill and our preferred fuel—hardwood charcoal—to build a two-level fire. We seasoned the butterflied meat with salt and pepper and, wary of flaming, used no oil. We placed the meat fat-side down over the coals, intending to brown it quickly over direct heat and then finish it over indirect heat.

The results dismayed us. The leg flamed and blackened. It was difficult to maneuver on the grill because of its size. The connective tissue in the shank retracted and curled so badly that eventually we had to cut it off and cook it longer. The rest of the leg cooked unevenly and tasted oily as well as scorched from the flame. Because it was so thin, it was difficult to carve into attractive slices.

We made up our minds to start from scratch and find out the best way to grill a butterflied leg of lamb. We had several questions: First, what's the best way to butterfly a leg of lamb? Is there a way to grill the shank attached to the leg, or must we always cut it off? Direct heat chars the leg more than we like, but how else can we grill it? Do we need

BUYING A LEG OF LAMB

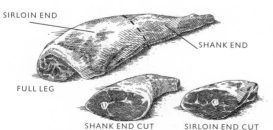

SIRLOIN END

SHANK END

FULL LEG

SHANK END CUT   SIRLOIN END CUT

When you go to the supermarket, you will probably be able to buy either a whole leg or a half leg. When buying a half, you can get either the sirloin (the upper half) or the shank (the lower half). Of the two, we prefer the sirloin end because it is slightly more tender.

BONING A LEG OF LAMB

1. Using the tip of a boning knife, make the first cut at the top of the shank, cutting around the knee cap, and continuing down one side of the leg bone.

2. Cut straight down to the leg bone with the tip of the knife, and, using the bone as a guide, cut until you reach the hipbone and must stop. Repeat on the other side.

3. Cut under and around the knee cap and along the side of the leg bone, loosening the meat from the bone as you go.

4. Cut around the hipbone to loosen the meat from the bone.

5. Using the tip of the knife, cut the meat away from the aitchbone (or pelvic bone). Use the tip of the knife to scrape the meat away from the bone.

6. At this point, the meat should be free from the leg bone (center), the aitchbone (lower left center), and the hip bone (lower right). The ball-and-socket joint is in the center.

7. Cut beneath the tarsal bone, keeping the knife right along the bone.

8. Lift the tarsal bone and continue scraping the meat away from the bone until you reach the ball-and-socket joint.

9. With the tip of the knife, scrape along and beneath the ball-and-socket joint to loosen it from the meat, and cut between ball and socket to loosen.

10. Snap the ball and socket apart and pull the tail-, hip-, and aitchbones away from the leg bone (save this piece for stock or discard).

11. Continue to cut beneath the leg bone, lifting it from the meat as you cut.

12. Lift the leg bone and cartilage around the knee cap to totally separate the leg and shank portion (if the leg came shank attached) and remove (save for stock or discard).

to cover the grill to control the flaming? And is it necessary to carve a leg of lamb across the grain for the sake of tenderness?

Our goal was to come up with a butchering technique that would yield an easy-to-manage piece of meat, thick enough to carve into attractive slices. And, as always when grilling, we wanted a crust that was caramelized but not blackened and a moist, tender interior.

To start, it helps to understand the structure of the leg, which consists of six different muscles: the meaty, dome-shaped top and smaller bottom rounds; the small cylindrical eye of round; the flat trapezoidal hip; the round knuckle; and the oblong shank. Restaurant chefs sometimes separate the muscles from one another (they pull apart very easily) and then cook and carve each separately because that allows each muscle to be cooked perfectly and carved across the grain into large slices for optimum tenderness. (After the meat is butterflied, the grain runs every which way, so it's impossible to carve against the grain.)

Cooking the muscles separately doesn't make sense for a home cook, particularly since people tend to turn to this cut when planning for a crowd. But we tried to adapt this technique by boning the leg and cooking it as is—with all the muscles intact and unbutterflied—planning to cut the muscles apart after cooking and carve each one separately. This time, to solve the flaming problem, we cooked the lamb entirely over indirect heat. It browned beautifully and didn't flame, but after 40 minutes it was clear that there wasn't enough heat to cook through the larger muscles (the top round and knuckle). We then turned our thoughts to butchering the leg to allow for more even cooking.

We were familiar with two methods of butterflying. One calls for cutting straight down into the meat and then spreading the meat open on either side of the cut. The second technique is to cut into the meat horizontally and then open it out like a book. We tried both and found that a combination of the two techniques worked best (see page 296). What we were after was a single piece of meat about three-quarter-inch thick. Traditional butterflying, as done by most butchers, produces a flat piece of

---

SIMPLIFIED BUTTERFLIED LEG OF LAMB

So you don't want to butterfly your own leg of lamb and just want to buy something straight from the meat case that can be seasoned and grilled? Here's how to adapt our recipe. The cooking times are the same, but note that you will probably have more gradations in the meat, with some parts more well-done and other parts rarer since a leg of lamb that is butterflied according to the traditional method usually has an uneven thickness.

Buy a 4 1/2- to 5-pound butterflied leg of lamb that has been divided into two equal pieces (this makes turning the lamb easier). The butterflied lamb should be about 1 inch throughout. If you cannot find this at your supermarket, we suggest that you buy a bone-in whole leg of lamb that weighs between 6 1/2 and 7 pounds and ask to have it boned and butterflied. Be sure to indicate that you want the meat to be about 1 inch thick throughout, and ask the butcher to divide the lamb into two pieces after butterflying. You may also find a boneless whole leg of lamb roast that has been rolled and tied. This roast simply needs to be butterflied. Again, you can ask your butcher to do this for you.

Because this recipe feeds a crowd (between 8 and 10 people), you may want to grill only half a leg of lamb. Supermarkets usually sell half legs of lamb, either the shank end or the sirloin end. Once again, you can purchase this cut of meat with the bone in and have it boned and butterflied by your butcher, again 1 inch thick throughout. Also remember to cut the ingredients in a marinade, if you are using one, by half.

---

meat, but it can be uneven in thickness. The butterflying method we adopted produces the evenness we wanted.

The butterflied leg was very large, however, so we cut it in half along a natural separation between the muscles. This enabled us to turn each piece with a single pair of tongs rather than struggle with a pair of tongs in each hand. This also made it more practical to buy, since you can freeze half if you are cooking for only four.

Satisfied with our butchering technique, we returned to the cooking. Working again over indirect heat, we grilled the butterflied leg pieces, cut-side up, for 5 minutes. Then we turned them 180 degrees and cooked them 5 more minutes to ensure that the meat cooked evenly all around. After 10 minutes the leg was well browned on the skin side, so we turned the pieces over and repeated the procedure, cooking the meat another 10 minutes, until it registered 130 degrees on an instant-read thermometer. We let the meat rest 10 minutes and then sliced into it. The outside crust was perfect, but inside we still had problems. While the meat in the center was a beautiful medium-rare, the perimeter of the leg was still pale because it needed more time to rest. And the shank meat was still undercooked.

The problem with the shank was easy enough to solve; we decided to cut it off and save it for another use. (Some supermarkets also sell the leg without the shank.) Then we tested resting times, letting the meat rest 15, 20, and 25 minutes, and found that 20 minutes was ample time for the juices to be redistributed throughout the leg. Finally, we experimented with carving to test for tenderness. We carved the meat into thin slices on the bias (for slices as large as possible) and actively disregarded slicing across the grain. As it turned out, this was a good decision. Although the different muscles varied in taste and texture, they were all plenty tender.

BUTTERFLYING A LEG OF LAMB

1. To butterfly, lay a large chef's knife flat on the center of the meat, at the thinnest part, parallel to the top round.

2. Keeping the knife blade parallel to the board, begin slicing through the muscle. Cut horizontally about 1 inch.

3. Begin to unroll the meat (it's like unrolling a carpet) with your other hand as you continue to cut into the muscle, always keeping the knife blade parallel to the board, cutting about 1 inch at a time, and unrolling as you cut.

4. Stopping about 1 inch from the end, unfold the edge of the meat and flatten it.

5. The butterflied muscle should be even in thickness.

6. Turn the board around and cut the knuckle muscle on the other side using the same method as in steps 1 through 4.

7. Near the center of the bottom round locate a hard thick section of fat. Using the tip of the boning knife, cut into the fat to locate the lymph node (a 1/2-inch round, grayish flat nodule). Carefully remove and discard.

8. Divide the butterflied meat in half by cutting between the eye and the bottom round.

9. Turn the pieces of meat over and use a boning knife to cut away the thick pieces of fat, leaving about 1/8-inch thickness for self-basting during grilling.

Charcoal-Grilled Butterflied Leg of Lamb

SERVES 8 TO 10

Be sure to have a spray bottle filled with water ready to dampen the flames, if necessary. See page 298 for tempting marinades.

1	leg of lamb (about 7 pounds), boned, butterflied, and halved between the eye and the bottom round (see the illustrations on pages 294 and 296)
1 ½	tablespoons extra-virgin olive oil Salt and ground black pepper

1. Light a large chimney starter generously filled with hardwood charcoal (about 6 quarts) and allow to burn until it is completely covered with a thin layer of gray ash. Build a modified two-level fire by spreading the coals over half the grill bottom. Set the cooking rack in place, cover the grill with the lid, and let the rack heat up, about 5 minutes. Use a wire brush to scrape clean the cooking rack. The grill is ready when the coals are hot. (See how to gauge heat level on page 34.)

2. Rub both sides of the lamb pieces with the oil and sprinkle generously with salt and pepper to taste.

3. Place the lamb pieces, fat-side down, on the side of the rack that is not directly over the coals but close to the fire. Grill the lamb, uncovered, for 5 minutes. Rotate the meat so that the outside edges are now closest to the fire. Grill until the fat side of the lamb is a rich dark brown, 5 minutes

longer. With tongs or a large meat fork, turn both pieces over. Cook, fat-side up, for 5 minutes, then move meat directly over the coals (they will have partially burned out by this point, putting out less heat), and cook until an instant-read thermometer inserted into the thickest part of each piece registers 125 to 130 degrees for medium-rare or 135 degrees for medium, 5 to 7 minutes longer.

4. Transfer the meat to a large platter or cutting board, tent loosely with foil, and let rest for 20 minutes. Slice thin on the bias and serve.

➤ VARIATION
Gas-Grilled Butterflied Leg of Lamb
Watch for flare-ups on the grill; use a spray bottle filled with water ready to dampen the flames as necessary.

1	leg of lamb (about 7 pounds), boned, butterflied, and halved between the eye and the bottom round (see the illustrations on pages 294 and 296)
1 ½	tablespoons extra-virgin olive oil Salt and ground black pepper

1. Preheat the grill with all burners set to high and the lid down, until very hot, about 15 minutes. Scrape clean the cooking grate with a wire brush. Leave one burner on high and turn the other burner(s) down to medium.

2. Rub both sides of the lamb pieces with oil and sprinkle generously with salt and pepper to taste.

3. Place the lamb pieces, fat-side down, over the burner(s) set to medium. Grill the lamb, covered, for 5 minutes. Rotate the meat so that the outside edges are now facing the hotter burner. Grill, covered, until the fat side of the lamb is a rich dark brown, 5 minutes longer. With tongs or a large meat fork, turn both pieces over. Cook, fat-side up, for 5 minutes, then rotate the meat 180 degrees to ensure even cooking. Continue grilling, covered, until an instant-read thermometer inserted into the thickest part of each piece registers 125 degrees for medium-rare or 130 to 135 degrees for medium, 10 to 12 minutes longer.

4. Transfer the meat to a large platter or cutting board, tent with foil, and let rest 20 minutes. Slice thinly on this bias and serve.

LEG OF LAMB: THE BONES

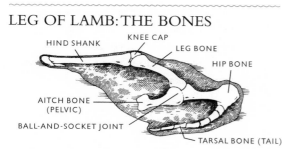

When boning a leg of lamb (see step-by-step illustrations on page 294), it is helpful to know the inner skeletal structure. In particular, note where all the bones come together in the center of the leg at the large ball-and-socket joint.

MARINADES FOR GRILLED LEG OF LAMB

Leg of lamb has a rich flavor that stands up well to a variety of marinades. To use any of these marinades, butcher the lamb as directed, place the lamb in a nonreactive large shallow pan or baking dish, and rub the marinade into all parts of the meat with your hands. Cover the pan with plastic wrap and refrigerate it at least 8 hours and up to 24 hours. Except for the Soy-Honey Marinade with Thyme, which is salty enough, season the marinated lamb with salt and pepper just before grilling, but do not oil the lamb.

Tandoori Marinade

ENOUGH FOR 1 BUTTERFLIED LEG OF LAMB

The yogurt forms an especially thick, browned crust when the lamb is grilled.

- 1/3   cup plain yogurt
- 5   medium garlic cloves, minced or pressed through a garlic press (about 5 teaspoons)
- 1   tablespoon grated fresh ginger
- 2   tablespoons juice from 1 lemon
- 2   teaspoons ground cumin
- 2   teaspoons ground coriander
- 1   teaspoon ground turmeric
- 1   teaspoon cayenne pepper
- 1/2   teaspoon ground cinnamon

Mix all of the ingredients together in a small bowl.

Lemon Marinade with Greek Flavorings

ENOUGH FOR 1 BUTTERFLIED LEG OF LAMB

If you like, use fresh oregano and thyme, doubling their amounts, in this marinade.

- 1/4   cup extra-virgin olive oil
- 2   tablespoons juice from 1 lemon
- 3   medium garlic cloves, minced or pressed through a garlic press (about 1 tablespoon)
- 1   tablespoon dried oregano
- 1   tablespoon dried thyme
-   Pinch sweet paprika

Mix all of the ingredients together in a small bowl.

Garlic and Rosemary Marinade

ENOUGH FOR 1 BUTTERFLIED LEG OF LAMB

A leg of lamb will be nicely flavored after just 3 hours in this marinade but can be marinated longer if you like.

- 6   medium garlic cloves, minced or pressed through a garlic press (about 2 tablespoons)
- 1 1/2   tablespoons minced fresh rosemary leaves
- 1/4   cup extra-virgin olive oil

Mix all of the ingredients together in a small bowl.

Soy-Honey Marinade with Thyme

ENOUGH FOR 1 BUTTERFLIED LEG OF LAMB

Minced fresh chile or hot red pepper flakes make a good addition to this marinade.

- 1/3   cup soy sauce
- 1/3   cup honey
- 2   medium garlic cloves, minced or pressed through a garlic press (about 2 teaspoons)
- 1   tablespoon grated fresh ginger
- 1   teaspoon minced fresh thyme leaves
-   Pinch cayenne pepper

Mix all of the ingredients together in a small bowl.

12

I WANT TO MAKE CHILI OR CURRY

I Want to Make Chili or Curry

DEFINED IN THE BROADEST POSSIBLE SENSE, a chili consists of meat, dried red chiles ground to a powder, and liquid and is more often than not seasoned with garlic, cumin, and oregano. But, of course, it's not that easy. Our research turned up numerous distinct styles of chili, the most prevalent of which were from Texas (chili con carne, with big chunks of beef and no beans) and Cincinnati (a sweeter, not terribly spicy version made with ground beef and served with spaghetti and beans). There's also the basic chili most Americans make that contains ground meat, canned tomatoes, and spices.

The term curry encompasses a wide range of dishes made throughout Asia. Almost any Indian stew can be called a curry, and the term is used throughout Southeast Asia, where the dish takes on many different forms. In this chapter, we focus on two basic styles of curry—classic Indian curry with garlic, ginger, and spices and Thai curry with coconut milk.

CHILI CON CARNE

A STRICTLY TEXAN CHILI, KNOWN AS CHILI con carne, depends on either pureed or powdered ancho chiles, uses beef, excludes tomato, onion, and beans, and features a high proportion of meat to chiles. We wanted a chili that would be hearty, heavy on the meat, and spicy but not overwhelmingly hot. We wanted a creamy consistency somewhere between soup and stew. The flavors would be balanced so that no single spice or seasoning stood out or competed with the chile or beef.

Because chiles are the heart of chili con carne, we had to learn about the different types. After considerable testing and tasting, we settled on a combination of ancho and New Mexico for the dried chiles (for more information on dried chiles see page 302), with a few jalapeños added for their fresh flavor and bite. Chilis made with toasted and ground whole dried chiles tasted noticeably fuller and warmer than those made with chili powder. The two main toasting methods are oven and skillet, and after trying both, we went to the oven simply

because it required less attention and effort than skillet toasting. The chiles will puff in the oven, become fragrant, and dry out sufficiently after five to six minutes. One caveat, though: Overtoasted chiles can take on a distinctly bitter flavor, so don't let them go too long.

With the chiles chosen and toasted, the next big question was how best to prepare them. The two options here are to rehydrate the toasted chiles in liquid and process them into a puree or to grind them into a powder. It didn't take long for us to select grinding as the preferred method. It was easier, faster, and much less messy than making the puree, which tasters felt produced a chili that was too rich, more like a Mexican enchilada sauce than a bowl of chili.

This felt like the right time to determine the best ratio of chile to meat. Many of the recipes we looked at in our research suggested that a tablespoon of ground chile per pound of meat was sufficient, but we found these chilis to be bland and watery. Three tablespoons per pound of meat, on the other hand, produced chili with too much punch and richness. Two tablespoons per pound was the way to go.

There was little agreement in the recipes we had collected as to the chile powder should be added. After running several tests, we found that sautéing the spices, including the chiles, is key to unlocking their flavor. We also discovered that blending the chili powder with water to make a paste keeps it from scorching in the pot; this step is advised.

Since chuck is our favorite meat for stewing, we knew it would work best in chili. Still, there were some aspects of the meat question that still had to be settled. Should the chuck be standard hamburger grind, coarser chili grind, hand-cut into tiny cubes, or a combination? The chili made from cubes of beef was far more appealing than those made from either type of ground beef; they both had a grainy, extruded texture. Most of the recipes we looked at specified that the meat should be cut into ¼-inch cubes. However, we found that larger 1-inch chunks gave the chili a satisfying chew. In addition, cutting a chuck roast into larger chunks was much, much faster and easier than breaking it down into a fussy, ¼-inch dice.

Next we set out to determine the best type, or

types, of liquid for the chili. The main contenders were water, chicken broth, beef broth, beer, black coffee, and red wine. We tried each one on its own, as well as in any combination we felt made sense. The surprise result was that we liked plain water best because it allowed the flavor of the chiles to come through in full force. Both broths, whether on their own, combined in equal parts with each other, or with water, muddied the chile flavors. All of the other liquids, used either alone or mixed with an equal part of chicken broth or water, competed with the chile flavor.

Another basic factor to determine was the garlic. Tasters agreed that three cloves were too few and eight were too many, so we settled on five. We found many recipes that called for powdered garlic rather than fresh. Out of obligation, we tested powdered versus fresh garlic and found fresh to be far superior.

Though common in modern recipes, Texas chili lore leaves tomatoes and onions out of the original formula. These two ingredients may break with tradition, but we found both to be essential. The acidity of the tomato and the sweetness of the onion, both used in small amounts, add interest and dimension to the chili. The batches we tested without them were decidedly dull. We tested various amounts and types of tomato products and determined that more than one cup pushed the flavor of the chili toward that of a spaghetti sauce. Products with a smooth consistency, such as canned crushed tomatoes or plain tomato sauce, helped create the smooth sauce we wanted.

We found that bacon lends the chili a subtly sweet, smoky essence that is most welcome. Other "secret" ingredients fell by the way side. Coke imparted a sourish, off taste. Brown sugar cut the heat of the chiles too much. An ounce of unsweetened chocolate gave the chili a rounder, deeper flavor, and 2 tablespoons of peanut butter made the sauce creamier and earthy tasting. Much as we liked both peanut butter and chocolate, we decided they were not essential.

Chili is generally thickened to tighten the sauce and make it smoother. Flour, roux (a paste of flour and melted butter), cornstarch, and masa harina (a flour ground from corn treated with lime, or calcium oxide) are the most common options. Dredging the meat in flour before browning and adding a roux along with the liquid were both effective, but these approaches made it more difficult to finesse the consistency of the finished product because both were introduced early in the cooking process. Roux added at the end of the cooking left a faint taste

---

INGREDIENTS: Dried Chiles

For the most part, chili con carne is based on fairly mild dried chiles. The most common of these are dark, mahogany red, wrinkly skinned ancho chiles, which have a deep, sweet, raisiny flavor; New Mexico Reds, which have a smooth, shiny, brick-red skin and a crisp, slightly acidic, earthy flavor; California chiles, which are very similar to New Mexico in appearance but have a slightly milder flavor; and long, shiny, smooth, dark brown pasilla chiles. Pasillas, which are a little hotter than the other three varieties, have grapey, herby flavor notes, and, depending on the region of the country, are often packaged and sold as either ancho or mulato chiles.

We sampled each of these types, as well as a selection of pre-blended commercial powders, alone and in various combinations in batches of chili. Though the chilies made with individual chiles tasted much more pure and fresh than any of the premixed powders, they nonetheless seemed one-dimensional on their own. When all was said and done, the two-chile combination we favored was equal parts ancho, for its earthy, fruity sweetness and the stunning deep red color it imparted to the chili, and New Mexico, for its lighter flavor and crisp acidity.

Chile heat was another factor to consider. Hotter dried chiles that appear regularly in chili include guajillo, de árbol, pequín, japónes, and cayenne. Though we did not want to develop a fiery, overly hot chili, we did want a subtle bite to give the dish some oomph. We found that minced jalapeños, added with the garlic to the chili pot, supplied some heat and a fresh vegetal flavor.

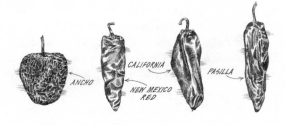

ANCHO CALIFORNIA NEW MEXICO RED PASILLA

of raw flour. We did prefer thickening at the end of cooking, though, because we could control the consistency by adding thickener gradually until the chili reached the right consistency. We like chili thick enough to coat the back of a wooden spoon, like the custard base of homemade ice cream.

Our first choice for thickening was masa harina, added at the end of cooking. Masa both thickened and imparted a slightly sweet, earthy corn flavor to the chili. If masa harina is not available in your grocery store and you'd rather not mail-order it, use a cornstarch and water slurry. It brings no flavor to the chili, but it is predictable, easy to use, and gives the "gravy" a silky consistency and attractive sheen.

One last note. Time and time again, tasters observed that chili, like many stews, always improved after an overnight rest because the flavors blended and mellowed. If you are able, cook your chili a day ahead. The result will be worth the wait.

Chili Con Carne

SERVES 6

To ensure the best chile flavor, we recommend toasting whole dried chiles and grinding them in a minichopper (see page 317) or spice-dedicated coffee grinder, all of which takes only 10 (very well-spent) minutes. Select dried chiles that are moist and pliant, like dried fruit.

To toast and grind dried chiles: Place the chiles on a baking sheet in a 350-degree oven until fragrant and puffed, about 6 minutes. Cool, stem, and seed, tearing the pods into pieces. Place the pieces in a spice grinder and process until powdery, 30 to 45 seconds.

For hotter chili, boost the heat with a pinch of cayenne, a dash of hot pepper sauce, or crumbled pequín chiles near the end of cooking. Serve the chili with any of the following side dishes: warm pinto or kidney beans, cornbread or chips, corn tortillas or tamales, rice, biscuits, or just plain crackers. Top with any of the following garnishes: chopped fresh cilantro leaves, minced white onion, diced avocado, shredded cheddar or Monterey Jack cheese, or sour cream.

3	tablespoons ancho chili powder, or 3 medium pods (about ¹/₂ ounce), toasted and ground
3	tablespoons New Mexico chili powder, or 3

	medium pods (about ³/₄ ounce), toasted and ground (see note)
2	tablespoons cumin seeds, toasted in a dry skillet over medium heat until fragrant, about 4 minutes, and ground
2	teaspoons dried oregano, preferably Mexican
¹/₄	cup plus 7 cups water
4	pounds beef chuck roast, trimmed and cut into 1-inch cubes (see the illustrations on page 148)
2	teaspoons salt, plus extra for seasoning
8	ounces (about 8 slices) bacon, cut into ¹/₄-inch pieces
1	medium onion, minced
5	medium garlic cloves, minced or pressed through a garlic press (about 5 teaspoons)
4–5	small jalapeño chiles, stemmed, seeded, and minced
1	cup canned crushed tomatoes or plain tomato sauce
2	tablespoons lime juice from 1 lime
5	tablespoons masa harina or 3 tablespoons cornstarch
	Ground black pepper

1. Mix the chili powders, cumin, and oregano in a small bowl and stir in the ½ cup water to form a thick paste; set aside. Toss the beef cubes with the 2 teaspoons salt; set aside.

2. Fry the bacon in a large Dutch oven over medium-low heat until the fat renders and the bacon crisps, about 10 minutes. Remove the bacon with a slotted spoon to a paper towel-lined plate; pour all but 2 teaspoons fat from the pot into a small bowl; set aside. Increase the heat to medium-high; sauté the meat in 4 batches until well browned on all sides, about 5 minutes per batch, adding 2 teaspoons additional bacon fat to the pot as necessary. Set the browned meat aside.

3. Reduce the heat to medium and add 3 tablespoons bacon fat to the now-empty pan. Add the onion and sauté until softened, 5 to 6 minutes. Add the garlic and chiles and sauté until fragrant, about 1 minute. Add the chili mixture and sauté until fragrant, 2 to 3 minutes. Add the reserved bacon and browned beef, crushed tomatoes, lime juice, and the remaining 7 cups water. Bring to a simmer.

Continue to cook at a steady simmer until the meat is tender and the juices are dark, rich, and starting to thicken, about 2 hours.

4. Mix the masa harina with ⅔ cup water (or the cornstarch with 3 tablespoons water) in a small bowl to form a smooth paste. Increase the heat to medium, stir in the paste, and simmer until thickened, 5 to 10 minutes. Adjust the seasonings generously with salt and ground black pepper to taste. Serve immediately or, for best flavor, cool slightly, cover, and refrigerate overnight or for up to 5 days. Reheat before serving.

➤ VARIATION

Smoky Chipotle Chili Con Carne

Grill-smoking the meat in combination with chipotle chiles gives this chili a distinct, but not overwhelming, smoky flavor. Make sure you start with a chuck roast that is at least 3 inches thick. The grilling is meant to flavor the meat by searing the surface and smoking it lightly; it is not a way to cook it.

1. To SMOKE THE MEAT: Puree 4 medium garlic cloves with 2 teaspoons salt. Rub the chuck roast with the puree, and sprinkle evenly with 2 to 3 tablespoons New Mexico chili powder; cover and set aside. Meanwhile, build a hot fire in the grill. When you can hold your hand 5 inches above the grill surface for no more than 3 seconds, spread the hot coals to an area about the size of roast. Open the bottom grill vents, scatter 1 cup soaked mesquite or hickory wood chips over the hot coals, and set the grill rack in place. Place the meat over the hot coals and grill-roast, opening the lid vents three quarters of the way and covering so that the vents are opposite the bottom vents to draw smoke through and around the roast. Sear the meat until all sides are dark and richly colored, about 12 minutes per side. Remove the roast to a bowl; when cool enough to handle, trim and cut into 1-inch cubes, reserving the juices.

2. To MAKE THE CHILI: Follow the recipe for Chili Con Carne, omitting the browning of the beef cubes and substituting 5 minced canned chipotle peppers in adobo sauce for the fresh jalapenos chiles. Add the grill-smoked meat cubes and the juice accumulated in the bowl with the cooked bacon.

CINCINNATI CHILI

REDOLENT OF CINNAMON AND WARM SPICES, Cincinnati chili is unlike any chili served in Texas—or the rest of the country, for that matter. On sight alone, its sauciness makes it look more like a Sloppy Joe filling or some strange sauce for pasta. One taste reveals layers of spices you expect from Middle Eastern or North African cuisine, not food from the American heartland.

Legend has it that Cincinnati chili was created in the 1920s by a Macedonian immigrant named Athanas Kiradjieff. He ran a hot dog stand called the Empress, where he served his chili over hot dogs. This deluxe hot dog eventually morphed into the "five-way" concoction beloved by locals.

Cincinnati chili is as much about the garnishes, or "ways," as the chili itself. On its own, it is merely one-way Cincinnati chili. Served over buttered spaghetti, it is two-way. Add shredded cheddar cheese and it becomes three-way. With chopped onions, four-way, and the final garnish, for five-way chili, is with warmed kidney beans.

To get a handle on this unusual chili, we tested a number of recipes, including one purporting to be from the original Empress Chili Parlor. We noticed two problems. First, most of the versions tested were much too greasy. Second, the myriad spices used in many recipes was overwhelming. Our goals were clear—cut the fat and figure out which spices were essential and which were not.

We focused on the meat element first. In most chili recipes, the meat is browned to build flavor and render some fat, which can be spooned off. Cincinnati chili is unique because it calls for boiling ground beef instead of browning it. The boiled meat had a texture described as "wormy" by most tasters, which, as odd as it sounds, pairs well with the pasta and the other accompaniments. But boiling the meat can make it difficult to rid the meat of excess fat, particularly since traditional recipes use the blanching liquid as the base for the chili.

We decided to try replacing ground chuck (80 to 85 percent lean), which is the usual choice for chili, with ground round (90 percent lean). This idea sounded great, but tasters felt that the flavor of the chili made with ground round suffered. Ground chuck has a beefier flavor, so we would have to figure out some way to eliminate the excess grease from the final dish.

For our next batch of chili, we added the beef to salted, boiling water and blanched it for three minutes, or until an unappetizing raft of oily meat foam had risen to the surface. We then drained the beef and discarded the water—along with the fat. The resulting chili was grease-free but lacked the body and flavor that fat provides. We had gone too far. Next, we cut the blanching time back to only 30 seconds, and the results were much better. The chili was rich and fully flavored, without being slick or greasy. This method also retained the traditional "wormy" texture of the meat.

Like curries in India, the spice mixture in Cincinnati chili varies from recipe to recipe (and house to house). Some mixes contain just two or three spices, while others embrace the entire spice cabinet and are more evocative of a Moroccan souk than an Ohio hot dog. We hoped to isolate the key flavors and create a streamlined spice mixture.

We had uncovered all kinds of incongruous combinations in our research, including one recipe that called for coriander, cardamom, turmeric, and nutmeg—a simply dreadful mixture. Tasters also objected to cloves and mace, both of which were deemed too overpowering. Chili powder, cinnamon, and cayenne pepper were essential, although

---

SCIENCE: How Come You Don't Think It's Hot?

One enduring mystery among those partial to spicy food is why people have such varying tolerances for the heat of chile peppers. As it turns out, there are several reasons why your dinner companion may find a bowl of chili only mildly spicy while the same dish causes you to frantically summon a waiter for a glass of milk to cool the heat before you expire. (Milk, not water, is the thing to drink when you want to cool the fire in your mouth.)

Your dining partner may be experiencing "temporary desensitization." The phenomenon, discovered by Barry Green of the Monell Chemical Senses Institute in Philadelphia, occurs when you eat something spicy hot, then lay off for a few minutes. As long as you keep eating chiles, their effect keeps building. But if you take a break—even for as few as two to five minutes, depending on your individual susceptibility—you will be desensitized when you go back to eating the chiles. In other words, a dish with the same amount of chiles will not seem as hot the second time around.

The more likely explanation, however, is that people who find chiles intensely, punishingly hot simply have more taste buds. According to Linda Bartoshuk, a psychophysicist at the Yale School of Medicine, human beings can be neatly divided into three distinct categories when it comes to tasting ability: unfortunate "nontasters," pedestrian "medium tasters," and the aristocrats of the taste-bud world, "supertasters."

This taste-detection pecking order appears to correspond directly to the number of taste buds a person possesses, a genetically predetermined trait that may vary by a factor of 100. Indeed, so radical is the difference among these three types that Bartoshuk speaks of them inhabiting different "taste worlds."

Bartoshuk and her colleagues discovered the extent of this phenomenon a few years ago when they carried out experiments using a dye that turns the entire mouth blue except for the taste papillae (structures housing taste buds and other sensory receptors). After painting part of subjects' tongues with the dye, they were rather stunned at the differences they saw. One poor taster had just eleven taste buds per square centimeter, while a supertaster had 1,100 in the same area.

Further experiments confirmed that the ability to taste intensely was in direct proportion to the number of taste buds. Researchers found that women were twice as likely as men to be supertasters, while men were nearly twice as likely as women to be nontasters.

What does this have to do with how hot you find chiles? It turns out that every taste bud in the mouth has a pain receptor literally wrapped around it. Along with the extra taste buds comes an extra ability to feel pain. As a result, supertasters have the capacity to experience 50 percent more pain from capsaicin, the chemical that gives chiles their heat.

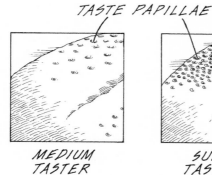

TASTE PAPILLAE

MEDIUM TASTER

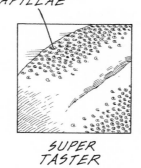

SUPER TASTER

the latter had to be used sparingly. Cincinnati chili should not be scorchingly hot.

Cumin, in addition to the small amount of cumin already blended into the chili powder, proved too much, so it was pulled. The cinnamon was not strong enough in early batches and was almost doubled in the final recipe. We were almost content with the basic spice mixture, but it needed a little more depth. After trying several ideas, a combination of black pepper and allspice proved winning. These spices added depth and, in conjunction with the rest of the spices, complexity.

Many recipes called for unsweetened chocolate, but we figured that cocoa powder would achieve much the same thing and would be easier to add along with the spices. (Further testing bore out the hypothesis.) Dried oregano rounded out our list of "spices." To further boost the flavors of our spice mixture, we toasted it in the oil before adding the liquid ingredients.

While the spices vary from recipe to recipe, the aromatics were consistently onion and garlic. Most recipes added them to the water with the meat. We decided to draw out a little more flavor and sweetness by sautéing them.

As far as the liquids go, most recipes call for tomato sauce and water. We tried to replace the generic canned tomato sauce suggested in most recipes with canned whole peeled tomatoes that we pureed in the blender. While the canned tomatoes made the chili taste a bit brighter, the chili made with canned tomato sauce was favored by most tasters.

Tasters felt that the water did little to improve the chili and wondered if it should be replaced. To add body, we tried using red wine as part of the liquid. We decided it was superfluous due to the strength of the rest of the flavors. In the end, we went with canned chicken broth for the sake of convenience. To keep the chicken flavor from dominating, we used half chicken broth and half water. A small amount of cider vinegar (very traditional) brightened the broth. Some brown sugar added the necessary sweetness to balance the vinegar and spices.

With our chili perfected, we turned our attention to the garnishes. After several tests, we realized it was best to leave tradition alone. Sure you could do without the beans or onions, but why compromise? Five-way Cincinnati chili is almost sacrosanct.

Cincinnati Chili
SERVES 6 TO 8

Choose a relatively plain can or jar of tomato sauce—nothing too spicy or herbaceous. To warm the kidney beans, simmer them in water to cover for several minutes and then drain.

CHILI

1 ½	pounds 80 percent lean ground chuck
2	teaspoons salt, plus more to taste
2	tablespoons vegetable oil
2	medium onions, chopped fine (about 2 cups)
2	medium garlic cloves, minced or pressed through a garlic press (about 2 teaspoons)
2	tablespoons chili powder
2	teaspoons dried oregano
2	teaspoons cocoa powder
1 ½	teaspoons ground cinnamon
½	teaspoon cayenne pepper
½	teaspoon ground allspice
¼	teaspoon ground black pepper
2	cups low-sodium chicken broth
2	cups water
2	tablespoons cider vinegar
2	teaspoons dark brown sugar
2	cups tomato sauce
	Tabasco sauce

ACCOMPANIMENTS

1	pound spaghetti, cooked, drained, and tossed with 2 tablespoons unsalted butter
12	ounces sharp cheddar cheese, shredded
1	medium onion, chopped fine (about 1 cup)
1	(15-ounce) can red kidney beans, drained, rinsed, and warmed

1. FOR THE CHILI: Bring 2 quarts of water and 1 teaspoon salt to a boil in a large saucepan. Add the ground chuck, stirring vigorously to separate the meat into individual strands. As soon as the foam from the meat rises to the top (this takes about 30

seconds) and before the water returns to a boil, drain the meat into a strainer and set it aside.

2. Rinse and dry the empty saucepan. Set the pan over medium heat and add the oil. When the oil is warm, add the onions and cook, stirring frequently, until the onions are soft and browned around the edges, about 8 minutes. Add the garlic and cook until fragrant, about 1 minute. Stir in the chili powder, oregano, cocoa, cinnamon, cayenne, allspice, black pepper, and remaining 1 teaspoon salt. Cook, stirring constantly, until the spices are fragrant, about 30 seconds. Stir in the broth, vinegar, sugar, tomato sauce, and water, scraping the pan bottom to remove any browned bits. Add the blanched ground beef and increase the heat to high. As soon as the liquid boils, reduce the heat to medium-low and simmer, stirring occasionally, until the chili is deep red and has thickened slightly, about 1 hour. Adjust the seasonings, adding salt and Tabasco sauce to taste. (The chili can be refrigerated in an airtight container for up to 3 days. Bring to a simmer over medium-low heat before serving.)

3. To SERVE: Divide the buttered spaghetti among individual bowls. Spoon the chili over the spaghetti and top with the cheese, beans, and onion. Serve immediately.

BASIC CHILI

LIKE POLITICS, CHILI PROVOKES HEATED debate. Some purists insist that a chili that contains beans or tomatoes is just not chili. Others claim that homemade chili powder is essential or that ground meat is taboo. But there is one kind of chili that almost every American has eaten (or even made) at one time or another. It's the kind of chili you liked as a kid and still see being served at Super Bowl parties. Made with ground meat, tomatoes, and chili powder, this thick, fairly smooth chili is spiced but not spicy. It's basic grub (and it can be great grub) that's not intended to fuel impassioned exchanges over the merits of ancho versus New Mexico chiles.

Although this simple chili should come together

easily, it should not taste as if it did. The flavors should be rich and balanced, the texture thick and lush. Unfortunately, many "basic" recipes yield a pot of underspiced, underflavored chili reminiscent of Sloppy Joes. Our goal was to develop a no-fuss chili that tasted far better than the sum of its common parts.

Most of the recipes for this plain-spoken chili begin by sautéing onions and garlic. Tasters liked red bell peppers added to these aromatics but rejected other options, including green bell peppers, celery, and carrots. After this first step, things became less clear. The most pressing concerns were the spices (how much and what kind) and the meat (how much ground beef and whether or not to add another meat). There were also the cooking liquid (what kind, if any) and the proportions of tomatoes and beans to consider.

Our first experiments with these ingredients followed a formula we had seen in lots of recipes: 2 pounds ground beef, 3 tablespoons chili powder, 2 teaspoons ground cumin, and 1 teaspoon each red pepper flakes and dried oregano. Many recipes add the spices after the beef has been browned, but we knew from work done in the test kitchen on curry that ground spices taste better when they have direct contact with hot cooking oil.

To see if these results would apply to chili, we set up a test with three pots of chili—one with the ground spices added before the beef, one with the spices added after the beef, and a third in which we toasted the spices in a separate skillet and added them to the pot after the beef. The batch made with untoasted spices added after the beef tasted weak. The batch made with the spices toasted in a separate pan was better, but the clear favorite was the batch made with spices added directly to the pot before the meat. In fact, subsequent testing revealed that the spices should be added at the outset—along with the aromatics—to develop their flavors fully.

Although we didn't want a chili with killer heat, we did want real warmth and depth of flavor. Commercial chili powder is typically 80 percent ground dried red chiles with the rest a mix of garlic powder, onion powder, oregano, ground cumin, and salt. To boost flavor, we increased the amount of chili powder from 3 to 4 tablespoons, added more cumin and oregano, and tossed in some cayenne for heat. We tried some more exotic spices, including cinnamon (which was deemed "awful"), allspice (which seemed "out of place"), and coriander (which "added some gentle warmth"). Only the coriander became part of our working recipe.

It was now time to consider the meat. The quantity (two pounds) seemed ideal when paired with two 16–ounce cans of beans. Tests using 90 percent, 85 percent, and 80 percent lean ground beef showed that there is such a thing as too much fat. Pools of orange oil floated to the top of the chili made with ground chuck (80 percent lean beef). At the other end of the spectrum, the chili made with 90 percent lean beef was a tad bland—not bad, but not as full flavored as the chili made with 85 percent lean beef, which was our final choice.

EQUIPMENT: Slow Cookers

Slow cookers (better known as Crock-Pots, a name trademarked by the Rival company) may be the only modern kitchen convenience that saves the cook time by using more of it rather than less. To see if these appliances could cook not just slowly but also well, we purchased five of them, all 6-quart oval cookers, a size and shape offering the most options in terms of the amount and type of food that can be prepared. The contestants included three "standard" cookers, the Rival Crock-Pot ($39.99), the Farberware Millennium Slow Cooker ($39.99), and the Hamilton Beach Portfolio Slow Cooker ($34.99); one with a new "programmable" feature, the Rival Smart-Pot ($49.99); and one with a completely revamped design, the West Bend Versatility Cooker ($54.99).

All five models had the standard slow cooker temperature settings of low, high, and keep warm. To test the functioning of each setting, we cooked the pot roast recipe (page 183) on low for eight hours and the basic chili recipe (page 307) on high for four hours; we then set each pot of chili on "keep warm" for two hours. All five cookers produced good renditions of the pot roast and chili, and all five kept the chili plenty warm for two hours. (The lowest temperature reached during warming was a piping-hot 187 degrees, by the West Bend cooker; the other four cookers maintained the chili at close to 200 degrees.)

What do we recommend? In the "standard slow cooker with no fancy features" category, both the Farberware Millennium and the Rival Crock-Pot performed admirably. The Hamilton Beach cooker showed slight scorching of the chili in the bottom corners of the crockery pot and so was slightly downgraded.

How did the two novel cookers fare? Rival's Smart-Pot is the only cooker on the market that lets you select a specific time and heat setting and then automatically shifts to the warm setting when the cooking time is up. Theoretically, this buys you a couple more hours at the mall or at work before you have to come home and tend the pot. Two hours after switching from high to warm, however, the Smart-Pot had brought the temperature of the chili down by just 10 degrees, from 205 to 195. We're not sure this feature is worth the extra money.

West Bend's Versatility Cooker is a standout because its pot is made from aluminum with a nonstick interior coating, which means you can use it to cook foods on the stovetop, just as you would any other conventional pan. Both our chili and pot roast recipes start out with instructions for browning on the stovetop, and it was nice to brown foods in the same pot we ultimately used for slow cooking. While a crockery-less crockery pot does seem a little odd, this expensive model does get the job done, and then some.

THE BEST SLOW COOKERS

The Farberware Millennium (left) and the Rival Crock-Pot (center) were the best basic models tested. The West Bend Versatility Cooker (right) has a stovetop-worthy pot made of aluminum rather than the classic ceramic.

We wondered if another type of meat should be used in place of some of the ground beef. After trying batches of chili made with ground pork, diced pork loin, sliced sausage, and sausage removed from its casing and crumbled, tasters preferred the hearty flavor and creamy texture of an all-beef chili. (The exception was one batch to which we added bacon; many tasters liked its smoky flavor, so we made a version with bacon and black beans as a variation on the master recipe.)

Some of us have always made chili with beer and been satisfied with the results. Nodding to the expertise of others, we tried batches made with water (too watery), chicken broth (too chicken-y and dull), beef broth (too tinny), wine (too acidic), and no liquid at all except for that in the tomatoes (beefy tasting and by far the best). When we tried beer, we were surprised to find that it subdued that great beefy flavor. Keep the beer on ice for drinking with dinner.

Tomatoes were definitely going into the pot, but we had yet to decide on the type and amount. We first tried two small (14-ounce) cans of diced tomatoes. Clearly not enough tomatoes. What's more, the tomatoes were too chunky, and they were floating in a thin sauce. We tried two 28-ounce cans of diced tomatoes, pureeing the contents of one can in the blender to thicken the sauce. Although the chunkiness was reduced, the sauce was still watery. Next we paired one can of tomato puree with one can of diced tomatoes and, without exception, tasters preferred the thicker consistency. The test kitchen generally doesn't like the slightly cooked flavor of tomato puree, but this recipe needed the body it provided. In any case, after the long simmering time, any such flavor was hard to detect.

We tried cooking the chili with the lid on, with the lid off, and with the lid on in the beginning and off at the end. The chili cooked with the lid on was too soupy, that cooked with the lid off too dense. Keeping the lid on for half of the cooking time and then removing it was ideal—the consistency was rich but not too thick. Two hours of gentle simmering was sufficient to meld the flavors; shorter cooking times yielded chili that was soupy or bland—or both.

Most recipes add the beans toward the end of cooking, the idea being to let them heat through without causing them to fall apart. But this method often makes for very bland beans floating in a sea of highly flavorful chili. After testing several options, we found it best to add the beans with the tomatoes. The more time the beans spent in the pot, the better they tasted. In the end, we preferred dark red kidney beans or black beans because both keep their shape better than light red kidney beans, the other common choice.

With our recipe basically complete, it was time to try some of those offbeat additions to the pot that other cooks swear by, including cocoa powder, ground coffee beans, raisins, chickpeas, mushrooms, olives, and lima beans. Our conclusion? Each of these ingredients was either weird tasting or too subtle to make much difference. Lime wedges, passed separately at the table, both brightened the flavor of the chili and accentuated the heat of the spices. Our chili was now done. Although simple, it is, we hope, good enough to silence any debate.

Beef Chili with Kidney Beans
SERVES 8 TO 10

Good choices for condiments include diced fresh tomatoes, diced avocado, sliced scallions, chopped red onion, chopped cilantro leaves, sour cream, and shredded Monterey Jack or cheddar cheese. If you are a fan of spicy food, consider using a little more of the red pepper flakes or cayenne—or both. The flavor of the chili improves with age; if possible, make it a day or up to 5 days in advance and reheat before serving. Leftovers can be frozen for up to a month.

2	tablespoons vegetable or corn oil
2	medium onions, chopped fine (about 2 cups)
1	medium red bell pepper, stemmed, seeded, and cut into 1/2-inch cubes
6	medium garlic cloves, minced or pressed through a garlic press (about 2 tablespoons)
1/4	cup chili powder
1	tablespoon ground cumin
2	teaspoons ground coriander

1   teaspoon red pepper flakes
1   teaspoon dried oregano
½   teaspoon cayenne pepper
2   pounds 85 percent lean ground beef
2   (15-ounce) cans dark red kidney beans,
    drained and rinsed
1   (28-ounce) can diced tomatoes
1   (28-ounce) can tomato puree
    Salt
    2 limes, cut into wedges

1. Heat the oil in a large Dutch oven over medium heat until shimmering but not smoking. Add the onions, bell pepper, garlic, chili powder, cumin, coriander, pepper flakes, oregano, and cayenne and cook, stirring occasionally, until the vegetables are softened and beginning to brown, about 10 minutes. Increase the heat to medium-high and add half the beef. Cook, breaking up the chunks with a wooden spoon, until no longer pink and just beginning to brown, 3 to 4 minutes. Add the remaining beef and cook, breaking up the chunks with the wooden spoon, until no longer pink, 3 to 4 minutes.

2. Add the beans, tomatoes, tomato puree, and ½ teaspoon salt. Bring to a boil, then reduce the heat to low and simmer, covered, stirring occasionally, for 1 hour. Remove the cover and continue to simmer 1 hour longer, stirring occasionally (if the chili begins to stick to the bottom of the pot, stir in ½ cup water and continue to simmer), until the beef is tender and the chili is dark, rich, and slightly thickened. Adjust the seasonings with additional salt to taste. Serve with the lime wedges and condiments (see note), if desired.

➤   VARIATION

Beef Chili with Bacon and Black Beans
Cut 8 ounces bacon (about 8 strips) into ½-inch pieces. Fry the bacon in a large Dutch oven over medium heat, stirring frequently, until browned, about 8 minutes. Pour off all but 2 tablespoons fat, leaving the bacon in the pot. Follow the recipe for Beef Chili with Kidney Beans, substituting the bacon fat in the Dutch oven for the vegetable oil and an equal amount of canned black beans, drained and rinsed, for the dark red kidney beans.

INDIAN CURRY

OUR GOAL IN CREATING A CURRY RECIPE was to translate the many dishes that earn this name (almost any Indian stew can be called a "curry") into a basic formula that could be easily adapted. In the process, we wanted to discover how to keep the flavors bright and clear. So many curries are dull and heavy-tasting.

Our usual resources were of little help. Cookbooks couldn't give us hands-on experience, explain why an ingredient was used this way in one recipe, that way in the next. Classic (that is, French) culinary training was worse than useless. Although we could pick out distinctly Indian cooking techniques, the food didn't seem to be inspired by technique. While a French (or any Western) stew follows a series of commands—brown, deglaze, emulsify—an Indian curry seemed to waft on the whim of the cook from one ethereal fragrance to the next.

Ultimately, we found our way into the kitchens of two extraordinarily gifted cooks in New York City, one Indian and one Pakistani. Their food defined two key elements of curry making. One was a mysterious, complex, and highly personal dance of spice, flavor, and fragrance that is the soul of the cuisine. The other was a simple, accessible technique that provided a structure within which we could dance. The marriage of these two elements resulted in a quick, elegant formula for curry, the mood of which can be endlessly varied by substituting ingredients and adjusting the form and quantity of spice.

To begin this quest, we studied a recipe for meat curry from a favorite Indian cookbook. The dish was essentially a meat stew, flavored with onion, garlic, fresh ginger, ground coriander, cumin, turmeric, and cayenne and simmered in water with chopped tomato. It used techniques familiar enough, following the predictable route of browning the meat, browning the onions, adding the spices, then cooking for a couple of hours with the liquid.

But looking in other books, we found similar meat curries that used less familiar techniques: Spices were added and cooked at different points depending on whether they were dry or wet, whole or ground, and the meat was added to the mixture partway through the cooking process with no preliminary browning. At a loss, we went to locate an Indian cook we could talk to.

We found Usha Cunningham, a Bombay-born home cook with no restaurant training. We laid out for her the two styles of curry we had found and asked her to cook a curry, in her own style, based on the ingredients in the meat curry recipe we had originally studied. Usha agreed but was a little hesitant about the recipe—it was such a plain dish, she said, like a plain roast chicken for an American; didn't we want her to show us something a bit more interesting? No, we assured her, we needed to start simple, to get our feet on the ground. Later, when we tasted her own cooking, we understood her reaction. Her food was astonishingly complex—bold, intense, and bright, each bite exploding in layers of distinct, individual tastes of sweet and sour, bitter, salty, and fragrant. When we had recovered sufficiently to ask her how she got this result, Usha shrugged and suggested that it might be in the way she used her spices—that is, with a heavy hand, as an Italian cook might use fresh herbs.

And so we began. She started work like a French chef, doing all her chopping and grinding first off; once we started cooking there would be no time for prep. And, as we pressed clove after clove of garlic through her press, it was clear that she did indeed flavor heavily: about one tablespoon each of ground coriander and cumin and pureed garlic and ginger per pound of meat, substantially more than the amounts used in the recipes we had found in cookbooks. Then Usha hit the stove.

First she heated a duet of whole spices—cinnamon and cloves—in hot oil until the cinnamon unfurled and the cloves popped. She explained that this step infused the oil with the fragrance of the spices, thus flavoring everything else that came in contact with the oil.

Next she added sliced onion and cooked it until translucent, just to evaporate out the moisture and set the sweetness. It was sliced, rather than pureed or chopped, she said, because slicing was easier. She explained that as a general rule she cooked onions translucent for a lighter-tasting sauce, such as the one we were making that day with tomatoes, or to a rich brown color for heavier sauces, such as those based on yogurt or bound by ground nuts.

The onions now cooked, she stirred in equal volumes of pureed garlic and ginger. Why pureed?

INGREDIENTS: Tomato Puree

In the family of canned tomato products, tomato puree is the neglected middle child, often overlooked in favor of its older sibling, whole peeled tomatoes, or its hotshot younger sibling, diced tomatoes. The reason is clear: While whole and diced tomatoes prove a passable substitute for fresh tomatoes (they are simply skinned and processed), tomato puree is cooked and strained, thereby removing all seeds and all allusions to freshness. That's not to say that tomato puree doesn't have a role in most kitchens, it's just that puree performs at best in long-cooked dishes where the thick, even texture of puree is important and fresh tomato flavor is not.

Although we haven't developed many recipes using tomato puree, we did find it to be necessary to achieve full tomato flavor and a smooth richness in our Beef Chili with Kidney Beans. But which brand is best? We gathered eight popular brands of tomato puree and tasted them plain. We then tasted the winner and loser of the plain tasting in our chili.

We had a tie in the straight puree tasting, with Progresso and

Hunt's sharing top honors. Hunts was praised for "layers of flavor," while Progresso won points for its "strong tomato flavor." Coming in last was Rienzi, unanimously criticized as too thin and watery, though a handful of tasters liked the "vegetal" flavor that one taster described as being like "wicked salty V-8."

For part two of our tasting, we pitted Progresso against Rienzi in our chili recipe. Although it was easy to judge the winners and losers of the straight puree tasting, we wondered how clear the differences would be once the puree had been simmered for two hours with a half dozen spices. The answer: not very clear. While some tasters found the batch made with Progresso "thicker" and "more full-flavored" and some found the batch made with Rienzi "slightly meatier" and "fresher and sweeter," most agreed with the taster who wrote, "I would use either one." Given that most recipes calling for tomato puree involve long cooking times and lots of ingredients, it's safe to say that using one particular brand over another is not going to make much of a difference in the final dish.

Usha maintained that chopping was Western. While every Indian household would have a grinding stone to grind spices daily, she pureed the garlic and ginger with a little water in an electric mini-chopper until smooth (see page 317) or pressed the garlic through a press. This choice was in part based on speed and convenience. In addition, experience had shown her that puree, with no surfaces to burn, cooked more evenly than a mince and melted into the sauce for a smooth finish. And because a puree is wet where a mince is dry, this method gave her a cushion against burning.

Now Usha added bone-in lamb shoulder to the pan (what, no preliminary browning?) and cooked it for about 10 minutes, stirring almost constantly, to evaporate all the moisture from the pan. As she stirred, she explained that the idea behind this traditional Indian technique was to release the flavors of the aromatic ingredients into the oil and cook them into the meat. If the meat were browned first, as in a French stew, the caramelized crust might inhibit the meat from absorbing the flavors.

Now we were ready to add the ground spices. Usha explained that she ground the coriander and cumin herself from whole seed for better flavor but contented herself with preground turmeric (a rhizome like ginger) and cayenne.

She mixed the ground dried spices with enough water to form a paste, then added the paste to the pan. Now she cooked, stirring, until enough moisture had been cooked out of the ingredients to allow the oil to separate out and pool around the clumps of meat, onion, and spice paste. This, Usha explained, was the secret to a well-made curry. The spices must fry in this hot oil, uninhibited by liquid, to release and develop their flavors. Once the final stewing liquid was added, the flavor of the spices would develop no further. (Spices may also be pan-roasted separately, ground, and then folded in at the end, but we will leave that option to another day.) Once the oil had separated, Usha turned the heat down and cooked everything for several more minutes.

The spices cooked, Usha finished the curry with lots of chopped tomato (no water) and a handful of dried fenugreek leaves. She didn't consider the fenugreek seeds to be right for this particular curry.

The leaves and seeds have different flavors, but their family resemblance is clear. Both are delicious with spinach, tomato, and sweet flavors.

We ate Usha's splendid curry with a pilaf of basmati rice, made with onion and whole spices. Usha showed us how to mash the curry and rice together with the tips of our fingers and then pop neat balls of the mixture into the mouth. (The less adventurous can mash with a fork as well.) The mashing opened up the flavors so effectively that the food had noticeably more flavor and fragrance than when eaten in the Western manner.

As we smelled the spices cooking in Usha's kitchen, we noticed that their fragrance had quite an effect on us. Whereas we like French food because it smells tasty in an earthy, comforting, body-satisfying way, we were entranced by Indian food because it was heady and dreamy. Sour, bitter, and sweet flavors that wouldn't appeal to us in French food (bitter fenugreek, for example) were exquisitely satisfying in Indian food.

We reasoned that it was this particular dreamy, foreign sensibility that Usha navigated while she cooked. (She herself described her experience in the kitchen as a sort of trance.) As we understood her, she improvised, associating to ingredients rather than building the dish within a formula so that she hardly knew at the beginning where she'd end up. Even the dishes we tasted from her refrigerator defied categorization. While her ethereal tomato-meat concoction was certainly a stew, such a term didn't begin to describe the experience of eating it. So even as we talked and cooked, we knew there was little hope of walking out of her kitchen with a formula that could map out such an intuitive journey. We took good notes and went back to our test kitchen.

We spent the next week or so cooking curries with Usha's approach. We tested her method against the technique used in the meat curry we had started out with and determined that Usha's method did infuse more flavor into the meat. With no browning in batches, it was easy, too. We also worked to educate our nose and palate to the taste and smell of properly cooked spices, tasting and smelling raw spices and noting how their acrid fragrance and flavor transformed and mellowed with frying (see page 317 for more information on the science of frying spices). We were getting very close; often our curries were delicious, but almost as often they came out heavy and muddy-tasting. We had no idea why.

As luck would have it, schedules and deadlines were such that we couldn't cook with Usha again. So we sought out another cook, this time a Pakistani woman named Samia Ahad, who had cooked extensively in New York restaurant kitchens and was trained in French cooking.

Samia's food defined the other end of the spectrum. While Usha's genius lay in the ecstatic dance of her bright, bold, and complex flavors, Samia's lay in the elegant and understated simplicity of the food. She used spices sparingly, particularly the dry ones, to produce in her curries a light, clean, aromatic, but everyday mood. Although the ingredients were the same, her curries were quite different from Usha's.

With Samia we found the cultural bridge we were looking for. Presumably, because her own restaurant work had required her to shuttle regularly between the cooking of two cultures, Samia had managed to translate the heady sensibility that inspired Usha's cuisine into a simple, accessible formula that invited endless variation. And she'd vastly condensed traditional technique as well.

Like Usha, Samia prepared all of her ingredients completely before cooking. Like Usha, she pureed garlic and ginger and sliced onion for convenience. She also ground her own cumin and coriander seed. However, she only used one third of Usha's liberal quantity of aromatics: about a teaspoon (rather than a tablespoon) of pureed garlic and ginger and ground coriander and cumin per pound of meat. Also like Usha, Samia started by frying sliced onion in oil until translucent. (And like Usha, she reserved browned onion for heavier sauces.)

Then, to our surprise, Samia added most of the rest of her ingredients: all of the spices she had prepared as well as a pound of boneless cubed meat, salt, and one half cup of chopped tomato. She cooked, stirring until the oil separated (about five minutes), and then cooked another 30 seconds to cook the spices completely. She explained, as had Usha, that this cooking of the spices was the heart of the dish.

Then she added two cups of water and a halved chile pepper (she liked the flavor of the fresh chile better than that of cayenne) and simmered until tender, about 40 minutes.

We asked Samia how she got away with condensing all the steps at the end. She explained that contrary to traditional technique, her experience was that as long as the oil separated, allowing the spices to fry in the oil for about 30 seconds, there was no need for the long cooking. She further explained that her formula could be used as the base for many, many flavor combinations. We could fry whole spices before adding onion, as Usha had done. We could add any number of cubed vegetables. We could cook beef, lamb, chicken, fish, or shrimp this way. We could reduce the recipe to its bare roots—a very simple stew of protein, onion, garlic, ginger, turmeric (for some reason she always uses turmeric, she said), and water—or embellish it with more spices, vegetables, or legumes.

We went back into the test kitchen and cooked a number of curries to test out what these two women had taught us.

First, we tested Usha's longer step-by-step cooking against Samia's condensed recipe and decided that, at least for this basic curry and for our taste buds, Samia's simplified method was as tasty, and far quicker. We also tried adding the tomato along with the water instead of reducing it with the spice; however, the reduced tomato in Samia's formula adds structure to the sauce, and we like the ease of adding everything at once.

We then tested a curry made with sliced onion against one made with chopped and found that slicing was vastly quicker. We also preferred the texture of the sauce with sliced onion.

We ran the same comparison between chopped and pureed ginger and garlic; not only was pureeing in a minichopper substantially easier than mincing, the wetness gave us a cushion against burning, just as Usha had explained.

Although up until now we had been cooking with bone-in lamb shoulder, we were sold on the ease of Samia's quicker-cooking boneless curries (40 minutes or fewer compared with 1½ to 2 hours), so we stuck to top sirloin and boneless leg of lamb.

We ran several experiments with spices: we compared a curry made with only ground spices with a curry using ground and whole spices. The comparison showed us that preground spices formed a kind of background wash; left whole, they came through as bright, individual flavors. (Thus, the cook can use the same spices to different effect.)

Then we cooked three curries to determine how long the combined ground spices needed to cook to develop their flavor: We tried 30 seconds, 5 minutes, and 10 minutes after the oil had separated. We found that 30 seconds was all it took. We also determined that the heavy, muddy taste of our early curries probably resulted from spices that had burned and turned bitter when they stuck to the bottom of the skillet. The spices were less likely to stick when cooked quickly, and the addition of yogurt or tomato obviated the need to make a paste.

Next we made a curry in which we added the stewing liquid before the oil had separated. Indeed, the curry tasted raw. Use your ear to help you recognize when the spices are frying in pure oil. The sound changes from the gentle sound of a simmer to the loud, staccato sound of frying.

Finally, we played around with the amount of spice. It seems that the quantity was more a matter of personal preference than of rule, more spice resulting in heavier flavor. For the master recipe that follows, we chose quantities that fell in between those given us by Usha and Samia simply because we liked that flavor. Precise quantities of wet spices are even less critical than of dry because their flavor is weaker, but we like equal quantities of garlic and ginger. In any event, the beauty of the formula is that it invites experimentation.

The master recipe that follows is largely the same as the one Samia demonstrated for us. As in standard French technique, it begins by heating the oil to provide a cooking medium. After that, however, it diverges completely from French style. Rather than browning the meat in the oil, we first sauté the whole spices, then the onions. The wet spices (ginger and garlic) are then added, along with the meat or fowl, and the moistening agent, either tomatoes or yogurt. All of these are cooked until the liquid evaporates, the oil separates, and

the spices begin to fry and become fully aromatic. Greens in the form of either spinach or cilantro are then added, along with water and chile peppers, and the whole is cooked until the meat is tender, at which point the vegetables are added and cooked until tender.

The ingredients in the recipe are completely interchangeable, depending on what result you're looking for. The whole spice combination (cinnamon, cloves, cardamom, peppercorns, and bay leaf) can be abbreviated to cinnamon and cloves or to cinnamon, cloves, and cardamom, if you like. The cumin and the coriander can also be used crushed, as in the Beef Curry with Crushed Spices and Channa Dal variation. Let yourself be drawn into the trance of the spices and improvise combinations from there.

Indian Curry
SERVES 4 TO 6

This recipe is a basic formula that can be altered in hundreds of ways, including omitting the whole spice blend. See the variations that follow for flavor combinations that work especially well. With all curries, gather and prepare all of your ingredients before you begin. Garlic and ginger may be pureed by hand or in a minichopper (see page 317). If pureeing by hand, use a garlic press, or mince the garlic and ginger with a knife on a cutting board, sprinkling with salt to break them down quite a bit. If using a minichopper, process the garlic and ginger with 1 to 2 tablespoons of water until pureed. You can substitute a scant ½ teaspoon cayenne pepper for the jalapeño, adding it to the skillet with the other ground dried spices. Feel free to increase the wet (garlic, ginger, onion, and jalapeño) or dry spice quantities. Serve the curry with basmati rice.

WHOLE SPICE BLEND

1 ½	(3-inch) cinnamon sticks
4	cloves
4	green cardamom pods
8	whole black peppercorns
1	bay leaf
¼	cup vegetable or canola oil
1	medium onion, sliced thin
4	large garlic cloves, pureed

1	(1 ½-inch) piece fresh ginger, peeled and pureed
1 ½	pounds top sirloin or boneless leg of lamb, trimmed and cut into ¾-inch cubes
2	teaspoons ground cumin
2	teaspoons ground coriander
1	teaspoon ground turmeric
½	teaspoon salt, plus more to taste
⅔	cup canned crushed tomatoes or ½ cup plain low-fat yogurt
2	bunches (1 ½ pounds) spinach, stemmed, thoroughly washed, and chopped coarse (optional)
1	cup chopped fresh cilantro leaves (optional)
2	cups water
1	jalapeño chile, stemmed and cut in half through the stem end
½	cup Indian split peas (channa dal), or 4 medium boiling potatoes, peeled and cut into ¾-inch dice, or 4 medium zucchini, cut into ½-inch dice, or 1 cup fresh or frozen green peas, thawed
2–4	tablespoons chopped fresh cilantro leaves (use the lesser amount if you've already added the optional cilantro)

1. If using, gather the ingredients for the whole spice blend in a small bowl. Heat the oil in a large deep skillet or sauté pan, preferably nonstick, over medium-high heat until hot but not smoking. If using the whole spice blend, add it to the oil and cook, stirring with a wooden spoon until the cinnamon stick unfurls and the cloves pop, about 5 seconds. Add the onion and sauté until softened, 3 to 4 minutes, or browned, 5 to 7 minutes, as desired. (If omitting whole spice blend, simply add the onion to the skillet and proceed with the recipe.)

2. Stir in the garlic, ginger, meat, ground spices, the ½ teaspoon salt, and tomatoes. Cook, stirring almost constantly, until the liquid evaporates, the oil separates and turns orange, and the spices begin to fry, 5 to 7 minutes. Continue to cook, stirring constantly, until the spices smell cooked, about 30 seconds longer.

3. Stir in the spinach and/or cilantro (if using). Add the water and the chile and season with salt to taste. Bring to a simmer, reduce the heat, cover, and simmer until the meat is almost tender, 30 to 40 minutes.

4. Add the vegetable of choice (except the green peas), cover, and cook until the vegetable and meat are tender, about 15 minutes. If using, add the peas and simmer 3 minutes more. Stir in the cilantro. Serve immediately, picking out and discarding the whole spices.

➤ VARIATIONS

Lamb Curry with Whole Spices
Yogurt creates a rich sauce in this recipe.

WHOLE SPICE BLEND

1 ½	(3-inch) cinnamon sticks
4	cloves
4	green cardamom pods
8	whole black peppercorns
1	bay leaf
¼	cup vegetable or canola oil
1	medium onion, sliced thin
4	large garlic cloves, pureed
1	(1 ½-inch) piece fresh ginger, peeled and pureed
1 ½	pounds boneless leg of lamb, trimmed and cut into ¾-inch dice
2	teaspoons ground cumin
2	teaspoons ground coriander
1	teaspoon ground turmeric
½	teaspoon salt, plus more to taste
½	cup plain low-fat yogurt
2	cups water
1	jalapeño chile, stemmed and cut in half through the stem end
4	medium red potatoes (about 1 ½ pounds), peeled and cut into ¾-inch dice
4	tablespoons chopped fresh cilantro leaves

1. Gather the ingredients for the whole spice blend in a small bowl. Heat the oil in a large deep skillet or sauté pan, preferably nonstick, over medium-high heat until hot but not smoking. Add the whole spice blend and cook, stirring with wooden spoon until the cinnamon stick unfurls and the cloves pop, about 5 seconds. Add the onion and sauté until softened, 3 to 4 minutes.

2. Stir in the garlic, ginger, lamb, ground spices, the ½ teaspoon salt, and yogurt. Cook, stirring almost constantly, until the liquid evaporates, the oil separates and turns orange, and the spices begin to fry, 5 to 7 minutes. Continue to cook, stirring constantly, until the spices smell cooked, about 30 seconds longer.

3. Add the water and chile and season with salt to taste. Bring to a simmer, reduce the heat, cover, and simmer until the meat is almost tender, 30 to 40 minutes.

4. Add the potatoes, cover, and cook until the potatoes and lamb are tender, about 15 minutes. Stir in the cilantro. Serve immediately, picking out and discarding the whole spices.

Lamb Curry with Figs and Fenugreek

The tomatoes and figs add a touch of sweetness to this recipe.

¼	cup vegetable or canola oil
I	medium onion, sliced thin
4	large garlic cloves, pureed
I	(1 ½-inch) piece fresh ginger, peeled and pureed
I ½	pounds boneless leg of lamb, trimmed and cut into ¾-inch cubes
2	teaspoons ground cumin
2	teaspoons ground coriander
I	teaspoon ground turmeric
½	teaspoon fenugreek leaves
½	teaspoon salt, plus more to taste
⅔	cup canned crushed tomatoes
2	cups water
I	jalapeño chile, stemmed and cut in half through the stem end
¼	cup dried figs, chopped coarse
4	tablespoons chopped fresh cilantro leaves

1. Heat the oil in a large deep skillet or sauté pan, preferably nonstick, over medium-high heat until hot but not smoking. Add the onion and sauté until softened, 3 to 4 minutes.

2. Stir in the garlic, ginger, lamb, ground spices, fenugreek, the ½ teaspoon salt, and tomatoes. Cook, stirring almost constantly, until the liquid evaporates, the oil separates and turns orange, and

the spices begin to fry, 5 to 7 minutes. Continue to cook, stirring constantly, until the spices smell cooked, about 30 seconds longer.

3. Add the water, chile, and figs and season with salt to taste. Bring to a simmer, reduce the heat, cover, and simmer until the meat is tender, 40 to 50 minutes. Stir in the cilantro. Serve immediately.

Beef Curry with Crushed Spices and Channa Dal

Channa dal is the name for yellow Indian split peas, available at Indian specialty food shops. Peeled, diced potatoes or regular green split peas may be substituted for the channa dal.

2	teaspoons whole coriander seeds
I	teaspoon cumin seeds
¼	cup vegetable or canola oil
I	medium onion, sliced thin
4	large garlic cloves, pureed
I	(1 ½-inch) piece fresh ginger, peeled and pureed
I ½	pounds top sirloin, trimmed and cut into ¾-inch cubes
I	teaspoon ground turmeric
½	teaspoon salt, plus more to taste
⅔	cup canned crushed tomatoes
2	cups water
I	jalapeño chile, stemmed and cut in half through the stem end
½	cup yellow Indian split peas (channa dal)
4	tablespoons chopped fresh cilantro leaves

1. Crush the coriander and cumin seeds in a mortar and pestle. Heat the oil in a large deep skillet or sauté pan, preferably nonstick, over medium-high heat until hot but not smoking. Add the coriander and cumin and cook, stirring with a wooden spoon, until fragrant, less than 5 seconds. Add the onion and sauté until softened, 3 to 4 minutes.

2. Stir in the garlic, ginger, beef, turmeric, the ½ teaspoon salt, and tomatoes. Cook, stirring almost constantly, until the liquid evaporates, the oil separates and turns orange, and the spices begin to fry, 5 to 7 minutes. Continue to cook, stirring constantly, until the spices smell cooked, about 30 seconds longer.

3. Add the water and chile and season with salt to taste. Bring to a simmer, reduce the heat, cover, and simmer until the meat is almost tender, 30 to 40 minutes.

4. Add the split peas, cover, and cook until the split peas and beef are tender, about 15 minutes. Stir in the cilantro. Serve immediately.

THAI CURRY

LIKE MOST THAI FOOD, THAI CURRIES embrace a delicate balance of tastes, textures, temperatures, and color that come together to create a harmonious whole. Thai curries (basically any spicy stew is called a curry in Thailand) are considered signature dishes of this cuisine. Thai curries have their antecedents in India. As with their Indian counterparts, the spices and liquid are simmered together to create a sauce, to which the protein and vegetables are added. There's no browning of meat or deglazing of pans. However, there are several major differences between Indian and Thai curries.

Thai curries almost always contain coconut milk, which not only blends and carries flavors but also forms the backbone of the sauce. While Indian curries rely on a mixture of ground spices and fresh aromatics (like ginger and garlic), the balance is tilted toward the fresh aromatics when making Thai curries. The aromatics are added in the form of a paste, which generally consists of garlic, ginger, shallots, and chiles. These pastes can be quite involved and may require an hour of preparation. The curries themselves come together rather quickly and simmer gently for far less time than Indian curries.

With these differences in mind, we set out to explore red curry paste, which is mostly commonly paired with meat. Our work was divided into three neat areas: developing recipes for the paste; cooking the paste to draw out its flavor (this would involve combining the paste with the other seasonings, such as coconut milk and fish sauce); and incorporating the meat and vegetables into the curry. We started with the paste.

Traditionally, ingredients for Thai curry pastes are pounded together in a mortar and pestle until smooth. Since this process can take up to an hour and requires a tool most American cooks don't own, we wanted to develop a paste recipe that could be assembled by other means. We tested a blender, food processor, and minichopper.

With its narrow base, a blender isn't the best tool for this job. The lack of liquid in the curry paste also presents a problem. Large chunks just sat on top of each other as the blade of the blender went round and round. We tried adding a little oil or water to help mix the ingredients, but this didn't work.

The food processor—though not perfect—did a much better job. You must make a lot of curry paste (two cups, enough for four curry recipes) when using the food processor. (Curry paste holds for a long time, so there's some logic to buying and preparing ingredients once and then enjoying curry on four different occasions.) With smaller batches, the blade simply wouldn't engage the ingredients. Even with more ingredients in the workbowl, we

EQUIPMENT: Minichopper
We spent a lot of time mincing and then pressing garlic and grating ginger until we gave in and bought a Cuisinart Mini-Mate Plus Chopper/Grinder. Although this machine would seem to be a luxury, it makes readying the ingredients for curries so much easier that it may make the difference, over time, between cooking them or not.

The motor and blade in the minichopper can handle garlic, ginger, and herbs, but don't expect much else. Don't try Parmesan cheese or nuts: They must be ground in the regular-size processor.

SCIENCE: Frying Spices
Why does an authentically prepared curry require that the spices in it be fried in oil or pan-roasted (as opposed to stewed, which leaves them tasting raw)? The answer is heat, which causes a madhouse of chemical reactions in foods, including spices. With high heat, the chemicals in the spices break down and re-form into totally different compounds with new tastes and aromas. Simmering in a liquid, a spice can be heated to a maximum temperature of 212 degrees. Oil, however, can heat the spices to more than 400 degrees and, depending on the metal, a dry skillet can get even hotter than that.

found that a little oil, or better yet, coconut cream, was needed to help bring the ingredients together. We also had the best results when we minced or cut the aromatics fairly small before adding them to the food processor. Although this increased the prep time, it yielded a better sauce. Note, though, that curry paste prepared in a food processor will be a tad grainy, not silky smooth like one ground in a mortar and pestle.

In further testing, we found that a minichopper works just as well as a food processor. Owing to its smaller bowl size, the minichopper will produce

MINCING LEMON GRASS

Because of its tough outer leaves, lemon grass can be difficult to mince. We like this method, which relies on a sharp knife.

1. Trim off all but the bottom 3 to 4 inches of the lemon grass stalk.

2. Remove the tough outer sheath from the trimmed lemon grass. If the lemon grass is particularly thick or tough, you may need to remove several layers to reveal the tender inner portion of the stalk.

3. Cut the trimmed and peeled lemon grass in half lengthwise, then mince fine.

about half as much curry paste as the food processor—enough for two of our curry recipes, not four.

It was time to test the ingredients themselves. Red curry paste relies on equal parts shallots, garlic and ginger and, of course, the chiles. Traditional recipes call for dried red chiles, soaked in hot water until softened. We found that pastes made with dried chiles alone were too thin and lacked proper body. A combination of soaked dried chiles and fresh red jalapeños provided the right combination of flavor and body. We found that any hot, small dried red chile will work in our recipe. Dried red Thai chiles, sometimes called bird chiles, are traditional, but japónes and de árbol chiles are equally hot and equally delicious.

Happy with our chile paste, we shifted gears and started to test ways to cook it. Our goal was to figure out the best way to unlock the flavors of the paste. Given our experience with Indian curry (see Frying Spices on page 317), we figured that frying the curry paste in fat would be key.

In our research, we ran across three different methods for cooking the curry paste—sautéing in oil, simmering in coconut milk, or cooking with the thick coconut cream that floats to the top of cans of coconut milk.

For our first test, we sautéed curry paste in peanut oil and then added the coconut milk. The aroma was good, but the sauce seemed thin and not as flavorful as we wanted. For our second test, we stirred curry paste into coconut milk and then brought the mixture to a simmer and let it cook until it thickened considerably. The flavors were subdued in this version, and the curry lacked the lustrous sheen we had come to expect. For our last test, we spooned off 1 cup of thick coconut cream from the top of a can of coconut milk. We mixed this cream with curry paste in a pan and then turned on the heat. After an average of 10 minutes, the fat in the coconut cream separated out and the paste began to fry in the oil. We let the curry paste fry in the oil until it was very aromatic, a process that took just one to two minutes. We added the remaining liquid ingredients, following with the protein and vegetables. The finished curry was thick and flavorful, with a glorious sheen.

Cooking the moisture out of the coconut cream is a somewhat magical process. At first the cream is bubbling away, but then it begins to separate into a solid mass that comes together like soft dough and a liquid oil (the color of the curry paste) emerges. Listen for the change that takes place as the gentle sound of liquid simmering becomes the louder, more staccato sound of oil frying.

The fat separates from the solids in the coconut cream at different rates, depending on the thickness of the coconut cream, how much is being cooked, and the amount of moisture in the curry paste. The thicker the cream, or the more cream in the pan, the longer the process takes. Dry store-bought curry pastes will speed up the process, while moist homemade pastes will slow it down.

Once the coconut oil separates out from the cream, the curry paste need only fry in the oil for a minute or two. The remaining coconut milk, fish sauce, and brown sugar (tasters found that this ingredient tempered the heat of the chiles better than granulated white sugar) are then added to the pot. We found that simmering the sauce for five minutes allowed the flavors to blend.

At this point, the meat and vegetables are added to the abundant liquid and cooked directly in the sauce. Aside from gauging the timing so that slow-cooking items, such as potatoes, go into the pot before quick-cooking items, such as snow peas, the process is very simple. Once the meat and vegetables are cooked, a final garnish of fresh herbs (we found that a combination of basil and mint best approximates the flavor of Thai basil) finishes the dish.

Thai curries are saucy and hot and require a nice cushion from rice. Jasmine rice is the most traditional option, but regular long-grain rice works fine. Rice noodles are another good idea. A pickled vegetable or cucumber relish will round out the meal.

INGREDIENTS: Lemon Grass

Visually akin to a scallion but longer, pale yellow-green in color, and extremely fibrous, lemon grass is an integral part of Southeast Asian cooking. It imparts a rich, ethereal, lemony essence not easily mimicked by lemon zest. Although even the woody upper portion of the stalk can be used, most often it is trimmed to the lower third, the tough outer leaves stripped away, and the soft inner core chopped or minced. If it is eventually to be removed, as in a broth, the stalk—leaves and all—can simply be bruised and used as is.

Fresh lemon grass is a staple in many Asian grocery stores, but it is not otherwise widely available. We did find it in both dried and water-packed form at our local grocer, however, and decided to investigate. We cooked them in broths and compared them with broths made with fresh lemon grass and lemon zest. Here are our findings.

Fresh lemon grass was the most aromatic, infusing the broth with a delicate, lemony freshness that made it the clear favorite. The next best was the water-packed lemon grass. Although it lacked the crispness and clarity of fresh, this version still maintained lemon grass characteristics. Grated lemon zest finished a remote third. Better zest than dried lemon grass, though. While the broth made with lemon zest was flat and one-dimensional compared with those made with fresh or water-packed lemon grass, it was still, at the very least, lemony. Dried lemon grass was the dog, with a dull, "off" herbal quality; the broth made with it lacked not only freshness but any lemon flavor.

Red Curry Paste
MAKES ABOUT 2 CUPS, ENOUGH TO PREPARE 4 CURRIES

Dried red chiles are traditionally used, but we found a combination of dried and fresh red chiles created a better texture. Red curry is delicious paired with beef and pork as well duck, chicken, and all types of seafood. This recipe is designed to be prepared in a food processor. Cut the quantities in half if using a minichopper. See the illustrations on page 318 for tips on handling lemon grass.

1/2   ounce dried small red chiles (Thai, japónes, or de árbol), stems snapped off, chiles broken in half, and seeds shaken out (about 1/2 cup)

20   medium garlic cloves, pressed through a garlic press or minced very fine (scant 1/2 cup)

1   teaspoon salt

2   tablespoons minced cilantro stems

2   tablespoons ground coriander

2   teaspoons ground cumin

1/2   teaspoon ground black pepper

4   large or 6 medium fresh red jalapeño chiles, stemmed, seeded, and chopped coarse (about 3/4 cup)

3   tablespoons minced fresh ginger

3–4 stalks lemon grass, outer sheath removed, bottom 3 inches trimmed and minced (about ½ cup)

4 teaspoons minced lime zest from 4 limes

1 small shallot, chopped coarse (about 3 tablespoons)

½ teaspoon shrimp paste or anchovy paste (optional)

2 tablespoons coconut cream or peanut or canola oil

1. Place the dried red chiles in a small bowl and pour hot water over to cover. Let stand until soft and rehydrated, about 30 minutes. Remove the chiles, discarding the liquid. Dry the chiles with paper towels.

2. Place all of the remaining ingredients in the workbowl of a food processor fitted with the steel blade and pulse 10 times, each pulse lasting 4 to 5 seconds; stop and use a spatula to push down the ingredients every few pulses. Once the ingredients begin to form a paste, process until smooth, stopping occasionally to push down the ingredients, about 3 minutes. Store in a covered glass container or bowl in the refrigerator for up to 1 month or in the freezer for several months. (If freezing, divide the curry paste into ½-cup amounts, so that one portion can be used for one curry recipe; freeze individually.)

Thai Curry

SERVES 4

This is more of a formula than a specific recipe. See the variations for combinations of meat and vegetables that we especially like. Adding the optional fresh chile will increase the heat. If you prefer milder food, reduce the amount of curry paste as desired. If you can find it, replace the basil and mint with 1 cup of Thai basil. Serve all Thai curries with jasmine rice or rice noodles.

2 (14-ounce) cans coconut milk, not shaken

½ cup Red Curry Paste (page 319) or 2 tablespoons store-bought

2 tablespoons fish sauce

2 tablespoons brown sugar

1 ½ pounds sliced meat Salt

5 cups sliced or chopped vegetables

1 fresh hot chile, stemmed, seeded, and quartered lengthwise (optional)

1 tablespoon lime juice from 1 lime

½ cup whole fresh basil leaves

½ cup whole fresh mint leaves

1. Carefully spoon off about 1 cup of the top layer of coconut cream from one can—this layer will be thick and possibly solid. Place the coconut cream and curry paste in a large Dutch oven and bring to a boil over high heat, whisking to blend, about 2 minutes. Maintain this brisk simmer and whisk frequently until almost all of the liquid evaporates, 3 to 5 minutes. Reduce the heat to medium-high and whisk constantly until the cream separates into a puddle of colored oil and coconut solids, 3 to 8 minutes. (You should hear the curry paste starting to fry in the oil.) Continue cooking until the curry paste is very aromatic, 1 to 2 minutes.

2. Whisk in the remaining coconut milk, fish sauce, and brown sugar. Bring back to a brisk simmer and cook until the flavors meld and the sauce thickens, about 5 minutes. Season the meat with salt to taste and stir it into the pot until the pieces separate and are evenly coated with the sauce, about 1 minute. Add long-cooking vegetables, such as eggplant, potatoes, and broccoli, and the fresh chile, if using, and simmer for several

INGREDIENTS: Coconut Milk

Coconut milk is an essential ingredient in Thai curries. We wondered if it mattered which brand we chose, so we went to a local Asian market and purchased several brands recommended in Southeast Asian cookbooks, including Chao Koh and Mae Ploy. We also purchased Thai Kitchen, Kame, and A Taste of Thai brands, all of which are sold in supermarkets and natural foods stores. With one exception, we found that all of these brands had a nice thick layer of solid coconut cream on top. The only brand we don't recommend is A Taste of Thai. The coconut cream in this can was not solid (the texture was akin to crème fraîche) and less plentiful—two-thirds cup, not the three quarters to one full cup of thick, almost solid cream we found in other cans the same size.

minutes. Add quick-cooking vegetables, such as bell peppers, snow peas, bamboo shoots, and mushrooms, and the fresh chile, if using, and continue to simmer until the meat and vegetables are cooked. (The total cooking time once the protein is added will range from 7 to 15 minutes.) Off heat, stir in the lime juice, basil, and mint. Serve immediately.

➤ VARIATIONS

Red Curry with Beef and Eggplant

This classic Thai curry is rich in flavors, textures, and colors. If the curry paste is purchased or prepared ahead of time, total cooking time is fewer than 30 minutes. Freeze the beef for 15 minutes to make it easier to cut.

2   (14-ounce) cans coconut milk, not shaken
1/2   cup Red Curry Paste (page 319) or
      2 tablespoons store-bought
2   tablespoons fish sauce
2   tablespoons brown sugar
1 1/2   pounds flank or skirt steak, trimmed of excess fat and sliced thin across the grain (see the illustrations on page 138)
      Salt
2   small eggplants (about 8 ounces total), halved lengthwise and sliced crosswise on diagonal into 1/4-inch-thick pieces (about 3 cups)
1   (8-ounce) can bamboo shoots, drained and rinsed

INGREDIENTS: Store-Bought Curry Pastes

In Thailand, many cooks rely on curry pastes purchased at food markets or in small shops. In the United States, supermarket shoppers may see small jars of Thai curry paste. How do store-bought pastes compare with homemade? We purchased red Thai Kitchen paste at the supermarket and several other brands at a local Asian market. All of these store-bought curry pastes were more potent than our homemade versions, so you must use far less. We found that all of the brands tested, including Thai Kitchen, which is nationally available, made good curries. The flavors were not as full as the recipes made with our homemade pastes, but the time saved is significant. So if you see Thai Kitchen curry paste in the supermarket, don't hesitate to buy this product and use it.

1   medium red bell pepper, stemmed, seeded, and cut into thin strips
1   fresh hot chile, stemmed, seeded, and quartered lengthwise (optional)
1   tablespoon lime juice from 1 lime
1/2   cup whole fresh basil leaves
1/2   cup whole fresh mint leaves

1. Carefully spoon off about 1 cup of the top layer of coconut cream from one can—this layer will be thick and possibly solid. Place the coconut cream and curry paste in a large Dutch oven and bring to a boil over high heat, whisking to blend, about 2 minutes. Maintain this brisk simmer and whisk frequently until almost all of the liquid evaporates, 3 to 5 minutes. Reduce the heat to medium-high and whisk constantly until the cream separates into a puddle of colored oil and coconut solids, 3 to 8 minutes. (You should hear the curry paste starting to fry in the oil.) Continue cooking until the curry paste is very aromatic, 1 to 2 minutes.

2. Whisk in the remaining coconut milk, fish sauce, and brown sugar. Bring back to a brisk simmer and cook until the flavors meld and the sauce thickens, about 5 minutes. Season the beef with salt to taste and stir it into the pot until the pieces separate and are evenly coated with the sauce, about 1 minute. Stir in the eggplant and bring to a brisk simmer over medium heat. Cook until the eggplant is almost tender, about 10 minutes. Stir in the bamboo shoots, bell pepper, and fresh chile, if using, and cook until the vegetables are crisp-tender, about 2 minutes. Off heat, stir in the lime juice, basil, and mint. Serve immediately.

Red Curry with Pork and Pineapple

Fiery red curry paste is delectable with pork and sweet pineapple. Red peppers and snow peas add some crunch and bright color to this classic combination. See the illustrations on page 405 for tips on preparing the pineapple.

2   (14-ounce) cans coconut milk, not shaken
1/2   cup Red Curry Paste (page 319) or
      2 tablespoons store-bought
2   tablespoons fish sauce
2   tablespoons brown sugar

1   large pork tenderloin (1 1/4 to 1 1/2 pounds),
    cut into thin strips (see the illustrations on
    page 141)
    Salt
3   cups pineapple chunks (1-inch cubes)
4   ounces snow peas, trimmed
1   medium red bell pepper, stemmed, seeded,
    and cut into thin strips
1   fresh hot chile, stemmed, seeded, and
    quartered lengthwise (optional)
1   tablespoon lime juice from 1 lime
1/2 cup whole fresh basil leaves
1/2 cup whole fresh mint leaves

1. Carefully spoon off about 1 cup of the top layer of coconut cream from one can—this layer will be thick and possibly solid. Place the coconut cream and curry paste in a large Dutch oven and bring to a boil over high heat, whisking to blend, about 2 minutes. Maintain this brisk simmer and whisk frequently until almost all of the liquid evaporates, 3 to 5 minutes. Reduce the heat to medium-high and whisk constantly until the cream separates into a puddle of colored oil and coconut solids, 3 to 8 minutes. (You should hear the curry paste starting to fry in the oil.) Continue cooking until the curry paste is very aromatic, 1 to 2 minutes.

2. Whisk in the remaining coconut milk, fish sauce, and sugar. Bring back to a brisk simmer and cook until the flavors meld and the sauce thickens, about 5 minutes. Season the pork with salt to taste and stir the pork and pineapple into the pot until the pieces separate and are evenly coated with the sauce, about 1 minute. Bring back to a brisk simmer over medium heat. Cook until the pork is almost done, about 4 minutes. Stir in the snow peas, bell pepper, and fresh chile, if using, and cook until the vegetables are crisp-tender, about 2 minutes. Off heat, stir in the lime juice, basil, and mint. Serve immediately.

13

I WANT TO BARBECUE SOMETHING SMOKY

I Want to Barbecue Something Smoky

BARBECUE IS THE TRADITIONAL LOW-AND-slow cooking method used with ribs of all kind, pulled pork (shredded Boston butt), and brisket. Because the goal is to impart as much smoke flavor as possible, a long cooking time over a relatively low fire is required. Barbecuing also provides ample time for fatty, tough cuts to become tender and palatable. To read more about barbecuing on both charcoal and gas grills, see pages 34 to 35.

BARBECUED SPARERIBS

WHEN PEOPLE USE THE WORDS "RIBS" AND "barbecue" in the same sentence, they are usually talking about pork spareribs. We wanted to know whether it is possible to produce authentic ribs (the kind you get at a barbecue joint) at home.

We started our tests by cooking one slab of ribs over indirect heat (the ribs on one side of the grill, the coals on the other), parboiling and then grilling another slab over direct heat, and cooking a third on our grill's rotisserie attachment (although reluctant to use this unusual bit of equipment, we thought, in the name of science, that we should give it a shot). All three tests were conducted over charcoal with hickory chips in a covered grill.

The ribs cooked over indirect heat were the hands-down favorite. Those cooked on the rotisserie were not nearly as tender, and the parboiled ribs retained the unappealing flavor of boiled meat. While the indirect method needed some refinement, we were convinced that it is the best way to cook ribs at home. It also comes closest to replicating the method used by barbecue-pit masters.

We tested a number of popular techniques for barbecuing ribs. Some experts swear by placing a source of moisture in the grill, most often an aluminum pan filled with water or beer. We filled a pan with water and put it next to the coals to create some steam. We couldn't taste the difference between the ribs cooked with and without the water. Next, we tested turning and basting. We found that for the even melting of the fat, it is best to turn ribs every half hour. Turning also ensures even cooking. It's important, though, to work as quickly as possible when turning the ribs to conserve heat in the grill.

Basting proved to be a bust. Tomato-based sauces burned over the long cooking time, and we didn't find the basted meat any more moist than meat that wasn't basted.

Under normal weather conditions, we found the ribs were done in two to three hours. Signs of doneness include the meat starting to pull away from the ribs (if you grab one end of an individual rib bone and twist it, the bone will actually turn a bit and separate from the meat) and a distinct rosy glow on the exterior. Because the ribs do not require an extended cooking time, there is no need to replenish the coals. A fire that starts out at 350 degrees will drop to around 250 degrees at the end of two hours.

At this point in our testing, we had produced good ribs, but they were not quite as moist and tender as some restaurant ribs. We spoke with several pit masters, and they suggested wrapping the ribs when they come off the grill. We wrapped the ribs in foil and then placed them in a brown paper bag to trap any escaping steam. After an hour, we unwrapped the ribs and couldn't believe the difference. The flavor, which was great straight off the grill, was the same, but the texture was markedly improved. The meat on the wrapped ribs literally fell off the bone.

We spoke with several food scientists, who explained that as the ribs rest, the juices redistribute throughout the meat, making the ribs more moist and tender. In fact, these ribs are so flavorful and tender that we consider sauce optional.

Barbecued Spareribs on a Charcoal Grill

SERVES 4

Hickory is the traditional wood choice with ribs, but some of our tasters liked mesquite as well. If you like, serve the ribs with barbecue sauce, but they are delicious as is. You will need a fair amount of heavy-duty aluminum foil and a brown paper grocery bag for this recipe.

2	full racks spareribs (about 6 pounds total)
¾	cup Dry Rub for Barbecue (page 397)
2	(3-inch) wood chunks or 2 cups wood chips
2	cups barbecue sauce (see pages 398–401), optional

1. Rub both sides of the ribs with the dry rub and let stand at room temperature for 1 hour. (For stronger flavor, wrap the rubbed ribs in a double layer of plastic wrap and refrigerate for up to 1 day.)

2. Soak the wood chunks in cold water to cover for 1 hour and drain, or place the wood chips on an 18-inch square of aluminum foil, seal to make a packet, and use a fork to create about 6 holes to allow smoke to escape (see the illustrations on page 35).

3. Meanwhile, light a large chimney filled a bit less than halfway with charcoal briquettes (about 2½ quarts or 40 coals) and allow to burn until covered with a thin layer of gray ash. Empty the coals into one side of the grill, piling them up in a mound 2 or 3 briquettes high. Keep the bottom vents completely open. Place the wood chunks or the packet with the chips on top of the charcoal. Put the cooking grate in place, open the grill lid vents completely, and cover, turning the lid so that the vents are opposite the wood chunks or chips to draw smoke through the grill. Let the grate heat for 5 minutes and clean it with a wire brush.

4. Position the ribs over the cool part of the grill. Barbecue, turning the ribs every 30 minutes, until the meat starts to pull away from the bones and has a rosy glow on the exterior, 2 to 3 hours. (The initial temperature inside the grill will be about 350 degrees; it will drop to 250 degrees after 2 hours.)

5. Remove the ribs from the grill and wrap each

slab completely in aluminum foil. Put the foil-wrapped slabs in a brown paper bag and crimp the top of the bag to seal tightly. Allow to rest at room temperature for 1 hour.

6. Unwrap the ribs and brush with the barbecue sauce, if desired (or serve with the sauce on the side). Cut the ribs between the bones and serve immediately.

➤ VARIATIONS

Barbecued Spareribs on a Gas Grill

If working with a small grill, cook the second slab of ribs on the warming rack.

Follow the recipe for Barbecued Spareribs on a Charcoal Grill through step 1. Soak 2 cups wood chips for 15 minutes in a bowl of water to cover. Place the wood chips in a foil tray (see the illustrations on page 35). Place the foil tray with the soaked wood chips on top of the primary burner (see the illustration on page 35). Turn all burners to high and preheat with the lid down until the chips are smoking heavily, about 20 minutes. Scrape the grate clean with a wire brush. Turn the primary burner down to medium and turn off the other burner(s). Position the ribs over the cool part of the grill and close the lid. Barbecue, turning the ribs every 30 minutes, until the meat starts to pull away from the bones and has a rosy glow on the exterior, 2 to 3 hours. (The temperature inside the grill should be a constant 275 degrees; adjust the lit burner as necessary.) Proceed with the recipe from step 5, wrapping and resting the ribs as directed.

Barbecued Spareribs with Hoisin, Honey, and Ginger Glaze

A combination of ground Szechuan and white peppercorns and coriander gives these ribs a complex peppery flavor. Use a spice grinder or coffee grinder to grind the peppercorns.

Mix 1½ tablespoons ground Szechuan peppercorns, 4 teaspoons ground white peppercorns, and 1½ teaspoons ground coriander together in a small bowl. Follow the recipe for Barbecued Spareribs (charcoal or gas), replacing the Dry Rub for Barbecue with the Szechuan peppercorn mixture. Grill as directed. When the meat starts to pull away from the bones, brush the ribs with ½ cup Hoisin,

THREE KINDS OF PORK RIBS

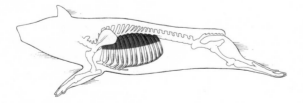

Baby back ribs (sometimes called back ribs or loin back ribs) come from the section of the rib cage closest to the backbone (the shaded area). Lean center-cut roasts and chops come from the same part of the pig, which explains why baby back ribs can be expensive and are prone to drying out when cooked. Spareribs are closer to the belly (just below the shaded area), which is also where bacon comes from. Spareribs are larger and fattier than baby back ribs. Meaty country-style ribs are cut from various parts of the pig and are usually cut into individual pieces before being packaged. Since these ribs are generally not sold in slabs we do not barbecue them.

Honey, and Ginger Glaze (page 401) and barbecue for another 15 minutes. Wrap and let the ribs rest as directed. Serve with more Hoisin, Honey, and Ginger Glaze, passed separately at the table. (Omit the barbecue sauce.)

Barbecued Spareribs with Mexican Flavors

Barbecue Sauce with Mexican Flavors (page 399) is ideal to serve with this recipe, although any barbecue sauce will taste fine.

Mix 2 tablespoons chili powder, 2 tablespoons ground cumin, 2 tablespoons dried oregano, 4 teaspoons ground coriander, 1 tablespoon salt, 2 teaspoons ground cinnamon, 2 teaspoons brown sugar, 2 teaspoons ground black pepper, and ¼ teaspoon ground cloves together in a medium bowl. Follow the recipe for Barbecued Spareribs (charcoal or gas), replacing the Dry Rub for Barbecue with the chili powder mixture. Grill, wrap, and rest the ribs as directed. Serve with a barbecue sauce of choice.

Oven-Roasted Ribs

BARBECUED SPARERIBS STRIKE A PRIMITIVE chord deep within all of us, excluding perhaps the most ardent vegetarian (although we suspect they have secret longings). The sweet and spicy crust and smoky, lush meat tempts us as few foods do. But we are the first to admit that hauling out the grill and stoking the slow fire necessary for sublime ribs can be inconvenient. And forget about barbecuing ribs during the winter in many parts of the country. Is there another way to achieve such bliss?

Most oven-roasted rib recipes we have tried turned out tough, stringy, and relatively flavorless meat, completely devoid of all the merits of barbecued ribs. Driven by the haunting flavor of great ribs, we thought we might create a recipe for oven-roasted spareribs that placed a close second to our barbecued ribs.

For the meat, there was little choice in the matter. Plain-old spareribs provided the best flavor and were the most economical. Two slabs of spareribs,

---

EQUIPMENT: Wood Chips and Chunks

Charcoal itself has some flavor (gas adds none), but the real smoky flavor of good ribs or brisket comes from wood chunks or chips. Chips will work on either a charcoal or gas grill, but chunks are suited to charcoal fires only, since to work they must rest in a pile of lit coals. (If placed on the bottom of a gas grill they will not get hot enough to smoke.)

Chips and chunks come from the same source—trees. The only difference between them is size. Chunks are usually the size of lemons or small oranges; chips are thinner shards, more like the fine wood chips you might spread over a garden bed.

Wood chips and chunks are made from hardwoods because they burn more slowly than softer woods. The most common choices are hickory, mesquite, and alder, although some stores may carry cherry or oak. Resinous woods, like pine, are not used for grilling because they give foods an off flavor.

Hickory is the most traditional wood used for outdoor cooking, but mesquite and oak have their advocates. In our tests, we found that any hardwood chunks or chips can be used. Frankly, the differences in flavor are minimal, especially if the food has been coated with spices.

Is there a difference in the results you get when using wood chunks versus wood chips? To find out, we tested the same amount by weight (eight ounces) of wood chips and wood chunks under the same conditions in a charcoal fire to see if one performed better than the other when barbecuing Boston butt to make pulled pork.

The wood chips were placed in a heavy-duty foil packet cut with holes that allow the smoke to escape and fill the grill, while the wood chunks were soaked for an hour and then drained. Each was then placed in a separate grill directly on top of 40 ignited coals. On each grill the lid was closed, the lid vents were opened halfway, and all other vents were left completely opened. The chips smoked for 30 to 35 minutes, while the chunks smoked twice as long, for one hour. As it turned out, the exposure to smoke for more than twice the amount of time had given the pork barbecued with wood chunks a greater concentration of smoky, grilled flavor than the pork cooked using the wood chips.

If you have a choice between wood chips and wood chunks, use the wood chunks. They deliver more smoky flavor. If you don't have a choice and must use wood chips, they make a perfectly acceptable substitute for chunks. You may even find them preferable if you prefer a lighter smoke flavor in your grill-roasted and barbecued food. For detailed instructions about using wood chunks and chips, see page 35.

about three pounds each, was enough to feed four people abundantly, and both slabs fit in the oven on one rack. We found that the meat needed little preparation outside of trimming any excessive fat.

One of the pluses of cooking ribs indoors is that the only equipment necessary is a pan in which to cook them. After roasting several batches of ribs in roasting pans and on baking sheets, we favored suspending the ribs on a sturdy flat rack over a shallow baking sheet so that no part of the meat would rest in the rendered fat. The baking sheet also allowed for the best circulation of heat.

To flavor the meat, we employed our Dry Rub for Barbecue (page 397). We found that the ribs needed to sit for a minimum of an hour coated in the rub for the spices to penetrate the meat. Refrigerating the spice-rubbed ribs overnight gave the meat the best flavor. If you can plan ahead, letting the rubbed meat rest in the refrigerator overnight is the best way to build flavor.

As any barbecue-pit master will tell you, the key to tender, falling-of-the-bones ribs is a steady fire and slow cooking. On a grill, the ribs are placed on the opposite side of the cooking grate from a small pile of banked coals. The temperature will fluctuate between 250 and 350 degrees—the lower the better. We experimented with oven temperatures ranging from 250 degrees to 350 degrees and found 300 degrees to be best. At 250 degrees, the ribs cooked for close to five hours before the meat had separated from the bone, and the outer meat was leathery. At 350 degrees, the ribs cooked too quickly and were tough and flabby with unrendered fat. At 300 degrees, they were fully done in 3½ hours; the meat had separated from the bone and was quite juicy. A lot of the fat had rendered out, too.

With an ideal oven temperature selected, we experimented with a variety of techniques to see if we could improve on the texture of the meat, if at all. Blanching, or parboiling, the ribs is a commonly employed technique that hastens cooking, but we found it yielded surprisingly tough, dry meat. We also tried adding a pan of water to the oven to increase the oven's humidity, but again the meat was tough in comparison with the dry-cooked meat. We then tried wrapping the ribs in foil to trap the steam. The wrapped ribs were paler but juicier

than unwrapped ribs. This inspired us to try wrapping the ribs for part of the cooking time and then uncovering them to attain the characteristic dark crust. We found that covering them for only the first hour of cooking yielded moist ribs with a thick flavorful crust.

The meat was sweet, savory, and succulent, but it lacked the smoky flavor and aroma essential to great ribs. We tried substituting ground chipotle chiles (smoked jalapeño peppers) for the cayenne pepper in our spice rub, but the smokiness of the chiles mysteriously disappeared among the other flavors. We then thought about adding barbecue sauce for its hickory flavor—a sensitive issue considering how quickly sugar-laden sauce burns. We first tried slathering sauce on after we took the foil off, one hour into cooking, and the sauce blackened and turned bitter. We then tried basting the ribs after three hours of cooking, and they remained wet and gummy when pulled from the oven half an hour later. Splitting the difference proved just right. When applied to the ribs after two hours of cooking (so the sauce cooked for 1½ hours), the sauce darkened but did not burn and reduced to a sticky, satisfying glaze.

The ribs disappeared from the test kitchen within minutes of coming out of the oven, but we were able to save a few and tried wrapping the ribs in foil and sealing them in a paper bag—the trick that had worked so well with our barbecued ribs. As we had expected, the ribs wrapped for an hour were juicier and more tender than ribs that were not wrapped.

While our oven-roasted ribs may not be quite as rarefied as those from a roadside shack in Kansas City, they are pretty close and infinitely easier than a trip to the Midwest.

Oven-Roasted Spareribs
SERVES 4

While the final step of wrapping the ribs in foil and putting them in a paper bag may seem eccentric, it is well worth it. We found the meat "finished" in this way to be extraordinarily succulent and tender. Although this recipe is very simple to prepare, you will need more than five hours to season, roast, and rest the ribs.

2   full racks spareribs (about 6 pounds total),
     trimmed of excess fat
¾   cup Dry Rub for Barbecue (page 397)
3   cups barbecue sauce (see pages 398 through
     401)

1. Rub both sides of the ribs with the dry rub and let stand at room temperature for 1 hour. (For stronger flavor, wrap the rubbed ribs in a double layer of plastic wrap and refrigerate for up to 1 day.)

2. Adjust an oven rack to the middle position and heat the oven to 300 degrees. Place the ribs, meaty-side up, on a heavy rack in a rimmed baking sheet, then wrap the pan with aluminum foil. Roast for 1 hour and remove the foil. Roast for another hour, then brush the meaty side of the ribs liberally with the barbecue sauce, about ¾ cup per slab. Cook for another 1½ hours, or until the bones have separated from the meat.

3. Remove the ribs from the oven and wrap each slab completely in foil. Put the foil-wrapped slabs in a brown paper bag and crimp the top of the bag to seal tightly. Allow to rest at room temperature for 1 hour.

4. Unwrap the ribs, cut between the bones, and serve immediately with the remaining barbecue sauce on the side.

BARBECUED BABY BACK RIBS

ON A HOT SUMMER'S DAY, LIFE DOESN'T get much better than a big, juicy, smoky slab of spicy, mouth-watering ribs. But more often than not, baby back ribs cooked at home come out tasting like dry shoe leather on a bone. Given the expense (two slabs, enough to feed four people, run about $24) and time commitment (many recipes require half a day), bad ribs are a true culinary disaster. Our goal was to produce flavorful, juicy, tender ribs that would be well worth the time, money, and effort.

Great baby back ribs start at the meat counter. We quickly learned that you have to shop carefully. Unfortunately, labeling of pork ribs can be confusing. Some slabs are labeled "baby back ribs," while other, seemingly identical ribs are labeled "loin back ribs." After a bit of detective work, we learned that the only difference is weight. Both types of ribs are taken from the upper portion of a young hog's rib cage near the backbone (see the illustration on page 326) and should have 11 to 13 bones. A slab (or rack) of loin back ribs generally comes from a larger pig and weighs more than 1¾ pounds; a slab of ribs weighing less is referred to as baby back ribs. (That said, most restaurants don't follow this rule, using the term baby back no matter what they've got because it sounds better.) During testing, we came to prefer loin back ribs because they are meatier.

There is one other shopping issue to consider. Beware of racks with bare bone peeking through the meat (along the center of the bones). This means that the butcher took off more meat than necessary, robbing you and your guests of full, meaty portions. Once you've purchased the ribs, there remains the question of whether the skin-like membrane located on the "bone side" of the ribs should be left on during cooking. One theory holds that it prevents smoke and spice from penetrating the meat, while some rib experts say that removing it robs the ribs of flavor and moisture. We found that the skin did not interfere with flavor; in fact, it helped to form a spicy, crispy crust.

It was time to start cooking. Our first step was to research the range of grilling times and techniques called for in other recipes. Most recommend a total cooking time of 1½ to 3 hours. Some use a very hot grill, while others use a moderate grill. We tested all of these recipes and found the resulting ribs to be extremely tough. High-heat cooking was particularly troublesome, as it quickly dried out the meat. Ribs cooked over moderate heat for three hours were better, but they were still too tough.

We realized that the only way to go was the classic "low-and-slow" method. We built a two-level fire, in which only half of the grill is covered with charcoal, thinking it would be best to smoke the ribs indirectly—on the coal-less side of the grill—to prevent overcooking. (Two full racks of ribs fit on one side of a 22-inch grill.) To add flavor, we placed soaked wood chunks on the bed of coals and then put the cooking grate in place and laid down the spice-rubbed ribs. Finally, we put the grill cover in place, with the vent holes over the ribs to help draw heat and smoke past the meat.

We found that maintaining a temperature between 275 and 300 degrees for four hours produced ribs that were tasty and tender, with meat that fell off the bone. Decent ribs could be had in less time, but they weren't as tender as those cooked for a full four hours. It's easy to tell when the ribs are ready—the meat pulls away from the bone when the ribs are gently twisted.

The problem was that the dry heat of the grill produced ribs that were not as moist as we would have liked. Our next test, then, was to cook the ribs halfway in an oven, using steam, and to finish them on the grill. These ribs were more moist, but now flavor was the problem; these ribs lacked the intense smokiness of ribs cooked entirely on the grill. Hoping to find another way to add moisture, we simmered the ribs in water for two hours. This robbed them of valuable pork flavor.

It then occurred to us that brining the ribs prior to cooking them might be the solution. We used our standard brining formula, which when applied to two 2-pound racks of ribs amounted to a two-hour immersion in four quarts of cold water mixed with two cups of kosher salt and two cups of sugar. This method produced, well, two very highly seasoned racks of ribs. Why? Ribs pack much more bone per pound than other cuts of meat, and all of the meat is right there on the exterior, so the brine doesn't have very far to go. We figured that a two-pound rack of ribs must soak up the brine much more quickly than an equal-size roast. We cut back the salt, sugar, and brining time by half, and the results were better, but the meat was still too sweet. We cut back the sugar by half once more, and this time the meat was both moist and perfectly seasoned.

These ribs were so good they didn't even need barbecue sauce, although you certainly could add some if you like. A quick rub with an easy-to-mix spice blend before going on the grill gave them just the right warm and savory touch.

Barbecued Baby Back Ribs on a Charcoal Grill
SERVES 4

For a potent spice flavor, brine and dry the ribs as directed, then coat them with the spice rub, wrap tightly in plastic, and refrigerate overnight before grilling. Serve with barbecue sauce (pages 398 through 401) if you like.

1   cup kosher salt or ¹/₂ cup table salt
¹/₂   cup sugar
2   full racks baby back or loin back ribs (about 4 pounds total)
¹/₄   cup Dry Rub for Barbecue (page 397)
2   (3-inch) wood chunks or 2 cups wood chips

1. Dissolve the salt and sugar in 4 quarts of cold water in a stockpot or large plastic container. Submerge the ribs in the brine and refrigerate 1 hour until fully seasoned. Remove the ribs from the brine and thoroughly pat dry with paper towels. Rub each side of the racks with 1 tablespoon of the dry rub and refrigerate the racks for 30 minutes.

2. Meanwhile, soak the wood chunks in cold water to cover for 1 hour and drain, or place the wood chips on an 18-inch square of aluminum foil, seal to make a packet, and use a fork to create about 6 holes to allow smoke to escape (see the illustrations on page 35).

3. Meanwhile, light a large chimney filled three quarters with charcoal briquettes (about 4½ quarts or 65 coals) and allow to burn until covered with a thin layer of gray ash. Empty the coals into one side of the grill, piling them up in a mound 2 or 3 briquettes high. Keep the bottom vents completely open. Place the wood chunks or the packet with the chips on top of the charcoal. Put the cooking grate in place, open the grill lid vents completely, and cover, turning the lid so that the vents are opposite the wood chunks or chips to draw smoke through the grill. Let the grate heat for 5 minutes and clean it with a wire brush.

4. Position the ribs on the cool side of grill. Cover, positioning the lid so that the vents are opposite wood chunks to draw smoke through the grill (the temperature inside the grill should register about 350 degrees but will soon start dropping).

Cook for 2 hours, until the grill temperature drops to about 250 degrees, flipping the rib racks, switching their position so that the rack that was nearest the fire is on outside, and turning the racks 180 degrees every 30 minutes. Add 10 fresh briquettes to the pile of coals. Continue to cook (the temperature should register 275 to 300 degrees), flipping, switching, and rotating the ribs every 30 minutes, until the meat easily pulls away from the bone, 1½ to 2 hours longer. Transfer the ribs to a cutting board, cut between the bones, and serve.

➤ VARIATION

Barbecued Baby Back Ribs on a Gas Grill

If you're using a gas grill, leaving one burner on and the other(s) off mimics the indirect heat method on a charcoal grill.

Follow the recipe for Barbecued Spareribs on a Charcoal Grill through step 1. Soak 2 cups wood chips for 15 minutes in a bowl of water to cover. Place the wood chips in a foil tray (see the illustrations on page 35). Place the foil tray with the soaked wood chips on top of the primary burner (see the illustration on page 35). Turn all burners to high and preheat with the lid down until the chips are smoking heavily, about 20 minutes. Scrape the grate clean with a wire brush. Turn the primary burner down to medium and turn off the other burner(s). Position the ribs over the cool part of the grill and close the lid. Barbecue, turning the ribs every 30 minutes, until the meat easily pulls away from the bones, about 4 hours. (The temperature inside the grill should be a constant 275 degrees; adjust the lit burner as necessary.) Cut the ribs as directed and serve.

Pulled Pork

PULLED PORK, ALSO CALLED PULLED PIG or sometimes just plain barbecue, is slow-cooked pork roast that is shredded, seasoned, and then served on a hamburger bun (or sliced white bread) with just enough of your favorite barbecue sauce, a couple of dill pickle chips, and a topping of coleslaw.

Our goal was to devise a procedure for cooking this classic Southern dish that was both doable and delicious. The meat should be tender, not tough, and moist but not too fatty. Most barbecue joints use a special smoker. We wanted to adapt the technique for the grill. We also set out to reduce the hands-on cooking time, which in some recipes can stretch to eight hours of constant fire tending.

There are two pork roasts commonly associated with pulled pork sandwiches: the shoulder roast and the fresh ham. In their whole state, both are massive roasts, anywhere from 14 to 20 pounds. Because they are so large, most butchers and supermarket meat departments cut both the front and back leg roasts into more manageable sizes. The part of the front leg containing the shoulder blade is usually sold as either a pork shoulder roast or a Boston butt and runs from six to eight pounds. The meat from the upper portion of the front leg is marketed as a picnic roast and runs about the same size. The meat from the rear leg is often segmented into three or four separate boneless roasts called a fresh ham or boneless fresh ham roast.

For barbecue, we find it best to choose a cut of meat with a fair amount of fat, which helps keep the meat moist and succulent during long cooking and adds considerably to the flavor. For this reason, we think the pork shoulder roast, or Boston butt, is the best choice. We found that picnic roasts and fresh hams will also produce excellent results, but they are our second choice.

To set our benchmark for quality, we first cooked a Boston butt using the traditional low-and-slow barbecue method. Using a standard 22-inch kettle grill, we lit about 30 coals, or close to two pounds, and cooked the roast over indirect heat (with the coals on one side of the grill and the roast on the other), adding about eight coals every half-hour or so. It took seven hours to cook a seven-pound roast. While the meat was delicious, tending a grill fire for seven hours is not something many people want to do.

In our next test we tried a much bigger initial fire, with about five pounds of charcoal. After the coals were lit, we placed the pork in a small pan and set it on the grate. The trick to this more intense method is not to remove the lid for any reason until the fire is out three hours later. Because you start

KEY STEPS TO PULLED PORK

1. If using a fresh ham or picnic roast (shown here), cut through the skin with the tip of a chef's knife. Slide the knife blade just under the skin and work around to loosen the skin while pulling it off with your other hand. Boston butt does not need to be trimmed.

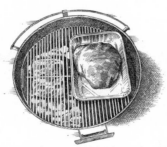

2. Set the unwrapped roast, which has been placed in a disposable aluminum pan barely larger than the meat itself, on the grill grate opposite the coals and the wood.

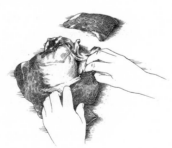

3. After cooking, as soon as the meat is cool enough to handle, remove the meat from the bones and separate the major muscle sections with your hands.

4. Remove as much fat as desired and tear the meat into thin shreds.

with so many coals, it is not necessary to add charcoal during the cooking time.

Unfortunately, the high initial heat charred the exterior of the roast, while the interior was still tough and not nearly fork-tender when we took it off the grill. So we tried a combination approach: a moderate amount of charcoal (more than in the low-and-slow method but less than in the no-peek procedure), cooking the pork roast for three hours on the grill and adding more charcoal four times. We then finished the roast in a 325-degree oven for two hours. This method produced almost the same results as the traditional barbecue, but in considerably less time and with nine fewer additions of charcoal.

We find it helpful to let the finished roast rest wrapped in foil in a sealed paper bag for an hour to allow the meat to reabsorb the flavorful juices. In addition, the sealed bag produces a steaming effect that helps break down any remaining tough collagen. The result is a much more savory and succulent roast. Don't omit this step; it's the difference between good pulled pork and great pulled pork.

As with most barbecue, pork roast benefits from being rubbed with a ground spice mixture. However, because the roast is so thick, we find it best to let the rubbed roast "marinate" in the refrigerator for at least three hours and preferably overnight. The salt in the rub is slowly absorbed by the meat and carries some of the spices with it. The result is a more evenly flavored piece of meat.

Barbecued Pulled Pork on a Charcoal Grill

SERVES 8

Pulled pork can be made with a fresh ham or picnic roast, although our preference is for Boston butt. Preparing pulled pork requires little effort but lots of time. Plan on 9 hours from start to finish: 3 hours with the spice rub, 3 hours on the grill, 2 hours in the oven, and 1 hour to rest. Hickory is the traditional choice with pork, although mesquite can be used if desired. Serve the pulled pork on plain white bread or warmed buns with the classic accompaniments of dill pickle chips and coleslaw. You will need a disposable aluminum roasting pan that measures about 8 inches by 10 inches as well as heavy-duty aluminum foil and a brown paper grocery bag.

I   bone-in pork roast, preferably Boston butt (6 to 8 pounds)

¾   cup Dry Rub for Barbecue (page 397)

4   (3-inch) wood chunks or 4 cups wood chips

2   cups barbecue sauce (see pages 398 through 401)

1. If using a fresh ham or picnic roast, remove the skin (see illustration 1 on page 332). Massage the dry rub into the meat. Wrap the meat tightly in a double layer of plastic wrap and refrigerate for at least 3 hours. (For stronger flavor, the roast can be refrigerated for up to 3 days.)

2. At least 1 hour prior to cooking, remove the roast from the refrigerator, unwrap, and let it come up to room temperature. Soak the wood chunks in cold water to cover for 1 hour and drain, or place the wood chips on an 18-inch square of aluminum foil, seal to make a packet, and use a fork to create about 6 holes to allow smoke to escape (see the illustrations on page 35).

3. Meanwhile, light a large chimney filled a bit less than halfway with charcoal briquettes (about 2½ quarts or 40 coals) and allow to burn until covered with a thin layer of gray ash. Empty the coals into one side of the grill, piling them up in a mound 2 or 3 briquettes high. Open the bottom vents completely. Place the wood chunks or the packet with the chips on top of the charcoal.

4. Set the unwrapped roast in the disposable aluminum pan and place it on the grate opposite the fire (see illustration 2 on page 332). Open the grill lid vents three quarters of the way and cover, turning the lid so that the vents are opposite the wood chunks or chips to draw smoke through the grill. Cook, adding about 8 briquettes every hour or so to maintain an average temperature of 275 degrees, for 3 hours.

5. Adjust an oven rack to the middle position and heat the oven to 325 degrees. Wrap the pan holding the roast with heavy-duty foil to cover completely. Place the pan in the oven and bake until the meat is fork-tender, about 2 hours.

6. Slide the foil-wrapped pan with the roast into a brown paper bag. Crimp the top shut. Let the roast rest for 1 hour.

7. Transfer the roast to a cutting board and unwrap. When cool enough to handle, "pull" the pork by separating the roast into muscle sections, removing the fat, if desired, and tearing the meat into thin shreds with your fingers (see illustrations 3 and 4). Place the shredded meat in a large bowl. Toss with 1 cup barbecue sauce, adding more to taste. Serve, passing the remaining sauce separately.

➤   VARIATIONS

Barbecued Pulled Pork on a Gas Grill
Follow the recipe for Barbecued Pulled Pork on a Charcoal Grill through step 2. Soak 4 cups wood chips for 15 minutes in a bowl of water to cover. Place the wood chips in a foil tray (see the illustrations on page 35). Place the foil tray with the soaked wood chips on top of the primary burner (see the illustration on page 35). Turn all burners to high and preheat with the lid down until the chips are smoking heavily, about 20 minutes. Turn the primary burner down to medium and turn off the other burner(s). Set the unwrapped roast in the disposable pan and position the pan over the cool part of the grill and close the lid. Barbecue for 3 hours. (The temperature inside the grill should be a constant 275 degrees; adjust the lit burner as necessary.) Proceed as directed from step 5 of the recipe.

Cuban-Style Barbecued Pork with Mojo Sauce
This pork is delicious served with rice and black beans. The use of wood for flavoring is not traditional in this dish and can be omitted if you prefer to keep the emphasis on the pork and seasonings.

Mix 9 medium garlic cloves, minced (about 3 tablespoons), 1 tablespoon ground cumin, 1 tablespoon dried oregano, 1 tablespoon salt, 1½ teaspoons ground black pepper, 2 teaspoons brown sugar, and 3 tablespoons extra-virgin olive oil together in a small bowl. Follow the recipe for Barbecued Pulled Pork (charcoal or gas), replacing the Dry Rub for Barbecue with the garlic mixture. Proceed with the recipe, but do not toss the pulled pork with barbecue sauce. To serve, pass Mojo Sauce (page 404) separately with the pulled pork.

BARBECUED BEEF RIBS

IN MOST PARTS OF THE COUNTRY, WHEN people say "ribs," they mean pork—that is, either spareribs or baby back ribs. However, beef ribs are another option worth considering. Barbecuing beef ribs is basically the same as barbecuing pork ribs. The goal is tender, smoky, red-tinged meat that almost falls off the bone. Because beef ribs are the bones included in prime rib, they are already tender and flavorful, so they require less cooking time than pork ribs. However, you don't want to cut the cooking time too much, because you still need to render excess fat and infuse the ribs with smoke flavor.

Butchers generally cut beef rib bones from the prime rib to make either boneless rib roasts or rib-eye steaks. If you don't see beef ribs in the meat case, ask your butcher if there are some unpackaged ribs in the back.

Prime rib has seven bones. Sometimes we found an entire slab of beef ribs with seven bones, but often we saw just a couple of ribs packaged together. As long as there are at least four ribs in a row, it's fine to barbecue them. These bones are quite large, so just a few make a serving. For us 12 bones (in either two or three partial slabs) are enough to feed four. When shopping, get the meatiest bones you can. We found that even the leanest ribs have more than enough fat to keep them moist during barbecuing. If you can only find ribs that are really fatty, trim away some surface fat before cooking them.

You will need a large kettle or gas grill to cook 12 beef ribs. It's fine if the ribs overlap slightly at the outset; we found that the meat quickly shrinks and that the ribs will fit in a single layer within 30 minutes or so. Don't try to cook more than 12 ribs at once; they just don't brown properly when stacked on top of each other.

Although some sources say that beef ribs can be quick-cooked on the grill, we thought ribs cooked this way were bland. Yes, they were tender, but we wanted more smoke as well as that red tinge you get from slow cooking on the grill. We ended up using the same method that worked with pork, with some modifications.

At first, we lit the same amount of coal we had used for pork spareribs, but we found that the beef ribs were getting too dark too quickly and that the ends were getting a touch burnt and dried out. So we reduced the number of briquettes from 40 to 30, with great results. The ribs were able to cook longer without burning, and some of the interior layers of fat now had time to render and drip off the ribs. When we let the ribs cook for only 1 hour and 15 minutes, we found them to be a little too fatty still. Barbecuing for 1 hour and 45 minutes to 2 hours produced better results.

As we had done with spareribs, we tested wrapping the beef ribs in aluminum foil and a paper bag for an hour; this method worked for us again. The wrapped beef ribs were more tender and moist throughout. When the ribs were taken straight off the grill and eaten, they were still delicious, but some of the meat on the ends of the ribs was a little dry and tough. Letting them rest in the foil and paper bag redistributed the moisture throughout the ribs, making them more appealing.

Barbecued Beef Ribs on a Charcoal Grill

SERVES 4

Beef rib bones are quite large, so you may need to arrange them carefully on the grill to make them fit. (You will need a large kettle grill for this recipe.) Don't worry if the ribs overlap a bit—they will shrink while cooking to fit comfortably in the grill. While a classic barbecue sauce can be used with beef ribs, tasters felt that a more acidic sauce best complemented the richness of beef. You will need plenty of heavy-duty aluminum foil and a brown paper bag for this recipe.

12	beef ribs in 2 or 3 slabs (about 5 pounds total), trimmed of excess fat if necessary
1/2	cup plus 2 tablespoons Dry Rub for Barbecue (page 397)
2	(3-inch) wood chunks or 2 cups wood chips
1 1/2	cups Sweet-Sour-Spicy Barbecue Sauce (page 400)

1. Rub both sides of the ribs with the dry rub and let stand at room temperature for 1 hour. (For stronger flavor, wrap the rubbed ribs in a double layer of plastic wrap and refrigerate for up to 1 day.)

2. Soak the wood chunks in cold water to cover for 1 hour and drain, or place the wood chips on an 18-inch square of aluminum foil, seal to make a packet, and use a fork to create about 6 holes to allow the smoke to escape (see the illustrations on page 35).

3. Meanwhile, light a large chimney filled one third with charcoal briquettes (about 2 quarts or 30 coals) and allow to burn until covered with a thin layer of gray ash. Empty the coals into one side of the grill, piling them up in a mound 2 briquettes high. Keep the bottom vents completely open. Place the wood chunks or the packet with the chips on top of the charcoal. Put the cooking grate in place, open the grill lid vents completely, and cover, turning the lid so that the vents are opposite the wood chunks or chips to draw smoke through the grill. Let the grate heat for 5 minutes and then clean it with a wire brush.

4. Position the ribs over the cool part of the grill. Barbecue, turning the ribs every 30 minutes, until the meat starts to pull away from the bones and has a rosy glow on the exterior, 1¾ to 2 hours. (The initial temperature inside the grill will be about 325 degrees and will drop to 250 degrees after 2 hours.)

5. Remove the ribs from the grill and wrap each slab completely in foil. Put the foil-wrapped slabs in a brown paper bag and crimp the top of the bag to seal tightly. Let rest at room temperature for 1 hour.

6. Unwrap the ribs and brush with some sauce. Serve, passing the remaining sauce at the table.

➤ VARIATIONS

Barbecued Beef Ribs on a Gas Grill

Keep an eye on the grill thermometer and adjust the lit burner as necessary to prevent the ribs from browning too quickly.

Follow the recipe for Barbecued Beef Ribs on a Charcoal Grill through step 1. Soak the wood chips for 15 minutes in a bowl of water to cover. Place the wood chips in a foil tray (see the illustrations on page 35). Place the foil tray with the soaked wood chips on top of the primary burner (see the illustration on page 35). Turn all burners to high and preheat with the lid down until the chips are smoking heavily, about 20 minutes. Scrape the grate

clean with a wire brush. Turn the primary burner down to medium and turn off the other burner(s). Position the ribs over the cool part of the grill. Barbecue, turning the ribs every 30 minutes, until the meat starts to pull away from the bones and has a rosy glow on the exterior, 2 to 2½ hours. (The temperature inside the grill should be a constant 275 degrees; adjust the lit burner as necessary.) Proceed with the recipe as directed from step 5.

Barbecued Beef Ribs, Chinese Style

Mix 1 tablespoon five-spice powder, 2 teaspoons garlic powder, 1 teaspoon ground white pepper, 1 teaspoon ground ginger, 1 teaspoon brown sugar, and ¾ teaspoon salt together in a small bowl. Follow the recipe for Barbecued Beef Ribs (charcoal or gas), replacing the Dry Rub for Barbecue with the five-spice powder mixture. Proceed with the recipe as directed, brushing the ribs with Sweetened Soy Glaze (page 401).

SHORT RIBS

SHORT RIBS ARE JUST WHAT THEIR NAME says they are: "short ribs" cut from any location along the length of the cow's ribs. They can come from the lower belly section or higher up toward the back, from the shoulder (or chuck) area or the forward midsection. There is no way to know, either by appearance or labeling, from where short ribs have been cut.

No matter what part of the rib section they come from, short ribs can be butchered in one of two ways. In most supermarkets, you will see English-style short ribs, in which each rib bone has been separated, with the thick chunk of meat attached, and the bone and the meat cut into manageable, rectangular chunks. In the other style of butchering, called flanken-style, the short ribs are cut into thin cross sections that contain two or three pieces of bone surrounded by pieces of meat.

Both styles of short ribs are fairly fatty, making them ideal candidates for the grill. Most cooks braise this cheap cut, which turns yielding and tender in a stew. However, the cook must jump through several hoops—trimming the excess fat

PREPARING ENGLISH-STYLE RIBS

Flanken-style short ribs are thin enough to marinate and cook as is. Thicker English-style short ribs must be opened up into a flatter piece of meat before being marinated.

1. With a paring or boning knife, trim off the surface fat and silver skin from each rib.

2. Right above the bone, make a cut into the meat. Continue cutting almost all the way, but not quite through, the meat.

3. Open the meat onto a cutting board, as you would open a book. Make another cut into the meat, parallel to the board, making the lower half of the section of meat that you are slicing about ¼ inch thick, cutting almost, but not all the way through, to the end of the meat. Open the meat again, like a book.

4. Repeat step 3 as needed, 1 or 2 more times, until the meat is about ¼ inch thick throughout. You should have a bone connected to a long strip of meat, about ¼ inch thick.

before cooking, draining off fat from the browned ribs, degreasing the stew liquid before serving—to keep the braise from tasting greasy. On the grill, the fat melts harmlessly into the fire and is not really an issue.

Although short ribs are similar to beef ribs in that each contains meat and bone, our research indicates that most cooks prefer to grill short ribs rather quickly. Given their diminutive size, this makes sense. If you gave a short rib enough time on the grill to truly barbecue it, it would shrink up to a tiny speck of meat.

Since English-style short ribs are more available, we started our tests with them. Our first efforts produced terrible results. At first, we burned the exterior before the thick middle portion of the meat was cooked through. We lowered the temperature and still found the interior to be tough by the time the exterior was charred. We figured maybe all the experts were wrong and that we should grill-roast English-style short ribs in a kind of compromise between barbecuing and grilling (see page 21 for a definition of grill-roasting). Although this method worked better, the meat became dry and stringy after half an hour of grill-roasting. Worse, there were several layers of unrendered fat throughout each rib that were flabby and unappealing.

Next, we tried simmering the ribs on the stovetop and finishing them on the grill. This method is tedious. First, you have to make a flavorful liquid for the meat to stew in, and then you have to cook the ribs down in the liquid for a few hours to make them tender. Finally, you have to finish by grilling the ribs until crisped and browned, which takes only eight minutes or so—not enough time to give them much smoke flavor. We'd rather spend all that time making braised short ribs, where you end up not only with tender meat but a great, satisfying, rich sauce that becomes a complete meal with mashed potatoes or noodles. It seemed like a waste to have to fire up the grill just to brown the ribs, after you'd spent three hours braising them. It made more sense to brown the ribs on the stovetop before braising them.

At this point, we decided to follow some Asian recipes in which short ribs are butchered further before being cooked. In effect, the meat is slit crosswise several times and opened up like a book until it is quite thin (between one quarter and one half inch thick), which makes it eligible for straightforward grilling. (See illustrations on page 336.) While this method worked well—the meat cooked quickly, it became tender, and the fat was easily rendered—there was a drawback: the need to butcher each short rib at home.

You can avoid this hassle by asking the butcher for flanken-style ribs. Because the meat is already cut thin and across the grain, flanken-style ribs are much easier to cook on the grill. While these ribs are not supertender (you have to work a little at eating them), they are juicy, rich, and packed with beefy flavor, especially near the bones, which are great to gnaw on. Furthermore, these ribs have a large surface area for caramelization, which makes for better flavor. When marinated, the ribs are infused with lots of good flavor because the meat is so thin.

When purchasing the ribs, try to get thinly sliced flanken-style ribs, which should be, on average, about one quarter inch thick. If you end up having to buy English-style, be sure that you get meaty ribs. We've seen ribs that are mostly bone. The meat should extend at least one inch above the rib bones. Also, in addition to butchering the ribs Asian-style, you will need to trim off the silver skin and fat on the surface of the ribs.

Grilling the ribs is extremely easy,, but you must have a fire that is hot enough to sear the meat. The meat is thin and cooks extremely quickly, making it impossible to go for medium-rare or even medium meat. You just want to have good caramelization to add a layer of sweet flavor on the surface of the ribs. We found that a medium-hot fire (a full chimney of hardwood charcoal) sears the meat in about five minutes. Because the ribs are so high in fat, be sure to have a spray bottle filled with water on hand to extinguish any flare-ups that might occur.

Charcoal-Grilled Beef Short Ribs

SERVES 4

If you are using English-style ribs, purchase only ribs with a good amount of meat on the bones; there should be at least 1 inch of meat above the bone. Keep a spray bottle handy to douse any flare-ups caused by this fatty cut of meat. Short ribs are delicious enough to eat when seasoned with just salt and pepper. The variations that follow offer more complex flavors. Note that because of the higher cooking temperature, these ribs are actually grilled rather than barbecued. Also, the higher cooking temperature means that wood, which would ignite very quickly, is not a practical option in this recipe. Rely on hardwood charcoal (rather than briquettes) to supply some smoky flavor.

2 ½ pounds flanken-style short ribs, about ¼ inch thick, or 3 pounds English-style short ribs, prepared according to the illustrations on page 336
Salt and ground black pepper

1. Light a large chimney full of hardwood charcoal (about 6 quarts) and allow to burn until covered with a thin layer of gray ash, about 15 minutes. Build a single-level fire by spreading the coals evenly over the bottom of the grill. Set the cooking rack in place, cover the grill with the lid, and let the rack heat up, about 5 minutes. Use a wire brush to scrape clean the grill. The fire is ready when the coals are medium-hot. (See how to gauge heat level on page 34.)

2. Season the ribs with salt and pepper to taste. Grill half of the ribs, uncovered and turning once, until richly browned on both sides, about 4½ minutes total. Transfer the ribs to a serving platter and cover with foil. Repeat with the second batch of ribs. Serve immediately.

➤ VARIATIONS
Gas-Grilled Beef Short Ribs
Preheat the grill with all burners turned to high and the lid down until very hot, about 15 minutes. Scrape the grill clean with a wire brush. Follow step 2 of the recipe for Charcoal-Grilled Beef Short Ribs and cook with the lid down.

Grilled Beef Short Ribs, Korean Style
This recipe is based on kalbi, a standard barbecued short rib dish from Korea. The sweet, salty marinade promotes excellent browning on the grill. Be sure to marinate the ribs for at least 4 hours or, preferably, overnight. If you

like, add ½ teaspoon or more red pepper flakes to the marinade. Serve with steamed rice and kimchee (spicy Korean pickled vegetables, available in Asian markets and some supermarkets).

I	medium, ripe pear, halved, cored, peeled, and cut into ½-inch pieces
6	medium garlic cloves, chopped
2	teaspoons chopped fresh ginger
½	cup soy sauce
2	tablespoons Asian sesame oil
6	tablespoons sugar
3	medium scallions, ends removed, green and white parts sliced thin
I	tablespoon rice vinegar
I	recipe Charcoal-Grilled or Gas-Grilled Beef Short Ribs (omit salt and pepper in step 2)

1. Place the pear, garlic, ginger, and soy sauce in the workbowl of a food processor fitted with the metal blade. Pulse until smooth, scraping down the sides of the bowl as necessary. Transfer the mixture to a medium bowl and stir in the sesame oil, sugar, scallions, and vinegar.

2. Place the ribs in a gallon-size, zipper-lock plastic bag and pour the soy sauce mixture over them. Seal the bag. Place the bag in the refrigerator and marinate the ribs for at least 4 hours or overnight.

3. Remove the ribs from the marinade and grill as directed.

Grilled Beef Short Ribs with Chipotle and Citrus Marinade

This marinade has some heat, smoky flavor, and acidity.

2	canned chipotle chiles in adobo sauce, minced, with 1 ½ teaspoons adobo sauce
3	tablespoons juice from 2 limes
6	tablespoons olive oil
I	tablespoon honey
6	tablespoons chopped fresh cilantro leaves
1 ½	teaspoons chili powder
1 ½	teaspoons ground cumin
4	medium garlic cloves, minced or pressed through a garlic press (about 4 teaspoons)
1 ½	teaspoons salt
1 ½	teaspoons ground black pepper

I	recipe Charcoal-Grilled or Gas-Grilled Beef Short Ribs (omit salt and pepper in step 2)
I	lime, cut into wedges

1. Mix the chiles and adobo sauce, lime juice, olive oil, honey, cilantro, chili powder, cumin, garlic, salt, and pepper together in a medium bowl.

2. Place the ribs in a gallon-size, zipper-lock plastic bag and pour the chile mixture over them. Seal the bag. Place the bag in the refrigerator and marinate the ribs for at least 4 hours or overnight.

3. Grill the ribs as directed, serving them with the lime wedges.

BARBECUED BRISKET

OUR FAVORITE WAY TO COOK BRISKET IS to barbecue it. When prepared correctly, the meat picks up a great smoky flavor and becomes fork-tender. Unfortunately, many a barbecued brisket ends up burnt, tough, or chewy. This is because brisket is so tough to begin with. Unless it is fully cooked, the meat is very chewy and practically inedible. Because brisket is so large (a full cut can weigh 13 pounds), getting the meat "fully cooked" can take many hours. Our goal was to make the meat as tender as possible as quickly as possible.

What does "fully cooked" mean when talking about brisket? To find out, we roasted four small pieces to various internal temperatures. The pieces cooked to 160 and 180 degrees were dry and quite tough. A piece cooked to 200 degrees was slightly less tough, although quite dry. A final piece cooked to 210 degrees had the most appealing texture and the most pleasant chew, despite the fact that it was the driest.

So what's going on here? Heat causes muscle proteins to uncoil and then rejoin in a different formation, which drives out juices in the same way that wringing removes moisture from a wet cloth. This process starts in earnest at around 140 degrees, and by the time the meat reaches 180 degrees, most of its juices have been expelled. This explains why a medium-rare steak (cooked to 130 degrees) is much juicier than a well-done steak (cooked to 160 degrees).

With tender cuts, like steak, the lower the internal temperature of the meat, the juicier and less tough the meat will be. However, with cuts that start out tough, like brisket, another process is also at work. Brisket is loaded with waxy-looking connective tissue called collagen, which makes the meat chewy and tough. Only when the collagen has been transformed into gelatin will the meat be tender. Collagen begins to convert to gelatin at 130 to 140 degrees, but the conversion process occurs most rapidly at temperatures above 180 degrees.

When cooking brisket, the gelatinization of collagen must be the priority. Thus, the meat should be cooked as fully as possible, or to an internal temperature of 210 degrees. The muscle juices will be long gone (that's why the sliced meat is served with barbecue sauce), but the meat will be extremely tender because all the collagen will have been converted to gelatin.

It is important to point out that moist-heat cooking methods (such as braising) are appropriate for cooking meats to such high internal temperatures because water is a more efficient conductor of heat than air. Meats cooked in a moist environment heat up faster and can be held at high internal temperatures without burning or drying out.

Given the fact that brisket must be fully cooked and that it can be so big, the meat needs 10 or 12 hours of barbecuing to reach the fork-tender stage. Even when butchers separate the brisket into smaller pieces, as is often the case, the cooking time is astronomical. Most cooks are not prepared to keep a fire going that long. To get around this tending-the-fire-all-day-long problem, we found it necessary to commit barbecue heresy. After much testing, we decided to start the meat on the grill but finish it in the oven, where it could be left to cook unattended.

We wondered how long the meat would have to

KEYS STEPS TO BARBECUED BRISKET

1. After barbecuing, place the brisket on two 4-foot sections of heavy-duty aluminum foil that have been sealed together to make a 4 by 3-foot rectangle. Bring the short ends of the foil up over the brisket and crimp tightly to seal.

2. Seal the long sides of the foil packet tightly up against the sides of the meat. Put the brisket on a rimmed baking sheet and put the sheet in the oven.

3. After the brisket comes out of the oven, use oven mitts to hold the rimmed baking sheet and carefully pour the juices into a bowl. Reserve the juices and defat if you like. They make a delicious addition to barbecue sauce.

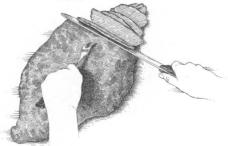

4. Since the grain on the two sections of the brisket goes in opposite directions, separate the cuts before slicing.

5. Carve the brisket on the bias across the grain into long, thin slices.

stay on the grill to pick up enough smoke flavor. In our testing, we found that two hours allowed the meat to absorb plenty of smoke flavor and created a dark brown, crusty exterior. At this point, the meat is ready for the oven. We found it best to wrap the meat in foil to create a moist environment. (Unwrapped briskets cooked up drier, and the exterior was prone to burning.) After barbecuing, a whole brisket requires three hours or so in a 300-degree oven to become fork-tender. Barbecue purists might object to our use of the oven, but this method works, and it doesn't require a tremendous commitment of hands-on cooking time.

Some further notes about our testing. Although many experts recommend basting a brisket regularly as it cooks on the grill to ensure moistness, we disagree. Taking the lid off wreaked havoc with our charcoal fire, and the meat didn't taste any different despite frequent basting with sauce. Likewise, we don't recommend placing a pan filled with water (we also tried beer) on the grill. Some barbecue masters believe that the liquid adds moisture and flavor to the meat, but we couldn't tell any difference between brisket cooked with and without the pan of liquid.

Brisket comes with a thick layer of fat on one side. We tried turning the brisket as it cooked, thinking this might promote even cooking, but we had better results when we barbecued the brisket fat-side up the entire time. This way, the fat slowly melts, lubricating the meat underneath.

Barbecued Beef Brisket on a Charcoal Grill

SERVES 18 TO 24

Cooking a whole brisket, which weighs about 10 pounds, may seem like overkill. However, the process is easy, and the leftovers keep well in the refrigerator for up to 4 days. (Leave leftover brisket unsliced, and reheat the foil-wrapped meat in a 300-degree oven until warm.) Don't worry if your brisket is a little larger or smaller; split-second cooking times are not critical because the meat is eaten very well done. Still, if you don't want to bother with a big piece of meat, barbecuing brisket for less than a crowd is easy to do. Simply ask your butcher for either the point or flat portion of the brisket (we prefer the point cut;

see page 192), each of which weighs about half as much as a whole brisket. Then follow this recipe, reducing the spice rub by half and barbecuing for just 1½ hours. Wrap the meat tightly in foil and reduce the time in the oven to 2 hours. No matter how large or small a piece you cook, it's a good idea to save the juices the meat gives off while in the oven to enrich the barbecue sauce. Hickory and mesquite are both traditional wood choices with brisket.

1	cup Dry Rub for Barbecue (page 397)
1	whole beef brisket (9 to 11 pounds), fat trimmed to ¼-inch thickness
2	(3-inch) wood chunks or 2 cups wood chips
3	cups barbecue sauce (see pages 398 to 401)

1. Apply the dry rub liberally to all sides of the meat, patting it on firmly to make sure the spices adhere and completely obscure the meat. Wrap the brisket tightly in plastic wrap and refrigerate for 2 hours. (For stronger flavor, refrigerate for up to 2 days.)

2. About 1 hour prior to cooking, remove the brisket from the refrigerator, unwrap, and let it come up to room temperature. Soak the wood chunks in cold water to cover for 1 hour and drain, or place the wood chips on an 18-inch square of aluminum foil, seal to make a packet, and use a fork to create about 6 holes to allow smoke to escape (see the illustrations on page 35).

3. Meanwhile, light a large chimney filled a bit less than halfway with charcoal briquettes (about 2½ quarts or 40 coals) and allow to burn until covered with a thin layer of gray ash. Empty the coals into one side of the grill, piling them up in a mound 2 or 3 briquettes high. Keep the bottom vents completely open. Place the wood chunks or the packet with the chips on top of the charcoal. Put the cooking grate in place, open the grill lid vents completely, and cover, turning the lid so that the vents are opposite the wood chunks or chips to draw smoke through the grill. Let the grate heat for 5 minutes and then clean it with a wire brush.

4. Position the brisket, fat-side up, on the side of the grill opposite the fire. Barbecue, without removing the lid, for 2 hours. (The initial temperature will be about 350 degrees and will drop to 250 degrees after 2 hours.)

5. Adjust an oven rack to the middle position and preheat the oven to 300 degrees. Attach 2 pieces of heavy-duty foil, 48 inches long, by folding the long edges together 2 or 3 times, crimping tightly to seal well, to form an approximate 48 by 36-inch rectangle. Position the brisket lengthwise in the center of the foil. Bring the short edges over the brisket and fold down, crimping tightly to seal. Repeat with the long sides of the foil to seal the brisket completely. (See illustrations 1 and 2 on page 339.) Place the brisket on a rimmed baking sheet. Bake until the meat is fork-tender, 3 to 3½ hours.

EQUIPMENT: Pepper Mills

A good steak needs some freshly ground pepper, but which mill? Most pepper mills work by similar means. Peppercorns are loaded into a central chamber through which runs a metal shaft. Near the bottom of the mill, the shaft is connected to a grinding mechanism that consists of a rotating, grooved "male" head that fits into a stationary, grooved "female" ring. Near the top of the male piece, the large grooves crack the peppercorns, then feed the smaller pieces downward to be ground between the finer grooves, or teeth, of the male and female components.

We tested a dozen mills and found four stand-outs. The Unicorn Magnum Plus managed an awesome output. In one minute of grinding, the Magnum produced an amazing average of 7.3 grams, or about 3½ teaspoons, of fine-ground pepper. By comparison, honors for the next-highest average output went to the Oxo Grind It, at 5.1 grams, while about half the pack came in around the 2-grams or less mark (which, at roughly 1 teaspoon in volume, is perfectly acceptable).

Grind quality and speed are only half the battle—especially if most of your peppercorns land on the floor when you try to fill the mill. So we appreciated mills with wide, unobstructed filler doors that could accommodate the tip of a wide funnel or, better yet, the lip of a bag or jar so that we could dispense with the funnel altogether. The East Hampton Industries (EHI) Peppermate took high honors in this category, with a lid that snaps off to create a gaping 3-inch opening, followed by the Zyliss, with a 2-inch opening, and the Oxo, with a wide-open 1³⁄₈-inch mouth. With its sliding collar door, the Unicorn Magnum Plus was also easy to fill. Along the same lines, the more peppercorns a mill can hold, the less often it has to be filled. The Zyliss held a full cup, and the Unicorn Magnum Plus trailed behind by just 1 tablespoon.

The ease of adjusting the grind was another factor we considered. Changing the grind from fine to coarse involves changing the tolerances of, or distances between, the male and female grinding components. The more space between them, the larger the pepper particles and the coarser the grind. Traditionally, a knob at the top of the mill, called the finial, is used to adjust the grind. This was our least favorite design for two reasons. First, the finial must be screwed down very tight for a fine grind, which not only requires significant finger strength but also makes the head (or the crank) of the mill more difficult to turn. Second, the finial usually has to be removed entirely to fill the mill, which means you have to readjust the grind with each filling. We preferred mills like the Unicorn Magnum Plus, which use a screw or dial at the base of the grinding mechanism.

THE BEST PEPPER MILLS
The Unicorn Magnum Plus (far left: $45) has a huge capacity and awesome speed. The East Hampton Industries Peppermate (second from left: $40) has a detachable cup that captures the ground pepper and makes measuring easy. The Oxo Good Grips Grind It (second from right: $20) is lightning-fast, but it can be tricky to adjust the grind on the mill. The Zyliss Large Mill (far right: $28) has a huge capacity and excellent range of grinds but it is slower than the other top models.

6. Remove the brisket from the oven, loosen the foil at one end to release steam, and let rest for 30 minutes. If you like, drain the juices into a bowl (see illustration 3 on page 339) and defat the juices in a gravy skimmer.

7. Unwrap the brisket and place it on a cutting board. Separate the meat into 2 sections and carve it on the bias across the grain into long, thin slices (see illustrations 4 and 5 on page 339). Serve with plain barbecue sauce or with barbecue sauce that has been flavored with up to 1 cup of defatted brisket juices.

➤ VARIATION
Barbecued Beef Brisket on a Gas Grill
You will need a pretty large grill to cook a whole brisket. If your grill has fewer than 400 square inches of cooking space, barbecue either the point or flat end, each of which weighs about half as much as a whole brisket. Follow the directions in the note on page 340 for cooking a smaller piece of brisket.

Follow the recipe for Barbecued Beef Brisket on a Charcoal Grill through step 2. Soak the wood chips for 15 minutes in a bowl of water to cover. Place the wood chips in a foil tray (see the illustrations on page 35). Place the foil tray with the soaked wood chips on top of the primary burner (see the illustration on page 35). Turn all burners to high and preheat with the lid down until chips are smoking heavily, about 20 minutes. Scrape the grate clean with a wire brush. Turn the primary burner down to medium and turn off the other burner(s). Position the brisket, fat-side up, over the cool part of the grill. Cover and barbecue for 2 hours. (The temperature inside the grill should be a constant 275 degrees; adjust the lit burner as necessary.) Proceed as directed from step 5 of the recipe.

14

I WANT TO COOK GROUND MEAT

I Want to Cook Ground Meat

GROUND MEAT IS A KITCHEN FAVORITE and with good reason. It can take on innumerable guises, from your all-American hamburgers and meatballs (with Italian or Swedish flavors) to tamale pie and tacos. This chapter demonstrates the versatility of ground meat. We've also included a few recipes that use shredded or diced meat, including a meaty tomato sauce made with ribs as well as corned beef hash. In these dishes, the meat functions like ground meat, losing its separate identify to create something with more flavor than just plain meat. See also the ham loaf recipe on page 384.

HAMBURGERS

AMERICANS PROBABLY GRILL MORE HAM-burgers than any other food. Despite all this practice, plenty of hamburgers seem merely to satisfy hunger rather than give pleasure. Too bad, because making an exceptional hamburger isn't that hard or time-consuming. Fast-food chains no doubt had good reasons when they decided against selling hand-formed, 100 percent ground-chuck burgers; home cooks, however, do not. If you have the right ground beef, the perfect hamburger can be ready in less than 15 minutes, assuming you season, form, and cook it properly. The biggest difficulty for many cooks, though, may be finding the right beef.

To test which cut or cuts of beef would cook up into the best burgers, we called a butcher and ordered chuck, round, rump, sirloin, and hanging tenderloin, all ground to order with 20 percent fat. (Although we would question fat percentages in later testing, we needed a standard for these early tests. Based on experience, this percentage seemed right.) After a side-by-side taste test, we quickly concluded that most cuts of ground beef are pleasant but bland when compared with robust, beefy flavored ground chuck. Pricier ground sirloin, for example, cooked up into a particularly boring burger.

So pure ground chuck—the cut of beef that starts where the ribs end and travels up to the shoulder and neck, ending at the foreshank—was the clear winner. We were ready to race ahead to seasonings, but before moving on we stopped to ask ourselves whether cooks buying ground chuck from the grocery store would agree with our choice. Our efforts to determine whether grocery-store ground chuck and ground-to-order chuck were even remotely similar took us along a culinary blue highway from kitchen to packing plant, butcher shop, and science lab.

According to the National Livestock and Meat Board, the percentage of fat in beef is checked and enforced at the retail level. If a package of beef is labeled 90 percent lean, then it must contain no more than 10 percent fat, give or take a point. Retail stores are required to test each batch of ground beef, make the necessary adjustments, and keep a log of the results. Local inspectors routinely pull ground beef from a store's meat case for a fat check. If the fat content is not within 1 percent of the package sticker, the store is fined.

Whether a package labeled ground chuck is, in fact, 100 percent ground chuck is a different story. First, we surveyed a number of grocery store meat department managers, who said that what was written on the label did match what was in the package. For instance, a package labeled "ground chuck" would have been made only from chuck trimmings. Same for sirloin and round. Only "ground beef" would be made from mixed beef trimmings.

We got a little closer to the truth, however, by interviewing a respected butcher in the Chicago area. At the several grocery stores and butcher shops where he had worked over the years, he had never known a store to segregate meat trimmings. In fact, in his present butcher shop, he sells only two kinds of ground beef: sirloin and chuck. He defines ground sirloin as ground beef (mostly but not exclusively sirloin) that's labeled 90 percent lean, and chuck as ground beef (including a lot of chuck trimmings) that's labeled 85 percent lean.

Only meat ground at federally inspected plants is guaranteed to match its label. At these plants, an inspector checks to make sure that labeled ground beef actually comes from the cut of beef named on the label and that the fat percentage is correct. Most retailers, though, cannot guarantee that their ground beef has been made from a specific cut;

they can only guarantee fat percentages. Because the labeling of retail ground beef can be deceptive, we suggest that you buy a chuck roast and have the butcher grind it for you. Even at a local grocery store, we found that the butcher was willing to grind to order. Some meat always gets lost in the grinder, so count on losing a bit (2 to 3 percent).

Because commercially ground beef is at risk for contamination with the bacteria E. coli, we thought it made theoretical sense for home cooks to grind their beef at home, thereby reducing their odds of eating tainted beef. It doesn't make much practical sense, though. Not all cooks own a grinder. And even if they did, we thought home grinding demanded far too much setup, cleanup, and effort for a dish meant to be so simple.

To see if there was an easier way, we tried chopping the meat by hand and grinding it in the food processor. The hibachi-style hand-chopping

SHAPING HAMBURGERS

1. With cupped hands, toss one portion of meat back and forth from hand to hand to shape it into a loose ball.

2. Pat lightly to flatten the meat into a 3/4-inch-thick burger that measures about 4 1/2 inches across. Press the center of the patty down with your fingertips until it is 1/2 inch thick, creating a well in the center. Repeat with the remaining portions of meat.

method was just as time-consuming and even more messy than the traditional grinder. In this method, you must slice the meat thin and then cut it into cubes before going at it with two chef's knives. The fat doesn't distribute evenly, meat flies everywhere, and, unless your knives are razor sharp, it's difficult to chop through the meat. What's worse, you can't efficiently chop more than two burgers at a time. In the end, the cooked burgers can be mistaken for chopped steak.

The food processor did a surprisingly good job of grinding meat. We thought the steel blade would raggedly chew the meat, but the hamburger turned out evenly chopped and fluffy. (For more information see Food Processor as Grinder on page 350.)

We figured the average chuck roast to be about 80 percent lean. To check its leanness, we bought a chuck roast-not too fatty, not too lean-and ground it in the food processor. We then took our ground chuck back to the grocery store and asked the butcher to check its fat content in the Univex Fat Analyzer, a machine the store uses to check each batch of beef it grinds. A plug of our ground beef scored an almost perfect 21 percent fat when tested.

Up to this point, all of our beef had been ground with approximately 20 percent fat. A quick test of burgers with less and more fat helped us to decide that 20 percent fat, give or take a few percentage points, was good for burgers. Any more fat and the burgers are just too greasy. Any less starts to compromise the beef's juicy, moist texture.

When to season the meat with salt and pepper may seem an insignificant detail, but when making a dish as simple as a hamburger, little things matter. We tried seasoning the meat at four different points in the process. Our first burger was seasoned before the meat was shaped, the second burger was seasoned right before cooking, the third after each side was seared, and the fourth after the burger had been fully cooked. Predictably, the burger that had been seasoned throughout was our preference. All the surface-seasoned burgers were the same. Tasters got a hit of salt up front, then the burger went bland. The thin surface area was well seasoned while the interior of the burger was not.

Working with fresh-ground chuck seasoned with

salt and pepper, we now moved on to shaping and cooking. To defy the overpacking and overhandling warning you see in many recipes, we thoroughly worked a portion of ground beef before cooking it. The well-done burger exterior was nearly as dense as a meat pâté, and the less well-done interior was compact and pasty.

It's pretty hard to overhandle a beef patty, though, especially if you're trying not to. Once the meat has been divided into portions, we found that tossing each portion from one hand to the other helped bring the meat together into a ball without overworking it.

We made one of our most interesting discoveries when we tested various shaping techniques for the patties. A well in the center of each burger ensured that they came off the grill with an even thickness instead of puffed up like a tennis ball. (See Shaping Hamburgers on page 346.) To our taste, a four-ounce burger seemed a little skimpy. A six-ounce portion of meat patted into a nicely sized burger fit perfectly in a bun.

Now nearly done with our testing, we needed only to perfect our grilling method. Burgers require a real blast of heat if they are to form a crunchy, flavorful crust before the interior overcooks. While many of the recipes we looked at advise the cook to grill burgers over a hot fire, we suspected we'd have to adjust the heat because our patties were quite thin in the middle. Sure enough, a superhot fire made it too easy to overcook the burgers. We found a medium-hot fire formed a crust quickly, while also providing a wider margin of error for properly cooking the center. Nonetheless, burgers cook quickly—needing only 2½ to 3½ minutes per side. Don't walk away from the grill when cooking burgers.

To keep the burgers from sticking to the grill, we coated it with oil. All you need to do is dip a wad of paper towels in some vegetable oil, hold the wad with long-handled tongs, and rub it on the hot grate just before adding the burgers.

One last finding from our testing: Don't ever press down on burgers as they cook. Rather than speeding their cooking, pressing on the patties serves only to squeeze out their juices and make the burgers dry.

Charcoal-Grilled Hamburgers
SERVES 4

For those who like their burgers well done, we found that poking a small hole in the center of the patty before cooking helped the burger cook through to the center before the edges dried out. See the illustrations on page 346 for tips on shaping burgers. See page 35 for details about grinding your own meat with a food processor.

1 ½	pounds 80 percent lean ground chuck
1	teaspoon salt
½	teaspoon ground black pepper
	Vegetable oil for grill rack
	Buns and desired toppings

1. Light a large chimney starter filled with hardwood charcoal (about 6 quarts) and allow to burn until all the charcoal is covered with a layer of fine gray ash. Spread the coals out evenly over the bottom of the grill. Set the cooking rack in place, cover the grill with the lid, and let the rack heat up, about 5 minutes. Use a wire brush to scrape clean the cooking grate. The grill is ready when the coals are medium-hot. (See how to gauge heat level on page 34.)

2. Meanwhile, break up the chuck to increase the surface area for seasoning. Sprinkle the salt and pepper over the meat; toss lightly with your hands to distribute the seasonings. Divide the meat into 4

PREVENTING BURGERS FROM STICKING TO THE GRILL

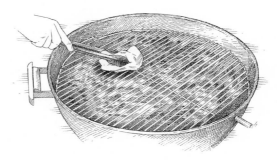

To keep burgers (as well as fish) from sticking to the grill grate, dip a large wad of paper towels in vegetable oil, grab the wad with tongs, and wipe the grate thoroughly to coat it.

equal portions (6 ounces each); with cupped hands, toss one portion of meat back and forth to form a loose ball. Pat lightly to flatten the meat into a ¾-inch-thick burger that measures about 4½ inches across. Press the center of the patty down with your fingertips until it is about ½ inch thick, creating a well, or divot, in the center of the patty. Repeat with the remaining portions of meat.

3. Lightly dip a wad of paper towels in vegetable oil; holding the wad with tongs, wipe the grill rack. Grill the burgers, divot-side up, uncovered and without pressing down on them, until well seared on the first side, about 2½ minutes. Flip the burgers with a wide metal spatula. Continue grilling to the desired doneness, about 2 minutes for rare, 2½ minutes for medium-rare, 3 minutes for medium, and 4 minutes for well-done. Serve immediately in buns with desired toppings.

➤   VARIATIONS

Gas-Grilled Hamburgers

Preheat the grill with all burners set to high and the lid down until the grill is very hot, about 15 minutes. Scrape the grill grate clean with a grill brush. Leave both burners on high. Follow the recipe for Charcoal-Grilled Hamburgers from step 2 and cook with the lid down.

Grilled Cheeseburgers

We suggest grating cheese into the raw beef as opposed to melting it on top. Because the cheese is more evenly distributed, *a little goes much farther than a chunk on top. Also, there's no danger of overcooking the burgers while you wait for the cheese to melt.*

Follow the recipe for Charcoal-Grilled Hamburgers or Gas-Grilled Hamburgers, mixing 3½ ounces cheddar, Swiss, Jack, or blue cheese, shredded or crumbled as necessary, into the ground chuck along with the salt and pepper. Shape and cook the burgers as directed.

Grilled Hamburgers with Garlic, Chipotles, and Scallions

Toast 3 medium unpeeled garlic cloves in a small dry skillet over medium heat, shaking the pan occasionally, until the garlic is fragrant and the color deepens slightly, about 8 minutes. When cool enough to handle, skin and mince the garlic. Follow the recipe for Charcoal-Grilled Hamburgers or Gas-Grilled Hamburgers, mixing the garlic, 1 tablespoon minced chipotle chile in adobo sauce, and 2 tablespoons minced scallions into the meat along with the salt and pepper. Shape and cook the burgers as directed.

Grilled Hamburgers with Cognac, Mustard, and Chives

Mix 1½ tablespoons cognac, 2 teaspoons Dijon mustard, and 1 tablespoon minced fresh chives together in a small bowl. Follow the recipe for Charcoal-Grilled Burgers or Gas-Grilled Burgers, mixing the cognac mixture into the meat along

---

SCIENCE: No More Puffy Burgers

All too often, burgers come off the grill with a domed, puffy shape that makes it impossible to keep condiments from sliding off. Fast-food restaurants produce burgers that are evenly shaped, but they are also extremely thin. We wondered if we could find a way to produce a meatier burger that would have the same thickness from edge to edge, giving the condiments a nice, flat top on which to sit.

We shaped 6-ounce portions of ground beef into patties that were 1 inch, ¾ inch, and ½ inch thick. Once cooked, all of these burgers looked like tennis balls, and it was nearly impossible to anchor ketchup and other goodies on top. After talking to several food scientists, we understood why this happens.

The culprit behind puffy burgers is the connective tissue, or collagen, that is ground up along with the meat. When the connective tissue in a patty heats up to roughly 130 degrees, it shrinks. This happens first on the flat top and bottom surfaces of the burger and then on the sides, where the tightening acts like a belt. When the sides tighten, the interior meat volume is forced up and down, so the burger puffs.

One of the cooks in the test kitchen suggested a trick she had picked up when working in a restaurant. We shaped patties ¾ inch thick but then formed a slight depression in the center of each one so that the edges were thicker than the center. On the grill, the center puffed up to the point where it was the same height as the edges. Finally, a level burger that could hold onto toppings.

with the salt and pepper. Shape and cook the burgers as directed.

Grilled Hamburgers with Porcini Mushrooms and Thyme

Cover ½ ounce dried porcini mushroom pieces with ½ cup hot tap water in a small microwave-safe bowl; cover with plastic wrap, cut several steam vents with a paring knife, and microwave on high power for 30 seconds. Let stand until the mushrooms soften, about 5 minutes. Lift the mushrooms from the liquid with a fork and mince, using a chef's knife (you should have about 2 tablespoons). Follow the recipe for Charcoal-Grilled Hamburgers or Gas-Grilled Hamburgers, mixing the porcini mushrooms and 1 teaspoon minced fresh thyme leaves into the meat along with the salt and pepper. Shape and cook the burgers as directed.

Pan-Seared Hamburgers

SERVES 4

A well-seasoned cast-iron pan is our first choice for this recipe, but any heavy-bottomed skillet can be used.

1 ½	pounds 80 percent lean ground chuck
1	teaspoon salt
½	teaspoon ground black pepper
	Buns and desired toppings

1. Break up the chuck to increase the surface area for seasoning. Sprinkle the salt and pepper over the meat; toss lightly with your hands to distribute the seasonings. Divide the meat into 4 equal portions (6 ounces each); with cupped hands, toss one portion of meat back and forth to form a loose ball. Pat lightly to flatten the meat into a ¾-inch-thick burger that measures about 4½ inches across. Press the center of the patty down with your fingertips until about ½ inch thick, creating a well, or divot, in the center. Repeat with the remaining portions of meat.

2. Heat a heavy-bottomed 12-inch skillet over medium-high heat. When the skillet is hot (drops of water flicked into it should evaporate immediately), add the patties, divot-side up. Cook the burgers, turning once, to the desired doneness, about 3 minutes per side for rare, 3½ minutes per side for medium-rare, 4 minutes per side for medium, and 5 minutes per side for well-done. Serve immediately in buns with desired toppings.

MEAT LOAF

NOT ALL MEAT LOAVES RESEMBLE MAMA'S. In fact, some ingredient lists look like the work of a proud child or defiant adolescent. Canned pineapple, cranberry sauce, raisins, prepared taco mix, and even goat cheese have all found their way into published recipes. Rather than feud over flavorings, though, we decided to focus on the meatier issues.

To begin with, we narrowed our testing to red meat. We had plenty of questions to answer: What meat or mix of meats delivers good mouthfeel and flavor? Which fillers offer unobtrusive texture? Should the loaf be cooked free-form or in a standard loaf pan, or are the new perforated pans designed for meat loaves worth the money? Should the loaf be topped with bacon, ketchup, both, or neither? Is it better to sauté the onions and garlic before adding them to the meat mix, or are they just as good raw and grated?

To determine which ground meat or meat mix makes the best loaf, we used a very basic meat loaf

COOKING BURGERS INDOORS

NOTHING BEATS A GRILLED HAMBURGER, but weather and circumstance (like living in a high-rise apartment) may not always permit outdoor cooking. So what's the best way to cook hamburgers in the kitchen?

Broiling and pan-searing are the two obvious choices. Even with the burgers very close to the heating element, we found that broiling did not create the kind of thick crust we wanted. We had much better results in a very hot pan (cast iron is ideal). And we didn't even need any fat in the pan to keep the burgers from sticking. All of the variations on pages 348 to 349 can be cooked according to the recipe that follows.

recipe and made miniature loaves with the following meat proportions: equal parts beef chuck and pork; equal parts veal and pork; equal parts beef chuck, pork, and veal; 2 parts beef chuck to 1 part ground pork and 1 part ground veal; 3 parts beef chuck and 1 part ground bacon; equal parts beef chuck and ham; all ground beef chuck; and all ground veal.

We found out that meat markets haven't been selling meat loaf mix (a mix of beef, pork, and veal, usually in equal proportions) all these years for nothing. As we expected, the best meat loaves were made from the combinations of these three meats. Straight ground veal was tender but overly mild and mushy, while the all-beef loaf was coarse-textured, liver-flavored, and tough. Though interesting, neither the beef/ham nor the beef/bacon loaves looked or tasted like classic meat loaf. Both were firm, dense, and more terrine-like. Also, as bacon lovers, we preferred the bacon's smoky flavor and crispy texture surrounding, not in, the loaf.

Although both of the beef/pork/veal mixtures were good, we preferred the mix with a higher proportion of ground chuck. This amount gave the loaf a distinct but not overly strong beef flavor. The extra beef percentage also kept the loaf firm, making it easier to cut. Mild-tasting pork added another flavor dimension, while the small quantity of veal kept it tender. For those who choose not to special-order this mix or mix it themselves at home, we recommend the standard meat loaf mix of equal parts beef, pork, and veal.

After comparing meat loaves made with and without fillers or binders, we realized that starch in a meat loaf offers more than economy. Loaves made without filler were coarse-textured, dense, and too hamburger-like. Those with binders, on the other hand, had that distinctive meat loaf texture.

But which binder to use? Practically every hot and cold cereal box offers a meat loaf recipe using that particular cereal. We made several meat loaves, each with a different filler. Though there was no clear-cut winner, we narrowed the number from 11 down to three. After tasting all the meat loaves, we realized that a good binder should help with texture but not add distinct flavor. Cracker crumbs, quick-cooking oatmeal, and fresh bread crumbs fit the bill.

Just as we found that we liked the less distinctly flavored fillers, so we preferred sautéed—not raw—onions and garlic in the meat mix. Because the meat loaf cooks to an internal temperature of just 160 degrees, raw onions never fully cook. Sautéing the vegetables is a five-minute detour well worth the time.

We found our meat loaves in need of some liquid to moisten the filler. Without it, the filler robs the meat dry. As with the fillers, we ran across a host of meat loaf moisteners and tried as many as made sense. Tomato sauce made the loaf taste like a meatball with sauce. We liked the flavor of ketchup but ultimately decided that we preferred it baked on top rather than inside. Beer and wine do not make ideal meat moisteners, either. The meat doesn't cook long enough or to a high enough internal temperature to burn off the alcohol, so the meat ends up with a distinctly raw alcohol taste.

As with many other aspects of this home-cooked favorite, we found that there is a good reason why the majority of meat loaf recipes call for some form of dairy for the liquid—it's the best choice. We tried half-and-half, milk, sour cream, yogurt, skim and whole evaporated milk, and even cottage cheese. Whole milk and plain yogurt ended up as our liquids of choice, with the yogurt offering a complementary subtle tang to the rich beef.

EQUIPMENT: Food Processor as Grinder

Even though we have a meat grinder in our test kitchen, we don't regularly grind meat ourselves. The setup, breakdown, and cleanup required for a 2-pound chuck roast is just not worth the effort. Besides, hamburgers are supposed to be impromptu, fast, fun food.

To our surprise, the food processor does a respectable grinding job, and it's much easier to use than a grinder. The key is to make sure the roast is cold, that it is cut into small chunks, and that it is processed in small batches. For a 2-pound roast, cut the meat into 1-inch chunks. Divide the chunks into four equal portions. Place one portion of meat in the workbowl of a food processor fitted with a steel blade. Pulse the cubes until the meat is ground, fifteen to twenty 1-second pulses. Repeat with the remaining portions of beef. Then shape the ground meat as directed in the recipe.

Cooks who don't like a crusty exterior on their meat loaf usually prefer to bake it in a loaf pan. We found that the high-sided standard loaf pan, however, causes the meat to stew rather than bake. Also, for those who like a glazed top, there is another disadvantage: The enclosed pan allows the meat juices to bubble up from the sides, diluting and destroying the glaze. Similarly, bacon placed on top of the meat loaf curls and doesn't properly attach to the loaf, and if tucked inside the pan, the bacon never crisps.

For all these reasons, we advise against the use of a standard loaf pan. If you prefer a crustless, soft-sided meat loaf, invest in a meat loaf pan with a perforated bottom and accompanying drip pan. The enclosed pan keeps the meat soft while the perforated bottom allows the drippings to flow to the pan below. While still not ideal for a crispy bacon top, it at least saves the glaze from destruction.

Ultimately, we found that baking a meat loaf free-form on a rimmed baking sheet gave us the results we wanted. The top and sides of the loaf brown nicely, and basting sauces, like the brown sugar and ketchup sauce we developed, glaze the entire loaf, not just the top. Bacon, too, covers the whole loaf. And because its drippings also fall into the pan, the bacon crisps up nicely.

Meat Loaf with Brown Sugar–Ketchup Glaze

SERVES 6 TO 8

If you like, you can omit the bacon topping from the loaf. In this case, brush on half of the glaze before baking and the other half during the last 15 minutes of baking. If you choose not to special-order the mix of meat below, we recommend the standard meat loaf mix of equal parts beef, pork, and veal, available at most grocery stores.

GLAZE

- 1/2   cup ketchup or chili sauce
- 4   tablespoons brown sugar
- 4   teaspoons cider or white vinegar

MEAT LOAF

- 2   teaspoons vegetable oil
- 1   medium onion, chopped (about 1 cup)
- 2   medium garlic cloves, minced or pressed through a garlic press (about 2 teaspoons)
- 2   large eggs
- 1/2   teaspoon dried thyme leaves
- 1   teaspoon salt
- 1/2   teaspoon ground black pepper
- 2   teaspoons Dijon mustard
- 2   teaspoons Worcestershire sauce
- 1/4   teaspoon hot pepper sauce, such as Tabasco
- 1/2   cup whole milk or plain yogurt
- 2   pounds meat loaf mix (50 percent ground chuck, 25 percent ground pork, 25 percent ground veal)
- 2/3   cup crushed saltine crackers (about 16) or quick oatmeal or 1 1/3 cups fresh bread crumbs (page 125)
- 1/3   cup minced fresh parsley leaves
- 8   ounces (8 slices) bacon, or more as needed (amount will vary depending on loaf shape)

1. FOR THE GLAZE: Mix all of the ingredients together in a small saucepan; set aside.

2. FOR THE MEAT LOAF: Heat the oven to 350 degrees. Heat the oil in a medium skillet. Add the onion and garlic; sauté until softened, about 5 minutes. Set aside to cool while preparing the remaining ingredients.

3. Mix the eggs with the thyme, salt, black pepper, mustard, Worcestershire sauce, hot pepper sauce, and milk in a medium bowl. Add the egg mixture to the meat in a large bowl along with the crackers, parsley, and cooked onion and garlic; mix with a fork until evenly blended and the meat mixture does not stick to the bowl. (If mixture sticks, add more milk, a couple tablespoons at a time, until the mix no longer sticks.)

4. Turn the meat mixture onto a work surface. With wet hands, pat the mixture into a loaf shape approximately 9 by 5 inches. Place on a foil-lined (for easy cleanup) rimmed baking sheet. Brush with half the glaze, then arrange the bacon slices, crosswise, over the loaf, overlapping slightly, to completely cover the surface of the loaf. Use a spatula to tuck the bacon ends underneath the loaf.

5. Bake the loaf until the bacon is crisp and the internal temperature of the loaf registers 160 degrees, about 1 hour. Cool at least 20 minutes.

Simmer the remaining glaze over medium heat until thickened slightly. Slice the meat loaf and serve with the remaining glaze passed separately.

TAMALE PIE

TAMALE PIE HAS ITS ROOTS IN SOUTHWEST–ern cooking. A mildly spicy ground meat filling is layered between a cornmeal crust and baked. Versions of this dish have been made throughout the past century. Although time and fashion have altered the recipe from decade to decade, the basic idea remains the same. A good pie contains a juicy, spicy mixture of meat and vegetables encased in a cornmeal crust that is neither too stiff nor too loose. Bad tamale pies, however, are dry and bland and usually have too much or too little filling.

Modern recipes often use cornbread for the crust. Many of these cornbread recipes skip the bottom layer of crust all together and just bake cornbread batter on top of the ground meat filling. More traditional recipes use cornmeal mush (cornmeal cooked with liquid, not unlike polenta) for both the bottom and top crusts. After several tests, we came to prefer a more traditional pie fully encased in cornmeal mush. Not only was this kind of tamale pie easier to serve, but its soft, polenta-like texture mixed nicely with the meat filling and was easier to eat.

We did have a number of questions about how to prepare the cornmeal mush. For starters, we tested finely ground cornmeal (such as Quaker, which is sold in most supermarkets) against coarser meals. As expected, the crust made with fine ground cornmeal was slightly smoother, but it was also bland in comparison with the toothsome crust made with coarse ground cornmeal. We made the mush with water and broth as well as with and without butter. Tasters preferred the clean, simple flavor of mush made with just water, salt, and cornmeal. The broth and butter added more flavor and fat to the crust than was necessary. We found 4 cups of water to 1½ cups cornmeal yielded a spoonable texture with enough structure to contain the meat filling.

Authentic and modern recipes use a variety of techniques to make the mush; some cook it slowly over low heat to keep it from burning, while others use the microwave. We found it difficult to keep an eye on the mush in the microwave, while cooking it low and slow was unnecessary. Using medium–high

---

INGREDIENTS: Ketchup

For many people, a burger isn't done until it has been coated liberally with ketchup. Ketchup is also an essential ingredient in many meat loaf recipes, including ours. This condiment originated in Asia as a salty, fermented medium for pickling or preserving ingredients, primarily fish. Early versions were made with anchovies and generally were highly spiced.

Tomato-based ketchup has its origins in nineteenth-century America. We now consume more than 600 million pints of ketchup every year, much of it landing on top of burgers. But as any ketchup connoisseur knows, not all brands are created equal. To find out which is the best, we tasted 13 different samples, including several fancy mail-order ketchups and one we made in our test kitchen.

It wasn't much of a surprise that the winner was Heinz. For all tasters but one, Heinz ranked first or second, and they described it with words like "classic" and "perfect." A tiny bit sweeter than Heinz, Del Monte took second place, while Hunt's (the other leading national brand, along with Heinz and Del Monte) rated third.

What about the mail-order, organic, fruit-sweetened, and homemade ketchups? Most tasters felt these samples were overly thick and not smooth enough. Some were too spicy, others too vinegary. Our homemade ketchup was too chunky, more like "tomato jam" than ketchup. In color, consistency, and flavor, none of these interlopers could match the archetypal ketchup, Heinz.

THE BEST KETCHUP
In a blind taste-test, Heinz beat 12 other samples, including several high-priced boutique brands. Panelists described it as "glossy," "balanced," and "smooth."

heat and a heavy-duty whisk, the mush took only 3 minutes to thicken to the right consistency.

With the cornmeal mush crust in place, we moved on to the filling. Most recipes use either ground beef or ground pork as the base, but we liked the flavors of both when mixed together. An all-beef pie turned out boring and tough, while an all-pork pie was light and mealy. A pie made with equal amounts of beef and pork turned out flavorful and nicely textured.

Most tamale pie fillings call for tomatoes, corn, and black beans. We found that this simple recipe easily accommodates canned and frozen vegetables with no ill effect on the final flavor. Seasoned with onion, garlic, jalapeño, and a little fresh oregano, the tamale filling tasted fresh and spicy.

Putting together the crust and filling was simple. We found that a deep-dish pie plate held the volume of this pie perfectly, and the sloped edges made it easy to spread the cornmeal mush over the bottom and up the sides evenly. A layer of cheese just under the top crust melts nicely without turning the top crust soggy or mixing prematurely with the filling. Sealed with a top layer of cornmeal mush, the pie needs only 30 minutes on the lowest oven rack in a 375-degree oven for the cornmeal to set and the pie to heat through. The pie will be easier to serve if you allow it to cool slightly before digging in.

Tamale Pie

SERVES 6 TO 8

We like coarse cornmeal (about the texture of kosher salt) for the crust. We had good results with Goya Coarse Yellow Cornmeal. To keep the cornmeal mush at a spreadable consistency, cover it while assembling the pie. If the mush does get too dry, simply loosen it with a little hot water.

FILLING

Butter for greasing pie plate

1 tablespoon vegetable oil

½ pound 90 percent lean ground beef

½ pound ground pork

1 large onion, chopped fine

1 medium jalapeño chile, stemmed, seeded, and minced

2 medium garlic cloves, minced or pressed through a garlic press (about 2 teaspoons)

1 teaspoon ground cumin

¼ teaspoon cayenne pepper

1 tablespoon chili powder

1 teaspoon salt

1 (14.5-ounce) can diced tomatoes

1 (15-ounce) can black beans, drained and rinsed

1 cup fresh or frozen corn

1 tablespoon minced fresh oregano leaves

Ground black pepper

2 ounces Monterey Jack cheese, shredded (about ½ cup)

CRUST

4 cups water

¾ teaspoon salt

1½ cups coarse cornmeal

1. FOR THE FILLING: Butter a 10-inch deep-dish pie plate (or similar casserole dish with 3-quart capacity) and set it aside. Adjust an oven rack to the lowest position and heat the oven to 375 degrees.

2. Heat the oil in a large skillet over high heat until hot, about 1 minute. Add the ground beef and pork and cook, breaking up large clumps of meat with a wooden spoon, until no longer pink and beginning to brown, about 4 minutes. Add the onion and chile and cook until just softened, about 3 minutes. Add the garlic, cumin, cayenne, chili powder, and salt and cook until aromatic, about 30 seconds. Add the tomatoes with their juice along with the black beans and corn. Simmer until most of the liquid has evaporated, about 3 minutes. Remove the pan from the heat and stir in the oregano and pepper to taste. Set aside.

3. FOR THE CRUST: Bring the water to a boil in a heavy-bottomed, large saucepan over high heat. Add the salt and then slowly pour in the cornmeal while whisking vigorously to prevent lumps from forming. Reduce the heat to medium-high and cook, whisking constantly, until the cornmeal begins to soften and the mixture thickens, about 3 minutes. Remove the pan from the heat.

4. TO ASSEMBLE AND BAKE: Spread two thirds of the cornmeal mixture (about 2½ cups) over the

bottom and up the sides of the buttered pie plate. Cover the pan with the remaining cornmeal mixture to prevent it from drying out. Spoon the beef mixture evenly into the dish and sprinkle with the cheese. Spread the remaining cornmeal mixture evenly on top of the cheese, spreading it out to the edges of the pie plate to seal in the filling.

5. Bake until the crust has set and the pie is heated through, 25 to 30 minutes. Remove the pie plate from the oven and let cool for 10 minutes. Spoon portions onto individual plates or into bowls and serve immediately.

SLOPPY JOES

EVERYONE LOVES A GOOD SLOPPY JOE. Spooned into a supermarket hamburger bun, the loose meat filling and ketchup-sweet sauce soak the bottom half of the bun, causing it to disintegrate and forcing diners to eat this informal sandwich with a fork. Sloppy Joe spice packages and canned premade filling can be found in supermarkets everywhere. But this quick-cooking sandwich tastes far better when made from scratch.

Most recipes call for the same few ingredients: ground meat, onions, garlic, some sort of tomato product, and seasonings. After making a few renditions of this recipe, we noted the keys to success include well-cooked but not overdone meat, an ample amount of slightly spicy/slightly sweet sauce, and a minimum of other seasonings. But a few questions remained: Which type of ground meat, which tomato products, and which seasonings?

Starting with the meat, we tried 95 percent, 90 percent, 85 percent, and 80 percent lean ground beef. The 95 percent and 90 percent lean had great meaty flavor but turned out dry and rubbery. At the other extreme, the 80 percent lean meat was too greasy. The 85 percent lean ground beef struck the perfect balance between meat and fat.

Although some recipes call for sauces made entirely from ketchup, we found them tart, vinegary, and lacking tomato flavor. We then tried combining the ketchup with tomato puree, crushed tomatoes, and tomato paste. The smooth, slightly thickened texture of pureed tomatoes worked well,

adding an honest tomato punch to the ketchup. We liked the balance of sweet and vinegar flavors when one half cup of ketchup was mixed with one cup of tomato puree. We then added one quarter cup of water to the sauce as it cooked, loosening it to the proper "sloppy" consistency.

To this ketchup-tomato puree, we tried adding numerous spices, including chili powder, Tabasco, Worcestershire, celery salt, garlic powder, dried onion, paprika, dry mustard, and sugar. While fresh onion and garlic tasted better than their stale, powdered counterparts, tasters disliked all other spices except small amounts of chili powder, Tabasco, and sugar. A little kick from the chili powder and Tabasco balanced lightly by brown sugar gave our Sloppy Joes a straightforward and simple flavor. The other spices were unanimously deemed out of place in this simple sandwich.

Sloppy Joes
SERVES 4

True to their name, these sandwiches are sloppy to eat: Serve them on plates, with forks and knives.

1	tablespoon vegetable oil
1	medium onion, minced
1	medium garlic clove, minced or pressed through a garlic press (about 1 teaspoon)
1/2	teaspoon chili powder
3/4	pound 85 percent lean ground beef
1/4	teaspoon salt
1/8	teaspoon ground black pepper
1	teaspoon brown sugar
1	cup tomato puree
1/2	cup ketchup
1/4	cup water
	Dash hot pepper sauce, such as Tabasco (optional)
4	hamburger buns

1. Heat the oil in a large skillet over high heat until shimmering, about 1 minute. Add the onion and cook, stirring often, until softened and browned around the edges, about 2 minutes. Add the garlic and chili powder and cook until aromatic, about 30 seconds. Add the beef, salt, pepper, and sugar and

reduce the heat to medium. Cook, using a wooden spoon to help break the meat into small pieces, until the meat is no longer pink, about 3 minutes.

2. Add the tomato puree, ketchup, water, and Tabasco (if using). Cook until slightly thickened, about 4 minutes. Adjust the seasonings with salt and pepper to taste. Spoon ½ cup of the meat mixture onto each hamburger bun and serve immediately.

TACOS

SO MAYBE THEY'RE NOT AUTHENTIC MEXICAN. They're Tex-Mex . . . maybe even gringo. But ground beef tacos have earned themselves a special place in the palates of at least a couple of generations. We recall our mothers ripping open the seasoning packet, the colorful array of toppings in mismatched bowls that cluttered the tabletop, and, of course, the first bite that cracked the shell and sent a trickle of orange grease running down the wrist. Indeed, there is something appealing about the silly taco. It's a mix of spicy ground beef, shredded cheese, sweet chopped tomatoes (or, as some would have it, jarred salsa), and cool iceberg lettuce. Those in favor of more toppings can always add chopped onions, diced avocado, and sour cream. All this contained in a crisp and corny taco shell. Seems hard to go wrong.

But when we sampled a few tacos made from supermarket kits in the test kitchen, our happy memories faded. The fillings tasted flat and stale, reeking of dried oregano and onion powder. The store-bought shells tasted greasy and junky—too much like unwholesome snack food to be served at the dinner table. There's no denying that these seasoning packets, along with prefab taco shells, make taco-making ridiculously easy, but with only a little more effort we thought that we could produce a fiery, flavorful filling and crisp, toasty taco shells—tacos that even adults could enjoy.

We began by trying fillings made according to the few cookbook recipes we uncovered. There were two approaches. The first had us brown ground beef in a skillet, add spices, sometimes chopped onion and garlic, and water and then simmer. The second directed us to sauté the onion and garlic before adding the beef to the pan, and this is the technique we preferred. Sautéing the onion softened its texture and made its flavor full and sweet, while a quick minute of cooking helped bring out the garlic's flavor. For a pound of ground beef, a small chopped onion was enough; as for garlic, we liked the wallop of a tablespoon, minced.

For burgers we prefer the relatively fatty 80 percent lean ground chuck, and we expected we would like the same for the taco filling. After testing them all, though, we were surprised that our tastes leaned toward the leaner types: Anything fattier than 90 percent lean ground beef cooked into a slick, greasy mess.

The labels on taco seasoning packets indicate a hodgepodge of ingredients, including dehydrated onion and/or garlic, MSG, mysterious "spices," and even soy sauce. However, they all include chili powder so we started with one tablespoon and then quickly increased the total to two for more kick. A teaspoon each of ground cumin and ground coriander added savory, complex flavors. Dried oregano in a more modest amount—½ teaspoon—provided herbal notes. For a little heat, we added cayenne.

The flavors were bold, but we wanted to make them fuller and rounder. From past experience we knew that exposing the spices to some heat—as often done in various types of ethnic cooking—makes their flavors blossom, so we tried this technique with our taco filling. In one batch we simply sprinkled the spices over the beef as it simmered, and in the second we added the spices to the sautéed onion along with the garlic and gave them a minute to cook. The difference was marked. The second batch was richly and deeply flavored and the spices permeated the beef. In the first, however, the flavors seemed merely to sit in the liquid that surrounded the meat, and the beef itself tasted rather dull.

Since the meat was lean and we needed a sauce to carry the flavors of the spices, the filling required some liquid. Many recipes call only for water, but water produced a thin, hollow-tasting mixture. We also tried canned chicken broth, canned plain tomato sauce, and a combination of the two. A combination was best—the chicken broth offered backbone while the tomato sauce added viscosity and liveliness.

The final flavor adjustments to the filling came in the form of sweet and sour. Tasters responded positively to a teaspoon of brown sugar—the slightest amount of sweetness expanded and enriched the flavor of the spices. Two teaspoons of cider vinegar picked up where the tomato sauce left off by adding just enough acidity to activate all the taste buds. Our taco filling was now "perfect," in the words of one taster. We moved onto the shell.

Store-bought taco shells are insipid (see page 357 for details on our tasting), although so convenient that many home cooks may opt for them. We wondered, however, if it was worth the trouble to purchase store-bought corn tortillas that could then be fried at home, thereby producing a superior, homemade, taco shell. The flavor of the home-fried shells we tried was a revelation, so we went on to perfect a technique.

We began testing with the choice of oil for frying. Vegetable and canola oils worked fine, but corn oil edged out in front—its sweet flavor matched that of the tortillas. An 8-inch skillet held a tortilla comfortably and required a minimum of oil. We found that the shells fried up cleanly (not greasy) and evenly in 3/4 cup oil heated to a temperature between 350 and 375 degrees. Cooler oil left the shells greasy and hotter oil browned them erratically and pushed the oil too close to the smoking point. Since the oil quantity was relatively small and the tortillas are fried one at a time, we settled on medium, instead of high, heat to maintain the correct oil temperature.

Because corn tortillas are like thin pancakes—they will not hold a shape—the question was how to fry them into the traditional wedge-shape used for tacos. The method we settled on was simple enough. We fried one half of the tortilla until it stiffened, holding on to the other half with tongs. Next, the other half was submerged in the oil while we kept the shell mouth open (about 2 inches wide), again using the tongs. Finally, we slipped the first half back into the oil to finish. Each shell took about 2½ minutes, not an unreasonable investment of time given the huge improvement in taste and texture that homemade taco shells offer.

Of course, what's offered as taco toppings is purely a matter of choice. Shredded cheese, however, is required—Monterey Jack and cheddar were the obvious picks. We bypassed jarred salsa in favor of some simple chopped tomato and onions because we preferred their fresher, brighter flavors and textures. Shredded iceberg lettuce was favored over romaine for its crispier crunch. Sour cream and diced avocado were the other often-requested toppings. Finally, chopped fresh cilantro—never an

MAKING YOUR OWN TACO SHELLS

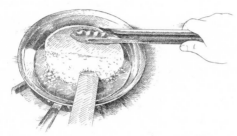

1. Using tongs to hold the tortilla, slip half of it into the hot oil. With a metal spatula in the other hand, submerge the half in the oil. Fry until just set, but not brown, about 30 seconds.

2. Flip the tortilla; using tongs, hold the tortilla open about 2 inches while keeping the bottom submerged in the oil. Fry until golden brown, about 1½ minutes. Flip again and fry the other side until golden brown, about 30 seconds.

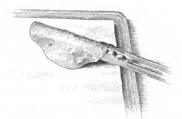

3. Transfer the shell, upside down, to the paper towel lined baking sheet to drain. Repeat with the remaining tortillas, adjusting the heat as necessary to keep the oil between 350 and 375 degrees.

option on our mothers' tables—was also welcomed. It helped to fast-forward the tacos of our pasts into the present. Truly these were tacos that tasted better than we remembered.

Beef Tacos

SERVES 4

Tomato sauce is sold in cans in the same aisle as canned whole tomatoes. Do not use jarred pasta sauce in its place. Taco topping are highly individual: You need not offer all of the ones that we suggest below, but cheese, lettuce, and tomatoes are, in our opinion, essential.

BEEF FILLING

2	teaspoons corn or vegetable oil
1	small onion, chopped small (about ²/₃ cup)
3	medium garlic cloves, minced or pressed through a garlic press (about 1 tablespoon)
2	tablespoons chili powder
1	teaspoon ground cumin
1	teaspoon ground coriander
¹/₂	teaspoon dried oregano
¹/₄	teaspoon cayenne pepper
	Salt
1	pound 90 percent lean (or leaner) ground beef
¹/₂	cup canned tomato sauce (not pasta sauce)
¹/₂	cup low-sodium chicken broth
1	teaspoon brown sugar
2	teaspoons vinegar, preferably cider vinegar
	Ground black pepper

SHELLS AND TOPPINGS

8	Home-Fried Taco Shells (recipe follows) or store-bought shells (warmed according to package instructions)
4	ounces cheddar or Monterey Jack cheese, shredded (about 1 cup)
2	cups shredded iceberg lettuce
2	small tomatoes, chopped small
¹/₂	cup sour cream
1	avocado, diced medium
1	small onion, chopped small
2	tablespoons chopped fresh cilantro leaves Hot pepper sauce, such as Tabasco

1. FOR THE FILLING: Heat the oil in a medium skillet over medium heat until hot and shimmering. Add the onion and cook, stirring occasionally, until softened, about 4 minutes. Add the garlic, spices, and ½ teaspoon salt; cook, stirring constantly, until fragrant, about 1 minute. Add the ground beef and cook, breaking the meat up with a wooden spoon and scraping the pan bottom to prevent scorching, until the beef is no longer pink, about 5 minutes. Add the tomato sauce, broth, sugar, and vinegar; bring to a simmer. Reduce the heat to medium-low and simmer uncovered, stirring frequently and breaking the meat up so that no chunks remain, until the liquid has reduced and thickened (the mixture should not be completely dry), about 10 minutes. Adjust the seasonings with salt and pepper to taste.

2. Using a wide, shallow spoon divide the filling

INGREDIENTS: Store-Bought Taco Shells

Prefab taco shells certainly simplify the process of taco-making, but we wondered if all shells were created equal. We conducted a tasting to find out, trying six brands of store-bought taco shells (warmed according to package instructions) as well as home-fried shells. The runaway winner was the home-fried shells. Uneven and imperfect, they looked charming and real, not manufactured. Most important, tasters preferred their clean, toasty corn flavor and crisp yet sturdy texture. One taster noted that the home-fried shells brought flavor and texture to the assembled taco, whereas most other taco shells seemed no more than convenient containers for the filling.

Rating the rest seemed more a matter of choosing the lesser of evils. Old El Paso Taco Shells finished a distant second. They

were described as "dry" and some tasters picked up "plastic" and "chemical" flavors, but a few appreciated their crispness and faint corn-y sweetness. El Rio Taco Shells and Ortega Taco Shells tied for third. The former were crisp but "too delicate" and "absolutely tasteless;" the latter were hard, dry, and tough, but some liked the "well-seasoned" corn flavor. Fourth place Taco Bell Taco Shells were bland with a decidedly stale texture. Bearitos Taco Shells, made with organically grown blue corn and costing almost a dollar more than some other brands, took fifth. Their color was off-putting and their texture too brittle and delicate to support the taco filling. Old El Paso White Corn Taco Shells came in sixth place, vetoed because of rancid flavor and stale texture.

evenly between taco shells; place 2 tacos on individual plates. Serve immediately, passing the toppings separately.

Home-Fried Taco Shells

MAKES 8 SHELLS

Fry taco shells before you make the filling, then rewarm them in a 200-degree oven for about 10 minutes before serving.

¾ cup corn, vegetable, or canola oil
8 corn tortillas (each 6 inches in diameter)

1. Heat the oil in a heavy-bottomed 8-inch skillet over medium heat to 350 degrees, about 5 minutes (the oil should bubble when a small piece of tortilla is dropped in; the tortilla should rise to the surface in 2 seconds and be light golden brown in about 1½ minutes). Meanwhile, line a rimmed baking sheet with a double thickness of paper towels.

2. Follow the illustrations on page 356 to fry the shells.

BOLOGNESE SAUCE

SCORES OF DELICIOUS MEAT-BASED SAUCES are made in Italy and elsewhere, but slow-simmering Bolognese (it comes from the city of Bologna, hence the name) is perhaps the best. Unlike meat sauces in which tomatoes dominate (think jars of spaghetti sauce with flecks of meat in a sea of tomato puree), Bolognese sauce is about the meat, with the tomatoes in a supporting role. Bolognese also differs from many tomato-based meat sauces in that it contains dairy—butter, milk, and/or cream. The dairy gives the meat an especially sweet, appealing flavor.

Bolognese sauce is not hard to prepare (the hands-on work is less than 30 minutes), but it does require hours of slow simmering. The sauce must be worth the effort. Bolognese should be complex, with a good balance of flavors. The meat should be first and foremost, but there should be sweet, salty, and acidic flavors in the background.

All Bolognese recipes can be broken down into three steps. First, vegetables are sautéed in fat. Ground meat is then browned in the pan. The final step is the addition of liquids and slow simmering over very low heat.

After an initial round of testing in which we made five styles of Bolognese, we had a recipe we liked pretty well. We preferred using only onion, carrot, and celery for the vegetable combination, and we liked them sautéed in butter rather than oil. We also discovered that a combination of ground beef, veal, and pork made this sauce especially complex and rich-tasting. The veal adds finesse and delicacy to the sauce, while the pork makes it sweet. Settling on the liquid element of the recipe, however, proved more difficult.

The secret to a great Bolognese sauce is the sequential reduction of various liquids over the sautéed meat and vegetables. The idea is to build flavor and tenderize the meat, which toughens during the browning phase. Many recipes insist on a particular order for adding these liquids. The most common liquid choices we uncovered in our research were milk, cream, stock, wine (both red and white), and tomatoes (fresh, canned whole, crushed, or paste). We ended up testing numerous combinations to find the perfect balance.

Liquids are treated in two ways. In the earlier part of the cooking process, liquids are added to the pan and simmered briskly until fully evaporated, the point being to impart flavor rather than to cook the meat and vegetables. Wine is always treated this way; if the wine is not evaporated, the sauce will be too alcoholic. Milk and cream are often but not always treated this way. Later, either stock or tomatoes are added in greater quantity and allowed to cook off very slowly. These liquids add flavor, to be sure, but they also serve as the cooking medium for the sauce during the slow simmering phase.

We tested pouring wine over the browned meat first, followed by milk. We also tried them in the opposite order—milk, then wine. We found that the meat cooked in milk first was softer and sweeter. As the bits of meat cook, they develop a hard crust that makes it more difficult for them to absorb liquid. Adding the milk first, when the meat is just barely cooked, works better. The milk penetrates more easily, tenderizing the meat and making it especially sweet.

We tried using cream instead of milk but felt that the sauce was too rich. Milk provides just enough dairy flavor to complement the meat flavor. (Some recipes finish the sauce with cream. We found that cream added just before the sauce was done was also overpowering.) So we settled on milk as the first liquid for the sauce. For the second liquid, we liked both white and red wine. White wine was a bit more delicate and is our choice for the basic recipe.

Then we moved on to the final element in most recipes, the cooking liquid. We did not like any of the recipes we tested with stock. As for tomato paste, we felt that it had little to offer; with none of the bright acidity of canned whole tomatoes and no fresh tomato flavor, it produced a dull sauce.

We tried tomatoes three more ways—fresh, canned diced, and canned crushed. Fresh tomatoes did nothing for the sauce and were a lot of work, as we found it necessary to peel them. (If not peeled, the skins would separate during the long cooking process and mar the texture of the sauce.) Crushed tomatoes were fine, but they did not taste as good as the canned whole tomatoes that we chopped. Diced tomatoes have an additional benefit—the packing juice. Because Bolognese sauce simmers for quite a while, it's nice to have all that juice to keep the pot from scorching.

Our recipe was finally taking shape, with all the ingredients in place. But we still wanted to know if it was necessary to cook Bolognese sauce over low heat and, if so, how long the sauce must simmer. When we tried to hurry the process by cooking over medium heat to evaporate the tomato juice more quickly, the meat was too firm and the flavors were not melded. Low simmering over the lowest possible heat—a few bubbles may rise to the surface of the sauce at one time, but it should not be simmering all over—is the only method that allows enough time for flavor to develop and for the meat to become tender.

As for the timing, we found that the sauce was too soupy after two hours on low heat, and the meat was still pretty firm. At three hours, the meat was much softer, with a melt-in-the-mouth

consistency. The sauce was dense and smooth at this point. We tried simmering the sauce for four hours but found no benefit. In fact, some batches cooked this long overreduced and scorched a bit.

Fettuccine with Bolognese Sauce
SERVES 4

Don't drain the pasta of its cooking water too meticulously when using this sauce; a little water left clinging to the strands will help evenly distribute the very thick sauce, as will adding 2 tablespoons of butter along with the sauce. If doubling this recipe, increase the simmering times for the milk and the wine to 30 minutes each, and increase the simmering time once the tomatoes are added to 4 hours.

5	tablespoons unsalted butter
2	tablespoons minced onion
2	tablespoons minced carrot
2	tablespoons minced celery
3/4	pound meat loaf mix or 1/4 pound each ground chuck, ground veal, and ground pork
	Salt
1	cup whole milk
1	cup dry white wine
1	(28-ounce) can diced tomatoes
1	pound fresh or dried fettuccine
	Freshly grated Parmesan cheese

1. Heat 3 tablespoons of the butter in a large Dutch oven over medium heat. Add the onion, carrot, and celery and sauté until softened but not browned, about 6 minutes. Add the ground meat and ½ teaspoon salt; crumble the meat into tiny pieces with the edge of a wooden spoon. Cook, continuing to crumble the meat, until it just loses its raw color but has not yet browned, about 3 minutes.

2. Add the milk and bring to a simmer; continue to simmer until the milk evaporates and only clear fat remains, 10 to 15 minutes. Add the wine and bring to a simmer; continue to simmer until the wine evaporates, 10 to 15 minutes longer. Add the tomatoes and their juice and bring to a simmer. Reduce the heat to low so that the sauce continues to simmer just barely, with an occasional bubble or

two at the surface, until the liquid has evaporated, about 3 hours (if the lowest burner setting is too high to allow such a low simmer, use a flame tamer). Adjust the seasonings with salt to taste. Keep the sauce warm. (The sauce can be refrigerated in an airtight container for several days or frozen for several months. Warm over low heat before serving.)

3. Meanwhile, bring 4 quarts water to a rolling boil in a large pot. Add 1 tablespoon salt and the pasta. Cook until al dente. Drain the pasta, leaving some water on the noodles. Combine the pasta, sauce, and remaining 2 tablespoons butter and toss well. Divide the pasta among individual bowls and serve immediately, passing the Parmesan separately.

➤ VARIATIONS

Fettuccine with Beef Bolognese Sauce

There is something very appealing about the simplicity of an all-beef sauce. While it may lack some of the finesse and sweetness of the master recipe, its pure beef flavor is uniquely satisfying.

Follow the recipe for Fettuccine with Bolognese Sauce, substituting ¾ pound ground beef chuck for the meat loaf mix.

Fettuccine with Beef, Pancetta, and Red Wine Bolognese Sauce

All ground beef (rather than meat loaf mix) works best with the pancetta in this sauce. If you can't find pancetta, use prosciutto, but don't use American bacon, which is smoked and will overwhelm the beef. We found that red wine stands up to the more robust flavors in this sauce better than white wine.

INGREDIENTS: Pancetta

Just like bacon, pancetta comes from the belly of the pig, but it has a very different flavor. American bacon is cured with salt, sugar, and spices and then smoked. Pancetta is not smoked, and is cured with salt, pepper, and, usually, cloves, but no sugar. As a result, pancetta has a richer, meatier flavor than bacon. Pancetta is rolled tightly, packed in casing, and then sliced thin or thick as desired.

Follow the recipe for Fettuccine with Bolognese Sauce, adding 2 ounces minced pancetta to the butter along with the vegetables, substituting ¾ pound ground beef chuck for the meat loaf mix, and substituting an equal amount of red wine for the white wine.

MEATY TOMATO SAUCE

BOLOGNESE IS THE KING OF ITALIAN MEAT sauces, but making it can be a labor of love. Many Italian cooks prefer a simpler, more rustic sauce made from canned tomatoes and a stray piece of meat. The meat (often a pork chop) is browned, the fat drained, and the sauce built in the empty pan. Then the browned meat is added back to the sauce, the pan covered, and the sauce simmered slowly until the meat is fall-off-the-bone tender. Finally, the meat is shredded and stirred into the sauce, which is then served over rigatoni with a good sprinkling of grated cheese.

When we began testing this sauce, it soon became clear that the choice of meat was the most important issue. We tried pork chops from the blade, loin, and sirloin. Even the fattiest chops were dry and tough after braising. We wanted the meat to almost melt when added to the tomato sauce. We needed a piece of meat with more marbling so that it would not dry out during braising.

We thought about a cut from the shoulder—either picnic or Boston butt—because this part of the pig has more fat than the loin, where most chops come from. The problem with these shoulder roasts was their size; the smallest at the market was four pounds. Nevertheless, we cut a pound of this meat into stew-like chunks and proceeded. This meat was more yielding when cooked and had a better flavor. However, the sauce tasted a bit wan; the meat had not done a really good job of flavoring the tomato sauce.

At this point, we turned to spareribs, which are fattier than roasts from the shoulder. The braised meat from spareribs was better than the Boston butt—it was unctuous, almost gelatinous. Best of all, the tomato sauce really tasted meaty. The bones had flavored the sauce in a way that meat alone couldn't. But spareribs are sold in an entire rack that weighs three or more pounds. We needed only four or five ribs for a batch of sauce. That meant spending $9 on a rack of ribs and using half for the sauce and freezing the rest. Was there a more economical way to make this peasant sauce?

We paid $1.99 per pound for country-style ribs and were able to find a small packet with just 1½ pounds of ribs—enough for one batch of sauce, with no leftovers. The sauce made with country-style ribs was similar to the spareribs sauce.

Next, we wondered if this sauce could be made with beef. Short ribs are roughly equivalent to spareribs and country-style ribs. (On the cow, ribs cut from the belly, called the plate, as well as those cut from the back are called short ribs.) The sauce made with short ribs was delicious, too. It's just important to remember that short ribs must be simmered longer than pork ribs because they are thicker.

Pasta and Rustic Slow-Simmered Tomato Sauce with Meat

SERVES 4

This sauce can be made with either beef or pork ribs. Depending on their size, you will need 4 or 5 ribs. To prevent the sauce from becoming greasy, trim all external fat from the ribs and drain off most of the fat from the skillet after browning. This thick, rich, robust sauce is best with tubular pasta, such as rigatoni, ziti, or penne. Pass grated pecorino (especially nice with pork) or Parmesan cheese at the table. The sauce can be covered and refrigerated for up to 4 days or frozen for up to 2 months.

1	tablespoon olive oil
1 ½	pounds beef short ribs, or pork spareribs or country-style ribs, trimmed of fat
	Salt and ground black pepper
1	medium onion, minced
½	cup dry red wine
1	(28-ounce) can diced tomatoes
1	pound pasta (see note above)
	Freshly grated Pecorino Romano or Parmesan cheese

1. Heat the oil in a heavy-bottomed 12-inch skillet over medium-high heat until shimmering. Season the ribs with salt and pepper to taste and brown on all sides, turning occasionally with tongs, 8 to 10 minutes. Transfer the ribs to a plate; pour off all but 1 teaspoon fat from the skillet. Add the onion and sauté until softened, 2 to 3 minutes. Add the wine and simmer, scraping the pan bottom with a wooden spoon to loosen the browned bits, until the wine reduces to a glaze, about 2 minutes.

2. Return the ribs and accumulated meat juices on the plate to the skillet; add the tomatoes and their juices. Bring to a boil, then reduce the heat to low, cover, and simmer gently, turning the ribs several times, until the meat is very tender and falling off the bones, 1½ hours (for pork spareribs or country-style ribs) to 2 hours (for beef short ribs).

3. Transfer the ribs to a clean plate. When cool enough to handle, remove the meat from the bones and shred it with your fingers, discarding the fat and

EQUIPMENT: Flame Tamer

A flame tamer (or heat diffuser) is a metal disk that can be fitted over an electric or a gas burner to reduce the heat output. This device is especially useful when trying to keep a pot at the barest simmer. If you don't own a flame tamer (it costs less than $10 and is stocked at most kitchenware stores), you can fashion one from aluminum foil. Take a long sheet of heavy-duty foil and shape it into a 1-inch-thick ring that will fit on your burner. Make sure that the ring is an even thickness so that a pot will rest flat on it. The foil ring elevates the pot slightly above the flame or electric coil, allowing you to keep a pot of Bolognese sauce at the merest simmer.

HOMEMADE FLAME TAMER
A homemade flame tamer made with aluminum foil keeps sauces, such as Bolognese, from simmering too briskly.

bones. Return the shredded meat to the sauce in the skillet. Bring the sauce to a simmer over medium heat and cook, uncovered, until heated through and slightly thickened, about 5 minutes. Adjust the seasonings with salt and pepper to taste.

4. Meanwhile, bring 4 quarts water to a rolling boil in a large pot. Add 1 tablespoon salt and the pasta. Cook until al dente. Drain the pasta well. Toss the pasta with the sauce. Serve immediately, passing the cheese separately.

➤ VARIATIONS

Pasta and Tomato-Pork Sauce with Rosemary and Garlic

Follow the recipe for Pasta and Rustic Slow-Simmered Tomato Sauce with Meat, using pork spareribs or country-style ribs. Substitute 3 medium garlic cloves, minced (about 1 tablespoon), for the onion, and add 2 teaspoons minced fresh rosemary leaves to the skillet along with the garlic; sauté until softened and fragrant, about 30 seconds. Proceed with the recipe.

Pasta and Tomato-Beef Sauce with Cinnamon, Cloves, and Parsley

Follow the recipe for Pasta and Rustic Slow-Simmered Tomato Sauce with Meat, using beef short ribs and adding ½ teaspoon ground cinnamon, a pinch ground cloves, and 2 tablespoons minced fresh parsley leaves to the softened onion; sauté until the spices are fragrant, about 30 seconds longer. Proceed with the recipe.

MEATBALLS, ITALIAN STYLE

MANY COOKS THINK OF MEATBALLS AS HAMburgers with seasonings (cheese, herbs, garlic) and a round shape. This is partly true. However, unlike hamburgers, which are best cooked rare or medium-rare, meatballs are cooked through until well done—at which point they've often turned into dry, tough hockey pucks. When this is the case, the dish can be so heavy that Alka-Seltzer is the only dessert that makes sense.

Our goal was to create meatballs that were moist and light. We also wanted to develop a quick tomato sauce that was loaded with flavor. We focused on the meatballs first. Meatballs start with ground meat but require additional ingredients to keep them moist and lighten their texture. Meatballs also require binders to keep them from falling apart in the tomato sauce. A traditional source of moisture in meatballs is egg. We tested meatballs made with and without egg and quickly determined that the egg was a welcome addition. It made the meatballs both moister and lighter.

The list of possible binders included dried bread crumbs, fresh bread crumbs, ground crackers, and bread soaked in milk. We found that bread and cracker crumbs soaked up any available moisture, making the meatballs harder and drier when cooked to well done. In comparison, the meatballs made with bread soaked in milk were moist, creamy, and rich. Milk was clearly an important part of the equation.

We liked the milk but wondered if we could do better. We tried adding yogurt (which works well in our favorite meat loaf recipe) but had to thin it with milk in order to mix it with the bread. Meatballs made with thinned yogurt were even creamier and more flavorful than those made with plain milk. We also tried buttermilk; the results were just as good, with no need to thin the liquid.

With the dairy now part of our working recipe, we found the meatball mixture a tad sticky and hard to handle. By eliminating the egg white (the yolk has all the fat and emulsifiers that contribute smoothness), we eliminated the stickiness.

It was finally time to experiment with the crucial ingredient: the meat. Ground round was too lean; we preferred fattier chuck. We tried blending in ground veal but decided it was not worth the bother; these meatballs tasted bland. Ground pork was another matter. It added a welcome flavor dimension.

With our ingredients in order, it was time to test cooking methods. We tried roasting, broiling, and the traditional pan-frying. Roasting yielded dry, crumbly meatballs, while broiling was extremely messy and also tended to produce dry meatballs. Pan-frying produced meatballs with a rich, dark crust and moist texture.

We wondered if we could save cleanup time and build more flavor into the tomato sauce by making it in the same pan used to fry the meatballs. We emptied out the vegetable oil used to fry the meatballs (olive oil is too expensive for this task and doesn't add much flavor), then added a little olive oil (olive oil is important to the flavor of the sauce) before adding garlic and tomatoes. Not only did this method prove convenient but it also gave the sauce depth, as the browned bits that had formed when the meatballs were fried loosened from the pan bottom and dissolved in the sauce.

Meatballs need a thick, smooth sauce—the kind produced by canned crushed tomatoes. Sauces made with whole or diced tomatoes were too chunky and liquidy; they didn't meld with the meatballs and also made them soggy.

Meatballs, Italian Style

SERVES 4 TO 6, MAKING ENOUGH TO SAUCE
I POUND OF SPAGHETTI

The shaped meatballs can be covered with plastic wrap and refrigerated for several hours ahead of serving time, if you like. Fry the meatballs and make the sauce at the last

BROWNING MEATBALLS

We found that meatballs taste best when browned evenly on all sides. Their round shape makes this a challenge. Our solution is to brown the two broader sides of the meatballs first, then use tongs to stand the meatballs on their ends. If necessary, lean the meatballs against one another as they brown.

minute. With a pound of spaghetti, this recipe will feed 4 to 6. You can also use the meatballs and sauce to make meatball sandwiches—just place several hot meatballs and a spoonful of hot sauce in a split hero roll, top with cheese (grated Parmesan and/or shredded mozzarella), and run under the broiler until piping hot.

MEATBALLS

2	slices white sandwich bread (crusts discarded), torn into small pieces
½	cup buttermilk or 6 tablespoons plain yogurt thinned with 2 tablespoons whole milk
I	pound ground meat, (preferably ¾ pound ground chuck and ¼ pound ground pork)
¼	cup finely grated Parmesan cheese
2	tablespoons minced fresh parsley leaves
I	large egg yolk
I	medium garlic clove, minced or pressed through a garlic press (about I teaspoon)
¾	teaspoon salt
	Ground black pepper
I–I ½	cups vegetable oil for pan-frying

SMOOTH TOMATO SAUCE

2	tablespoons extra-virgin olive oil
I	medium garlic clove, minced or pressed through a garlic press (about I teaspoon)
I	(28-ounce) can crushed tomatoes
I	tablespoon minced fresh basil leaves
	Salt and ground black pepper

1. FOR THE MEATBALLS: Combine the bread and buttermilk in a small bowl. Let sit for 10 minutes, mashing occasionally with a fork, until a smooth paste forms.

2. Place the ground meat, Parmesan, parsley, egg yolk, garlic, salt, and pepper to taste in a medium bowl. Add the bread-milk mixture and combine until evenly mixed. Shape 3 tablespoons of the mixture into a 1½-inch-round meatball. (When forming meatballs, use a light touch. If you compact the meatballs too much, they can become dense and hard.) You should be able to make about 14 meatballs.

3. Pour vegetable oil into a 10- or 11-inch sauté pan to a depth of ¼ inch. Turn the heat to medium-high. After several minutes, test the oil with the

edge of a meatball. When the oil sizzles, add the meatballs in a single layer. Fry, turning several times, until nicely browned on all sides, about 10 minutes (see the illustration on page 363). Regulate the heat as needed to keep the oil sizzling but not smoking. Transfer the browned meatballs to a plate lined with paper towels and set aside.

4. FOR THE SAUCE: Discard the oil in the pan, but leave behind any browned bits. Add the olive oil for the tomato sauce along with the garlic and cook over medium heat, scraping up the browned bits on the pan bottom, just until the garlic is golden, about 30 seconds. Add the tomatoes, bring to a simmer, and cook until the sauce thickens, about 10 minutes. Stir in the basil and salt and pepper to taste. Add the meatballs and simmer, turning them occasionally, until heated through, about 5 minutes. Serve. (Leftover meatballs can be refrigerated in leftover sauce for 1 day. Warm the meatballs and sauce in a covered saucepan over medium-low heat until piping hot.)

SWEDISH MEATBALLS

SWEDISH MEATBALLS ARE TRADITIONALLY flavored with nutmeg and allspice and served with a lightly sweet cream sauce (and lingonberry preserves) during a celebratory Smorgasbord. They also can be served for dinner with a side of egg noodles or mashed potatoes. For many of us, however, their mention brings to mind dreadful, lead sinkers swimming in condensed cream of mushroom "gravy" in a chaffing dish. Wanting to rectify our embarrassing American rendition of this classic, we set out in search of the real thing.

Examining several authentic Swedish recipes, we were surprised to find how similar they were to our Italian-style meatball recipe. Most used a combination of ground pork and beef, added bread that had been soaked in some sort of dairy for tenderness, and pan-fried them in a skillet. Using our Italian recipe as the basis for our testing, we simply stripped out the Italian flavors of garlic and Parmesan and added a pinch of nutmeg and allspice for our first test. With a tender texture and delicate flavor, tasters found only a few improvements were needed.

Besides finding their size a bit too large, the consistency of the cooked meatballs was a bit mushy while their flavor was too tangy. Taking a closer look at the Italian ingredients we had left out, these comments quickly made sense.

The omission of the Parmesan had thrown off the balance of wet and dry ingredients, leaving the meatball mixture too wet. The flavorful, Italian meatballs had also benefited from the tangy flavor of buttermilk or yogurt (mashed into the bread), however, these flavors did not work with the more delicate Swedish seasonings. Replacing the original one half cup of buttermilk in our Italian meatballs with one quarter cup of heavy cream gave our Swedish the desired mild flavor and cohesive texture. Reducing the size of the meatballs to a more appropriate size was easy. Using a generous tablespoon measurement, we found the recipe yielded roughly 30 meatballs.

We wanted to add some onion flavor in place of the missing garlic and tried several ways to incorporate it into the meat mixture. Adding raw minced onion produced a stinky, steamed onion flavor and the bits of onion ruined the smooth texture of the meatballs. Sautéing the minced onion before adding it into the meat mixture tasted good, however, it was a bit of a pain. Grating the raw onion against the large holes of a box grater quickly broke the onion down to a mild-tasting, pulpy mush that was easily incorporated into the ground meat. This method was the clear winner.

Most authentic recipes use the pan drippings left over from frying the meatballs to make an accompanying creamy sauce with a slightly sweet flavor. This sauce is usually made with chicken broth and either sour cream or heavy cream. We first tried reducing broth in the pan with the drippings, then whisking in some sour cream and herbs. This, however, produced a watery, hollow-tasting sauce. Lightly thickening the broth with some flour and butter (a roux) produced a better consistency, while some bay leaves and brown sugar boosted the flavor of the sauce. Tasters liked sauces finished with either sour cream or heavy cream. With just a brief window in which to serve the sour cream sauce before it separated (thus taking on an ugly curdled appearance), we chose to go with the heavy cream.

Seasoned with a sprinkling of fresh dill and squirt of lemon juice, this flavorful sauce tastes great over a bed of egg noodles, yet is sturdy enough to withstand a few hours in a chaffing dish if need be.

Swedish Meatballs

SERVES 4 TO 6 AS A MAIN COURSE, MORE AS AN APPETIZER

The meatballs and sauce can be served with a pound of egg noodles or with mashed potatoes for dinner. To serve as an appetizer, keep the meatballs and sauce warm in a chafing dish. Over time, the sauce will thicken but can be thinned with a little milk or water.

MEATBALLS

2	slices white sandwich bread (crusts discarded), torn into small pieces
1/4	cup heavy cream
8	ounces ground chuck
8	ounces ground pork
1	large egg yolk
1	small onion, grated on the holes of a large box grater
1/8	teaspoon grated nutmeg
1/8	teaspoon ground allspice
	Salt and ground black pepper
1–1 1/2	cups vegetable oil for pan-frying

SAUCE

1	tablespoon unsalted butter
1	tablespoon all-purpose flour
1 3/4	cups low-sodium chicken broth
1	tablespoon dark brown sugar
2	bay leaves
2	tablespoons lemon juice from 1 lemon
1/2	cup heavy cream
1	tablespoon minced fresh dill

1. FOR THE MEATBALLS: Combine the bread and cream in a small bowl, mashing occasionally with a fork, until a smooth paste forms, about 10 minutes.

2. Place the ground meats, egg yolk, onion, nutmeg, allspice, 1/2 teaspoon salt, and 1/4 teaspoon pepper in a medium bowl. Add the bread-cream mixture and combine until evenly mixed. Shape a generous 1 tablespoon of the mixture into a 1-inch-round meatball. You should be able to make about 30 meatballs.

3. Pour vegetable oil into a 10- or 11-inch sauté pan to a depth of 1/4 inch. Turn the heat to medium-high. After several minutes, test the oil with the edge of a meatball. When the oil sizzles, add the meatballs in a single layer. Fry, turning several times, until lightly browned on all sides, 7 to 10 minutes. Regulate the heat as needed to keep the oil sizzling but not smoking. Transfer the browned meatballs to a plate lined with paper towels and set aside.

4. FOR THE SAUCE: Discard the oil in the pan but leave behind any browned bits. Add the butter and return the pan to medium-high heat. When the butter is melted, stir in the flour and cook for 30 seconds. Add the broth, sugar, and bay leaves, and bring to a simmer, scraping up the browned bits on the pan bottom. Cook until the sauce thickens, about 5 minutes. Add the cream and meatballs and simmer, turning them occasionally, until heated through, about 5 minutes. Remove pan from the heat and discard the bay leaves. Stir in the lemon juice and dill and season with salt and pepper to taste. Serve.

LAMB PATTIES

WHETHER YOU CALL IT KEFTA, KIBBE, KOFTA, or simply ground meat patties, lamb-based patties appear all over the Middle East. Generally the bastion of street vendors, the patties are stuffed into sandwiches with any number of toppings, from incendiary sauces and exotic pickles to a simple tahini or yogurt-based sauce and lettuce. We think these sandwiches make an exotic weeknight dinner. Middle Eastern spices and ground lamb turn an otherwise prosaic meatball sandwich into something special.

The sandwich is composed of three parts: the meat, the garnishes, and the bread, The patty recipes we researched ran the gambit as far as flavor and technique. Some included a long list of ingredients that necessitated a great deal of effort, while others kept the flavors simple and preparation brief. A quick taste test of extremes suggested we needed to find a comfortable medium. The simplest versions tasted bland and the fancy versions buried the meat under an inordinate amount of spices and took entirely too long to assemble.

After looking at numerous ingredient lists, we broke the patty down into three components—the meat, the binding, and the seasoning. Unlike ground beef, ground lamb is normally only available in one unspecified fat content. You could ask your butcher to grind fresh meat for you, but we found it unnecessary: additional fat renders out. (Much of lamb's somewhat "gamey" flavor is located in the fat, so we found leaner meat tasted milder, if this is a concern.)

In contrast to European-style meat patties, most Middle Eastern recipes do not contain much binding, relying instead on tight packing of the patty or an occasional handful of bulgur or bread crumbs. Most tasters found the authentic texture on the dense side, and suggested bread crumbs and dairy to help tenderize the meat and prevent the patties from drying out while frying. Just one slice of bread yielded all the crumbs necessary. For dairy, a little milk worked fine, but keeping in the spirit of things, yogurt proved the best choice as its sharp tang and rich flavor worked well with the robust lamb flavor.

Many recipes we researched contained a long list of spices. Patties from Morocco employed the spice blend call ras el hanout, which includes up to twenty spices, while recipes from Lebanon and Syria were more restrained, including cinnamon, allspice, cumin, cayenne, coriander, or turmeric. In an effort to keep things simple, we opted to use cumin for a deep musky flavor, and cayenne for bright heat. And to round out the flavorings, a handful of chopped cilantro brought a pleasant sharpness. The resulting patties tasted distinctly Middle Eastern and full flavored, all with a minimum of ingredients and labor.

Traditionally, the patties are grilled on skewers, but for the sake of convenience we opted for pan-frying. Broiling would have been the logical indoor replacement for grilling, but we found pan-frying offered more control and the patties developed a crisper crust—a definite bonus according to most tasters. All of the patties could fit into a large skillet at one time and were cooked through in less than 10 minutes. After a quick blot on paper towels, they were ready to eat. We briefly chilled the patties prior to frying. The cold firms them up and helps them retain their definition.

To finish the sandwich, though, we needed the sauce, lettuce, and the bread. Yogurt-based sauces appear throughout the Middle East and were a perfect accompaniment to lamb as the yogurt's sharpness cuts the lamb's richness. To keep the ingredient list brief, we chose to reuse some of the ingredients in the patties, including cilantro for brightness and cayenne for spiciness. To add pungency, we included minced garlic—just one clove so as to not overwhelm the other flavors.

Any mild, sweet lettuce will do, but tasters most enjoyed romaine for its sturdy leaves and crisp bite. And for bread, your favorite pita is perfect—just pick up the largest size you can find and cut off the top corner to facilitate filling.

Middle Eastern–Style Lamb Sandwiches with Yogurt Sauce
SERVES 4

If you would like to include more garnishes, tomato, pickled red onions, cucumber slices, and even sliced pickled pepperoncini would be appropriate. If you do not like cilantro, feel free to substitute fresh mint. If you don't have sandwich bread, one quarter of a large pita will do as a binder for the patties. Simply crumble it roughly and pulse it in a food processor until reduced to coarse crumbs. You will need large pita pockets—at least 8 inches in diameter—to hold the amount of filling per sandwich.

1	pound ground lamb
	Salt
1	teaspoon ground cumin
1/4	teaspoon cayenne pepper, plus additional to taste
3	tablespoons chopped fresh cilantro leaves
1	cup plus 3 tablespoons plain yogurt
1	slice white sandwich bread, crumbled into rough crumbs
1	small garlic clove, pressed through a garlic press or minced to a puree (see the illustrations on page 30)

3   tablespoons vegetable oil
4   large pita breads, top ½ inch sliced off each
4   cups coarsely chopped romaine lettuce

1. With your hands, mix the lamb, 1 teaspoon salt, cumin, cayenne, 2 tablespoons of the cilantro, the 3 tablespoons yogurt, and white bread crumbs together in a medium bowl. Divide the mixture into 12 equal pieces and roll them into balls. Gently flatten the balls into round disks, 1½ to 2 inches thick. Place the shaped patties on a large plate or baking sheet and place in the freezer for 5 minutes.

2. While the patties are chilling, combine the remaining 1 cup yogurt, remaining 1 tablespoon cilantro, garlic, and salt and cayenne to taste in a small bowl. Set the sauce aside.

3. Heat the oil in a large nonstick skillet over medium-high heat until shimmering. Using a spatula, place the patties in the skillet in a single layer and cook until well browned, about 2 minutes. Flip the patties, reduce the heat to medium, and cook until well browned on the second side, about 6 minutes. Transfer the browned patties to a plate lined with paper towels.

4. Divide the patties evenly among the pita rounds and stuff each with 1 cup lettuce and a spoonful of the yogurt sauce. Serve immediately, passing the remaining yogurt sauce at the table.

SHEPHERD'S PIE

NOTHING MORE THAN A RICH LAMB STEW blanketed under a mashed potato crust, shepherd's pie is a hearty casserole originally from the cool climes of sheep-centric northern Britain. Today, it is as much a part of American cookery as British, best eaten on a blustery winter day sidled up to a roaring fire with a frothy pint of stout. It's arguably America's favorite lamb dish.

Like numerous other dishes in this book, shepherd's pie was a meal made Monday with Sunday night's leftovers—the remnants of the roast, vegetables, and mashed potatoes. In this day and age, few of us have such delicious Sunday dinners, much less leftovers, so we aimed to create an assertively flavored shepherd's pie from scratch.

Our first step was to figure out what cut of lamb worked best. To save on prep time, we hoped to use ground lamb. Shepherd's pie made with ground lamb tasted OK, but it was somewhat bland. If pinched for time, ground lamb is a decent choice, but we prefer our favorite cut of lamb for stewing, shoulder chops. It is easy to cut the meat off the bone and into cubes, and, after searing, the meat delivers a rich lamb flavor without tasting gamey or greasy, as lamb often does. While many of the recipes we gathered specified minced lamb, we preferred larger, more toothsome chunks.

Choosing vegetables to flavor the lamb proved easy. Sautéed carrots and onions added sweetness and depth. A touch of garlic added a little zest, and sweet frozen peas—characteristic of many British-style meat stews—brought bright color to an otherwise drab-looking dish. For herbs, we wanted big flavors strong enough to stand up to the lamb's richness. Rosemary and thyme are traditional lamb flavorings, and they tasted great in this instance. Fresh, not dried, herbs provided the best flavor.

As for the liquid in the stew, we settled on chicken broth enriched with red wine. Beef broth clashed with lamb's earthy flavors, while chicken broth was neutral. After testing a variety of red wines, we liked a medium-bodied Côtes du Rhône best because it is well rounded, low in tannins, and not oaky, all traits that allowed it to marry well with all the flavors in the dish. In addition to the broth and wine, we added a little Worcestershire sauce for its sweetness and savory tang.

With the stew assembled and cooked, we were ready to top it off with a mashed potato crust. We quickly found out that simple mashed potatoes would not do; they crumbled and broke down while baking. We started our adjustments by reducing the amount of butter and dairy we usually add to mashed potatoes. To give the potatoes some structure, we then added egg yolk, turning the mashed potatoes into what is known as duchesse potatoes in France. The yolks did the trick; the potatoes retained their shape and texture and picked up a little more richness in the bargain. (Given the added richness of the yolks, we felt that whole milk, rather than half-and-half, was the better dairy choice.) The yolks also gave the potatoes a slight golden hue that complemented the deep brown of the stew beneath.

We tried a variety of methods for assembling the casserole and were most pleased with the simplest route. The stew fit into either a 13 by 9-inch baking dish or, more snugly, into a 10-inch pie plate, which made for a more attractive presentation than the rectangular dish. A large, rubber spatula was the best tool for spreading the potatoes evenly across the top of the stew. It was important to cover the stew completely and seal the edges of the pan with the potato topping; otherwise the stew sometimes bubbled out of the pan.

Because the lamb is already tender when it goes

MAKING PIE-SHAPED SHEPHERD'S PIE

The filling and potato topping for our shepherd's pie fit nicely in a standard 13 by 9-inch baking dish. But for a fancier presentation, we like to bake the pie in a 10-inch pie plate. The mashed potato topping rises high above the filling, much like a lemon meringue pie or baked Alaska. If you want to try this presentation, follow the steps below.

1. Place the filling in a 10-inch pie plate and then drop spoonfuls of mashed potatoes around the perimeter of the pie plate.

2. Use a rubber spatula to attach the potatoes to the rim of the pie plate. It's important to seal the edges this way to prevent the filling from bubbling out of the pie plate in the oven.

3. Drop the remaining mashed potatoes in the center of the pie plate and then smooth the top with the spatula. Because the topping rises so high, we recommend baking the pie on a rimmed baking sheet to catch any spills.

into the casserole, the baking time is short. Once the potato crust turns golden brown, the shepherd's pie is ready to come out of the oven.

Shepherd's Pie
SERVES 6 TO 8

Diced lamb shoulder chops give the filling a much richer flavor than ground lamb. If you prefer to use ground lamb, see the variation that follows. This recipe includes basic assembly instructions in a 13 by 9-inch baking dish. For a fancier presentation in a 10-inch pie plate, see the illustrations at left.

FILLING

3	pounds lamb shoulder chops (4 chops), boned and cut into 1-inch pieces (should yield about 1 1/2 pounds meat)
1 1/2	teaspoons salt
1	teaspoon ground black pepper
3	tablespoons vegetable oil
2	medium onions, chopped coarse
2	medium carrots, cut into 1/4-inch slices
1	medium garlic clove, minced or pressed through a garlic press (about 1 teaspoon)
2	tablespoons unbleached all-purpose flour
1	tablespoon tomato paste
2 1/4	cups low-sodium chicken broth
1/4	cup full-bodied dry red wine
1	teaspoon Worcestershire sauce
1	teaspoon chopped fresh thyme leaves
1	teaspoon chopped fresh rosemary
1	cup frozen peas, thawed

TOPPING

2	pounds large russet potatoes, peeled and cut into 2-inch cubes
1	teaspoon salt
6	tablespoons unsalted butter, softened
3/4	cup whole milk, warmed
2	large egg yolks
	Ground black pepper

1. FOR THE FILLING: Season the lamb with the salt and pepper. Heat 2 tablespoons of the oil in a 12-inch skillet over medium-high heat until shimmering. Add half of the lamb and cook, stirring

occasionally, until well browned on all sides, 5 to 6 minutes. Remove the lamb from the pan and set aside in a medium bowl. Heat the remaining 1 tablespoon oil in the pan. Add the remaining lamb and cook, stirring occasionally, until well browned on all sides, 5 to 6 minutes. Transfer the lamb to the bowl.

2. Reduce the heat to medium and add the onions and carrots to the fat in the now-empty pan. Cook until softened, about 4 minutes. Add the garlic, flour, and tomato paste and cook until the garlic is fragrant, about 1 minute. Whisk in the broth, wine, and Worcestershire sauce. Stir in the thyme, rosemary, and browned lamb. Bring to a boil, reduce the heat to low, cover, and simmer until the lamb is just tender, 25 to 30 minutes.

3. FOR THE TOPPING: Meanwhile, put the potatoes in a large saucepan; add water to cover and ½ of the teaspoon salt. Bring to a boil and continue to cook over medium heat until the potatoes are tender when pierced with a knife, 15 to 20 minutes. Drain the potatoes well and return them to the pan set over low heat. Mash the potatoes, adding butter as you mash. Stir in the warm milk and then the egg yolks. Season with the remaining ½ teaspoon salt and pepper to taste.

4. TO ASSEMBLE AND BAKE: Adjust an oven rack to the middle position and heat the oven to 400 degrees. Stir the peas into the lamb mixture and check the seasonings. Pour the lamb mixture evenly into a 13 by 9-inch baking dish. With a large spoon, drop spoonfuls of the mashed potatoes over the entire filling. Starting at the sides to ensure a tight seal, use a rubber spatula to smooth out the potatoes and anchor them to the sides of the baking dish. (You should not see any filling.) Bake until the top turns golden brown, 20 to 25 minutes. Let rest for 5 to 10 minutes and serve.

➤ VARIATION

Shepherd's Pie with Ground Lamb
Follow the recipe for Shepherd's Pie, substituting 1½ pounds ground lamb for the shoulder chops. Cook, one half at a time, until well browned, about 3 minutes for each batch of lamb. Proceed with the recipe as directed, reducing the simmering time in step 2 to 15 minutes.

CORNED BEEF HASH

CORNED BEEF HASH, IN PARTICULAR, CAN be traced back to New England ingenuity and frugality. What was served as boiled dinner the night before was recycled as hash the next morning. All the leftovers—meat, potatoes, carrots, and sometimes cabbage—would be fried up in a skillet and capped with an egg. This being a dish of leftovers, we found traditional recipes to be few and far between, as if corned beef hash were a common-sense dish, unworthy of a recipe. And the recipes we did find produced starchy, one-dimensional hash that was light on flavor. Knowing most people do not have leftovers from a boiled dinner sitting in their refrigerator, we set out to create a flavorful hash with fresh ingredients that was easy to prepare.

Meat and potatoes are the heart and soul of this dish—everything else is just seasoning. While leftover beef from the boiled dinner on page 194 is ideal, we found that deli-style corned beef can be satisfying. At first, we diced the meat into pieces equivalent in size to the potatoes, but this led to tough and chewy meat that sharply contrasted with the potato's velvety softness. Mincing the beef kept it tender and imparted a meatier flavor to the hash. There is no need for a uniform mince; we coarsely chopped the meat and then worked our knife back and forth across the rough dice until it was reduced to ¼-inch or smaller pieces.

Potatoes were an easy choice. Texture being foremost, we knew we wanted starchy potatoes that would retain some character but that would soften and crumble about the edges to bind the hash together. We quickly ruled out anything waxy, such as red potatoes, because they remained too firm. Russets were our top choice.

Prior to being combined with the beef, the potatoes must be parboiled. (If you have leftover boiled potatoes, you can skip this step.) While we generally boil our potatoes whole and unpeeled so they don't absorb too much liquid, we discovered that dicing the potatoes prior to cooking worked fine in this instance. And they cooked more quickly, too. To echo the flavors of the corned beef, we added a couple of bay leaves and a bit of salt to the cooking water. About four minutes of cooking after the potatoes had come to a boil yielded perfect potatoes—soft but not falling apart.

Onions and garlic sharpened the dish and a minimum of thyme added an earthiness that paired well with the beef. Although the potatoes loosely bound this mixture, most recipes call for either stock or cream to hold the ingredients more firmly together. We tested both and preferred the richness of the cream. A little hot pepper sauce added with the cream brought some spice to the dish.

After cooking several batches of hash at varying temperatures and with differing techniques, we realized that a fairly lengthy cooking time was crucial to flavor. The golden crust of browned meat and potatoes deepened the flavor of the hash. Recipes we tried dealt differently with the crust: Some preserved the crust in one piece, cooking both sides by flipping the hash or sliding it onto a plate and inverting it back into the skillet; and other recipes suggested breaking up the crust and folding it back into the hash. After trying both styles, tasters preferred the latter, feeling that it had a better overall flavor. We lightly packed the hash into the skillet with the back of a wooden spoon, allowed the bottom to crisp up, and then folded the bottom over the top and repeated the process several times. In this way, the crisp browned bits get evenly distributed.

Tasters agreed that the eggs served with hash need to be just barely set, so that the yolks break and moisten the potatoes. While poaching is the easiest technique for preserving a lightly cooked yolk, it can be a hassle. We found that we could "poach" the eggs in the same pan as the hash by nestling the eggs into indentations in the hash, covering the pan, and cooking them over low heat.

Corned Beef Hash

SERVES 4

A well-seasoned cast-iron skillet is traditional for this recipe, but we preferred a nonstick 12-inch skillet. The nonstick surface leaves little chance of anything sticking and burning. We like our hash served with ketchup. If you have leftover potatoes and corned beef (see the recipe on page 194), use them in this recipe and skip step 1.

2   pounds russet potatoes, peeled and cut into 1/2-inch dice
1/2 teaspoon salt
2   bay leaves
4   ounces (4 slices) bacon, diced
1   medium onion, diced
2   medium garlic cloves, minced or pressed through a garlic press (about 2 teaspoons)
1/2 teaspoon minced fresh thyme leaves
1   pound corned beef, minced (pieces should be 1/4 inch or smaller)
1/2 cup heavy cream
1/4 teaspoon hot pepper sauce, such as Tabasco
4   large eggs
    Salt and ground black pepper

1. Bring the potatoes, 5 cups of water, the salt, and the bay leaves to a boil in a medium saucepan over medium-high heat. Once boiling, cook the potatoes for 4 minutes, then drain and set aside.

2. Place the bacon in a nonstick 12-inch skillet over medium-high heat and cook until the fat is partially rendered, about 2 minutes. Add the onion and cook, stirring occasionally, until the onion has softened and browned about the edges, about 8 minutes. Add the garlic and thyme and cook until fragrant, 30 seconds. Add the beef and stir until thoroughly combined with the onion mixture. Mix in the potatoes and lightly pack the mixture into the pan with a spatula. Reduce the heat to medium and pour the heavy cream and hot pepper sauce evenly over the hash. Cook undisturbed for 4 minutes, then, with the spatula, invert the hash, a portion at a time, and fold the browned bits back into the hash. Lightly pack the hash into the pan. Repeat the process every minute or two until the potatoes are thoroughly cooked, about 8 minutes longer.

3. Make 4 indentations (each measuring about 2 inches across) equally spaced on the surface of the hash. Crack 1 egg into each indentation and sprinkle the egg with salt and pepper to taste. Reduce the heat to medium-low, cover the pan, and cook until the eggs are just set, about 6 minutes. Cut into 4 equal wedges, making sure each wedge includes an egg, and serve immediately.

15

I WANT TO COOK HAM, SAUSAGES, OR BACON

I Want to Cook Ham, Sausages, or Bacon

THE PORK CHOPS AND ROASTS WE TEND to grill, sauté, or roast come from the shoulder or mid-section of the animal. A variety of other products come from other cuts, including ham, sausage, and bacon.

Ham is the hind quarter of a pig. There are two general categories, which are referred to by butchers and people in the business as country and city hams. Country hams are salted and aged by a process known as dry-curing. City hams are brined in a salt solution (like pickles) by a process known as wet-curing. The former method results in salty, firm, dry meat, like prosciutto or the famed serrano ham of Spain. The latter process is used to make moister slicing hams, the kind sold in supermarkets, including our favorite, a spiral-sliced ham. Many markets also sell fresh ham, which is cut from the same part of the animal but is not cured.

Sausages can be made from almost any meat but pork sausages are a favorite, including kielbasa and bratwurst. Bacon is cut from the belly of the pig, then cured with salt and sugar before being smoked. These pork products can be used to make a variety of recipes, as demonstrated in this chapter.

SPIRAL-SLICED HAM

WE'VE ALWAYS BEEN FOND OF HAM. WE love its toothy, meaty chew and its unique flavor combination of sweet, salt, and smoke. Despite this devotion, we have to admit that the versions appearing on most holiday tables are far from ideal. Very often they are dry as dust or mushy as a wet paper towel. We decided to find the best possible way to prepare a precooked supermarket ham so that it could live up to its full potential.

Hams vary in terms of the amount of water added during the curing process. A ham that has no added water is labeled just plain "ham." While some manufacturers still make these hams, they are very hard to find in supermarkets. "Ham with natural juices" (as the label would state) has 7 percent to 8 percent water added; "ham–water added" has 12 percent to 15 percent water added; and "ham and water product" contains more than 15 percent added water. The more water a ham contains, the

less expensive it is per pound. They also vary in terms of bone. They maybe boneless, semiboneless, or completely bone-in.

Our tasting results were pretty predictable: more bone and less water seemed to make for the tastiest hams. Boneless and semiboneless hams had "compressed" textures that we did not like, and the hams with most water added had the most diluted ham flavor. Bone-in, spiral-sliced hams with natural juices were the favorite in our tasting. They were neither overly pumped up with water nor packed into a cylindrical loaf shape. They were also the favorite of the test kitchen staff in terms of convenience. After having to carve many of the hams in the testing, they were quite happy to meet up with a ham that had been carved for them. Spiral-sliced hams were hands-down the most convenient of the bone-in choices.

"Cooking" (really, only heating) these fully cooked hams is a no-brainer, which is why, we'll bet, that these hams are so popular around the holidays. The problem is that heating instructions for spiral-sliced hams differ from package to package. To add to the confusion, there are discrepancies in recommended final internal temperatures. Such imprecision wouldn't be such an issue if these hams didn't readily dry out and turn to jerky when heated improperly.

One factor that had to be decided at the outset was the internal temperature to which the ham should be heated. Spiral-sliced hams are fully cooked, and so long as the sell-by date hasn't come and gone, the ham can be served straight out of the package. While most cooks would still elect to heat the ham before serving, there is no consensus as to what temperature it should reach before being brought to the table. The label of one package said 120 degrees. The National Pork Producers Council said 140 degrees. Two manufacturers didn't include a temperature in their heating directions, so we called to inquire and were told 150 degrees by one and 155 degrees by the other. This discrepancy is unfortunate, because heating the ham to the proper internal temperature is critical to helping it retain its juices.

When we heated a ham to 140 degrees it lost a large amount of liquid and was dry. Heating to 130 degrees was an improvement, but we found

CHOOSING A HAM

Shank End   **Butt End**

For easy carving, look for a shank-end ham (left), which has a tapered, pointed end opposite the cut side. The sirloin, or butt, end (right) has a rounded, blunt end.

that taking the ham to only 100 degrees was better yet. The outer inch of the ham registered at about 145 degrees, and residual heat caused the internal temperature to continue rising as the ham rested, covered, after coming out of the oven. After 40 minutes it peaked at 115 to 120 degrees, which had been our original goal. Though this may sound like a low temperature, the ham was warm to the touch and, most important, had remained moist and juicy. And, after all, we are dealing with a precooked cut of meat here.

Having settled on the final temperature, we needed to figure out exactly how to get there. Our first task was to determine the proper oven temperature. We quickly found that a high (400 degrees) or even a moderate (325 degrees) oven was no good. Though the hams were covered with foil for protection, when subjected to these temperatures they lost an astounding amount of liquid (up to 2 cups); the meat was dry and leathery and the slices curled and splayed.

We then began experimenting with low oven temperatures. These worked much better, but the cooking time now became an issue. At the low end of the scale, an average nine-pound ham heated in a 225-degree oven was both juicy and moist and held its shape, but it took a grueling 3¼ hours to heat up. In a 250-degree oven, the ham was just as good, but it heated in 2¾ hours, shaving 30 minutes off the cooking time.

Although easy, this was still a long process, so

we sought means to speed it up. We tried different combinations of high and low temperatures, but they were either detrimental to the moistness of the ham or did nothing to speed its heating.

Someone in the test kitchen then suggested a plastic oven bag instead of the foil cover. Quite to our astonishment, this simple, flimsy-looking accouterment trimmed a few minutes per pound. While this may sound insignificant, it can translate into a 20- to 30-minute differential when cooking a piece of meat the size of a ham. How did it work? We posited that the oven bag, wrapped tightly around the ham, eliminated the air space—an insulation of sorts—formed between the foil and the ham, thereby giving the ham direct exposure to heat and speeding its heating. Another step that speeds the heating process is letting the ham stand at room temperature for 90 minutes before putting it in the oven. This, too, takes off a couple of minutes per pound. By using an oven bag and letting the ham stand at room temperature, we had whittled the heating time down to about 2 hours, with a 40-minute rest out of the oven. Protracted though this process may seem, it's great in that it frees the oven for other last-minute cooking tasks.

With the cooking method in place, we now had two more points to consider: making the sauce and carving the ham. We wanted to come up with something better than the gooey glaze that comes in a packet with many hams. And we wanted to see which of the two cuts of spiral-sliced ham available—the shank or the sirloin—would be easier to carve.

TRIMMING THE OVEN BAG

Use scissors to trim the oven bag, leaving 1 inch above the tie.

Most spiral-sliced hams come with an enclosed packet of glaze. We tossed them all aside because we have found that glazes, whether prepackaged or homemade, do little to enhance this kind of ham. Instead, they tend to sit on the surface like a layer of gooey candy. Although this may appeal to children, we much prefer to make an interesting, flavorful sauce. The sauce, since it doesn't use any pan drippings, can be made ahead and reheated. It dresses up the ham, making it look and taste more elegant, and it also adds moisture to carved ham slices, which tend to dry out somewhat as they sit uncovered on a serving platter.

We also discovered that the shank end of the ham is substantially easier to carve than the sirloin, or butt, end because of the bone configuration. The packages aren't labeled as such, but the shank can be identified by the tapered, more pointed end opposite the cut side. The sirloin, on the other hand, has a very blunt, rounded end. If you can't find a shank half, however, don't despair; both halves taste equally good. Your knife will just encounter a few more bumps and curves when you carve the sirloin half.

Spiral-Sliced Ham

SERVES 20 TO 30

You can put the ham in the oven cold, bypassing the 90-minute standing time. If you do, add a couple of minutes per pound to the heating time. If using an oven bag, cut slits in the bag so it does not burst. Allow about 3 to 4 servings per pound for a bone-in ham. We recommend buying a shank portion because the bone configuration makes it easier to carve; look for the half ham with a tapered, pointed end.

I   **spiral-sliced bone-in half ham (7 to 10 pounds), preferably shank end**

1. Unwrap the ham and remove and discard the plastic disk covering the bone. Place the ham in a plastic oven bag, pull tightly for a close fit, tie the bag up, and trim the excess plastic (see the illustration on page 374). Set the ham cut-side down in a 13 by 9-inch baking dish and cut 4 slits in the top of the bag with a paring knife. Alternatively, place

CARVING A SPIRAL-SLICED HAM

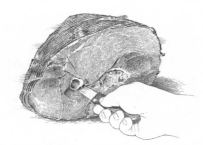

1. With the tip of a paring or carving knife, cut around the bone to loosen the attached slices.

2. Using a long carving knife, slice horizontally above the bone and through the spiral-cut slices, toward the back of the ham.

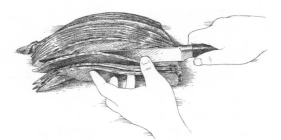

3. Pull the cut portion away from the bone and cut between the slices to separate them fully.

4. Beginning at the tapered end, slice above the bone to remove the remaining chunk of meat. Flip the ham over and repeat the procedure for the other side.

the unwrapped ham cut-side down in the baking dish and cover tightly with foil. Let stand at room temperature for 90 minutes.

2. Meanwhile, adjust an oven rack to the lowest position and heat the oven to 250 degrees. Bake the ham until the center of the ham registers about 100 degrees on an instant-read thermometer, 1½ to 2½ hours (about 14 minutes per pound if using a plastic oven bag, about 17 minutes per pound if using foil), depending on the size of the ham.

3. Remove the ham from the oven and let it rest in the baking dish in the oven bag or with the foil cover until the internal temperature registers 115 to 120 degrees on an instant-read thermometer, 30 to 40 minutes. Cut open the oven bag or remove the foil, place the ham on a carving board, and slice according to the illustrations on page 375. Serve immediately with one of the following sauces, if desired.

Dried Cherry and Stout Sauce with Brown Sugar and Allspice
MAKES ABOUT 4 CUPS

Stout is a strong, dark beer made from toasted barley. It makes a rich sauce with smoky notes and an appealing bitter finish.

1	cup low-sodium chicken broth
2	tablespoons cornstarch
2	tablespoons unsalted butter
3	medium shallots, chopped fine
⅛	teaspoon ground allspice
4	cups stout
⅓	cup packed brown sugar
1	cup dried tart cherries (about 5 ounces)
1 ½	tablespoons balsamic vinegar
	Salt and ground black pepper

1. Whisk the broth and cornstarch together in a small bowl; set aside. Heat the butter in a 12-inch skillet over medium heat until foaming; add the shallots and cook until softened, about 3 minutes. Stir in the allspice; cook until fragrant, about 30 seconds. Add the stout, brown sugar, and dried cherries; increase the heat to medium-high, bring to a simmer, and cook until slightly syrupy, about 10 minutes.

2. Whisk the broth and cornstarch mixture to recombine, then gradually whisk it into the simmering liquid; return to a simmer to thicken, stirring occasionally. Off heat, stir in the balsamic vinegar; season with salt and pepper to taste. (The sauce can be cooled to room temperature and refrigerated for up to 2 days. Reheat in a medium saucepan over medium-low heat.) Serve with ham.

INGREDIENTS: Spiral-Sliced Hams

Spiral-sliced hams offer the best combination of flavor, texture, and convenience when it comes to slicing, but are all spiral-sliced hams the same? To find out, we rounded up the five most widely available spiral-sliced bone-in hams. All were heated according to our recipe and served plain (without a sauce or glaze).

We found a wide variety in both flavor and texture. The Cook's Spiral Sliced Hickory Smoked Honey Ham ($2.29 per pound) was the clear winner. Almost all tasters appreciated this ham's clean and meaty flavor, though a few were left wanting stronger sweet, salt, smoke, and spice flavors. Overall, it was declared an "honest ham" that "doesn't seem processed" or "taste as if it's pumped full of chemicals."

The Hillshire Farm Spiral Sliced Brown Sugar Cured Ham ($1.79 per pound) also received mostly positive comments. Most tasters noted a pleasant balance of salt and sweet, but others thought the flavor insubstantial and "lacking much assertion." As for the texture, many found it a bit chewy and dry, while a couple of tasters said these qualities made it a "real man's ham."

The other hams in the tasting did not fare as well. Almost every taster remarked on the pock-marked meat of the Hillshire Farm Spiral Sliced Honey Cured Ham ($1.79 per pound). Its appearance, coupled with the rubbery, wet, very "pumped" texture, made this very sweet ham "look and taste like a sponge." Tasters could not get too enthused about the Colonial Spiral Sliced Ham ($2.69), either, finding it spongy and soft. The most expensive ham in the tasting, the Carando Spiral Sliced Hickory Smoked Ham ($3.99 per pound), landed at the bottom of the rankings. Sold under the Farmland label in the Midwest and on the West Coast, this ham elicited comments such as "sour," "acidic," and "musty" from tasters. The meat verged on dry, with a coarse, crumbly, "fall-apart" quality.

Mustard Sauce with Vermouth and Thyme

MAKES ABOUT 3 ½ CUPS

The Dijon mustard lends a creaminess to this sauce, while the whole-grain mustard adds texture and visual appeal.

1 ½	cups low-sodium chicken broth
2	tablespoons cornstarch
2	tablespoons unsalted butter
3	medium shallots, chopped fine
2	cups dry vermouth
1	tablespoon packed brown sugar
½	cup Dijon mustard
¼	cup whole-grain mustard
1	tablespoon chopped fresh thyme leaves
	Salt and ground black pepper

1. Whisk the broth and cornstarch together in a small bowl; set aside. Heat the butter in a 12-inch skillet over medium heat until foaming; add the shallots and cook until softened, about 3 minutes. Stir in the vermouth and sugar; increase the heat to medium-high and simmer until the alcohol vapors have cooked off, about 4 minutes.

2. Whisk the broth and cornstarch mixture to recombine, then gradually whisk it into the simmering liquid; return the sauce to a simmer to thicken, stirring occasionally. Off heat, whisk in the mustards and thyme; season with salt and pepper to taste. (The sauce can be cooled to room temperature and refrigerated for up to 2 days. Reheat in a medium saucepan over medium-low heat.) Serve with ham.

COUNTRY HAM

MOST COUNTRY HAMS ARE MADE IN SMALL batches on farms in Virginia, the Carolinas, Kentucky, and Tennessee. Unless you live in the South, you won't see country hams in markets, but they can be ordered by mail or through your local butcher.

Country hams are cured in salt or a mixture of salt and sugar for several weeks, usually about five. During this dry-curing period, the meat must lose at least 18 percent of its fresh weight. (Many country hams shed 25 percent of their weight, for an even saltier, more concentrated ham flavor.) By law, a country ham must also absorb at least 4 percent salt. At this level, the salt acts as preservative and prevents any bacterial growth during the long aging process that follows.

Once a country ham has been cured, it's smoked (over hardwoods like hickory or apple) for two to six days, rubbed with black pepper, and then aged, at least 60 days and up to a year or more in some cases. Country ham can be eaten raw (it's fully preserved), but the custom in the United States is to cook ham. The most famous country hams come from the small Virginia town of Smithfield. By law, Smithfield hams must be dry-cured and then aged a minimum of six months.

The flavor of a country ham is always intense and often quite salty. Good country ham has a complex smoky flavor with hints of blue cheese, nuts, wood, and spice. In general, the longer a ham has been aged, the stronger the flavors will be. When buying country ham, decide how strong and intense a flavor you like and then buy according to age. Most novices will find a 15-month ham overpowering and are probably better off with a shorter-cure ham. Southerners who grew up on good country ham may find a three-month ham insipid.

Many people believe that soaking a country ham is essential to its final edibility. The theory is that soaking causes the meat to lose some of the salt with which it was cured, as the salt naturally moves from places of greater concentration (in the ham) to places of lesser concentration (the soaking water). As salt migrates out of the ham, water replaces some of it, a process that helps soften the ham's texture and prevents excessive dryness.

Our testing supported this theory but also showed that the process doesn't happen as quickly as you might think. Only when we soaked a year-old ham for a full 36 hours could we detect any change in texture compared with a similar ham that was not soaked. The soaked ham was just a bit less dry and a bit less salty.

In our tests, we found that hams subjected to cures of less than six months are rarely so salty that they need soaking. But a ham cured for more than

PREPARING A COUNTRY HAM

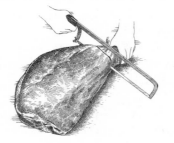

1. If necessary, use a hacksaw to remove the hock so that the ham will fit into a large stockpot.

2. Simmer the ham as directed in the recipe. As soon as the ham is removed from the simmering water, let stand until cool enough to handle, then remove the rind and most, but not all, of the fat. Start by slicing into the rind with a sharp knife.

3. Peel away the rind and discard. With a knife, trim the remaining fat to a thickness of about ¼ inch.

4. Score the fat: Use a sharp paring knife to cut down into the fat, making sure not to cut into the meat. Cut parallel lines across the ham, spacing them about 1 ½ inches apart. Make a series of perpendicular lines to create a diamond pattern in the fat.

a year needs at least three days in cold water before cooking to become edible. Hams cured for six to 12 months need to be soaked for 36 hours.

Many recipes suggest adding ingredients, especially sweeteners, to the soaking liquid. We found that sugar, Coca-Cola, and white vinegar (all recommended by various sources) have no effect on a country ham, which is covered with a very thick rind.

The next step is to cook the ham. We tried baking the ham in a 325-degree oven and liked the results quite a lot. The ham is dry and salty. However, this method is for ham lovers only. Many ham novices were put off by the strong flavor. Simmering the ham tames some of the salt and is the best bet when preparing ham for a holiday crowd. Simmering also adds a little moisture to the ham, making it easier to carve in thin slices. (Country ham is too rich and salty to be sliced into thick slabs like a city ham.)

We tried all kinds of simmering regimens and found that cooking the ham at the barest simmer is better than boiling. Gentle heat ensures that the outside layers of meat don't cook too fast. As for the timing, we found that 10 minutes per pound is a decent barometer. Better still, use an instant-read thermometer and pull the ham out of the pot when it reaches 120 degrees.

At this point, the rind and most of the fat need to be removed. The ham can then be scored, glazed, and put into the oven just to set the glaze, the best option when serving the ham as the centerpiece of a holiday meal. A simmered country ham can also be cooled, boned, weighted, and then sliced into very thin chunks and served as part of a buffet with biscuits.

Baked Country Ham

SERVES ABOUT 30

We tested nine brands of mail-order country hams. All but one of the hams was deemed good or excellent. We particularly liked the Wigwam ham from S. Wallace Edwards & Sons (800-222-4267). Any size dry-cured ham can be adapted to this recipe; just adjust the cooking time as needed to reach the internal temperatures listed below. Country ham is best served in very thin slices over biscuits or in rolls. It's much too rich and salty to serve in thick slices. Leftover bits of ham can be used to flavor cooked greens, eggs, pasta, or rice. If removing the hock, save it to flavor soup or beans. We don't like to chew on whole cloves so we don't stud the ham; we prefer adding the flavor of cloves to the glaze. Don't baste the ham with any of the pan juices. They are too salty and intense.

1	country ham (14 to 15 pounds)
1	cup glaze (recipes follow)

1. Scrub the mold off. If necessary, remove the hock with a hacksaw (see illustration 1 on page 378). If the ham has been aged less than 6 months, proceed with step 2. If the ham has been aged more than 6 months, place the ham in a large stockpot filled with cool water. Place the pot in a cool place and change the water once a day. Hams aged 6 to 12 months should be soaked for 36 hours. Hams aged more than a year should be soaked for 3 days. Drain the ham and scrub again.

2. Place the ham in a large stockpot and cover with fresh water. Bring to a boil, reduce the heat, and simmer until an instant-read thermometer inserted into the thickest part of the ham registers 120 degrees, 2 to 3 hours. Transfer the ham from the pot to a large cutting board. (The liquid in the pot can be reserved and used to cook greens or rice or to flavor soup.)

3. Adjust an oven rack to the middle position and heat the oven to 325 degrees. When the ham has cooled just enough to handle, peel away the rind and most of the fat (see illustrations 2 and 3. Discard the rind and fat and score the remaining fat (see the illustration 4).

4. Place the ham on a flat rack in a large roasting pan lined with a double layer of aluminum foil. Pour 2 cups water into the pan. Using a rubber spatula, smear the glaze onto the exterior of the ham. Bake until an instant-read thermometer inserted in several places in the ham registers 140 degrees, about 1 hour. Transfer the ham to a cutting board and let rest about 15 minutes. Carve into very thin slices and serve.

Orange Juice and Brown Sugar Glaze for Ham

MAKES ABOUT 1 CUP

For a sweeter, glossier glaze, brush the ham with a little honey about 30 minutes before it is ready to come out of the oven.

1 ¼	cups packed light brown sugar
3	tablespoons juice from 1 medium orange
½	teaspoon ground cloves

Mix the sugar, orange juice, and cloves together in a medium bowl to form a thick paste. Set the mixture aside until ready to glaze the ham.

Mustard and Brown Sugar Glaze for Ham

MAKES ABOUT 1 CUP

For a sweeter, glossier glaze, brush the ham with a little maple syrup about 30 minutes before it is ready to come out of the oven.

1 ¼	cups packed light brown sugar
¼	cup Dijon mustard
½	teaspoon ground cloves

Mix the sugar, mustard, and cloves together in a medium bowl to form a thick paste. Set the mixture aside until ready to glaze the ham.

ROAST FRESH HAM

ALTHOUGH THIS ROAST IS CALLED A HAM, it gains much of its undeniable appeal from the fact that it's not really a ham at all—or at least not what most of us understand the term to mean. It's not cured in the fashion of a Smithfield ham or salted and air-dried like prosciutto. It's not pressed or molded like a canned ham, and it's not smoked like a country ham. In fact, the only reason this cut of pork is called a ham is because it comes from the pig's hind leg.

Even before we began roasting, we had decided that a full fresh ham, weighing in at about 20 pounds, was too much for all but the very largest feast. So we decided to use one of the two cuts into which the leg is usually divided—the sirloin, which comes from the top of the leg, or the shank, from the bottom of the leg (see below). We also decided that we wanted our ham skin on (we couldn't see giving up the opportunity for cracklings). Fortunately, this is how these roasts are typically sold.

From our experiences with other large roasts, we knew what the big problem would be: making sure the roast cooked all the way through while the meat stayed tender and moist. In our first set of tests, then, we wanted to assess not only the relative merits of sirloin and shank but also the best oven temperature and cooking time.

Early on in this process, we determined that the roast needed to be cooked to a lower final internal temperature than some experts recommend. We found that we preferred the roast pulled from the oven at 145 to 150 degrees—at this point, the meat is cooked to about medium and retains a slight blush. While the roast rests, its residual heat brings the temperature up to approximately 155 to 160 degrees.

That determined, we started testing different oven temperatures. First to come out of the oven was a ham from the sirloin end of the leg that we had roasted at a high temperature, 400 degrees, for its entire stay in the oven. Carving this ham was akin to whittling wood—Olympics-worthy agility with the carving knife was required to gut around the aitchbone (part of the hip), the cracklings were more suited for tap shoes than consumption, and the meat was dry, dry, dry. We moved on to roasting a shank-end ham at a low heat the whole way through. This ham tasted like a wrung-out washcloth, with no cracklings in sight. What we did appreciate was the straightforward bone composition of the shank end, which simplified carving and convinced us to use this end of the fresh ham for the remainder of our tests.

Next we roasted a shank-end ham by starting it at a low temperature (325 degrees) and finishing it at a higher one (400 degrees), hoping to end up with both moist meat and crispy cracklings. To our dismay, this ham was also rather dry, which we attributed to the ham's long stay in the oven, made necessary by the low cooking temperature. What's more, the brief hike in the temperature at the end of cooking didn't help to crisp the skin.

Again, we figured we ought to try the opposite: starting the ham at a high temperature to give the meat a head start and get the skin on its way to crisping, then turning down the heat for the remainder of the roasting time to cook the meat through. Although meat cooked according to this method was slightly chalky and dry, the skin was close to our goal, crispy enough to shatter between our teeth yet tender enough to stave off a trip to the dentist. We decided that this would be our master roasting method.

Hoping to solve the dry meat dilemma, we brined a shank-end ham, immersing it in a solution of saltwater and spices to tenderize and flavor it. More than slightly biased from the positive results we achieved in past brining experiments with turkey, chicken, shellfish, and other cuts of pork, we expected brining to make the meat incredibly juicy. The salt in a brine causes the protein structure in meat to unravel and trap water in its fibers; brining also encourages the unwound proteins to gel, forming a barrier that helps seal in moisture. Together, these effects allow the cook to increase the roasting temperature, thus speeding the roasting process without fear of drying out the meat. Our estimations proved accurate: the brined shank emerged from the oven succulent and flavorful, with meat tender enough to fall apart in your mouth.

BUYING FRESH HAM

SIRLOIN END

SHANK END

Fresh ham comes from the pig's hind leg. Because a whole leg is too large for most occasions, it is usually cut into two sections. The sirloin, or butt, end, is harder to carve than out favorite, the shank end. Either way, make sure to buy a fresh ham with skin, which will protect the meat and keep it moist.

Just when we thought the ham couldn't possibly get any better, we decided to try roasting one shank face-down on a rack set in a roasting pan rather than letting it sit directly in the pan. This adjustment kept the cut end from becoming tough and leathery from direct contact with the hot pan. Rack roasting also allowed the heat to circulate around the ham constantly, promoting faster and more even cooking.

With our temperature firmly in place, we turned to tweaking the flavor of the roast and obtaining the type of cracklings we had heard of but never really tasted. Not content with the infusion of flavor from the brine, we turned to spice rubs to further develop the flavor of the roast. Fresh thyme, sage, rosemary, garlic, brown sugar, cloves, dried mustard, juniper berries, peppercorns, and salt were all given an equal opportunity to complement the pork. We liked the combination of sage's earthy sweetness and garlic's pungent bite as well as the edge of fresh parsley, peppercorns, and kosher salt. Since our composed rub didn't lean strongly on any one particular spice, we were left with a wide-open field of glazing options.

While some recipes we tried called for simply basting the roast in its own drippings, we veered in the direction of sugary glazes, opting for sugar's ability to crisp, caramelize, and sweeten the skin. But the intermittent encounters between glaze, brush, and ham were still under negotiation: Exactly when should we glaze? Throughout the roasting period? If so, at what intervals? Since part of the beauty of this pork roast is that it can be left in the oven mostly unattended, we didn't want glazing to complicate the process. Starting the ham at 500 degrees negated glazing it at the outset—the sugary glaze would definitely char black before the roast had been in the oven very long. We decided to let the roast cook unglazed at 500 degrees for the first 20 minutes. We then turned the oven temperature down to 350 degrees and began to brush it liberally with glaze. We continued to do so in 45-minute intervals, which amounted to three bastings during the roasting period. This ham was the one: flavorful meat with sweetened, crunchy skin.

More than one person in the test kitchen proclaimed this ham to be the best roast pork they'd ever eaten. Rich and tender, with an underlying hint of sweetness, the meat had the power to quiet a room full of vocal, opinionated cooks and editors. Perhaps even better is the sweet, slightly salty, crisp and crunchy skin that intensifies to a deep crimson by the time the roast is done. It was attacked with precision and proprietary swiftness during our trials in the test kitchen. Unbelievably succulent, tender, and uncomplicated, this culinary gem will leave you wondering how you could have gotten along so far without it.

Roast Fresh Ham

SERVES 8 TO 10

Fresh ham comes from the pig's hind leg. Because a whole leg is too large for most occasions, it is usually cut into two sections. The sirloin, or butt, end, is harder to carve than our favorite, the shank end. If you don't have room in your refrigerator, you can brine the ham in a large insulated cooler or a small plastic garbage can; add 5 or 6 freezer packs to the brine to keep it well chilled.

ROAST
- 1 fresh bone-in half ham with skin (6 to 8 pounds), preferably shank end, rinsed

BRINE
- 4 cups kosher salt or 2 cups table salt
- 3 cups packed dark or light brown sugar
- 2 heads garlic, cloves separated, lightly crushed and peeled
- 10 bay leaves
- 1/2 cup black peppercorns, crushed

GARLIC AND HERB RUB
- 1 cup lightly packed sage leaves from 1 large bunch
- 1/2 cup parsley leaves from 1 bunch
- 8 medium garlic cloves, peeled
- 1 tablespoon kosher salt or 1 1/2 teaspoons table salt
- 1/2 tablespoon ground black pepper
- 1/4 cup olive oil

GLAZE
- 1 1/3 cups glaze (recipes follow)

1. Following the illustration below, carefully slice through the skin and fat with a serrated knife, making a 1-inch diamond pattern. Be careful not to cut into the meat.

2. FOR THE BRINE: In a large (about 16-quart) bucket or stockpot, dissolve the salt and sugar in 1 gallon hot tap water. Add the garlic, bay leaves, peppercorns, and 1 gallon cold water. Submerge the ham in the brine and refrigerate 8 to 24 hours.

3. Set a large disposable roasting pan on a baking sheet for extra support; place a flat wire rack in the roasting pan. Remove the ham from the brine. Rinse under cold water and dry thoroughly with paper towels. Place the ham, wide cut-side down, on the rack. (If using the sirloin end, place the ham skin-side up.) Let the ham stand, uncovered, at room temperature 1 hour.

4. FOR THE RUB: Meanwhile, adjust an oven rack to the lowest position and heat the oven to 500 degrees. In the workbowl of a food processor fitted with the metal blade, process the sage, parsley, garlic, salt, pepper, and oil until the mixture forms a smooth paste, about 30 seconds. Rub all sides of the ham with the mixture.

5. TO BAKE AND GLAZE THE HAM: Roast the ham at 500 degrees for 20 minutes. Reduce the oven temperature to 350 degrees and continue to roast, brushing the ham with glaze every 45 minutes, until the center of the ham registers 145 to 150 degrees on an instant-read thermometer, about 2½

hours longer. Tent the ham loosely with foil and let stand until the center of the ham registers 155 to 160 degrees on thermometer, 30 to 40 minutes. Carve, following the illustrations on page 283, and serve.

➤ VARIATION
Cola Ham
Although cooking with Coke may seem humorous and unsophisticated, you haven't lived until you've tried cola pork. Cola pork was born when one of our staff members mentioned the southern tradition of Coca-Cola glaze and joked that we should try brining the meat in it. After giving this joke fair consideration, we dumped six liters of Coca-Cola Classic into a brine bucket, added kosher salt, and let the ham soak in this foamy concoction overnight. The next day we cooked it according to our recipe. The outcome was the talk of the kitchen. It was juicy, it was unusual, it was fantastic. The Coke had added its own unique flavor to the ham while tenderizing the meat even more than our regular brine. The meat was falling off the bone and unbelievably tender throughout.

Follow the recipe for Roast Fresh Ham, substituting 6 liters Coke Classic for both the hot and cold water in the brine, omitting the brown sugar, and reducing the salt to 3 cups kosher salt or 1½ cups table salt. Proceed as directed, rubbing the ham with the garlic and herb mixture and using the Coca-Cola Glaze with Lime and Jalapeño (page 383).

SCORING THE SKIN

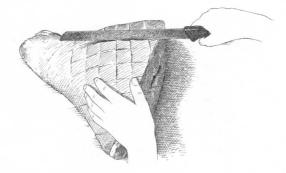

Without cutting into the meat, slice through the skin and fat with a serrated knife, making a 1-inch diamond pattern.

Apple Cider and Brown Sugar Glaze

MAKES ABOUT 1 ⅓ CUPS, ENOUGH TO GLAZE
1 FRESH HAM

1   cup apple cider
2   cups packed dark or light brown sugar
5   whole cloves

Bring the cider, brown sugar, and cloves to a boil in a small nonreactive saucepan over high heat. Reduce the heat to medium-low and simmer until syrupy and reduced to about 1⅓ cups, 5 to 7 minutes. (The glaze will thicken as it cools between bastings; cook over medium heat about 1 minute, stirring once or twice, before using.)

Spicy Pineapple-Ginger Glaze

MAKES ABOUT 1 1/3 CUPS, ENOUGH TO GLAZE
1 FRESH HAM

1   cup pineapple juice
2   cups packed dark or light brown sugar
1   (1-inch) piece fresh ginger, peeled and grated
    (about 1 tablespoon)
1   tablespoon red pepper flakes

Bring the pineapple juice, brown sugar, ginger, and red pepper flakes to a boil in a small nonreactive saucepan over high heat. Reduce the heat to medium-low and simmer until syrupy and reduced to about 1⅓ cups, 5 to 7 minutes. (The glaze will thicken as it cools between bastings; cook over

---

CARVING THE TWO CUTS OF HAM

Shank End

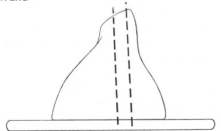

1. Transfer the ham to a cutting board and carve it lengthwise alongside the bone, following the two dotted lines in the illustration above.
2. Lay the large boneless pieces that you have just carved flat on the cutting board and slice into ½-inch pieces.

Sirloin End

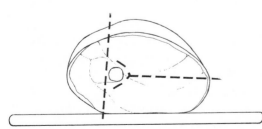

1. Transfer the ham to a cutting board and carve into three pieces around the bones along the dotted lines in the illustration above.
2. Lay the large boneless pieces that you have just carved flat on the cutting board and slice into ½-inch pieces.

---

medium heat about 1 minute, stirring once or twice, before using.)

Coca-Cola Glaze with Lime and Jalapeño

MAKES ABOUT 1 1/3 CUPS, ENOUGH TO GLAZE
1 FRESH HAM

1   cup Coca-Cola
¼   cup juice from 2 limes
2   cups packed dark or light brown sugar
2   medium jalapeño chiles, stemmed, seeded,
     and cut crosswise into ¼-inch-thick slices

Bring the Coca-Cola, lime juice, brown sugar, and chiles to a boil in a small nonreactive saucepan over high heat. Reduce the heat to medium-low and simmer until syrupy and reduced to about 1⅓ cups, 5 to 7 minutes. (The glaze will thicken as it cools between bastings; heat over medium heat about 1 minute, stirring once or twice, before using.)

Orange, Cinnamon, and Star Anise Glaze

MAKES ABOUT 1 1/3 CUPS, ENOUGH TO GLAZE
1 FRESH HAM

1   tablespoon grated zest and 1 cup juice from 2
     large oranges
2   cups packed dark or light brown sugar
4   pods star anise
1   (3-inch) cinnamon stick

Bring the orange zest and juice, brown sugar, star anise, and cinnamon to a boil in a small nonreactive saucepan over high heat. Reduce the heat to medium-low and simmer until syrupy and reduced to about 1⅓ cups, 5 to 7 minutes. (The glaze will thicken as it cools between bastings; cook over medium heat about 1 minute, stirring once or twice, before using.)

HAM LOAF

ALTHOUGH LESS POPULAR THAN ITS KIN,
meat loaf, ham loaf is traditional in many parts of
the country. In our test kitchen library, homespun
cookbooks from Down-East Maine to southern
California all contain variations. Like red beans
and rice, ham loaf supposedly originated as a
Monday night dinner based on Sunday's leftovers.
And like too many recipes based on leftovers, there
are some pretty poor versions out there—from
greasy, overseasoned logs to sticky-sweet creations
closer to dessert in flavor. We were not sure what
our ideal ham loaf would be, but we were certain
that we could do better than most of the recipes
we tested.

Heading into testing, we knew there were two
ways to approach ham loaf: We could use flavors
associated with baked ham, like fruit or warm
spices, or we could choose ingredients common in
meat loaf recipes, such as garlic, herbs, and bread
crumbs. We tried loaves topped with fruit, loaves
enriched with nuts and spices, and simple pork
variations on meat loaf. The meat loaf style won
unanimously. Tasters agreed that fruit flavorings
and lots of spices belong on whole hams, not in
ham loaves.

Ham loaf provides the perfect use for the leftover
bits and trimmings of a ham that might otherwise
go begging. If you do not have leftovers and still
hanker for a ham loaf, ham steaks work well, too.
We discovered that about a pound of ham supplied
enough flavor for one loaf without making the loaf
too salty or overwhelmingly "hammy." We chose
readily available standard ground pork to mix with
the ham. A blend of half ham and half ground pork
delivered good flavor and yielded a loaf that could
serve six to eight.

Ground pork can go into the ham loaf as is, but
the ham needs to be broken down somehow. We
found that grinding the ham to the proper size in a
food processor proved crucial to the loaf's texture.
If it was too coarse—¼-inch and larger bits—the
loaf was marred by an unpleasant chewiness. When
the ham was ground too fine—almost to a paste—
the loaf was mealy. About ¹⁄₁₆-inch bits, or bread-
crumb size, provided the best texture, reminiscent
of meat loaf.

For seasonings, we were able to apply findings
from our meat loaf recipe (see page 349). Sautéed
onions and garlic tasted as good in the ham loaf as
in the meat loaf, adding a pleasing sweetness and
depth. A little mustard and hot pepper sauce added
piquancy that cut the ham's richness, and parsley
and thyme brought freshness and color. A pinch
each of allspice and cloves reaffirmed the ham flavor.

To bind the loaf, tasters favored fresh bread
crumbs above cracker crumbs and oatmeal, both of
which had worked well in our meat loaf recipe. In
ham loaf, the cracker crumbs and oatmeal adversely
affected the texture of the loaf, making it too loose.
We found that the ham loaf required more crumbs
than meat loaf because the ham, which is already
cooked, does not bind the way uncooked beef does.
Bread crumbs, and lots of them, are the best binder
for the job.

To keep the meat moist while cooking, we tried
a variety of liquids, including wine, broth, and different dairy products. Wine lent the loaf a decidedly
acidic flavor, and broth took over. Plain whole milk
yogurt was the crowd pleaser for the way its lactic
tang offset the ham's potent smokiness.

Although we liked the terrine-like formality of
the ham loaf baked in a standard loaf pan, it did not
have the crispy exterior we desired. And fat and
juices rendered from the loaf pooled in the pan,
effectively steaming the meat. Unless you have
a dedicated meat loaf pan with holes perforating
the bottom, we think the best way to cook a ham
loaf (or meat loaf, for that matter) is free-form on
a rimmed baking sheet lined with aluminum foil.
Excess juices and fat run off the loaf, allowing the
sides and top to crisp nicely.

To add a little more crispness to the loaf's exterior, we appropriated the bacon topping from our
meat loaf recipe. Tasters liked the texture and the
way it introduced a third pork flavor to the loaf.

We also loved the sweet tomato-based glaze
on our meat loaf and wanted a similar glaze that
would complement the pork. Ham and mustard
are a natural combination, and honey has a unique
flavor that works well with both. A healthy dose of
freshly ground black pepper cut the honey's sweetness. We put the glaze underneath the bacon, the

same technique we use for the meat loaf, but we also added more glaze at the end of cooking to "candy" the bacon and make the loaf look glossier.

The results were stunningly attractive. The bacon picked up a mahogany glow, and the interior, in stark contrast to meat loaf, retained an attractive rosy pink flecked with herbs.

Baked Ham Loaf

SERVES 6 TO 8

Use either a pound of boneless ham (from a leftover roast) or ham steaks. If using the latter, we had good results with ham steaks from Cook's, a company that also makes a favorite spiral-cut ham.

1/2	cup honey
1/4	cup plus 2 teaspoons Dijon mustard
3/4	teaspoon ground black pepper
2	teaspoons vegetable oil
1	medium onion, diced
2	medium garlic cloves, minced or pressed through a garlic press (about 2 teaspoons)
2	large eggs, lightly beaten
1/4	cup minced fresh parsley leaves
1	teaspoon minced fresh thyme leaves
1/4	teaspoon hot pepper sauce, such as Tabasco
	Pinch ground cloves
	Pinch ground allspice
1/2	cup plain whole milk yogurt
1	pound ground pork
1	pound ham, ground to 1/16-inch bits (resembling bread crumbs) in the workbowl of a food processor fitted with the metal blade
2	cups fresh bread crumbs (page 125)
8	ounces (8 slices) bacon, or more as needed (amount will vary depending on loaf shape)

1. Adjust an oven rack to the middle position and heat the oven to 350 degrees.

2. For the glaze, mix the honey, the 1/4 cup mustard, and 1/4 teaspoon of the pepper together in a small saucepan over low heat just until combined; set aside.

3. Heat the oil in a medium skillet over medium heat. Add the onion and cook until softened, about 5 minutes. Add the garlic and cook until fragrant,

about 30 seconds longer. Remove the pan from the heat.

4. In a large bowl, mix together the eggs, remaining 2 teaspoons mustard, remaining 1/2 teaspoon pepper, parsley, thyme, hot pepper sauce, cloves, allspice, and yogurt. Add the ground pork, ham, bread crumbs, and cooked onion and garlic, and mix everything together, with your hands or a wooden spoon, until it no longer sticks to the side of the bowl (if it does stick, add another 1 to 2 tablespoons yogurt). Turn the mixture onto a foil-lined rimmed baking sheet and pat into roughly a 9 by 5-inch loaf shape. Brush the loaf with half of the reserved glaze, then arrange the bacon slices, crosswise, over the top, overlapping slightly, to cover the surface of the loaf completely. With a spatula, tuck the ends of the bacon strips under the loaf.

5. Bake the loaf until the bacon is crisp and the internal temperature of the loaf registers 160 degrees, about 1 hour. Remove the loaf from the oven, increase the oven temperature to 450 degrees, and coat the loaf with the remaining glaze. Return the loaf to the oven and bake until the glaze bubbles and turns golden, about 5 minutes. Remove the loaf and let it stand at least 20 minutes before serving.

FRIED HAM STEAK WITH CIDER GRAVY

WITH CRISPY BROWN EDGES AND SWEET, nutty-tasting meat, pan-fried ham steaks are a Southern treat. Luckily, when the craving hits, they cook in minutes. For this version, we chose to gussy ham steaks up a bit with a cider-based gravy—nothing too fancy—just a little something to moisten the meat and to use for dunking biscuits.

Ham steaks are sold in two sizes-small, individual portions and large-size slices obviously cross-cut from a whole ham. Initially, we were attracted to the individual portions, but quickly found that their flavor paled in comparison to the larger steaks. And the texture was significantly tougher. On close inspection, they appeared to be cut from pressed or canned hams (bits of ham trimmings packed together) rather than whole large hams. Clearly large steaks were the way to go—portioning would be done after cooking. Most large ham steaks weigh in between one and 1½ pounds. Some companies do produce extra-thick steaks closer to two pounds, but we found that these are best reserved for other purposes, like baking or grilling, as they take too long to heat through in the skillet. Premium ham steaks (which we recommend) are cut from the center of the ham, the leanest section, though it can be hard to tell unless specifically marked on the package.

Admittedly, frying ham steaks is not rocket science. The meat is already cooked; it is just a matter of heating the meat through and creating a well-browned crust. We tried temperatures from low to high heat and found medium-high yielded the best results with well-browned, crisp edges. Butter proved a better bet than oil as a frying medium because it made for a richer crust.

With the steak fried and resting in a warm oven, we tackled the gravy. The recipes we found included everything from cider thickened with flour to a complicated sauce worthy of a three-star restaurant. We aimed for a middle ground—full flavored, but not requiring inordinate effort; it was a simple ham steak, after all.

The steak left a thick fond that started the gravy off right. We deglazed the skillet with cider, vigorously scraping the bottom with a spoon to free the brown bits firmly affixed to it. The issues we needed to solve were how much cider to start with and how much to reduce it by. When it boiled down too far, the resulting gravy was sickly sweet to most tasters—more like the base for a dessert sauce. Too little and the gravy was bland. After several tests, we found reducing two cups of cider to one cup yielded a slightly viscous liquid with a strong apple flavor that was not too sweet—just what we wanted. In fact, we had to add a pinch of brown sugar to appease some tasters.

Despite the cider's syrupy texture, most tasters desired a slightly thicker gravy, so we needed to add a thickener. Flour imparted pastiness, but cornstarch was flavorless and added an appealing luster. A scant ¾ teaspoon packed all the thickening

power necessary for a glossy gravy just substantial enough to nap the ham. And to add a little more character to the gravy, we looked for a seasoning or two complementary to the ham's sweet flavor. After sampling a few, tasters agreed on thyme for earthiness and mustard for an assertive punch.

~

Fried Ham Steak with Cider Gravy

SERVES 3 TO 4

The size of the ham steak ultimately determines the serving size. We were able to feed 4 from 1 large steak (with a couple of side dishes), but feel free to fry 2; you will need to reduce the skillet's temperature to medium for the second steak. You may want to taste a small bite of the cooked ham steak before adjusting the gravy's seasoning to prevent oversalting—some brands of ham steaks are be saltier than others. Ideal accompaniments would be biscuits and either a leafy salad or cooked greens.

¾	teaspoon cornstarch
½	teaspoon brown sugar
I	teaspoon Dijon mustard
2	cups plus I tablespoon cider
I	tablespoon unsalted butter
I	large ham steak (about I ½ pounds), patted dry with paper towels
2	sprigs fresh thyme
	Salt and ground black pepper

1. Adjust an oven rack to the middle position and heat the oven to 200 degrees.

2. Whisk the cornstarch, brown sugar, mustard, and the 1 tablespoon cider together in a small bowl.

3. Heat the butter in a 12-inch skillet over medium-high until the foaming subsides. Add the ham steak and cook, without moving, until browned, 3½ to 4 minutes. Using tongs and a large spatula, flip the steak and cook on the second side until browned, about 3 minutes. Transfer the ham steak to an ovenproof plate or baking sheet and place it in the oven.

4. Return the skillet to medium-high heat and add the remaining 2 cups cider and thyme sprigs,

scraping the pan bottom with a wooden spoon to release any browned bits. Cook until the cider is reduced by half, about 6 minutes. Whisk in the cornstarch mixture and cook, stirring frequently, until the sauce is thickened, about 2 minutes. Remove and discard the thyme sprigs and adjust the seasonings with salt and pepper to taste.

5. Cut the ham steak into 3 or 4 pieces and place a piece on individual plates. Spoon some cider gravy over each ham steak and serve immediately.

SAUSAGE AND PEPPER SANDWICHES

A STANDARD OF STREET FAIRS AND BALL parks, sausage and pepper sandwiches are street food at its very best. An authentic sausage and pepper sandwich is nothing more than bell peppers, onions, and sausage packed into a chewy roll, with spicy mustard on the side. It's best consumed with a cold beer and a stack of napkins.

So why would we want to bring it into the home kitchen? Because the sandwiches can be made quickly and, despite the charm of eating the sandwich at the source—fresh from the vendor's cart—some things can be made even better at home. Our idea was to stay as true to the vendor's version as possible and keep effort to a minimum. As far as cooking the sausage and peppers, we chose a large skillet to replace the vendor's griddle; there was more than enough room to cook both the peppers and sausages simultaneously.

The peppers and onions were first into the pan. More often than not, green bell peppers are the norm, despite their bitter, vegetal flavor. For the sake of authenticity, we gave them a whirl, and, predictably, tasters disapproved. Red bell peppers were preferred, though Italian frying peppers, also known as cubanelle peppers, scored high, too. Cubanelles are pale green to yellow in color and are mild tasting and sweet, less assertive than red bell peppers. Combined, red and cubanelle peppers provided the best flavor and pleasing visual contrast. For onions, we stuck with plain, yellow onions; red onions were too sweet.

For once, slow and steady did not win the race. Over low heat, the peppers softened too much and provided little contrast to the soft roll. Tasters wanted a bit more of a bite, so we increased the heat to medium-high, which yielded well-browned peppers and sweetly caramelized onions with some texture.

Depending on where you live in the country, the sausage used in this sandwich can vary quite a bit. In some areas, Italian hot and sweet sausage are king, while others favor garlicky kielbasa. When we tried both in the test kitchen, tasters favored the latter for its assertive flavor, chewy texture, and moistness—the sausage exuded quite a bit of juice to flavor the peppers and onions. A big bonus was the fact that kielbasa is sold precooked so it only needed to heat through. This saved on total cooking time and meant that the pepper mixture could stay in the pan, pushed to the cooler edges while the sausages were heated. Italian sausage necessitated removing the vegetables from the skillet as the links had to cook through rather than just heat.

A crusty, chewy roll is the only bread cut out for the task. We had good luck with basic submarine or hoagie rolls from our local bakery and recommend the same—just avoid anything that looks too spongy or fragile. The roll has to be substantial enough to soak up the juices from the sausage and vegetables. Tasters favored briefly toasted rolls, just enough to crisp up the crust.

Sausage and Pepper Sandwiches
SERVES 4 TO 6

If you cannot find cubanelle peppers, also called Italian frying peppers, use all red bell peppers, or substitute yellow bell peppers for visual contrast. Leftovers reheat well; you can also use them as an unusual and delicious omelet filling.

2   tablespoons olive oil
1   large onion, halved and cut into 1/4-inch-thick slices

2   medium red bell peppers (about $^3/_4$ pound),
    stemmed, seeded, and cut into $^1/_4$-inch-thick
    slices

2   medium cubanelle peppers (about $^3/_4$ pound),
    stemmed, seeded, and cut into $^1/_4$-inch-thick
    slices
    Salt

1   pound kielbasa sausage, split in half length-
    wise, then halved crosswise to yield 4 pieces
    Ground black pepper

4–6 sandwich rolls, split open
    Spicy brown mustard (optional)

1. Adjust an oven rack to the middle position and heat the oven to 400 degrees.

2. Heat the oil in a large skillet over medium-high heat until shimmering. Add the onion, peppers, and 1 teaspoon salt and cook, stirring occasionally, until very soft and beginning to brown, 9 to 10 minutes. Reduce the heat to medium and, using a wooden spoon, push the vegetable mixture to the edges of the skillet. Place the sausage, cut side down, in the center of the pan, and cook until lightly browned, about 3 minutes. Flip the sausages and cook until heated through, 2 to 3 minutes longer. Adjust the seasonings with salt and pepper to taste.

3. Meanwhile, place the rolls, split-side down, on a rimmed baking sheet and toast in the oven until lightly crisped, about 5 minutes.

4. Divide the peppers and sausages evenly among the rolls and serve immediately, with by the mustard, if desired.

SPANISH-STYLE BRAISED LENTILS WITH SAUSAGE

THE PAIRING OF BEANS WITH CURED MEAT is common in many cuisines. Think Cuban black beans, split pea soup, even Boston baked beans— all have rich ham, bacon, or sausage as a prime ingredient. The beans absorb the robust flavor and stretch the meat so a small amount can feed more people. For quick one-pot meals, the pairing makes perfect sense. Fast-cooking legumes, like lentils, cook within the hour and are a perfect foil to hearty sausage. Because of the meat's assertive flavor, the dish requires few additional ingredients, which limits both preparation and shopping time. Inspired by a classic Spanish dish of green lentils flavored with paprika and morcilla, or blood sausage, we wanted to develop a recipe that would cook as quickly as possible and taste authentic. Morcilla is rarely available in the United States, so a less exotic sausage would have to be substituted.

Our first step was to evaluate the traditional recipes we found and uncover where time might be trimmed in cooking and preparation. Recipes required slow simmering—that is, braising—in the oven with aromatics and sausage, a method that took hours. We didn't want to spend this much time preparing something so simple, so we opted to give the lentils a head start on the stovetop while we assembled the remaining ingredients. Then, once the lentils were almost tender, we combined all of the dish's components and finished it in the oven. This final step reduced the cooking liquid to a glossy glaze and browned the sausage, lending flavor that stovetop cooking alone could not accomplish.

Glossy green lentils du Puy were our bean choice for this dish. Their firm texture—they retain their shape better than other lentils—and hearty flavor are ideal with sausage. For the fullest flavor, we simmered them in diluted chicken broth flavored with a bundle of fresh thyme leaves; the whole herbs imparted a great deal of flavor with no preparation required. In 20 to 25 minutes, the lentils were just shy of tender—the perfect state for finishing in the oven.

We knew the lentils needed flavor help from aromatics like onion and garlic. The traditional recipes included these as well as tomato and, after testing several, we saw no reason to alter the ingredient list. The onions and garlic gave the lentils sweetness and depth, while the tomato provided fruitiness and acidity. Our only change was to toast the garlic in olive oil to a light golden color for the roundest flavor. Once the aromatics were sautéed, we added the lentils to the skillet (its greater surface area relative to the saucepan in which the lentils were simmered made for faster cooking in the oven), and the dish was ready for the oven—with the addition of sausage, of course.

As for spices, paprika—smoked paprika, in particular—gave the dish all the punch it needed. Produced only in the Vera region of Spain, smoked paprika is made from pimiento peppers that are slowly smoked over oak prior to crushing. The flavor is intensely smoky and comes in three grades: sweet, hot, and bittersweet. Despite its localized Spanish production, smoked paprika is widely available in specialty stores and large markets. For this dish, we favored bittersweet paprika, as sweet was too mild and hot numbed the palate. For the best flavor, we found it important to toast the smoked paprika briefly in the skillet before adding liquid—the heat activates the volatile oils.

Replacing morcilla sausage was a tall order. We opted for convenience rather than authenticity and tried a wide range of readily available sausages, including chorizo, linguiça, hot and sweet Italian sausage, and kielbasa. The latter won out for its smoky, sweet flavor and compact texture. In addition, kielbasa is sold ready to eat, which meant it just needed to heat through and brown a little for flavor.

As the sausage was already cooked, the dish's stay in the oven could be fast and furious. High heat quickly reduced the cooking liquid and browned the sausage—just what we wanted. Temperatures ranging from 400 to 500 degrees all worked fine, but 475 degrees produced the most consistent results. In 10 to 15 minutes, the lentils were glossy, the cooking liquid had evaporated, and the sausage was lightly browned but still juicy.

Our final touch, though nontraditional, was to scatter thinly sliced scallions over the lentils. Tasters enjoyed the piquant scallion punch and the added visual appeal.

Spanish-Style Braised Lentils with Sausage

SERVES 4

Inspect the lentils carefully for small pebbles and other detritus; lentils almost always have foreign matter that needs to be removed. A white plate or bowl makes the bits easy to see (see the illustration on page 178). Smoked paprika is available in many specialty stores. Be sure to choose the bittersweet variety unless you have a penchant for very spicy food; hot smoked paprika is exactly that. You can use regular paprika if you can't find smoked; the difference is, of course, that regular paprika lacks smokiness. If you like your lentils on the mushy side, leave them in the oven for an additional 5 minutes. The dish reheats well and may even be eaten at room temperature with a drizzle of lemon juice or sherry vinegar.

1	cup lentils du Puy, picked over and rinsed
5	sprigs fresh thyme, tied together with kitchen twine
1 3/4	cups low-sodium chicken broth
2	tablespoons extra-virgin olive oil
4	medium garlic cloves, slivered
1	medium onion, diced
	Salt
1 1/4	teaspoons smoked bittersweet paprika or regular sweet paprika
1	(14.5-ounce) can diced tomatoes, drained
8	ounces kielbasa, split in half lengthwise, then halved crosswise to yield 4 pieces
	Ground black pepper
2	medium scallions, sliced thin on the bias

1. Bring the lentils, thyme sprigs, broth, and 1½ cups water to a boil in a medium saucepan over medium-high heat. Reduce the heat to medium-low and simmer until the lentils are almost tender but still a little crunchy, 20 to 25 minutes.

2. Meanwhile, adjust an oven rack to the middle position and heat the oven to 475 degrees. Heat the oil and garlic in an ovenproof 12-inch skillet over medium-high heat. As the oil begins to sizzle, shake the pan gently back and forth to prevent the garlic from clumping (stirring with a spoon will cause the garlic slivers to stick together). When the garlic turns a very light golden brown, after 2 to 3 minutes, add the onion and ½ teaspoon salt and cook, stirring occasionally, until the onion softens, about 4 minutes. Add the paprika and cook until aromatic, about 1 minute. Stir in the tomatoes. (If the lentils are not ready, set the skillet aside.)

3. When the lentils are ready, add them and any liquid in the pan to the skillet and arrange the kielbasa, cut-side up, across the surface. Transfer the skillet to the oven and cook until the liquid has evaporated and the lentils are soft, 10

to 12 minutes. Remove the skillet from the oven and let cool for at least 5 minutes. Discard the thyme, adjust the seasonings with salt and pepper to taste, and garnish with the scallions. Serve immediately.

ONE-PAN BRATWURST AND SAUERKRAUT

SOME MIGHT CALL THE DISTINCT FLAVOR OF sauerkraut an "acquired" taste, but it is a healthy and traditional foundation for several classic German and Alsatian meals. Bratwurst and sauerkraut may be the best known. Well-browned, flavorful sausage nestled into meltingly soft sauerkraut—what's not to love? Unfortunately, the dish traditionally relies on a long list of ingredients and a slow simmer in the oven for its full flavor. Despite the hurdles, we sensed the dish was ripe for a quick-cooking makeover.

We were not out to reinvent the dish, just to find a way to cook it quickly without compromising the essential flavors. This meant employing our deductive skills and examining the classic technique and flavors to find shortcuts and the core ingredients. Our first realization was that surface area was crucial to cooking the sauerkraut quickly, so we ditched the conventional Dutch oven in favor of a large (12-inch diameter), heavy-bottomed skillet with a lid. There was plenty of surface area for the sauerkraut to cook. The fond that developed when the sausages browned would in turn flavor the sauerkraut.

Browning the sausages was the first step, just a minute or two per side to intensify flavor and develop fond to flavor the sauerkraut. Bratwurst is the classic choice, though knockwurst follows closely; feel free to combine them if you like. Authentic bratwurst is made from a combination of pork and veal seasoned with a variety of spices, including ginger, nutmeg, and caraway. Knockwurst (or knackwurst) are a combination of beef and pork flavored with cumin and garlic. Both are fresh sausages and must be thoroughly cooked. Browning gets things started and steaming

in the sauerkraut finishes the task. While we recommend a trip to your local German butcher for the best-quality sausages, your local market should carry them, if not in the meat section, in the deli department—sometimes side-by-side with bags of sauerkraut.

With recipes dating to the early Middle Ages, sauerkraut has a long lineage. At its very simplest, sauerkraut is nothing but thinly sliced cabbage tightly packed with salt and slowly fermented. Depending on the temperature at which the cabbage is stored, fermentation may take up to a year before the sauerkraut is ready. Rarely does it go this long—one to two months is more conventional. Clearly our aim was not to make our own—store-bought would have to do. And, luckily, all the brands we tested were perfectly acceptable, especially when well rinsed to remove the potent brine.

To boost the flavor of the sauerkraut, we stuck to conventional flavorings like onion, carrot, and apple. Apple and carrot (grated coarsely on a box grater) cooked the fastest, breaking down to enrich the sauerkraut. We tried grating the onions but found they did not brown as well as when sliced and the sauerkraut suffered, lacking depth. Despite the sweetness provided by the onion, carrot, and apple, tasters agreed that the sauerkraut needed more. While white sugar worked adequately, brown sugar lent a new dimension to this dish. A scant tablespoon was all that was necessary.

For liquid, everything from cider and beer to chicken stock and water was common in our researched recipes. Cider made the cabbage taste too sweet and fruity for most tasters, even when partially diluted with water. Beer added a malty note that some tasters enjoyed but the majority felt clashed with the sauerkraut's tang, so we skipped it. Water lent little, so chicken broth (for convenience) was it, adding richness and depth without altering the dish's balanced flavors.

In the recipes we consulted, traditional seasonings included sage, caraway seeds, garlic, cloves, bay leaves, and juniper berries. We tried most of them—solo and in tandem—but tasters most enjoyed the woodsy, almost camphor-like flavor of the juniper as it added complexity without competing with the

EQUIPMENT: Large Skillets

Have you shopped for a skillet recently? The choices in material, weight, brand, and price—from $10 to $140—are dizzying. Preliminary tests on a lightweight discount store special selling for $10 confirmed our suspicions that cheap was not the way to go. But how much do you need to spend on this vital piece of kitchen equipment? To find out what more money buys, we zeroed in on a group of eight pans from well-known manufacturers, ranging in price from $60 to more than twice that, and sautéed our way to some pretty surprising conclusions.

All of the pans tested had flared sides, a design that makes it easier to flip foods in the pan (accomplished by jerking the pan sharply on the burner). Oddly, this design feature has created some confusion when it comes to nomenclature. Different manufacturers have different names for their flare-sided pans, including sauté pan, skillet, frypan, chef's pan, and omelette pan. In the test kitchen, we refer to flare-sided pans as skillets and to pans with straight sides (and often lids as well) as sauté pans. All of the pans tested also fall into a category we refer to as traditional—that is, none of the pans were nonstick.

The pans tested measured 12 inches in diameter (across the top) or as close to that as we could get from each manufacturer. We like this large size in a skillet because it can accommodate a big steak or all of the pieces cut from a typical 3½-pound chicken. Because the pan walls slope inward, the cooking surface of each pan measures considerably less than 12 inches. In fact, we found that even ¼ inch less cooking space could determine whether all of the chicken pieces fit without touching and therefore how well they would brown. (If a pan is too crowded, the food tends to steam rather than brown.) For instance, the All-Clad, with its 9¼-inch cooking surface, accommodated the chicken pieces without incident, whereas the 9-inch cooking surface of the Viking caused the pieces to touch.

Skillet construction also varies, and our group included the three most popular styles: clad, disk bottom, and cast. The All-Clad, Viking, Calphalon, Cuisinart, and KitchenAid units are clad, which means that the whole pan body, from the bottom up through the walls, is made from layers of the same metal that have been bonded under intense pressure and heat. These layers often form a sandwich, with the "filling" made of aluminum—which has the third highest thermal conductivity of all metals, behind silver and copper—and each slice of "bread" is made of stainless steel—which is attractive, durable, and nonreactive with acidic foods but is a lousy heat conductor on its own.

In the disk bottom construction style, only the pan bottom is layered and the walls are thus thinner than the bottom. In our group, the Farberware has an aluminum sandwich base and the Emerilware has disks of both aluminum and copper in its base.

Casting is the third construction style, represented here by Le Creuset, in which molten iron is molded to form the pan, body, and handle alike. Cast-iron pans are known to be heavy, to heat up slowly, and to retain their heat well. The French Le Creuset pans are also enameled, which makes them nonreactive inside and out.

Did our testing uncover any significant differences in performance based on these three construction styles? Although some manufacturers tout the benefits of cladding, our kitchen testing did not support this. The two skillets with disk bottoms, the Farberware and the Emerilware, did heat up a little faster than the rest of the field, but it was easy to accommodate this difference by adjusting the stovetop burner.

The weight of the pans turned out to be more important than construction, especially in our solder tests. The lightweight (1 pound, 1 ounce) aluminum budget pan was the quickest to reach 361 degrees, at an average of 2.8 minutes, while the heavy 6.5-pound Le Creuset was the slowest, at an average of 10.1 minutes. The lightweight pan performed poorly in kitchen tests, while Le Creuset did well. Still, cast iron does have its disadvantages. The heavy Le Creuset pan is difficult to lift on and off the burner and to handle while cleaning. If your strength is limited, these factors can mean a lot. In addition, the pan's iron handle gets just as hot as the rest of the pan, so it's necessary to use a potholder both during and just after use.

We concluded that a range of 3 to 4 pounds is ideal in a 12-inch skillet. The medium-weight pans (especially those from All-Clad, Viking, and Calphalon) brown foods beautifully, and most testers handled them comfortably. These pans have enough heft for heat retention and structural integrity but not so much that the they are difficult to lift or manipulate.

THE BEST LARGE SKILLETS
The All-Clad Stainless 12-Inch Frypan (top: $125) took top honors in our testing. The Calphalon Tri-Ply Stainless 12-Inch Omelette Pan (bottom right: $65) and the Farberware Millennium 18/10 Stainless Steel 12-Inch Covered Skillet (bottom left: $70) were rated best buys, costing about half as much as the winning pan.

assertive spiciness of the sausage.

One final though crucial lesson we learned was the importance of pricking the sausages prior to cooking. Without a liberal pricking, the sausages were prone to exploding—an unsightly mess to say the least. A skewer or the tip of a thin paring knife worked perfectly.

One-Pan Bratwurst and Sauerkraut

SERVES 4

Don't be alarmed when the grated apple rapidly oxidizes, the brown color won't impact the finished dish. The dish may be prepared ahead of time and reheated, but add water or chicken broth to keep the sauerkraut moist. An ideal accompaniment would be potatoes, either mashed or boiled.

1	tablespoon unsalted butter
4	bratwursts or knockwursts, punctured liberally with a small skewer
1	small onion, halved and sliced thin
10	whole juniper berries
1	medium carrot, peeled and grated on the large holes of a box grater
	Salt
2	pounds packaged sauerkraut, well rinsed and drained
1	medium Granny Smith apple, peeled and grated on the large holes of a box grater
1	tablespoon brown sugar
1 3/4	cups low-sodium chicken broth
	Ground black pepper

1. Heat the butter in a 12-inch skillet over medium-high heat. Once the foaming subsides, add the sausages and reduce the heat to medium. Cook until well browned, 1 to 1½ minutes. Using tongs, rotate the sausage one-quarter turn and brown the next side, about 1 minute. Repeat 2 more times until browned all sides (about 4 minutes total.) Transfer the sausages to a plate.

2. Add the onion, juniper berries, carrot, and ¼ teaspoon salt to the now-empty skillet. Cook, stirring frequently, until the onion softens, about 3 minutes. Stir in the sauerkraut, apple, sugar, and

broth, increase the heat to medium-high, and bring to a simmer. Nestle the sausages into the sauerkraut, evenly spacing them around the skillet. Cover, reduce the heat to low, and simmer until the liquid is almost evaporated, about 30 minutes. Adjust the seasonings with salt and pepper to taste. Transfer to a platter, arranging the sausages on the sauerkraut, and serve.

BACON

MANY HOME COOKS NOW USE THE MICRO-wave to cook bacon, while others still fry bacon in a skillet. In restaurants, many chefs "fry" bacon in the oven. We decided to try each of these methods to find out which worked best.

For each cooking technique, we varied temperature, timing, and material, cooking both a typical store-bought bacon and a thick-cut mail-order bacon. The finished strips were compared in terms of flavor, texture, and appearance, while the techniques were compared for consistency, safety, and ease.

While the microwave would seem to have the apparent advantage of ease—stick the pieces in and forget about them—this turned out not to be the case. The bacon was still raw at 90 seconds; at two minutes it was medium-well-done in most spots, but still uneven; but by two minutes and 30 seconds the strips of bacon were hard and flat and definitely overcooked. The finished product didn't warrant the investment of time it would take to figure out the perfect number of seconds. Microwaved bacon is not crisp, it is an unappetizing pink/gray in color even when well-done, and it lacks flavor.

The skillet made for a significantly better product. The bacon flavors were much more pronounced than in the nuked version, the finished color of the meat was a more appealing brick red, and the meat had a pleasing crispness. There were, however, a number of drawbacks to pan-frying. In addition to the functional problems of grease splatter and the number of 11-inch strips you can fit into a 12-inch round pan, there are problems of consistency and convenience. Because all of the heat comes from below the meat, the strips brown on one side before the other. Moreover, even when using a cast-iron pan, as we did, heat is not distributed perfectly evenly across the bottom of the pan. This means that to get consistently cooked strips of bacon you have to turn them over and rotate them in the pan. In addition, when more strips are added to an already-hot pan, they tend to wrinkle up, making for raw or burnt spots in the finished product.

The best results from stovetop cooking came when we lowered the heat from medium to medium-low, just hot enough to sizzle. The lower temperature allowed the strips to render their grease more slowly, with a lot less curling and spitting out of the pan. Of course, this added to the cooking time, and it did not alleviate the need for vigilance.

Oven-frying seemed to combine the advantages of the microwaving and pan-frying while eliminating most of the disadvantages. We tried cooking three strips in a preheated 400-degree oven on a 12

EQUIPMENT : Chef's Knives

A good chef's knife is probably the most useful tool any cook owns. So what separates a good knife from an inferior one? To understand the answer to this question, it helps to know something about how knives are constructed.

The first pieces of cutlery were made about 4,000 years ago with the discovery that iron ore could be melted and shaped into tools. The creation of steel, which is 80 percent iron and 20 percent other elements, led to the development of carbon steel knives (the standard for 3,000 years. Although this kind of steel takes and holds an edge easily, it also stains and rusts. Something as simple as cutting an acidic tomato or living in the salt air of the seacoast can corrode carbon steel.

Today, new alloys have given cooks better options. Stainless steel, made with at least 4 percent chromium and/or nickel, will never rust. Used for many cheap knives, stainless steel is also very difficult to sharpen. The compromise between durable but dull stainless steel and sharp but corrodible carbon steel is a material called high-carbon stainless steel. Used by most knife manufacturers, this blend combines durability and sharpness.

Until recently, all knives were hot drop forged—that is, the steel was heated to 2000 degrees, dropped into a mold, given four or five shots with a hammer, and then tempered (cooled and heated several times to build strength). This process is labor intensive (many steps must be done by hand), which explains why many chef's knives cost almost $100.

A second manufacturing process feeds long sheets of steel through a press that punches out knife after knife, much like a cookie cutter slicing through dough. Called stamped blades, these knives require some hand finishing but are much cheaper to produce because a machine does most of the work.

While experts have long argued that forged knives are better than stamped ones, our testing did not fully support this position. We liked some forged knives and did not like others. Likewise, we liked some stamped knives and did not like others. The weight and shape of the handle (it must be comfortable to hold and substantial but not too heavy), the ability of the blade to take an edge, and the shape of the blade (we like a slightly curved blade, which is better suited to the rocking motion often used to mince herbs or garlic than a straight blade) are all key factors in choosing a knife.

When shopping, pick up the knife and see how it feels in your hand. Is it easy to grip? Does the weight seem properly distributed between the handle and blade? In our testing, we liked knives made by Henckels and Wüsthof. An inexpensive knife by Forschner, with a stamped blade, also scored well.

Buying a good knife is only half the challenge. You must keep the edge sharp. To that end, we recommend buying an electric knife sharpener. Steels are best for modest corrections, but all knives will require more substantial sharpening at least several times a year, if not more often if you cook a lot. Stones are difficult to use because they require that you maintain a perfect 20-degree angle between the stone and blade. An electric knife sharpener (we like models made by Chef's Choice) takes the guesswork out of sharpening and allows you to keep edges sharp and effective.

THE BEST CHEF'S KNIVES
The Henckels Four Star (bottom) and Wüsthof-Trident Grand Prix (center) are top choices, but expect to spend about $80 for one of these knives. The Forschner (Victorinox) Fibrox (top) is lighter but still solid and costs just $30.

by 9-inch rimmed baking sheet that would contain the grease. The bacon was medium well-done after 9 to 10 minutes and crispy after 11 to 12 minutes. The texture was more like a seared piece of meat than a brittle cracker, the color was that nice brick red, and all of the flavors were just as bright and clear as when pan-fried. Oven-frying also provided a greater margin of error when it came to timing than either of the other methods, and, surprisingly, it was just about as easy as microwaving, adding only the steps of preheating the oven and draining the cooked bacon on paper towels. Finally, the oven-fried strips of bacon were more consistently cooked throughout, showing no raw spots and requiring no turning or flipping during cooking. Because the heat hits the strip from all sides, there is no reason for the bacon strips to curl in one direction or another, and when the strips do curl, the ruffled edges cook as quickly as the flat areas.

Our last test was to try 12 strips of bacon—a pretty full tray—in a preheated oven. This test was also quite successful. The pieces cooked consistently, the only difference being between those in the back and those in the front of the oven; we corrected for this by rotating the tray once from front to back during cooking. That was about the limit of our contact with the hot grease.

⤜✦⤏

Oven-Fried Bacon
SERVES 4 TO 6

Use a large, rimmed baking sheet that is shallow enough to promote browning, yet deep enough (at least ¾ inch in height) to contain the rendered bacon fat. If cooking more than 1 tray of bacon, exchange the positions of the trays in the oven about halfway through the cooking process.

12   slices bacon, thin- or thick-cut

Adjust an oven rack to the middle position and heat the oven to 400 degrees. Arrange the bacon slices, without overlapping, in a rimmed baking sheet or other shallow baking pan. Roast until the fat begins to render, 5 to 6 minutes; rotate the pan front to back. Continue roasting until the bacon is crisp and brown, 5 to 6 minutes longer for thin-sliced bacon, 8 to 10 minutes longer for thick-cut. Transfer the bacon with tongs to a plate lined with paper towels to drain. Serve.

16

RUBS, SAUCES, SALSAS, AND GRAVY

Rubs, Sauces, Salsas, and Gravy

This chapter includes spice rubs, sauces, salsas, and one all-purpose gravy, any of which can be used with the recipes in this book. Most of the combinations that follow are staples—recipes that you will make over and over again.

Spice Rubs

A MIXTURE OF DRY SPICES, CALLED A RUB, is often used to coat foods before barbecuing. Rubs encourage the formation of a deeply browned crust filled with complex, concentrated flavors. Like marinades, spice rubs add flavor to foods before cooking, but we think rubs and pastes have several advantages over marinades.

Because rubs are composed almost solely of spices and herbs, they provide stronger flavor than marinades. (Marinades consist mostly of oil with an acidic liquid added, such as lemon juice or vinegar.) Rubs also adhere to foods more than marinades do—after all, rubs are massaged directly into foods before grilling. The better the adherence the better the flavor. Finally, because of the oil in marinades, there can be flare-ups. On the other hand, spice rubs can be left on foods for several hours without causing fires.

Spice rubs can be used on just about any type of food you want to barbecue. In general, you can freely mix and match rubs and pastes on different foods. That said, it is still worth observing a couple of useful guidelines: First, consider matching the strength of the rub or paste with the nature of the food being cooked. For example, earthier spices are better with meat: lighter spices and herbs with fish and chicken. Also keep in mind that spices like cumin and paprika are good "bulk" spices, while aromatic spices like cinnamon and cloves should be used sparingly so as not to overwhelm.

We find that bare hands—not brushes—are the best "tools" for applying rubs. Use a bit of pressure to make sure that the rub actually adheres to the food. Although rubs can be applied right before cooking, we've discovered that the flavor of the spices penetrates deeper into the food if given time to develop. Refrigerate rubbed meats for at least a few hours to maximize the return.

Dry Rub for Barbecue
MAKES ABOUT 1 CUP

You can adjust the proportions of spices in this all-purpose rub or add or subtract a spice, as you wish. For instance, if don't like spicy foods, reduce the cayenne. Or, if you are using hot chili powder, eliminate the cayenne entirely. This rub works well with ribs and brisket as well as with Boston butt for pulled pork (page 332).

4	tablespoons sweet paprika
2	tablespoons chili powder
2	tablespoons ground cumin
2	tablespoons dark brown sugar
2	tablespoons salt
1	tablespoon dried oregano
1	tablespoon granulated sugar
1	tablespoon ground black pepper
1	tablespoon ground white pepper
1–2	teaspoons cayenne pepper

Mix all of the ingredients together in a small bowl. (The rub can be stored in an airtight container at room temperature for several weeks.)

Simple Spice Rub for Beef or Lamb
MAKES SCANT ¼ CUP

This fragrant rub is good on most cuts of beef and lamb, especially flank steak, shoulder steak, lamb shoulder chops, and butterflied leg of lamb.

1	tablespoon black peppercorns
1	tablespoon white peppercorns
1 ½	teaspoons coriander seeds
1 ½	teaspoons cumin seeds
½	teaspoon red pepper flakes
½	teaspoon ground cinnamon

1. Toast both the peppercorns and the coriander and cumin seeds in a small skillet over medium heat, shaking the pan occasionally to prevent burning, until the first wisps of smoke appear, 3 to 5 minutes. Remove the pan from the heat, cool the spices to room temperature, then mix them with the pepper flakes and cinnamon.

2. Grind the spice mixture to a powder in a dedicated spice grinder or coffee mill. (The rub can be stored in an airtight container at room temperature for several weeks.)

BARBECUE SAUCES AND GLAZES

OF ALL THE SAUCES AND GLAZES USED FOR barbecuing, barbecue sauce is the most common. Almost all of these sauces and glazes, however, contain ingredients such as tomatoes or a sweetener that will cause them to burn if left on grilled foods for any length of time. For this reason, these sauces are usually brushed on grilled foods during the last few minutes of cooking and are also served at the table.

Classic barbecue sauce, we discovered, is relatively easy to make. The combination of tomato sauce and whole tomatoes in juice cooks down to a thick, glossy texture. Vinegar, brown sugar, and molasses add the sour and sweet notes, while spices (paprika, chili powder, black pepper, and salt) round out the flavors. For some brightness, we added a little fresh orange juice as well. The only downside to this sauce is that it takes at least two hours of gentle simmering for the flavors to come together and for the tomatoes to break down into a sauce of the proper consistency.

Was there a way to shorten up on the cooking time? The answer was yes. The first thing we had to do for quick barbecue sauce was abandon the canned whole tomatoes—they took too long to cook down. So we tried all tomato sauce (and no fresh tomatoes), which made a sauce that seemed more appropriate for pasta. We then tried ketchup and had better luck because it is already sweet, tart, and thick.

The only other major obstacle we encountered when developing our quick rendition of barbecue sauce was the onion. After two hours of simmering in our classic barbecue sauce, the onion became, not surprisingly, very soft. In our quick-cooked version, though, it remained crunchy. We tried

---

INGREDIENTS: Bottled Barbecue Sauce

Despite the best of intentions, there's not always time to make barbecue sauce. It's no surprise that many cooks turn to bottled sauces.

We wondered if some brands of bottled barbecue sauce were much better than others. Are the "gourmet" brands worth the extra money, or will a supermarket brand suffice? We tasted 12 samples to find out. We limited the tasting to tomato-based sauces because they are far and away the most popular and represent what most Americans picture when they think "barbecue sauce."

In general, tasters were not overly impressed with these bottled sauces. Most were much too sweet and had an overly thick, gummy texture. The ingredients responsible were high-fructose corn syrup and food starch. We did find one sauce that everyone agreed was quite good and another three sauces worth considering. Three of these four sauces were more expensive "gourmet," organic offerings, so, at least when it comes to barbecue sauce, more money does buy a better product.

Our favorite sauce is Mad Dog, a boutique brand from Boston. Although the ingredient list is mercifully short (many other sauces have long lists of hard-to-pronounce ingredients), tasters thought this sauce was more complex and balanced than the rest of the pack. It also contained less sugar than most brands and no corn syrup, an ingredient found in all but three of the sauces tested.

Bull's Eye, Sweet Baby Ray's, and Muir Glen received decent scores and mixed comments. Like most supermarket offerings, Bull's Eye is very sweet and has a thick, glossy consistency, but it also delivers a decent hit of smoke, something missing from other mass-market sauces. Tasters liked the strong molasses flavor in the Sweet Baby Ray's and Muir Glen sauces, although neither was an overwhelming favorite. The rest of the sauces were so bad that tasters felt they harmed rather than improved the flavor of plain broiled chicken. With one exception then, this tasting did not uncover products about which we could get enthused.

As with homemade barbecue sauce, bottled sauces are finishing sauces, not basting sauces. They all contain sweeteners and tomatoes, which will cause foods to burn within minutes after application. Foods destined for the grill should not be marinated in barbecue sauce. The food will burn and taste awful. Just brush a little sauce on during the last two or three minutes of the cooking time, and then brush again just before serving.

---

pureeing the quick sauce after it had cooked, as we did with our classic sauce, but the quick sauce lost its glossy texture and turned grainy. One of our test cooks then suggested using onion juice—made by pureeing raw onion with water—to give the sauce some onion flavor without texture. This worked liked a charm.

At this point, it was only a matter of adding flavors. Worcestershire sauce and Dijon mustard contributed instant depth. The usual spices—chili powder, cayenne, black pepper—provided more flavor and heat.

In the event classic or quick barbecue sauce is not for you, several specialized barbecue sauces, with distinct flavor profiles, are also included in the following pages.

Classic Barbecue Sauce
MAKES 3 GENEROUS CUPS
Brush this sauce onto chicken parts during the last minute or two of grilling or serve at the table with ribs, brisket, or pulled pork.

2	tablespoons vegetable oil
1	medium onion, minced
1	(8-ounce) can tomato sauce
1	(28-ounce) can whole tomatoes with juice
3/4	cup distilled white vinegar
1/4	cup packed dark brown sugar
2	tablespoons molasses
1	tablespoon sweet paprika
1	tablespoon chili powder
2	teaspoons liquid smoke (optional)
1	teaspoon salt
2	teaspoons ground black pepper
1/4	cup orange juice

1. Heat the oil in a large, heavy-bottomed saucepan over medium heat until hot and shimmering (but not smoking). Add the onion and cook, stirring occasionally, until golden brown, 7 to 10 minutes. Add the remaining ingredients. Bring to a boil, then reduce the heat to the lowest possible setting and simmer, uncovered and stirring occasionally, until thickened, 2 to 2½ hours.

2. Puree the sauce, in batches, if necessary, in a blender or the workbowl of a food processor fitted with the steel blade. Transfer the sauce to a bowl and use immediately or let cool, then store in an airtight container. (The sauce can be refrigerated for 2 weeks or frozen for several months.)

➤ VARIATIONS
Barbecue Sauce with Mexican Flavors
A few ingredients added to basic barbecue sauce give this recipe a south-of-the-border flavor.

Follow the recipe for Classic Barbecue Sauce, stirring 1½ teaspoons ground cumin, 1½ teaspoons chili powder, 6 tablespoons juice from 3 limes, and 3 tablespoons chopped fresh cilantro leaves into the finished sauce.

Barbecue Sauce with Asian Flavors
Soy sauce, ginger, and sesame oil give this tomato-based sauce an Asian flavor.

Follow the recipe for Classic Barbecue Sauce, stirring 1 tablespoon minced fresh ginger, 6 tablespoons soy sauce, 6 tablespoons rice vinegar, 3 tablespoons sugar, and 1½ tablespoons Asian sesame oil into the finished sauce.

Barbecue Sauce with Caribbean Flavors
When you brush foods with this sauce, serve Black Bean and Mango Salsa (page 403) on the side.

Follow the recipe for Classic Barbecue Sauce, stirring 2 tablespoons pineapple juice, 2 tablespoons dark rum, 1 tablespoon Caribbean hot sauce, 2 teaspoons sugar, and a pinch ground allspice into the finished sauce.

Quick Barbecue Sauce
MAKES ABOUT 1½ CUPS
Classic barbecue sauce must simmer for a long time in order for the whole tomatoes in it to break down. However, we found that starting with ketchup can shortcut the process. Use this sauce as you would any another barbecue sauce—either brushed on foods during the last minutes of grilling or served at the table as a dipping sauce with ribs or brisket.

1	medium onion, peeled and quartered
1/4	cup water

1 cup ketchup

2 tablespoons cider vinegar

2 tablespoons Worcestershire sauce

2 tablespoons Dijon mustard

5 tablespoons molasses

1 teaspoon hot pepper sauce, such as Tabasco

1/4 teaspoon ground black pepper

1 1/2 teaspoons liquid smoke (optional)

2 tablespoons vegetable oil

1 medium garlic clove, minced or pressed through a garlic press (about 1 teaspoon)

1 teaspoon chili powder

1/4 teaspoon cayenne pepper

1. Process the onion with the water in the workbowl of a food processor fitted with the steel blade until pureed and the mixture resembles slush, about 30 seconds. Strain the mixture through a fine-mesh strainer into a liquid measuring cup, pressing on the solids with a rubber spatula to obtain 1/2 cup juice. Discard the solids.

2. Whisk the onion juice, ketchup, vinegar, Worcestershire, mustard, molasses, hot pepper sauce, black pepper, and liquid smoke (if using) together in a medium bowl.

3. Heat the oil in a large nonreactive saucepan over medium heat until shimmering but not smoking. Add the garlic, chili powder, and cayenne; cook until fragrant, about 30 seconds. Whisk in the ketchup mixture and bring to a boil; reduce the heat to medium-low and simmer gently, uncovered, until the flavors meld and the sauce is thickened, about 25 minutes. Cool the sauce to room temperature before using. (The sauce can be refrigerated in an airtight container for 1 week.)

Sweet-Sour-Spicy Barbecue Sauce

MAKES ABOUT 1 1/2 CUPS

We developed this highly acidic sauce for beef ribs. The vinegar, tomato paste, and spices balance the richness of the beef. It is quite strong, so brush only a little bit of it on the ribs to start. If you like your sauce especially spicy, add another 1/2 teaspoon of cayenne pepper.

1 cup distilled white vinegar

1/4 cup tomato paste

2 tablespoons salt

1/2 cup sugar

2 tablespoons sweet paprika

2 teaspoons dried mustard

2 teaspoons ground black pepper

1/2 teaspoon cayenne pepper

1/2 teaspoon onion powder

1/2 teaspoon garlic powder

1/2 teaspoon chili powder

4 tablespoons vegetable oil

1. Mix the vinegar, tomato paste, salt, and sugar together in a medium bowl. In another bowl, combine the paprika, dried mustard, black pepper, cayenne, onion powder, garlic powder, and chili powder.

2. Heat the oil in a small saucepan over medium heat. Add the spice mixture and cook until sizzling and fragrant, 30 to 45 seconds. Stir in the vinegar mixture and increase the heat to high. Bring to a boil, reduce the heat to low, and simmer for 5 minutes. Remove the pan from the heat and cool to room temperature. (The sauce can be refrigerated in an airtight container for 1 week.)

Eastern North Carolina–Style Barbecue Sauce

MAKES 2 CUPS

This sauce contains no tomato but is rich with heat and vinegar. It is traditionally served with pulled pork (page 332) but can also be brushed onto ribs or brisket.

1 cup distilled white vinegar

1 cup cider vinegar

1 tablespoon sugar

1 tablespoon red pepper flakes

1 tablespoon hot pepper sauce, such as Tabasco
Salt and ground black pepper

Mix all of the ingredients, including salt and pepper to taste, together in a medium bowl. (The sauce can be refrigerated in an airtight container for several days.)

Mid–South Carolina Mustard Sauce

MAKES 2 ½ CUPS

Here is another classic sauce for pulled pork (page 332) that works well with other cuts of grilled pork, too.

I	cup cider vinegar
6	tablespoons Dijon mustard
2	tablespoons maple syrup or honey
4	teaspoons Worcestershire sauce
I	teaspoon hot pepper sauce, such as Tabasco
I	cup vegetable oil
2	teaspoons salt
	Ground black pepper

Mix all of the ingredients, including black pepper to taste, together in a medium bowl. (The sauce can be refrigerated in an airtight container for several days.)

Sweetened Soy Glaze

MAKES I GENEROUS CUP

This Asian sauce is more traditional than Barbecue Sauce with Asian Flavors on page 399 because it does not contain any tomato. It is great on beef ribs.

½	cup soy sauce
¼	cup water
¼	cup sugar
I	tablespoon rice vinegar
2	teaspoons minced fresh ginger
I	medium garlic clove, minced or pressed through a garlic press (about 1 teaspoon)
2	teaspoons cornstarch dissolved in I tablespoon cold water
I	teaspoon Asian sesame oil
I	medium scallion, sliced thin

1. Bring the soy sauce, water, sugar, vinegar, ginger, and garlic to a boil in a medium saucepan over medium heat. Whisk in the cornstarch mixture and cook for 1 minute.

2. Remove the pan from the heat and whisk in the sesame oil and scallion. (The glaze can be refrigerated in an airtight container for a day or two.)

Hoisin, Honey, and Ginger Glaze

MAKES ABOUT I ½ CUPS

This sweet and thick glaze is great on spareribs or any other cut of pork.

½	cup soy sauce
¼	cup ketchup
¼	cup honey
2	tablespoons brown sugar
2	tablespoons juice from 1 lemon
I ½	tablespoons hoisin sauce
2	teaspoons vegetable oil
I	teaspoon minced fresh ginger
2	medium garlic cloves, minced or pressed through a garlic press (about 2 teaspoons)

1. Mix the soy sauce, ketchup, honey, brown sugar, lemon juice, and hoisin sauce together in a medium bowl.

2. Heat the oil in a small saucepan over medium-high heat until shimmering. Add the ginger and garlic and cook until fragrant but not browned, about 30 seconds. Add the soy mixture and bring to a boil. Cook for 1 minute and remove the pan from the heat. Cool to room temperature. (The glaze may be refrigerated in an airtight container for 1 week.)

PEELING GINGER

Because of its shape, ginger can be difficult to peel, especially if using a knife. Try this method to reduce waste. Use the bowl of a teaspoon to scrape off the knotty skin from a knob of ginger. The spoon moves easily around curves in the ginger, so you remove just the skin.

SALSAS AND SAUCES

THE CONDIMENT-LIKE SALSAS, RELISHES, and sauces in this section are served at the table with meats. Many are made with raw ingredients; the rest are lightly cooked. Most can be made in advance and refrigerated for several days and brought to room temperature before serving.

Classic Red Table Salsa

MAKES ABOUT 5 CUPS

Our Mexican-style salsa is equally good with fajitas or tortilla chips. To reduce the heat in the salsa, seed the chile. This recipe can be cut in half if desired.

3	large, very ripe tomatoes (about 2 pounds), cored and diced small
1/2	cup tomato juice
1	small jalapeño chile, stemmed, seeded if desired, and minced
1	medium red onion, diced small
1	medium garlic clove, minced or pressed through a garlic press (about 1 teaspoon)
1/2	cup chopped fresh cilantro leaves
1/2	cup juice from 4 limes
	Salt

PREPARING AN AVOCADO

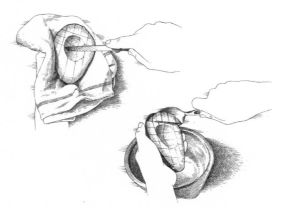

1. Use a dish towel to hold the pitted avocado half steady. Make 1/2-inch crosshatch incisions in the flesh of each half with a dinner knife, cutting down to but not through the skin.
2. Separate the diced flesh from the skin, using a spoon inserted between the skin and the flesh, gently scooping out the avocado cubes.

Mix all of the ingredients, including salt to taste, together in a medium bowl. Refrigerate the salsa in an airtight container to blend the flavors at least 1 hour or up to 5 days.

Chunky Guacamole

MAKES 2 1/2 TO 3 CUPS

Guacamole is an essential accompaniment to fajitas with grilled flank steak. To minimize discoloration, prepare the minced ingredients first so they are ready to mix with the avocados as soon as they are cut. Ripe avocados are a must. To test for ripeness, flick the small stem off the end of the avocado. If it comes off easily and you can see green underneath it, the avocado is ripe. If it does not come off or if you see brown underneath, the avocado is not ripe. The guacamole can be covered with plastic wrap, pressed directly onto the surface of the mixture, and refrigerated for 1 day. Return the guacamole to room temperature, removing the plastic wrap just before serving.

3	ripe medium, avocados (preferably pebbly-skinned Hass)
2	tablespoons minced onion
1	medium garlic clove, minced or pressed through a garlic press (about 1 teaspoon)
1	small jalapeño chile, stemmed, seeded, and minced
1/4	cup minced fresh cilantro leaves
1/4	teaspoon salt
1/2	teaspoon ground cumin (optional)
2	tablespoons juice from 1 lime

1. Halve 1 avocado, remove the pit, and scoop the flesh into a medium bowl. Mash the flesh lightly with the onion, garlic, chile, cilantro, salt, and cumin (if using) with the tines of a fork until just combined.

2. Halve and pit the remaining 2 avocados. Make 1/2-inch crosshatch incisions in the flesh of each avocado half with a dinner knife, cutting down to but not through the skin (see the illustration at left). Separate the diced flesh from the skin using a spoon inserted between the skin and flesh, gently scooping out the avocado cubes (see illustration 2). Add the cubes to the bowl with the mashed avocado mixture.

3. Sprinkle the lime juice over the diced avocado and mix the entire contents of the bowl lightly with a fork until combined but still chunky. Adjust the seasonings with salt to taste, if necessary, and serve.

PREPARING A MANGO

1. With a sharp paring knife, remove a thin slice from one end of the mango so that it sits flat on a work surface.

2. Hold the mango, cut-side down, and cut off the skin in thin strips, working from top to bottom.

3. Once the skin has been completely removed, cut down along the side of the flat pit to remove the flesh from one side of the mango. Remove the flesh on the other side in the same manner.

4. Trim around the pit to remove any flesh that remains. The flesh can be chopped or sliced as needed for recipes.

Black Bean and Mango Salsa
MAKES 2 ½ CUPS

This Caribbean-inspired mixture is great with grilled pork.

½	cup cooked black beans
1	medium mango, peeled, pitted, and cut into ¼-inch dice (see the illustrations at left)
¼	medium red bell pepper, stemmed, seeded, and diced small
¼	medium green bell pepper, stemmed, seeded, and diced small
¼	medium red onion, diced small
6	tablespoons pineapple juice
¼	cup juice from 2 limes
¼	cup chopped fresh cilantro leaves
1	tablespoon ground cumin
½	small jalapeño chile, stemmed, seeded, and minced
	Salt and ground black pepper

Mix all of the ingredients, including salt and pepper to taste, together in a medium bowl. Refrigerate the salsa in an airtight container to blend the flavors at least 1 hour or up to 4 days.

Mango Salsa
MAKES ABOUT 2 CUPS

This salsa goes especially well with pork.

2	medium mangoes, peeled, pitted, and cut into ¼-inch dice (see the illustrations at left)
½	medium red onion, minced
2	scallions, sliced thin
½	medium jalapeño chile, stemmed, seeded, if desired, and minced
1	tablespoon juice from 1 lime
2	tablespoons minced fresh cilantro leaves
	Salt and ground black pepper

Mix all of the ingredients, including salt and pepper to taste, together in a medium bowl. (The salsa can be refrigerated in an airtight container for several days.)

Pineapple Salsa

MAKES ABOUT 2 ½ CUPS

This sweet and spicy salsa works well with pork. You will need to prepare it shortly before serving to prevent discoloration of the banana and avocado.

¼	small pineapple, peeled, cored, and cut into ½-inch dice (about 1 ¼ cups, see the illustrations on page 405)
1	small barely ripe banana, peeled and cut into ½-inch dice
½	cup seedless green grapes, halved or quartered
½	firm avocado, peeled, pitted, and cut into ½-inch dice (see the illustrations on page 402)
4	teaspoons juice from 1 lime
1	medium jalapeño chile, stemmed, seeded, and minced
1	teaspoon minced fresh oregano leaves
	Salt

Combine all of the ingredients, including salt to taste, in a medium bowl. Let stand at room temperature for 30 minutes. (The banana and avocado will darken if the salsa is prepared much further in advance.)

Peach Salsa

MAKES ABOUT 2 ½ CUPS

Nectarines can be substituted for the peaches. This salsa works well with pork or lamb.

2	ripe but not mushy peaches, pitted and chopped coarse
1	small red bell pepper, stemmed, seeded, and diced
1	small red onion, diced
¼	cup chopped fresh parsley leaves
1	medium garlic clove, minced or pressed through a garlic press (about 1 teaspoon)
¼	cup pineapple juice
6	tablespoons juice from 3 limes
1	medium jalapeño chile, stemmed, seeded, and minced
	Salt

Mix all of the ingredients, including salt to taste, together in a medium bowl. Cover and refrigerate to blend the flavors at least 1 hour or up to 4 days.

Mojo Sauce

MAKES 1 GENEROUS CUP

This Cuban citrus sauce is delicious with pork.

½	cup extra-virgin olive oil
6	medium garlic cloves, minced or pressed through a garlic press (about 2 tablespoons)
½	teaspoon ground cumin
½	cup juice from 2 oranges
¼	cup juice from 2 limes
1	teaspoon salt
½	teaspoon ground black pepper

1. Heat the oil in a small, deep saucepan over medium heat until shimmering. Add the garlic and cumin and cook until fragrant but not browned, 30 to 45 seconds.

2. Remove the pan from the heat and add the orange juice, lime juice, salt, and pepper carefully. Place the pan back over the heat, bring to a simmer, and cook for 1 minute. Remove the pan from the heat and cool the sauce to room temperature. (The sauce can be refrigerated in an airtight container for 3 days.)

Quick Onion and Parsley Relish

MAKES GENEROUS ¾ CUP

Serve with lamb or beef.

½	medium red onion, diced small
½	cup chopped fresh parsley leaves
¼	cup extra-virgin olive oil
¼	cup juice from 2 lemons
	Salt and ground black pepper

Mix the onion, parsley, oil, and lemon juice together in a small bowl. Season with salt and pepper to taste. (The relish can be covered and set aside at room temperature for several hours.)

Salsa Verde

MAKES GENEROUS ¾ CUP

A slice of sandwich bread pureed into the sauce keeps the flavors balanced and gives the sauce texture. Toasting the bread rids it of excess moisture that might otherwise make a gummy sauce. Salsa verde is excellent with grilled or roasted meats as well as with boiled dinners such as Bollito Misto (page 196). It is best served immediately after it is made, but can be refrigerated in an airtight container for up to 2 days. If refrigerated, bring the sauce to room temperature and stir to recombine it before serving.

1	large slice white sandwich bread
½	cup extra-virgin olive oil
2	tablespoons juice from 1 lemon
2	cups lightly packed fresh parsley leaves
2	medium anchovy fillets
2	tablespoons drained capers
1	small garlic clove, minced or pressed through garlic press (about ½ teaspoon)
⅛	teaspoon salt

1. Toast the bread in a toaster at low setting until the surface is dry but not browned, about 15 seconds. Cut the bread into rough ½-inch pieces (you should have about ½ cup).

2. Process the bread pieces, oil, and lemon juice in the workbowl of a food processor fitted with the steel blade until smooth, about 10 seconds. Add the parsley, anchovies, capers, garlic, and salt. Pulse until the mixture is finely chopped (the mixture should not be smooth), about five 1-second pulses, scraping down the bowl with a rubber spatula after 3 pulses. Transfer the mixture to a small bowl and serve.

Parsley Sauce with Cornichons and Capers

MAKES ABOUT 1¼ CUPS

This sauce pairs perfectly with beef tenderloin (cooked in the oven or on the grill).

¾	cup minced fresh parsley leaves
12	cornichons, minced (6 tablespoons), plus 1 teaspoon cornichon juice
¼	cup drained capers, chopped coarse
2	medium scallions, white and light green parts, minced
	Pinch salt
¼	teaspoon ground black pepper
½	cup extra-virgin olive oil

Mix all of the ingredients together in a medium bowl. (The sauce can be covered and set aside at room temperature for several hours.)

Chimichurri

MAKES 1 GENEROUS CUP

Like a loose, fresh salsa in consistency, this mixture is a common accompaniment to sautéed, roasted, and grilled meats in South America. For best results, use flat-leaf parsley. This sauce works well with beef, especially mild

PREPARING A PINEAPPLE

1. Start by trimming the ends of the pineapple so it will sit flat on a work surface. Cut the pineapple through the ends into quarters.

2. Place each quarter, cut-side up, on the work surface, and slide the knife between the skin and flesh to remove the skin.

3. Stand each peeled quarter on end and slice off the portion of the tough, light-colored core attached to the inside of each piece. Discard the core sections. The peeled and cored pineapple can be diced or sliced, as desired.

filet or tenderloin. Although this sauce tastes best the day it is made, any that is left over can be refrigerated for several days.

1   cup packed fresh parsley leaves, preferably
     flat-leaf parsley
5   medium garlic cloves, peeled
1/2 cup extra-virgin olive oil
1/4 cup red wine vinegar
2   tablespoons water
1/4 cup finely minced red onion
1   teaspoon salt
1/4 teaspoon red pepper flakes

Process the parsley and garlic in the workbowl of a food processor fitted with the steel blade, stopping as necessary to scrape down the sides of the bowl with a rubber spatula, until the garlic and parsley are chopped fine (twenty 1-second pulses); transfer to a medium bowl. Whisk in the remaining ingredients until thoroughly blended. Let stand for 30 minutes to allow the flavors to develop before serving.

ALL-PURPOSE GRAVY

GRAVY, BY DEFINITION, IS A THICKENED sauce made of meat juices and pan drippings, usually left over from a roast. But what if you don't have a roast on hand and want gravy for some mashed potatoes or pork chops? What if you are limited to just some canned broth and a few vegetables? The problem is that a roast provides concentrated flavor through the fond, the browned bits at the bottom of the roasting pan. Without these small flavor jewels, a professional chef would say that any gravy is a lost cause. However, being fond (no pun intended) of lost causes, we set out to create a top-notch all-purpose gravy that could be made quickly, without one special ingredient, including a roast.

Our first thought was to turn to the supermarket shortcuts for making gravy, including products such as Kitchen Bouquet and Gravy Master. The results were unacceptable (see page 408 for details). Next, we researched gravy recipes that can be made without a roast and without homemade stock. They ran the gamut—from a six-minute gravy prepared in the microwave to one that had more than 20 ingredients and took 1½ hours to make. The flavors were, to say the least, disappointing. Most were thick and bland with no meat flavor; others were just downright frightening with oddly out-of-place Asian overtones.

What we did learn from all this testing was that some combination of supermarket broth and sautéed vegetables thickened with flour was the likely solution, given the fact that this approach seemed to deliver the most authentic, richest flavor. We began our recipe development with the liquid base. We quickly ruled out both water and vegetable broth because they made flavorless gravies. Bouillon cubes were also disappointing because their high salt content was oppressive. This left us with three options: chicken broth, beef broth, or a combination of both. Using a base recipe (some sautéed vegetables and flour), we prepared two batches of gravy, one using beef broth, the other using chicken. Tasters agreed that the beef broth gravy was acidic and contained a metallic aftertaste. On the other hand, the chicken broth was well liked, although the strong poultry flavor was inappropriate for all-purpose gravy. Finally, we tried equal amounts of chicken and beef broth and found that combination to be a winner.

Many gravy recipes include wine in addition to broth, so we tried substituting one half cup of both red and white wine for that amount of broth. Not a single taster felt that this was an improvement—the resulting gravy was tart and sour. Other liquids, such as sherry and cider—ingredients we had found in other recipes—fared no better.

It was time to focus on the vegetables. We had started with a standard mirepoix (a mixture of onions, carrots, and celery) that was lightly sautéed in oil. While this combination of vegetables lent the gravy a balanced sweetness and body, it failed to accent the gravy's meatiness or impart any roasted flavor. We replaced the mirepoix in our basic recipe with a cup of mushrooms in one test, and two cups of onions lightly caramelized in a second test. The gravy made with the mushrooms was a complete miss. Both the color and the appearance became muddy and the overall flavor was bland and vegetal. The caramelized onions didn't perform much better. One taster thought that the gravy tasted like French onion soup.

However, we did learn an important lesson from these tests. The process of caramelizing onions creates a fond on the bottom of the pan—not unlike the fond created after roasting meat—which gave the gravy an appealing nutty-brown color; we could also detect the hint of a pleasant roasted essence. It occurred to us that the development of a vegetable fond might be the key to increasing the gravy's flavor. We went back to the original mirepoix and merely extended the cooking time until the vegetables were well browned. This meant cooking the vegetables in butter (for more flavor) over medium-high heat for about seven minutes. As we had hoped, the gravy had a more pronounced roasted, meaty flavor. Much to our delight, we also found that if we chopped the vegetables in the food processor, we not only saved time but also created a better-tasting fond in less time due to the smaller pieces.

The last step in gravy making involves thick-ening. Our basic recipe called for browning the vegetables in butter and then sprinkling flour over them to create a roux, the classic combination of fat and flour that thickens liquids. We then whisked in the broth and simmered the gravy until thickened, after which time the raw flour taste had dissipated. We also tested other thickeners (cornstarch and arrowroot) and thickening techniques (making a paste of butter and flour that is added to the gravy at the end of the cooking time). Believe it or not, we also tried gingersnaps, as suggested in one of the initial test recipes.) Each of these options (even the gingersnaps) thickened the gravy to a similar consistency, but they created other problems. The cornstarch and arrowroot variations tasted fine but had an unappealing, translucent quality; the gingersnaps, meanwhile, produced a gravy that tasted like cake batter. All in all, the butter-based roux produced a superior gravy.

Still short in terms of depth of flavor, we thought to employ a technique used by Creole cooks in

INGREDIENTS: Black Pepper

For a spice that we use just about every day, and with a wide variety of foods, it's hard not to wonder if we have taken pepper too much for granted. Although most of us tend to think that one jar of black pepper is the same as another, several varieties exist. The most readily available include Vietnamese pepper, Lampong (from the island of Sumatra), and Malabar and Tellicherry (both from India). Among spice experts, each has gained a reputation for its particular attributes. Perhaps we should be seeking out black pepper from a particular region of a particular country.

Or, at the other end of the spectrum, perhaps all this fuss over grinding fresh whole peppercorns is nonsense, not really providing any improved flavor. We decided to hold a blind tasting to sort it all out. We included in our tasting the two preeminent national supermarket brands as well as the above-mentioned varieties, which were ordered from specialty spice and gourmet stores.

All of the peppers were offered plain but with the option of being tasted on plain white rice. Overall, our tasting confirmed that freshly ground pepper is far superior to pepper purchased already ground. The latter carried minimal aroma and tended to taste sharp and dull, lacking in complexity. Those whole peppercorns that were fresh ground just before the tasting contained bold as well as subtle flavors and aromas that were both lively and complex.

As for differences between the varieties of whole peppercorns

that were tasted fresh ground, we found them to be distinct yet subtle. All were appreciated for their particular characteristics, receiving high scores within a close range of one another. Based on these results, we concluded that what is important is not so much which variety of pepper you buy but how you buy it.

Why did we find the most noticeable differences in pepper to be between fresh-ground whole pepper and commercially ground pepper? When a peppercorn is cracked, the volatile chemical components that give pepper its bold aroma as well as its subtle characteristics immediately begin to disperse. These more subtle flavors often include pine and citrus. So with time (and cracking), what remains is the predominant nonvolatile compound in black pepper, piperine. Piperine is the source of black pepper's renowned pungency and is what gives it its characteristic hot, sharp, and sting-ing qualities. It is also said to stimulate saliva and gastric juices, creating the sensation of hunger.

THE BEST BLACK PEPPER

McCormick Whole Black Peppercorns beat out the rest of the supermarket competition as well as several mail-order brands. Note that this "premium" product, sold in glass bottles, also fared better than McCormick peppercorns sold in plastic bottles. This brand is sold under the Schilling label on the West Coast.

making gumbo and cooked the roux until it was the color of milk chocolate, far beyond the pale blonde color of previous tests. Much to our amazement, this simple technique substantially boosted the flavor of the gravy, helping to develop complex flavor elements in our simple recipe. In conjunction with the caramelized vegetable fond, the toasted flour provided an unexpectedly rich roasted flavor as well as a bold meaty flavor—exactly what we had been looking for. And the gravy's color was now a rich, deep brown as well.

We were close, but we still wanted to test some of the more unusual flavor-building ingredients, including miso (which made the gravy taste like a stir-fry sauce), coffee (which colored the gravy but added no flavor), and molasses (which thickened the gravy but made it sweet and bitter). Instead, we opted for a more classic combination of dried thyme, bay leaf, and peppercorns. Not only did this traditional trio round out the flavor of the gravy but they were all items found at arms' length in most kitchens.

All-Purpose Gravy
MAKES 2 CUPS

This gravy can be served with almost any type of meat and with mashed potatoes as well. The recipe can be doubled. If doubling it, use a Dutch oven so that the vegetables brown properly, and increase the cooking times by roughly 50 percent.

I	small carrot, peeled and chopped into rough $1/2$-inch pieces (about $1/2$ cup)
I	small celery rib, chopped into rough $1/2$-inch pieces (about $1/2$ cup)
I	small onion, chopped into rough $1/2$-inch pieces (about $3/4$ cup)
3	tablespoons unsalted butter
$1/4$	cup unbleached all-purpose flour
2	cups low-sodium chicken broth
2	cups low-sodium beef broth
I	bay leaf
$1/4$	teaspoon dried thyme
5	whole black peppercorns
	Salt and ground black pepper

1. In the workbowl of a food processor fitted with the steel blade, pulse the carrot until broken into rough $1/4$-inch pieces, about five 1-second pulses. Add the celery and onion; pulse until all the vegetables are broken into $1/8$-inch pieces, about 5 one-second pulses.

2. Heat the butter in a large heavy-bottomed saucepan over medium-high heat. When the foaming subsides, add the vegetables and cook, stirring frequently, until softened and well browned, about 7 minutes. Reduce the heat to medium; stir in the flour and cook, stirring constantly, until thoroughly browned and fragrant, about 5 minutes. Whisking constantly, gradually add the broths; bring to a boil, skimming off any foam that forms on the surface. Reduce the heat to medium-low and add the bay leaf, thyme, and peppercorns. Simmer, stirring occasionally, until thickened and reduced to 3 cups, 20 to 25 minutes.

3. Strain the gravy through a fine-mesh strainer into a clean saucepan, pressing on the solids to extract as much liquid as possible; discard the solids. Adjust the seasonings with salt and pepper to taste. Serve hot.

INGREDIENTS: Gravy Additives

In our research for all-purpose gravy, we had found several recipes that had called for the use of Kitchen Bouquet or Gravy Master. Although, we had heard of these ingredients, we had never before cooked with them. A trip to the supermarket revealed that these were not the only gravy "additives" that are available.

These products, which primarily consist of caramel or caramel coloring, vegetable extracts, salt, and preservatives, are made to impersonate fond—the little flavor-packed bits left in the pan after roasting meat. Since fond was exactly what we were trying to replicate in our all-purpose pantry gravy, we thought these items might be the key to the best recipe.

We choose four gravy additives, two powders and two liquids, and prepared four gravies following the instructions on each of the packages. Overall results were dismal and tasters all complained that the gravies tasted fake and artificial. While the theory behind the supermarket additives—a store-bought replacement for the time-consuming fond—was right on, the results were off base. Our suggestion: Build your own fond, with fresh vegetables and leave these items on the shelf.

INDEX

V

Veal:
  breast roast, 11
    Bollito Misto, 195–97
  buying, 10–11
    five primal cuts, 10
    milk-fed vs. natural, 10
    retail cuts, 11
  chops, 81, 109–12
    best cuts for grilling, 88
    loin, 11
    rib, 11
    shoulder (round bone chops or
      shoulder arm chops), 11
  Chops, Breaded, 110–12
  Chops, Grilled, 88–90
    on Bed of Arugula, 90
    best cuts for, 88
    on Charcoal Grill, 88–89
    on Gas Grill, 89
    with Mediterranean Herb
      Paste, 89
    Porcini-Rubbed, 89
  Chops, Pan-Seared, 109–10
    with Wilted Spinach and
      Gremolata, 110
  cutlets, 115, 122–30
    Breaded, 125–27
    breading, 126
    buying, 122
    cutting, 122
    Milanese, 127
    with Olive, Anchovy, and
      Orange Sauce, 124
    Parmesan, 127–28
    Saltimbocca, 124–25
    Scaloppine, 122–24
    with Tomato and Caper Sauce,
      123–24
    Wiener Schnitzel, 128–30
  ground
    Fettuccine with Bolognese
      Sauce, 358–60
    Meat Loaf, 349–52
  Milanese, 127
  milk-fed vs. natural, 10
  optimum internal temperatures
    for, 19
  Parmesan, 127–28
  Saltimbocca, 124–25

Veal (cont.)
  Scaloppine, 122–24
  shanks, 11
    Osso Buco, 205–7
  shoulder roast (rolled veal roast),
    11
    Italian Veal Stew, 164–65
    Veal Stew with Fennel,
      Tarragon, and Cream,
      162–64
  stews, 162–65
    with Fennel, Tarragon, and
      Cream, 162–64
    Italian, 164–65
  top round roast (leg round roast),
    11
  Vitello Tonnato, 130–32
    Cold Tuna Sauce for, 132
  Wiener Schnitzel, 128–30
Vegetable(s):
  and herb bouquet, making, 159
  in stir-fries, 135
Vermouth, Mustard Sauce with
    Thyme and, 377
Vindaloo, Pork, 170–72
Vinegar:
  Balsamic, Braised Shoulder Lamb
    Chops with Red Peppers,
    Capers and, 107
  Pork Chops with Bell Peppers
    and, 95–97
  Red Wine, Sautéed Pork
    Tenderloin Medallions with
    Warm Spices, Raisins and,
    121
Vitello Tonnato, 130–32
  Cold Tuna Sauce for, 132

W

Wagyu steaks, 13
Warm-Spiced Parsley Marinade with
    Ginger, 69
West Indian Flavors, Grilled Pork
    Kebabs with, 75
Wet-curing, 373
Wet spice rubs:
  Asian, 290
  Caribbean, 290
  Mustard, Garlic, and Honey, 290

  Orange, Sage, and Garlic, 290
White beans, in Cassoulet, 176–80
Wiener Schnitzel, 128–30
Wine:
  red
    Barolo, Beef Braised in, 188–90
    Beef, and Pancetta Bolognese
      Sauce, Fettuccine with, 360
    Beef Burgundy, 155–59, 221
    Braised Shoulder Lamb Chops
      with Tomatoes and, 107
    Lamb Shanks Braised in, 204–5
    Madeira Pan Sauce with
      Mustard and Anchovies, 50
    Marsala, in Veal Scaloppine, 123
    Pan Sauce, Classic, 47–50
    Pan Sauce, Roasted Racks of
      Lamb with Rosemary and,
      272
    Port, Sautéed Pork Tenderloin
      Medallions with Dried
      Cherries, Rosemary and, 120
    Pot Roast with Mushrooms,
      Tomatoes and (Stracotto),
      188
    Sauce for Beef Wellington,
      247–48
    Short Ribs Braised in, with
      Bacon, Parsnips, and Pearl
      Onions, 201–2
    Vinegar, Sautéed Pork
      Tenderloin Medallions with
      Warm Spices, Raisins and,
      121
  red, tastings of
    for beef Burgundy, 158
    for cooking, 51
    for stew, 151
  white, in Veal Scaloppine, 123
Woks, 135
  electric, 144
Wood chips, 35, 327
Wood chunks, 327

Y

Yogurt Sauce, Middle Eastern–Style,
    366–67
Yorkshire Pudding, Individual,
    236–38